PROBLEMS OF A MATURE ECONOMY

Problems of
a Mature Economy

A TEXT FOR STUDENTS OF
THE BRITISH ECONOMY

F. V. Meyer, D. C. Corner
and J. E. S. Parker

MACMILLAN

ST MARTIN'S PRESS

First published 1970 by
MACMILLAN AND CO LTD
London and Basingstoke
Associated companies in New York Toronto
Dublin Melbourne Johannesburg and Madras

Library of Congress catalog card no. 79-123635

SBN (boards) 333 04240 9
(paper) 333 11315 2

Printed in Great Britain by
ROBERT MACLEHOSE AND CO LTD
The University Press, Glasgow

Contents

PART II

Industrial Organisation

PART III

Incomes: A Macro-Economic Survey

Contents

Preface

The origin of this book lies in discussions between the three authors on the current state of the British economy. Although they specialise in different aspects of the economy and use appropriately different techniques, their conclusions were broadly and consistently similar. There seemed to be a case for presenting these conclusions to a wider public. The results are set out in the following pages. They are addressed to students of the British economy, who are familiar with the basic techniques and jargon used by economists. At university level this means second-year honours or third-year general degree students.

J. E. S. Parker's contribution is mainly, though not exclusively, in Part I, D. C. Corner's in Part II, and F. V. Meyer's in Parts III and IV. In the course of writing, much help was received from a number of academic and business experts, and also from recent students. None of those who helped are, however, in any way responsible for the final version (which none of them has seen) or for any of the errors of fact and exposition which may have remained despite their help.

Special thanks are due to Sir Ralph Hawtrey for detailed comments on an earlier version of the chapter on 'Sterling'. His thorough knowledge of monetary history and theory helped to avoid many pitfalls. Valuable advice on current monetary facts and history was received from Mr C. J. Wiles and Dr L. S. Pressnell. Mr G. Teeling-Smith and Mr M. R. Wickens read, and passed valuable comments on, an earlier version of the chapter on 'Invention, Innovation and Growth'. On invisible trades, most helpful expert advice was received from Mr T. S. Donaghy, Mr R. E. Liddiard and Mr O. K. Oliphant. The authors' colleagues in Exeter have been most patient throughout the two and a half years it took to write this book. Mr V. H. Beynon commented on points relating to rent and food prices; Professor J. Black on profitability, profits and invisible trades; Mr H. Burton on sterling; Mr A. R. Culyer on the whole of Parts III and IV; Mr A. Maynard on wages; and Professor David Walker on problems of industrial research and development.

Throughout, the authors have received helpful research assistance from Mr R. Davies, especially for Parts II, III and IV. In the early stages Mr G. Cole and Mr D. E. Gamble helped with collecting material for Parts I and II respectively; and in the final stages Miss Gill Brady and Mr J. Mercer helped with Part II, and Mr D. R. Beasley with Parts II and III.

University of Exeter   F. V. Meyer
July 1969   D. C. Corner
                                                             J. E. S. Parker

1 The Plan and Purpose of the Book

From any vantage point of earlier history, the 1950s and 1960s would have seemed a golden era. Economic progress proceeded at a faster rate than at almost any other time in recorded British economic history. Incomes, output and exports all reached a record level. Most people were better fed, clad and housed than ever before. They had more consumer goods and more leisure. Above all there was more security of employment than at any other time since industrialisation began.

Yet there was disquiet and discontent, and not all of this was due to man's insatiable wants and forgetfulness of past achievement. If the British economy did well, others did better. If there was more economic stability in the United Kingdom than elsewhere, there were faster growth rates in other industrial economies. Eventually this showed in the balance of payments. Corrective measures were taken, and these often further retarded British economic growth.

In this book an attempt is made to put some of the current economic problems into perspective. There are four parts. Part I is concerned with the growth of individual firms. The discussion is conducted at a micro-level. The prosperity of the economy is closely linked to the performance of constituent companies. An effort is therefore made to discover the main determinants of company growth. Part II adopts a wider approach. The labour and capital markets are described in some detail. A case-study approach is then adopted to illustrate some problems of industry and industrial organisation. The engineering, chemicals and gas industries are taken as major examples of activity in an industrial economy. The importance of monopoly and restrictive practices is also discussed. Part III examines the distribution of the national income. Part IV broadens the approach still further, and deals with problems of the whole economy. The pattern of international trade and the valuation of a currency are seen to have a major influence on internal development. The special circumstances of a mature economy are described. In the process the problems which appear to confront the British economy with increasing regularity are put into perspective.

The intention of this book is to stimulate thought on some of the major problems of the economy. The authors do not pretend to have discovered the answers. In fact they are aware of several limitations. Coverage of a number of issues is limited. Furthermore there are a number of matters of economic importance which have been omitted or given scant treatment. Such omissions and curtailed treatment have been made either on practical grounds of almost complete lack of information, or in the belief that inclusion would not add significantly to the discussion. The cumulative effect of these omissions may, however, be that some interrelationships are not appreciated and thus diagnosis may be affected.

A further shortcoming of the book may be an overemphasis on the role of innovation. The development of new products and processes, and their diffusion, form only a relatively small part of current economic activity. Firms are for the most part concerned to repeat what they have done in the past. New products and processes are probably not, quantitatively, very important. Nevertheless these have been stressed in this book, on four main grounds. First, innovations tend to be the growth points in companies' turnover. Second, innovations induce changes in production functions. These changes breed other changes. A chain reaction is generated, so that the effects of an initial innovation may be spread throughout the economy. Over time the whole level of performance of industrial sectors may be upgraded, and growth potential thus enhanced. This may happen even when the originating change was quantitatively almost insignificant, in terms of current contribution to the national income. Third, innovations usually generate sophisticated goods. These are readily exportable to high-income economies. They therefore provide a potential route away from balance-of-payments problems for the British economy. Consequently, although innovations may appear to be marginal activities, nevertheless they may help to lift one of the constraints on the growth of the economy. Fourth, innovations may be a means of factor saving, in a situation where there is an absolute scarcity of factors. This is particularly important to a mature economy.

One advantage of the mixed approach in this book is that economy-wide aggregates are related to the contribution of individuals, firms, industries and sectors. If the approach of this book had been entirely micro in character, the importance of factor saving to the economy may not have emerged. At the level of the individual firm, factors of production do not appear all that scarce. Companies usually manage to secure all the instruments of production they require. Once the problem is viewed from an industry and economy level, the absolute scarcity of factors becomes apparent. Firms are competing for extra resources which, to the whole economy, are very restricted in supply.

This book attempts to diagnose the major problems of the British economy in the 1950s and 1960s. Conditions are now very different from those experienced before the war. Causal relationships and relative magnitudes have changed. Some inherited theories must be changed. If the diagnosis here puts some current issues into perspective, allays disquiet and stimulates discussion on solutions to the real problems, the major purpose of the book will have been served.

Part I

THE GROWTH OF FIRMS

2 The Environment

Firms are the constituent producing elements of the economy. They can be of all sizes, ranging from one-man businesses to giant corporations. They are managed by all manner of men, with motives of operation ranging from ambition to expand their activities to contentment with their present lot. Some succeed in making the best of their opportunities, others fail. The sum total of their achievements is the national output of commercial goods and services. Any inquiry into national economic performance must therefore include a consideration of the influences which make firms grow and improve their commercial performance.

Part I of this book attempts to identify the main determinants of company growth. To this end a number of studies analysing the process are examined. One difficulty with this approach is that the complications of the real world must be taken into account. In a purely theoretical world the environment may be completely specified. In the highly complex real world this may not be done. Interpretation must, therefore, proceed on knowledge and assumptions, some of which may prove fallible. Consequently it is important to make explicit what is assumed to be the central features of the environment in which companies operate.

The following assumptions are made about the salient features of the present-day commercial environment. The majority of companies are assumed to be multi-product in character. Competition is assumed to vary with the type of product and over time. The pricing of goods is taken to be related to the nature of the prevailing competition. Lastly, growth is assumed to be an important motivation in companies. In what follows the consequences of these assumptions are enumerated. It becomes clear that the commercial environment differs considerably from that embodied in traditional models of company activity. Commercial rivalry takes new forms and is not necessarily less active.

In the modern world companies are typically multi-product in character. They may encompass a wide range of economic activities. Furthermore some firms are now so large that their decision-making centres are outside the influence of any one industry. Conglomerate companies are examples. They have interests that are spread so wide that this special term has been coined to describe them. They do not belong to any one industry. They are economic units which are spread right across the economy. The concept of an industry is becoming increasingly difficult to apply in modern economic conditions. Summary description of industrial conditions is likely to be misleading where multi-product firms operate. Competitive conditions vary from product to product. The terms monopoly, oligopoly, monopolistic competition and perfect competition become of limited usefulness because of the problem of identifying firms with particular industries. These models of economic activity were constructed on the assumption of single-product firms, operating wholly within a particular industry. Matters become more complex when firms spread activities across industries. Current usage of the models of market behaviour has therefore become circumspect. The models are now used either in a wide sense to describe the general character of the business environment facing companies, or in a highly specific way and confined entirely to particular products and not to firms. By confining the analysis to specific products, the problem of the product mix of companies is avoided. When used in this way, the unit of competition relates to particular activities and not necessarily to whole firms.

Competitive conditions may vary widely between different sections of companies' turnover. Individual companies may be the sole manufacturers of one product, and merely one of thousands in another. Competitive conditions may also vary with the continuing process of innovation and differentiation. Products may be genuinely new as a result of innovative effort. They may be varied slightly and thus differentiated from rivals' products, or, as a result of a change in selling effort, they may be altered in the eyes of the consumer. Differentiation and selling effort directed at creating a new image are really minor forms of innovation. Innovation is more than the development of physical inventions. It includes the way in which a product is brought to the market and presented to consumers. Differentiation and innovation are distinguished, however, because of the different effect on the nature of products. Differentiation refers to achieving small alterations. These may come from different branding, new selling effort or a minor alteration in the physical nature of goods. Innovation is more fundamental and involves major changes. Once innovation and differentiation are recognised as an essential feature of commercial life, then competition comes to mean product as well as price competition. Emphasis is given to the variation in the character of goods, as an important element in commercial rivalry. Emphasis is also given to selling costs. Firms must inform potential customers of the advantages of their products, and establish a market so that the advantage of volume production may be secured quickly.

It is useful to distinguish between 'product competition' and 'innovative competition'. Both of these types of competition emphasise the qualitative aspects of the products concerned. Innovative competition is used to refer to rivalry between firms, based on securing significant steps forward in their products. Product competition is used to distinguish a market situation which emphasises differentation. Minor improvements in products are used to enhance the competitive position of individual firms. Innovative competition is usually associated with technologically advanced industries, whose products are relatively new. Examples are pharmaceuticals, electronics and jet aviation. These industries spend considerable sums on research and development and are generally growing fast. Industries where product competition is typical probably include tobacco, footwear and furniture. Such industries rely on minor alterations of the product to achieve an advantage. In their case dramatic alterations in the nature of the product are rare, and research and development expenditures are not high.

The pricing of products under present-day conditions, where competition tends to emphasise the quality and not the selling price of products, is fairly complex. The advantages to a company of marketing distinctive products are considerable. Because products are no longer homogeneous between different sellers, there is no longer a unique price-for-a-product relationship. Instead there are bands of prices within which companies operate. Companies do not have complete freedom in what they charge for products. Upper and lower limits to prices will be influenced by considerations such as the price of the nearest substitute products, and a desire to dampen the encroachment of rivals. The width of these bands will be influenced by the quality differential which a company can maintain, and the sales image which it may project. As will be argued later, distinctive goods, particularly those associated with innovative competition, tend to have low price elasticity of demand and high income elasticity. Costs of production may also decline with rising output, and profit potential is therefore likely to be considerable. This is not an unmixed blessing. Good profits will attract rivals. Such profits may not therefore be long-lived.

Competition will fluctuate with the continuing process of innovation, differentiation and emulation. Any competitive advantage secured through innovation and differentiation will tend to be temporary. Once a new product, or a variant of a new product, is seen to be successful, rivals will respond. Companies are therefore only likely to retain their advantage through continual change. Competition of this form is likely to be dynamic process hinged around creating and retaining consumer loyality.

The commercial history of a product may be divided into three phases according to the character of competition. Phase I relates to new products, phase II emphasises price competition, and phase III stresses a lack of rivalry where monopoly and cartel may be prevalent. In phase I the product is new. The innovating company has a considerable advantage. There are virtually no close substitutes, and the demand for the good tends to be price-inelastic and income-elastic. Demand is not likely to be greatly influenced by price considerations. There is sufficient novelty to make price merely one of a number of determinants of sales. Such products tend to be fairly sophisticated in character, and associated with economies which enjoy an advanced standard of living. Demand is likely to be related to income and increases in income (see Chapter 24). A new product is likely to be priced on an average cost basis. As output expands, overhead costs incurred in development and production start up, and are spread over greater turnover. Average cost per unit probably declines. Marginal cost pricing will not recoup total costs; average cost pricing will. There is likely to be considerable freedom in setting the price: there are no close rivals, so price will either be set by reference to demand or average costs. If linked to demand, price may be pitched at what the market will bear. This means that price is set at a level equal to the nearest substitute product, plus an addition for the quality differential. If linked to costs, price will be related to average costs, for the reasons argued above.

Phase I competition may gradually change over to phase II. Phase II, is more traditional-type competition, with emphasis on price rivalry. Potential competitors, realising the advantage that the innovating company has secured, will emulate their product. As more companies enter the field, the commercial freedom of the innovator is constrained. Customers have the choice of close substitutes, and so will tend to buy on price consideration. Individual companies have to accept the selling price which is largely determined by rivals' prices. Output is thus adjusted to price per unit, and once the production process becomes settled and economies of scale fully exploited, pricing is based on marginal cost. The way in which a market will move towards this price-type competition will vary according to circumstances. A new good may either stimulate product or innovative competition. If the technological possibilities in the field are great, and also the demand prospects, competitors may react not by emulation but by improvement and modification of the original product. Innovative competition will result. The technological possibilities and revenue prospects encourage rivals to seek substantial steps forward in the products. The technology will advance rapidly. If the technological possibilities are not great, or revenue prospects apparently do not justify the expense of developing a significant step forward, product competition may emerge. Rivals aim for minor modifications of the new product. These are not very costly to achieve, and may give some degree of commercial advantage. The technology of the product will not advance fast and competition will be of the product variety.

Whether phase I competition will actually move all the way into phase II (price-type) competition depends on the extent to which the production process has stabilised, the cost structure of major competitors and the number of companies involved. If the technological possibilities of the production process have largely stabilised, then companies will attempt to minimise costs in relation to the market-determined price. Competition will become largely based on price considerations, although an element of differentiation is likely to remain.

The numbers of companies involved and their cost structures are also important. With large numbers of companies of similar cost structures, the market form is likely to approximate to perfect competition. Differentiation will become too costly in relation to price, and the product will sell almost entirely on price considerations. If the cost structures of companies are not similar and there is an element of asymmetry in this sense, the type of competition may move to phase III, namely monopoly or cartel. If there are large companies amongst manufacturers of this hypothetical product, they may be in a position to monopolise the market. Sheer size may confer sufficient economies of scale to drive other rivals out of business. Alternatively such large concerns may not have a cost edge, but may still be able to eliminate rivals. By cross-subsidising this product from other activities in their turnover, they may be able to under-cut rivals for sufficient time to bankrupt them. A cartel or monopoly situation may result. This is not meant to imply that monopoly or cartel is necessarily unfavourable. If prices are forced too high, new entrants may be attracted. Knowledge that this may happen may therefore limit exploitation of the market. Cartelisation of markets can result from over-fierce competition. A cartel may be formed to defend the capital costs of the production process involved. Sulphuric acid provides an example, which is described in Chapter 16 of Part II.

This classification of the history of a product is highly schematic. No particular product may conform to the pattern. It is useful, however, in that it stresses even further that the working of the competitive process must be viewed at the individual product level. Industries and firms tend to cover a wide range of activities. The type of competition can vary between products and over time as the processes of innovation, differentiation and emulation proceed. Examples of the various types of competition are given in the case studies of individual industries, in Part II.

Unless companies are producing phase III products (monopoly or cartel), commercial success will tend to be temporary. As a consequence they will do their utmost to achieve an element of security. The incursions of rivals may be reduced by a number of commercial devices. These may include interlocking directorates; part-ownership of competitors; trade investments; conditional purchase arrangements like tie-in sales or full-line selling; quantity discounts; conditional or exclusive marketing arrangements; and so on. Companies may also achieve an element of commercial security by becoming large and multi-product in output. One means to achieve this end quickly is a high rate of growth.

By becoming large and having a wide enough range of products to absorb fluctuations within overall results, companies may to some extent stabilise their performance. Successes and failures in various lines of production may balance each other. Once companies become multi-product in character, their commercial results are no longer so dependent on a limited range of particular goods. Instead activities are spread across a wide field of interest, and thus company results are not so dependent on particular ventures. As will become clear later, such companies tend to be large. Companies seeing the advantages of stable results have a very considerable incentive to become large and multi-product in character. The faster their rate of growth, the earlier will they achieve this.

Growth is a major motivation. It is a means of securing sufficient size to stabilise commercial results. It allows a company to extend its range of activities and achieve a degree of commercial influence. Growth is also required by shareholders, particularly the ordinary shareholders. A major reason for holding equities or ordinary shares is for capital gain and as a hedge against inflation. Over the long term, ordinary shareholders expect their shares to increase in value. Unless this expectation is realised at an adequate rate, there may be very serious consequences for lagging companies. Inflation erodes the purchasing power of a given sum of money. Unless capital gains compensate for inflation, and also provide a real, and not an inflationary, reward for holding the securities, the ordinary shares are unlikely to be popular on the Stock Exchange. The end-result may well be take-over. Thus management, particularly in public-quoted companies, has a considerable incentive to ensure that their companies grow.

Fortunately, there may be no limit to the size of firms. Growth may continue from year to year. Traditional U-shaped average cost curves imply that there may be an optimum size for firms. Expansion beyond this optimum may carry cost penalties. This may act as an effective restraint on companies' ambition. However, firms tend to be multi-product and diversified in character. The overall cost pattern thus represents a weighted average of the cost pattern of all products. Firms will adjust output according to cost and demand relevant to individual products. New products may enjoy decreasing costs as more is sold. These sorts of products are likely to have L-shaped cost schedules. Eventually costs may rise, even with new products as economies are exhausted, and competition begins to emphasise price, as in phase II. But this does not mean that the size of the company will be constrained. It may have a number of other new products to provide further growth points. Multi-product companies are therefore unlikely to have an optimum size. Companies with vested interests in new products will always attempt to market goods with expanding demand. The economic success of these new products allows lagging products to be withdrawn. This constraint on size and growth may be avoided, even if average costs of individual goods eventually rise. By the time this happens, others will be found to provide further growth impetus. As long as there is a succession of new products, there need be no limit to the size of the firm.

While there may be no optimum size for companies, there may be a most favourable rate of growth. The expansion process involves a net addition to productive capacity. New factors must be absorbed within companies. New management personnel, capacity, products and so on have to be integrated into the existing organisation. These take time to shake down and make a full contribution to output. If new ventures are taken on too fast and too great a rate of expansion is attempted, the consequences may be serious. Disruption of existing output may result from commercial indigestion. Too great a proportion of key personnel's time may be absorbed, so that current activities suffer. The production rate may decline and so may profits. The investment effort involved may make the company very vulnerable to changes in current business conditions. If sales slow down, revenue generation may be insufficient to support the rate of expansion to which the company is now committed. Supplementary funds may be available only at penal rates. The very livelihood of the company may thus be jeopardised. Too slow a rate of expansion, on the other hand, may also have serious consequences. Companies may lose profitable opportunities to rivals. This lack of ambition may frustrate the dynamic and thrusting members of management. They may leave and join rivals, thus enhancing their competitive strength. Too slow a rate of expansion may mean that the product mix remains unchanged. Rivals may gradually encroach upon the markets of this stagnant company. Commercial influence and consumer goodwill may suffer, and eventually the very existence of the company may be threatened. These potential effects of too fast and too slow growth suggest that there may be an optimum rate of expansion for companies.

Growth should proceed at a rate to avoid the consequences which may occur at these limits. An intermediate rate is indicated. This may be what has been called a balanced or sustainable growth rate. (1) At a balanced rate of expansion, a company can repeat its growth rate from year to year. The process is sustainable and not discontinuous. Growth proceeds smoothly. In this way expansion is maintained. There is not a burst of growth, followed by a period of stagnation, during which time commercial indigestion is cured. Instead there is a gradual and smooth process, whereby each year's performance generates the basis for next year's step forward. Management training, forward planning, adjustment of capacity and redeployment of the work force, all proceed in an orderly fashion. The effect is to generate an attitude conducive to change. This becomes normal. Of course, it is unwise to maintain that a balanced growth rate is necessarily the optimum. Circumstances vary greatly between firms as also do the opportunities for expansion. For example, take-over is a powerful means of achieving fast growth for the individual company. But unless there is a succession of victims, it is unlikely that the expansion rate can be maintained. Circumstances which make take-over favourable are not wholly within the control of individual firms. Hence take-over activity will tend to be spasmodic. Furthermore it may only be under very special circumstances that balanced growth is appropriate. The general nature of business organisations may be such that resources are freed for a further bout of expansion only after a period of consolidation. If this is so, the optimum growth rate may not be balanced or sustainable but discontinuous instead.

The environmental factors enumerated above suggest that commercial rivalry may become limited. Companies appear to have considerable market influence and to be anxious to avoid direct price competition. In a theoretical business world, where perfect competition rules everywhere, factors move to their best use quickly. Returns on all forms of activity move to equality, and no improvement in earning power may be secured by switching assets. In the real world there are manifold complications. Competition is not perfect, as has already been indicated. Every company is in a position to secure an element of market power. Innovation and differentiation enable consumer loyalty to be generated. Downward-sloping demand curves are typical. Furthermore resources do not appear to have this capacity to shift employment rapidly. Capital equipment is often fixed in character, and very specific to its current task. Labour and management are frequently immobile. Economic forces alone do not dictate where and in what employment factors will be used. In practice, however, there is a fair degree of mobility of resources and there are also forces which prevent markets becoming completely monopolised. Additions to the stock of factors have a high degree of mobility. For example, current uncommitted business savings are potentially employable anywhere. These may be deployed to new uses quickly. Even resources already committed to use may be moved fairly rapidly, through the device of take-overs and mergers. In this way existing assets may change hands and be used more effectively under new management.

The 'real world' competitive process should favour companies that are making above-average use of resources. Such companies should be able to secure more resources than companies which are less successful. If their profit figures are good, then these should provide an immediate source of funds for plough-back. In addition, good profits are evidence of high commercial skill, and thus should be a good basis for securing credit and further capital from outside sources. Furthermore good profits, allied to the borrowing power that these confer, should provide sufficient cash for success in the field of take-overs. Thus companies that do well should enjoy the benefit of what has been called the transfer machine. (2) Companies that do badly should also suffer from the mechanism working in the other direction. Markets are unlikely to be monopolised, however, by the successful company because forces are set in motion to reduce their economic power. Products are emulated, new firms enter markets with new products, and existing firms switch their lines of business towards the demonstratively lucrative ventures. This is probably simple for highly diversified companies, who may well have a field of activity very close to those which have proved successful. Companies that are doing badly suffer a commercial shock. Losses may make them improve performance, and reverse the trend of their fortunes; what is known as the innovation mechanism begins to operate. (3)

Notice the stress given to innovation in this representation of the competitive mechanism. Innovation is a means of reversing the trend of industrial fortunes. Companies may revamp their output. New companies may be founded to produce new products. Differentiation and innovation may secure for each company a degree of market influence. They are weapons which may be used to reduce the power even of market leaders. They lessen the impact of price competition, but they do not necessarily reduce commercial rivalry. This now takes the form of innovative and product competition. The appeal of a particular product becomes a function of a combination of factors besides price. These include the distinctive qualities, service, selling and advertising effort associated with the good.

Evidence that these new forms of competition are active is difficult to assess. However, there are a number of key measures which suggest that competition, even in these forms, is in practice viable. There are reasonably strong correlations between profitability and growth, and improved efficiency and growth, of individual companies. (4) These associations suggest that companies which are on average successful in terms of increased efficiency and profit-making secure more resources than others. Rapid changes in company fortunes measured by market shares, rank changes and changes in earnings growth suggest also that the new competition is alive. (5) Predictions based on past company results have only limited success. An above-average rating on a wide variety of measures in one period of time is a limited guide to what will occur in the succeeding time period. Apparently there are forces in operation which make repetition of past results the exception rather than the rule.

A further manifestation of these forces in action is the tendency for rates of return earned on industrial activity to move towards equality over time. (6) Above-average returns tend to attract resources, and below-average to repel them. Assets move between employment as the classic distribution theory would predict. The net effect is a continual tendency for wide disparities in rates of return to be narrowed. Lucrative activities attract resources, with the result that returns are competed down. Activities earning low returns, on the other hand, do not attract uncommitted capital and may well cause existing factors to move to alternative employment. Resources employed in such activities will tend to be reduced, and thus returns improve through the consequent reduction in supply.

The fact that price competition is now less important does not necessarily hinder the movement of factors towards better uses. Present-day industrial competition is complex. It must take account of a wide variety of business facts of life. These will include innovation, differentiation, selling costs and growth motivation. The latter includes a desire for large absolute size, commercial security, diversified output and a constant desire to dampen the encroachment of rivals. All of these factors resolve themselves into a form of competition which may not emphasise price as the main commercial weapon. What empirical evidence there is available suggests that this form of competition is active. Inequalities of returns do not long continue. New companies enter, new products are produced, old products are refashioned. Returns move towards equality over time.

In the following chapters of this part of the book some influences on the growth of firms are examined. These include the size of companies, finance, dividends, profitability, take-over and merger, invention and innovation, and management. Each of these is examined in an attempt to explain and clarify company growth. Considerable emphasis is given to innovation both in this part and throughout the whole book. Innovation is stressed because it results in new products and processes. For the individual firm these are often the growth points in their turnover. For an economy, particularly a mature economy, where there is absolute scarcity of the factors of production, new goods and methods are particularly important (see Part IV). They are a means to achieve factor saving and a higher overall growth performance. They are also important to the balance of payments. Goods with technological edge sell readily in advanced economies, and therefore provide a potential route away from balance-of-payments problems. In absolute terms, new products are probably not responsible for a high proportion of national income. But in terms of their impact on the growth performance of firms and the economy, their importance can hardly be understated. This is why such emphasis has been put on innovation in this book.

3 Size and Growth of Firms

It is often inferred that large firms are the growth firms, and that the economy's overall performance could be accelerated if companies were made larger. The following will show that such reasoning is either plain wrong or confuses cause and effect. Large firms may be those which have grown most in the past. Alternatively they may be the oldest and have achieved their present size by very slow growth over the years. Even if size and growth are linked, causation may not be evident. Large size may cause fast growth, or fast growth large size. Equally plausible is the existence of some third factor which provides the true explanations. Both of the variables may be related to this key factor, and thus any link between growth and size may be spurious in terms of indicating the economic forces explaining growth.

The approach in this chapter is micro-economic and emphasises the growth of individual firms. There are, however, macro-economic implications. The causes of general economic growth must lie in part with the commercial performance of individual firms making up the private-enterprise sector. Even if no clear relationship can be established between the growth of the whole economy and the growth of individual firms, it can be safely asserted that overall economic performance will represent the net effect of changes within that economy. An attempt will be made to assess the importance of each individual factor in company growth. This procedure will not of course prove any of the hypotheses in an absolute sense; it will merely indicate whether they are consistent with the facts.

Large firms should benefit from economies of scale, and therefore it is reasonable to assume that there will be a connection between the absolute size of firms and their rates of growth. Long runs of production should mean low costs per unit and, other things being equal, high profitability. High profitability implies a large supply of finance for further investment and therefore high growth. Other possible advantages of size relate to borrowing power, risk minimisation by spreading activities across a multi-product output, the power to carry a considerable research programme and the goodwill which is associated with an established company with considerable market influence. In practice, economies of scale are important in industries like book-printing, steel, oil refining (1) and motor-car manufacture. For example, in the United States output per man is four and a half times as great as in the United Kingdom in automobile manufacture. (2) A large part of this difference can be directly attributed to the size of the production units and final markets.

An alternative way of illustrating the advantages of large size is to indicate the penalties of being small. Two studies have shown that profit rates of small quoted companies tend to fluctuate much more than those of large companies. (3) Large companies tend to be more diversified and thus losses in one sector may be offset by profits in another. The Small Business Survey carried out at the Oxford University Institute of Statistics in 1956, covering 49 unincorporated businesses and 286 private companies, showed small companies to be more dependent on short-term credit and finance than large companies. (4) These findings are firmly established by the Board of Trade's more recent stratified random sample covering 1,941 private exempt companies. (5) Similar conditions also hold for the United States. For example, in 1963 firms with assets of less than $1 million financed more than one-third of assets with short-term credits, compared with about one-sixth in the case of larger companies. Also such small companies tended to use twice as much trade credit as companies with assets of more than $5 million. (6) In effect small companies are penalised by the form in which they typically finance their activities. Using a relatively large proportion of short-term credit and finance, they have rather more working capital tied up in the form of cash or liquid assets to service this debt than have the larger companies. Furthermore this method of financing may actually help to generate the fluctuations in profit rates mentioned above. Working capital tends to fluctuate widely with trading conditions. Current liabilities are part of working capital. Profitability is defined in the two studies (7) as profits as a percentage of net assets. Net assets are total assets less current liabilities. If the value of current liabilities and therefore net assets varies widely with trading conditions, the resultant profit rates will also fluctuate. Large firms which rely less on short-term credit and finance are thus likely to have profit rates which fluctuate less under the same business conditions. In addition their wider spread of commercial activities should also dampen fluctuations in results. If small firms are genuinely at a disadvantage, this should show in their profit and growth performance. The following attempts to examine the issue.

In fact there appears to be no appreciable difference in the profit performance of large firms compared with small. If profits are normalised, by expressing them as a ratio of capital utilised by individual companies, then large companies are, in general, no more profitable than small companies. Scatter diagrams of size and profitability reveal no positive association between the variables. A similar lack of association is also found between size and the rate of growth of companies. There are numerous studies examining these issues. (8) The main procedure in these is to correlate the variables to gain some indication of the strength of the relationships. By and large the degree of correlation appears to be zero. There are many problems in the handling of company data, such as the accuracy of figures for capital and the maintenance of consistency in definitions between companies. (9) Nevertheless the weight of the evidence indicates that there appears to be no general link between growth and size, and profitability and size.

At first sight the conclusion that neither profitability nor growth is associated with the size of companies is rather surprising. These findings would appear to deny the existence of economies of scale. In view of the advantages which large companies appear to enjoy, it is not unreasonable to expect them to be more efficient and to grow faster. Yet the facts suggest that this is not the case. What, therefore, is the explanation, and why do economies of scale, which are known to exist in practice, not lead to greater profitability and greater growth of large companies?

The explanations are numerous. The absence of a link between size and the two variables does not, in reality, imply that economies of scale are fictitious. Large firms may have achieved their present size because of their efficiency in the past. The basic costs of processing may decrease because of larger-scale operation, but administrative costs may well rise as the market becomes sated with their major products. If large firms tend to be multi-product in character, then above-average efficiency of various sectors may be absorbed by their other, less successful trading activities. Small firms, on the other hand, may gain economies of scale by being highly specialist even in a very limited market. There is no reason why there should even be a direct relationship between the size of firms and efficiency. In other words size must not be measured in absolute terms. There are other factors to be considered, namely the size of the market and the number of other firms competing in it. Large size may lead to low costs of production, but if there are a number of competing firms then this competition may reduce margins over cost so that high profitability may not result. Economies of scale exist in practice. But they may not be used by management to enhance growth. Rather they may be absorbed in the survival and perpetuation of firms, particularly where growth motivation is not strong. Any of these reasons, let alone a combination of them, may help to explain the absence of a link between size and growth, and size and profitability.

Empirical studies, examining the relationship between size and growth, are handicapped by the paucity of data. Often they have to rely on crude ranking of absolute capital values. Absolute size is, however, meaningful only when used in the context of a particular firm in a particular industry in a particular market. For example, the British Leyland Motor Corporation may appear to be a very large company by the standards of the United Kingdom. In terms of United States motor-car manufacturers the situation is different. Another difficulty arises because the studies so far available are confined either to quoted or non-quoted companies, and none includes both types of companies. Consequently one major aspect of size may thus be ignored. When companies achieve sufficient status to receive a Stock Exchange quotation, further growth is facilitated. Once firms have a quotation, they have access to a ready market for funds, and it can be presumed that this may remove a major constraint on growth. Yet another difficulty is that if greater profitability and enhanced growth are expected of large companies, then the studies are using the variable size as a proxy for efficiency and high growth motivation. Since absolute size or the ranking of companies by size are not reliable indicators of the causes of growth, other and more direct measures must be sought. One possible indicator is suggested by the positive association between increased efficiency and the growth of companies. (10) It will be argued below, however, that companies enjoying either increased or high levels of efficiency are not necessarily the large ones, though they will tend to be the companies that are becoming larger.

None of the studies available gives a full account of the association between company size and growth. However, their results exhibit one important economic truth: economies of scale may be important but they do not by themselves necessarily enhance company profitability or growth. Other factors are involved. The motivation to grow, future prospects and the supply of management skill are examples. If larger size always meant improved industrial performance, then the economy would ultimately be run by a single giant firm. (11) If larger companies were always more efficient than smaller companies, then the better firm would always be a larger firm. Ultimately all industrial resources and activities would be concentrated in one vast firm. In effect, then, it is implied by the findings that the optimum-sized firm is not always the largest firm. This may be interpreted to mean either that there is no such thing as the 'optimum' firm, or, in practice, that the optimum firm varies in size with particular circumstances to such an extent that no pattern of advantage emerges. However, the real point of the studies is their effect in stressing that increased size does not automatically generate faster growth or higher profitability. These arise from improved industrial performance, and may be achieved by companies of *any* size.

The apparently random character of firm size and growth has led to the suggestion that the growth process is stochastically determined. Chance, it is argued, is the major factor in explaining the pattern of expansion. In 1931 R. Gibrat proposed that this type of model may be relevant to companies. (12) There is an enormous range of factors which affect company growth. These vary from factors within the control of individual firms, such as the range of products and the quality of management, to factors beyond their control, such as the activities of rivals and political upheavals. On balance, the effect over time may be that the pattern of growth is such that the probability distribution is the same for all companies of all sizes. In effect, then, it is implied that proportionate change in the size of firms is independent of their absolute size, or that the probability of the proportionate change in size during a specific period, is the same for all firms regardless of their size.

The lack of association between size and growth seems to establish what has become known as Gibrat's Law or the Law of Proportionate Effect. However, this lack of association does not in reality establish the working of the law. There could be a complex relationship which has not been identified by the statistical tests. Or, more pertinently, there are requirements of the law which do not appear to hold in practice. If the growth of firms is determined by chance and the probability of growth is independent of the size of firms, this would imply two things: first, firms of different size would have the same average growth rate, and second, the dispersion of growth rates about the average would be the same for all sizes. (13) In a study of approximately 450 companies quoted in the United Kingdom (in the food, clothing and footwear, shipbuilding and non-electrical engineering and tobacco industries), it has been found that one of the requirements is not met. (14) The average growth rates in different-sized classes are on the whole very similar to each other, but dispersions of growth rates are not. In statistical terms the dispersion of growth rates is expressed in standard deviations. Larger companies tend to have lower standard deviations. Variations in growth rates tend to decline with the increasing size of companies. Thus although there is no positive association between the rate of growth and size, Gibrat's Law or the Law of Proportionate Effect appears not to apply. There is a tendancy for growth to become more 'uniform' as size increases.

There must be some advantages of larger size to provide motivation for company growth. Growth means companies of larger size, and the faster growth is, the more quickly will any advantages be realised. But what tangible form do these advantages take? The arguments so far advanced suggest that large companies should enjoy enhanced profitability and growth. Neither of these propositions has been supported by the facts. Instead there is a greater degree of 'uniformity' of growth rates. In addition it has been found that profitability exhibits a similar pattern. (15) As company size increases, the dispersion of profit rates decreases. There are some indications, although weak, that the profitability of companies may even decline with increased size. (16) Effectively there may be a trade-off between lower profit rates and the higher security of these earnings. Statistically these findings are not well established, but they may well be of some economic importance. Thus large size may tend to be associated with more 'uniform' growth and more 'certain' profit rates. As size increases, activities are diversified across many industries and growth proceeds in a more even fashion. Changes in market fortune and sales outlets appear to balance out within overall performance. Investment leading to growth is less dependent on

B. M.P.M.E.

the success of single markets, so that large size offers increased security of profits and growth. The actual size at which these advantages begin to accrue is of course extremely difficult to identify. Nevertheless it has been found that, in a large sample, firms with net assets of more than £1 million in the period 1948-54, and with assets of more than £500,000 in the period 1954-60, have an appreciably greater uniformity of growth rates than firms below this size. (17)

A convenient way of summarising the evidence is to say that the expected advantages of size are not realised in an obvious way. Overall, there is no positive correlation between either size and growth or size and profitability. Large size may confer greater security in terms of lower fluctuations in industrial performance, but large size does not automatically generate improved profits or growth. For improved profits and growth there must be management skill and motivation, and also future market opportunities. Thus from the point of view of the aims of the present study an important point emerges: large size is no panacea for enhanced growth. This comes from other factors. Of course, large firms are very important in the economy. Major firms are often trend-setters in their industries. Their growth will greatly affect expectations in those industries. Research and development benefits from large industrial units which have profits which are large and stable enough to support viable research and development programmes. Even so, the point is made. From a policy angle, improved economic growth will not necessarily result from creating large industrial units. Advantages of size are only potentials. They will only be realised if the energy, skill and know-how of management and workpeople are deployed to commercial effect.

There is a mixture of relief and concern at these findings. Relief comes from the lack of association between size and growth and the weak nature of the evidence suggesting that profitability and size are negatively related. Apparently there is no such thing as an optimum-sized firm. Size may increase without significant penalty either to growth or profitability. Of course there may still be an optimum for *plant* sizes, determined by technical production characteristics, but there is no reason why this should apply to firms. Firms are units which organise, co-ordinate and control plants. They are not necessarily subject to the same forces which specify plant size. If there is no such thing as an optimum-sized firm, this implies that companies are unlikely to be constrained in their growth performance by becoming too large. Growth necessitates an increase in size. If there were an optimum size for firms, then growth would ultimately be constrained as this is reached. A negative association between growth and size would be revealed if enough companies were at this stage. Of course this pattern may be disguised, if only a few companies are near the optimum. However, as much of the data for the studies has been drawn from United States data, where firms have achieved greater size than in Britain, this suggests that in practice there is no optimum-sized firm. Thus public concern for continuing and faster company growth does not appear to be at variance with the economic facts of life. Apparently there is no practical limit to the size of firms.

Concern at the results arises on three grounds. Firstly, that the motivation for growth may be dampened once large size is achieved. Secondly, that cross-subsidisation of activities within diversified firms may continue to the detriment of resource allocation. Thirdly, that large firms may make a smaller contribution to national growth than a number of separate firms which in aggregate are equivalent to the large ones. The large firms' motivation to grow may be damped, once the advantages of size are achieved. Once increased security of earnings and stability of growth is realised, management's urge to grow may be lessened. Only if commercial results are continually challenged will motivation remain high. Large firms are almost always highly diversified. This gives them great powers of survival. Effectively, the allocation mechanism operates with less force on these concerns. Successful projects may offset failures. Cross-subsidisation of activities may mean that only when a large proportion of activities becomes unsuccessful will commercial survival be at stake. Large diversified firms may therefore be the vehicles of mediocrity. Their less good ventures, instead of being strictly disciplined by the market, may instead continue almost indefinitely, because the overall results achieved by the corporation are not determined by them alone. Effectively a change in these sections of activities becomes discretionary. They do not have to change for the better. Nothing has to be done so long as there are other ventures doing well. The pressure of the market is softened. Decision-making within such institutions may thus lose its commercial purpose. Resource allocation may suffer and so also may growth and profit potential. The remaining worry is also related to growth and profit potential. The economic performance of large firms should be compared with what *might* have been achieved by a smaller number of firms which, in aggregate, are equivalent to the large ones.

There should be concern that the overall use of assets may be better in a different form of organisation. The effort to which large companies go to simulate the autonomy of small companies, in the organisation of their sub-sidiaries, suggests that this is considered a very real problem. Inevitably they cannot fully emulate the commercial pressure which is present in a small concern. Local autonomy will be constrained within certain limits. Rules of action will only be rules, rather than axioms of necessity. The existence of group resources are bound to cushion any changes caused by a local reversal of fortune. Of course it is admitted that large-sized firms may confer very considerable benefits. Increased stability of results may allow a more rational investment programme and a larger research and development effort. However, the grounds for concern expressed above may be real. An all-out policy to create large firms may carry dangers and these should be appreciated.

4 Finance and Growth

Sources of finance to promote growth are current earnings, the proceeds from the sale of assets not required for present operation, and outside or 'external' moneys raised from shareholders, private individuals and institutions. These sources are strongly influenced by the legal status of companies, their size, past record, gearing and future prospects. For example, non-quoted companies may not offer their shares for sale to the general public. Therefore external sources of finance tend to be rather restricted. Placings may be arranged through brokers for shares, but such companies may not use the more usual procedures of public issues or offers for sale. (1) By and large, of course, non-quoted companies tend to be small, and so do not usually require sums sufficiently large to warrant the use of normal Stock Exchange mechanisms. However, as the number of shareholders is restricted by law to not less than two and not more than fifty, issues to members of the companies may provide a very limited source of external capital. Coming away from the special problems of the non-quoted companies, all concerns are competing for capital and thus have to justify their use of it. Without a good past record of profitability, all forms of capital will be severely limited. Retentions of profit will not yield large sums, and shareholders will be unwilling to lend liberally on the basis of a poor rate of return in the past. Absolute size is also important. Large companies will have more assets to offer as security for loans, and their very size is some indication of commercial success in the past.

The various sources of money capital to United Kingdom quoted companies have been thoroughly examined for the years from 1948 to 1953, and compared with the uses to which these funds have been put. (2) It emerged that retained profits were the most important source of funds to companies. The self-financing ratio which relates net savings to net investment over the period 1948-53 was about two-thirds. The smaller quoted companies tended to be rather more self-financing. Those up to £250,000 in size financed about four-fifths of their activities out of their own resources. Faster-growing companies, however, tended to be less self-financing and made more use of the new-issue market. (3)

Further studies for the years following 1953 reveal that retained profits remained by far the most important source of funds for quoted companies. (4) Smaller and non-quoted business companies still tend to be more self-financing than their public quoted counterparts. For example, one study (5) found that about one-third of non-quoted companies were almost completely self-financing. (6) The form in which finance was raised was also different from public quoted companies. There was a noticeably greater use of hire-purchase finance, directors' loans and leasings. (7) More pertinently, however, the faster-growing companies were also less self-financing. (8) Thus the evidence of the various studies available adds weight to the plausible hypothesis that the faster the rate of growth, the less self-financing companies become. Firms' very ambition may force them to seek outside finance. Effectively, therefore, the explanation for different companies achieving different degrees of self-finance, lies in their different propensities to invest and their legal status.

The relationship between growth and the use of outside funds is low and positive. 'Growth influences the extent to which external financing is used; apparently some relationship exists but this relationship provides for less than a total explanation of inter-industry differences in the use of outside money.' (9) To meet market demand or advance the plans of management, ambitious firms borrow ahead of their internally generated funds. The statistical evidence on the growth of the firms and the use of external funds suggests, however, that this tendency is not so strong as to amount to a 'rule' of growth. Analysis of a sample of United States companies on an industry basis has revealed a correlation coefficient between growth and external finance of 0.30. (10) Although fast-growing industries include slow-growing companies, similar results apply on an individual firm basis. According to one calculation relating to the years from 1948 to 1960, this was found to be so. The relationship between growth and the use of internal funds was such that $r = -0.35$. (11) There was a tendency for faster growth to be associated with proportionally less use of internal funds. External funds become of greater importance as firm growth increases. If the relationships had been very strong, this would have indicated that so many firms follow the pattern that, effectively, external funds would be obligatory to high growth. Not surprisingly this is not the case. Companies vary greatly in their liquidity positions. Some companies have considerable funds available for growth, others are constrained, perhaps by a previous burst of growth. Thus there is a tendency, rather than a uniform pattern, for companies to rely on external funds when high growth is required. It has been said that 'the faster the rate of growth of the firm, the less likely is it that financing can be achieved from internal sources'. (12) Ambitious firms cast their net wider than the funds available from retained profits. They make considerable use of capital issues to raise these external funds. Effectively, therefore, ordinary unambitious companies exhibit a bias in favour of internal funds, unless they are strongly motivated to do otherwise. Fast-growing firms tend to be so motivated. For example, between 1948 and 1953 about three-quarters of the very fast-growing companies (net assets increased by over 100 per cent) made capital issues, compared with about one-third for all companies. (13) These issues represented over two-fifths of their growth in net assets, compared with just over one-quarter for all companies. Specific reasons for this overall bias in favour of internal funds are given below in the section covering distribution policy.

Further investigation has added considerable weight to the argument that fast-growing companies tend to use external funds to a greater extent than their more staid counterparts. The simple correlation coefficients cited above suffer from the disadvantage that a relationship between any two indicators may be caused by an association with a third variable. No conclusion may be drawn about any *independent* association between indicators of company performance, based on simple correlation coefficients alone. A more powerful statistical technique is required to identify any genuine link which is not a result of a common association with another indicator. One such technique is partial correlation. This has been used to calculate the partial correlation coefficent, or first-order correlation coefficient, between growth and internal financing, with profitability held constant. (14)

Both the internal use of finance and the growth of companies are correlated reasonably strongly with profitability. Thus the simple correlation coefficient between growth and the use of internal funds may be a result of the common association with profitability. The partial correlation coefficient between growth and the internal use of funds, with profitability held constant, is the simple correlation coefficient between the residuals from the linear regression equation relating growth to profitability, and the residuals from the linear regression equation relating the internal use of funds to profitability. This may be interpreted as the simple correlation between the two variables with profitability held constant. In this way any independent association between the indicators is identified. In the case of growth and internal finance, the first-order correlation coefficient, with profitability held constant, is -0.68 for all the industries concerned. (15) This means that there is a tendency for fast growth to be associated with a proportionately decreasing use of internal funds, when profitability is held constant in this sense.

Another interesting feature of fast-growing companies is the tendency for the retention ratio to increase. As expansion proceeds, these companies exhibit a pattern, albeit weak, for retained profits to increase as a proportion of retained profits plus ordinary dividends. The simple correlation coefficient between the retention ratio and growth is 0.25. (16) Fast-growing companies are so 'capital hungry' that they tend both to retain a larger proportion of profits and also to raise more external finance than slow growers. In this instance the partial correlation coefficient between growth and the retention ratio, with profitability held constant, is 0.18. (17) Admittedly this is weak, but by industry over the two sub-periods covered, the sign of the regression coefficients is always positive, and moreover individual industries have values which are considerably higher than the overall figure. Again specific reasons will be given in the chapter on distribution policy, explaining how fast-growing companies are able to retain a higher proportion of their profits without alienating shareholders.

For any individual company there are a number of strategic decisions which have to be made in order to obtain finance. The company's management must decide on the best form in which to raise capital and how to improve growth without jeopardising the liquidity position of the concern. These decisions are often summarised in one question, namely, what is the optimal finance function? This may relate to a number of desirable ends, such as maximising the flow of funds or maximising the capital value of shares. To achieve the chosen ends, there are a number of variables about which managers must make decisions. For instance, what is the appropriate level of gearing or how much of profits should be distributed? These are the sorts of decisions which concern management in the pursuit of the aims in view. They are important because they affect such issues as the marketability of shares, the liquidity of current operations and the sources of finance. For convenience, the specific problem of the level of distributions will be dealt with later. The remaining items covered by the term 'financing mix' will be discussed now.

An element of gearing or leverage may significantly reduce the cost of capital. Gearing is the fixed-interest element in the total issued capital of a company. Debenture interest in the United Kingdom is deductible as an expense against corporation tax (preference interest is not). Potential holders of fixed-interest stocks may be prepared to pay more for a unit of such capital because it is regarded as safer than ordinary shares. As a prior charge on a company this capital is more senior, and in the event of liquidation it is paid off before the ordinary shares. If it is issued shrewdly, this may increase the earnings on the equity shares. For example, debentures or preference shares may be issued at 7 per cent, while 20 per cent may be earned by the company on the capital raised in this way. The 13 per cent difference is available for the equity shares. Debenture and preference capital have the further advantage that it normally involves no alteration in the voting rights. Debentures have no voting rights. Preference shares have these only under certain circumstances, for example when their dividend is in arrears or where the Articles of Association make specific provision. (18) Also if stock is issued with a definite redemption period and there is inflation between issue and redemption, the real value of the debt will be significantly reduced by the time of maturity. All of these reasons suggest that it will be to a company's advantage to have at least some gearing. However, gearing may carry its dangers. If too high a proportion of any profit earned is pre-empted for the fixed-interest securities, then the position of the equity shareholders deteriorates. Too large a share of profits must be used to pay the senior capital, so that the ordinary dividend is reduced or may have to be omitted altogether. Should the value of the ordinary shares consequently fall too much on the Stock Exchange, a take-over may follow and control pass to others. Thus there may be an 'appropriate' level of gearing or leverage, and this is likely to be somewhere between the following limits. The lower limit is set by the desire to reduce capital costs, and the upper limit by the desire to avoid loss of control of the company. (19)

The appropriate level of gearing or leverage may vary significantly between fast- and slow-growing companies. It may also vary widely between industries which are risky and those which are safe. Firms which are likely to face large fluctuations in profits would be unwise to adopt as high a percentage of prior-charge capital as companies in comparatively safe and stable industries. It is not unusual for fixed-interest securities to be of the form where unpaid charges accumulate against future profits. Thus a severe downturn in profits may constrain the future operation of such companies by generating a debt against future revenue. The actual level of gearing may be measured in a number of ways:

1. <u>Nominal value of fixed-interest securities</u>
    Nominal value of total issued capital

2. <u>Fixed-interest payments</u>
      Total profits

3. As (1) above, but the nominal value of fixed-interest securities has liquid assets deducted. (20)

Liquid assets (being cash and near cash) are deducted from the third measure, because they amount to negative gearing. In other words they could be used to pay off fixed-interest securities. In practice shareholders probably measure gearing in the second way. To them, any downturn in profits represents an increase in gearing and so is likely to lead to a downward adjustment in share values because holders feel relatively less covered. A further factor likely to be relevant to gearing is the absolute size of companies and the form in which they hold their tangible fixed assets. A large company is more likely to be able to attract fixed-interest shareholders simply because it is better known and has more security to offer. Moreover, if much of productive assets are in property, land and buildings, this will have a high resale value compared with most fixed industrial equipment, whose value in alternative uses is low.

Experience supports this reasoning. 'Reliance on debentures is on the whole a feature of large and stable companies whose financial status is such that they can raise money at or near gilt-edged rates.' (21) But not all investigators have found a link between size and gearing. (22) It is probably not so much size alone which affects gearing, but stability of earnings. The emphasis in the quotation above is thus on 'large and stable' companies. Where earnings are not stable and commercial uncertainty high, gearing is likely to be low. Gearing appears to reflect the degree of risk involved. For example, in the cotton textile industry, which is considered 'risky', ordinary shares account for a high proportion of issued capital. In the brewing industry, on the other hand, gearing tends to be high. (23) The industry's profits tend not to fluctuate widely, and property has a high resale value and is an important proportion of fixed assets. Family control has also been an important feature of ownership. Debentures do not reduce the extent of control and thus tend to be favoured in such industries. Chapted 12 gives figures for quoted companies and also explains further measures of gearing.

Growth industries which face considerable risk are unlikely to be highly geared. When growth has taken place, and the industry's future becomes less uncertain, the situation may change. It has been said that 'where lies the risk there the control lies also'. (24) The capital structure of Independent Television provides an example of this principle in operation. In the early years operations were almost entirely equity-financed. Later, when success had been achieved and the industry became established, more gearing was adopted. However, in some industries which are regarded as both progressive and risky the accounts do not reveal low gearing. For example, in the electronics, chemical and aircraft industries gearing does not vary much from the normal. The reasons may be partly economic and partly statistical.

. The chief economic reason is that growth industries are not necessarily in risky activities. Furthermore growth and commercial success may enable companies to organise their activities on a broad base. This may reduce the effect of fluctuations in particular activities. The greater regularity of income may make such companies attractive to the purchasers of fixed-interest securities. If so the companies concerned may enjoy all the benefits of a normal level of gearing in spite of considerable interests in 'risky' fields.

The chief statistical reason arises from the classification of industries, which may obscure the position of the growth sectors. Industry-wide classification is such that many individual companies may not operate wholly within the industry concerned. Any relationship between gearing and growth may be disguised because of the wide variety of companies and activities included within the industries. Even so, the particular industrial environment probably has a significant effect. For example, 'the lower gearing ratios in engineering may be due to the more cyclical nature of demand and profits in the industry which makes fixed-interest obligations inadvisable'. (25) But to class the electronics, chemicals and aircraft industries as high-growth and risky, and then expect lower gearing ratios, is to generalise too far. A uniform pattern is unlikely to be exhibited when gearing is subject to these statistical and economic influences. Much the best approach is to examine the position of individual firms. Fast-growing companies are likely to incur greater risks than more staid concerns. To some extent this logic is established by the relationship between the level of gearing and the rate of growth of *individual* companies. The higher the rate of growth of individual firms, the lower tends to be the level of gearing. The association is not strong, however. The correlation coefficients are of the order of − 0.32. (26)

The association is not strong, for the simple reason that high growth is not necessarily linked with large profit fluctuations and high risk. Were this the case, even a normal level of gearing would be too high. Nevertheless there is some tendency, however weak, for high growth to be associated with a level of risk which managements and shareholders regard as higher than usual. At any rate, a sufficient number of firms act as if this were the case. Approximately 10 per cent of the variation in the use of fixed-interest securities may be statistically accounted for by variations in the growth rate. Linking the two properties exhibited by fast-growing companies, namely the tendency to use less fixed-interest securities and more external finance, gives some indication of the form this finance will take. If gearing is reduced and yet more external funds are used, then the latter are likely to be raised through the issue of equities. For what are deemed to be risk situations, such a bias is to be expected.

Company decisions concerning the financing mix must also take account of the preservation of liquidity. Unless operations are managed wisely, companies may find themselves in a dilemma: business may be expanding, overall profitability rising, and yet, in the short term, there may be insufficient cash and liquid assets to meet all current liabilities due. Technically such companies could be made bankrupt. This particular problem may be acute especially for companies which are growing fast. Companies often have to sell on credit to customers, and as a widely quoted investigation has found, growth usually necessitates the granting of additional net trade credit to customers. (27) Hence the amounts received as credit by growing companies tend to be less than the amounts granted. For the static, non-growing companies, however, trade credit received may be greater than trade credit granted, so this will be a source of funds. A grant of credits equal to one-tenth of net assets would normally be regarded as substantial. Very fast-growing companies, however, often have to give much more credit. In their case more than one-quarter of net assets were involved. These fast-growing companies also tended to have large bank overdrafts and to be highly illiquid at the end of the period investigated. Presumably bank overdrafts were secured to help cover the granting of trade credit, and the net effect was that the companies became highly illiquid. Thus it would appear that commercial success in the form of high growth may carry a considerable risk. Companies may find themselves in the position of effectively having to grant trade credit to improve sales. In consequence, when turnover rises they have to find additional finance.

If additional finance is found in the form of short-term funds such as bank overdrafts the liquidity of the firm may suffer. Current liabilities, or money lent to the firm on short notice, may be larger than current assets, thus putting management in a vulnerable position. Technically, the 'quick assets' ratio may suffer. This ratio relates current assets, minus stocks and work in progress, to current liabilities. The result is a better measure of the liquidity position of a firm than a straight comparison of current assets with current liabilities, because stocks and work in progress will not generate cash until they are actually sold. Therefore to count them as freely available to meet current liabilities is not altogether realistic.

Although correlation analysis has not revealed any significant tendency for high growth to be associated with either decreasing liquidity or a tendency to grant increasing amounts of net trade credit, the absence of such statistical correlation does not disprove the importance of the financial problems imposed by growth. (28) If increasing sales necessitate the granting of more trade credit, then funds tied up here are not available for other functions. Growth could be constrained. Rather than risk liquidity problems, firms may deliberately limit expansion. Alternatively, the lack of association between growth and decreasing liquidity may merely indicate that fast-expanding companies have been successful in controlling these financial problems. Other firms may have been constrained and thus remain amongst the plodders. More specifically, the results may be due to the industrial composition of whatever sample is investigated. Trade credit given and received varies considerably from industry to industry. Some of the variations are probably due to the different customs and traditions in different industries and even within industries. Other variations may perhaps be explained by reference to the position of industries in the chain of production. For example, suppliers of intermediate goods are more likely to have to extend larger amounts of net trade credit than companies retailing actual finished goods to the final consumer. To achieve expansion in industries such as wholesale distribution, building and contracting, electrical engineering and iron and steel is likely to involve extending substantial net trade credit. For other industries, such as clothing and footwear, food and retail distribution, growth may not carry a similar obligation. In their cases sales tend to be made for spot cash and credit received for stocks of goods. The pattern of credit behaviour tends to vary from industry to industry. The granting of net trade credit is not necessarily a function of expansion. The fast-growing firm will not always be obliged to extend net trade credit. This is partly influenced by current practice in the activity concerned, and also by the companies' skill in managing finance. Even within industries which, by tradition, grant large amounts of net trade credit, growth may not imply a deteriorating liquidity position. Companies may be successful in controlling the unfavourable tendencies.

There are ways of avoiding decreasing liquidity and the consequent constraint on growth. One of these escapes is to use external sources of finance. This implies a substitution of long-term funds for short-term debt. As already pointed out, there is some tendency for fast-growing companies to do this. They use capital issues to finance a higher proportion of their growth than do staid concerns. Another is to improve cash generation. This may well happen with growth and thus counter-balance the increasing volume of funds that may be committed in the form of trade credit. As will be explained later, high growth is usually associated with high profitability, so that the undesirable financial effects may be mitigated. 'Firms whose growth is constrained by the available supply of internal funds normally have low or falling profits. . . .' (29) As the major source of funds, profits play a key role. Good profits provide a borrowing base. Poor profits limit companies' ability to seek outside funds.

Yet another way to side-step liquidity problems, which is much used in the United States, is factoring. Essentially the problem of a successful company is to avoid the liquidity consequences of having to supply goods to distributors ahead of sales. Factoring enables companies to do this. By selling their commercial debt of 'accounts receivable' to a merchant for spot cash, the lag in the generation of cash between supply and sale is thus eradicated. The merchant now becomes responsible for the collection of debts. There is, of course, a charge for this service, and this usually takes the form of a discount on the face value of the debt. In principle the operation is very similar to taking out a bill of exchange. The process enables the seller of the goods to get immediate cash. The effect on a growing company could be very marked. The cash realised is available for other purposes. A greater rate of turnover may now be financed with the same quantity of cash. Most factoring is done on a non-recourse basis, which means that any bad debt becomes the liability of the factor. There is no 'recourse' to the firm that originally sold the article. Thus firms may no longer be so immediately concerned with the bad debts of their customers. This risk is carried by the factor. In export markets this form of insurance for the sellers has advantages. Sometimes the identity of the factor is not disclosed. (30) If so, this is known as undisclosed factoring. The advantage of such an arrangement is that the goodwill between firms and customers is preserved. Customers have no knowledge of the identity of the agent who is collecting the accounts. Typical charges for the factoring range from 10 to 15 per cent according to Bank Rate and the bad debt record of firms' customers. This is relatively cheap when it is set against the savings in other costs. For example, bank overdrafts are presumably reduced and thus bank charges as well. The factor does the invoicing, and so firms' paper-handling departments involved with credit control, sales accounting and collection may now be reduced or still cope when sales are very much larger. Fairly large turnovers are required by factors before they are prepared to accept business. Naturally they will not accept specific sections of firms' business where bad debt is high. Minimum turnover required is usually of the order of £100,000. Effectively, therefore, this is a service not available to the smallest firms.

Factoring is not used at present by many companies in the United Kingdom, but nevertheless is quickly achieving recognition. Such a device for releasing cash has, however, an obvious attraction to firms who have already found their growth performance constrained by liquidity problems. More important, many firms may have maintained a slow rate of growth because of fear of such liquidity difficulties. Once this device becomes more widely known, then one constraint on their potential growth may be lifted. Finance may no longer be an active limit to growth and thus overall performance may be raised. Hence there are likely to be benefits from the rapid acceptance of the principle involved, namely, the sale of commercial debt to an agent. Basically this amounts to more specialisation. Firms are no longer so concerned with the collection of debt, whether at home or overseas. This would be left to the factor.

In a way factoring is a minor form of merchanting. The traditional British merchants fulfilled the intermediary function. They acquired ownership over goods produced by a large number of small firms, and then sold the goods to distributors the world over. With the growth of large business units, covering both production and distribution, this role declined. A revival of this intermediary function might help firms with their growth problems. Factoring concentrates largely on debt collection. Merchanting has a somewhat wider function. Both of these arrangements release significant sums of finance for alternative uses by companies. In this way they may make a contribution to growth.

5 Dividend Policy

Distribution policy is part of the finance function. Managements make explicit decisions about the level of dividends to be paid to shareholders. These decisions have a direct influence on the liquidity of companies and the quantity of finance available for expansion. It has been said that 'pay-out, under an ideal dividend policy in a growth situation, should not exceed the minimum amount necessary to maintain the market position and integrity of existing debt and equity issues and of issues contemplated in the near future'. (1) Companies concerned to grow must respect shareholders, preserve the market position of their shares, service existing debt and adjust dividend policy to potential issues of capital.

The actual level of dividend payments must be within certain limits. The upper limit is set by the current investment needs of the firm; the more it pays out in dividends, the less it has left for plough-back. The lower limit is set by future investment needs; a firm that pays no dividend at all would retain all internal funds for investment, but would prejudice the market for its shares and also the prospect of obtaining external funds later on. Somewhere between these limits lies an appropriate policy.

Shareholders require a reward for holding the shares of a particular company as opposed to those of any other. This reward may take the form of a dividend payment and/or capital gains. Whether the payment is for risk-taking, sacrifice of personal liquidity or to compensate for a time preference in favour of present consumption, is of small practical concern. More important in the present context may be that managements are aware that a change in ownership may involve a change in management. There is always the possibility of a take-over when market values of ordinary shares are low. To prevent this, management will try to ensure an adequate market value by paying acceptable dividends. What constitutes an 'acceptable' dividend varies with the extent to which there is a trade-off between potential capital gains and current dividends, and with the payments made by other concerns. Some companies, with an excellent growth record, may pay a small dividend. This low pay-out is compensated for by the prospect of good capital gains. Others, without such a record, may pay more generously and thus also secure reasonable immunity from take-over. Of course, companies which are very closely controlled or non-quoted will not be so concerned with the level of dividends. Even so, the opportunity cost of holding shares in such companies will mean that there is a reward of some kind inducing continuing loyalty. This may take the form of commercial independence, power, wages and so on. For example, it was found in the Small Firm Survey that over half of the companies in the sample paid no dividend, and a further one-fifth of companies paid dividends equivalent to less than 30 per cent of net profits. These figures do not illustrate thriftiness, but rather the high proportion of profits taken out as income by directors. (2)

It is arguable that investors should not prefer dividends to retained earnings, since 'retained earnings can be regarded as equivalent to a fully subscribed, pre-emptive issue of common stock'. (3) In other words ordinary shareholders should regard ploughed-back profits as a fully paid-up issue whose benefits are earmarked for them. Retained earnings are used for plough-back, thus increasing the asset backing for the equity shares and also, it is assumed, the trading strength of companies. However, in practice ordinary shareholders appear to prefer dividends to retained earnings. (4) Dividends are capitalised at a much higher rate than undistributed profits. In other words a unit of dividends has a greater effect on share prices than a unit of undistributed profits. Furthermore variations in the last declared dividend, per share, explain a considerable variation in corresponding share prices. There is a reasonably strong positive correlation between the dividend return on equity assets and what is called the valuation ratio. Dividend on equity assets is dividends gross of tax as a per-centage of the average assets attributable to the ordinary shares (5) The valuation ratio is a measure of the stock market rating of companies' ordinary shares in relation to the book value of the corresponding assets. The value of the ordinary shares on the market is related to the book value of the equity assets as in the accounts. The more highly priced are a company's ordinary shares, the higher will be the valuation ratio. The correlation indicates that companies which pay a high dividend in relation to the book value of equity assets have, by and large, a high valuation ratio.

The question arises as to why the level of dividend payments should affect share prices and, furthermore, why variations in share prices should be associated with variations in dividend. Share prices are affected by dividends for a number of reasons. The current level of payment is often taken as a signal of manage-ments' views on future company prospects. A change in the level of payment may alter investors' expectations about the future and effectively change the risk class of the shares. An actual reduction in dividends, made to increase retentions and the present value of future dividends, may cause a downward revision in the current share price. Shareholders' time preference for current consumption may operate against such a substitution of future for present income. In addition a difference between tax rates on income and capital gains may affect shareholders' valuation of current income in the form of dividends. (6)

The generally accepted view that ordinary shareholders value dividends more highly than retained earnings has been questioned. (7) The argument is that the various studies made contain a number of biases, which arise from the variables omitted or assumed constant, and also from the weight given to extreme observations by the regression procedure, random variations of income, measurement problems and problems of causation. Examples of omitted variables or of variables which are assumed constant are risk and expectations. 'In view of what we know about managerial desire to avoid dividend cuts, it certainly seems logical to expect that companies facing greater uncertainty about future profit performance would adopt lower current dividend pay-out as a means of hedging the risk of being forced to cut their dividends. Thus high risk may result in both low pay-out and low price—earnings ratios, whereas low risk may result in high pay-out and high price—earnings ratios. Consequently omission of a risk variable from the regression equation could conceivably impart a substantial upward bias to the dividend coefficient, depending upon both the extent to which risk varies between companies and the strength of risk in determining current pay-out.' (8)

Regression weighting may also bias the results. Extreme observations tend to be important in determining the value of the correlations. These extreme observations may be those where high dividends and high share prices are typical. Random variations in company income may bias results in favour of dividend pay-out influences. This may happen where share prices are related to normal rather than currently reported income. Income measurement errors could have the effect of biasing the measurement of retained earnings in a downward direction.

Finally there may be dual causation. Dividends may affect share prices and share prices dividends, so that conclusions based on one-way causality may misrepresent the role of dividends. Attention has been drawn also to the peculiarity of the behavioural assumptions, implied by a state of affairs where a unit of dividend has a much greater influence on ordinary share prices than a unit of retained earnings. (9) Firstly a market reaction of this sort implies that investors have a strong preference for a current income at the margins of their portfolios. Secondly, shareholders view the expected increase in earnings from plough-back as involving greater risk than at present incurred on corporate assets. Thirdly, from a shareholder's viewpoint the profitability of additional company investment is considered low, compared with yields available on assets of other companies in the stock market.

These behavioural assumptions may be at variance with observed market behaviour. Shareholders may favour capital gains to income (10) if they have a stronger preference for future gains than for current income. This preference may be caused by, or reinforced by, a potential tax advantage, as long as realised long-term capital gains are taxed at a lower rate than the standard rate on income charged on dividends. Where surtax is paid on dividends, the difference is, of course, more evident. Marginal profit rates in a number of industries appear quite high, and therefore additional company investment ought to be attractive to shareholders.

As a result of these behavioural assumptions and the possible statistical biases, it is alleged that there is an error in the studies showing shareholders' preference for dividends. When an attempt is made to correct for the biases, the resulting conclusions do not bear out the customary view. This is that a unit of dividend has considerably more impact on share prices than a unit of retained earnings. There is some indication that in non-growth industries as a whole a somewhat (but only moderate) higher investor valuation may be placed on dividends than on retained earnings within the range of pay-out experienced, but that the opposite may be true in growth industries. The difference in behaviour between growth and non-growth industries probably relates to the advantages to be gained from plough-back. Growth industries are, on the whole, relatively profit-able, and therefore retentions should enhance share prices because the internal return is greater than the minimum rate required by shareholders. Non-growth industries, on the other hand, can 'purchase' shareholder loyalty with larger pay-outs. These conclusions are tenuous, because of the limited coverage of industries and time periods studied. Further research is required to modify the established position that dividends have a considerable effect on ordinary share prices. Nevertheless, some doubt has been cast on the currently held belief in the predominant effect of dividends on share prices.

Management may believe that shareholders value dividends more highly than retained earnings, and yet ploughed-back profits or retentions remain the largest single source of funds. There is an apparent contradiction and this must now be dealt with. Presumably it would benefit companies to pay large dividends and recoup funds via issues. If this is not always done, the reason must lie mainly with managements' attitude to external finance and other general constraints on dividend policy.

There are disadvantages in raising capital from shareholders. Shares are issued in exchange for funds. If shares carry voting rights, there may be a change in the balance of control. Major shareholders may not have the money to take up their 'rights', in which case their voting power will suffer a relative decline. (11) Even if the new shares do not carry voting rights, there is still a problem. The exercise is basically an exchange of a lump sum of current funds from shareholders for the future expectation of dividends from the company; thus in raising capital, companies are creating an explicit future obligation. This normally amounts to at least maintaining the old rate of dividend on the increased number of shares. Effectively, therefore, companies are expected by shareholders to match the level of profit which has already been achieved per £100 invested. There may be a short period, when the new shares do not rank for dividends, in order to give management time to employ the new funds. In contrast, retaining funds from profits does not create an explicit obligation. The number of shares remains the same; management does not have a larger number of shares on which an accepted dividend is expected, so that even if the capital ploughed back is not employed very successfully, the current rate of dividend is unlikely to be cut. Effectively, therefore, the ambitious and successful companies are the ones most likely to employ external funds. This has already been established earlier. By offering shares to members at a price, companies are subjecting themselves to the vetting procedure of the market. Shareholders are faced with an immediate decision whether to take up the shares or renounce them. Price movements, following the announcement of a rights issue, then reflect a summary of the weight of market opinion on the terms and prospects of the issue. In addition to creating extra obligations on future earnings, raising capital on the market involves costs which are not incurred when profits are merely ploughed back. Details of the issue must be printed, shareholders circularised, and underwriting expenses may be involved.

Fast-growing companies tend to combine two features: they tend to use more external finance, and they tend to retain a greater proportion of their disposable profits. After paying tax, meeting depreciation and the interest on prior-charge capital, they are able to retain a higher proportion of the remaining profits to plough-back. One crucial question is how such companies are able to do this without unfavourable implications for dividends. There seem to be three possible explanations. Firstly, it may be that ordinary shareholders are prepared to accept lower dividends and thus permit a higher retention ratio because of the favourable prospects of future capital gain. Secondly, growing companies may be able to pay dividends which match those of other companies and yet represent a smaller proportion of disposable profits, because they may have a lower level of gearing and therefore less total revenue pre-empted for fixed-interest securities. Thirdly, they may be able to pay matching or even higher dividends because their profits are greater than other companies'. This third explanation is probably the most important. As will be shown later, growth and profitability are fairly strongly related. In addition, growth and dividend return on equity assets are also associated. The correlation coefficient between the level of dividend pay-out on equity assets and growth is 0.34. (12) This association, however, almost certainly arises from a common link of both the variables with profitability. When the data are tested for any association independent of the effect of profitability, the results are for the most part not significant. Where they are significant, a weak tendency is indicated that with profitability held constant, dividends on equity assets are reduced with increasing growth. (13) In effect, growing companies are able to pay higher dividends because of their superior commercial performance. Only if all companies made the same level of profits, would higher retentions imply a low level of dividends. Shareholders in growing companies do not necessarily have to accept lower levels of dividends than those obtainable elsewhere, even in exchange for good prospects of capital gain. Such companies tend to have good profit records and are therefore able to retain a higher proportion of their profits and still pay acceptable dividends.

Other considerations also affect dividend policy. For convenience of exposition, these are put into three groups of associated causes: firstly, gearing and the nature of the industry; secondly, the nature of the assets, depreciation, and taxation; and thirdly, the general philosophy of dividend payments. These will be dealt with in order.

First, the value of payments to the fixed-interest capital affects the level of dividends paid to the ordinary shares. As prior charges, debentures and preference shares are paid before the ordinary. Thus it would appear that the higher the gearing, the lower is likely to be the percentage appropriation of income to the equity or ordinary shares. This does not follow, however, because gearing is to some extent related to the nature of the industry concerned, as is distribution policy. For example, in brewing, where gearing is high, so also is the allocation to dividends. (14) In contrast gearing in cotton textiles is low, and so is the dividend pay-out. Brewing is a relatively stable industry. Profitability does not fluctuate widely. There is no great obsolescence problem in keeping up to date with machinery. In cotton textiles, on the other hand, profitability is generally low and fluctuates widely. Obsolescence of machinery is also a greater problem. For these reasons appropriations to ordinary shares tend to be a small percentage. In general, dividend policy seems to be related to industrial requirements. (15) It is determined by the whole trading environment surrounding companies and industries.

The second group of causes concerns the nature of assets, depreciation, inflation and taxation. The brewing industry has been particularly favoured. Because of the nature of a large part of the assets, replacement-cost depreciation is not necessarily appropriate. Land and buildings are exceedingly long-lived and generally increase in value along with inflation. For other industries, where depleting assets are the rule, the situation is different. Inflation necessitates replacement at enhanced prices. Moreover technological change means that frequently such machinery has to be replaced before the end of its working life. If depreciation provisions are not based on replacement cost and amortisation is not based on technological advance, net profits will appear larger than they really are. Consequently taxable profits, net of depreciation, and therefore possibly also the dividend distribution, will be larger than appropriate. The same sort of argument applies to inventories. It has been found that 'a really serious degree of over-estimation of profits and over-taxation has occurred through including in profits the rise in value of inventories due entirely to changes in prices'. (16) The problem is more important the faster is the rate of inflation, and the greater is the rate of technological change. In progressive high-growth industries, where techniques are advancing at a fast pace, this problem will be more important than for more staid industries. It has been found that rates of depreciation increased markedly from slow- to fast-growing companies. (17) the explanation may be that fast-growing companies are likely to derive an unusually large benefit from the various types of investment allowances. Another explanation seemed to be that slow-growing companies tend to have fixed assets largely in the form of buildings, on which depreciation is low. Fast-growing industries, on the other hand, tend to be those where plant and machinery is more important. Depreciation is much higher on plant and machinery than on buildings. Another explanation may be added: slow- and fast-growing companies probably adopt different policies towards depreciation. Fast-growing companies may be fully convinced of the importance of replacement-cost depreciation. Their management may be more aware of the implications of rising replacement costs. For instance, between 1954 and 1963 there was a 40 per cent rise in the price indices for a wide variety of industrial plant; this meant that replacement cost had increased correspondingly. For specific types of plant the increase has been well over 50 per cent. (18) In other words historical cost has been inadequate as a basis for recouping moneys to replace plant. The use of historical costs could well mean that over such a period there would be a 40 per cent shortfall in the actual sums required for replacement. It has been succinctly put that 'a firm which does not cover the cost of replacing expired materials and services as well as the taxes imposed upon it, is necessarily in the process of liquidation'. (19) For growing companies which are continually acquiring extra industrial capacity, this problem is basic. If they do not use replacement-cost depreciation, their profits may be overstated. If they are overstated, tax charges and dividend payments may be too high.

Company taxation is an important constraint on dividend policy. Disposable profits are reduced and dividends may be relatively expensive to maintain at the accepted level. Because taxation amounts to an appropriation of funds, there is less available for distribution. Under corporation tax, there is discrimination against distributed profits. At the time of writing, 45 per cent is levied on profits and, in addition, income tax is payable on dividends. (20) The discrimination takes two forms. One is that a company only incurs income tax if dividends are distributed. The other is that some companies may find it more expensive to maintain their existing level of dividends compared with the previous system of taxation. Under the old system the standard rate was levied on taxable profits, plus 15 per cent profits tax. The official aim of the discrimination is to encourage companies to finance growth through internal expansion. The effect may, however, be perverse. Growth companies may deem it wise to maintain dividends even if they are now more expensive, for they can recoup funds through capital issues on the Stock Exchange. The net effect could be to encourage, rather than discourage, the use of external funds. Whether this will actually happen is largely a question of company philosophy towards dividends. This is the third factor affecting policy.

Company philosophy towards ordinary dividends may be determined by essentially long-run considerations, or it may treat them as a residual after the desired level of internal finance has been deducted from earnings. An investigation of a sample of United States companies shows that long-run considerations predominate. (21) Dividend policy is conservative, in that managements tend to alter dividends by only a part of the change indicated by current financial conditions. The dependent variable in the decision-making process is the change in the existing rate and not the amount of the newly established rate. The current liquidity position acts as a buffer between dividend policy and current investment opportunities. Investment requirements as such have little direct effect in modifying dividend behaviour. If this latter point were true of the United Kingdom, then the corporation tax may well have the perverse effect mentioned above. It has been suggested, however, that in the United Kingdom 'the common attitude of managements to dividends expresses no obvious relation between dividends and current profits, but treats dividends rather as a residual after the decision as to the volume of internal finance of growth has been taken'. (22) If so, dividends, and not liquidity, are represented as the buffer.

Investigations into the behaviour of British companies do not support the view that dividends are the residual. There appear to be three possible dividend policies: (23) the required reinvestment type, the fair or fixed shares, and the stable-rate type. The required reinvestment type relates to a situation where a definite proportion of earnings may be required for investment. Here dividends vary directly with earnings and the attained rate of return. For example, three percentage points may always be set aside for reinvestment and the remainder distributed. Technically, therefore, shareholders are rewarded after reinvestment requirements are met and dividends are treated as a residual. The fair or fixed-share type is a policy where the proportion of earnings split between dividends and retentions is kept at a fixed proportion throughout. The stable rate represents the situation where the dividend payment is held at a constant level over time. The observations from quoted companies investigated suggest that, in general, the most usual policy is a compromise between the application of the fixed-shares and the stable-rate principle. By and large dividends are characterised by a considerable degree of stability. Perhaps the interpretation of these findings is that dividend payments are pitched at a conservative level where downward revisions are unlikely and where adjustments to current profitability are only fractional. Whether this is still true of present-day conditions is difficult to infer. The investigation was made at a time when dividend restraint was government policy, and when taxation rates discriminated heavily against distributions. Thus dividend-rate stability was encouraged.

Evidence for the pre-war period (24) also suggests that business saving rather than dividends are 'the' residual item. For example, in the downswings of 1921, 1929-32 and 1938 net business savings fell more sharply than dividends and increased more in the upswings that followed. Evidence from the recent past indicates that firms are anxious not to upset existing levels of dividends, and that company savings are a residual after meeting dividend payments which have effectively become obligatory. (25) 'The average dividend return and its dispersion are much the same in different industries and over different periods of time. It is also worth noting that the dispersion of dividend return between firms is relatively much lower than the dispersion of profitability or growth between firms. It would therefore appear that in spite of very considerable differences in average profitability, firms try to maintain a similar dividend on equity assets.' (26) Another study, admittedly confined to the brewing industries, indicates that 'dividends represent the primary and active decision variable in most situations'. (27) Other evidence from the current period is somewhat broad, but points in a similar direction. From 1947 until 1958 the rate of tax charged on distributed profits was higher than on retentions. In 1955 the difference in the rates was at a maximum of eleven times. (28) Nevertheless the proportion of profits paid as dividends increased over the period. This occurred against a background of rising profits but slowly declining rates of return. (29) In 1958 discrimination against distributed profits ended and the proportion of profits distributed as ordinary dividends increased from approximately one-quarter to approximately one-third in 1965 (30). With the coming into operation of the corporation tax in 1966, discrimination has been reintroduced. However, previous experience suggests that with a relatively favourable trading background managements do not actually reduce the percentage paid to dividends because of discrimination. Thus the effect of corporation tax may not be to increase the savings—income ratio or the amounts invested from internal sources. If trading conditions are not favourable, however, the situation may be very different. At such times companies' savings intentions may well dictate that financing growth out of retained earnings is a priority, and not the current level of dividends. On balance, however, the weight of the evidence on dividend policy suggests that companies are reluctant to depart from distribution levels that have become accepted. 'Under such circumstances, the investment outlay on fixed and working capital seems, in the short run, most plausibly treated as a residual defined to be the difference between total net flow of funds realised from current operations less the established or conventional dividend payment.' (31) The 'residual funds' theory, where investment is the dependent variable and dividends are the independent variable, apparently operates. Managements consider that dividends are so important that they are not completely adjusted to current trading results. In this way, when profits are improving, only a fraction of the improvement is put to dividends. Similarly when profits turn down, dividends do not necessarily have to be reduced because such a contingency has been anticipated by the existing level of payment.

It is interesting to speculate on the official belief that raising the savings–income ratio is likely to increase company growth. It is generally true that fast-growing companies tend to have a high savings–income ratio, but this is almost incidental. It does not mean that to induce a high rate of growth the use of internal funds should be encouraged. Fast-growing firms happen to have a high proportion of internal funds, for three possible reasons: they are generally pretty profitable, there is probably a trade-off between the level of dividends and prospective capital gains, and also dividend payments are probably based on fractional adjustment to current trading conditions. Hence cash generation tends to be good, and if dividends are not completely adjusted to current profitability, the proportion of retentions to earnings appears high. As pointed out before, high-growth companies tend also to raise money externally more than slow growers. Thus they have a high savings–income ratio, and they typically use the stock market more. Their growth is made possible because they can secure funds both internally and externally in considerable amounts, and not because the ratio of internal funds to income is high.

To come back to the main argument: for a variety of reasons, companies exhibit a prejudice for internal funds. Raising funds externally creates explicit obligations. The type of assets used influences depreciation provisions, particularly so if replacement-cost procedures are followed. Company philosophy is probably very conservative and thus distributions are pitched at a level which is maintainable over the likely range of business fluctuations. Current taxation policy discriminates against distributions, and while this may not appear to cause a reduction in the proportion distributed as dividends, nevertheless it is part of a pressure favouring retentions as a major source of funds. Fast-growing companies, on the other hand, are somewhat different. It is true that they appear to rely heavily on internal sources of funds, because their savings–income ratio tends to be higher than that of slow-growing companies. But as already pointed out, this ratio may be misleading. In other words the relevant ratio is that of investment to income, and not savings to income.

How is the difference in the source of funds between slow- and fast-growing companies related to observed dividend payments? Fast-growing companies do not necessarily exhibit a particular distribution pattern. There is no obligatory relationship between dividend payments and the rate of growth. The correlation coefficient found is $r = 0.34$, (32) and this is not strong enough to amount to a rule of growth. Some high growers appear to follow a generous distribution policy, others do not. The reason for this lack of strong pattern is probably that the flow of funds to such companies is not greatly influenced by dividend policy. A successful company will secure funds because it is successful, and not because of a particular dividend policy. The ability of companies to secure finance is largely determined by their reputation. There is thus a choice of dividend policy. To grow fast, companies do not find themselves forced by market pressure into adopting a set pattern of distributions. The conjectured pay-off between dividends and capital gains probably operates. The partial correlation coefficients between growth and dividends on equity assets, when profitability is held constant, help to establish this. When significant, they tend to be negative, indicating that fast-growing companies may be able to reduce their rate of dividends on equity assets presumably without prejudicing the market for their shares. (33) Distribution policy is thus a decision which is not prescribed by capital requirements, but related more to the attitude of managements and their success within particular industries.

6 Profitability

The preceding discussion has indicated that the status of companies may be important to their supply of funds. Companies with Stock Exchange quotations have ready access to a large and well-developed market for industrial capital. The ways in which non-quoted companies typically finance operations suggested that they may be at a disadvantage. But in practice most funds are generated within companies. Growth is thus likely to be more closely aligned to the opportunities for profitable investment than to technical considerations relating to the supply of external capital. Put bluntly, profits are the major source of funds, and thus companies are likely to relate their investment programmes to their current earnings. The quality of investment in the financial sense may therefore be a determinant of growth. If so, there should be some link between company growth and company profitability. The size and importance of any such link will be the concern of this chapter.

Profitability is the ratio relating profits to capital. The ratio form is used in order to standardise profits and thus make them independent of firms' size. Absolute profit figures provide no guide to the quality of company performance because large firms tend to make large profits while the opposite is true of small firms. When the profits earned by each company are related to the capital used by each company, then some useful basis for comparison is established. Profitability figures indicate the amount of revenue and costs which have been generated in relation to the capital employed. The level of the profitability figures is likely to have a considerable influence on internally financed growth potential. Externally financed growth potential will also be affected by the level of profitability. High profitability means, in general, a large pool of profits from which further investment may take place. High profitability also provides a dual incentive for shareholders in companies to retain their holdings. They either receive large dividend pay-outs or high 'cover' for a smaller distribution. Cover is the number of times by which profit attributable to the ordinary shares is greater than the ordinary dividend. This high cover may give promise of larger future distributions or, in times of recession, greater safety for shareholders' income. Consequently a successful company tends to have a considerable advantage. The firm's disposable income may be supplemented by further issues of shares. These issues are virtually ensured success (in the sense that they will be taken up by the market), because of the past record of the company. An unsuccessful company or one which has poor profitability is clearly at a disadvantage here. While its successful rival may draw heavily upon its shareholders and also distribute relatively little, the unsuccessful company is in the opposite position. Its growth potential is therefore likely to be less.

The level of profitability is thus a useful proxy for the supply of finance. Actual growth potential is influenced by the availability of internal and external funds and the whole range of problems discussed before, such as company status, gearing, trade credit and so on. Even so the level of profitability is likely to be a major determinant of growth potential. As an index of achieved results, it is likely to influence managements' attitude towards future prospects. At the same time shareholders and potential shareholders will be influenced in their assessment of companies by the profits generated on capital employed.

If profitability is a good indicator of the supply of funds to companies, then there ought to be some link between company profitability and growth. Various studies have examined this hypothesis. (1) They are nearly all concerned with public quoted companies. Such quoted firms have already achieved a measure of success. They have crossed the barrier which divides non-quoted companies from the rest. However, one advantage of such companies is that their motives and aspirations are probably fairly homogeneous. Each has a broadly similar shareholding structure, and each is subject to the same criteria of success which shareholders apply. Once a company turns public, decisions are less likely to be influenced by the desire to retain family control or to limit the size of the firm. Instead there are the impersonal requirements of the shareholders to consider. If so, presumably growth and increasing profits thus become major motives in the operation of these companies. The studies bear this out, in so far as they reveal a reasonably strong degree of association between the two major variables. The correlation coefficients which measure the strength of the association vary between approximately 0.5 and 0.7. This means that between 25 and 49 per cent of the variation in the dependent variable is statistically accounted for by variation in the independent variable. The measures used are mean growth and mean profitability over the time periods concerned, and not year-to-year figures. On a year-to-year basis there is apparently no link between the variables. (2) But once a longer-term view is taken, and average growth and average profitability related, then there is a fairly strong degree of association between them.

This link between company growth and profitability is probably the most important single relationship in the growth process. The relationship, however, requires very careful interpretation, as will be explained below. Companies exhibit a bias in favour of internally generated funds. Retentions are the largest single source of capital for expansion. The achieved level of profits, therefore, has a direct effect on funds available for expansion. The higher the level of profitability, the more funds are available. Actual investment is probably related to the level of profits which businessmen believe will continue. The nature of the relationship is, however, of considerable importance. If this were known with accuracy, prediction of companies' performance might be much improved.

The correlation coefficients measure the degree of linear association between two variables. This procedure implies that companies' response to changes in growth or profitability levels is constant throughout the whole range of possible values. In technical terms, the slope of the regression coefficient is the same for all ranges of values of the variables. For example, if the regression coefficient of growth on profitability is 0.7, then a 1 per cent change in profitability is on average associated with a 0.7 per cent change in the growth rate, regardless of the actual level of profitability. This does not seem very plausible. Effectively, companies earning very high rates of profit are assumed to respond in exactly the same way to a given change in that level of profits as companies which are earning very low returns. A more plausible representation of the pattern of association between the variables may be one where there is a varying response to a given change in profitability at different levels of profitability. Under such circumstances a 1 per cent change in profitability when profits are at, say, 13 per cent could lead to a more than 0.7 per cent increase in growth rate. An increase from a low level of profits, such as 4 per cent, could alternatively be associated with a much smaller change in the growth rate, say of 0.4 per cent. Fig. 6.1 illustrates three possible types of relationship.

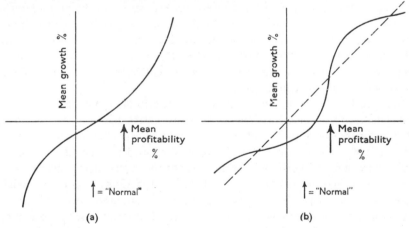

Fig. 6.1 Representation of three possible types of regression line between mean growth and profitability, of a large number of individual companies (3)

The diagram represents three general types of regression lines which may be fitted to scatter diagrams of the mean growth and mean profitability, over a number of years, of a large number of individual companies. In (a) growth is represented as cumulating downwards at an ever increasing rate as losses increase. In the opposite direction, as companies become increasingly successful in raising profit levels above 'normal' (indicated with an arrow), so growth cumulates upwards. In (b) the representation is more complex. Basically companies' response to growth is such that expansion cumulates upwards in the area where positive profits are being earned, but are below the average or 'normal'. Above the 'normal', growth still increases for a given change in profitability, but soon the response is not greater than the change in profitability. Of the two, (b) is probably the more realistic. It is unlikely that growth will continue to cumulate upwards as profits increase above the 'normal' or average as represented in (a). A position will probably be reached where managements believe it is unlikely that the current very high profits are maintainable, and thus will not instigate the growth rate suggested in (a).

It seems reasonable to postulate that response hinges around the 'normal' or average profitability and also companies' expectations about their ability to maintain or better existing profits performance. Therefore even if a company is earning above the 'normal' or average, it is unlikely that the very ambitious expansion programme suggested by (a) will in fact be instigated, unless it has strong expectations of maintaining this performance. Notice that in both (a) and (b) the postulated curvilinear relationships do not pass through the origin. Both have been drawn with a positive intercept. At zero growth, profit rates are represented as positive. This accords with the concept of an opportunity-cost rate of return, i.e. unless companies are earning a rate of return which at least justifies their present employment of the factors involved, growth is unlikely to occur. It is unlikely that there will be the incentive and means to grow when profits are not adequate in this sense.

Statistical evidence on the form of the relationship and the value of the intercept is not conclusive. Investigators are aware that the pattern of the relationship between the variables may be non-linear, but the problem is to identify just what the pattern is. There is some evidence that the relationship may be curvilinear. (4) However, this does not mean that it is inappropriate to use a linear approximation. The problem of specifying a correct model is statistically complex. Furthermore a linear relationship may be a good approximation to reality over the *whole* range of observations. For example, in (b) a linear line of 'best fit' may be an excellent approximation to the overall situation. However, the effect of such an approximation may be to disguise the pattern within a limited range of values. This may explain why investigators do not always find a value for the intercept such that zero growth is registered with positive profits. Observations either side of these values may influence the line of best fit, so that it passes through the origin. Hence the fact that the intercept is not significantly greater than zero is therefore probably the consequence of statistical techniques, and does nothing to refute the opportunity-cost argument. More research will have to be done before it will be possible to specify the form of the relationship with greater accuracy. This is unlikely to be a once-and-for-all task, for there are probably inter-industry and inter-temporal variations which may upset any generality.

The full meaning of the correlation coefficients between growth and profitability requires very careful interpretation for a number of reasons. They point to the importance of profitability in the growth process. But this conclusion must be tempered by the fact that correlation analysis says nothing about causation. It does nothing to distinguish cause and effect, nor does it indicate whether there is any *real* association. High profitability may cause high growth or vice versa. High growth may be an equally plausible explanation of high profitability. For example, a considerable improvement in turnover may generate high profitability and thus the cash for future investment. Alternatively the relationship between growth and profitability may be caused by some association with a common third factor. Or again, the relationship may be just a statistical freak, resulting from the form in which the indicators are measured. In the present context this last point may have very considerable weight. Both the indicators (profitability and growth) have the same common denominator, namely capital. The indicators are mean $\frac{P}{C}$ per cent and the mean percentage change in capital. Capital is used as a denominator in both the ratios. Adopting a ratio form of this character gives rise to the fear that a correlation coefficient will result which is just a product of the measures used and therefore without economic significance. Under these conditions a spurious correlation coefficient of up to 0.5 can sometimes be expected. (5) If this is likely to occur, the significance of the results must be carefully considered. There are two main points in support of the results. First the two ratios, profitability and growth, each have economic significance of their own. Any correlation revealed between them is not necessarily spurious in an economic sense. Second, the conditions under which a 'spurious correlation' is likely to arise involve ratios of the general form $\frac{A}{B}.\frac{C}{B}$ where A and C are uncorrelated. In the present context A (absolute growth) and C (absolute profits) are likely to be highly correlated. In simple terms big firms tend to make large absolute profits and grow by large absolute amounts. Dividing through by B (capital) is a deliberate attempt to remove this obvious correlation. By standardising or normalising both profits and growth in relation to capital, an effort is made to determine a relationship which is independent of firms' absolute size. Since the initial condition for a spurious condition is unsatisfied, this largely answers the objection that the association between growth and profitability is spurious. Any remaining doubts are dispersed by turning to the economics of the case. In these terms the results are both useful and significant.

The arguments supporting a link between growth and profitability are convincing. Profits are a condition of survival in the business world and also a major source of finance for investment. The higher are profits, the higher is likely to be the rate of investment. But the actual direction of causation remains unspecified by the studies so far available. It has not yet been possible to present strong evidence establishing which factor is the independent variable. In Fig. 6.1 (a) and (b) the horizontal axis has been labelled 'profitability'. By convention, this axis is reserved for the independent variable. However, the very schematic relationships put forward in these diagrams are not meant to imply anything about causation. In practice this is not known. The most plausible hypothesis represents profits as a springboard for growth. The better firms are at generating funds for investment, the greater is likely to be their growth potential. But when the argument is reworded, with growth as the catalyst, it also has a ring of conviction. For example, improved cash generation may be dependent on raising turnover and the physical capacity to produce this. Here improved profitability follows improved growth and not vice versa. Unfortunately simple lagging of the variables to establish which is the 'follower' and which the 'leader' reveals no obvious pattern. The absence of any obvious lagged relationship is probably due not only to variation in the direction of causation in different circumstances, but also to variations in the period of the lag. There is unlikely to be any simple rule that, for instance, profitability is always the independent variable and growth follows improved profits performance in a predetermined manner. The business decision-making process is probably far more complex than this. The determinants are probably highly interrelated. The level of management motivation to grow, business conditions, the current phase of the trade cycle and existing profit levels are all likely to affect firms' response to changes in growth or profitability. Of course figures of mean profitability and mean growth are very summary measures of business performance. Disguised within these measures are determinants which will clearly affect decision-making. The trend of profits, whether falling or rising, and the dispersion of results, namely the fluctuation in year-to-year performance, are bound to influence managements. This is yet another reason why causation is not readily determined from the growth and profitability studies.

In relation to Fig. 6.1 (a) and (b), the direction of causation may well be affected by the companies' position in the overall pattern. For companies earning poor profits or making losses, survival is probably the prime motive. Any growth is therefore likely to be profit-constrained. Companies which are making average profits are less likely to be so concerned with mere survival. In the commercial sense they are established and unlikely to go bankrupt, as long as their present commercial performance continues. In such instances growth may be the motor variable. By increasing industrial capacity, they are probably able to sell all the extra they can produce. In this sense profitability may follow growth. In the case of companies with exemplary commercial performance, with both high expansion rates and excellent revenue figures, causation may revert to being profit-determined. Management may deem it prudent to make the present level of growth dependent on the continuance of the excellent profit figures. So long as these continue, expansion is likely to remain above average. Inevitably these representations of company response are very schematic, but they help to emphasise that causation is unlikely to be simple or constant. The fact that no studies so far available have managed to establish the direction of company response is fairly strong evidence of the complexity of the problem.

The second reason why these results need very careful interpretation is their apparent clash with other empirical studies. An examination has been made of the problem of whether growth in one period of time is likely to lead to further growth in a succeeding period. The title of the relevant article, 'Higgledy Piggledy Growth', aptly summarises the findings. (6) Using Moodies' card data and correlation analysis, there appears to be no link between companies' pre-tax equity earnings growth performances in one year to that in another. In a further investigation, it is again found that there is virtually no tendency for growth trends over any period of time to repeat themselves. (7) Thus from these two studies it would appear that the future growth of companies cannot be predicted from past results. This conclusion may seem puzzling. As mentioned above, average growth and average profitability are associated, and yet, when equity earnings performance in one period is related to that in another, there appears to be no connection.

Apparently, successful management does not continue to do well. More specifically, successful companies appear to be unlikely to differ from the average in a succeeding period. Not enough companies succeed in returning above-average growth of earnings for a sufficiently long period to establish significant correlations. Investors on the stock market are thus mistaken in their belief that there is sufficient constancy in the results of companies to provide a reliable basis for prediction of future performance.

Possible explanations of this apparent contradiction between the various studies turn on the definitions used and the aims involved. The profitability and growth studies use company assets to determine the average level of the variables. The 'Higgledy Piggledy Growth' studies, on the other hand, use a completely different measure, namely *changes* in earnings per equity assets to indicate growth. These measures are so fundamentally different that no comparison can really be drawn. 'An increase in assets is very different from an increase in earnings per share, adjusted for capital changes. A company which grows rapidly in asset size may have no increase in earnings per share. It can grow by borrowing or by buying other companies for an issue of shares.' (8)

Even the aims of the studies are different. One series of studies is effectively asking whether it is generally true that those companies which have grown the fastest were also on average the most profitable over the same period. Put differently, the question is whether as a point of historical fact companies which have achieved a high level of average profitability over a period also achieve a high level of average growth in that same period. The other series of studies associated with the 'Higgledy Piggledy' theories has a different aim, namely to determine whether growth in equity earnings in one period is likely to be repeated in a succeeding period. The latter ask, does growth breed growth? The lack of persistency of growth of earnings per share leads the authors to argue that there is either no continuity of good or bad management, or that there is no such thing as good or bad managment. However, these conclusions only hold in the context of their measures of the quality of management. If good management is defined as the maintenance of an above-average *growth* of earnings per share, then in these terms their studies reveal an important point. Management apparently does not succeed in maintaining an above-average growth of earnings per share. However, as soon as a different criterion of the quality of management is substituted, then good or bad management may be identified. If the maintenance of an *above average level* of profitability is set up as an alternative criterion, then firms exhibit some consistency. This is the more usual and meaningful criterion of management success. For example, companies may achieve a magnificent earnings growth record and yet be making a miserably low average level of profits. In terms of the *average* level of profitability, there is some persistence between periods. (9) Effectively, therefore, there is no clash in the findings. Earnings per share can fluctuate widely and yet average profitability and growth still be related.

Reasons explaining the wide fluctuations in earnings growth probably include the operation of random processes, rapid change of management, the trade cycle, the power of competition and organisational 'slack'. (10) Good or bad luck can affect all firms. A high turnover of senior posts can alter the quality of management very quickly. Trading conditions can vary widely over the trade cycle. Competition can erode success and spur failure. Organisational slack, which is a measure of management potential, may vary widely. Company results may oscillate from bad to very good according to management response to the stimulus of degrees of success. Companies which have achieved succes may, in a sense, rest on their laurels, organisational slack may develop and competition may gradually erode away their supremacy. Eminence is lost and ordinary or poor results appear. On the other hand companies which have poor results are likely to shed some fat in an effort to improve their performance. The picture set up is that of company 'snakes and ladders', where position changes are constantly occurring and today's leaders become tomorrow's laggards. The 'Higgledy Piggledy' evidence is in a sense some support for this oscillatory-type behaviour, since there is no generally established tendency for previous behaviour to be repeated in the future.

Reconciliation of the 'Higgledy Piggledy' results with the growth and profitability studies is just a matter of recognising the nature of the exercises and the measures used. There is no clash. Companies earning exemplary profit returns and growing furiously can have a growth of earnings which fluctuates widely or is not repeated from year to year. On one criterion management is good, and on another not good. Of course both groups of studies are examining general trends and are not attempting to comment on individual firms. These may exhibit patterns of behaviour which are at variance with all the results. It is just that, on balance, not enough companies repeat earnings growth, and at the same time sufficient numbers do exhibit a reasonably strong association between the average level of growth and profitability.

The third reason why the association between profitability and growth needs careful interpretation is on the grounds of its generality. The relationship may have resulted from the particular characteristics of the industries investigated or the size of the firms or the particular years concerned. If so, then it does not necessarily follow that there is a general relationship which most companies obey. With one exception, however, all the available studies cover a reasonably wide range of industries. Only one is restricted in coverage to two industries, namely engineering and food processing. When the growth rate figures of these industries were tested, it was found that only a small part of these differences could be attributed to size or to the trade in which the firm operates; most of the differences are differences between firms in comparable situations. (11)

Investigators using a wider sample found on the other hand that there was a considerable difference between coefficients and the degree of explanation of growth obtained for different industries. (12) Furthermore the relationship between profitability and growth may change substantially over time within individual industries. (13) In other words the closeness of the association varies between industries and over time, and also the slope of the lines of 'best fit'. It is hardly surprising that both the strength of the association and the values for the regression coefficient vary between industries. Different trading environments and varying elements of risk will obviously have an effect on companies' views about the required levels of profitability to sustain expansion. Financing practices may also vary. If self-financing is favoured within certain industries,

C. M.P.M.E.

then expansion is likely to be very directly linked to the level of internally generated funds. Where more external funds are used, then expansion will be less constrained by current levels of profitability. In addition, firms' investment response to varying levels of achieved profitability may alter over time. Even if profitability is suffering a decline, firms may maintain investments and adjust to these lower returns. It is interesting to note that the largest firms show a weak tendency not to exhibit the inter-industry and inter-temporal differences in the regression coefficients. (14) Very large firms are probably members of many industries, in the sense that they have a wide spread of products and commercial interests. Thus they are unlikely to be greatly affected by the pattern evident in particular industries. Similarly, because they tend to be multi-product in character, fluctuations in trading fortunes may be ironed out within group activities. Such firms are therefore less likely to be greatly affected by large variations in trading fortunes within particular industries over time. The large firms in this context are those with assets of more than £2 million between 1948 and 1960. (15)

On the major argument, however, there is complete agreement between the studies investigating the relationship between average growth and profitability. All of them establish that there is a reasonably strong association between the variables. The pattern holds true for all industries and through time. Values for explanatory power (r^2) vary, and also the particular way in which the relationship holds, but in all cases the overall pattern is revealed. Growth and profitability are linked. There is sufficient degree of agreement on this major point to dismiss the possibility that the studies are not representative. Enough companies follow the pattern to make this a rule of 'growth'. The association is not special to particular industries, but holds right across all commercial activities. As argued earlier, the motives and aspirations of public quoted companies are probably fairly homogeneous. Each company is subject to the same criterion of success which shareholders apply. Growth and profitability are common motives of operation.

There is also evidence that the same is true for non-quoted companies. An inquiry almost entirely confined to non-quoted companies finds the established pattern. (16) Intuitively, it is reasonable to suppose that non-quoted companies may not behave like their quoted counterparts. Control is usually held closely by a few shareholders. Frequently it is asserted that the 'quiet life' may be an important motive of operation. Nevertheless the evidence available suggests that even so, the expected pattern of behaviour is revealed. On reflection this is hardly surprising. The reason is that even for non-quoted companies 'profits remain a condition for survival, a social (as well as economic) test of success and of influence, and a means to even more extensive accomplishment'. (17) Growth and profitability appear to be linked throughout the industrial world irrespective of corporate status.

The fourth qualification to the overall interpretation of the relationship between profitability and growth relates to special sorts of non-quoted companies which are often subsidiaries. Until the 1967 Companies Act came into force, incorporated non-quoted companies were basically of three sorts, the non-quoted public company, the private exempt and the private non-exempt company. As a general rule all companies were required to file annual returns with the Registrar of Companies, but private companies could, until January 1968, claim exemption from filing a copy of their accounts with their returns. If, however, a private concern had another company as a shareholder, or nominee shareholders, then this exemption from filing the accounts was not allowed. The logic behind these conditions was to prevent public companies hiving off activities into private concerns which did not have to submit accounts. It was these non-exempt non-quoted companies which were often subsidiaries. From January 1968 private exempt companies have been abolished and thus all private companies must lodge a copy of their accounts with the Registrar of Companies. Exemption is still retained, however, for partnerships. In a study by the Board of Trade, the accounts of a number of non-quoted companies were analysed. (18) These were all 'non-exempt', as the accounts of exempt companies were not available. Of the 460 accounts analysed, 202 were subsidiaries of, or controlled by, overseas companies, and thirty were subsidiaries of companies whose shares were quoted in the United Kingdom. In short, the majority were subsidiaries. This is important because subsidiary organisation may mean that the normal circumstances which constrain autonomous companies in their commercial policies need not apply with such rigour.

There is some evidence that subsidiaries are peculiar in this sense. (19) Companies are usually organised on a group basis and subsidiaries are merely part of the group. In their early years of operation it is parent company funds which are used to establish and sustain operations. Immediate profitability is not therefore of such pressing concern. The usual circumstances which normally constrain ordinary companies in their investment programme may not apply with much force. The parent company know-how, injections of capital, and the protection which a subsidiary enjoys from the full rigour of the competitive process, all would suggest that such companies are different. Newly established subsidiaries may achieve 'take-off' even with unpromising profits. They may be able to grow to a viable size under conditions where normal firms would be constrained by lack of finance. Evidence is drawn from foreign-owned subsidiaries in the United Kingdom. All the correlation coefficients relating growth and profitability are extremely low. Apparently for such companies this association is not a 'rule of growth'. Seemingly they are not constrained to such an extent as normal independent companies. The low correlation coefficients may thus be interpreted as a measure of the strength of the parent company power.

Subsidiary performance may vary widely from normal because of the influence of parent company backing. Of course these results could have arisen because of the extreme youth of many of the companies included. New companies are likely to exhibit peculiar results until they are well established. Some attempt has been made to test for this, by correlating the observations for quoted subsidiaries only, and also those companies which have been operating for at least five years. (20) Quoted subsidiaries are usually foreign companies which are so well established in the United Kingdom that they now raise capital locally through the Stock Exchange. Alternatively they are former United Kingdom quoted companies which have been taken over, but have retained their quotations even though they are now foreign-owned. Neither of these tests of independence from parent company backing revealed a different pattern. The association between growth and profitability was still almost zero. Another reason explaining the peculiar results is the poor quality of the data. As will be made clear below, figures from the accounts of subsidiaries may be extremely misleading. The results may therefore be entirely a product of the data and not reflect any economic meaning at all. This is indeed a possibility and must be recognised in the interpretation of the results. However, the lack of association between growth and profitability of subsidiaries has an intuitive appeal, since subsidiaries are not like ordinary autonomous concerns. They have parent company backing which must make some difference to their operation. On balance, therefore, the results probably illustrate an economic fact, namely that subsidiaries are peculiar and are not constrained by their growth or profits performance like ordinary companies.

Subsidiaries highlight the fifth qualification of the results, namely the use and interpretation of company accounting data. In 'autonomous concerns' the accounts are a reasonable guide to trading results. By law, all activities are consolidated into one account. Raw materials and management are acquired at market prices, and the majority of costs and benefits are reflected in the annual accounts. There are, of course, well-known problems of the book valuation of the assets. Assets are recorded in the accounts either at their acquisition price or at a revaluation figure. There is inevitably a mixed age composition of assets, and so total book values represent a mixture of price levels. However, by and large, capital figures are a reasonable indicator of companies' potential revenue-generating power, and thus ratios expressing profits to capital are not too bad as indicators of the returns being earned on the assets employed. With subsidiaries, these normal problems are compounded by many more. The accounts of such concerns are not a consolidation of group activities but a representation of branch activities only. The consequences of artificially isolating such companies from their groups is to create a whole series of problems which make interpretation of any ratios extremely difficult. Separate accounts are presented for subsidiaries either because they have retained their status and legally have not been fully merged with a home parent company, or because they are foreign owned and are thus required to lodge their accounts with the .Registrar of Companies. The special interpretation problems are that subsidiaries often market products which have been proven by the parent company. They have a fund of know-how and management ability available from the parent company and they may receive this at less than market cost. Often, especially when they are newly established, premises are rented and thus do not appear in the book values in the accounts. Later, with establishment, premises may be bought and manufacturing capacity developed.

The effect of all these factors may be to make subsidiaries appear highly successful. The return on capital employed or profitability is likely to be very high. However, it is clear that often this apparent success is the result of the technical characteristics of subsidiaries. With proven products, profit figures tend to be overstated because development costs and many other costs have been incurred elsewhere. With a fund of management ability and know-how available from parent companies, again the effect is likely to lead to an overstatement of revenue. Subsidiaries do not have to compete in the open market for these things, but may receive them from the group organisation. Similarly on the capital side the effect is likely to be to cause high profitability. Capital involvement is likely to be understated either because many assets are rented or because the subsidiaries are acting as selling agents for the parent company. The manufacturing capacity is not fully represented in the accounts, either because it is rented or because the parent company has done the processing and the subsidiaries are merely selling.

Unfortunately a straightforward conclusion that subsidiaries are likely to be highly profitable is upset by a number of circumstances. These are the period of establishment and inter-company pricing arrangements. Basically, the longer subsidiaries have been established, the more likely they are to develop their own manufacturing capacity and to incur most of their costs locally. Thus the interpretation problems should ease with the passage of time. This may be so, but the development of greater autonomy does nothing to help the inter-company pricing problem. The charges parent companies make to subsidiaries for their products or raw materials may range from zero to way above the costs or even market price. Consequently it is within the power of parent companies to adjust the cost to subsidiaries of these materials and products to such an extent that their profitability may be made to appear almost at any level.

Where subsidiaries are foreign-owned, there are advantages in using inter-company pricing arrangements to minimise group taxation, tariff burdens and exchange risks. Where there are tariffs and differences in the level of company taxation between the countries concerned, it will be of obvious benefit to arrange inter-company pricing so that profits accrue where they are taxed least and tariffs have the smallest effect. For instance, where subsidiaries are operating in countries with high profits tax it pays parent companies to charge very heavily for products and raw materials supplied. In this way higher profits will accrue in the country with lower taxes. Subsidiaries will have relatively high costs and thus a lower tax burden. Inter-company pricing may be used in this way in order to avoid rules forbidding or limiting dividend repatriation. Instead of repatriating dividends, the parent company may charge highly for supplies, thus generating the profits at home and avoiding the necessity for dividend repatriation from abroad. This device could be particularly powerful where subsidiaries are operating in countries which have weak currencies and strict exchange-control regulations. By avoiding the necessity of dividend repatriation, the parent company side-steps the problem of converting currencies which are not readily acceptable internationally. In this country the Inland Revenue has powers of investigation to ensure that subsidiaries are not avoiding taxation by such pricing arrangements. Nevertheless the problems of establishing 'proper' inter-company pricing relations are such that only the most blatant evasion could be spotted. Of course, adjusting pricing arrangements to maximise group profits is eminently sensible and illegal only where it is used to thwart the law. However, it does make interpretation of profitability figures very difficult. There is not likely to be any consistency between subsidiaries. Parent—subsidiary cost relationships vary so widely, as also do tax, tariff, dividend repatriation and exchange rules. Hence no uniform and predictable effect is likely to occur.

There are further problems involved in interpreting the profitability of subsidiaries. Such companies may tend to cluster in newer industries where plant and process obsolescence is high. In addition, where such companies are new, most of their assets will be at current or near-current book values. Higher gross profits are therefore required on two counts, one for the lower pay-back period and the other for the high value of the assets. In addition, companies are likely to require higher net profits to continue in industries where change is rapid. Whether high gross and net profits are actually achieved is of course another matter. However, if plant and process obsolescence is genuinely high, then for investment to continue, at least high gross profits must be eventually achieved. Unfortunately, even if excellent profits are achieved, they may not be apparent from the accounts. Because book values are likely to be a reasonable indicator of the current acquisition price of new assets in recently established companies, profitability may not appear high in comparison to other older and longer-established companies. As explained before, normal book values tend to be a mixture of assets of varying ages. With inflation proceeding, the overall effect is probably for capital values in accounts to be below current values. Thus profitability of older companies tends to be exaggerated, so that newer companies may appear relatively less profitable than in fact they are.

The basic problem with subsidiaries is to adjust the data for their particular circumstances. Adjusting profitability figures is difficult. Costs incurred by parent companies may be deducted from the profits of subsidiaries. (21) Appropriate definitions of capital 'employed' may be chosen to minimise the effect of parent company loans in the profitability calculations. (22) Even so, these adjustments are unlikely to be satisfactory. Any results based on such unreliable data must be interpreted with great caution. One precaution is to avoid basing conclusions on profitability figures alone. For instance, the pharmaceutical industry in the United Kingdom is largely composed of foreign-owned subsidiaries, and it has been subject to a great deal of criticism based largely on such figures. Commentators have been unaware, or have forgotten, that such figures require great discretion in their use.

So difficult are the data to handle that the apparent lack of association between growth and profitability amongst subsidiaries may be entirely due to the shortcomings of the figures. But the results have an intuitive appeal, namely that subsidiaries are likely to be shielded by parent companies. Nevertheless this may not be verified by the full facts simply because the data may not represent them.

With all of these five qualifications in mind, what then is the full meaning of the association found between company growth and company profitability? Basically the evidence indicates either that profitability is an important ingredient in the growth process or that growth has a significant influence on profitability. 'This evidence is interesting for showing that firms do not typically neglect current profits as a signal of profitable growth opportunities . . . '. (23) The lack of correlation between year-to-year figures of growth and profitability also perhaps indicates that management reaction is cautious. (24) Immediate action is apparently not taken on a particular set of figures. The strength of the correlation coefficients when such longer-term evidence is used indicates, however, that there are other factors besides companies' profit performance which may influence growth. In statistical terms, only between 25 and 49 per cent of the variation of the chosen dependent variable has been accounted for. The remaining 75 to 51 per cent needs explanation. The explanation must lie with the forces affecting and inducing firms to grow. Not all firms wish to grow. The 'quiet life' may still be a relevant factor, even with managers of public quoted companies. But given that firms wish to grow, they may be hindered by relative market positions and technical factors. Other influences may have the opposite effect and induce a rate of growth in excess of that implied by a firm's profitability. Some firms may require growth for its own sake. In this context entrepeneurial ability is an obvious example. As attracters and users of funds, some men have great success. Through their special skill they mav be able to support a rate of growth in excess of that indicated by their profits. There are technical influences which may also induce high rates of growth. Some firms with high unit costs have a powerful incentive to expand and realise further economies of scale. In addition, mergers and take-overs are not necessarily closely related to the profitability of the units inducing the commercial nuptials (see Chapter 7). Thus the general answer to the question why growth is not dominated completely by cost and revenue considerations is that inducements and ability to grow vary from firm to firm. Even if all firms were equally profitable, differences in entrepreneurial ability, uncertainty, relative market and technical positions, business fashions, influential friends, government aid, subsidiary organisation and shareholders' faith in the future of companies would help to explain inter-firm differences in growth rates.

If the association between growth and profitability is a 'rule of growth', this ought to be an aid in the prediction of future company performance. Achieved levels of profits or expansion should provide reasonable indicators of forth-coming performance. Prediction models, hinged around this major association, have been conducted with the future growth of firms represented as a function of achieved profitability in the past. (25) Unfortunately the results of such prediction models are rather disappointing. The same is true of more complex models. Even with eight explanatory variables, only 16 per cent of the variance of growth is 'explained'.

This poor predictive power stresses that the relationship between growth and profitability may change radically over time. There is still an overall relationship between time periods, but the particular form it takes may vary to such an extent that prediction based on past performance yields results of limited power. 'In spite of this it is worth noting that past profitability seems to provide a better explanation of future growth than the past growth of the firm taken by itself.' (26) In terms of predictive power, it would seem that past profitability may be a more important causal factor than past growth. It is tempting to extend this conclusion to say that profitability is the major cause of growth. This would be over-bold, but nevertheless it is evidence pointing in this direction.

In the long run the relative profitability of firms is one measure of the quality of management. High profitability implies good revenue-earning ability and/or low unit costs. With freedom of entry and exit, resources may be switched between activities. Thus a company which maintains an above-average return on capital over a period of years may be deemed to be well endowed with manage-ment ability and/or good luck. This does not apply where there is a monopoly position and no freedom of entry. Monopolies may be able to earn high rates of return merely by exploiting their market power. In a competitive economy, therefore, a large part of the key to high profitability lies in the skill of management in deploying the resources at their disposal. Thus the association found between growth and profitability actually lays emphasis on the central role of management in the growth process. What matters in determining the rate of return on capital is the quality of investment in the commercial rather than the technical sense. The task of management is to strive for improvements in companies' performance. The means at their disposal and the way in which these are employed will be discussed in Chapter 8.

7 Take-over and Merger

Take-overs and mergers are means towards achieving large size. These, together with the raising of funds on the Stock Exchange, are external methods of expansion. 'Internal' expansion, via plough-back of profits, is generally thought to be more important to the growth process. For example, it has been found that in the period 1949-53, (1) 85 per cent of expansion was accounted for by internal expansion. For the following period, 1954-61, acquisitions paid for in cash and by shares accounted for 26 per cent of the growth of public quoted companies. (2) For the United States, internal development is also responsible for the major extent of growth. (3) However, the distinction between internal and external expansion is not altogether clear-cut. Cause and effect in the process cannot be sharply distinguished. An amalgamation between two companies may enhance subsequent growth. Any improved performance, following amalgamation, is neither purely internal nor external but mixed in character. While it may be true that overall expansion is more frequently achieved via internal development, nevertheless external means are very important. A single transaction, involving a take-over, may raise the whole level of subsequent growth because the asset mix is now more appropriate. Technically the enhanced growth may be classed as internal, because it has been achieved through plough-back of improved profits following the transaction. In practice, without the take-over this improvement may not have come about. Thus it is likely that figures apportioning expansion between 'internal' and 'external' understate the importance of mergers and take-overs. Even if the percentage attributable to external development were actually smaller than is in fact the case, take-overs and mergers would still be important in the growth process for reasons which will become clear later.

Conventionally, the distinction between a take-over and a merger rests on the level of agreement between the parties to the transaction. When the control is exchanged amicably, then this is known as a merger. Usually there is not an 'aggressor' who swallows another company; instead, interests are amalgamated. Take-overs, on the other hand, usually imply a struggle for control, and not infrequently a loss of identity for the acquired company. Take-overs may be achieved by a straight purchase of company assets, by a general offer to shareholders, by a deal with the existing board of directors who sell their shares and may resign their posts, or by acquisition of sufficient shares on the Stock Exchange to replace existing management. The key to success in any take-over bid lies in securing legal control. This is achieved by securing a majority of the voting shares.

Mergers are effected by three general procedures. First, a new concern, usually in the form of a holding company, may be formed. This is normally a non-trading concern whose function is to control the major decisions of the group. Second, there may be a complete amalgamation of the assets of the constituent companies. Identities of the original companies are merged either into a new company or into an existing one. Third, there may be general pooling arrangements. These may cover, for example, joint marketing or research units. (4) There are, of course, many methods whereby companies may become connected. Royalty and licensing payments, interlocking directorates, trade investments, jointly owned suppliers and retail outlets, and the acquisition of minority interests are examples. These, however, do not usually amount to mergers or amalgamations, but merely represent links of mutual benefit. For convenience, from now on the terms 'take-over' and 'merger' will be used in the general sense that they are both means of external expansion available to companies. No distinction will be drawn between them unless there is a specific purpose.

Of more interest than methods of take-over and mergers are the motives lying behind them. There is a wide variety of reasons which induce firms to acquire fellow companies. These motives have relevance to the growth process because they may indicate the intended use of the assets. They may be split broadly between efficiency and technical considerations. Where a company grows 'externally' in order to secure the advantages of large size and multi-product operation, to secure distribution and advertising economies and to secure the financial advantages of enhanced size, these motives are basically concerned with raising efficiency. Where, on the other hand, take-overs are instituted for tax advantages or for the gain of promoters, they are more technical in nature. However, the distinction is not sharp. Regardless of the overriding motives at the time of the deal, the outcome may be enhanced efficiency. For example, is a take-over designed to secure a tax advantage really technical in nature? By acquiring a company which has accumulated considerable losses, group performance may improve. The 'tax loss' thus acquired may be set against group profits for tax purposes and so improve overall liquidity. There are some motives which are prima facie difficult to classify. Where the limitation of competition or securing of patents is the main aim, it is not at all clear into which class they fall. If take-overs are used to maintain a monopoly position, then this may be far removed from efficiency considerations. Or if patents are acquired and then deliberately not used, the same may also be true. In both instances, however, the opposite could be the case. Maintaining monopoly could amount to defending the advantages of large-scale operation, or acquiring patents could mean that they are to be used more efficiently in their new hands.

Take-overs and mergers are sometimes described in terms of their effect on the scale of output and the range of products of companies. Vertical, horizontal, diagonal, lateral and conglomerate are the usual forms of classification. Vertical integration usually involves spreading the processes undertaken by companies forward towards the final consumer and/or backward towards the sources of supply. A large vertically integrated unit describes a company which is directly involved in most of the stages of production, from collection of raw materials right through to the marketing of the final manufactured product. Horizontal types of mergers and take-overs involve companies which operate at similar stages of production. A combination of two companies which both specialise in the production of a similar good is an example. The range of firms' activities remains unchanged, but the scale of operation is increased. Lateral integration consists of the 'combination of processes which may not be related directly to the same productive process'. (5) Firms extend their range of products in this way.

Lateral integration is a common way by which firms diversify. A greater number of products is added to their output. Diagonal integration is similar to lateral integration in that diversification of products is involved, but in this case the specific meaning refers to the adding of auxiliary goods and services to a firm's existing activities. Conglomerate mergers or take-overs relate to companies which already have a very wide range of products at varying stages in the manu-facturing process. Integration of two holding companies which control a large number of firms covering a very wide range of products would be classified as a conglomerate merger or take-over.

Basically, horizontal and vertical integration involves adding to the scale of production or becoming involved in more of the processes leading to a final product. Companies do not usually extend their range of final products. Diversification is not usually involved. Lateral, diagonal and conglomerate mergers, on the other hand, involve diversification. Companies' range of products is extended.

Each of the types of merger has particular economic advantages. Vertical integration is usually aimed at security of supply, rationalisation of linked production processes and a greater control of market outlets. Raw-material sources come under the industrial user's control. They are no longer separately owned and so security of supply is ensured. Production efficiency should be improved through rationalisation of stock holding and output volume. There is a direct unified link between the final market for the product at the one end and the source of raw materials at the other. Furthermore, because sales outlets may also be controlled, market coverage is known and may be more secure.

The main economies to be secured from horizontal integration are basically those associated with increased scale of production. By remaining specialists but increasing output potential, horizontally integrated firms should benefit from economies of scale.

Diversification is usually involved in lateral and diagonal integration and often brings a degree of commercial security. The same is likely to be true of conglomerate mergers. A firm with a wide range of products is less prone to the effects of a downturn in one particular trade. Such a company is in a position to offset losses by gains elsewhere within its turnover. The overall profit results of the group are less susceptible to the whims of fortune than a highly specialist unit whose profits will inevitably be affected by current trading conditions in its particular field of operation. The lower standard deviation of profitability figures of large companies (6) is probably a direct result of the advantages to be gained from having wide commercial interests. The majority of large companies are probably fairly diversified, and so fluctuations in their profitability are reduced. Of course the really large company should be in a very strong position. It can take advantage of both diversification and scale economies. Member units of the group can be large and highly specialist units. In this way they can take advantage of economies of scale. At the same time all of the units which form part of the group can cover a very wide range of commercial interests.

Some economies may be achieved regardless of the type of merger. Management and finance economies are probably the main examples. Here it is the size of companies rather than their industrial composition which is crucial. Large size ought to improve the quality of management and the supply of finance. Large companies should have more 'asset backing' as security for borrowing, and sheer size should also give greater confidence to borrowers simply because of the degree of market influence. The efficiency of management should improve. Large companies tend to pay better salaries than small ones. They should therefore be able to attract management of high quality and thus effect considerable improvements in their decision-taking and organisation. These advantages in management and the supply of finance may accrue independently of the type of business and the range of activities. They are an effect of size. Any type of take-over or merger which leads to the formation of a large company should achieve at least these sorts of economies. Other economies relating to production, research, marketing, purchases and so on will be more dependent on the type of business concerned. They may also be more difficult to achieve. (7)

One problem arises with conglomerate mergers. Here the emphasis in acquisitions may be primarily financial rather than industrial. If the shares of a conglomerate group (8) can achieve a reputation for capital gains, then a high price—earnings ratio will result. The stock market will price the shares favourably. In this way a conglomerate group will be well placed for further take-overs. As will be shown later in the chapter, shares are nearly always part of the payment for companies, and thus a high market rating will reduce the cash content of a bid. The emphasis in these acquisitions may be financial rather than industrial. If so, after a successful bid financial surgery will follow. The less successful activities are cut out or severely restricted. As a result higher profitability will be achieved almost immediately and the financial position of the whole group enhanced. This gives the stock market capitalisation of the conglomerate a further boost. One difficulty with this procedure is that this increase in profitability could be achieved by practically any company. Almost inevitably, if less successful ventures are cut out, the short-term effect is improved profits. But what of the long term? This sort of financial surgery may be very short-sighted. It may represent the only management skill of the group. Other management skills, such as improving efficiency, reorganisation, and the development of new products, may be entirely neglected in the pursuit of high stock market capitalisation through take-over activity. The real concern is that it is difficult to disentangle the effects of improved profitability which result from this surgery, from those which arise from internal growth and improved industrial housekeeping within the group. Provided a conglomerate has sufficient victims, it is possible for it to appear a very 'efficient' commercial group without conventional management skills. Continued acquisitions of any sort of companies, regardless of their commercial interests, can give this effect. The criterion for the selection of victims emphasises the financial terms on which they can be acquired, rather than the compatibility of their commercial activities with group interests. Management of the group may in fact be poor. There may be no effort to improve the use of their existing facilities. 'Growth' or improved profits will result from acquisitions followed by surgery.

This representation of the activities of conglomerates has been deliberately accentuated to emphasise their financial character. There is, however, public concern on these issues. The problems of disentangling internal and organic growth resulting from better housekeeping, from 'growth' induced by acquisitions, are very real. The enthusiasm of the stock market for capital gains confers a great advantage to companies through their share rating. If once the acquisition process falters and results become dependent on the normal management skills, a nasty crash might result. The investigations by the Federal Trade Commission in the United States, and the concern with conglomerates of the British Monopolies Commission, suggest that these fears are not groundless.

Take-overs and mergers represent an extremely powerful method of growth for the individual company. With one transaction, group assets may be substantially increased. The physical assets, labour and management team of the acquired company are immediately available. Instead of having to create these, they are an already co-ordinated unit which may be absorbed into group operations. Particularly where physical capacity is at a premium, a take-over is a really effective means of securing increased production power almost immediately. The acquired company switches its capacity to the production of group products and thus helps to reduce the excess demand. From a national point of view, this mere change of ownership does not represent growth. All that has been effected is a change in legal ownership. There is no more productive capacity available to the economy as a whole. This is a paper transaction which has left the real situation unchanged. If, however, the assets acquired through merger or take-over have been diverted to a more efficient use, then improved growth for the group, and possibly the economy, may follow. As a result of the combination, the earning power of the assets may be revitalised. With a more appropriate distribution of resources, the overall level of group performance may be raised. Take-overs and mergers are thus part of the 'transfer' process whereby assets may move towards a better use. (9)

Imagine a theoretical economy where there are no voting shares and where there is a level of workable competition. Because there is no possibility of take-overs, the allocation mechanism would operate only through agreed mergers, losses and new funds. Companies making continuing losses will go out of existence because suppliers will not give credit indefinitely and workpeople will not suffer long arrears of wages. Companies which are doing extremely well, on the other hand, will secure a higher proportion of new funds than ordinary performers, because they have a larger pool of profits to plough back. Moreover, because their record is evidence of ability, they are able to raise new moneys from outsiders on favourable terms. But without the possibility of take-overs there is no mechanism which forces companies to be even normally profitable. As long as they are just breaking even, such concerns may continue in existence. Only if competitors erode their markets to such an extent that losses are made will the resources be switched to alternative uses. However, once take-overs are part of the transfer process, the situation is very different. There is now a mechanism which imposes a real obligation on companies to be at least normally profitable. Unless companies achieve this norm, then their assets may become attractive to a take-over raider. Their shares may be undervalued in relation to the physical assets which they control. Shareholders may be open to the blandishments of an offer and thus control may pass. Losses do not have to be made for a bid to succeed. The raider has merely to persuade the holders of the voting shares that their prospects would be better under his control.

This simple analysis serves to illustrate the importance of take-overs in the allocation mechanism. It is the possibility or threat of a take-over which should apply pressure for companies to conform. The mere threat of loss of control should normally be sufficient in the real world to ensure that companies are pressured into an adequate performance. Only where they actually fail in this, or shareholders can be persuaded by a raider to relinquish control, will a take-over or merger ensue. Consequently take-overs which actually take place may be a signal of failure in this respect. These occur where a threat has been insufficient to improve company performance. Consequently the actual figures, which attempt to isolate 'external' expansion in company growth, understate the role of take-overs and mergers in the allocation of resources. They are exceptionally important to the process and particularly important to growth. They are part of a mechanism which, even in the imperfect real world, guides assets towards more effective economic use.

As already pointed out, not all take-overs and mergers are motivated by efficiency considerations. Furthermore companies effecting take-overs need not necessarily be more efficient than those they are acquiring. It has been found that take-overs may succeed for reasons which are not closely related to the success or failure of the individual business. (10) The successful company is not always more profitable than the firm it is absorbing. (11) Furthermore the company being acquired is not necessarily earning profits which are below the average for the industry concerned. Take-overs can succeed under such circumstances because ultimately it is economic power at the strategic moment of the bid which determines the outcome. Economic power and efficiency need not coincide. For example, sheer size can be important. The Board of Trade find that the 'very large companies were able, because of the greater marketability of their shares and of the "premium" they can command over the shares of smaller acquiring companies, to finance a higher proportion of their acquisition expenditure by the issue of shares'. (12) The result was that only 36 per cent of such expenditures had to be found in cash, compared with 55 per cent for other companies. This advantage of size may have little to do with economic efficiency. Thus take-overs may occur which do not necessarily involve switching assets to a better use.

Another reason why in practice the take-over mechanism may not operate to full effect occurs in the private company sector. Private companies are controlled by not less than two and not more than fifty shareholders, and by law may not invite the general public to become shareholders. Basically these companies are closely controlled, and little is known of their financial performance. (13) Because they are closely controlled, and because there is no open market for their shares, this sector of the company world approaches fairly closely that of the model of an economy operating without possibility of take-over. Motives such as retention of family control and the preservation of commercial independence, even if it be at the expense of low returns, assume greater importance than in the more ruthless quoted company sector. Non-quoted companies can be taken over, but this is only achieved with the agreement of the controlling group. The allocation mechanism is thus working in a truncated form. Loss-making causes assets to switch. Profitable private companies will grow because they can raise money on reasonable terms and also plough back their sizeable profits. But companies which are neither loss-makers nor highly profitable, and which also do not earn a normal return, can survive. The threat of take-over is very modified and so these concerns will continue so long as their proprietors are satisfied. Practical evidence for the existence of such companies is exhibited in the retail trade. There are many corner shops which just pay the owner a living wage, but which probably earn nothing like their opportunity-cost return.

In practice, then, the take-over mechanism is modified by the real world. Other considerations besides efficiency may influence the allocation of resources. Nevertheless the mechanism is important. It causes managements to be aware that mediocre performance can be sanctioned. Where shares are widely distributed, take-over is always a possibility. Managements can, however, secure a degree of immunity by ensuring good financial results. Thus even though take-overs may succeed for a very wide variety of reasons, they nevertheless provide an incentive to maintain and improve efficiency.

This simple analysis helps to explain, in economic terms, the prejudice which exists against non-voting ordinary shares. Devices which deliberately limit the dissemination of control, as, for example, non-voting A ordinary shares, are in effect a means of reducing the likelihood of take-over. The analysis also illustrates the importance of the Stock Exchange in the economy. By providing a free market in securities, take-overs are facilitated. Not only does the analysis stress the importance of a market in shares, but it also highlights the pricing and valuation process. If share prices do not reflect past economic performance or give a guide to future results, then the allocation of resources to a better use may be frustrated. Should the Stock Exchange valuation of shares be perverse, then companies may be taken over by others which are economically inferior. Resources may move to a less good use, simply because control is determined by securing a majority of the voting shares and not by being economically superior. Hence the way in which the Stock Exchange values companies is crucial to the allocation mechanism. It has been found that the Stock Exchange assessment of shares does not provide a successful means of predicting future earnings growth. In addition 'it does not tend to establish high yields for companies which are going to do best or vice versa. The market is a neutral arbiter.' (14)

Although the market is apparently poor at predicting the future performance of companies, at least in terms of their earnings growth, nevertheless share prices are linked to the past performance of companies. As pointed out earlier, dividend payments and ordinary share prices are positively related. In addition there is an association between the valuation ratio of companies and their current profitability. (15) The valuation ratio is a measure of the value of the ordinary shares in relation to the book value of the assets owned by companies. This ratio brings together the market valuation of the equity of a company as determined by the Stock Exchange, and the value as entered in the accounts of the assets such as factories, plant and equipment which companies use for trading purposes. The closer the relationship between companies' ability to use their assets and the valuation ratio, the more closely will current economic performance be reflected in share prices.

The book value of assets has a number of limitations as an indicator of the assets at the disposal of companies. Inflation means that almost inevitably there is a gap between original or book-value prices and current prices. The age composition of individual company assets is largely unknown, so no simple adjustment procedure is likely to be effective. Periodic revaluations do take place in some companies. These clarify the position in such cases, but do nothing to relieve the problem of companies which never or very rarely revalue. For all these limitations, the book value of assets is one of the most widely used indicators of the 'real value' of companies. Calculations of asset backing or realisation value are made by stockbrokers for their clients. These calculations are based on the assumption that in the event of liquidation the assets could at least be sold for their original purchase price. This is probably not unrealistic. If shareholders take note of the assets employed by companies, it is probable that the valuation ratio has some economic meaning. The comparison of the book value of assets and the market valuation of the ordinary shares amounts to an assessment of the way in which it is anticipated particular companies will use the assets concerned. A high valuation ratio implies that shareholders collectively expect an above-average use of the assets concerned to generate profits. A low valuation ratio implies the opposite. One of the key indicators guiding shareholders in their opinion of companies is likely to be past performance. Central to this opinion is likely to be the profitability of operations.

There is a connection between the market rating of companies and their past performance. The correlation coefficients between profitability and the valuation ratio of companies range from 0.35 to 0.47. (16) These correlations are strong enough to dispel any fears that Stock Exchange valuations are perverse. Current economic performance and the valuation of companies by the market are linked. One powerful explanation of this link is a degree of persistence of company results at least in terms of profit figures. There is some evidence that on average, companies tend to repeat their results. In a recent investigation, a correlation of approximately 0.60 has been found between rates of return on net assets between the two time periods concerned. (17) Past trading results apparently provide some guide to likely future performance.

Companies may therefore secure a degree of immunity from take-over by exhibiting economic excellence. The more successful a company, the more highly will its assets be valued by the market. Take-over becomes more costly, and shareholders less susceptible to the blandishments of raiders, because of the excellence of the performance achieved by their own company. There is some tendency for the rates of return earned by companies to influence the bid price made in take-over. (18) The more successful a company, the greater is the premium over the book value of its equity assets which has to be paid to secure control. In this sense the market is certainly not a neutral arbiter. Good performance is rewarded and poor performance penalised. Managements are well aware that should they turn in poor results, then the market may arbitrate against them. Performance will be reflected in the share price and the likelihood of take-over affected. Thus although the stock market may not be a good predictor of future company earnings growth performance, it nevertheless provides a mechanism to reward excellence and sanction mediocre and poor performance.

Although the pricing of shares on the stock market appears not to clash with the requirements of the allocation mechanism, it is not at all clear that assets are ultimately diverted to a more efficient use by take-over and merger. As mentioned earlier, the motives of take-over and merger are varied and need not serve the ends of improving efficiency. Furthermore it is difficult to assess the effects of company amalgamation. The 'true effects' (19) can only be guessed at. These are the contrast between what has happened with what might have happened without the mergers. No satisfactory technique exists for forecasting what might have happened.

Although the 'true effects' of mergers are difficult to assess, the ultimate or final effects are probably the same as those that would be achieved without mergers. For example, ultimately greater efficiency, rationalisation and the elimination of excess capacity may be achieved in a given industry by competitive elimination of firms. The contrast, however, lies in the timing. Mergers may allow the achievement of greater efficiency more quickly. In the example given, mergers may alter the timing of a given change, but the final outcome remains the same. (20) If this argument is accepted as generally true, then only where take-overs or mergers allow the achievement of any change more quickly will allocation improve. The prescription that assets should be diverted to a more efficient use thus has two meanings. First, that their earning power should be greater in their new employment, and second, that this enhanced performance should be achieved more quickly. If take-over slows the achievement of higher earnings, then some other form of adjustment will be more appropriate. It is impossible to lay down general rules indicating where take-over and merger will always be successful in these terms. Take-overs and mergers are merely instruments of change. They do not cause improvements in efficiency. These have to be realised by management efforts. Take-overs and mergers may affect the speed at which change may be implemented. Improvements will not accrue without management effort and skill.

Acquisitions and amalgamations are the only speedy method of creating large units. However, it is by no means tautologous that the fastest-growing companies rely most heavily on them. What is of concern is sustainable or high average growth per annum. A once-and-for-all expansion via acquisition which is not maintained in subsequent years is unlikely to be fast growth in this sense. Companies which grow by acquisition and merger may take a great deal of time to recover their liquidity position and reorganise. However, evidence from the United States lends support to the thesis that high growth and the frequent use of acquisition and merger are associated. (21) In the United Kingdom the fast-growing companies' more frequent use of external funds also points in the same direction. It is likely that acquisitions are partly financed by the issue of shares. Thus where external finance is important, this perhaps suggests that acquisitions and mergers are a significant element in the growth process.

The possible advantages of increased size via acquisitions and merger are well recognised. The Industrial Reorganisation Corporation has the power to make £150 million available to induce mergers. The National Plan also laid some stress on the role of mergers and amalgamations as a means to concentrate and rationalise. (22) The recently formed Industrial Mergers Ltd, a subsidiary of the Industrial and Commercial Finance Corporation, is designed to help businesses choose the right moment, terms and partner in the company marriage market. Until the I.C.F.C. formed this subsidiary, it had been handling around thirty mergers a year, but essentially on an ad hoc basis. The function has now been fully recognised in this new subsidiary. There is no lower limit to the size of companies with which Industrial Merger Ltd will deal, and fees charged vary according to the work involved. Public policy also recognises the power of mergers to create monopolies. The Monopolies Commission has already prevented amalgamations between the Ross Group and Associated Fisheries; Montague Burtons and United Draperies; District, Lloyds and Martins Banks; and Rank Organisation and De La Rue. These proposed mergers were found to be against the public interest. The effect of this power to investigate is to stress the importance of planned mergers, with the emphasis on efficiency rather than market power.

Private enterprise has not been slow to recognise the advantages of planned mergers. There are now a number of merger brokers. Chesham Amalgamations, and Singer and Friedlander's Merger Register, are examples. There are advantages to firms seeking partners or wishing to reorganise their subsidiaries. Discussion can take place, privately, between interested parties without any publicity.

Mergers and realliances can be organised coolly, with the really important issues well to the fore. The compatibility of organisations, the complementarity of manufacturing capacity and the ultimate effect on joint efficiency can be given proper consideration. Mergers need no longer go astray because the full implications are not considered at the time of the deal. Charges for the services range from ½ per cent to 3 per cent of the selling price involved. 'Mergers in future will not be the plain marriage of balance sheets, but inspired by industrial integration, the pooling of research costs and the rationalisation of products. The better planning of mergers owes a little to the role of the merger broker. It is to be hoped that in future the expertise in particular fields of brokers will limit the number of misalliances.' (23)

The pace of acquisitions is quickening, and concentration and rationalisation are proceeding too, (24) but are they proceeding in the right places? From a public policy point of view, where should government effort be directed? To date, considerable emphasis has been given to the declining industries. Declining industries have a slow rate of change of productivity, and individual firms have survived relatively long periods of adverse trading conditions. In some of them, market forces have failed to restructure the industries into a viable form. Ship-building and cotton are two examples. With both these industries the government has provided incentives to reduce capacity, regroup and raise efficiency. The example of these industries is enough to bring into question the efficiency of market forces in improving industrial performance. Even under the impetus of very stiff competition, mainly from overseas, government help has been necessary to reshape the industries and provide funds for improving efficiency. The explanation for the failure of market forces to revitalise these industries lies in part in the way in which the mechanism works, and in part with the particular circumstances of the industries. When industries are prosperous, funds are available for growth and improving efficiency. When competition becomes stiff, 'an industry weakened by surplus capacity can muster neither the will nor the resources to scrap and re-equip at the necessary scale or speed'. (25) Take-overs and mergers are a possible way of revitalising the earning power of assets. By regrouping within the industry concerned or merging with firms outside the industry, trading prospects can be improved. But while the threat of take-over may be present to the firms in the industry, bidders may not in fact appear because of the highly specific nature of the assets and their particular geographical location. This is particularly relevant to cotton and shipbuilding; moreover, competition is determined only partly by market forces. Political and strategic motives of foreign competitors reinforce it. Former customers have established industries behind tariff barriers and now compete in the world market, usually with a government subsidy of some sort. Thus the allocation mechanism may well not operate via take-overs, simply because outside firms do not want highly specific assets which have few alternative uses, and insiders cannot muster the funds to achieve adequate rationalisation. In instances like this there is a case for government intervention.

Considerable state intervention also occurs where the cost of projects is so high and the risk so great that private enterprise would not undertake them. Atomic energy and aircraft are two examples. But for other industries, what should guide the state in its efforts to secure greater efficiency and faster growth? In any economy there are certain industries which supply intermediate products to other industries which then produce the final articles. Industries which are not completely vertically organised thus have a proportion of the cost of their final articles predetermined. By influencing efficiency in the intermediate industries, the state would therefore be in a very powerful position to have a considerable effect on a very wide range of final manufacturing costs. Already, of course, the state uses this device to spread its influence on total costs. Nearly all of the nationalised industries produce intermediate products. However, as far as inducing improved efficiency in the private sector via take-over and mergers is concerned, intermediate goods are the obvious candidates. The I.R.C. is well aware of this. Its interest in micro-circuitry is an example. Micro-circuitry may soon be the key component in atomic equipment, tele-communications, computers, radio, domestic appliances and motors. Thus any satisfactory concentration of assets and ability within this field may have a very widespread effect. This is the sort of field in which the state should concentrate its efforts.

Discussion in Chapter 2 has indicated that perhaps there is no limit to the size of firm. This implies that there may be no 'optimum-sized' firm. This may be true, but yet does not deny the existence of an optimum at the level of the individual plant. Production efficiency is largely determined at plant level, and marketing efficiency lies with securing sales to serve plant capacity. Merely creating large firms may have very little to do with improving industrial efficiency. Forming large groups may have the effect of protecting a number of small and inefficient units which otherwise would have been forced out of existence. In fact mergers and acquisitions only serve the ends of efficiency if they permit the reorganisation of production capacity so that plant 'optimums' are more nearly approached and give firms sufficient marketing power to utilise this capacity. In other words public policy must advocate acquisitions and merger because this is the only speedy method of creating large units. However, this support for larger units must proceed in the realisation that large size only facilitates improved efficiency; it by no means causes it.

Take-overs and mergers have a part to play in improving industrial efficiency. But merely creating large units is no panacea for improving growth. Large firms can be comprised of tiny units which are, for example, very 'one-off' and jobbing in nature. There is no obvious relation between size and growth. Size is only a vehicle to produce a sufficient concentration of assets to promote efficiency. The two are by no means automatically linked. Size, if it is to have a definite meaning, must be related to the optimum plant. Only to the extent that large plant is required are large-sized firms prescribed for improved efficiency. Take-overs, however, can only be effective in allocation where company control is not held very tightly and where the assets concerned are not highly specific to a particular industry and do not suffer under a level of competition which is almost destructive in force. With these qualifications, take-overs and mergers are a very important instrument facilitating the growth process.

8 Invention, Innovation and Growth

1 INVENTION AND INNOVATION

Firms continually adjust themselves to change. The preceding chapter has shown how they can do so through take-over and merger. The present chapter will examine what they will have to adjust themselves to. In the broadest sense, this will include adjustment to all environmental changes, be they technological, social or political. Here, however, attention will be confined to the major influences inducing technological change at the level of the individual firm.

Technological change is at the heart of the growth process. Major elements inducing technological change are invention and innovation. The result is new products and processes. Production functions, which represent the ways in which inputs are combined to produce outputs, respond. New products and methods of production alter cost and revenue relationships. Changes in production methods and output mix become inevitable. These changes may be internally generated by firms themselves or externally induced. In either event there has to be an adjustment of the production functions.

Empirical studies of technological change tend to be applications of the theory of innovations to particular situations. Briefly, this theory asserts that economic growth depends on producing in new ways. (1) These new ways may be the application of a new invention or the application of an old invention where it has not been applied before. The key to growth is not just invention, but its application, and such application is known as innovation. This means a combination of factors of production in new ways so that they can create either more known goods or entirely new ones.

Invention must precede innovation. But invention by itself only fills the pages of learned journals. Its application, in the form of an industrial innovation, is the task of business firms. The latter may be aware that expenditure on research can lead to more inventions and so raise the possibility of more innovations, and they may finance their own research establishments or subsidise the universities. None the less, it does not follow that there must always be a direct link between inventor and innovator, nor that inventions are always readily taken up.

An extreme example of an unwanted invention is Leonardo da Vinci's flying machine. The market was not ready for it, and no one was willing to incur the development expenditure needed to turn this invention into a marketable product. Half a millennium elapsed before flying machines were reinvented and became accepted as commercial propositions. Even then it took half a century before air transport was sufficiently developed to become widely used. Along the road of development of the aircraft industry substantial further discoveries were made, and are still being made. Concorde is an example. This aircraft is a mixture of new discoveries and developments of the simpler aircraft of the past.

The line between discovery and development is never easy to draw, especially since any development expenditure can lead to new discoveries. The purpose of development expenditure is innovation, but its results may be path-breaking and in the nature of inventions. Moreover development expenditure may lead to innovations in the manufacture of products other than the one it was originally intended to improve. There may be a 'fall-out', of benefit to entirely new industries. For instance, the fall-out of the aircraft industry has led to ball-pens and space flight.

As there is no clear-cut distinction between inventions and innovations, there can be no clear-cut distinction between research expenditure (which is incurred with a view to inventions) and development expenditure (which is incurred with a view to innovations). What matters to industrial enterprises is innovation, and if this leads to inventions as well, there may be benefit later on. From the point of view of an industrial firm, research and development expenditure (R. & D.) are best treated together, bearing in mind that usually the immediate purpose is development towards improved application of former inventions.

Improved application is the essence of technology. It has a direct bearing on the production function of any one firm, and so is part of the entrepreneurial function of management. It includes any development of scientific and economic knowledge, and affects product mix, economies of scale, management techniques, staff organisation and any other conceivable aspect of a firm's structure and organisation.

Stages in the process of technological change are invention, followed by investigation of the economic feasibility of the new idea, development work, commercial production, and finally diffusion to other firms, industries and economies. The term 'innovation' covers all these stages except invention. Diffusion is part of the process and relates to the spread of an innovation through adoption, imitation and emulation. Development up to the first production in the originating concern is sometimes called the 'point' or initial innovation. Another term with the same meaning is 'autonomous innovation'. The subsequent spreading of the new technical knowledge, with modifications and improvements, is the later part in the overall process of innovation. It has been found that 'diffusion within a nation often takes twenty years and rarely fewer than ten'. (2) In the plastics industry, even though the pace of change is fast, between five and twelve years usually elapse between research and normal commercial production. A further period, ranging from two to three years for the United States and Germany, to more than twenty years in some cases, is required for diffusion from the originating country. (3)

Although the present concern is with individual firms, it may be mentioned that the macro-economic consequences of an innovation will be greater if this occurs at an early stage in the chain of production. Whenever there is an innovation at any one stage in the chain of production, succeeding stages experience changes in relative factor cost. The firms at later stages then rearrange their production functions to make use of the factors that have become more effective, or cheaper. These induced changes have a major impact on an economy. They represent the spreading of the *effects* of an innovation. In the present context, however, diffusion is used in a narrower sense. It represents the spread of the physical usage of the product or process, rather than its effects. For example, cheaper electricity, through the use of newly invented turbo-generators, will have a significant impact on the whole economy. The effects will be spread through practically every form of commercial activity and will induce a whole range of changes in production functions. Such induced effects are not included in the meaning of diffusion as used in this chapter. Here diffusion is confined to the spread of the innovation amongst users. The reason for this particular definition is that most studies examining diffusion adopt this approach. They do so because it is relatively easy to trace the adoption of an innovation, but much more difficult to assess its effects.

2   INNOVATION AND THE FIRM

For an individual firm, technological progress means more knowledge about useful goods and how to make them. (4) During recent years 'economists have shown that product diffusion and the use of new knowledge are more important for the growth of ouput per head than is the accumulation of physical capital'. (5) Technical knowledge increases as a result of invention and innovation. New methods of production and new goods are the outcome. As these are diffused through the economy, industrial performance improves. As shown before, the distinction between invention and innovation relates to the difference between discovery and application. Invention is an 'activity directed towards the discovery of new and useful knowledge about products and processes'. (6) Innovation on the other hand relates to the 'introduction of new and improved products into the economy'. (7) Innovation covers 'all activities of a business enterprise in developing a product or production method to the point at which it gives reliable services and allows sales at a price greater than cost'. (8) Innovation is thus the activity which applies inventions and brings them into the production process. The term 'innovation' covers all the stages beyond invention. The purpose of innovation is to bring new knowledge to bear upon production functions and to spread the benefits through the economy. Inventions are rarely immediately applicable. Further investigation is usually needed to establish the economic feasibility of the new idea. There has to be development work leading eventually to commercial production. This is costly and takes time. The cost has to be recouped by the innovating firm. The eventual benefit, however, accrues not only to the innovating firm but to imitators and emulators as well. They will also gain as the innovation is diffused.

From a commercial point of view there is no benefit from an invention until it is part of the process of production. Once this has been achieved (if United States experience is any guide), the benefits may be considerable. Both growth and profitability of firms are affected. In a sample from the steel and petroleum industries, innovations have apparently raised the growth rate by anything between 4 and 13 per cent. (9) Prior to the introduction of the innovations, the firms concerned exhibited no tendency to grow more rapidly than their counterparts. Successful innovation also tended to be very profitable.

The experience of two United States industries cannot easily be translated into precepts for British firms. Unfortunately the majority of empirical studies on the subject of innovation are based on United States data. There are dangers in assuming that the results apply to the British economy, but for the most part this has to be done. In the absence of local information, the next-best approach is to draw on experience which has been subject to empirical study. The procedure is justified on the grounds that the industrial environment in the two countries is not dissimilar at the level of the individual firm, and that the United States influence in the British economy in terms of investment and techniques is significant. With the dangers of this procedure kept in mind, it may be argued that successful innovation will have a very considerable impact on the growth and profit performance of individual companies in the United Kingdom.

3 THE MEASUREMENT OF INVENTIVE AND INNOVATIVE ACTIVITY

There are considerable difficulties in measuring the level of inventive and innovative activity. These difficulties are important because they affect the interpretation of empirical studies. Before developing the argument of this chapter further, it is important to show what sort of information is available and what its limitations are. The major sources of information include lists of inventions, figures for research and development expenditure, numbers employed in research and patent numbers. Each of these indicators of inventive and of innovative activity will be dealt with in turn.

Lists of inventions are available for a few industries. (10) There are, however, several problems of interpretations. The lists do not directly indicate the level of inventive activity. They merely set out the major steps in the development of the technology of the industries concerned. No indication is available of the importance of particular inventions. It is never easy to discern what impetus to further developments an invention may have provided. It is not always easy to distinguish between the relative importance of an original invention and successive modifications. Despite these difficulties, such lists probably provide the best available measure of inventive activity.

Where no lists have been compiled, alternative indicators, surrogates or proxy variables have to be used. The level of research and development expenditure, the numbers of research and development employees and the number of patents have been mentioned as examples. These again are only indicators of the level of the activity lying behind them. Expenditure and numbers employed in R. & D. are measures of inputs devoted in search of new ideas, methods, processes and products. They are not concrete measures of their output. The way in which money is spent, and the quality of the research personnel, will affect the output. Patent numbers, on the other hand, are indicators of inventive output. After all, patents are not granted unless they relate to new ideas, products or processes. Once again, however, patent registrations are only indicators of the level of technical activity. Not all inventions are patented, and there are also wide differences in their economic significance. Furthermore by no means all patents are developed to the stage of commercial exploitation. Fortunately there is probably a close association between the inputs, namely expenditure and numbers employed in research and development, and the subsequent ouput measured by the numbers of patents. It has been shown that amongst some of the largest United States firms, the correlation coefficient between R. & D. expenditure and patent numbers was 0.85. (11) The period between expenditure and patenting was lagged by four years in line with the average period between invention and the subsequent issue of patents. The correlation coefficient between numbers employed and patents was also 0.85. (12) Thus if patents are considered a good measure of inventive ouput, the indication is that expenditure and numbers employed in research and development are also reasonably good.

In the estimates of R. & D. inputs there is no distinction between activities devoted to invention and innovation. As mentioned before, such a distinction is difficult to draw in practice. Even if the intention is to finance development, the result may be an invention, and where the aim is to finance invention, the ouput may be an innovation which develops an old invention rather than a new one. Patent numbers, on the other hand, are an output measure. These are usually regarded as an index of invention. In practice, however, they may also be an index of innovation. Patents are applied for and granted with a view to commercial development. These patents may have arisen from development work in bringing a particular idea to the market. Thus patent numbers measure either invention or innovation, just as research and development expenditure does. Often it will not matter whether input or output data are used, since they tend to support one another and there is substantial overlap in what they are measuring. Logically, patent numbers are perhaps the better indicator of achieved invention, and research and development expenditure of the intention to invent or innovate. The following will conform with this general assumption. Throughout, however, it should be borne in mind that invention precedes innovation and that invention only assumes commercial significance when transformed into an innovation.

4   INCENTIVES TO INNOVATE

Technological progress comes about through invention and innovations. The benefits are spread through the economy in the form of new processes and products. These new processes and products may improve productivity and the standard of living. Two questions thus become relevant. One relates to the amount of resources that can be devoted to such activities, the other to what precisely encourages firms and individuals to innovate.

The volume of resources available for innovation depends on the present state of knowledge, the level of talent and the incentive to search for more knowledge. The economic incentive to innovate, on the other hand, depends on the expected money value of the solution to technical problems. These prospective valuations largely determine the current level of research and development work. The decision to invent and innovate is primarily an economic one. Unless there are prospects of a pay-off, technological activity by firms and individuals is unlikely to be forthcoming in significant quantities. It has been shown that research and development expenditure of large firms is considerably affected by profit expectations. (13) In addition it has been shown that the amount of invention, as opposed to expenditure on research and development, is governed by the extent of the market. Apparently even inventive activity is heavily influenced by considerations of profitability. Inventive interest declines 'because of the decline not in the technical possibilities of the field, but in its economic pay-off'. (14) Using the example of the horseshoe, J. Schmookler shows how the annual number of American patents rose, and then, as the 'steam traction engine and later the internal combustion engine began to displace the horse, inventive interest in the field began to decline . . . '. (15) As the technical possibilities in horseshoe manufacture were by no means exhausted, it was the decline in the prospects of the industry that explained the reduction in inventive activity. Further tests are carried out to establish whether revenue or cost considerations are supreme in determining technological activity within an industry. By examining industries which rely on several technologies, the primacy of value over cost is established. There are two assumptions in the procedure. One is that the cost of a given advance varies between technologies used within an industry, the other that the different technologies are unlikely to approach perfection together and thus exhaust the need for further invention at the same time. If these assumptions are true of the world, then the proposition is established. The close association exhibited between the time series of patent numbers of the different technologies within given industries indicates that some overriding force is in action. Patent numbers are used to indicate inventive activities. The close correspondence in the time series shows that prospects overrule differences in the cost of development, as well as in the state of perfection of the various techniques. So powerful is the influence of prospects that there are almost parallel movements in the time series of inventive activity in different technologies used within a given industry. (16)

If the series of patent numbers did not correspond closely, then this would imply that inventive activity in the relevant technologies would continue independently of the demand situation for the end-product concerned. Techniques would continue to be developed until they reached their own state of perfection at different times. Alternatively varying costs of development would regulate inventive activity and no correspondence would be evident in the series. Thus the tests indicate pretty convincingly the ascendancy of value over costs in the inventive process, and the major importance of the expected value of the solution to technological problems as a motive inducing invention.

In practice costs and the state of perfection of technologies within a given industry are likely to differ. The pattern exhibited by the time series showing inventive activity in the respective technologies must therefore indicate some overriding economic force. This is so powerful in operation that inventive activity is regulated by it. Differing costs and the state of perfection of the techniques are subservient. The result is the almost parallel movement in series already referred to. The determining force must be demand, operating through realised and expected sales in the industries concerned.

This conclusion is based on an analysis of patent numbers. Patent numbers are used as indicators of inventive activity. Clearly the findings will apply to innovation, because innovation is the process specifically aimed at making inventions commercial. The development of inventions to the stage of commercial exploitation is bound to be market-orientated. However, because innovation is likely to be so geared to economic prospects, the limitations of patent numbers as indicators of *inventive* activity must be remembered:

Firstly, patent numbers may not segregate inventive from innovative activity. Secondly, the *level* of inventive activity may also not be reflected. Large numbers of patents in a particular industry may be a result of secondary invention. These are specifically aimed at improving on the primary inventions which have established the basic technique in the industry. Examples of primary invention are steam propulsion and heavier-than-air flight. Secondary invention is therefore very akin to innovation in that effort is unlikely to be forthcoming unless the commercial prospects are attractive. Thirdly, patents may arise as a by-product of increasing development and innovational expenditures. These again are likely to be incurred only if prospects are good. Fourthly, there is no really satisfactory means of weighting patents to establish their relative importance. A rise in patent numbers may therefore be misleading. Patent numbers may rise at a later stage in an industry's development, when secondary inventions or innovations are patented. The few patents which lay the foundations of the industry's technology may well have represented a much more significant level of inventive activity. Fifthly, the early inventions may have occurred almost entirely by chance. Once it is realised that they have a demand potential, then research and patents may follow. This later activity is more likely to be demand-related than the initial discoveries. However, given these shortcomings, J. Schmookler's findings are of major importance. They mean that, in an economic sense, 'demand induces the inventions that satisfy it', (17) and technological progress in an industry slows down because it becomes less valuable and not because it becomes more costly.

The pharmaceutical industry provides an example of how expected future demand may influence the pattern of inventive activity. In a broad sense, demand for future products is indicated by those suffering from diseases which are currently incurable. Any company which invents a cure will have a market which is already specified. Numbers presently suffering indicate likely demand. This may have the effect of guiding research effort into these areas. With most other industries future demand is specified in less obvious ways. Unless the invention is likely to establish a new industry or replace existing market leaders, then assessment of market potential requires great skill in forecasting. Likely market capture, the rate of consumer acceptance and rival firms' reactions are amongst the uncertainties which make future demand so difficult to assess. Even so the decision to devote resources to invention and innovation will be heavily influenced by the prospective pay-off. If the invention of a particular new product or process is deemed worthless, then it is unlikely to attract the effort. The major impetus to change within an industry is economic opportunity.

Commitment to research and development varies widely between industries. In an Organisation for European Co-operation and Development study, industries are classified in order of research intensity. (18) Group A industries have a much greater commitment to research and development than those in group C. In 1964, in the United Kingdom, expenditure in group A industries (aircraft, electronics, chemicals and allied machinery, vehicles and instruments) was £405 million. Excluding aircraft, this figure was £266.4 million. In group C (food, textiles, timber, furniture and other manufacturing) expenditure amounted to £33.8 million.

A study based on United States data shows the varying impact of technological change within particular industries. Inter-industry differences are examined by correlating patents on sales. (19) The difference in the correlation between industries reflects the 'technological push' which tradition and the type of activity will impart, and the 'demand pull' on behalf of consumers. Technological push is a reflection of the opportunities. Demand pull is the pressure consumers exert influencing technological activity. This is likely to be highest where technological change is occurring very rapidly. An example is the electrical equipment and communications industry. In this case technological push and consumer pull operate strongly and the relationship between patenting and sales is very close. The propensity to patent can, however, affect the correlations. For instance, in the United States aircraft and parts industry the relationship is surprisingly low. (20) This is probably due to the influence of the United States Government contracting system. Exclusive rights in the form of patents are not usually granted for these contracts. With this proviso, where the relationship between patenting and sales is close, industries are so geared to technological change that any firm operating wholly within them will find itself practically forced to innovate in order to survive. Individual firms can, however, to some extent escape such pressure by belonging to many industries. The more widespread are a firm's activities, the less will a particular industry's technological pressure affect its research. This is why it is important to discuss invention and innovation at the level of the individual firm. In addition there are factors which influence research and development which are also best handled at the level of the individual firm. These include the size of companies, the type of competition or market form and the degree of diversification.

5   THE SIZE OF FIRMS

The advantage of large firms in invention and innovation is likely to be most marked in terms of their ability to meet the high costs of research, to bring new products or processes to the market quickly and profitably, and to carry the risks involved. Large size should ensure that new projects are only part of a considerable effort, so that failures may be carried by successes. Most investigators accept the assumption that there is a minimum size required for research activity. Large companies have wider sources of funds. For example, it is argued that in the United Kingdom the new-issue market is not suitable for issues smaller than £50,000 or for companies with assets smaller than £100,000. (21) Companies below these 'threshold levels' effectively have to rely on other means of raising capital. Large companies can afford to have viable research units, because the cost of carrying these is spread over large turnovers. With an element of market domination, large firms should be able to secure high returns on innovations and thus recoup research and development expenses relatively quickly. Moreover, because of their position in a market, any innovational edge should not be eroded too quickly by competition. Other arguments which favour large companies relate to the advantages of multi-product output. Highly diversified companies are likely to be able to produce and market 'a high proportion of unexpected inventions which are the almost inevitable outcome of research'. (22)

These arguments are persuasive. R. & D. expenditure is an investment in the future. Most modern inventions take a considerable time to become commercially viable. The average lag between invention and innovation has been eleven years in the petroleum industry and fourteen in others. (23) It is probably shortest in mechanical innovations. (24) There is also some indication that the lag is tending to decrease with more modern inventions, but this tendency is by no means well-established. (25) But regardless of the type of research activity, there is always a considerable delay between expenditures and receipts of revenues. Furthermore R. & D. costs may bear no relation whatsoever to the earning power of the final innovations. Uncommitted funds are therefore a prerequisite to engaging in this sort of activity. Such funds are more likely to be generated by large companies with a degree of market control. The following will summarise the results of empirical investigations, in an endeavour to answer the question whether size is a significant determinant of R. & D. effort.

One investigation (26) has found that the percentage of companies undertaking research increases steadily with the size of the firm. As already mentioned, there is a close relationship between patent outputs and R. & D. inputs. (27) Thus the larger a company, the more likely is it to undertake research, and the greater the R. & D. expenditure, the greater is likely to be the number of patents forthcoming. Neither of the relationships so far, however, describes whether large firms actually carry out more research. What matters is not so much that large companies do more research than small firms, but that they do relatively more. In both the United States and the United Kingdom large firms dominate industrial research. But it is hardly surprising that the largest companies spend more on research and development than the smallest. The relevant question is whether the largest companies spend more on research and development than the next largest, and so on. It would appear that this holds up to a certain size, but beyond that size research expenditure ceases to rise. If so, there may be an optimum firm in terms of research inputs. There have been a number of studies concerned with this problem. (28) Their findings have been summed up as follows:

'At least beyond a certain size level, the ratio of research and development expenditure to some index of firm size does not increase significantly with size, and may not increase at all.' (29) And in greater detail: 'Up to a certain size, innovational effort increases more than proportional to size: at that size, which varies from industry to industry, the fitted curve has an inflection point and among the largest few firms innovational effort generally does not increase and may decline with size.' (30) Thus in terms of inputs (R. & D. expenditure) there is some relationship between size and willingness to put resources at risk in the search for new processes and products. The form of the relationship is such that the very largest companies may devote proportionately less to R. & D. than the not so large. The optimum size, in this sense, varies between industries. This is hardly surprising, because what is a large company in one industry may, in absolute terms, be small in another. For example, the top company in terms of asset size in footwear would appear well down the list in chemicals. What matters is size in relation to the particular industry and markets served. Also a research effort which is appropriate in one industry may be totally inadequate in another. The technological pressure varies between industries, and so does the level of research effort associated with the optimum firm. Overall, the relationship between firm size and research input is weak, and not uniformly demonstrated. A large part of the explanation probably lies in varying conditions between different industries.

The relationship between firms' size and research has been examined from the viewpoint of innovations actually introduced. The study covers the United States iron and steel, petroleum-refining and bituminous coal industries. (31) It ranks in the order of importance the processes and products introduced since 1918. The results are examined to determine whether the four largest firms in each sector introduced a disproportionately large share of the innovations. A disproportionate share is defined as where a firm's share of innovations is greater than its market share. It was found that the largest firm did not always introduce a disproportionate share of innovations. In the petroleum and coal industries the four largest companies introduced more innovations than their market shares, but in the steel industry they did not. In steel the firms appeared too large relative to the innovations introduced. From this it might be concluded that dissolution of these companies would have a positive effect on the rate of innovation. This does not necessarily follow. Fragmentation of the industrial leaders might increase the average delay in utilising the innovations, if the largest firms are the prime movers in the process. This could be costly. Whatever the details in respect of these United States industries, there appear to be three general conditions which favour the largest companies. (32) First, where the innovation required a large investment compared with the size of the potential user. Second, the minimum size of the firm that could use the innovation was large compared with the average firm in the industry. Third, the average size of the largest four firms in the industry concerned was much greater than the average size of all firms which may use the innovation.

In all the empirical studies the major difficulty lies with the data. If the samples cover only a limited range of company sizes, then a wide variety of findings are consistent with the overall pattern. If only small companies are investigated, no relationship may be revealed. If only the very largest are covered, then innovation may appear to decline with size. Only if a wide range of companies is selected may a general pattern be revealed. Even if the samples cover the whole range of sizes, no general pattern may be exhibited because it is probably not so much the size of companies as such which is important, but the possible consequences of size. The problem is to separate out and identify just what are the advantages of size in R. & D. effort. Among the possible benefits put forward are a degree of monopoly and diversified output. But large size in itself does not necessarily imply either of these. Firms may be large in absolute terms and yet have little power in the market. Large firms may not necessarily have uncommitted profits, and they may be very specialist in their output. Thus unless the samples include everything that may induce increased research effort, the expected pattern may not be exhibited. The following will consider whether it is size by itself which induces increased R. & D. effort, or whether other causes are important.

6 MARKET FORM

Research costs, like other costs, have to be financed out of sales revenue. Currently incurred research costs do not, however, help to generate present revenue. Such expenditures are aimed at future process or product benefit. Research may not be obligatory to commercial survival. Unless profits are greater than required to pay acceptable dividends, service the debt capital and meet replacements of capacity, research within firms may not take place.

Under perfect competition, profits of this level may not be generated for a sufficient period of time. Competitors in such a close market will imitate any change almost immediately. There is no incentive for the entrepreneur to seek new processes or products. There is unlikely to be sufficient 'priority in time' for the initiator to recoup his research expenses. There are no restrictions on entry and no legal protection of the property rights in new processes or products. The innovating firm will effectively pass the fruits of research straight on to competitors at no charge. All firms within the market will immediately adopt the new technology and thus destroy any further incentive for an individual firm to innovate. Only if imitation is slow enough to allow sufficient profits to reward the venture will it be undertaken. But under perfect competition imitation will be quick because other companies will not have the research costs to meet. Should the price associated with the new technology be sufficient to allow the pioneer firm to recoup all its research costs, then this would represent a 'super-normal' level of profits for every other company. In addition firms outside the industry would be induced to enter and so the price would drop, leaving the initiating firm with unrecouped research costs.

The perfectly competitive market situation provides no mechanism for the individual firm to undertake research. This is hardly surprising. The model was constructed to analyse the nature of the cost and pricing process. It was not designed to analyse shifts in companies' production function brought about through technological change, nor to highlight the central features in company growth. For research to be accommodated in the model, modifications of the basic assumptions would have to be made. These may include restrictions on entry of new firms, a tax on the super-normal profits of imitating firms to discourage them from driving the price below the recoupment level, collective research by all the members of the industry, licensing or pricing arrangements to make imitators contribute towards the original research costs, patent protection which amounts to a legally enforceable period of priority in time, and research executed by some body outside the industry which then makes the outputs available to all members on appropriate terms. This outside body could of course be the Government. All of these modifications basically amount to curbing the rigour of the competitive process in order to provide an incentive to devote resources to research.

The perfectly competitive model is far removed from the real world. In today's market conditions, new products are continually being produced. The product, rather than the price, is intended to be the attraction. The problem now is no longer how to get new customers for the same product, but how to attract customers away from old products into markets for new ones. In short, the problem is one of 'innovative' and 'product' competition. In consequence, a model that merely indicates the working of price competition is now of limited value. All this does is to indicate that fierce price competition is likely to be inimical to research. In the real world competition has for long been modified by patent laws designed to protect the inventor. Patents confer limited property rights in ideas. The purpose is to raise the incentive to invent. Once a patent has been granted by the Patent Office, the initiator of the idea enjoys a monopoly for sixteen years. Without such protection the returns to invention would probably be much lower. Only where new processes could be kept secret or the costs of imitation were high would the inventor be free from rapid imitation by rivals. Under a patenting system a firm which succeeds in developing a patent to the stage of commercial exploitation becomes a monopolist of the new product or process.

The emphasis in the patent system is not, however, intended to be restrictive. For when patent protection is granted, the details become public knowledge. Thus patents involve disclosure of the principles of invention. A high proportion of patents are allowed to lapse after four years, when the renewal fees become payable, and many others are in fact available on licence. (33) The Comptroller-General of Patents also has the power to grant compulsory licences, if it is shown that a patentee is using his monopoly to the detriment of industry.

However, because development tends to be costly, it may be that patent protection is more important to innovation than invention. An American study (34) estimates that the costs of the research and development leading to an invention are typically only about 10 to 15 per cent of total costs. The remainder is accounted for by innovation and manufacturing start-up expenses. Experience in the United Kingdom appears to be similar. Research involved in the inventive step is rarely more than 5 per cent of the total cost before a product reaches the market. (35) Effectively, development tends to be much more costly than invention. If these figures may be taken as typical, it would appear that innovation is much more costly than invention. 'It is at the point where a firm has to decide whether or not to attempt to develop a discovery into a marketable commodity that patent protection becomes of crucial importance. Development is a high-cost and high-risk process, and the promise of a guaranteed period of protection for any successful product must be important in creating an atmosphere conducive to its being undertaken. A surplus must be gained from the sale of any successful products, not only to earn a fair return on their development costs, but also to cover the losses incurred on the failures.' (36) Whether the likely effect of fierce price competition on research and development expenditure actually establishes the case that monopolies are the best market form to induce high-level R. & D. is another matter. Immediate earnings, above the normal or opportunity-cost level, are required, and so is a degree of protection from the incursions of rivals to allow recoupment of cost devoted to invention and subsequent development. But it will now be argued that the evidence does not necessarily support the case for monopoly.

Monopolies are in a position to earn above-normal profits. They are therefore likely to have uncommitted funds which could be devoted to research. These are a prerequisite to engaging in such a highly uncertain activity as research. It has been found (37) that there is a positive association between R. & D. to sales ratios and weighted concentration ratios. The R. & D. to sales ratios are used as indicators of research effort. The concentration ratios, or percentage of sales, accounted for by particular firms are used as indicators of market power. This association was not, however, particularly strong. Only 30 per cent of the R. & D. variance could be statistically explained by industrial concentration. 'Hence though a positive association between R. & D. and industrial concentration apparently exists, it must be described as weak, as must also be the case for industrial concentration as a stimulus to R. & D. both in absolute and relative terms.' (38) There are disadvantages of using concentration ratios. They are not particularly good indicators of monopoly power or the likelihood of monopoly profits. There is a considerable variation in profits in industries having the same concentration ratios. However, even if the indicators were complete measures of monopoly power, there would still be reasons why the association between industrial concentration and R. & D. is unlikely to be strong. Monopolies may not exercise their market power to earn large profits. Instead they may deliberately not exploit their position. Even if large profits are earned, these may not be used to finance large R. & D. expenditures. There are many ways of using surplus funds. R. & D. is only one. Furthermore monopoly domination of markets may not induce a high-level motivation towards research. Competitors are, by definition, not a serious threat to commercial existence. The incentive for continuous improvement of product or process range may be damped by the commercial success which monopolies have already achieved. Uncommitted funds are required for research to be carried out, but this does not necessarily mean that monopoly is appropriate. Such funds may also be generated under oligopoly or monopolistic competition. What is required may be a temporary product or process benefit. Under monopoly, profits may be too permanent to provide an adequate stimulus to continuing effort. Furthermore 'what is needed for innovation is a situation in which firms that fail to innovate get hurt and get hurt badly'. (40) In addition what is required are conditions which are most favourable to innovative competition. As argued in Chapter 2, this form of competition may induce major steps forward in products and processes, and encourage rivalry along these lines. This is contrasted with product competition, where minor improvements are sought. In these terms, what is needed is competitive oligopoly which emphasises innovative competition. Innovation may be most rapid in industries with a few large firms, provided they are kept under pressure. A compromise seems to be implied whereby the disadvantages of fierce competition are avoided, as also are those of monopoly. Competitive oligopoly, that is a market structure where there are a few large firms competing with each other, may be more favourable to research. Above-normal profits may be earned by companies in this market form but the force of competition is such that their continuance depends upon retaining a competitive edge. The word 'competition' is included in the description of the market form to stress that there must be rivalry between companies and that competition must be effective in inducing innovation. Oligopoly must not be collusive. The major companies in the industry must not work in concert. If they do, then the effects on motivation may be similar to that of monopoly.

Companies under competitive oligopoly should have a sufficient degree of influence to bring the market for new products quickly to 'criticality'. (41) This means that there should be sufficient 'priority in time' to earn profits which are large enough to recoup research expenses and provide adequate returns. Competitors faced with the success of a rival should have the resources to mobilise assets to emulate or improve on the new product. This should occur quickly enough to persuade management that the record of successes and failures of new products or processes shows research expenditure to be worth while, and yet that the benefits from any one advance will not be permanent. Continuing research and development should therefore be thought necessary to maintain commercial eminence and induce innovative competition. Under monopolistic competition these conditions may not be fulfilled. There are many companies producing differentiated products. Each individual company is probably too small for an effective research programme. Where a successful product is developed, the market influence of the innovating company may be insufficient to recoup costs before rivals emulate. The pressure to emulate is likely to be great, especially if companies do not have much consumer loyalty. Thus even if the innovating company does create a market quickly, it is likely that companies will emulate very fast so that the originating company may not recoup costs.

Another factor supporting a market form which lies between competition and monopoly is the direction of causality between research and development expenditure, increased productivity and profitability. From a sample of eighteeen chemical companies and five in pharmaceuticals in the United States, it has been concluded that 'causality runs from R. & D. to productivity and finally to profitability'. (42) In other words, present profitability is the result of past R. & D. activity rather than the other way round. The link is not the expected one, whereby profitability determines R. & D. expenditure and thus changes in productivity. Instead the direction of causality seems to run the other way. This finding may be important as a guide to the R. & D. decision-making mechanism. If this is true of most industries, then the motivation for research may come not from the existence of high profits, but rather from the desire to enhance the present level of profits. Thus high-level or monopoly profitability may not be the best precondition for R. & D. A level of profits which is just adequate to support a viable research programme may provide a much stronger management motivation to research. This level of profits is more likely to be associated with an intermediate market form than monopoly. As argued above, competitive oligopoly may be suitable.

These sorts of arguments are persuasive, but there are complications. These are multi-product output, the type of research, the sources of ideas and the patent law. As argued in Chapter 2, companies tend to be multi-product in character. Consequently descriptions of market forms must either confine themselves to the particular products and not firms, or merely be a broad classification of the general type of business environment. In line with this reasoning, the case for competitive oligopoly must be restated. Competitive oligopoly must either relate to the general commercial environment encompassing the whole of companies' turnover or to the specific conditions facing particular products. The case for competitive oligopoly is now as follows: Innovative competition may be fostered by active rivalry between relatively few companies. This may occur because the general ethos facing these concerns encourages expenditure on R. & D. The general commercial atmosphere affects companies' attitude towards research and change. This must allow sufficient market power, at least in some areas of turnover, to generate enough profits to carry viable research and development effort.

The type of research may also affect the case for competitive oligopoly. Research is conventionally classified into two types, basic and development. Basic research is concerned with the investigation of fundamental knowledge and principles in a given field. Development research is more concerned with the application of the knowledge which basic research has yielded. Typically, basic research is carried out by universities and government institutions, and development research by firms and commercial institutions. This division is based on the principle that it is appropriate to apply commercial criteria in development and not in basic research. At the development stage the potential commercial benefits of an idea may be weighed against the costs. At the earlier or basic research stage such pressures are inappropriate, particularly if they are pressures for high returns over short periods. The search for new knowledge is more of an academic than a business exercise. This distinction between basic and fundamental research is akin to that between invention and innovation. Basic research may lead to invention and development research to innovation. As mentioned earlier, it has been found that patenting is influenced considerably by demand prospects. (43) But this does not necessarily mean that it would be appropriate to organise basic research in a fully commercial atmosphere. The reasons are as follows:

Although many patents result from basic research, it is not normally the main aim of this type of activity to secure immediate commercial benefit. It has been found that 'patenting is related most closely to development and least to basic research', (44) and that patentable inventions emerge from the final stages of the

R. & D. process. Basic research is the area of investigation which precedes development, and is therefore not necessarily very closely linked to patenting. Direct classification of research activities by type reveals that companies do little basic research. Presumably prospective pay-offs are too distant. (45) Firms typically concentrate on short-term research activities which are likely to yield commercial results within five years or less. (46) Furthermore evidence from the United States suggests that the effect of commercial pressure is not only to concentrate research activity on 'short-reach' projects, but also to bias activities towards new products rather than processes. (47)

Emphasis is on new or improved products rather than new processes which may affect the costs of production of existing goods. Businessmen believe that new products are likely to secure them greater profits. A new product is considered to be commercially more valuable than a new process. The overall effect of commercial pressure is therefore to divert effort towards short-term research to secure new products. This may cause neglect of longer-term projects and those aimed at new processes. Basic research organised under similar conditions of competitive pressure might also exhibit such a bias, which could be costly to the economy. This pattern may not be true of the United Kingdom. There is, however, some evidence to the effect that there is a tendency for companies to concentrate on short-term projects. (48) However, there is no information on the balance of effort between process and product innovation. It is often argued that British firms are less market-orientated than their American counterparts. (49) This attitude may relieve them from the bias towards new products. However, in the absence of empirical information it is difficult to be conclusive.

Basic research is research for its own sake. This form of research is expensive and hazardous. Such fundamental research is 'so unpredictable as to time of result that only companies with very large capital can afford to gamble with it'. (50) Governments are well placed to undertake this sort of research.

The plan to build an atomic accelerator, although subsequently withdrawn, is an extreme example of a risky project which governments are in a position to take. The construction costs were estimated to be £150 million, and these were to be shared by the Governments of the United Kingdom, France and Germany. With this machine there was a chance that physicists would break through to a much more profound understanding of matter. The final benefit to mankind could have been great. Equally this project could have led to a series of experimental results which might be of no use in application. Governments are in a position to take these sorts of risks. When commercial concerns undertake basic research, they have to take a very long view as to the likelihood of recouping costs. This sort of research is not of the specifically commercial type; rather a search is being made for fundamental principles which may ultimately prove valuable. Clearly this sort of research is only likely to be carried out by companies which feel sufficiently secure in their trading position to take a long view. These circumstances are more likely to be those of monopoly than oligopoly. The arguments advanced so far in favour of competitive oligopoly amongst large firms, to induce innovative competition, are thus seen to apply to short-term development research and not to basic research. Basic research is unlikely to benefit from competitive pressure. This sort of pressure is only likely to bring advantages when applied to development research. This is a specifically commercial process. Basic research is not. Thus it is unlikely to be carried out in the commercial world except by monopolies or firms acting in co-operation either through industrial research laboratories or through information-swapping arrangements. In summary, 'the closer one moves to basic research, the greater the probable benefits from co-operation, and the closer one moves to actual innovation, the greater the desirability of competition'. (51)

Other complications to the simple proposition that competition of an intermediate form, such as oliogopoly, will be best suited to encourage research, are the widespread sources of ideas and the effects of the patent law. The inventive genius may be employed anywhere. The impetus that such an individual gives to R. & D. may occur in any type of firm. He may be self-employed or work part-time for a number of companies. The large firm will not necessarily employ more of these individuals than the small concern. A study of sixty-one major inventions, between 1900 and 1950, indicated that over half came from individuals not engaged in company-directed research. (52) Nor will the force of competition necessarily make these individuals gravitate towards certain sorts of companies. The inventive genius may set up his own company to develop his ideas rather than continue in his present employment. Commercially this may be astute. If he is granted patent protection, he has a monopoly. The law is designed to protect the property rights in ideas. Tiny companies within a given industry may be monopolists of their own products or processes. Because ideas may come from a wide variety of sources and the patent law is designed to reward inventive effort by granting a temporary monopoly, the case for competitive oligopoly does not look particularly strong. However, there are weighty arguments in favour of such a market structure which encourages development rather than basic research. They recognise two major points. These are the tendency for inventive activity to become dominated by team research organised within firms and institutions, and the weakness of patent protection.

It has been argued (53) that invention has changed from an activity overwhelmingly dominated by individuals, to one less overwhelmingly dominated by business enterprise. There has been a shift in the occupational characteristics of the inventing group. The trained technologist forming part of a research team, rather than an independent individual, is now much more important. Because of the complexity of modern research and the high costs of developing ideas to a marketable stage, the role of the individual inventor is now less marked. He is by no means extinct, but his role is now more limited. Examples of areas of investigation, which are still well suited to his activities, include design improvements suggested by working experience, or new consumer goods which require neither complex scientific knowledge and equipment nor large-scale operations. Also the individual inventor may still flourish, even though the large company is increasingly dominating research activities. Some companies permit individuals limited patent rights, in recognition of their contribution to a discovery. Alternatively the individual may license or sell his patent to a company, after the early work has been completed. In this way he avoids the necessity of establishing production capacity himself and at the same time benefits from the transaction. However, by and large the role of the individual in research is probably becoming smaller.

The other factor favouring the larger commercial institution is the weakness of patent protection. Patents are intended to give a degree of protection to the inventor. In this way resources are more likely to be put at risk to develop ideas to a marketable stage. This should also hurry the process of the application of ideas. In addition, complementary inventions arising out of an original patent should be speeded up because patents involve disclosure of the principles involved. But to exploit his ideas, the individual inventor must have funds to develop them into marketable products. Often, however, patents are 'regarded as little more than licences to sue'. (54) The individual may not have the funds to develop his inventions or protect them in the courts. Thus unless patents are allied to economic power, their real protection may in practice be minimal. The descriptions filed with the Patent Office may well give rivals enough knowledge of the ideas to copy them and add just sufficient modifications so that no legal infringement will occur. As pointed out earlier in this chapter, it is at the development stage that patent protection is probably of greatest importance. Development is often a high-cost and high-risk business. Because of the weakness of patent protection, the private individual is at a disadvantage. Large firms are more likely to have the funds to undertake development and also defend their patents in the courts. This does not mean that an individual may not gain by his inventive genius, nor is it intended to give the impression that patent protection is without value. For all their weaknesses, patents may be a major inducement to technological change. In particular they may be especially important to the small firm and private individual. These units do not have the resources to mobilise productive capacity quickly. The possibility of legally enforceable rights to a patent may be a very real incentive. However, it appears that the balance of factors is weighted in favour of the bigger corporation. Both the tendency for research to become a team activity and the weakness of patent protection amount to such a bias. Thus the choice of the most suitable commercial environment between monopoly and other market forms remains important. The complicating factors of patent protection, the widespread sources of ideas and the effects of commercial pressure on the type of research imply, however, that no clear-cut overall policy recommendation may be given. The most suitable market form may only be prescribed when the specific circumstances within industries are known. For example, if it is intended that all basic research is to be carried out by government institutions and development activities by firms, then an intermediate market form may be appropriate. Alternatively, if basic research is also to be carried out by companies, then monopoly may be more appropriate.

7   DIVERSIFIED OUTPUT

Continuing with the factors which may induce increased research effort, diversified output may mean that a higher proportion of unexpected research findings may be utilised. There is a greater chance that the findings may be in line with existing activities. The knowledge may be used in the production of more than one product. If firms cover a wide range of activities, they may be more likely to apply innovations earlier. Firms covering a wide range of activities may also be more likely to operate in one or more progressive industries. All of these are potential advantages of diversified output. The unexpected invention, which is almost inevitable from research activity, has a greater chance of being employed by firms which have a wide range of products and whose technological base is wide. Firms whose technology may have stabilised may benefit from having other activities in newer and more dynamic fields. Demand may be growing fast in these areas, and the profit potential may be such that research activity is stimulated. (55) These arguments are persuasive, but do they in fact mean that diversified companies carry out more research and are more effective in the employment of the results? It has been found, that 'diversification is not per se a structural condition necessarily favourable to patentable inventions'. (56) Instead the data illustrate the favourable effect of operating in dynamic industries by firms whose base was not conducive to patentings and research and development. Firms with an interest in other industries besides their main one may be considerably influenced in their inventive output, particularly if the other industries are dynamic. Diversification was thus not necessarily favourable to research and development, but potentially could be.

One major problem with this sort of exercise is to separate the effects of size from diversification. Large firms may tend to be highly diversified. They have sufficient size to make operation in many spheres economically possible. Production units can be of a viable size even though activities are widely spread.

Firms of large size can comprise specialised production units in many fields. The organisation can be such that production units are linked with others only through common ownership. Day-to-day operation in each unit may continue unaffected by the vast range of goods which the firm as an aggregation of all these activities covers. If the largest firms tend to be the most diversified, then any statistical exercise designed to test the effects of widely spread activities may in fact reflect the consequences of size. It is only if size and diversification are not highly correlated that some idea of the separate effects may be accurately assessed.

8 SCALE EFFECTS

Apart from the effects of market power and diversified output, the question arises about further possible advantages associated with a particular size of firm in their innovational effort. Do the largest firms necessarily have an advantage in the organisation of their research? Do economies of scale exist in commercial research? Specifically, is a unit of research effort more productive when carried out in a large or a small firm? Alternatively, in firms of a given size is a greater research effort associated with greater research output? These are organisational questions aimed at establishing the effects of varying research expenditure on research output in firms of a similar size, and the effectiveness of a unit of research expenditure in terms of subsequent output in firms of varying size. An examination of these two issues in the United States has revealed that, holding firm size constant, the number of significant inventions seemed to be influenced by the amount of research and development expenditure. (57) However, there was only a more than proportional increase in inventive output in one of the industries concerned, namely chemicals. In that case there was evidence that there were economies of scale in research expenditure. This perhaps indicates that there are no marked advantages of the largest-scale research activities over medium and large ones. On the second issue, the average productivity of a unit of research expenditure in terms of inventive output, proved to be negative in relation to firm size. The inventive output per unit of R. & D. expenditure seemed to be lower in the largest firms compared with the medium and large ones. Apparently a given sum spent on research is not necessarily more effectively employed in the largest companies. There were indications that the problems of organisation and control were such that the relationship was negative. Apparently there are two conflicting forces in operation within firms; these are the advantages of more expenditure on R. & D. within firms of a given size, and the disadvantages in terms of average productivity per unit of expenditure of organising research within the largest firms. The results perhaps indicate that the arguments on size, research and development and inventive output may be ones of degree. The largest firms may well have passed the optimum size in terms of efficiency and effectiveness of R. & D. expenditure. On these criteria, it may be possible to be too large.

The advantage of this empirical approach lies in the deliberate attempt to highlight the effects of size; the disadvantage is that the relevant information is available only for major firms. This implies a certain element of market power. It is also likely that these companies are highly diversified and thus encouraged in their research effort through wide outlets for any potential discoveries. Size alone is thus unlikely to be the complete explanation of the observed differences in the behaviour pattern. Nevertheless it is reasonable to postulate that size has played some part. It would be unwise, however, to generalise these findings too much. As already pointed out, the degree of technological push varies between industries, as does the economic meaning of large size. In addition United States experience may be different from that of the United Kingdom.

Fortunately there are factors in most industrial economies which make the search for the optimum-sized firm less crucial. These include patents, the wide-spread sources of ideas, industrial research laboratories, contracted or sponsored research, licensing arrangements and a wide range of government institutions. The most insignificant firm has always the chance of becoming the sole owner of a patent. Small firms may have access to large research through collective research laboratories organised, for example, through trade associations. Or again research may be contracted by a small firm to a big firm, with an agreement to apportion the benefits of any results between them. New products may be manufactured under licence from the patentee. There is the power under the Patents Act for the Government compulsorily to license manufacture by other companies besides the patentee. The National Research and Development Corporation is an institution whose aim is to carry development risks and provide finance in return for a levy on profits or turnover on any commercially viable output. These arrangements probably do not completely balance the advantages enjoyed by large companies in research processes. Nevertheless they make the establishment of an optimum-sized firm in terms of research less crucial.

9   DIFFUSION

The discussion so far has leaned heavily towards the impact of structural influences on the level of point or initial innovation. An attempt has been made to isolate the effects of market form, diversification and size as such. The success of the exercise has been limited. Of parallel importance to point innovation is the strength of the mechanism which spreads change throughout an economy. Diffusion may be even more important than the origination of new products or processes. Unless these are spread through the economy, the benefit will remain localised and may so have a small impact on overall economic performance. One writer is of the opinion that 'in principle, a country has a much greater opportunity to gain an advantage in the growth rate race by reducing the gap between average and best practice than by advancing the frontiers of knowledge'. (58) This viewpoint is persuasive. A considerable part of the 'late starter' thesis, used to explain the relative demise of the leaders in the world's industrial revolution, turns on the advantages which developing nations have in adopting the knowledge and technique which have been proved by advanced countries. Only if a country is responsible for a very high proportion of the output of the world's innovation and is also dependent upon these for its export performance, is the argument that diffusion is more important than point innovation likely to be upset. In this case the supply of new ideas is likely to be crucial in economic performance. However, regardless of the particular situation of individual countries, diffusion of innovation is quite clearly of exceptional importance in the process of technological change. Factors which hinder the spread of new processes and products will be responsible for slowing improvements in living standards.

The process of productivity and technological change has been analysed on the basis of performance data. (59) The results illustrate the gap between best practice and the average techniques within given industries. This gap is a measure of the delay in utilisation of new techniques. A similar analysis of twelve innovations in four industries in the United States shows that average time between first use and use by half of the ultimate users was 7.8 years. (60) Ten more years passed before 90 per cent of the ultimate acceptance was reached. The time between first use and use by half of the final consumers varied between industries.

Diffusion is thus a lengthy process with considerable variation in the speed of operation. Studies of diffusion have so far been confined to producer goods. Consumer goods or final products have not been included. In practice this is unlikely to matter too much. In both instances firms are involved in the decision-making process. Furthermore there is unlikely to be a great contrast in the character of decisions to produce a new product or an existing product with a new technique. General considerations which delay adoption are the existence of fixed capital equipment, business secrecy, poor communications, management inertia, labour fears and patents. The effect of fixed capital may need elaboration. Fixed capital equipment 'inhibits immediate adjustment to a flow of new techniques'. (61) Long-lived and with few alternative uses, such assets will remain employed so long as they cover the supply prices of transferable factors like labour, raw materials and those parts of the investment which could be changed to alternative employments. Furthermore, if their original cost has already been recouped, such machines may continue in employment for the period of their physical lives.

Other forces affecting the gap between best and average performance within industries are the intensity of competition, relative price movements, the expected value of any change and the elasticity of substitution of new for old capital and capital for labour. The last point may require clarification. If the elasticities of substitution can be increased, the change to new techniques is facilitated. For example, if a particular industry is in a phase of expansion where gross investment is high, it is likely that the elasticity of substitution will also be high. New capital equipment with greater productive capacity may be incorporated, both as part of replacement and expansion. Labour is unlikely to be laid off, even though such new plant may be very labour-saving. Alternatively, in a downward phase the opposite forces may be in operation. These sorts of considerations have led to the suggestion that high gross investment may induce high growth. (62) On this view, investment is the engine of technological change, inducing greater efficiency and growth. A high rate of gross investment allows new techniques to be 'embodied' in the production process and the capital stock to be updated. The lag between the use of advanced techniques and average ones may thus depend on the rate of gross investment.

An individual company faced with the problem of adjusting to technological change, is likely to assess each alteration in its products and processes in terms of a number of major considerations. These include, first, the long-run advantages of the innovation; second, the transition costs and frictions of any potential change-over; third, the risks involved in not adopting the innovation; fourth, doubts about the superiority of the new product or process; and fifth, the ease of overcoming these. (63) A firm will probably be favourably disposed to the change if it seems highly profitable, if capital costs and labour displacement are low, if the innovation is not replacing existing goods, and if uncertainties of its potential market may be assessed by a limited trial. Even if all these favourable circumstances are present, firms will vary greatly in their speed of response. Managements' general attitude to change will be important. Dynamic executives, technically advanced and conversant with new developments, are likely to thrust their companies amongst the ranks of the innovators. Conservative, entrenched and satisfied managements are more likely to be laggards. One author has suggested a standard nomenclature to describe companies' reaction to technical change. Companies are classified as innovators, early adopters, early majority, late majority and laggards, according to their speed of reaction to change. (64) These attitudes to change influence companies and industries in the diffusion process. Competition is rarely so stringent that companies must adopt the current 'best' techniques rapidly or be eliminated. Managements have a large element of discretion. It is possible to belong to the laggard group for generations and still survive.

There is little evidence on the diffusion process in British industry so that United States experience must be relied on. This is drawn from a study of twelve innovations in four industries. (65) Each of the twelve innovations required substantial investment, and diffusion was not impeded by patents. The information relates to the rate at which firms imitated innovators. The figures do not cover the rate at which new techniques displaced old ones, nor the rate at which new techniques increased. The study is conducted in terms of the rate at which firms begin using an innovation. The major hypothesis tested is that the probability of a firm adopting a new technique is an increasing function of the proportion of firms already using it and the profitability of doing so, but a decreasing function of the size of the investment required. This model of the imitation process within industries stands up well to testing. Apparently the larger the proportion of firms using a new technique, the greater is the probability that an individual firm will adopt it. The greater the profitability, the greater also is the likelihood that imitation will take place. The size of the investment required apparently has an inverse relation to adoption. The smaller the sum involved, the faster is imitation likely to be. This behavioural model ignores variations over time in the profitability of introducing an innovation, sales and promotional efforts, and the degree of risk firms believed they faced when they first introduced innovation. The coverage of the sample is limited; all the firms are large and none was in a new industry with a rapidly changing technology. However, the model is helpful as a guide to the rate of imitation. The major influences in the process are highlighted. These are the profitability of the innovation, the size of the investment required and the proportion of firms using the new technique.

Another study examines the economic characteristics of firms which are relatively quick and relatively slow to begin using new techniques. (66) Here the emphasis is on the economic features of companies and their influence on the speed at which new techniques begin to be used. For example, are large companies with high profits and dynamic managements those which are always quick to adopt innovations? It was found that the central feature in the imitation process is the expected value to the firm of using the innovation. The greater the commercial stimulus in terms of improved revenue, the more quickly are firms likely to change. In this context profitability is potential profitability. Companies in a decision-making situation can only assess the advantages of any change. They will not necessarily be able to repeat the profit experience of those earlier in the field. However, the more successful are their predecessors, the more tempted will they be to try. It is found that for individual companies the wait before using new techniques is inversely related to the profitability of the particular invention. In addition the size of companies is inversely related to the wait involved before adoption. Holding firm size constant and also the profitability of the particular invention, there is no significant tendency for the length of wait to be related to the overall profitability of individual companies, the profit trend, growth rate, liquidity or age of the companies' chairman. Liquidity is used as a proxy for the availability of funds. Past growth and the age of company chairmen are used as proxies for the dynamism of management. The past profit trend is used as an indicator of the pressures to adopt new techniques. For example, if the trend has been downwards, then there might be a strong impetus to search for alternative techniques. No particular group of firms exercised technological leadership for long periods, and there was no evidence that increases in size lead to sluggish performance in the introduction of innovations. The implications are as follows: profitability is essential to the imitation process. Profitability does not mean the *overall* financial health of companies; rather it means the extent to which a particular innovation offers an economic stimulus in the form of profits. The speed of firms' response is related to this stimulant. The greater the profitability of a particular innovation, the shorter is likely to be the wait before introducing the new product or process. Financial health, in terms of liquidity and overall profitability, bears no close relationship to the wait. It is the impetus of the profitability of a specific innovation which is important in the imitation process. The larger the company which assesses a specific innovation, the faster is likely to be the speed of introduction. Amongst the reasons are likely to be the following: Large firms often enjoy financial stability. They frequently cover a wide range of activities and thus have a better chance of applying innovations earlier. At any moment of time large firms are more likely to have products or machinery that need replacing and therefore they may be in a position to adopt innovations earlier. In addition, a change may involve large investment. Within large firms this may be less inhibiting. Another important implication is that general classifications of firms into groups like 'pioneers' and 'laggards' is likely to be misleading. It was found that individual companies which are quick to adopt innovation at one time will not necessarily repeat this performance.

10   INTRA-FIRM DIFFUSION

Diffusion has so far been discussed in terms of the speed at which firms begin to use an innovation. Another part of the process, known as intra-firm diffusion, is the rate at which firms substitute a new product or technique for an old one, once they have begun to use the new one. In engineering, for example, lathes are used to turn out a wide variety of products. Once a firm has installed an improved lathe with, for example, a numerical control system, then the rate at which the new machines subsequently displace the old ones is the rate of intra-firm diffusion. An examination of the speed of intra-firm diffusion in the United States railroad industry over the period 1925-61 (67) was concerned with the rate at which diesel traction displaced steam traction within each firm. The rate of intra-firm diffusion is defined as the time it took thirty randomly chosen firms to increase their diesels from 10 per cent to 90 per cent of their total locomotive stock. The 10 per cent figure is taken as the time when the firm 'began' to dieselise, and the 90 per cent figure as the time when the process is completed. The specific figures of 10 per cent and 90 per cent are arbitrary, but nevertheless should span the period which extends beyond experimentation and up to effective completion of the change to diesels for each company. The model, which attempts to explain variations in the rates of intra-firm diffusion, includes the profitability of replacing a steam locomotive with diesel, the age distribution of firms' steam locomotives, the apparent riskiness involved at the time of the investment, the size of the firm and its liquidity at the time when the firm 'began' to dieselise. The model has considerable explanatory power. About 70 per cent of the inter-firm variation in the rate at which diesels replaced steam can be statistically accounted for. Although this study covers only one industry, it probably has general relevance. As its author points out, the model is similar to that used for testing diffusion among firms, which has been described earlier. Apparently there is a similarity in the factors inducing these two sorts of diffusion. This would suggest 'that there exists an important economic analogue to the classic psychological laws relating reaction time to the intensity of the stimulus. The profitability of an investment opportunity acts as a stimulus, the intensity of which seems to govern quite closely a firm's speed of response. In terms of the diffusion process, it governs both how rapidly a firm begins using an innovation and how rapidly it substitutes it for older methods.' (68) Techno-logical change occurs through invention and innovation. The benefits are spread through the economy by diffusion both amongst and within firms. The major impetus to invention and point innovation is also market-orientated, namely the expected value of the solution to technological problems. (69) Structurally, both processes may be fostered by intermediate competition. Fierce competition may reduce the expectations of profit and therefore the pressures to invent and innovate. Sufficient relative price and factor movements are required to spread change, and yet there must be good prospects to encourage research and development.

11   THE COMMERCIAL ENVIRONMENT

Imagine a successful innovation which will ultimately displace the existing technology of an industry. In order to speed the diffusion process, there must be
high potential rewards to the innovators, the early adopters and perhaps the
early majority. At the same time the competitive process should operate to force
the remaining groups (the late majority and the laggards) to follow on quickly.
This may be effected through reduced returns on their present technology, thus
making imitation relatively attractive. Not only should there be high potential
rewards to those companies early in the field, but these rewards should be
ranked according to the degree of uncertainty faced by companies making the
decision. Companies adopting early are not in a position to assess market
potential by reference to achieved results. They are pioneers breaking new
ground with as yet unknown potential. They face a situation of greater risk than
a laggard who is adopting a product which has become commercially established.
For such pioneers the market is unmapped. Furthermore future modifications of
the product or process by other companies may quickly erode the impact they
hoped to achieve by being early in the field. If the innovation is to be diffused
with any rapidity, the profit potential must be greater for those who are
prepared to carry such risks. If this is not the case, it might pay companies to be
slow. The market form may influence the potential return and therefore the
speed of reaction. Competitive oligopoly might give this ranking of potential
returns. Companies early in the field should achieve considerable market impact
and thus enjoy sizeable demand potential. They should derive advantages from
'learning by doing', as the improved expertise which results from familiarity with
the production process has its effect on costs. (70) 'Priority in time' should not
be eroded too quickly. Companies should be able to establish and keep some
consumer loyalty as a result of their market success. Late comers in the field will
be unlikely to achieve such market impact. In their case the change-over to the
new product or process may be 'forced' by relative price and factor movements,
to the detriment of their existing product and process mix. They may be so
averse to risk-taking that any change is probably commercially defensive rather
than aggressive.

   This representation of diffusion under competitive oligopoly is highly
schematic. As argued in Chapter 2, with multi-product companies the concept of
an industry is difficult to apply. The market forms should now relate to particular activities and/or stress the general commercial environment. Nevertheless it
serves to stress the central requirements for innovation and diffusion in a given
industry. Innovating companies have no foreknowledge that their ambition will
be rewarded. However, they must be induced to continue devoting resources to

research. The ranking of ventures according to companies' responsiveness to change will not necessarily occur for each and every innovation. The working of the market form must, however, on balance reward the venturesome companies. 'On balance' in this context means that over the years returns from successful ventures must compensate for the inevitable failures. The compensation must be at a level which is sufficient to maintain the incentive to change.

Despite the potential advantages of being an innovator, there is always the danger that imitators might enjoy higher profitability. Unless imitation is as costly as the original R. & D., or the innovating company already has such market power that competitors are of small consequence, the fruits of research may pass straight to rivals. Such a reordering of potential returns may be prevented by patents. Patents amount to a recognition of the arguments that innovators require special treatment and that there should be penalties for being 'second in the field'.

Evidence of a general character exists supporting the contention that large firms with an element of market power should be beneficial to technological change. In both the United States and the United Kingdom, industries with high concentration or large factories appear to enjoy greater technological change. Technological change is defined in terms of the increase in output per employee-hour. (71) Of course this measure includes all factors which go towards improving efficiency, such as innovation and diffusion as well as improved use of existing facilities. This evidence, together with that cited earlier on the importance of the stimulus of profits, helps to dispel any fears that the structural requirements of the various stages in the innovation process are at variance with each other. Industries which have larger establishments and/or high concentration ratios tend to have an above-average rate of increase in productivity. Large size and an element of market power are apparently not harmful to technological change. The association between the measures is, however, not particularly strong, but at least it does not contradict expectations.

Large firms thus appear to play an important part in the process of technological change, but they must be kept under commercial pressure. This adds weight to the assertion that competitive oligopoly may be the most suitable market form to foster technological change. The case in favour of large firms, however, is not so well founded as to provide strong grounds for deliberately creating such units. Instead it supports arguments for mitigating the disadvantages faced by small companies in the process of technological change.

12   THE INDIVIDUAL FIRM

To return to the main theme of the individual firm, what is the link between company growth and R. & D.? It has been found that corporate profits are related positively in normal times to inventive output (72), and that regardless of size the technically progressive firm is generally better managed in all respects than the unprogressive firm. (73) Moreover 'it may also be true that rapidly growing and profitable firms will be more innovation-prone'. (74) The returns to research and development are high, and furthermore the impact of successful innovation on company growth is considerable. Seemingly, high-growth, high profits and high inventive output are all positively associated. This is eminently plausible. However, one puzzling feature remains. This is the high level of returns associated with R. & D. (75) If these are typical, they suggest that perhaps there is under-investment in R. & D. With more firms and greater quantities of finance devoted to seeking new products and processes, presumably the returns would not be so high nor the effect on firm growth so great. Why, therefore, do returns remain at such high levels and why is there this degree of 'under-investment'? The answer is perhaps due to a number of inhibiting factors which influence research and development: first, the risks involved in R. & D. projects; second, the cost of research facilities; and third, the advantages of being 'second in the field'.

Research and development is admitted to be a risky process. There is no certainty that funds employed in the search for new products and processes will result in end-products. For example, of the inventions submitted to the National Research Development Corporation from publicly supported bodies, 48 per cent were accepted for attempted exploitation, 11 per cent secured licence arrangements and 4.5 per cent became revenue-earners. (76) Success is not achieved by merely raising R. & D. spendings. This is borne out by the nature of the association between growth, profitability and research inputs. There is some link between these factors, but it is weak. (77) The explanation lies of course in the simple fact that R. & D. spending does not ensure that commercial innovations will result. Effectively, R. & D. spending is a poor guide to growth potential and profitability. Even if research spending was an excellent indicator of innovative output, there would still be a further complicating factor. The competence of management varies between firms. The supervision of new products and processes to the market is a multi-stage process, which is very demanding in management ability. Companies' response to the challenge of technological change, therefore, varies not only with their research spending but also with their ability to manage. One very important management problem involved in innovation is the estimation of returns. The relationship between actual and estimated yields on capital projects which for the most part involved an element of innovation tends to be low. In one study the correlation was only 0.13. (78) Over-estimation and under-estimation was equally likely in the examples studied. Unforeseen changes in demand seem to be the factor most frequently responsible for the divergences. Differences in the cost of investment, followed by the technical possibilities involved, were the other two factors responsible.

Research facilities are expensive. Estimates of the average cost per qualified man in industrial research vary between £3,000 to nearly £9,000 per annum. (79) Some firms in the chemical industry argue that an effective research and development department will involve at least twenty qualified scientists and cost £100,000. (80) The effective size of a research team varies between industries; nevertheless the high absolute costs of an effective research effort will act as a 'threshold effect'. Small firms are unlikely to be able to carry such expenditures within their turnover. As a consequence, research at least of the formal kind, with laboratory facilities and scientifically qualified full-time personnel, is likely to be confined to the large and well-established companies.

Even where companies are involved in R. & D., the costs of developing inventions beyond the discovery stage to a marketable product may inhibit them. As mentioned earlier, it is the development stage which tends to be the most costly. The effect of the expense, allied to the uncertainty of the commercial value of any output, may be to reduce the potential inputs. The advantages of being 'second in the field' may also have a similar effect. If companies are in a position to copy a new product without incurring any of the research costs and risks involved, then this may bias effort towards imitation rather than innovation. The innovating company carries all the risks, establishes a market and then finds that other companies jump on the bandwagon. Graphically, the situation may be represented as in Fig.8.1

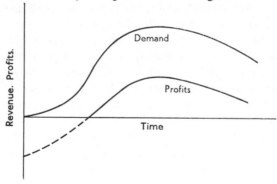

Fig. 8.1 Demand and profits patterns over time for a new product

The demand pattern over time for a new product may often take the general form of an initial slow take-off, followed by a rapid increase as consumer acceptance is established, and then a flattening of the steep increase as market absorption is reached and demand tends to come from replacement rather than new customers. The profits profile association with this demand pattern over time, may show an initial loss and then a rapid increase and finally a flattening-out or even a decline in profits as market absorption is reached. Obviously any company intending to rely on imitation rather than innovation will attempt to add this hypothetical product to its output during the period when profits are rising strongly. In this way good returns will be secured with very little uncertainty. 'Under-investment' in R. & D. may therefore arise because attractive profits may be earned by copying rather than initiating the development of products. These profits may not be as high as those earned by the innovating company; nevertheless they may be high enough to dampen the incentive to be first in the field and to carry out research and development.

In practice it is difficult to judge whether there is under-investment in R. & D. The presumption that not enough resources are being devoted to research arises from the theoretical proposition that returns will tend to move to equality. Good profits attract investment, poor profits repel it. The net effect should be movement of factors between various employments until rewards are brought to equality. If returns remain persistently high in particular employments within such a theoretical system, this implies either that factors are not free to move, or that the premium return above the normal is justified for some reason. It is sometimes argued that high returns to R. & D. may not imply under-investment, but rather that they reflect the level of uncertainty faced by venturesome companies. These high returns may remain in the system because other companies are inhibited by the commercial risks involved. As argued above, this inhibition may be reinforced by practical reasons like the advantage of copying rather than initiating and the effective absence of small companies in research and development because of the absolute costs involved.

In practice, uncertainty involved in R. & D. may not be very high. Admittedly research and development for military purposes seems to carry high risk. One study shows that cost estimates were almost always below the true subsequent costs and, on average, were out by 40 per cent. (81) Not only were costs out, but also completion times. Both costs and completion times were influenced by the extent of the technological advance involved. Where a big step forward was being taken, the errors tended to be greater than with a small advance. Industrial research, on the other hand, probably carries less risk. It is often argued by businessmen that putting money into research provides no guarantee of a saleable output. Strictly this is correct for any *particular* firm, but as a general rule there is a reasonably strong correlation between the overall R. &

D. expenditure by firms and subsequent output in terms of patents (82) Whether these patents have any commercial value is, of course, another matter. Furthermore there is limited evidence that the risks involved in industrial R. & D. projects may not be very great. A study of one important United States company in electrical equipment, electronics and appliance manufacture found that failure of a particular project was often due to the firm diverting attention elsewhere or time schedules not being met, rather than an absolute failure in the sense of being thwarted by technical difficulties. (83) In a survey of seventy applied R. & D. projects undertaken by this firm, three-quarters had an estimated probability of success of 0.80. Even if the bias towards optimism caused by professional researchers' need to convince management is removed, the probability of success is still estimated as 0.50. When the outcome of these projects is checked, about 50 per cent were a success on the criteria of the project evaluation group within the firm. Only 16 per cent were a failure due to technical difficulties. The rest had not come to fruition because of delays or attention being diverted elsewhere. Effectively, therefore, this corporation faced a relatively low level of risk. The overall chance of success averaged 0.75. The majority of failures were man-made rather than due to the cussedness of technology. Some of the reason for the low level of risk is probably due to the concentration of research effort. The majority of projects were expected to be completed in less than four years, and application of the results was seldom expected to take more than a year. Furthermore most projects did not appear to involve great technological risk, presumably because large advances were not being aimed for. Generalisation of the findings of the studies to the United Kingdom would be rash, but nevertheless there is probably a moral here. If effort is devoted to short-reach projects within a particular field, the risk of genuine failure through being thwarted by technology is probably not high. Technology is not so ill-natured as might be thought.

If the risks associated with R. & D. are genuinely low, why then do high returns still persist? Part of the answer may lie with the factors which determine the research programme of individual firms. There is a study of the influences which determine the overall size of research spending by firms and the allocation of expenditures to specific research projects. (84) Overall spending is explained in terms of average expected profitability of projects in hand, the profitability of alternative uses of funds, and the size of firms. Adjustments to the desired level of R. & D. programmes seem to be made in a fractional manner. This is done in order to maintain stability and avoid the cost of sudden changes in research programmes. Allocation of funds to particular research projects within the firm under review appeared to follow a profit-maximisation model. Expenditure on a project is increased to the point where the increase of the *probability* of success is no longer worth the cost. Profit expectations are important, but can only explain about half the variation in the allocation of funds. The remaining variation may be explained by factors like intra-firm politics, the persuasiveness of particular individuals, the desire to satisfy scientific as well as commercial objectives, and a preference for safe over risky projects for a given estimated profit level.

In effect, then, the allocation of resources to research is not entirely dependent on profitability. Other factors operate in determining the distribution of resources to R. & D. These include the size of firms and the alternative use of funds. One alternative use of funds already mentioned is copying or imitating rather than initiating. This, in particular, could be a powerful inhibiting factor in the R. & D. process.

Two important points need to be made here. First, the estimates for probabilities of success relate to technical and not commercial success. (85) There could be a great deal of difference between the two meanings of success. Technical success means achieving the aims of a project. Commercial success, on the other hand, means achieving a profitable market. Thus true risk could still be high, even though research projects come to fruition with relatively low failure rates. Secondly, the data on the probability of success are drawn from one very prominent United States company. This company evidently uses a fairly sophisticated screening procedure to select R. & D. projects. By continuous appraisal of progress and a strict check on expenditures, management probably reduces the level of uncertainty involved. A contributory factor may be a concentration on short-reach projects which do not strive for large technological advances. In contrast the majority of companies, particularly in the United Kingdom, may be less well versed in the control and assessment techniques involved in research and development. They may believe that the chances of technical success are poorer than suggested by this study. If true, this will be reflected in their investment in R. & D. The net effect of such a situation may be that the majority of companies require higher rates of return on their R. & D., either because commercial risk is generally high or because they believe it to be so. On the other hand highly competent managers should be able to secure excellent returns because of their ability to control and assess research projects, and also because the overall level of research carried out by other companies may be inhibited.

In practice it is difficult to be definite about the level of risks involved in industrial research and development. The contrast between technical success and final commercial achievement is vital. In a similar way, it is difficult to establish whether there is 'under-investment' in R. & D. Factors of significance are the degree of commercial risk, the level of management competence in allocating funds to R. & D., general influences such as the size of companies and their ability to carry research within their turnovers, the effectiveness of patents and the advantages of being second in the field. A general presumption that high returns to R. & D. implies under-investment is too naïve. Allocation of resources in the real world is complicated. Profits are not the sole guide to the movement of factors into and out of research.

13   THE ROLE OF THE GOVERNMENT

The role of the Government in inducing technological change is basically to mitigate the weaknesses displayed by the market mechanism, to supplement research efforts in order to induce a higher rate of growth of the economy, and to ensure that the balance of government research is appropriate to the require-ments of the United Kingdom economy. There is no doubt whatsoever that technological advance in developed nations is the most significant factor in the growth process. If technological advance were to dry up, the United Kingdom economy would soon reach a limit in terms of income per head. Admittedly new techniques could always be borrowed from other countries, but it would be a serious matter if local research activity were to cease.

The weaknesses displayed by the market mechanism are as follows: First, a tendency for firms to concentrate their research effort in short-term development work, with an emphasis on products rather than processes. This means that very little basic research is done by companies.

Second, large firms probably have an advantage in research expenditure, but unless these can be kept under competitive pressure, the motivation to continue the search for new products and processes may be damped. The phenomenon known as 'risk aversion' may operate. (86) Small firms and individuals probably need some form of encouragement to preserve as large a 'think' potential as possible and also to remain as potential competitors to the industrial giants.

Third, sometimes the working of the price mechanism can cause a large gap between public and private returns. An example is research expenditure on defence. The public return in the form of greater security is probably larger than the private return in the form of marketable products. Admittedly there are likely to be commercial 'spin-offs', such as improved navigation systems and industrial explosives, but these would be unlikely to evoke the required level of defence research effort from private sources. Other examples may occur where technological change is very rapid within an industry, or where intermediate goods result from research effort. Where technological change is very rapid within an industry, the life of new products can be so short in terms of sales that returns to research for individual companies are reduced to low levels. From the public viewpoint it is very desirable that the pace of technological change does not slacken. Export potential is enhanced where goods are technologically ahead of those available in other countries, and so public returns to R. & D. may be above private returns. Where an industry supplies intermediate products, a similar gap may arise. The effect on the prosperity of the industry producing the final product may be dramatic. For example, a great deal of the technology which has revolutionised textiles has evolved in the chemical industries. Unless the inter-industry pricing arrangements are appropriate, a situation may well arise where the public return in terms of greater prosperity for textiles is greater than the private return secured by the innovators in chemicals.

Fourth, diffusion of innovations is often a lengthy process. In economic terms it is not necessarily inefficient to use techniques which are outmoded. Provided opportunity costs of the marginal firm are being covered, then their employment of resources is justified. However, in terms of growth potential the situation can be different. With new techniques the whole level of returns of companies within an industry may be raised sufficiently to support research programmes. The effect on the rate of growth and technological change could be dramatic.

Fifth, market pressures to violate patent rights of a successful product or process are considerable. Unless the patent law is strictly enforced, the incentive to innovate may be damped. On the other hand, if the patent law is too rigid the process of diffusion may be slowed. Government policy must arrange a compromise.

Faced with these weaknesses, government policy is specified in a broad fashion. Long-term basic research requires financing. The risks tend to be too high for this sort of activity to thrive under market pressure. Large firms have a considerable advantage in research and development. Small firms require encouragement. Collective research laboratories, contract or sponsored research schemes, piggy-back systems where ideas originating in small firms may be developed in conjunction with large firms and institutions like the National Research Development Corporation, are all examples. In these ways small companies have an increased chance of adding to the impetus of technological change without being swamped by the advantages which accrue to larger companies. The gap between private and public returns to innovation needs to be narrowed. Patents are devices which are intended to make sure that the innovator catches a large share of the benefits, and thus bias effort towards initiating rather than imitation. But as already pointed out, there are weaknesses in the patent system. Supplementary means of stimulating innovation may be required, particularly where patent avoidance within the law is relatively easy. Government research grants may reduce some of the pressure to imitate. With grants, not all research funds have to be generated by sales and thus commercial pressure may be reduced. They may also help companies over the initial hurdle of establishing research facilities and so provide an impetus for them to search for their own products instead of imitating those of others. Research grants may also have the effect of extending the time horizon of projects, and thus lessen the pressure to recoup expenses over a short period. Where patents are capable of being strictly enforced to the detriment of the economy, the Government may use devices which help speed up the diffusion process. Legally enforceable sub-licensing arrangements, government powers of negotiation of royalty payments; these are the sorts of devices whereby the over-restrictive effects of patents may be lessened.

General taxation policy may also help to add to the impetus of technological change. If taxation of profits is too great, uncommitted surplus funds may not be available for research. The net of tax reward may be too small to recompense the initiating firms for the costs of being first in the field. This may be relevant to the United Kingdom. The paucity of really large international research-based United Kingdom firms may be partly due to the level of taxation. It is probably true that where it is active, the competitive process works very rapidly. Resources will move into lucrative fields quickly and thus prevent returns staying too high. Alternatively the process probably does not work nearly so rapidly in the downward direction. Where returns are poor, enough firms may not leave the field to restore earnings to a level sufficient to carry a viable research effort. Unless technological pressure is particularly great in an industry, research need not be undertaken and firms may merely survive by stagnating. What technological change does take place will probably take the form of imitation. If the competitive process is asymmetrical, in this sense, then a uniform level of company taxation may slow down the transition of assets to more lucrative fields. The logic of the present system of company taxation, with uniform rates applied to all levels of profits, implies that either there is no asymmetry in firms' reaction to profit levels or that assets will move out of relatively unprofitable areas quickly. A tax structure more in line with the asserted working of the competitive process may be one which applies relatively lower percentage rates of tax to higher levels of profit performance. The effect of such a system would be a bias in favour of improved performance on two accounts. Firstly, poor profits would be penalised relatively heavily. Secondly, good profits would be rewarded by lower rates of taxation. Such a system would recognise the need to 'force' assets from mediocre employment, and also at the same time provide the incentive to shift and reorganise assets to improve efficiency and thus achieve lower tax rates. In addition it would recognise that good profits from successful innovation are likely to be temporary, and so not penalise companies for their success. This may be particularly important if companies are to be induced to have a large R. & D. programme to maintain a stream of new products.

The major problems of such a system would lie in establishing measures of profit performance and also preventing monopoly being rewarded by lower tax rates. If high profit rates have the effect of attracting assets very quickly, then it is unlikely that monopoly power will be a major problem. Consistency in accounts and means of measuring industrial performance will be more tricky. This is a serious objection. However, the purpose of the analysis is to stress that the working of the tax system, together with competition, may mean that returns to innovation are low. One way of encouraging a greater commitment to research and development may be to offer a tax bonus in the form of lower rates. Government grants to individual companies are available for research, but these do not necessarily encourage research where the funds are likely to be well used. With a performance-rated system as suggested above, an impetus to R. & D. and more rapid adoption of new methods may result. Companies which have proved their worth in terms of performance will benefit. Others which have not may be induced to greater efforts. In particular, shareholders may become active and stir up lagging managements. Provided that there is this asymmetry in the operation of the competitive process, and that competition remains at adequate levels, then the proposal may help to improve the level of company performance, particularly in respect to technological change.

Governments may help speed up the diffusion process in a number of ways. Examples are improved communications between basic research centres and industry; the use of government purchasing power to stimulate industrial experimentation with new products and processes; arrangements to allow firms a limited trial of equipment on a sale or return basis; and financing an industrial extension service to keep firms up to date with changes so that they will be better equipped to assess technical literature.

Actual schemes in operation along these lines are the trial-period arrangement organised for numerically controlled machine-tools by the National Research Development Corporation; information services provided by the Ministry of Technology on recent industrial development, particularly those originating abroad; and the provision of investment grants. The information services are intended to speed up the rate of spread of knowledge. The trial-period scheme is meant to break down resistance to this new type of machine-tool by allowing companies to assess their potential without committing themselves to purchasing the equipment. Investment grants are intended to stimulate the level of gross investment and thus the rate at which new techniques are embodied in the production process. The indications are, however, that these grants have only limited success. (87) The N.R.D.C. scheme has enjoyed some success, but the principle has not yet been used extensively.

Public policies are required to ensure that individual firms are quick to adopt new techniques and are anxious to join the ranks of the initiators. If both point innovation and diffusion are to be fostered via innovative competition, a delicate balance is required between adequate profits to reward risk-taking and a degree of competition which prevents success being followed by a relaxation of commercial aspiration. Competitive oligopoly may provide this balance. The hypothesis that inventive output ought to increase with industrial concentration is modified to recognise the potential benefits of competitive oligopoly. (88) In these terms the function of the Monopolies Commission is to ensure that oligopoly amongst the leading industrial firms does not degenerate into per se monopoly. The case, however, in favour of the degree of industrial concentration associated with competitive oligopoly is not so strong as to support an all-out government policy designed to create big industrial units. Instead a policy is indicated of protecting small firms from any discrimination in the system which favours research in large companies. The purpose is to preserve as large a 'think' potential as possible, and widen the pool from which the industrial leaders of the future may be drawn.

Basic research is carried out by few firms. In the United Kingdom, universities, technical colleges and government research institutes specialise in this sort of research. Development work is more the function of the individual firms. As a result of this specialisation, there may be a neglect of what is termed the middle ground between academic science and product development. (89) This is why improved communications between basic research centres and industry have been advocated. With better information services, industry will become acquainted with developments in scientific thinking earlier. As a result the industrial potential of any breakthrough in basic thinking may be realised much quicker, and thus become part of the production process that much earlier.

The work of the National Research Development Corporation comes close to meeting these requirements. This institution fosters inventions from individuals, firms and publicly supported bodies by providing finance and arranging research facilities. In this way the special risks associated with development research are catered for. The output of basic research centres is brought to the attention of the commercial world. Ventures are jointly financed by the National Research Development Corporation and private companies and thus the risks of development are spread. Where successful products result, the National Research Development Corporation recoup costs by means of a levy on turnover or by licensing arrangements. Cephalosporin is the most successful example. This originated at Oxford University between 1949 and 1952, and was jointly sponsored by the National Research Development Corporation and Glaxo. This now has world sales of approximately £25 million.

The remaining function of the Government is to ensure that the balance of research in the economy is in some sense 'correct'. This balance concerns the disposition of resources between basic and development research. The

Government is responsible for financing the great proportion of basic research carried out in the United Kingdom. This research tends to be expensive both in terms of monetary expenditure and scientific personnel used. This raises the question whether these resources are well employed. In particular it is important to know whether the use of such highly qualified personnel in government research activity might be better employed in industry. The concern arises on three grounds; first, a belief that the United Kingdom is over-committed in government basic research. (90) For example, the United Kingdom spends a larger percentage of national expenditure on basic research than the United States. This arises in part from defence and the aircraft industries. Second, the results of basic research are free goods internationally. The general principles of research findings are usually published in academic journals and are therefore readily available. The exceptions are findings important for defence purposes. As a consequence there may be no association between the country originating an idea and the country subsequently developing it into a marketable product. It has long been argued that the United Kingdom has been particularly good at invention but bad at development. The effect of this has often been that products with great market potential have been developed abroad when the ideas have originated here. Part of the reason may be insufficient resources devoted to development work and too many to the gratuitous activities of basic research. Third, it is argued that the United Kingdom could reduce its commitment to government-financed basic research simply because in aggregate terms the country's spending is small in world terms. Russia and the United States together account for more than three-quarters of the world's expenditure. In quantitative terms it would appear unlikely that a reduction of the United Kingdom's contribution would make a significant difference to the sum total of knowledge. Fourth, the supply of scientists and technologists, particularly engineers, is relatively fixed and the market for such persons has such imperfections that the price mechanism, which would normally operate by establishing salary differentials, does not work effectively to allocate these scarce resources. Furthermore, because effective salary differentials are not established, the future long-term supply of scientists and engineers is presumably affected. The monetary incentive to recruit tomorrow's scientific personnel is not being signalled strongly enough by today's salaries.

The effect of these arguments has been to question the present size of the Government's basic research effort. A transfer of some of the highly qualified personnel employed by the Government could, it is argued, have a considerable impact on the level and quality of industrial research in the United Kingdom. (91) At the same time it is unlikely that the United Kingdom would suffer greatly from the effects of reducing its basic research. Of course it is not suggested that government basic research should be run down to an insignificant level. But it is suggested that the major function of basic research could be achieved with a smaller share of scarce resources. These arguments are plausible and highlight one of the problems the Government must face. This is that government basic research is not immediately concerned with securing a commercial benefit but that indirectly any imbalance of the disposition of resources can have serious repercussions on research in the industrial sector of the economy. This arises because the Government and firms are competing for the same scarce resources. The solution to the problem can only be indicated in general terms. In view of the likely benefits to be secured from increasing industrial research, government expenditures on basic research should be reduced to a level which is just large enough to allow its major functions to be accomplished. In summary, it is argued that the Government must be aware of the implications of its own basic research programme. If a redeployment of scientific manpower resources can be effected without jeopardising the aims of this basic research, the net effect may be a significant contribution to the technological thrust injected by industry into the United Kingdon economy.

Another aspect of the balance of research is the disposition of the aid which Government gives to industry. This takes the form either of grants to industrial research associations or development loans and contracts to individual firms. It has been pointed out that until recently government support of industrial research seemed to be concentrated on industries where its impact is unlikely to be most effective. (92) Government support has tended to be biased towards industries which are not particularly research-intensive. A classification of industries by their degree of research intensity into classes A, B and C shows that government support has tended to go to groups B and C. Such support might well have been better employed on the A-class industries. These industries tend to make intermediate producer goods like electronics, chemicals, machinery and vehicles. Improvements in their products affect productivity in other industries which use them. The impact of the benefits of research in A-class industries are likely to be spread quickly throug the economy. The Ministry of Technology now appears to appreciate this argument. Additional forms of aid have been devised. These are better suited to the dynamic industries which are dependent on industrial research. Development loans and contracts have been introduced which may benefit individual companies. The Industrial Reorganisation Corporation has been set up. This has powers to make research funds available to individual companies. Both of these new forms of aid are better suited to the aggressive go-ahead type of company. Grants to industrial research associations are still used, but these are unlikely to be suitable for A-class industries. Firms in such industries are more interested in conducting their own research programmes and are unlikely to benefit greatly from association research. The organisation of research in associations may be such that projects will be selected that suit the

E. M.P.M.E.

majority of members and will be aimed at minor improvements which have a strong chance of being realised simply because of the collective pressure exerted by members for tangible results in exchange for the money they have expended. Potentially, industrial research associations could be centres of basic research. Each individual member's risk is limited and yet a sizeable research budget is available in aggregate from all members. In practice, however, the emphasis appears to be towards development research which involves steps forward of a minor nature. (93)

14   SUMMARY

Technological progress is a major cause of growth, and comes about through invention and innovation. Invention is concerned with discovery and innovation with application. Diffusion and imitation are part of innovation. The term 'point' innovation refers to development up to first production in the originating concern. Diffusion tends to be a lengthy process. Successful innovation has a very considerable impact upon companies' performance. The level of inventive and innovative activity is difficult to measure. The level of R. & D. expenditure is greatly affected by profit expectations.

Invention is also market-orientated and heavily influenced by revenue prospects. Latent or potential demand is an important force allocating inventive effort. Industries vary considerably in their involvement with technological change. At the level of the individual firm a number of factors are of importance. These include the size of companies, the type of market form and the degree of diversification.

Empirical investigation suggests that large companies do enjoy some advantages in the R. & D. process. But the relationship between firm size and research inputs and outputs is not at all strong. Fierce competition may be inimicable to research. Monopoly may also not provide a strong motivation to carry out R. & D. Intermediate market forms may in fact provide the industrial atmosphere most conducive to research. Innovative competition may be fostered best under competitive oligopoly. There are complications, however, to this proposition. These are multi-product output, the type of research, the sources of ideas and the patent law.

Multi-product output means that the market form relates not to an industry but to the general commercial atmosphere surrounding company activities. A commercial atmosphere is more suited to development than to basic research. Patents confer monopoly rights. These may be important to the private individual who does not have the economic power enjoyed by companies, especially large companies.

Diffusion is important. The rate at which firms begin using an innovation is influenced by the proportion of firms using it, the profitability of the change and the size of the investment required. The main economic feature which characterises slow and fast adopters is not the overall financial health of companies but rather the extent to which a particular innovation offers an economic stimulus in the form of profits. The size of companies also has some effect.

Intra-firm diffusion, or the rate at which a new product or process is substituted for an old one, is also influenced by the potential profitability of the change. Patents are a means of biasing effort away from imitation towards invention. High returns to R. & D. do not necessarily imply under-investment. R. & D. expenditure is inhibited by the risk, the cost and the advantages of being 'second in the field'.

A case study of one prominent American company in electrical equipment, electronics and appliances manufacture suggests that the risks involved in R. & D. probably tend to be overestimated. But risk here refers to the likelihood of being thwarted by technology, and not to the chances of achieving commercial success. Allocation of funds to R. & D. in the firm seem to follow a profit-maximisation model. A number of other factors are, however, of considerable importance.

The role of the Government in inducing technological change is to mitigate the weakness displayed by the market mechanism, to ensure that the balance of research under its control is appropriate to the requirements of the economy, and to speed up the diffusion process.

15 CONCLUSION

The pace of change is accelerating. In Britain there are many industries which were virtually unknown before the war. Nuclear power, electronics, pharmaceuticals, jet aviation, computers and hovercraft are examples. All of these industries are based on research effort, and their prosperity is dependent on continuing improvement of their products. Research represents a deliberate attempt to modify and create new products and processes. The impetus to seek new processes and products is generated by opportunity on the one hand and pressure on the other. Opportunity is potential profits. Pressure comes from commercial rivalry. Unless the forces of economic selection are allied to those of technological change, progress may be delayed. Innovative competition fosters technological rivalry between companies. The most suitable commercial environment to induce this type of competition, may be competitive oligopoly. Successful innovation has a considerable impact on both the profits and growth of individual firms. It also has a significant impact on economies. As new products and processes are diffused, productivity and living standards improve. Inventions and the application of inventions are central to improving the performance of both firms and economies.

9 Management

A firm's management has to co-ordinate the factors of production at its disposal. In the private-enterprise sector of the economy, staying in business should involve earning at least the opportunity-cost rate of return. A management that fails in this task brings take-over or bankruptcy near. Losses arising from business are borne by the owners. Managers may be owners, but owner-managers have now become rare. More frequently nowadays, managers are salaried employees. This has the result that the major decisions are taken by individuals whose personal fortunes are not at stake in the company concerned. They do have an interest, however, in the profits of the firm. Bankruptcy would spell loss of employment. Take-over would not necessarily do likewise, but it would at least involve some changes in management personnel. Success of the firm, on the other hand, means greater salary prospects in present or alternative employment. The widespread divorce of the managerial function from ownership thus makes the profit motive in decision-making more indirect. Nevertheless, it remains powerful.

The role of profits is an admixture of rewards for uncertainty bearing, ensuring commercial survival and a springboard for further investment and growth. Management makes decisions under conditions of uncertainty. Uncertainty relates to situations where the probability distribution of outcomes is not known with any accuracy. Where the distribution is known with certainty, then this is called actuarial risk. The degree or amount of actuarial risk is determined by the variance or standard deviation of the probability distribution. This sort of risk is known as variability risk. The degree of uncertainty faced by an enterprise with a particular venture is determined by the level of knowledge of the distribution of possible outcomes. Where there is complete ignorance, this is known as pure uncertainty. The function of uncertainty bearing therefore covers situations where a degree of ignorance exists. It does not include situations of actuarial risk. These may be covered by insurance policies and so carry no uncertainty in the technical sense. (1) The influence of uncertainty on company operations may be observed in the financial decisions with respect to liquidity, leverage and portfolio balance. (2)

There are a number of conventional financial ratios which management find prudent to maintain at accepted levels. (3) Companies which habitually violate these may be more prone to bankruptcy than those which do not. (4) The uncertainty of business operations means that contingencies must be met. As pointed out earlier, the finance function involves compromises. For instance, high cash balances represent safety from short-term claims, but they also represent a sacrifice of the earning power of that cash. Or again, high growth may represent an improvement in long-run company profitability, but may jeopardise current liquidity in the short run. The pressures to maintain these ratios may not be such as to amount to 'homeostasis of the balance sheet'. (5) Nevertheless companies which do not conform may invite unfavourable comment from the financial press and come under selling pressure on the Stock Exchange. Whether these ratios are considered as goals or constraints of operation will be important in the growth process. Fast growth may involve violating the conventions. As already seen, fast-growing companies favour issues of capital and tend to be illiquid. In their case it is likely that the accepted ratios are merely part of the range of goals and are not an active constraint. The sluggards, on the other hand, may not be sufficiently strongly motivated towards growth, and fear of possible violations of the conventions may provide a justification for their lack of ambition.

Unfortunately little is known about the actual motivation of managers or their aims of operation. In economic theory a variety of assumptions are used. These range across such motives of operation as profit, sales and utility maximising and satisficing behaviour. Satisficing is a general term describing non-maximising behaviour. For example, company management may aim for results which are 'good enough' in their particular industry. Emphasis is placed on securing a satisfactory but not maximum performance. (6) However, in the real world the predominant motive of operation matters. Presumably fast-growing concerns are distinguished by the strength of their motivation towards expansion. But the factors which bring about this motivation are not clearly understood. The growth process is not mechanistic. The strength of the association between profitability and growth shows this. Because a company achieves a certain level of success, it does not automatically generate further growth. A continuing management effort is required for continuing growth. In terms of human psychology, a special motivation is required. This will deny the temptation to relax when the obvious goals of salary and status are achieved. Instead the decision-makers in firms must be instilled with a 'divine discontent' which spurs them on to further achievement. Managers must become identified with the firm and link their personal performance with that of the firm. (7) This peculiar psychology may be instilled by the force of competition and encouraged in management by performance-rated means of payment. Competition implies that success may only be temporary. Even the star companies must feel that only continuing efforts ensure their eminence. If managers' salaries are also based on achieving certain standards of company performance and there is competition within the management hierarchy for posts, then this sort of motivation is plausible. If responsibility is apportioned according to ability and not seniority, then thrusting junior management provides yet another spur for continuing effort from senior executives in addition to that provided by rival business concerns. Where nepotism operates, such 'internal' competition for posts is limited. Senior executive positions are earmarked for persons with family connections. Within public-quoted concerns, however, nepotism is less likely to operate. They are no longer completely controlled by family groups, and thus executive selection is open to the pressure of internal competition.

Whilst it is easy for the outside observer to specify the management psychology required for continuing high-level growth, it is quite another matter actually to identify firms which have good management and high growth potential. Any such assessment is based on surmise. Firms which have achieved success in the past are assumed to have good management; alternatively, firms which employ the latest techniques in decision-making are assumed to have good management. However, both of these criteria may be misleading. The trappings of good management, as shown in sophisticated decision-making procedures, may avail little if their outcome is a continuing trading loss. Equally, firms which may have achieved success in the past may not continue to achieve this in the future. For example, it has been found that a prediction model which includes a wide variety of the known financial characteristics of firms does not perform even moderately in explaining company growth. (8) The problem is therefore basically one of identifying in an objective way the factors which point to commercial success.

Now that 'management' has become accepted as a subject capable of being taught, the problem is partly solved. There exist a number of management tools which are designed to improve the quality of decision-making within the firm. Examples are operations research, decision theory, linear programming and cost benefit. Firms which do not avail themselves of these techniques do so at their own peril and may eventually join the ranks of loss-makers. An attempt has been made to identify thrusting or sleeping management. (9) Managements are classed as thrusters if they submit to regular financial appraisal, if they organise an export sector, and if they tend to make what could be sold rather than sell what the firm could make. Test sectors used to establish 'attitudinal ratings' of managements include the objective of firms, sales promotion, attitudes to unions and competition, the quality of the personnel function and the use of operational research techniques and budgetary control systems. A correlation is found between financial results and the attitudinal ratings displayed. However, it must be pointed out that this correlation is an impression formed by the investigators and not a result of a direct testing of the data using regression analysis. No direct indication of the strength of the association between the quality of management and financial results is therefore available.

Mere knowledge of advanced management techniques will not ensure success, but it could at least ensure that firms are not unnecessarily handicapped by ignorance. Unfortunately the more sophisticated tools of management are not always widely known or employed. For example, discounted cash flow was 'hailed as a new discovery of the fifties' (10) when in fact it has a record which goes back into antiquity. Or again, in 'Investment Appraisal' the National Economic Development Office set out the effects of calculating profits net of tax and also of using discounted cash flow in appraising investment allowances. (11) Presumably this would not have been done had it been thought that these particular techniques were widely known. Because these techniques are still not widely known, some space will be given to discussing them. It is not intended to make a close examination of all the various management decision techniques. Details may be found in specific references. (12) Instead some attention will be given to the general principles involved in discounting procedures and their use in practice, with reference to their importance in the growth process.

Factors of production are scarce, so that the procedures used in their allocation matter. If 'best use' is not made of them, there is a real sacrifice of benefit both to the firm and to the economy as a whole. Managements require a basis for accepting or rejecting capital expenditure programmes. They also require to rank these in order of attractiveness. The most commonly used procedures are the pay-back period and the average return on capital. The pay-back period is the time taken to recover the costs of the project. The average return on capital involves a comparison of profits in relation to the capital employed over the period of the investment. Projects with the shortest pay-back period, or highest average rate of return, will be placed top of the list of possible capital expenditures. Others, with less promising figures, will be ranked lower in the list of potential investments. Both of these procedures are useful enough. However, the pay-back criterion implies that the sooner invested capital is recouped by earnings, the more attractive is the scheme. The average return procedure, in its turn, implies that schemes with the highest overall return, regardless of the time period concerned, are to be preferred. Neither of the criteria gives enough emphasis to the time value of money. This is important for the following three reasons. One is that all investment projects have a cost over time. Even if the funds come out of firm's own resources (and so are not borrowed), alternative uses are forgone. Once the investment decision is carried into effect, alternative plans can no longer be financed. The second reason is that funds kept idle are funds wasted. The existence of a rate of interest indicates that the future is discounted. More value is attached to £100 now than £100 in the future. Moreover, with inflation proceeding, a third consideration comes into play. This is the erosion of capital. Unless earnings are at least equivalent to the enhanced purchase price of the equipment at the time of replacement, a company will effectively be in the process of liquidation.

Two procedures specifically allow for the time value of money. They are the present-value and the marginal efficiency of capital methods. These are sometimes referred to as the discounted cash flow and the internal rate of return respectively. (13) These two procedures allow the time-adjusted rate of return on projected capital expenditure to be calculated. The project concerned should be adopted if the discounted cash flow is positive, or the rate of discount which brings the expected earnings into equality with the cost of the investment under scrutiny is greater than the relevant rate of interest. The procedures amount to an application of the familiar 'marginal cost equals marginal revenue' rule, with a time-discount modification.

As mentioned earlier in this chapter, these techniques have not been widely used in the United Kingdom. The cost of this neglect could be high. For example, the two simple criteria of pay-back and the average rate of return may signal acceptance of certain projects. Under discounted cash flow or marginal efficiency of capital techniques, either the order on the scale of attractiveness could be altered, or even their rejection signified. It may happen that a project is adopted on the grounds of one of the 'simple' criteria. This may well jeopardise the commercial performance of the companies concerned.

Perhaps the two terms 'the rate of discount' and 'the ruling rate of interest' should be explained. Overall, managements must ensure that the assets under their control earn their opportunity-cost rate of return. However, from a decision-making point of view investment that has been made in the past may be treated differently from that contemplated in the future. In manufacturing industry, investments already made usually take the form of highly specific fixed capital, which has very few alternative uses. The minimum operating criterion on this type of equipment will be to cover the prime costs of operation. This may imply a short-term return of less than the opportunity cost of all the funds tied up. (14) In contrast, *new* investment must show promise of covering its opportunity cost. Until funds are committed to a particular use, they may be deployed anywhere, and thus should be employed as effectively as any others. The means of testing this is the rate of discount or the ruling rate of interest. The actual level of these rates applied is very heavily influenced by three factors: the uncertainty of the investments, the availability of capital, and the availability of managerial resources. In addition inflation is another complicating factor. Uncertainty has an obvious influence on the 'cut-off' returns required by management on new investment. For no involvement or effort, funds may earn a yield roughly equivalent to Bank Rate, if used to purchase dated government bonds. There is no question of the Government failing on their redemption. The only chance element in the whole transaction is price movements following purchase of the bonds. Even this may not apply if the holders wait until redemption, which is at par. At slightly more risk a firm may purchase 'blue chip' equities. These are ordinary shares of quoted companies of very high commercial standing, who have not passed a dividend for a considerable number of years. By and large such a purchase should earn a reasonable return. Consequently uncertainty has a definite meaning in terms of the yield required at the planning stage of investment within companies. There is a spectrum of assets into which managements can put funds. These range from virtually riskless government paper, through 'blue chips' right up to casino-like ventures. Within this spectrum there is, of course, the possibility of ploughing back funds into the businesses themselves. In hard cash terms, this therefore means that the internal use of funds should be expected to yield a greater monetary return than could be obtained elsewhere for no involvement beyond the provision of finance. In practice, money is ploughed back into firms for other motives besides the purely commercial. Pride in the corporation and preservation of the business are examples; but in the harsh competitive world where take-overs are a possibility, this sort of opportunity-cost calculation is relevant. Thus at the planning stage managements should require the 'blue-chip return plus'. In other words they should require an overall rate of return greater than that available to the private individual with funds on the Stock Exchange.

Some indication of minimum expected returns may be inferred from the cost of equity capital. Shareholders require some compensation for holding their shares. They will only retain shares in a particular firm so long as they are in some sense 'satisfied'. If capital gains and dividends are insufficient, shares will be sold, with adverse effects on the market valuation of the company. There is thus an implicit cost of capital, equal to the yield available on the shares. This yield consists of dividends and capital gains. It should be noted that this implicit cost of capital is not the cost of raising new capital but the cost as indicated by the yield available to shareholders from existing shares on the Stock Exchange. No company should accept projects which promise to yield less than this implied cost of capital. To do so would be to violate the basic commercial principle of attempting to earn more than costs. This implicit cost of equity capital is likely to set the minimum target rate for capital vetting. The actual rate applied by companies is likely to be above this for reasons which will be made clear below. In the years from 1956 to 1966, investors on the Stock Exchange earned on average 6.4 per cent a year in real terms net of all taxes. In money terms, ignoring the changing purchasing power of money, the equivalent return was 9.6 per cent per annum. (15) In money terms companies are likely to use a test rate above the yields already mentioned. For these yields are on average available to anyone with funds who is prepared to purchase equity capital. Management decisions to invest capital in their own firms will carry a greater degree of risk. Capital invested in firms is often converted into specific assets which have limited alternative uses. Equity investors, on the other hand, are usually not so heavily committed. Through the facilities offered by the Stock Exchange, they are in a position to switch their holdings very quickly. By spreading holdings widely and being prepared to switch shares, private individuals may face less risk of loss than managements in individual firms. Managements are therefore likely to seek returns greater than the implicit cost of equity capital, to compensate for this higher level of uncertainty. This argument is reinforced by the practice of nationalised industries. They are now required to apply a 10 per cent test rate when discounted cash flow is used for investment appraisal, 'risk being separately allowed for'. (16) If 10 per cent is considered to be an appropriate rate of discount when risk is separately allowed for, then it is plausible to argue that private firms will probably apply a rate well above this level in an attempt to allow for this uncertainty.

Unfortunately the fact that firms should expect to earn comparatively high returns on new capital gives no guide as to how uncertainty should be allowed for in the capital-vetting procedure. This does not imply that higher rates of discount should necessarily be applied to projects with high uncertainty. It is true that companies require the incentive of high returns to induce them to be venturesome. But the application of high rates of discount to uncertain projects will do very little to ensure these returns. Uncertainty involves varying degrees of ignorance of probability distributions. The application of progressively higher discount rates to projects of increasing uncertainty will do nothing to relieve this ignorance. All that such a procedure will establish is that the estimated revenue and cost flows do, or do not, meet the test criterion. The company will be no wiser on the likely outcome of adopting such projects. What is required are means of reducing the uncertainty. Ignorance of the probability distribution must somehow be reduced. Often this may be achieved by improved market research, experimentation, limited market trials, pilot production projects, parallel research efforts and so on. In practice there is no single way of allowing for uncertainty. There are many methods which are intended to guide the firm in the decision-making process. (17) But none of these is a substitute for more knowledge on the distribution of likely outcomes. Results from discounted cash flow or the internal rate of return procedures may be tested for their sensitivity by applying ranges of costs and revenues instead of single values. Alternatively cost and revenue figures may be weighted by the likelihood of their occurrence, but by definition knowledge of the probabilities involved is likely to be poor.

Even with these modifications, the procedures do not reduce the uncertainties involved in a given decision-making situation. What they provide, however, is a means of comparing projects with varying time patterns of cost and revenue flows. They are an advance on the average return procedure and payback period method, because they explicitly recognise the time value of money. They are not a cure-all, however, and are no substitute for greater knowledge of the likely outcome of capital projects.

The availability of capital and management resources also has an effect on the 'cut-off' rate applied by management at the planning stage. If capital is scarce, then only those projects showing the highest potential returns will be put into operation. This is particularly relevant when companies are loath to use outside finance to supplement their disposable funds. Again, if management resources are scarce, and should not be stretched beyond some optimum, only projects which are within their immediate capability will be adopted. Needless to say, these of course are the projects with the most attractive returns. Inflation is also a complicating factor. If there is a differential rate of inflation, such that replacement of capital goods increases in cost faster than the price of the firm's products, this may make business less profitable. If, on the other hand, the firm's products increase in price faster than capital goods employed in production, the opposite effect may occur. Businesses may become more profitable. Inflation thus adds to the complications of investment appraisal. Not only has management to assess future cash flows from various projects but it also has to take a view on the future effects of inflation. To make investment appraisal less fallible, tests should be carried out on the effects of varying rates of inflation on revenue flows and costs. These tests may cause a re-ordering of projects and a rejection of some that were previously attractive.

The combined effects of uncertainty and the limited availability of management and capital resources is to raise the return required on projects well above the ruling rate of interest. Even if companies do not use discounted cash flow or the marginal efficiency of capital methods, high returns are probably required on new projects for the reasons already indicated. The overall effect is to reduce the volume of investment in industry. This might have a considerable influence on the growth of the economy. It is only dynamic managements which are prepared to find the capital and put forward the extra effort to take on schemes which do not yield such high returns. These companies come near to applying the theoretical criterion that investment should proceed until extra revenue is equal to extra cost. Their investment effort is greater and so, other things being equal, is their growth.

This cursory discussion of some of the capital-vetting systems lays stress on the importance of management motivations. The techniques available to help the decision-making process are increasing in number and sophistication, but effort is needed to acquire and use them. To some extent the learning process can be short-circuited by the employment of specialists such as management consultants. However, for really effective use of the techniques management should at least be familiar with them and know their limitations. Competition may have the effect of forcing their adoption, but in practice the firms which are strongly motivated towards improving their performance are most likely to use them. An exhaustive account of the supply of management effort would fill a tome on business administration. Here discussion must be limited. Forms of organisation structure may be devised to leave top management with the job of managing. Delegation, the use of specialists and the 'span of control' affect an organisation in its day-to-day working and influence the time available for analysis and reappraisal of performance by managements. One fascinating theory on the effect of growth on the supply of management effort is as follows: Growth is constrained by the limited availability of personnel to plan and execute the process, and constraints become more noticeable with a faster rate of expansion. Although recruitment may offer one way round this bottleneck, new personnel may be only gradually absorbed into a firm. There must be time for training and settlement. This diverts effort from the immediate task of expansion. Only when the new recruits have settled to their jobs is the aggregate supply of management effort increased. Effectively, therefore, there is a 'receding managerial limit'. (18) Once the immediate growth effort is over, there are management resources available for further expansion. This idea of an immediate bottleneck, followed by a lessening of the constraint as personnel is absorbed and the immediate expansion is achieved, helps to explain why some firms are 'fliers' and others 'sluggards'. Any expansion programme beyond the immediate capabilities of present management requires a considerable effort both in terms of outlay and the absorption of new personnel. Companies not strongly motivated towards growth will not institute such programmes. Other companies may. Their reward, after the initial period of adjustment and constraint is a receding managerial limit. They then have disposal over a supply of managerial effort for further growth in a succeeding period. If so, their commercial performance may be cumulatively superior to that of their less ambitious rivals.

Another idea relevant to the supply of management is 'organisational slack'. (19) A large number of organisations are probably operating below potential, and are doing so for considerable periods of time. This may change when new talent is engaged or the company does badly. The fear of the penalties which accrue to an overtly second-rate performance may force management to work to the limits of its potential, in the hope that the position may be rectified. Competition may administer such a shock to complacency. If competition is weak, such a shock may never fall upon a company. The latter may continue quietly returning adequate profits without really utilising its full management ability. If so there is a case for competition to ensure managerial efficiency.

The supply of management effort has a major impact on the growth of individual firms. Change is management-intensive. Examples of change which inevitably absorb management effort are as follows: the addition of new products to the existing range of outputs, the extension of production capacity and the absorption of recently acquired companies. The attitude of management towards change is important. Companies with traditional, conservative and satisfied management are likely to avoid activities which demand extra effort. Thus major motives of operation may be the maintenance of the status quo and the preservation of existing markets. The above examples of change do not appeal to such companies. Under these conditions management tends to become mere supervision. Dynamic management acts differently. Greater emphasis will be placed on enhanced commercial performance. This will involve a continuing process of appraisal and re-appraisal of the firm's existing lines of business. Thought will be given to future markets, new products, capital expenditure in anticipation of future demand, the advantages of any technological change and so on. These activities represent the entrepreneurial function. Much has been made of the fact that in modern companies, where salaried managers take the decisions, the person of the entrepreneur is rarely indentifiable. This may be of small practical concern. The function of management involves both entrepreneurship and supervision of the production process. In dynamic companies the entrepreneurial function is likely to take up a major proportion of management time. In addition such companies are likely to ensure that a good supply of entrepreneurial ability is available for the future from within their own ranks. Training schemes and management development programmes will be in evidence. These are activities which less active managements tend to neglect. They are very demanding in that they involve a concern for future performance rather than mere repetition of what has already been achieved.

Companies that aim to maintain the status quo still bear uncertainties. They are making a decision to the effect that no change is to the advantage of their company. In practice this may not prove to be the case. The example of the two extreme types of management is meant to stress the contrast in the way in which time and effort may be spent. There is a sharp distinction between the purpose of each activity. Supervision is intended to ensure that existing activities are not hampered. The entrepreneurial function is much more concerned with the future. In some companies this is explicitly recognised, in that corporate planning committees are set up. It is this aspect which should take up most of the time of top management.

The preceding chapter has shown how growth depends on innovation and diffusion of new products and processes throughout the economy. The present chapter has drawn attention to the role of management in promoting change through investment and the supply of effort. Attitudes to change can have a considerable effect on the speed at which production functions are adopted to new techniques and products. The process of technological change is very management-intensive. It involves continuing reassessment of research and development expenditures, keeping up to date with new developments and integration of these into existing production facilities. Few firms can escape the consequences of technological change. Such is the pressure generated by new products and processes that even the laggards in the process will eventually have to change. But even so management attitudes are very important. They affect the level of pressure within a firm for change. The 'pushes and pulls' represent the external forces generated by the industrial environment. Management attitudes, however, determine the character of the response to these stimuli. Because the process of technological change is so management-intensive, once again the importance of the supply of management effort is stressed. If too much of management's time and effort is devoted to routine matters, then forward thinking and planning may suffer. There may be an 'entrepreneurial gap'. For example, it is sometimes alleged that the British economy is good at invention but slow at applying new products and processes. (20) Whether this is true or not, more application of new products and processes could accelerate the economy's rate of growth. Whether it can or will be done depends on the quality of managers. By and large, development of invention is a management problem. Market potential must be recognised and enough resources applied to bring invention to a marketable stage quickly. If this does not occur, then promising inventions may be developed overseas. The alleged slowness of British industry to take advantage of new inventions may be a direct outcome of such an 'entrepreneurial gap'. This gap is generally agreed to be a crucial management problem (21) and may be directly linked to an overemphasis on routine management and a neglect of the really important function of thinking and planning for the future.

The attitude of management towards technological change affects the rate of company growth. It will govern individual companies' commitment to change. Firms which have their own R. & D. departments have deliberately set up an organisation within themselves to generate new products and processes. Others which have not must rely entirely on emulation to keep up with progress. The management of research and development is an activity which epitomises the entrepreneurial function. R. & D. is an explicit commitment to change. The nature of the process is such that it is very demanding of management effort for two reasons:

Firstly, innovation is aimed at future product and process benefit. It is an investment process with a difference. It is intended to upset settled production processes and displace established products. Inevitably R. & D. will involve alteration in the running of companies. For example, new products will require a redisposition of productive capacity. Not only will production be altered but also the whole attitude of management. The R. & D. department must not be treated like an autonomous unit free from commercial pressures. R. & D. must be managed. Considerations of profit and loss must impinge upon research budgets and personnel. '. . . the function of industrial research and development is not simply to advance knowledge or to follow the imaginative urges of designers, but to create new products or methods of production that are commercially sound'. (22) One of the most satisfactory means of ensuring this aim is to integrate research into management. This usually involves having scientists and engineers as board members and not merely as specialist boffins available for technical advice. If so the whole attitude of management must change.

Secondly, the risks associated with R. & D. expenditure are usually greater than those encountered with ordinary investment. The level of risk will vary with the aim and type of research involved. Fundamental industrial research is usually aimed at a big step forward in technology. Ordinary industrial research is less ambitious. In both cases risk will be related to the character and aims of research. There is no assurance that new products and processes will materialise. Even if they do, assessment of market potential is difficult. This will be related to a large number of influences, which will include the superiority of the innovations, rivals' reaction, the securing of patents and their defence, and likely market capture. Rivals may react with superior innovations which render the initial change obsolescent. The length of market life of a product is therefore another unknown which is part of the uncertainties involved. Calculation of the prospective returns to R. & D. is more than usually difficult. Accurate assessment of all the unknowns will be very dependent on the quality of management decision-taking processes. Real-world verification of the uncertainties involved in R. & D. comes from a deliberate policy of companies to limit R. & D. expenditure. For example, in the United Kingdom pharmaceutical industry most companies keep research within 10 per cent of their turnover. (23)

Technologically progressive companies are aware of the special problems involved in the management of research and of keeping abreast of change. Management for innovation is very important. Certain characteristics distinguish such companies. (24) Amongst these are a deliberate and periodic survey of potential ideas arising from all sources, the high status of science and technology in the firm, a consciousness of costs and profits in research and development departments (if any), a rapid replacement of machines, a sound policy on recruitment of management and training of staff, the use of management techniques, good-quality high and intermediate management, the use of scientists and technologists on the board of directors, a high rate of expansion and an effective selling policy. Unprogressive companies for the most part lack these characteristics. One interesting feature which apparently does not affect the technical progressiveness of firms is membership of an industry with a strong scientific or technological background. Advanced industries contain a high proportion of progressive firms, but the converse does not hold. Traditional industries are not necessarily populated by backward firms.

The preceding discussion has stressed that the adoption of change will be heavily influenced by management attitudes. The colourful picture of a red-hot research team producing a series of brilliant innovations and then being frustrated by timid decision-taking is perhaps rather fanciful. But it draws attention to a crucial point: good management is vital to rapid application of results. Successful innovation requires a mixture of bold decision-taking coupled with judicious caution which arises from an appreciation of the difficulties involved in assessing market potential. An innovation may be years ahead of its time. Automatic transfer machines were such an example. Full utilisation of their potential had to await commensurate advances in ancillary technologies such as hydraulics and pneumatics. An innovation may also not be compatible with the aims and objectives of a company. The investment involved may be too great, especially for companies without a Stock Exchange quotation. Capital in sufficient quantities may just not be available. If independence and family control are primary goals of operation, then such a change will not be undertaken.

As already pointed out, there is a widely held belief that there is an 'entrepreneurial gap' in the United Kingdom. One of the most disturbing manifestations of this apparent timidity are the many examples of British inventions which have been developed overseas even when home industries had first option. This has also been referred to as a 'development gap'. (25) Unfortunately it is difficult to establish how real these gaps are. Overseas development of a home invention may in practice merely be an example of specialisation. Often development tends to be more costly that invention. Overseas fostering of an invention may in fact mean that a marketable product results more quickly than if home capital had been absorbed in the process. The overseas country, for example the United States, may have larger volumes of capital and also greater expertise for the purpose. Of course some overseas development of British inventions may reflect the timidity and short-sightedness of British management, but not necessarily all. There may be very good economic arguments supporting foreign development of home inventions. Royalty and licence payments for the final product may well represent an extremely good bargain, particularly for companies with small financial resources who are anxious to be amongst the pioneers of new products. However, the establishment of the Ministry of Technology is partly a reflection of the general concern that the United Kingdom may in fact be missing oppor-

tunities to develop home inventions. This Ministry implies a decision to give
greater emphasis to the role of the state in enforcing a more rapid application of
science and technology in industry. (26) The United Kingdom's overall record,
summarised by what is sometimes referred to as the 'technological balance of
payments', (27) appears relatively good. Aggregate payments for know-how,
techniques and new products in the form of royalties, licences and fees are less
than aggregate receipts. In these terms there is a surplus on the technological
balance of payments. Interpretation of the meaning of this surplus is difficult.
There are too many complications, like companies operating international joint
ventures, foreign-owned subsidiaries in the United Kingdom, the fact that world
patent protection is particularly poor and thus much usage of technology will
not be reflected, and the implied assumption that payments for technology in
some sense reflect the economic worth involved. This last assumption is unlikely
to be true because payments between companies are complicated by tax
differences and tariff difficulties. If however the obvious interpretation is
accepted, namely that the United Kingdom sells more technology than it
receives, then this perhaps reflects to the credit of British research effort and
management. But in order to stress that this is a tentative conclusion, it has to be
pointed out that the world's leading industrial nation, namely the United States
of America, runs a deficit on this account. Furthermore this surplus on the
technological balance of payments does not absolve management from the
charge that there is a 'development gap'. The United Kingdom's position could
be that much stronger, given greater effort to develop home inventions.

The ideas of the receding managerial limit, organisational slack and the
development or entrepreneurial gap are evocative, but they are not much help to
management in the practical problem of how to improve company performance.
A more effective procedure is to point to eminently successful industrial concerns, draw the contrast and analyse the reasons. Typically this has been done by
setting up American industry as the model. Where this is done, (28) the result
usually points to the greater economic efficiency of American industry. However, the facts revealed are not always easy to interpret. The studies do not
always compare like with like, and it is not always clear whether less efficient
British performance is 'avoidable'. Explanations for the difference in performance turn around the size of the home market, standardisation of products,
capital superiority and the quality of management. The extent to which
American methods should be adopted in this country is, however, difficult to
infer and is in part determined by environmental factors. In many instances such
procedures would be inappropriate to the British market structure. For example,
the difference in the capital intensity of production in the manufacturing sector
may be a reflection of different labour costs. (29) In the context of the United
States market, high wages may be a pertinent explanation of the greater use of

capital in production. However, even with these problems of interpretation the impression of overall superiority of American industry remains. The implication, therefore, is that to some extent United Kingdom industry would benefit by adopting some American methods.

A more satisfactory procedure than inter-country comparisons is to study the efficiency of United States companies working in the United Kingdom. In this way common factors may be more easily isolated. A direct comparison of factors relevant to efficiency is then possible. One widely quoted comparison of the economic performance of the United States subsidiaries in the United Kingdom has been made. (30) By pairing companies according to their competitive counterparts, a direct comparison is possible. On most of the counts the United States companies exhibit superior efficiency. Subject to two reservations, the conclusion has been suggested that these concerns demonstrate the superiority of American management. The two reservations are a likely bias in the sample and the problems of interpreting figures from subsidiaries. The bias in the sample may arise because it is quite probable that only dynamic and enterprising American companies will set up this country. These may not be representative of typical United States companies. Whilst this may be true, it does nothing to lessen the impact of the findings. Their purpose is constructive, namely to exhibit the contrast even if it does happen to be with the best of American companies. The problems of comparing subsidiaries with financially independent United Kingdom companies is more difficult. (31) Subsidiaries are only part of companies. Indicators of efficiency will in part reflect the benefit of parent companies in the background. For example, profit figures are likely to appear high in relation to capital employed because costs and capital involvement tend to be understated in the company accounts. Marketing a product proven in the parent's home market, and imported in a semi-finished state or very cheaply, will complicate profitability comparisons. Research and development costs of the product do not have to be met by the subsidiary. Fixed assets in the form of manufacturing plant may be at a minimum if the concern is merely acting as a selling agency. Thus some of the apparently superior figures registered by the American companies may in fact merely be a reflection of the advantages of subsidiary organisation. These advantages are extremely difficult to disentangle. An attempt has been made to do this by adding back development costs to some of the figures of the subsidiary. However, overall it is extremely difficult to challenge the findings of the study. On a very wide variety of ratios the American companies proved superior. Thus even in the United Kingdom environment, United States firms exhibit better management. These findings, and those of the inter-country studies, amount to a considerable body of evidence all pointing in the same way, namely that on the whole American management achieves superior results. In practical terms there is a direct message for British management. There would be benefits from adopting American management methods where these are compatible with the United Kingdom trading environment.

So far this chapter has considered the role of management in improving company performance. Emphasis has been given to the problems involved in investment decision and technological change. Problems raised by industrial relations have been ignored. The implicit assumption has been made that industrial relations have been sufficiently good not to hinder change. This is an over-simplification. Without good industrial relations, alteration in work methods and adjustments to technological advance will be hindered. There is a vital link between inproved productivity and industrial relations. Management is in large part responsible for the smooth running of businesses. The level of employee motivation, the adequacy of communications between shop floor and the decision-making echelons and the willingness to change, all reflect the company environment. It is not intended to discuss the subject, but a brief survey of the attitude of trade unions to technological change and also an outline of the recent statutes may help to remind readers of the burden which is imposed upon industrial relations by modern business conditions.

Management is faced on many occasions with manpower problems, especially in those cases of technical improvements involving labour-saving plant and machinery. The successful redeployment of displaced labour may be a more difficult problem for managements than the straight decision to go ahead with the installation of new plant and equipment of a labour-saving nature solely on financial grounds. The impact of technological change on workers and management depends on the kind of change. The introduction of integrated handling equipment, for example, eliminates many jobs filled by unskilled workers, but simultaneously increases the number of opportunities open to semi-skilled workers. The introduction of automatic control may lead to a reduction in the number of inspection staff, but at the same time lead to increased employment of maintenance workers to supervise the control mechanisms. Changes in product design will frequently involve alterations in the occupational structure of a firm's labour force. For example, the use of printed circuits in the electronics industry reduces the need for solderers and other types of skilled labour. Sometimes technological change will involve a decline in labour engaged on direct production but increase the amount of indirect labour. Such changes will also tend to alter the proportion of skilled to unskilled workers in an industry.

In recent years the Ministry of Labour, now the Department of Employment and Productivity, has made a number of manpower studies of the occupational impact of technological change. Inquiries have proceeded not simply into the effects of technological change in manufacturing industries such as electronics, but into a number of service industries such as the use of computers in offices and food retailing. The electronics study, published in 1967, provides a particularly apposite example of the manpower planning problems involved, since, as the report states, 'the range of technological innovation is outstanding even for a science-based industry'. (32) This study involved estimates of changes in occupational structure between 1965 and 1970. Because the industry has been, and still is, an expanding one, innovations involving relative occupational shifts may nevertheless require additional workers to be trained for and employed in those occupations showing relative declines. The burden of adjustment with redundancies caused by technological change is naturally heavier in a stationary or declining industry. Thus in another study an overall fall in office employment was anticipated on account of the introduction of computers. This was likely to be compensated for by an increase in administrative and technically qualified workers, especially in the maintenance field. However, during the 1960s unemployment as a result of automation has become much more of an issue in the United States than in the United Kingdom.

Technological change has had an important impact on the attitudes of trade unions to collective bargaining. There is clearly a conflict between the forces of economic change and security of employment. Memories of the heavy cyclical and structural unemployment in the United Kingdom during the 1930s still persist in the minds of many trade union leaders, and the restrictive practices which grew up during those years have subsequently proved difficult to break down. From the union standpoint, employment changes arising from technical innovations or from government decisions relating, for example, to the future of various military projects or organisation of nationalised industries have resulted in greater preoccupation with the principles governing the manpower policy of individual firms. Unions have been taking the line that, in cases of redundancy, dismissals should take place on a 'last in, first out' basis. This is considered to have the advantage that older workers, who generally find job opportunities more limited than younger workers, are given some form of protection. It is also considered that where retraining may be necessary in consequence of technological unemployment, younger workers are more adaptable. Union bargaining with individual companies has also taken the line that wherever possible a first approach to redundancy should be a gradual running-down of the labour force through the non-replacement of workers retiring on reaching the age limit. Premature retirement with appropriate benefits has also been urged as a partial solution and has been seriously tried in the coal industry and in railway workshops.

The introduction of new plant and equipment has also been the occasion for the introduction of productivity deals, discussed later in Chapter 13. Apart from including clauses relating to increased pay as a result of increased output per worker, such deals have frequently involved agreements relating to the redeploy-

ment within the works of labour made redundant on account of the introduction of labour-saving equipment in one particular workshop. The opportunities for such transfer of labour between departments may involve some
degree of retraining of transferred workers, either on the job or under specially
designed retraining schemes run by the company concerned. Problems involved
in such transfers of workers are easier when the size of the company is large, and
companies operating a number of plants may be able to close down the
inefficient ones which utilise the older plant and move labour to the more
up-to-date plants. Such moves are not, however, always possible. New technologies, for example in brick-making, may involve employing a new labour
force trained not in traditional brick-making skills, but having an entirely
different technological background. Original brick-making skills might prove a
positive hindrance to the operation of automated plant.

In order to minimise the adverse impact of technological change on workers,
management needs to look more ahead with regard to manpower policy and
requirements. Relatively few firms engage in a positive manpower policy, and it
is rare even for those firms which do to plan labour requirements for as long as
five years ahead. Plans involving manning requirements are more generally on a
one- or two-year basis. Mobility as a result of technological change may also be
hampered by the all too frequent lack of transferability of pension rights
between companies and occupations. To assist in successful manpower planning,
the Manpower Research Unit of the Department of Employment and Productivity published during 1968 a booklet entitled 'Company Manpower
Planning'. (33) This dealt with recruitment training, management development
schemes, the estimation of labour costs, accommodation requirements and productivity bargaining. Successful manpower planning involves the clarification of
the company's objectives, the correct forecasting of future shortages or surpluses
of particular skills and occupations, including the level of skill, and decisions on
where the company should concentrate its efforts.

During the 1960s in particular, attempts have been made by successive
Governments to ease the impact of technological change on the working
population. This has involved statutory attempts both to improve training
facilities and to provide a financial cushion for those declared redundant whilst
they seek new openings. The importance of advance warning of termination of
employment was stressed in the Contracts of Employment Act, 1963, which laid
down requirements relating to the amount of notice which must be given to
employees. Some individual industry agreements, such as those in cement, glass
processing, pottery and printing, also contain long notice clauses in the terms of
employment.

The Industrial Training Act of 1964 instituted a series of industrial training
boards whose operations are paid for by firms in the industry concerned under a

system of levies and grants. Firms who do no training are thereby obliged to contribute towards the training schemes of those which do, the argument being that in the last resort all draw their labour supplies from a common source of trained manpower. Consequently all firms should participate. Up to the end of 1968 twenty-six industrial training boards had been established. Finally the Redundancy Payments Act, 1965, specifying the payment of redundancy grants, graduated according to length of time with the current employer, was also aimed at improving the position of workers with long service. Payments made during the first year of operation indicate that claims were most numerous in engineering and electrical goods, construction, the distribution trades and vehicles.

Throughout this chapter it has been assumed that for improving company performance the onus is squarely on management's shoulders. In fact company performance is in some degree the responsibility of every member concerned. However, it is management that takes the major decisions which are central to a company's health. If immediate performance is poor, resources may be switched into more lucrative lines, production may be reorganised and so on. Thus company results are basically a direct reflection of the quality of management, because it is management that is responsible for the decisions which are most directly related to these results. To improve company results is a management problem.

To improve the United Kingdom economic growth performance is also a management problem. From the Government's point of view the difficulty is to motivate sufficient companies into making the greater efforts required. A drastic way, and one with considerable risk, is to make the economy more open to international competition. A less drastic way is by education, appeals and blandishments. In the 1960s the approach has been mixed; tariffs were reduced and approaches made to widen free trade. At the same time increasing amounts of public money were spent on management education and the provision of inducements to acquire more up-to-date machinery. Neither approach can yield quick results. Raising the overall performance of companies is a long-term project. In the short term, however, results may be improved by greater efforts on the part of management. The way in which companies frequently improve from a trading shock shows that results are not entirely exogenously determined. Companies can always do better, but motivation may only be strong when survival is threatened. To maintain this level of motivation during normal trading conditions is the Government's aim. To respond to this is management's duty.

Summary and Conclusions

The importance of technological change in upgrading company performance is central to the growth process. New products may confer considerable advantages to innovating companies. Demand may not be particularly price-elastic and may be more dependent on income levels and income growth (see Part IV). Rivals may react by improving upon innovations, and this may result in 'innovative competition'. Development of techniques or products may be hustled forward through the impetus of competition. Lagging companies may be forced to adopt their production functions, and the whole standard of performance of companies may be upgraded. Competitive oligopoly may be the commercial environment most suitable to achieve these desirable results.

Adjustment to technological change usually involves capital deepening. Known methods of production are not merely duplicated as in capital widening. Instead new methods are adopted. These are often more capital-intensive at the margin (see Part IV) and are usually more productive in terms of output per man or revenue generation. Profits should improve or be maintained. Fast-growing companies probably have a higher proportion of new products and processes within their turnover than stagnant firms. Their profitability also tends to be greater. Knowledge of the statistical association between profitability and growth should not, however, be misused. A bald prescription that companies should somehow be arbitrarily made more profitable to boost their growth would be nonsense. For example a reduction in the rate of tax on profits would immediately improve companies' net return on capital employed, but would not necessarily lead to improved performance. The process of company growth is complex and is ultimately related to skill in the use of scarce resources. It is therefore unlikely that a change of such appealing simplicity will elicit the desired response.

One important method of improving the use of scarce resources is to speed up the rate of diffusion. Competition is rarely so stringent as to force all companies to adopt innovations immediately. Companies have considerable discretion. This is where the role of management is most evident. Growth and expansion is management-intensive. This applies particularly to R. & D. and its application. A great part of the explanation of varying growth rates between companies must relate to the quality of management personnel and the supply of management effort devoted to inducing change. Individual company growth is a function of the opportunities to expand, the finance to facilitate this, and the quality of management to induce, motivate and co-ordinate the process. The past performance of companies, their size, legal status, and the nature of their commercial environment, all of these may be constraints on growth potential.

Fast-growing companies are distinguished by their emphasis on change, slow-growing companies by their conservatism. To upgrade the average level of performance of firms within the British economy requires a greater emphasis on change. This is largely a management problem.

Part II

INDUSTRIAL ORGANISATION

10 The Size of Firms and Business Concentration

1 THE SIZE DISTRIBUTION OF COMPANIES

In modern industrial societies economies of scale assume great importance. Their existence may be traced to discussions amongst early economists, such as Adam Smith, of the division of labour. In essence the advantages derived from the division of labour, coupled with an increasing size of market, have made for the highly uneven size distribution of companies in the modern world. One such distribution is shown in Table 10.1, which relates to the world's largest industrial corporations of the mid-1960s. Amongst the giant corporations with sales of over $250 million in 1965, the top five, or 1½ per cent of the total of almost five hundred companies, accounted for a sixth of their total sales. These companies were General Motors, Standard Oil of New Jersey, Ford Motor Company, Royal Dutch-Shell and Unilever. Amongst the five hundred giant corporations, motors and petroleum tend to dominate the overall sales position. Three-fifths of the large corporations had their headquarters in the United States, one-seventh in the countries of the European Economic Community, and one-ninth were domiciled in the United Kingdom. Of the remaining companies, only those domiciled in Japan, Canada and Switzerland formed any significant part of the total. The dominance of the United States amongst the world's leading corporations is even more marked when the percentage of total sales is considered rather than the number of companies, whilst the importance of giant companies domiciled in the United Kingdom, Japan and Canada is somewhat diminished.

The enormous size of the world's top five industrial companies may be inferred from the following considerations. General Motors employs 735,000 people, as many as the whole population of Manchester, and its sales in 1965 were equal to the whole of the British Government's income from taxation in that year. Standard Oil of New Jersey and Ford Motor Company were about half the size of General Motors in 1965, whilst the largest European-based companies, Royal Dutch-Shell and Unilever, were only about a quarter of the size of General Motors.

Distributions of companies by size, similar to that for the world's leading

Table 10.1 Size Distribution of Industrial Companies by Sales, 1965

Sales (S m.)	Number of companies								Percentage of total	
	U.S.A.	Canada	U.K.	E.E.C.	Switzerland	Japan	Other	Total	Companies	Sales
20,000 and over	1							1	0.20	5.22
10,000 and under 20,000	2							2	0.40	5.79
5,000 ,, 10,000	2		1	1				4	0.81	5.99
2,500 ,, 5,000	10							10	2.02	8.63
1,000 ,, 2,500	45		6	16	1	2		70	14.14	26.76
500 ,, 1,000	74	4	16	24	2	10	7	137	27.68	24.79
228 ,, 500	161	10	33	29	5	22	11	271	54.75	22.83
Total	295	14	56	70	8	34	18	495	100.00	100.01
Percentage of companies	59.60	2.83	11.31	14.14	1.62	6.87	3.64	100.01		
Percentage of sales	67.11	1.59	9.63	14.20	1.13	4.23	2.11	100.00		

Source: Calculated from 'Fortune Magazine' (July-Aug 1966).

corporations, may be produced for manufacturing activity as a whole in the United Kingdom, and for a large number of individual industries. It is necessary at this stage to distinguish between the concept of the 'business enterprise' used by the Board of Trade in the last full Census of Production, and the 'establishment'. The latter refers to a separate factory or workshop, whilst the former refers to individual companies and may include a number of different establishments operating under the same trading name.

Table 10.2 shows the distribution of enterprises by size and numbers employed, and also that for establishments for 1961. The data relate only to what are known by the census authorities and the Department of Employment and Productivity as 'larger establishments'. The number of enterprises with under 25 employees is unfortunately not given. The size distribution of business enterprises and establishments is remarkably similar. Around three-fifths of both enterprises and establishments are small (under 100 employees); around a third are of medium size (between 100 and 500 employees); with the remainder being large (between 500 and 1,000 employees) and very large (1,000 employees and over).

Concentration of numbers employed amongst large concerns is naturally greater for enterprises than for establishments. About three-fifths of total employment in larger establishments is concentrated in very large enterprises, compared with about a third of total employment concentrated in very large establishments. Just over one-fifth of employment is concentrated in medium-

Table 10.2 Size of Enterprises and Establishments in Manufacturing
Industry in 1958 and 1961

Size (numbers employed)	Numbers of enterprises/establishments				Employment ('000)			
	Enterprises, 1958		Establishments, 1961		Enterprises		Establishments	
	Number	%	Number	%	Number	%	Number	%
10,000 and over	74	0.31	19	0.06	1,863	26.39	261	3.65
5,000 and under 10,000	106	0.45	65	0.19	709	10.05	439	6.13
1,000 ,, ,, 5,000	777	3.31	1,144	3.37	1,547	21.91	1,954	27.29
500 ,, ,, 1,000	993	4.24	1,532	4.51	687	9.73	1,043	14.57
100 ,, ,, 500	7,240	30.88	11,446	33.72	1,509	21.38	2,427	33.90
25 ,, ,, 100	14,257	60.81	19,734	58.14	744	10.54	1,035	14.46
Total	23,447	100.00	33,940	99.99	7,059	100.00	7,159	100.00

Sources: Board of Trade Census of Production, 1958; 'Ministry of Labour Gazette' (Apr 1962); 'Annual Abstract of Statistics'.

size enterprises, compared with a third of total employment in medium-size establishments.

The reason for these differences lies in the large number of multi-establishment enterprises as the size of the enterprise increases. Thus in 1958 enterprises in manufacturing industry with 10,000 employees and over had an average of 30 establishments each; those between 5,000 and 10,000 employees had 14.8 establishments each; those between 1,000 and 5,000 had 5.4 establishments each; those between 500 and 1,000 had 2.8 establishments each; those between 100 and 500 had 1.6 each; and those under 100 only 1.2 each. Establishments belonging to an individual enterprise may be of different size groups, depending on the nature of the enterprise's output, whether it manufactures its own components, the nature of the productive processes involved, and so on. The phenomenon of a small number of large or very large enterprises and establishments accounting for a large proportion of the total numbers employed is widespread throughout the world's manufacturing industry, as well as between industries within the manufacturing sector of each country.

Two measures of the size of companies and establishments have now been presented, namely sales and employment. Size can also be measured in terms of output (net value added in the Board of Trade's Censuses of Production) or according to net assets employed. Details for publicly quoted companies are to be found in a series of Board of Trade publications entitled 'Company Assets and Income'. The ranking of companies according to net assets employed and income, defined as 'trading profit (after deducting directors' fees and emoluments, pensions to past directors, superannuation payments, compensation for loss of office, auditors' fees, etc.) and other income (from investments and securities and other sources) before allowing for depreciation and other provisions' may enable individual companies to be identified. The Census of Production material, however, is so aggregated that this is never possible. The ranking of individual companies will naturally vary according to the method employed. Those companies, for example, where net assets employed per person are high may rank differently on an assets or numbers employed basis. But whichever measure of size is used, the same overall results emerge: a small number of very large concerns, a larger number of large ones, a still larger number of concerns of medium size, and a very large number of small ones.

This part of the present book is concerned primarily with manufacturing activity, and references will have to be made to individual industries within this sector of economic activity. Manufacturing activity may be viewed as essentially a transformation process, raw materials being transformed by a variety of processes either into final products for the individual consumer or into intermediate products which are bought by other firms and used as components in an assembly process, or are subject to further transformation processes before reaching the final consumer. To a large extent the classification used by the Board of Trade in preparing its Census of Production material is based on the physical characteristics of industrial output. Essentially the transformation process is based on a number of raw materials, for example primary metals, clay, stone, wood, fibres and oil. Primary metals are used as a base for a whole range of engineering products, clay and stone are used for building materials and pottery, wood for the furniture and paper industries, fibres for textiles and clothing, and oil for a major section of the chemical industry. In a number of important instances the manufacturing process is a refining process rather than a constructional one. This is largely the case with food-processing industries, oil refining and the primary metal industries. The competitive position between outputs of similar products using different raw-material bases tends to be neglected, although it is of considerable concern to the economist. These considerations must be borne in mind when using the Census of Production data to assess the degree of competition existing in the economy.

In order to gain uniformity in discussion of industrial problems and to relate output to manpower, the Standard Industrial Classification (S.I.C.) was introduced in 1948 and revised to take account of changing technological conditions in 1958. Current details are given of large numbers of products classified according to S.I.C. and of products included in each S.I.C. heading in a 'Blue Book'.

2. THE SIZE OF PLANTS AND ENTERPRISES

Large-size firms or enterprises are clearly of great importance in the industrial structure of the economy. They account for a major share of total capital assets in manufacturing activity, employ a large proportion of the total labour force and produce a large amount of total output. The influences which make for their existence are usually considered under the broad heading of economies of scale. Strictly speaking, arguments concerned with economies of scale should consider what happens to costs per unit of output when the proportions of all factors of production remain constant. In general, however, an increase in the size of a firm will lead to a change in the proportion of factors employed. This makes it difficult to identify economies of scale. Discussions relating to economies of scale have been at the core of most writings in the field of industrial organisation from Adam Smith, through Marshall in both his 'Principles of Economics' and 'Industry and Trade', to more modern writers. (1) Such discussions have frequently, although not exclusively, been orientated towards the elusive concept of the optimum firm. They have also made use of Marshall's distinction between internal and external economies, namely economies which arise from actions associated with the managerial actions of the individual firm, and those associated with the broad spectrum of actions taken by managements in the industry as a whole. Recent contributions to the theory of the firm have tended to stress the impact of growth as a managerial objective on the firm's organisation. (2) As a result, the stationary concept of the optimum firm has been jettisoned and replaced by theories connected more with managerial attitudes and organisational theories.

The technical factors giving rise to economies of scale have naturally varied according to the state of the arts, though new innovations which affect the scale of the individual plant may be capital-using and labour-saving or *vice versa*. Consequently, where the size of plant or firm is measured by employment or capital employed, bias may be introduced. A capital-intensive brickworks of automated design may produce three times the output of bricks as a works of older design using coke-fired furnaces, but with no difference in the numbers of the labour force. The use of numbers employed as a measure of size is none the less a good first approximation.

Frequently non-technical economies become important only when the available technical economies of scale have been fully exploited. Examples of non-technical economies are economies of a financial nature. They too can result in an increase in the size of the firm attainable with a further decrease in costs per unit of output, or they may act as a restraint to further growth. Technical economies come first, but they are more important in some industries than in others. Some guide to the importance of technical economies of scale is the presence of large establishments in certain industries, while lack of technical economies accounts for much of the predominance of small establishments in other industries.

Taking numbers employed as a measure of the size of plant and enterprise, small plants/enterprises may be regarded as those employing fewer than 100 persons, medium-sized plants/enterprises as employing between 100 and 500 persons, and large ones as employing 500 persons or more. In British manufacturing industry as a whole in 1958, about half the number of employees were to be found in large plants, while around one-third were in plants of medium size. This suggests that important technical economies of scale exist in manufacturing industry as a whole.

The position with regard to individual trades is indicated in Table 10.3. The average size of plant and enterprise is shown separately according to numbers of trades. In only 7 per cent of trades was the average size of plant large, although 13 per cent of trades had a large average size of enterprise. About 40 per cent of trades had a medium size of both plant and enterprise. Technical economies of size relating to plant appear to be of importance in locomotives and railway-track equipment, man-made fibres, mineral-oil refining, aircraft, telegraph and

Table 10.3 Size of Plant and Enterprise in Trades
in Manufacturing Industry, 1958

Size of plant/enterprise (average employment)	Number of trades	
	Plants	Enterprises
2,000 and over	0	2
1,000 and under 2,000	3	5
750 ,, ,, 1,000	0	3
500 ,, ,, 750	5	5
400 ,, ,, 500	3	3
300 ,, ,, 400	5	8
200 ,, ,, 300	13	12
100 ,, ,, 200	27	26
75 ,, ,, 100	11	11
50 ,, ,, 75	19	15
25 ,, ,, 50	28	24
Under 25	6	5
Total	120	119

Source: Calculated from Board of Trade Census of Production, 1958.

telephone apparatus, industrial engines, tobacco, and iron and steel (general). In some instances even the Board of Trade definition of a census trade may be insufficiently narrow to permit more than tentative inferences to be drawn from such data. For example, the presence of component manufacturers in the 'motor vehicle manufacturing' trade affects the average size of both plant and enterprise considerably (307 and 360 respectively). It should not be confused with the motor vehicle assembly trade, which it includes.

The size of enterprise is affected more by non-technical economies than technical ones; the latter affect principally the size of plant. Thus to those trades where the average size of plant is large for technical reasons must be added a number of other trades where average size of the enterprise is large for non-technical reasons. These are explosives, insulated wire and cables, railway carriages, sugar, cement, linoleum and coke ovens. Where the limits to technical economies of scale have been approached, a firm may duplicate or otherwise increase the number of plants in order to take advantage of non-technical economies. Some indication of the importance of non-technical economies may be estimated from the ratio of average employment per enterprise ($\bar{X}_e$) to the average size of plant ($\bar{X}_p$). Table 10.4 shows the results of such a calculation for the Board of Trade 'larger' establishments and enterprises (being those with 25

Table 10.4 Ratio of Average Size of Enterprise to Average Size
of Plant in Manufacturing Industry, 1958

Index $(\overline{X}_e / \overline{X}_p) \times 100$	Number of trades
300 and over	5
250 and under 300	2
200 ,, ,, 250	8
175 ,, ,, 200	6
150 ,, ,, 175	28
125 ,, ,, 150	51
Under 125	20
Total	120

$\overline{X}$ = arithmetic mean size; e = enterprise; p = plant.

Source: Calculated from Board of Trade Census of Production, 1958.

or more employees). They are the same trades as those appearing in Table 10.3. Non-technical economies would appear to be important in some 21 trades, but should not be ruled out entirely in others. To the 15 trades with large size of enterprise, non-technical economies could be of importance in spirit distilling, coal-tar products, chemicals (general), steel tubes, ordnance and small arms, radio and other electronic apparatus, spinning and doubling of cotton, bricks, milk products, brewing and soft drinks.

Three main methods have been used to investigate the existence of technical economies of scale and the impact of non-technical economies. The first method consists of cross-section studies within industries and seeks to draw conclusions regarding the existence of economies of scale from a comparative performance of existing plants. Here direct comparisons of actual costs of plants and firms of different sizes are made. A major objection to this method is that actual costs may be valued by accountants in a number of different ways, so that unless some standardised system of cost-accounting can be introduced for studies of this kind, the final measure of efficiency will be biased. Differences in product mix may also produce important cost divergences which may invalidate straight inter-firm and inter-plant comparisons, and a very large number of firms are multi-product. A variant of this method is to use rates of return on capital employed. The historical time at which valuations of capital employed are made is crucial for the success or failure of the rate of return method. Unless all firms in the comparison value their capital employed on the same basis and at the same time, and unless they constantly revalue their assets, rates of return will not be strictly comparable. Furthermore each cost—size observation is meant in theory to represent a point on the long-run average-cost curve, but the data often refer to different states of technology for various plants. (3)

The second method is a technological approach to the existence of economies of scale. It is based on fairly precise engineering estimates of the operating costs of plants of given size, at a particular moment in the state of technical knowledge. To these estimates are added a series of non-precise 'guestimates' for non-technological data, based on management's assessment of associated marketing costs, transport costs and changes in labour costs. Each element of the productive process is studied by production engineers, with a view to quantifying the relationship between inputs and outputs for plants of varying size. These kinds of engineering estimates are frequently undertaken by firms contemplating expansion or replacement of existing plant and equipment. (4) As a result a fair amount of data is generally available in the archives of individual firms and scattered amongst the literature of the technological journals and trade magazines. The use of this approach has almost, though not entirely, replaced the cross-sectional type of study during the last decade. (5)

A third method is known as the 'survivor principle'. (6) This method is based on a consideration of the structure of a trade or industry at different dates. A comparison is made of the most popular size of plant/firm at each date, and the method is based on the argument that the plants which have the lowest costs will be those which have survived into the next period. If plants of a given size are increasing their share of the trade's total output, it is argued that this represents the new 'optimum' size of the plant. The basis of this approach rests on the argument that the existence of competition ensures that the most efficient plants/firms survive through time. Although the optimum size of plant may be revealed at a given time, the method tells little about the influences making for that optimum. In an imperfectly competitive world, firms or plants may survive for reasons other than that they are the most efficient; and although take-over bids may be a means of getting rid of some inefficient firms, there is no guarantee that this method will ensure that only the most efficient firms survive. All three methods clearly have their limitations, but where two or all of the methods point to the same conclusions for a particular industry, it seems reasonable to regard this as evidence for the existence of economies of scale in that industry.

The following will consider evidence relating to the existence of economies of scale in three different industries. The industries selected for detailed discussion are ones which include as their leaders some of the largest of the world's firms shown in Table 10.1. They are the motor industry, the oil-refining industry and the steel industry. Of the 28 firms in the United States with $2 billion turnover a year or more in 1965, 17 were in the three industries selected, and they accounted for 70 per cent of the turnover of these 28 firms. Outside the United States, firms in these three industries accounted for half the total number of firms with turnover of $1 billion or more in 1965 (14 out of 30), and they accounted for half the total turnover.

(a)   The Motor-car Industry
Cross-sectional studies of economies of scale in the motor industry are rare. The earliest relates to 1935, (7) and indicated that output per man in the United States industry was around three times that for the United Kingdom. One technological-type study has been made for the United Kingdom, (8) and this may be compared with information from the United States. (9) Evidence for the existence of considerable economies of scale may also be found in the use of the survivor technique. (10) In the motor industry the existence of economies of scale is bound up with the extent of vertical integration. During the 1930s and 1940s the British motor industry moved away from vertically integrated car plants towards assembly and production of engines only, buying in bodies and other components from other specialist manufacturers. From 1953 onwards the movement has been reversed, with the acquisition by Ford Motor Co. of Briggs Motor Bodies and by British Motor Corporation (B.M.C.) of Fisher and Ludlow in that year. The process has been extended further, so that the major British assemblers of motor vehicles possess body-making subsidiaries, B.M.C. (now merged with Leyland) further acquiring Pressed Steel in 1965, Standard Motor Co. (now in turn a subsidiary of British-Leyland Motor Corporation) acquiring Mulliners and the Rootes Group acquiring British Light Steel Pressings. During this period too, small assembly producers have gradually been absorbed, and around 90 per cent of the market is now supplied by the British firms, British Leyland and Rootes (American-linked with Chrysler), and the American subsidiaries, Ford and Vauxhall (the latter being a subsidiary of General Motors). In 1961 Leyland Motor Corporation acquired Standard Motor Co., and in 1967 it took over Rover before finally merging with B.M.C. in 1968 Similarly Jaguar was merged into the larger B.M.C. to form British Motor Holdings (B.M.H.) in 1966, and Singer was acquired by Rootes in the 1950s. There appear to be different technical economies of scale and optimum sizes of plant for different kinds of operation in the motor industry. Large economies exist for the pressing of bodies, in the engine shops and in assembly itself. Except in a few cases, such as some electrical equipment, the major assembly firms still tend to 'buy out' components from special producers where the technical optimum size of plant is small. During the post-war period the optimum size of assembly plant has risen from around 100,000 vehicles a year to somewhere in the region of 500,000

vehicles a year. Economies of scale have arisen in the engine shops through the introduction of special-purpose machines. This in turn involves concentration on engines of given capacity which may be fitted into a variety of vehicles. Thus the B.M.H. brand of British Leyland puts a standardised 1098-c.c. engine into its '1100' range and into the former Morris '1000' – in all, four different models with a further five variations. Nevertheless in 1967 B.M.H. still manufactured nine different sizes of engines for thirty-one different models, of which twelve were identical in all but name. As will be seen from Table 10.5, B.M.H. had a variety of engine plants of different size, and the same is true of body pressings where substantial economies are available by concentrating on long runs of a particular model. To some extent a relatively low number of pressings per year can be compensated for by retaining a model in production over a longer period of time. Thus a two-year life of model is usual in the United States, and a five- to seven-year life in the United Kingdom. In an industry where international competition is often based on model changes, a long run per year has considerable advantages.

(b) The Oil-Refining Industry

Petroleum companies feature amongst the very large companies, by size of sales and assets, both within the United States and in the rest of the world. In 1965 there were seven United States oil companies with a turnover of over $2,000 million: Standard Oil of New Jersey, Socony Mobil Oil, Texaco, Gulf Oil, Shell Oil, Standard Oil of Indiana, and Standard Oil of California, with a combined turnover of $32,000 million. Outside the United States two companies had a turnover of $2,000 million or over. They were Royal Dutch-Shell and British Petroleum, with a combined turnover of $9,000 million. All exhibited a high

Table 10.5 Size of Plant of British Motor Holdings, 1967*

Number of employees		*Assembly*	*Engines*	*Bodies*	*Transmission, radiators, carburettors*	*P.S.V.†*	*Total*
20,000 and over		1					1
10,000 and under 20,000				1			1
7,500 „ „ 10,000		1		1			2
5,000 „ „ 7,500			1	1			2
2,500 „ „ 5,000		2	2	1	2	1	8
1,000 „ „ 2,500			2			1	3
Under 1,000		1			1		2
Total		4½	5½	4	3	2	19

Derived from 'Autocar', 10 Aug 1967.
* Prior to merger with Leyland Motor Corporation.
† Public service vehicles.

degree of vertical integration, including within their operations prospecting, crude oil production, transportation of crude oil by tankers and pipelines, the refining process, distribution of the finished product and ownership of retail outlets. As side activities they also engage in the production of petrochemicals. The actual oil-refining process is thus only one branch of their activities. From the standpoint of technical economies of scale it is nevertheless an important one, in that oil refining is fairly typical of the other important chemical process industries.

The technical economies governing the oil-refining process cannot, however, be considered without reference to the location of refineries. If refineries are located away from the source of crude oil, then the ability to maintain a constant flow of crude oil, either by pipeline or tanker, becomes important in balancing technical economies of refinery operation against those of tankers and port installations. The size of oil refineries is thus determined by the availability of crude resources. The length of sea routes, depth of water at oil jetties and increasing size of tankers all help to determine the actual size of refineries. Another major consideration affecting technical economies of scale is the size of the local market. This in turn includes considerations relating to the yield pattern for different types of crude oil, and the pattern of demand for yields of different kinds.

The production process in oil refining consists of splitting carbon and hydrogen molecules present in the crude oil by the process of distillation. Hence oil-refinery capacity is measured in terms of distillation capacity. The process plant consists essentially of a pipe still and distillation column, with a variety of additions of plant for the desulphurisation of gas-oil, bitumen production and catalytic cracking. Fixed costs are important, and the evidence points to a greater effect of idle capacity on small refineries than on large ones. Technical engineering-type studies show a clear gain in terms of rapidly falling costs as refinery size increases from 1 to 2 million tons a year throughput of crude oil, with a proportionately smaller fall in costs as capacity expands from 2 to 5 million tons throughout a year. (11) This point was underlined by the Vice-Chairman of Shell-Mex and B.P., when he stated in 1966 that the capital costs per ton of a refinery with a capacity of 5 million tons a year were only half those of a refinery with a capacity of 1 million tons a year. Estimates similar to American ones were produced for United Kingdom refinery operating costs in 1958. (12)

The size of sub-markets for finished products is of considerable importance in determining the capacity of oil refineries in both the United Kingdom and the United States. In the United States it was found that, whereas the optimum size of oil refinery of efficient scale might account for only 1¾ per cent of national output, this could rise to between 4.3 per cent and 11.5 per cent in the four

Table 10.6 Capacity of E.E.C. and U.K. Oil Refineries, 1966

Capacity ('000 barrels per day)	Belgium	Holland	France	Germany	Italy	U.K.	Total	% total capacity
			Number of refineries					
300 and over		1					1	4.6
250 and under 300							—	—
200 „ „ 250			1			2	3	9.4
150 „ „ 200	1	1	1		2	3	8	19.0
100 „ „ 150			2	1	5	3	11	17.9
75 „ „ 100	1	1	6	8	2	—	18	21.1
50 „ „ 75		1	2	10	5	1	19	15.0
25 „ „ 50	1		4	4	6	2	17	8.6
10 „ „ 25	1		2	3	5	1	12	2.6
Under 10	2	1		6	11	6	26	1.7
Total	6	5	18	32	36	18	115	99.9

Derived from 'World Petroleum' (July 1966).

regional sub-markets. (13) In local markets an oil producer would need to be assured of 4 per cent of total sales if he were to operate a refinery of optimum size. Because of segmented markets and the high cost of transporting products, it is no longer economical to build extremely large single units. There has been a big shift from the giant crude-based refineries of Abadan in Iran (412,000 barrels a day, or over 20 million tons a year) and Amuay Bay (Creole Petroleum Corporation in Venezuela, 368,000 barrels a day) to refineries which are market-orientated. This has been partly induced by the post-war demands of European governments to save foreign exchange, but it has been reinforced by rising distribution costs for finished products and falling transportation costs for crude oil. Thus the optimum size in European oil refineries differs according to market fragmentation, as may be seen in Table 10.6. The major part of German production comes from refineries much smaller than those in the United Kingdom, the Netherlands or Italy. The German optimum size also reflects her lack of deep-water jetties for large tankers. The largest European refineries are to be found in the neighbourhood of areas of densest population in the Low Countries and South-east England. There is some evidence from both United States data and British data, using the survivor technique, that the optimum size of refinery has been increasing in the post-war period. Thus Table 10.7 gives an example of the survivor technique applied to data for refineries in the United Kingdom between 1938 and 1965. The optimum size of refinery in the United Kingdom in 1965 would appear to be somewhere between 9 and 12 million tons a year (or 180,000 to 240,000 barrels a day), going well beyond the optimum

158   *Industrial Organisation*

level suggested only a few years earlier. (14) As Table 10.7 shows, by 1965 over half of the refinery capacity in the United Kingdom was accounted for by four refineries with a crude throughput of 9 million tons a year and over.

Table 10.7 Oil Refinery Capacity in the U.K., 1938-65
(number of refineries and percentage of total capacity)

Capacity ('000 tons per year)	1938		1950		1955		1960		1965	
	No.	%	No.	%	No.	%	No.	%	No.	%
12,000 and over										
9,000 and under 12,000							2	42	4	56
6,000 ,, ,, 9,000					1	24	1	15	2	20
4,000 ,, ,, 6,000					2	32	2	20	2	13
2,000 ,, ,, 4,000			2	45	3	29	3	18	1	4
1,000 ,, ·,, 2,000			4	45	2	10	1	3	3	6
500 ,, ,, 1,000	1	36	–	–	–	–	–	–	–	–
250 ,, ,, 500	–	–	–	–	–	–	–	–	2	1
Under 250	7	64	7	10	7	4	7	2	4	1
Total	8	100	13	100	15	99	16	100	18	101

Source: Ministry of Fuel and Power, 'Digest of Statistics'.

(c) The Steel Industry

The steel industry, like the motor-car and oil-refining industries, is characterised by the large physical size of its plants. The majority of plants in the steel industry are engaged in the finishing processes, and only a minority is concerned with the primary processes of producing pig-iron and its conversion into crude steel. Attention will be confined mainly to the economies achieved in the steel-making process, but since integrated works now produce the bulk of crude steel output in the United Kingdom, economies in the pig-iron process cannot be neglected.

Steel furnaces use a mixture of three inputs, namely hot metal (iron), cold pig-iron and scrap. Combinations of these inputs can be varied according to the availability of each and according to relative price movements, especially between iron ore and scrap. There is a variety of steel-making processes available, but in 1960 open-hearth basic furnaces produced the bulk of crude steel in the United Kingdom. In 1965 this method still remained the principal method of producing steel, but its share had dropped from around 80 per cent to 60 per cent, whilst the new L.D. Kaldo and rotor converter methods had come up from a mere 2 per cent to 20 per cent of the total, with the production of crude steel from electric arc furnaces increasing from 7 per cent to 13 per cent.

Technical studies prepared for the Economic Commission for Latin America have shown how blast-furnace production costs fall as capacity increases. Between a furnace capacity of 100,000 and 200,000 tons a year they fell by 30 per cent, by a further 30 per cent between 200,000 and 500,000 tons a year, and by half as much again once the 1,000,000 tons a year mark was reached. The findings of these technological-engineering studies are in keeping with the large increase in size of blast furnaces in the United Kingdom during the period 1950-1965.

In the case of steel-making processes, the bulk of United Kingdom production now comes from large integrated works. (15) Cross-industry and plant studies carried out by the Anglo-American Productivity team in the early 1950s had highlighted the economies to be obtained by concentrating output in the large integrated United States steelworks as compared with those obtained in existing plants in the United Kingdom. Iron and Steel Board operating costs for furnace capacity heats fall rapidly (by 30 per cent) as the size of the furnace heat doubles from 75 to 150 tons. (16) Increasing the size of the furnace heat to 400 tons brings operating costs down by half as much again. Economies of scale in integrated works have risen because of heat conservation due to hot instead of cold rolling, the new process of continuous casting, the ability to make better use of materials-handling equipment such as cranes and conveyor belts, which form up to 35 per cent of capital costs in an integrated works, economies from larger rolling mills installed alongside the larger furnaces, and the ability to make more use of sintering plant, only available to integrated works.

The trend towards a higher optimum size of furnace may be traced in Table 10.8, relating to the capacity of open-hearth basic steel furnaces in the United

Table 10.8 Capacity of Open-Hearth Basic Steel Furnaces, 1950-65

Furnace capacity per heat (tons)	Percentage of industry capacity				Number of furnaces			
	1950	1955	1960	1965	1950	1955	1960	1965
Under 60	14.3	9.6	4.4	2.0	90	73	36	13
60 and under 80	19.9	11.5	11.2	8.3	90	62	66	39
80 „ „ 100	20.9	12.4	7.7	8.5	73	52	35	31
100 „ „ 120	8.4	13.7	13.9	8.7	24	47	52	26
120 „ „ 160	8.6	12.2	15.7	13.6	19	33	46	32
160 „ „ 200	6.3	7.5	2.9	3.2	11	16	7	6
200 „ „ 250	2.9	11.9	23.5	28.0	4	20	43	41
250 „ „ 300	8.7	7.3	5.4	3.3	10	10	8	4
300 and over	10.0	13.9	15.3	24.4	9	15	18	23
Total	100.0	100.0	100.0	100.0	330	328	311	215

Source: Annual Statistics of the Iron and Steel Board and the British Iron and Steel Federation.

Kingdom between 1950 and 1965. Whereas in 1950 about 55 per cent of the industry's capacity of open-hearth basic steel furnaces was in furnaces of less than 100 tons capacity by 1965 almost a quarter of the total capacity was to be found in furnaces of 300 tons per heat or over, and over half was to be found in furnaces of 200 tons per heat or more. Small furnaces, of below 100 tons per heat, had been replaced both absolutely in terms of falling numbers and proportionally in their share of total capacity, which by 1965 had fallen to under 20 per cent.

The above survey of scale in three industries shows that in each case there are important economies of scale. The evidence of the technological-engineering studies and of the survivor technique for locating economies of scale are entirely consistent and point to the same conclusions.

3   MEASURES OF CONCENTRATION

The study of the economics of large-scale production in three trades has shown the predominant size of plant and enterprise to be large. This also applies to a number of other trades, especially in manufacturing industry. Where it applies, the large-scale enterprises employ a large proportion of the labour force. In the following, the relationship between the numbers of firms of given size in a trade and the proportion of the trade's total labour force which they account for, will be examined with reference to a trade's industrial structure and its competitive structure. If a few large plants and/or a few large firms dominate total employment and output in a given trade, this may provide a guide to the competitive structure of the trade and the pricing policy of the firms of which it is comprised. Such a situation as the one described would lead one to suspect the existence of oligopoly or some other form of imperfect competition. Consequently various attempts have been made to measure the degree of concentration existing in different trades.

There are two principal approaches to the measurement of concentration of employment or output in the hands of a relatively small number of firms in an industry, namely the statistical approach and the enumerative approach. Both methods have their own limitations. The concentration of economic power which gives a firm's management the ability to control the volume of output which it produces or the price at which units of that output will be sold, reflects the competitive structure of the industry, and may itself be looked upon as concentration of employment, output or capital in the hands of a few firms. Frequently, but not invariably, a high degree of concentration of the total employment of a given trade amongst a few firms will also be an indication that a similar degree of concentration will exist if this is measured in terms of output or capital. It also happens that the statistical and enumerative approaches to the measurement of concentration are more applicable to one of the indicators of competitive structure than to the other two. Each of the two methods of measuring concentration is now considered in turn.

(a)   The Statistical Approach

The statistical measures of concentration most commonly employed stem largely from the work of Pareto, Lorenz and Gini. For the complete success of this method, a knowledge of the relevant indicator of size (employment, output or capital) is required for *each* productive unit, plant or enterprise in the trade concerned. Such information is seldom available and thus statistical measures of concentration are often confined to the indicator 'capital employed'. Even here, where the sizes of individual firms can readily be ascertained from company accounts (which must be registered with the appropriate authorities such as the Board of Trade in the United Kingdom), the firms themselves may operate in a number of different industries, and capital employed may be revalued at different times by different companies. Again, although information relating to capital employed may easily be available for quoted companies, such data have been more difficult to obtain for the (usually small) unquoted companies. Each of the other two indicators for concentration has some drawbacks. Where employment is the indicator used to measure the degree of concentration, the true degree of concentration will be understated if the largest firms in the industry use more capital-intensive methods of production. If output is taken as the indicator, this may be taken either gross or net. The degree of concentration will be overstated for gross output if the trade in question produces a large number of semi-manufactures and/or engages in a high degree of vertical integration. The use of net output will again overstate the degree of concentration if there are a large number of inter-plant transfers of material and semi-finished products.

On the assumption that exact information concerning the relevant indicators is available, the Lorenz–Gini method of measuring the degree of concentration may be illustrated as follows. Fig. 10.1 shows Lorenz curves of the cumulative percentages of sales taken by the cumulative percentages of the hundred largest non-financial firms in the United States and Europe. Complete equality is indicated by the diagonal line, so that 10 per cent of firms would account for 10 per cent of total sales, 25 per cent of firms would account for 25 per cent of sales, and so on. The actual divergence of the curved lines from the diagonal is a measure of the departure of firms measured in terms of sales from complete equality. In the example given, the largest United States company, General Motors, accounted for 10.74 per cent of total sales for the hundred largest

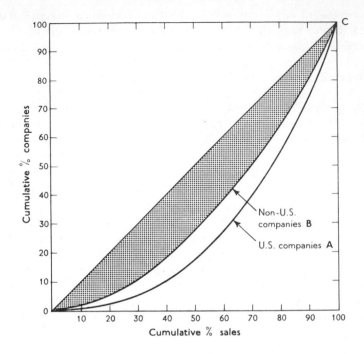

Fig. 10.1 Lorenz curves of industrial concentration of sales, 1965.

A = 100 largest U.S. firms
B = 100 largest non-U.S. firms

Source: Calculated from data in 'Fortune Magazine' (July – Aug 1966).

United States companies in 1965; and the two largest, General Motors and Ford Motor Co., accounted for 16.72 per cent. The fact that Fig. 10.1 shows the Lorenz curve of United States firms to lie wholly outside that of the non-United States firms indicates a greater degree of inequality or concentration of sales amongst the largest United States firms than for non-United States firms. A more exact measure of inequality, used particularly where comparisons are required between two cumulative distributions of firms according to size, is the Gini coefficient. This measure is the proportion of the area under the diagonal *OC* covered by the divergence from the diagonal of the area enclosed by the Lorenz curve, being the hatched area in Fig. 10.1. A small hatched area, giving a low coefficient, indicates a low degree of concentration. In the present case the non-United States firms have an estimated Gini coefficient of 15.2 per cent, whereas that for the United States firms is 27.7 per cent.

(b) The Enumerative Approach

Because of difficulty in obtaining data, the more commonly used method of measuring industrial concentration is the enumerative approach. The method is a two-way one. It may be inquired what proportion of total employment, output or capital of a given trade is accounted for by the three or four largest plants or firms, or it may be asked how many plants/firms account for a given percentage of employment and so on. Data are more normally available in the form of the percentage of employment or output accounted for by the three or four largest firms. In this approach no information is revealed about individual firms. The first type of enumerative approach is the one most workers in the field use to measure the degree of concentration in British industry, and it has frequently been used in the United States. Such a concentration ratio has been $C = \dfrac{E_3}{E_n}$ and this has been used to measure the degree of concentration of employment in some 220 trades, where C is the concentration ratio, E_3 the number of workers employed by the three largest firms (business units), and E_n the total employment of all firms in the trade. (17) The coefficient is usually expressed in percentage terms. A further measure, useful in studying the structure of different trades, and using the same kind of technique, is the size ratio of units, $W = \dfrac{W_3}{W_n}$. This compares the average size of the three largest units with the average size of all units. The use of the enumerative method makes it possible for research workers to use Census of Production data. Whereas it is illegal for the census authorities to reveal material relating to individual firms, or publish data in such a way that information relating to individual firms may be deduced, the combination of information relating to the three or sometimes four largest firms meets this objection.

A number of difficulties arise in the use of Census of Production data for investigating the degree of concentration in different trades. These relate largely to the manner in which such data are collected. In the United Kingdom the Board of Trade classifies industries largely on a technological basis, and little importance appears to be attached to market conditions or cross-elasticities of demand. Again, many of the establishments classified as belonging to a particular trade are multi-product, and produce goods which are 'characteristic' of other trades. Occasionally the output of a 'non-characteristic' product of a trade could be an important source of supply of the output of another trade. It could sometimes falsify conclusions arrived at from census data concerning the degree of concentration in that trade. This would be especially important in cases where the 'non-characteristic' producer was in fact one of the major suppliers of a product characteristic of another trade. Hence on occasions the classification of an establishment or business unit to a particular trade on the basis of its principal products might give a misleading view of the importance of its overall activities.

4 THE EXTENT OF CONCENTRATION IN BRITISH AND AMERICAN MANUFACTURING INDUSTRY

A major study of concentration of employment and output in the British economy for 1951 (18) produced evidence relating to the degree of concentration in 220 trades in manufacturing industry. Taking 67 per cent and over as indicating a high employment concentration ratio, 23 per cent of all trades were to be found in this category, but they accounted for only 10 per cent of the total employment in all 220 trades. The most trades (46 per cent of the total) were found to have a low employment concentration ratio (33 per cent and under), and they accounted for two-thirds of the total employment.

Technological conditions of production may well account for the high degree of concentration exhibited in fifty trades. They include many of the trades which had a high average size of plant and enterprise in 1958. They include mineral-oil refining, explosives and fireworks, and cement. On the other hand large size of plant and sometimes enterprise should not invariably be taken to mean that the trade will exhibit a high employment concentration ratio. The size of the market for the products of the trade may be such that a relatively large number of large plants and enterprises can be accommodated. Locomotive manufacture, steel sheets, electric wire and cables, aircraft manufacture and repair and motor bodies all exhibited only a medium degree of concentration, whilst iron and steel (smelting and rolling) and railway carriages and wagons both displayed a low degree of concentration.

Generally speaking, trades with a high employment concentration ratio are also ones with a high output concentration ratio. Employment and output concentration ratios are in fact highly correlated. For some trades where company activities are generally confined to a fairly narrow field, it is possible to make a comparison of employment and output concentration ratios with financial concentration ratios in terms of assets employed. In all ten trades where such a comparison was possible, concentration measured in terms of assets (net capital employed) was greater than that measured by either output or employment. Three trades, distilling, cement and tobacco, all had a high degree of concentration no matter what indicator was taken. Four trades, cottons, woollen and worsted, hosiery and brewing, all had a low degree of concentration however measured. On the other hand concentration in the cocoa, chocolate and sugar confectionery trade was of medium degree when measured in terms of output or employment, but 'high' in terms of assets. Whilst in newspapers and carpets concentration when measured in terms of assets was sufficient to class these two low output/employment concentration ratio trades into the medium range. In both trades the assets concentration ratio was 9 per cent higher than the higher of the output/employment concentration ratios.

Some comparison is possible between the extent of concentration in Britain and the United States. A number of technical problems arise when such international comparisons are made. Even when the Census of Production data are the same, narrower definitions of a trade in one country than in the other will tend to yield a higher concentration ratio in the country having the narrower trade definition. It has already been pointed out in the case of open-hearth steel furnaces and oil refining that subdivisions of a trade (for example on a geographical basis) will result in a higher optimum size of plant and frequently a higher degree of concentration of output amongst plants of optimum size. A further difficulty is that one country may give data referring to the three largest business units, whereas the other country may relate such information to the four largest units. When due allowance is made for such differences by applying appropriate statistical techniques, the evidence available suggests that the overall degree of concentration in manufacturing industry in the United Kingdom was rather lower than in the United States during the early 1950s. It was later found that, whereas 20 per cent of United Kingdom employment in trades common to the United Kingdom and the United States had a concentration ratio of 50 per cent and over, the corresponding figure for the United States was 27 per cent. (19) Again, 7.3 per cent of comparable British industries had a concentration ratio of 60 per cent or more compared with 12.4 per cent of United States industries. Despite a fair number of divergences, in the majority of cases industries with a high concentration ratio in one country also showed a high concentration ratio in the other. A similar conclusion is reached by another writer. (20) This differs from the position in the mid-1930s, when it was found that the concentration ratio was rather greater in the United Kingdom than in the United States. (21) Observations concerning changes in the degree of concentration over time will be considered in Chapter II.

5   CONCENTRATION AND COMPETITIVE POWER

The final problem to be considered in this chapter is whether any inferences can be drawn from concentration ratios about the competitive structure of the economy. The time spent on calculating and comparing concentration ratios can only be justified if it helps towards a greater understanding of the forces determining industrial structure and the degree of competition, or lack of it, displayed by an economy. Initially a number of different competitive situations may be implied in a high concentration ratio. For example, in an industry with a concentration ratio as high as 70 per cent, the three largest business units could have output or employment amongst them divided in such a way as to imply almost complete monopoly with considerable price leadership. The top business unit might conceivably account for 60 per cent of total output and the other two units only 5 per cent each, the remaining 30 per cent being shared between a very large number of small producers. Alternatively the three largest units might share the 70 per cent equally with 23 per cent each, indicating the possible existence of an oligopoly situation. Equally a moderate concentration ratio of 48 per cent might be indicative of an oligopoly situation, each business unit having 16 per cent of total output, with the next three business units having 15 per cent each, the remainder of total output, 7 per cent, being accounted for by small units. The chief weakness of the enumerative approach to business concentration lies in the fact that it is usual for only one absolute concentration ratio to be given by the census authorities, though employment and output are sometimes also given. One method of improving reliance on one absolute concentration ratio is to use additional information relating to size of plant, yielding useful information concerning the existence of economies of scale. Thus a size ratio of business units may be suggested along similar lines to the employment or output concentration ratio. (22)

Despite important qualifications, high concentration ratios must be taken as an important bench-mark in the sense of suggesting that further studies of a given trade should pay attention to price leadership, barriers to entry and the general absence of competition. A high concentration ratio is almost certainly incompatible with the existence of a very large number of important sellers, let alone the economist's concept of a perfectly competitive situation. In considering the control of oligopoly and other forms of imperfect competition, the existence of a high concentration ratio in a trade may be taken as an indicator that the trade in question should be given priority treatment in official investigations. From the early 1950s onwards there was plenty of work for the Monopolies Commission and the future Restrictive Practices Court to do. Monopoly situations probably existed in only about 7 per cent of total employment in the 220 trades which they investigated. But there was a good deal of evidence for the existence of oligopoly, accounting for some 21 to 28 per cent of total employment. A highly competitive position probably existed in about one-third of the 220 trades, covering 25 per cent of total employment, whilst some degree of monopolistic competition probably existed in the remaining trades, accounting for 40 per cent of total employment. The next chapter examines attempts to regulate the imperfectly competitive position found to exist in British manufacturing industry. (23)

11 The Control of Monopoly and Restrictive Practices

1 THE GROWTH OF MONOPOLY AND RESTRICTIVE PRACTICES

The previous chapter has shown how technical and other economies of scale favour large enterprises in a number of industries; and where the size of the market is given or cannot expand proportionately, this implies concentration of output amongst a few firms. If that sort of situation prevails, it frequently gives rise to near monopoly with price leadership, where one firm practically controls the market; or it may give rise to the existence of oligopoly, where a few sellers are in a position to determine price or output. During the severe slump of the 1930s, when the unemployment rate was high and there was much excess capacity, firms would amalgamate and merge with the object of closing down at least part of the excess capacity. This process had the result of increasing the degree of concentration of output in several industries into the hands of a smaller number of producers, and led in turn to an organised decrease in competition. While this applied to most industries, it did not apply to all. Where economies of scale are not overriding, concentration would be less. Overall, however, it has been found that between 1935 and 1951 an increase in principal product concentration occurred in more trades than did a decrease. (1) It is also probable that the period saw a decrease in the amount of competition in the economy as a whole, but more especially in manufacturing industry.

There were several influences at work during the sixteen years from 1935 to 1951 making for an increase in concentration in British manufacturing industry. Because of the existence of heavy unemployment during the 1930s, the Government of the day, along with most other governments of the Western world, started to pursue highly protectionist policies with regard to competing imports. As an accompaniment to the protection granted to manufacturers, the Government set out and implemented various schemes for reducing the amount of excess capacity in a number of industries, of which the most notable was the cotton textile industry. The general procedure was to cut out the smaller and usually less efficient plants, and to concentrate output on the larger, more efficient ones. The process came to be known as 'rationalisation'. Other examples were in the steel and shipbuilding industries. In some industries, however, the effects of the various government schemes served mainly to induce concerted action through trade associations rather than by mergers of individual firms. War-time restrictions on the production of civilian goods, the introduction of 'utility' schemes especially in the field of clothing and footwear, and the operation of rationing schemes further reduced the number of firms in some industries, though they may have facilitated the entry of new firms into some other industries, where licences were not required for output below a given size. The other major form of government intervention between 1935 and 1951 which made for an increase in concentration in the economy as a whole was the nationalisation of the coal-mining industry, railways, road transport (above a given size of operator), gas and electricity (and for a brief period steel, though because the firms retained their identities during this interlude the first steel nationalisation hardly affected concentration).

The tendency towards increased concentration of output and employment amongst the larger units of industry was also fostered by a number of technical innovations which made for considerable economies to be achieved through large-scale production. Some important instances have already been seen in the previous chapter in motor-vehicle production, where mass-assembly lines were already in operation during the late 1930s; in steel production, where size of furnace was important; and in the introduction of the continuous strip mill in the allied tinplate industry, especially in South Wales. Again, wrought-iron and steel tubes were subject to similar economies of scale, and their efficient production involved the closing-down of small, inefficient plants. Increased concentration in mineral-oil refining between 1935 and 1951 came about through the establishment of what was virtually a new industry for the United Kingdom. Before the war, oil refining within the United Kingdom had been on a small scale. The need to save foreign exchange, and the growing importance of consumer markets, led to the establishment of 'large' oil refineries in Europe, using techniques already in use either by British companies in the Middle East or by Dutch and American companies in the American Gulf and Venezuela. Other details of factors lying behind important mergers and amalgamations during this period in the engineering industries are given in Chapter 14.

War-time pledges to maintain full employment, and its subsequent achievement after the war, weakened one of the main arguments in favour of state support for mergers and monopolistic arrangements, with the seeming exception of the nationalised industries. There were demands to curb the power of large-firm monopolies and oligopolies, the nationalised industries 'naturally' exempted. Considerations following from pre-war theoretical static analysis of imperfect competition lent the weight of academic opinion to such demands. The argument was that competitors could be made to behave in accordance with the dictates of a perfectly competitive economic system, which in itself would automatically ensure maximum welfare and returns from the economy's productive resources. If so, there was a case for some control over monopoly, oligopoly and restrictive practices in general. These points, coupled with political mistrust of big business, led to the introduction of the first piece of British legislation designed specifically to deal with the problem of the control of monopoly in the private sector of the economy.

2 POST-WAR LEGISLATIVE ACTION

The following paragraphs will outline the main changes and provisions of Parliamentary legislation relating to the control of monopoly and restrictive practices. Subsequent sections of this chapter will deal with the subject in an analytical rather than historical fashion, and will be followed by an assessment of the extent to which legislation in this country appears to have been successful in curbing the power of monopolies and reducing the extent of restrictive practices.

At the end of 1968 there were statutory provisions of monopoly and restrictive practices legislation relating to a fairly wide range of situations. They covered the existence of monopoly situations themselves, defined as concentration of one-third of the total supply of a product in the hands of a single producer or group of producers, with a recent extension to cover the case of conglomerates extending over two or more industries. They also covered the possibility that a merger between two or more suppliers of a commodity might result in the subsequent existence of such a situation; the control of a defined and registrable list of restrictive trading practices and agreements; and the enforcement of resale price maintenance by individual as well as collective suppliers.

The initial post-war legislation dealing with the problem was the Monopolies and Restrictive Practices (Inquiry and Control) Act of 1948, which set up the Monopolies and Restrictive Practices Commission with investigational powers to be carried out at the request of the President of the Board of Trade. The commission was charged with ascertaining:

(a) whether a monopoly situation did or did not exist, and
(b) whether, if such a situation did exist, its working was against or not against the public interest.

A great deal depended on how 'the public interest' was defined. Further discussion of this problem will be deferred until later in this chapter. Meanwhile it is sufficient to note that the Commission was enjoined to take into account a number of specific matters in reaching their decision. Once the Commission had carried out its inquiry and made its reports with appropriate recommendations, if any, it was left to the appropriate Minister to take action, such as the drafting of a Parliamentary order which would have the force of law once Parliamentary consent had been given. Having published its report, the Commission had no further responsibility in the matter unless specifically requested to carry out a further investigation by the President of the Board of Trade. A further Act followed in 1953, which had the major effect of enlarging the size of the Commission from ten to twenty-five members.

In 1956, following a general report of the Monopoly and Restrictive Practices Commission into the nature and extent of a wide range of restrictive practices such as exclusive dealing, collective boycotts, aggregated rebates and other forms of collective discrimination (Report 11, June 1955), the Restrictive Trade Practices Act provided for the registration and judicial investigation of certain restrictive trading agreements, and for the prohibition of such agreements when found contrary to the 'public interest'. It also prohibited the 'collective enforcement of conditions regulating the resale price of goods'. Judicial investigation was to be carried out by a new branch of the High Court, with an innovation in the form of non-legally trained judges in addition to judges of the High Court. Henceforth the old Monopolies and Restrictive Practices Commisssion was to deal solely with cases of monopoly, and was renamed the Monopolies Commission. In 1964 the Resale Prices Act also provided for the registration of individual agreements and their prohibition unless found to be in the public

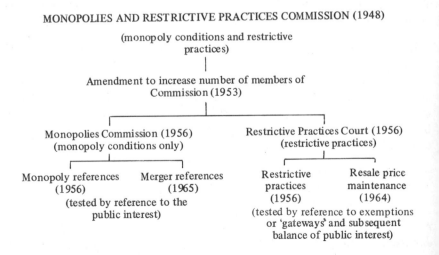

MONOPOLIES AND RESTRICTIVE PRACTICES COMMISSION (1948)

(monopoly conditions and restrictive practices)

Amendment to increase number of members of Commission (1953)

Monopolies Commission (1956)
(monopoly conditions only)

Monopoly references (1956)   Merger references (1965)
(tested by reference to the public interest)

Restrictive Practices Court (1956)
(restrictive practices)

Restrictive practices (1956)   Resale price maintenance (1964)
(tested by reference to exemptions or 'gateways' and subsequent balance of public interest)

Figure 11.1

interest by the Restrictive Practices Court. Lastly, the Monopolies and Mergers Act of 1965 made provision for the investigation of prospective mergers, which could be prohibited if it were considered by the Monopolies Commission that they would result in the formation of monopoly supply conditions, and that the resultant merger would also be against the public interest under the terms of the 1948 Act.

Fig. 11.1 is a 'family tree' of monopolies and restrictive practices legislation to the end of 1967, in terms of the institutions set up and their spheres of interest.

Discussion on the work of the Monopolies Commission and the Restrictive Practices Court will centre largely on the economic principles, or lack of them, lying behind their respective findings and recommendations.

3 THE MONOPOLIES COMMISSION

(a) Economies of Scale and Restrictive Practices
Trades chosen for reference by the Board of Trade to the Monopolies Commission for investigation have mostly had fairly high concentration ratios, whether measured in terms of gross or net output or employment. Concentration ratios were available from the 1951 Census of Production data, and an analysis of 25 trades (out of 34 investigated by the Monopolies Commission to the middle of 1967) has shown the following results. (2) Of these 25 trades, 14 (56 per cent) had a high concentration ratio (67 per cent or over) for either gross or net output or employment, 10 (40 per cent) had a medium concentration ratio (33-66 per cent); and only one trade had a low concentration ratio. Three-quarters of the 25 trades had at least one of the concentration ratios of 50 per cent or over. After the Restrictive Practices Court had been set up in 1956, the Commission ceased to be concerned with restrictive practices. It then concentrated on monopolies and oligopolies. Eleven such cases were referred to it before 1956 and had been reported on by 1967. Seven of these references concerned trades which had high concentration ratios. One concerned a trade with a medium concentration ratio, and in three cases no concentration ratios were publicly available. Prior to the establishment of the Restrictive Practices Court, the Commission had also had referred to it some cases which would have been dealt with more appropriately by the Restrictive Practices Court, and most of the trades with low or medium concentration ratios would in all probability have come within this category.

Monopolies Commission procedure may be dealt with briefly. Once a reference has been made by the Board of Trade to the Commission, it advertises its willingness to receive evidence from interested persons and holds informal meetings with any trade associations concerned, receiving evidence from those operating monopoly practices. Evidence of complaints about the abuse of a firm's or firms' monopoly position is then gathered from consumers, independent concerns, government departments and other interested parties. Moreover the Commission will frequently engage in a series of factory visits to obtain an idea of the industry's method of work. It is then normal practice for the accountancy staff of the Commission to carry out a costing investigation, frequently with the objective of trying to discover whether profits are too high in relation to capital employed, and so to provide evidence regarding the existence or non-existence of monopoly profits. At this stage a first draft of the Commission's report, embodying factual information, is presented to the industry for its comments. This is followed by formal hearings between the members of the Commission and the trade associations or firms concerned, which at this stage are usually represented by counsel; after which the final report, complete with recommendations, is drawn up.

In reaching its recommendations, the Commission has first to decide on the factual question as to whether monopoly conditions prevail. If the commission is satisfied that they do prevail, it has to reach conclusions regarding the public interest. Even if such conditions, as defined in various Acts, do prevail, it is open to the Commission to declare that none the less the position should not be altered, since the existing situation is not against the public interest. Alternatively the Commission may come out with some recommendations which the industry should comply with so that the public interest is safeguarded. The 'public interest', as defined in the various Monopolies Commission Acts, is somewhat wider than the conditions which have to be considered by the Restrictive Practices Court. It is required to take into account four main considerations: the most efficient means of production for home and overseas markets and their reflection in prices; the encouragement of new enterprises; the optimum distribution of the country's resources and the development of technical improvements; and the expansion of existing markets and the opening-up of new ones.

Monopolies Commission reports and investigations have generally been extremely thorough, akin to reports of Royal Commissions. They have frequently taken a long time to appear from the time when the reference was first made, as may be seen from Table 11.2. Half the total number of 35 reports issued from the time the Commission started work to mid-1967 took 31 months to appear, and a quarter of them took 40 months. The speed of reporting was particularly slow during the early years of the Commission's work, though a relatively large number of references were made, as may be seen from the figures in Table 11.1.

Table 11.1 References Made to and Reports Issued by the
Monopolies Commission, 1949-66

	Number of references made	*Number of reports issued*
1949-51	9	3
1952-4	11	6
1955-7	5	12
1958-60	1	2
1961-3	3	2
1964-6	11	7

Following the split of work between the Commission and the Court after 1957, when the Commission became concerned almost exclusively with monopoly and oligopoly situations arising from economies of scale, and the Court took over that part of the Commission's activities which had previously been concerned with restrictive practices, the number of references to the Commission fell away greatly, only to see a large increase between 1964 and 1966 and a subsequent falling-off during 1967 and 1968. In mid-1967, for example, reports had still to be received from the Commission on six of the eleven references made to the Commission between 1964 and 1966.

Table 11.2 Time taken by Monopolies Commission
to Issue Reports (to December 1968)*

Months taken	*Number of reports*
72 and over	1
60 and under 72	0
54 ,, ,, 60	4
48 ,, ,, 54	2
42 ,, ,, 48	0
36 ,, ,, 42	6
30 ,, ,, 36	8
24 ,, ,, 30	8
18 ,, ,, 24	3
Under 18	6
Total	38

* Excluding 'services' references.

At times the Commission has functioned as a single entity, with all its members working on one or more references at the same time. At other times the Commissioners have split into smaller groups of eight or so members each, out of the Commission's total membership of eighteen at 31 December 1966. But however the Commission has been organised, each group carrying out an investigation has contained at least one academic economist. The chairman of the Commission has invariably been a member of the legal profession.

Appendix 1 to this chapter gives the titles of the inquiries, dates of references and publication of reports, the name of the chairman and academic economist(s) signing the report, whether monopoly conditions were found to exist, and if so, whether they were agains the public interest or otherwise.

Before the Restrictive Practices Court started to operate in 1958, a number of the inquiries carried out by the original Monopolies and Restrictive Practices Commission were into the existence of restrictive practices rather than monopoly or oligopoly situations arising from the existence of economies of scale. Thus the Commission's inquiries into the supply of buildings in the Greater London area (Report 9, ref. March 1953), into the supply of sand and gravel in central Scotland (Report 13, ref. December 1953), standard metal windows and doors (Report 18, ref. February 1954) and hard fibre cordage (Report 14, ref. July 1953) were all concerned with the operation of price agreements, aggregated rebates and exclusive dealing, matters which since 1956 would be more likely to have been referred to the Restrictive Practices Court.

In practice the Commission has frowned on the existence of five types of restrictive practices, in addition to the 'pure monopoly' case arising largely from the existence of one or a few firms with major economies of scale operating in one market. The first type of restrictive practice generally held by the Commission to operate against the public interest has been the establishment of common or minimum prices and the existence of discussions on price levels and charges. Such conditions were found to operate in 14 out of the 38 specific cases reported on by the Commission to the end of 1968. In 12 out of these 14 cases the Commission found that the practice operated against the public interest; but the two cases where the Commission found that it did not — standard metal windows and doors, and linoleum — prove the assertion that the Commission takes into account the circumstances under which the restrictive practice operates, rather than the straight nature of the practice and proof that it exists.

Only one example exists of the second type of practice frowned on by the Commission, that of level tendering in the report on the supply of buildings in the Greater London area. There have been two examples of the third type of disapproved practice, namely discount rebates, including loyalty and aggregated and quantity rebates. These conditions were found to exist in the cases of hard fibre cordage, and the supply and export of certain semi-manufactures of copper and copper-based alloys.

The Commission found 12 cases of the fourth set of disapproved practices, namely exclusive dealing, collective boycotting and the establishment of 'approved lists'. Of these, two, namely restrictive outlets for infant milk foods and cigarettes, were found not to be against the public interest. The fifth type of disapproved practice is pool quota schemes. Only two cases have been before the Commission, namely insulated wire and cables and hard fibre cordage, both being found to be against the public interest.

Lastly, there is the case of monopoly control stemming essentially from the existence of economies of scale. The Commission found 11 instances of this, of which 5 were found where the firms concerned were not exploiting their monopoly position to the detriment of the public. It was found that in those cases the public benefited from prices lower than they would have been obliged to pay had there been more suppliers, none of which could have fully exploited the economies of scale available to the industry. These were cigarettes and tobacco, chemical fertilisers, insulin, electrical equipment for land vehicles, and electric wiring harness for vehicles. In general the benefits to be obtained from a small number of firms supplying the whole output for a market, where economies of scale were large and where the firms concerned have been able to prove that they have not unduly exploited the resultant monopoly/oligopoly position, has impressed the Commission more than any of the arguments in favour of the other five types of restrictive practice. In some instances it will be seen from Appendix 1 that industries or firms have been operating more than one type of restrictive practice, or have operated such a practice as well as possessing monopoly power. The Commission has also generally been more willing to find situations of monopoly control not to be against the public interest where there has also been evidence of countervailing power available in the guise of large buyers for the product in question, and where those buyers fix prices at a level which reduces the amount of monopoly profits earned by such firms to a reasonable rate of return on capital employed, such as found in similar industries where such monopoly conditions do not prevail.

Where conditions in a trade have been found to operate against the public interest, the Commission, and subsequently the Government, in the form of the particular department principally concerned with the trade, has tended to be satisfied with written assurances concerning future behaviour of the monopoly firms or trade associations, and has been reluctant to take direct action, especially where this would involve the breaking-up of existing firms. Thus in the case of industrial and medical gases (Report 17), the Commission found that British Oxygen Co. had deliberately sought to control the provision of oxygen plant to maintain its monopoly supply conditions and had been making excessive profits in the region of 23 to 25 per cent on capital employed on an historical-cost basis, and that the profits remained excessive even allowing for a revision of capital employed on a replacement-cost basis. Nevertheless the Commission simply recommended that British Oxygen should be left with as much freedom as possible compatible with a safeguard of the public interest, and that the Board of Trade should review the situation from time to time, having access to all relevant cost and profits data. But there was, and still is, no legislation to enforce such arrangements, and as a result little appears to have been done in this direction. Again, in the case of cigarettes and tobacco (Report 24), where the Commission decided that the monopoly position of Imperial Tobacco Co. did not operate against the public interest, the degree of concentration in the industry was such that the retention by Imperial Tobacco Co. of its holding in Gallaher might be expected to operate against the public interest. Yet the Government was reluctant to enforce the sale by Imperial Tobacco of its shareholding in Gallaher. Assurances were given by Imperial regarding the abandonment of its practice of granting a bonus to distributors for granting display facilities.

(b) Merger References

One of the principal complaints about the working of the 1956 Act was that neither the Monopolies Commission nor the Board of Trade had powers to deal with merger situations which were prospectively of a monopoly character. The amalgamation or merger had to have taken place, with all the difficulties attendant on the unscrambling of merged companies, before the situation could be referred to the Commission for investigation. This situation was rectified by the 1965 Act, which permits references to be made to the Commission where it is considered that the resultant merger would create 'monopoly' conditions as laid down in the 1948 Act. References may also be made where the value of the assets taken over exceed £5 million. Whenever a reference is so made, the Commission is obliged to report its findings within a period of six months. Special provisions are contained in the Act regarding newspaper mergers.

Between the passing of the Act in 1965 and the end of 1968, ten references had been decided on in respect of mergers, of which one was within the special field of newspapers, namely 'The Times' and the 'Sunday Times'. The ten references are set out in Appendix 2. Of the ten references, three proposed mergers were found to be against the public interest, though sometimes by a majority decision. In general the Commission has had very much in mind the weighing-up of any savings which might be attained by the ability to achieve greater economies of scale as a result of the proposed merger, and the extent to which such savings might be passed on to the final consumer even though the degree of competition may be reduced considerably. It has also had in mind the results which might be achieved in increasing export markets by reducing duplication of sales efforts in particular. In three cases out of the ten the mergers were allowed to proceed after written assurances had been obtained by the Commission from the companies concerned regarding such matters as pricing policy, access to supplies and the like. In the case of the proposed merger between the Ross Group and Associated Fisheries, which was not allowed to proceed, the Commission decided that the economies of scale which were expected as a result of the merger were small and that the merger itself would do little to reduce the considerable fragmentation of the industry and might well result in an increase in prices. Furthermore it was not possible to devise a series of written assurances whereby the public interest might be safe-guarded.

Rather more than in the non-merger cases which it has considered, the Commission appears to have been impressed with arguments designed to show that the resulting merger would be beneficial to exports. For example, in the merger reference relating to British Insulated Callender's Cables and Pyrotenax, the Commission concluded that 'It may turn out that the most valuable result of the merger for the public interest will be that it will make possible a more rapid increase in exports' (para. 160). In the same paragraph they raise a problem consistently in the minds of a number of companies when considering mergers. (3) 'Its high profits enabled Pyrotenax to finance the rapid growth of mineral insulated cable in this country, but it could not readily find the money to mount the effort required for intensive promotion in more than a few over-seas markets. The need for skilled technical salesmen has also set a limit to both companies' efforts. Since, therefore, the resources available prevent an adequate effort being made by the two companies separately in all the markets that appear ripe for development, it seems to make better sense for them to combine and co-ordinate their resources, rather than to continue to compete with each other in the same markets, as had been happening before the merger.' Again, in merger reference 5, Between Guest, Keen and Nettlefolds Ltd and Birfield Ltd, G.K.N. considered that 'the public interest' in this merger lay in the enhance-ment of British international competitive power that it would bring about (para. 103). International competitive operations on the scale required to sell in world markets 'demanded the resources, resilience and organisational powers of big battalions'! And in considering the merger as a whole, the Commission stated, in para. 154, that the company (G.K.N.) 'has stressed its desire to increase its export and other overseas trade and, above all, to use Birfield's established footholds in Europe for selling on a much larger scale the products of the merged company. We cannot of course say whether G.K.N. will succeed in these aims, but we have little doubt that its success would be to the national advantage.'

There appears to be some tendency then for the Monopolies Commission to be giving rather more prominence to the benefits to be obtained from economies of scale, either as arising from straight 'monopoly' situations or prospective economies of scale to be obtained from mergers. Provided that prices are not raised to the disadvantage of the consumer as the result of a prospective merger, that the benefits of cost reductions either from prospective mergers are passed on to the consumer or the country as a whole in the form of an expected increase in exports, or that some form of countervailing power in the form of large purchasers can put pressure on a 'monopoly' company so that it is unable to 'exploit' its monopoly position in the form of higher prices and profits than might be expected to prevail under more competitive conditions, or written assurances are given that such a position will not be exploited, the Commission has been inclined more recently to recommend that no further action should be taken.

Towards the end of the 1960s attention was focused on a form of industrial organisation relatively new to the United Kingdom. This was the formation of 'conglomerates', a term used to describe the existence of parent companies based on a number of subsidiaries unrelated from the industrial standpoint. Such acquisitions of companies by an agressor firm may be regarded as carrying a policy of diversification of interests and risk minimisation to its penultimate. The conglomerate should be distinguished from the form of organisation known as a holding company, which is principally a device for maintaining financial control of a number of subsidiaries which may or may not be related on an industrial basis. The conglomerate merger does not necessarily involve the setting-up of a new holding company.

In the United States conglomerate mergers have been seen to have a snowball effect, and in recent years as having unsound financial structures because of the pyramiding of share and loan capital. In the United Kingdom conglomerate mergers have been increasing in number, and the sheer size of the resultant firms has led government to consider the advantages and disadvantages of such mergers. In particular, two such cases were referred to the Monopolies Commission during 1968-9 under the heading of 'financial assets'. In considering the proposed mergers between Unilever Ltd and Allied Breweries Ltd, and between the De La Rue Co. Ltd and Rank Organisation, the Commission was faced with the task of defining more precisely its own attitude towards conglomerate mergers. No clear guidelines existed for deciding whether such mergers were in or against the public interest, since the normal criteria concerning monopoly situations did not apply.

It was with the intention of providing some guidance on these and related matters that the Board of Trade published during the summer of 1969 a guide to its practice in considering prospective mergers. The decision to refer to the Commission the two proposed mergers mentioned above, appears to have been taken on grounds of sheer size of the resultant firm; they were to be regarded as test cases. On the other hand the 'mergers' booklet does concede that there is nothing intrinsically undesirable about rapid growth and large size, taken in isolation. But it went on to list in para. 58 half a dozen considerations which appeared to be relevant in assessing whether such mergers were or were not in the public interest.

(c) Types of Collective Discrimination and their Extent

In December 1952 the Board of Trade referred certain 'specified practices' to the Monopolies and Restrictive Practices Commission for general investigation. These 'specified practices' were collective discrimination by sellers (category I) in the form of price discrimination and/or exclusive dealing; collective discrimination by sellers in return for exclusive buying (category II); collective agreements to adopt and enforce conditions of sale, resale price maintenance (category III) and methods of enforcement (category IV); collective discrimination by buyers in the form of exclusive buying (category V); and aggregated rebates (category VI). A good deal of evidence on the existence, operation and effect of such practices had been available for some time in the United States of America, (4) which described evidence relating to price leadership by large corporations or trade associations; pooling agreements; price discrimination, especially in the form of the basing-point system used in the steel, cement and sugar industries; and drew attention to the widespread nature of the important practice of non-price competition. No such inquiry in depth had been attempted for the British economy, though a good deal of scattered evidence was in existence indicating that such practices were by no means confined to the North American continent. The findings of some of the early inquiries of the Monopolies and Restrictive Practices Commission, especially those on dental goods, cast-iron rainwater goods, electric lamps, insulated wires and electric cables, and to a lesser extent insulin, had suggested that the time was ripe for a general inquiry into the practices outlined above.

Some attempts had been made during the middle of the nineteenth century to establish a few of the specified practices, but in the years before 1914 'the main emphasis seems to have been on the prevention of retail price-cutting and the method chosen was the collective enforcement of resale price-maintenance by means of stop lists'. (5) Many of the pre-war agreements collapsed under the economic pressures of the 1920s and more especially the severe slump of 1929-32. During the later 1930s many of the practices appear to have been revived, especially those aimed at enforcing manufacturers' common prices, as well as the growth of a new practice, exclusive dealing arrangements. The basis of each of the 'specified practices' is set out in paras 30 to 37 of the 'Collective Discrimination' report, and the reader may wish to make direct reference to them. Indeed, a reading of the whole of this report is an important prelude to a study of the work of the Restrictive Practices Court, whose establishment it presaged.

The width and range of the 'specified practices' in British industry in 1953, when the major part of the empirical work of the Commission's inquiry was carried out, may be judged from Table 11.3. A large part of the empirical work of the Commission was carried out through the offices of various trade associations, and Table 11.3 indicates the proportion of trade associations which

Table 11.3 Proportion of Trade Association Describing the Existence
of Specified Discriminating Practices in 1953.

Industry	Number of associations contacted	Percentage describing specified practices
Fishing	2	100
Mining and quarrying	4	0
Non-metalliferous manufacturers	36	64
Chemicals and allied trades	31	29
Pharmaceutical preparations, toilet goods, etc.	9	67
Metal manufacture	16	69
Engineering	15	40
Electrical engineering	23	70
Vehicles	10	100
Other metal goods	40	65
Precision instruments, etc.	6	33
Textiles	17	59
Leather and leather goods	2	0
Clothing	19	42
Food, drink and tobacco	20	55
Wood and Cork	4	0
Paper (including some building materials)	9	78
Printing and publishing	11	13
Other manufacturers	16	56
Total	290	57

Source: Monopolies and Restrictive Practices Commission, 'Collective Discrimination', Cmnd 9504 (H.M.S.O., June 1955) para. 20, p. 9.

made statements to the Commission describing practices coming within the reference. Despite the possibility of a certain amount of double-counting, where trades with a number of associations operating a particular agreement all described that agreement, the table gives a fair indication of the way in which industries differed in their operation of discriminating practices. Industries particularly prone to the operation of restrictive trading practices in 1953 appear to have been in metal manufacture and the engineering industries in general (electrical engineering, vehicles and other goods), though not in mechanical engineering, paper and printing and pharmaceuticals.

4   THE RESTRICTIVE PRACTICES COURT

(a)   The Nature of the Court

The Monopolies and Restrictive Practices Commission's report on collective discrimination appeared in June 1955, and the drafting of new legislation to deal with the type of restrictive practices which it had found to be widely prevalent in British industry finally received Parliamentary assent in the Restrictive Practices Act of 1956. As outlined in a previous section of this chapter, this Act provided for the setting-up of the Restrictive Practices Court as distinct from the Monopolies Commission; the Court was to deal with a variety of practices which would henceforth be registrable compulsorily with a new Registrar of Restrictive Practices, who would have the duty of deciding in which order cases should be sent to the Court for trial.

The establishment of the new Court broke two major traditions in English and Scottish law. First, although the President of the Court was to be a member of the judiciary, along with two other judicial members, there were to be four additional non-judicial members who would have equal weight with their legal brethren. It has not been the practice for all seven members of the Restrictive Practices Court to be present at all hearings, and this division of the High Court has tended to follow the precedent set by other divisions in the sharing-out of the work to be done. However, in the first two cases heard, all seven members of the court took part; six heard the third case, and thereafter the usual number of members of the Court sitting on any one hearing has generally been four, though occasionally three or five. The second break with the normal tradition of English and Scottish law is that the onus of proof lies with the defendant, who must satisfy the Court that the registered practice is not against the public interest. It will be immediately apparent that the Court is engaged not with investigating monopoly and restrictive practices in a whole industry, as had been the case with the Monopolies and Restrictive Practices Commission prior to 1956, but with deciding whether a particular practice is or is not against the public interest. The

Court also has the power to enforce its decisions by injunctions, should such action prove necessary.

(b)   Agreements to be Registered

The agreements which are required to be registered with the Registrar of Restrictive Practices are essentially those examined in the report of the Monopolies and Restrictive Practices Commission into collective discrimination, namely (i) common prices; (ii) terms or conditions of sale; (iii) level or agreed tendering; (iv) the granting of preferential terms; and (v) the confining of supplies to certain persons or traders.

The 1964 Resale Prices Act also added resale price maintenance on the part of individual suppliers. Some doubts have been expressed as to exactly what is an agreement and whether the term included 'oral' agreements as well as 'recommendations'. In general it has been decided that 'information agreements', the equivalent of open-price agreements, which could be the vehicle for understandings amongst manufacturers in a given trade with regard to price leadership, are not registrable under the 1956 Act. Similar considerations apply to 'gentlemen's agreements' which often exist under oligopoly conditions and may lead to parallelism of price movements. Investigations into such situations have been left to the Monopolies Commission.

Because of the length of time taken to obtain the requisite information, the restrictive practices register was not open for public inspection until April 1959. By the end of December 1959, 2,240 agreements had been registered of which 1,630 (73 per cent) were concerned with some form of control over prices; 1,100 (49 per cent) were concerned with standard terms and conditions of sale; 300 (13 per cent) with persons; another 300 with the area supplied; 275 (12 per cent) with discriminatory discounts; 200 (9 per cent) with the kind of goods supplied; and a further 200 with quantities. Any of the 2,240 agreements might of course contain more than one type of restriction, so that the categories are not mutually exclusive, and the percentages consequently add up to more than 100 per cent. But they give some indication of the relative importance of agreements of different types.

(c)   The Justiciability Issue

A good deal of discussion took place during the Parliamentary debates relating to the passing of the 1956 Act as to whether a court of law was the proper instrument for making decisions of what were thought to be essentially industrial matters, but the subsequent experience of the working of the Court in establishing case law has tended to quell doubts on this important issue. (6) The issue still, however, remains in being, especially since the passing of the 1965 Monopolies and Mergers Act, where the control of monopolistic and restrictive practices and the safeguarding of the competitive system in this country has been further divided between two different decision-making bodies; political where the appropriate Minister has the final word in the case of monopolies and mergers resulting from economies of scale, and judicial in the case of other forms of restrictive practice. The principal issue in the justiciability debate has been whether the problems in question, namely whether or not certain restrictive practices are or are not against the public interest, are capable of being decided by the judicial process. Some of the matters before the Court are regarded as being questions of economic policy, and as a result are outside the normal function of English or Scottish courts of law, since in reaching their decisions the judges have to engage in predictions of what would happen if particular lines of action were pursued, and in particular the likely course of events in an industry if a registered restrictive practice were abandoned. But as the President of the Court stated in his summing-up in the Chemists' Federation case, the first to be heard by the Court, 'Our task is the ordinary task of a court of law to take the words of the Act according to their proper construction and see if upon the facts proved, the case falls within them'. (7) In general the court has not seen fit to discuss the desirability or otherwise of competition, though as will be discussed below, the Court has been obliged to come to some conclusions regarding the usefulness of economic models in helping it to reach its conclusions.

(d)   The 'Public Interest'

If control over competition and restrictive practices is to be undertaken by a court of law, then the matters over which it must exercise its 'justiciability' must be drawn up as clearly and as tightly as possible. The Restrictive Trade Practices Act of 1956 thus sought to define the 'public interest' much more closely than had been the case in the Acts establishing the Monopolies Commission. The appropriate section of the 1956 Act is section 21, 'Presumption as to the Public Interest'. All registrable restrictive practices were declared to be illegal under the terms of the 1956 Act unless they could be shown by the defendants to come within the provisions of section 21. The provisions of the various subsections of section 21, frequently referred to in the literature on the operation of the Restrictive Practices Court as 'gateways', through which an agreement must pass if it is to stand a chance of being declared not to be against the public interest, may be summarised as follows: (8)

21 (a) The restriction is necessary to protect the public from injury.
   (b) It confers specific and substantial benefits on the public.
   (c) It is reasonably necessary to counteract other restrictive measures.
   (d) It is necessary to enable the parties to the agreement to negotiate on fair terms with a strong buyer or seller.

(e) The removal of the agreement would be likely to have a serious and persistent adverse effect on the general level of employment in an area.

(f) Its removal would be likely to cause a substantial reduction in the volume or earnings of exports.

(g) It is required to maintain another agreement which has been shown not to be against the public interest.

Even where the agreement is accepted by the Court as passing through one of these seven gateways, it also has to satisfy what has become known as the 'detriment tailpiece', whereby the Court must be satisfied that the advantages shown by the defendant to exist under sections 21(a) to (g) outweigh any disadvantages or 'detriment' caused by the operation. In other words the Court is required to perform a balancing act in the true legal tradition of the scales of justice, as for example in assessing civil damages. The general practice of the Court has been such that the onus of proof in sections 21(a) to (g) of the Act has lain with the defendants, but that the onus of proof in the 'detriment tailpiece' has lain with the Registrar of Restrictive Practices, who has been required to produce evidence to the effect that, on balance, the upholding of the restrictive practice would do more harm than good to the public as a whole.

Under the terms of the Restrictive Practices Act of October 1968, a further gateway (h) was added to those listed above.

(h) The 'restriction does not directly or indirectly restrict or discourage competition to any material degree in any relevant trade or industry and is not likely to do so' (section 10).

During the short period between October and December 1968 this clause had not been pleaded before the Court.

(e)   The Work of the Court: Decisions on Cases, 1958-66
Between 1958, when the Court started work on the first case presented to it by the Registrar of Restrictive Practices, and the end of 1966, it had dealt with 35 cases. These are listed in Appendix 3, which gives the short title of the case, the type of agreement before the Court, the gateways pleaded under section 21 of the Act, the decision of the Court and the presiding judge. It is possible to divide the type of agreements before the Court on a rather narrower basis than the division given under agreements to be registered. The types of agreements are listed in Table 11.4.

It will be seen that price restrictions in some form or other account for 26 out of the 35 agreements before the Court, which is almost three-quarters of the total. Compared with the Monopolies Commission, the Court has dealt with a far

Table 11.4 Categories of Agreements dealt with by the
Restrictive Practices Court, 1958-66

Sales restrictions, including retailers' lists and outlets	4
Minimum prices	12
Recommended prices, including resale price maintenance	3
Fixed prices	11
Description of goods	1
Boundary agreements	1
Contract sharing, including level tendering	2
Buying pool	1

greater number of cases per year, an average of 4½ a year. In sheer terms of the length of hearings the cost of defending an agreement before the Court is heavy. Up to June 1964 over half the hearings before the Court had lasted over 16½ days, and a quarter lasted 23 days or more, with only a quarter lasting for a period of less than 10½ days. The cost of engaging leading counsel, expert witnesses and the actual preparation of the defence of such cases has frequently meant the abandonment of agreements which might otherwise have succeeded in passing through one of the gateways, plus the detriment clause. It has often been the case that only the richer trade associations or groups of firms have been able to defend their agreements, and to this extent the 1956 Act discriminates in favour of the larger and better-off associations.

Successes under section 21 of the Act are indicated in Table 11.5. The first three cases all went against the defendants; indeed, out of the first eight cases only one, that of the water-tube boilermakers, was found to be not contrary to the public interest, and the Court soon acquired a reputation for toughness.

Table 11.5 Successes under Section 21 of the Restrictive Practices Act

Clause pleaded	Number pleaded	Successes
21 (a)	4	0
(b)	32	8
(c)	2	1
(d)	6	1
(e)	3	0
(f)	8	1
(g)	10	9

Of the 35 cases before the Court to the end of 1966, 12 agreements passed through one of the gateways and were held not to be contrary to the public interest. In many instances more than one gateway was pleaded, and indeed in only one case (No. 33) was section 21(g) pleaded on its own, and that successfully. The majority of successes were a combination of 21(b) and (g), being the clause relating to specific and substantial benefits under this agreement or tied to it. So far the Court has refused to accept 21(a), the protection from injury clause, or 21(e) the employment clause. Manufacturers before the Restrictive Practices Court have also done rather badly on 21(f), the export clause, the second most popular clause under which to appeal. On the other hand the Monopolies Commission has been more prepared to accept arguments stemming from economies of scale, especially in improving export prospects either by firms being in a better position to hold prices steady or even to reduce them, or as a result of the sharing of sales facilities in overseas markets.

Gradually more agreements were passed. The watershed would seem to be around 1962. (9) In that year three major agreements had got past the Court, permanent magnets, metal windows and the net book agreement. In fact in 1962 all three agreements before the Court succeeded. In 1963, however, only one out of six was successful, with one being held not to be an agreement within the terms of the Act. Comparing the years before 1962 with the five following (including 1962 itself), of the 17 cases heard in 1958/9-1961, only 3 succeeded in passing through one of the gateways, whilst during the period 1962-6, 9 cases (plus the one judged not to be an agreement within the terms of the Act) succeeded out of a total of 18 cases. An examination of the successful cases from 1962 onwards, compared with failures and successes before 1962, leads not so much to the conclusion that the Court had 'gone soft' but that counsel were becoming far more sophisticated in presenting their arguments, more used to presenting expert witnesses in the best light, and had learned the type of arguments which the Court would and would not accept. One argument in particular has failed to impress the Court, namely the 'quality defence', where counsel has argued that a reduction in quality would follow the abandonment of the agreement. Similarly arguments that the abandonment of an agreement would lead to a reduction in research and development expenditure has not in general been accepted, though it has been more readily accepted by the Monopolies Commission.

(f) The Economics Applied by the Court

Discussion concerning the arguments which the Court will and will not allow leads to a consideration of whether the Court has evolved an economic model of its own, and whether it uses this model as a means of examining and reaching conclusions on particular lines of defence. The presumption of the 1956 Act is in favour of competition except where special circumstances exist. The general presumption of the Act is that competition is to the consumer's advantage, but that on occasions restrictions by manufacturers and others may protect him. The Court's interpretations of the Act depends on how it views 'competition'. Should a perfectly competitive situation always be interpreted to mean competition through price, as in the economic model of perfect competition? If it followed this model, the Court might look at evidence of price movements, freedom of entry into the market, the extent of consumers' knowledge and all the other appurtenances of perfect competition. (10)

That model is a static one, where market size is given, competition is for a share in the market, and firms are working under conditions of diminishing returns and marginal-cost pricing is consequently appropriate. In a dynamic situation the model has to be adjusted. For instance, there may be economies of scale arising for technological reasons. This implies further capital investment and falling unit costs, so that for a time marginal costs are below average costs. Marginal-cost pricing would then lead to bankruptcy of enterprising firms. By some means or other the differences between marginal cost and average cost must be charged. To protect the consumer by enjoining marginal-cost pricing would be an appropriate solution in a static economy, but this may preclude economic growth.

A court that sides with price competition (which implies marginal-cost pricing) is thus more interested in spreading present economic welfare than in increasing its future size. This emphasises the difference between an economic organisation favouring consumers and one favouring producers. Hence models applicable to both are needed. To date the Court has sided more with the consumers than with the producers; its general rules apply to consumers, and producers' interests are admitted only through the gateways. In many of the cases before the Restrictive Practices Court (and in many of the investigations carried out by the Monopolies Commission) the consumer in question is in fact another producer. The Court has experienced some difficulties in assessing 'substantial benefits' for the producer—consumer.

Neither the Court nor the Commission has openly and concisely stated the economic model of competition which it is following, and especially in the case of the Court, its general view can be constructed only from detailed study of its judgements in very many cases. Competition may mean one thing at one time and another thing on another occasion. Nor does the Court always appear to have been consistent as between presiding judges, although a few cross-references to other judgements of the Court have at times been made in the summing-up. The Court is a court of lawyers and businessmen who are not necessarily trained in the principles of economic analysis. In many instances cross-examination of 'expert' witnesses, whether in the form of economists or accountants put up both by counsel for the defence and for the Registrar, has not been the most fruitful way to elicit the right sort of evidence on which the Court may act. The addition of an economist to the Court might have saved time taken in proceedings simply because lawyers are not used to analysis for predictive purposes. Yet just that is required if the effects of the abandonment of restrictive agreements are to be assessed. An economist might act as a technical assessor, as appears to happen in inquiries carried out by the Commission.

To the Court, competition appears to mean essentially 'price competition'. This was thought to promote efficiency. Such at any rate was the attitude of the Court in its early days, and it coincided with the views expressed by the Commission in the cases of calico printing and hard fibre cordage. According to the general views of the Court, the more efficient firms will tend to obtain a larger share of the market and force out the less efficient. Thus in the case of the water-tube boilers, the Court stated that 'In the ordinary case . . . the normal results of competition will come into play. The more efficient tenderers will gradually obtain a larger share of the market and will drive the less efficient out of business. That is as it should be. . . .' (11) Again, in the phenol case it was argued that 'lower prices can generate new users and new demand'. (12) Where there is the possibility of having a high-quality product at a high price, and a lower-quality product at a lower price, the public should have the choice. Hence the 'quality defence' argument has failed to impress the Court. The concept of product competition has also failed to make much impression on the Court. This sort of competition may result from the existence of oligopoly-type situations or cartelisation of an industry. Here price is held steady, common prices prevailing, and competition takes place through product variations and advertising. (13) It has also tended to reject the argument for innovative competition namely that such a situation may have strong innovatory tendencies. Arguments based on the necessity of keeping abreast of competitors, even in the international field, through heavy expenditures by trade associations on research and development have also tended to be discounted as justifying common prices or level tendering. At times trade associations have attempted to stress co-operation in those matters as providing a specific advantage to the public under section 21(b). Such agreements have been regarded by the associations as providing some additional security against risk, and they have argued that the absence of the relevant agreement would inhibit the exchange of technical information. Such a narrowing of one type of business risk follows from the high degree of uncertainty as to markets and the successful outcome of innovational activity. The Court's attitude, however, has tended to be that if such co-operation is profitable it will continue even in the absence of the agreement. Occasionally, however, the Court has allowed this agreement to stand, as in the cases of tiles, magnets and windows.

On some occasions the Court has thought along lines of 'reasonable prices'. Whether prices are reasonable or not depends to a large extent on costing methods and the appropriateness of rates of return on capital employed. Criteria used by the Court in assessing 'reasonable prices' in relation to costs have varied from case to case. In the judicial summary of the water-tube boilermakers' case, the Court defined 'really competitive and keen prices' as 'prices which cover overheads and allow a small, but only very reasonable margin, of profit'. (14) But a different interpretation appeared in the transformers' case. Some of the Court's difficulties have clearly arisen from a failure to understand the nature of imputed costs in multi-product firms. Unfortunately in many instances the defendants themselves have failed to use standard costing systems. The Commission has been more aware of the nature of this problem and has frequently stated its dissatisfaction with the methods by which agreed or common prices have been reached, as for instance in rainwater goods and calico printing. Although of importance to economists, and still of considerable use despite doubts about the state of 'competitive' and other models of the firm, the concept of price elasticity of demand has been used explicity in only five cases — black bolts and nuts, transformers, cement, tiles and scrap iron — but even here there has been no reference to the elasticity of demand curves facing individual firms.

Frequently what matters in determining whether prices are 'reasonable' or not is the long-run elasticity of demand. The Court has generally set its face against long-run forecasts of what would happen in the absence of an agreement, complaining in the case of the water-tube boilermakers that such matters were 'speculative', but that it would have to engage in some long-run estimates. The possibility of new entrants is of importance in deciding the correct degree of capacity in an industry relative to prices and output. The possibility of new entrants coming about through the switching of some part of production of already existing firms to new, though related, products, should profit margins become excessive for those firms already producing the good in question, has tended to escape the notice of the Court, though less so that of the Commission. Discussions of capacity have played some part in the yarn spinners' and heavy steelmakers' cases, but the Court has not seen fit to place such emphasis on this problem in relation to a long-run decline in demand in the former case compared with other factors, or fluctuating demand, in the case of the latter.

Strangely enough, most of the successful cases of defendants before the Court have been oligopolistic-type industries, frequently with price leadership stemming from one or two large firms. This has applied in those cases where the successful defendant has been a cartel, since the cartel's policy in turn has been dominated by two or three major firms. This has certainly been so in the cases of the water-tube boilermakers, black bolts and nuts, steel scrap, tiles, magnets and metal windows. They are cases where the Court does not appear to have appreciated the nature of oligopolistic instability, and that in the case of industries investigated by the Commission the abandonment of some agreements has led to a considerable degree of price leadership. Again, part of the success of these associations and firms before the Court is that counsel has stressed the positive advantages obtained by the public from the existence of the agreements rather than that their abandonment would make the public worse off. In sum, the Court's use of economic model and concepts, even where applicable, has been on a somewhat unsophisticated level and has resulted in a number of seemingly contradictory judgement statements. This is not to say that the Court has been lacking in securing equal and consistent treatment for defendants, but that in paying great attention to the legal interpretation of the gateways clause of the 1956 Act, and to the arguments put forward under this section, it has been less able to take a general view of the whole nature of the competitive process. Perhaps the original critics of the 'justiciability issue' were correct, and greater guidance should be given to the Court in a series of amendments to section 21, particularly in the definition of competition, difficult though this is, and in the treatment of oligopoly situations.

(g) The Effectiveness of the 1956 Act

An attempt must now be made to sum up the effectiveness of legislation relating to monopoly and restrictive practices. The 1965 Act with its inclusion of merger references has dealt with one of the main criticisms of the 1956 Act, namely that although the Commission could investigate monopoly situations, it had no power to prevent them coming into being. Similarly the 1964 Act will in time be able to deal more thoroughly with cases of individual resale price maintenance, and has already resulted in the abandonment of some agreements.

Of the 34 investigations carried out by the Commission to mid-1967, there are nine where it is possible to make a comparison between 1951 concentration ratios and those in the 1958 Census of Production. The lack of the full results of the 1963 census even at the end of 1968 is a serious drawback to assessing the impact of the work of the Commission on concentration in British industry. Of the nine cases where comparisons can be made, four industries in fact showed an increase in concentration ratios between 1951 and 1958, two showed no change or a minor change, and three showed a decrease, though one case (No. 30) must be discounted since the reference was made after 1958. On the whole it seems doubtful whether the work of the Commission has resulted in any reduction in the degree of concentration in British industry. On the other hand some industries have given written assurances regarding their pricing and supply policies, and the impact of the Commission has probably been felt in the more subtle form of loosening-up of monopoly and oligopolistic power, and engendered a feeling that any attempts at too overt an exploitation of the final consumer or intermediate buyer would result in the rigours of an inquiry by the Commission with the publicity which such a reference involves.

Some of the impact of the work of the Restrictive Practices Court is more readily assessable on a statistical basis. By 31 December 1959 the Registrar of Restrictive Practices in his first report (January 1961, Cmnd. 1273) disclosed that there were some 2,240 agreements on the register, of which half covered the United Kingdom as a whole and half related to local arrangements. Eighteen months later he reported that some 590 agreements had been abandoned, and a further 475 revised so as not to come within the terms of the 1956 Act. A large number of the cases abandoned had been of the local variety following the adverse judgement of the Court in the Doncaster and Retford Co-operative Society's case (No. 10, 31 October 1960). The report to 30 June 1963 (January 1964, Cmnd. 2246) gave the following information, the most comprehensive to the end of 1967:

Agreements ended	1,000
Agreements varied so as to be excluded from the operation of the Act	525
Agreements subject to consideration under section 12	185
Cases referred to the Court or in preparation	160
Agreements dependent on those coming to the Court	150
Balance of agreements to be dealt with	430
Total	2,450

Considerable interest has naturally centred on what has happened to industries when agreements have been abandoned or declared contrary to the public interest. After several years' working of the Act, there is scope for a full-scale investigation of this problem by the Monopolies Commission. So far however only one major study of this important matter has been attempted (15). In a private inquiry, without the backing of the Commission to obtain information compulsorily, a detailed investigation was carried out by means of interviews and questionnaires into the effects of the abandonment of agreements by trade associations and firms. At the time the survey was carried out, some 1,100 registered agreements had been abandoned. Out of 734 associations and firms contacted, 220 sent in detailed replies. Around 32 per cent claimed that they would have suffered less competition had the agreements to which they were parties not been cancelled, and 67 per cent stated that competition was about the same. Allowing for all non-respondents to claim that competition had not increased would lower the increase in competition on an agreement or trade basis to around 16 per cent, and it was thought that the true proportion was likely to be around 24 per cent (being mid-way between 16 per cent and 32 per cent). Industries suffering the greatest increase in competition in the form of lower prices, attributable to the abandonment of agreements, were engineering (48 per cent), metal manufacture (44 per cent), chemicals (43 per cent) and food, drink and tobacco (37½ per cent). Paper and printing (20 per cent), distribution (20 per cent) and wood and cork (11 per cent) suffered far fewer price cuts than the average as a result of the abandonment of agreements. The main effect of the abandonment of agreements appears to have been on prices.

One important way round the 1956 Act has been the establishment of 'open-price agreements'. These were not registrable under the Act. (16) Associations have had to be more careful in the manner in which information agreements, open to all members of a trade and frequently to major customers, have been framed and published since the 'basic slag' case, which went as far as the Court of Appeal in July 1963. This decision tightened up the position with regard to open-price agreements. The Court decided that such an agreement would be registrable (a) if a firm A makes representation as to its future conduct expecting other firms to follow suit, (b) if such representation were communicated to firm B, and (c) that A's conduct operates as an inducement to B to follow suit. (17) Of information agreements 'in force' before the basic slag case, it has been estimated (18) that half were concerned with an exchange of price information only, 21 per cent covered prices, costs and turnover combined, 9 per cent were concerned with prices and turnover, and a further 9 per cent with turnover alone. The remaining combinations formed an insignificant proportion of all such agreements. The estimation of the effectiveness of price cuts on firms as a result of the abandonment of agreements is complicated by the fact that many of the firms concerned were multi-product firms, some of whose products had not been subject to agreements. In general specialist firms appear to have been harder hit by the abandonment of agreements than diversified companies.

In some instances the abandonment of agreements has led to an increase in the number of mergers and amalgamations of firms formerly parties to such agreements. These appear to have been largely of a horizontal nature, with firms producing the same line of products having a greater tendency to merge than those at different stages of the productive process. This would fit in with amalgamations in food, drink and tobacco, where competition during the early 1960s was particularly severe; and it might also account for the greater willingness to merge shown by firms in electrical engineering. But in both cases other important factors have been at work in fostering take-overs and amalgamations, apart from the effect of the abandonment of agreements subject to restrictive practices legislation, and it is doubtful whether this factor can be separated from the remainder.

In the field of resale price maintenance, to which the Court turned most of its attention during 1967 and 1968, a few major decisions of an adverse nature have banished this practice from a wide range of products. These cases, not listed in Appendix 3 because of their small number, have been into chocolate and sugar confectionery (July 1967), footwear (May 1968) and tobacco products (September 1968). The adverse judgements given in these cases led to the freeing of a large number of other products from resale price maintenance. Subsequent to these decisions many manufacturers simply decided that it was no longer worth attempting to claim exemption for their products and no longer sought to defend their practices before the Court.

It seems possible, then, that one of the results of the 1956 and 1964 Acts has been to create a more competitive climate throughout industry, but that many manufacturers and their legal counsel are resourceful in devising methods of getting round some aspects of the Acts. In particular, it may well turn out that one major effect of the success achieved by the Restrictive Practices Court in discouraging the retention of price and other restrictive agreements may be to encourage more mergers, eventually creating more work for the mergers section of the Monopolies Commission. (19)

Appendix 1

Reports of the Monopolies Commission

P = 'Monopoly' conditions proved. NP = 'Monopoly' conditions not proved.
A = Conditions found to be against the public interest.
NA = Conditions *not* found to be against the public interest.
Type of restrictive practice:
1. Common prices, minimum prices, discussions on price levels and charges.
2. Level tendering.
3. Discount rebates, including loyalty and aggregated and quantity rebates.
4. Exclusive dealing, collective boycotting or 'approved lists'.
5. Pool quota schemes.
6. Monopoly control from economies of scale.

No.	Short title	Date of reference	Date of publication of report	Chairman and economist(s)	Conditions and restrictive practice	Public interest
1.	Dental Goods	Mar 1949	Dec 1950	Sir A. Carter; Joan Robinson	P 4	A
2.	Cast Iron Rainwater Goods	Mar 1949	Apr 1951	Sir A. Carter; Joan Robinson	P 4	A
3.	Electric Lamps	Mar 1949	Nov 1951	Sir A. Carter; Joan Robinson, G. C. Allen	P 4	A
4.	Insulated Electric Wire and Cables	Mar 1949	July 1952	Sir A. Carter; G. C. Allen, Joan Robinson	P 1,4,5	A
5.	Insulin	Dec 1950	Oct 1952	Sir A. Carter; G. C. Allen, Joan Robinson	P 6	NA

6. Matches and Match Making Machinery	Mar 1949	May 1953	Sir A. Carter; G. C. Allen, Joan Robinson	P 4	A
7. Imported Timber	Oct 1951	Oct 1953	Sir A. Carter; G. C. Allen	P 4	A
8. Calico Printing	Apr 1951	Apr 1954	Sir A. Carter; G. C. Allen, Sir A. Plant	P 1	A
9. Building in the Greater London Area	Mar 1953	Sep 1954	D. Cairns; G. C. Allen, Sir A. Plant	P 2	A
10. Certain Semi-manufactures of Copper and Copper-based Alloys	Dec 1950	Sep 1955	Sir D. Cairns; G. C. Allen	P 1,3	A
11. 'Collective Discrimination: A Report on Exclusive Dealing, Collective Boycotts, Aggregated Rebates and other Discriminating Trade Practices'	Dec 1952	June 1955	Sir D. Cairns; G. C. Allen, Sir A. Plant	—	
12. Pneumatic Tyres	Sep 1952	Dec 1955	Sir D. Cairns; G. C. Allen, r A. Plant	P 6	A
13. Sand and Gravel in Central Scotland	Dec 1953	Mar 1956	Sir D. Cairns; G. C. Allen	P 1	A
14. Hard Fibre Cordage	Jul 1953	June 1956	Sir D. Cairns; G. C. Allen	P 1,3,5	A
15. Certain Rubber Footwear	Apr 1954	Jul 1956	Sir D. Cairns; G. C. Allen	P 1,4	A
16. Linoleum	Sep 1953	Sep 1956	Sir D. Cairns: Sir A. Plant	P 1	NA

No.	Short title	Date of reference	Date of publication of report	Chairman and economist(s)	Conditions and restrictive practice	Public interest
17.	Certain Industrial and Medical Gases	Feb 1954	Jan 1957	Sir D. Cairns; Sir A. Plant	P 6	A
18.	Standard Metal Windows and Doors	Feb 1954	Jan 1957	Sir D. Cairns; Sir A. Plant	P 1	NA
19.	Tea	Sep 1955	Jan 1957	Sir D. Cairns; Sir A. Plant	P 1	A
20.	Electrical and Allied Machinery and Plant	Apr 1952	Feb 1957	Sir D. Cairns; Sir A. Plant	P 1	A
21.	Electronic Valves and Cathode Ray Tubes	Dec 1954	Feb 1957	Sir D. Cairns; G. C. Allen	P 1,6	No opinion to be expressed
22.	Imported Timber Xb (2) (Compliance Inquiry)	Feb 1957	July 1958	R. F. Levy; G. C. Allen	———	
23.	Chemical Fertilisers	Oct 1955	Feb 1960	R. F. Levy; G. C. Allen	P 6	NA
24.	Cigarettes and Tobacco and Cigarette and Tobacco Machinery	Nov 1956	July 1961	R. F. Levy; G. C. Allen	P 4,6	4A, 6NA
25.	Electrical Equipment for Mechanically Propelled Land Vehicles	Apr 1957	Dec 1963	R. F. Levy; (G. C. Allen)	P 6	NA
26.	Wallpaper	Sep 1961	Jan 1964	R. F. Levy, T. Barna	P 4,6	A
27.	Petrol	Sep 1960	July 1965	R. F. Levy; T. Barna	1,4	A
28.	Colour Film	Mar 1963	Apr 1966	A. Roskill; T. Barna	P 6	A

29.	Electrical Wiring Harness for Motor Vehicles	July 1965	June 1966	W. E. Jones; A. Silberston	P 6	NA
30.	Household Detergents	May 1963	Aug 1966	B. Davidson; T. Barna	P 6	A
31.	Films for Exhibition in Cinemas	Sep 1964	Oct 1966	A. Robin; T. Barna	P 6	A
32.	Aluminium Semi-manufacturers	July 1965	Dec 1966	A. Roskill; T. Barna	NP	—
33.	Infant Milk Foods	Feb 1966	Feb 1967	J. M. A. Smith; T. Barna	P 4	NA
34.	International Motor Insurance Cards	May 1966	June 1967	A. Roskill; B. Yamey	P 1	A
35.	Flat Glass	July 1965	Feb 1968	A. Roskill; A. Silberston	P 6	NA
36.	Man-made Cellulosic Fibres	July 1965	Mar 1968	A. Roskill; T. Barna	P 6	A
37.	Men's Haircutting Services	Feb 1967	June 1968	A. Roskill; B. Yamey	NP	—
38.	Electric Lamps: Second Report	Feb 1966	Dec 1968	A. Roskill; A. Silberston	P 1,3,4	A
39.	Clutch Mechanisms for Road Vehicles	Dec 1966	Dec 1968	A. Roskill; T. Barna	P 1,6	A

Appendix 2
Monopolies Commission: Merger References

No.	Proposed Merger	Reference	Report	Chairman and economist(s)	Public interest (subject to)
1.	British Motor Corporation	Aug 1965	Jan 1966	R. F. Levy; A. Silberston	NA (assurances)
2.	Ross Group Ltd and Associated Fisheries Ltd	Feb 1966	May 1966	A. Roskill; A. Silberston	A
3.	Dental Manufacturing Co. Ltd, or Dentists' Supply Co. of New York and Amalgamate Dental Co. Ltd.	Feb 1966	Aug 1966	A. Roskill; B. Yamey	NA
4.	'The Times' and the 'Sunday Times'	Aug 1966	Dec 1966	A. Roskill; B. Yamey	NA (assurances)
5.	Guest, Keen and Nettlefolds Ltd and Birfield Ltd	July 1966	Jan 1967	A. Roskill; T. Barna	NA
6.	British Insulated Callender's Cables Ltd and Pyrotenax Ltd	Dec 1966	May 1967	A. Roskill; A. Silberston	NA (assurances)
7.	Montague Burton Ltd and United Drapery Stores Ltd	May 1967	Sep 1967	A. Roskill; T. Barna, B. Yamey	A
8.	Thomson Newspapers Ltd and Crusha and Son	Sep 1967	Jan 1968	A. Roskill; B. Yamey	NA
9.	Thorn Electrical Industries and Radio Rentals	Feb 1968	June 1968	A. Roskill; T. Barna, B. Yamey	NA
10.	Barclays Bank Ltd, LLoyds Bank Ltd and Martins Bank Ltd	Feb 1968	July 1968	A. Roskill; R. Opie, B. Yamey, R. S. Sayers*	A

A = Against the public interest.
NA = Not against the public interest.

* Special member for this inquiry only.

Appendix 3

Summary of Cases heard before the Restrictive Practices Court (omitting R.P.M. references after 1964)

No.	Judgement date	Short title	Type of agreement	Clause(s) pleaded (Gateways, §21(1))	Judgement (Contrary (C) or not contrary (NC) to public interest. If NC, successful clause given.)	Presiding judge
1.	3 Nov 1958	Chemists' Federation	Sales restriction (outlets)	(a)(b)	C	Devlin
2.	2 Feb 1959	Yarn Spinners	Minimum price	(b)(e)	C	Devlin
3.	23 Mar 1959	Blankets	Minimum price	(b)	C	Devlin
4.	31 July 1959	Water-Tube Boilers	Contract sharing	(b)(d)(f)	NC(f)	Upjohn
5.	23 July 1959	Scottish Bakers	Minimum price	(b)	C	Cameron
6.	16 Dec 1959	Multiple Bakers	Minimum price	(b)	C	Pearson
7.	21 Dec 1959	Carpet Manufacturers	Fixed price	(b)(f)	C	Upjohn
8.	7 Apr 1960	Phenol Producers	Fixed price	(b)	C	Pearson
9.	15 July 1960	Black Bolt and Nut	Fixed price	(b)(g)	NC(b)(g)	Diplock
10.	31 Oct 1960	Co-operatives	Trading boundary agreement	(b)	C	Diplock

No.	Judgement date	Short title	Type of agreement	Clause(s) pleaded (Gateways, §21(1))	Judgement (Contrary (C) or not contrary (NC) to public interest. If NC, successful clause given.)	Presiding judge
11.	9 Dec 1960	Wholesale Confectioners	Recommended prices	(b)	C	Russell
12.	21 Dec 1960	Motor Vehicles	R.P.M. and lists	(a)(b)(e)	C	Diplock
13.	16 Mar 1961	Cement Makers	Fixed price	(b)(g)	NC(b)(g)	Diplock
14.	24 Mar 1961	Transformer Manufactures	Minimum price	(b)(d)(f)	C	Russell
15.	24 Mar 1961	Bottles	Minimum price	(b)	C	Russell
16.	22 June 1961	Linoleum	Minimum price	(b)(f)	C	Russell
17.	27 July 1961	Newspaper Distribution	Sales restriction (lists)	(b)	C	Diplock
18.	7 June 1962	Magnets	Minimum price	(b)(f)(g)	NC(b)(g)	Mocatta
19.	17 July 1962	Metal Windows	Minimum price	(b)(g)	NC(b)(g)	Megaw
20.	30 Oct 1962	Books	R.P.M.	(b)(f)(g)	NC(b)(g)	Buckley
21.	15 Mar 1963	Tyres	Sales restrictions (outlets)	(a)	C	Buckley
22.	26 Mar 1963	Jute	Minimum price	(b)(e)	C	Cameron
23.	10 Apr 1963	Building	Contract sharing (tendering)	(b)	C	Mocatta
24.	29 Apr 1963	Paper and Board	Waste paper price	(b)	C	Megaw

			Description of goods	(b)	Not a restriction within §6 of Act	Megaw
25.	29 Apr 1963	Waste Paper		(b)		Megaw
26.	12 July 1963	Sulphuric Acid	Buying pool	(d)(g)	NC(d)(g)	Megaw
27.	17 Jan 1964	Floor Tiles	Fixed price	(b)	NC(b)	Buckley
28.	27 Jan 1964	Scrap Iron	Fixed price	(b)(g)	NC(b)(g)	Mocatta
29.	22 July 1964	Heavy Steelmakers	Maximum (fixed) price	(b)(f)	C	Megaw
30.	21 Dec 1964	Wire Rope	Fixed price	(b)(d)(f)(g)	C	Megaw
31.	30 Apr 1965	Retail Newsagents etc.	Sales (distribution) restriction	(d)	C	Buckley
32.	4 Oct 1965	Finance Houses Association	Hire-purchase commission restrictions	(b)	C	Megaw
33.	21 Dec 1965	Black Bolt and Nut	Fixed price	(g)	NC(g)	Mocatta
34.	16 Nov 1966	Sulphuric Acid	Common delivered prices	(b)(c)(d)(g)	NC(d)(g)	Megaw
35.	10 Nov 1966	White Fish	Minimum price	(b)	NC(b)	Megaw

12 The Market for Long-term Industrial Capital

1 SOURCES OF COMPANY FINANCE

The market for industrial capital is an important one for the individual company. The problems faced by the individual firm in raising finance have already been discussed in Chapter 4. This chapter is concerned not with those problems, but with the efficient working of the capital market and the firms and institutions which comprise it. The providers of industrial capital are important in their own right, as well as acting as intermediaries between savers and investors, between the ultimate suppliers of new capital and those who use it. Competitive forces are at work leading to the amalgamation of such institutions and the entry of new ones. Important barriers to entry may exist, creating imperfections in certain branches of the capital market. This does not mean that competition does not exist between the institutions of the capital market, but that it is limited. In contrast to the position in industrial activity and distribution, the most important measures of size of firm are not numbers employed or net output, but net capital employed or assets controlled.

The plan of this chapter will be along the following lines. The present section will recapitulate, in a rather differently orientated form, those aspects of the capital market relating to individual firms previously studied in Chapter 4. The next section will be concerned with the major markets for existing industrial capital, namely the various United Kingdom stock markets. This will be followed by a discussion of the methods by which firms obtain new long-term capital, and the institutions whose role is to fulfil that demand, that is to say, the new-issue market. Lastly there will be a discussion of the provision of finance for takeovers and mergers, a subject which has become of increasing importance during the last decade; and this is linked with the forces making for change in industrial structure outlined in Chapter 10. In an age of rapid technological change there must be continuous availability of capital to finance the expansion of business, and this requires an appropriately organised capital market.

How firms obtain capital depends to a large extent on the activities they are concerned with. For industries differ considerably in the manner in which capital employed in the business is financed. At the end of 1967, for example, loan stock represented just over one-quarter of the nominal value of capital employed by United Kingdom registered and managed companies quoted on the London Stock Exchange. Preference capital represented just under one-tenth and ordinary capital a little under two-thirds. Banks, discount houses and rubber companies are financed almost entirely in terms of equity capital, and their prior charges in terms of fixed-interest outgoings from income are kept low. This reflects their relative lack of tangible assets. In contrast, property companies, breweries and distilleries tend to have a high proportion of loan and preference capital, and the equity proportion is correspondingly low. In most instances loans can be easily raised and secured against tangible assets, frequently in the form of land or buildings. Thus money can be raised by breweries against the mortgage or secured loan against their ownership of public houses.

As indicated in Part I, gearing may be calculated in a number of ways. An additional complication arises from the contrast between nominal and market values. The difference made to the calculation of gearing according to the method of valuation is illustrated in Table 12.1. Gearing is calculated by dividing the value or percentage value of ordinary shares into the total valuation of all securities. Zero gearing (where the total value of capital is equal to the value of the ordinary share capital, there being no prior charges) is equal to 100 on this basis. It will be seen that gearing on a market-value basis is considerably less than on the basis of nominal values. In terms of the calculations of prior charges, nominal-value gearing is more important to a company than market-value gearing. As the market values of loan and preference capital have fallen during the post-war period, while those of ordinary share capital have risen, market-value gearing has declined considerably. There has also been some decline in nominal-value gearing. Under conditions of rising prices of equities and falling prices of loan stock, companies have generally been able to persuade their shareholders to subscribe further capital by way of rights issues of ordinary shares,

Table 12.1 Nominal- and Market-Value Gearing of
Company Securities, 1964

Type of security	*Percentage of nominal value*	*Total valuation (market value)*
Loan stock	16.8	5.3
Preference shares	12.4	3.6
Ordinary shares	70.8	91.1
Gearing (total ordinary)	141.1	109.5

Source: 'Stock Exchange Official Year Book, 1965.'

rather than in terms of loan or preference stock. In order to restore gearing, companies have also resorted to the issue of convertible debentures (loan stock which may be converted into ordinary shares at fixed prices at predetermined dates in the future). The change-over to the system of corporation tax, in lieu of profits and income tax, in 1965 has been a force favouring increased gearing. The nominal-value gearing of United Kingdom registered and managed companies rose from 147 to 156 between 1965 and the end of 1967. Market-value gearing, however, remained virtually constant at 113. The overall gearing of United Kingdom registered and managed companies is slightly higher than that for all company securities quoted on the London Stock Exchange.

An alternative way of considering sources of company finance is to examine the distribution of capital employed between 'own' capital (ordinary and preference), loan capital and reserves. There was a big swing towards the finance of companies through ordinary and preference capital, especially during the second half of the 1950s, and a corresponding decline in reserves, with loan stock rising slightly. Since 1965 loan capital has come to represent a higher proportion of total net assets, while the proportion represented by ordinary and preference capital has fallen considerably. This again reflects the change-over to the corporation-tax regime. Corporation-tax considerations are, however, only part of the decision to raise capital in the form of loan stock. For in times of industrial stagnation when growth prospects for equities are not good, firms may find it more appropriate to issue fixed-interest securities. Both forces operated during 1966 and 1967. But when stock market conditions are buoyant, the arguments in favour of equity issues appear to be overriding. These conditions applied in 1968.

The most important source of funds to companies is their own savings out of income received — in other words, retentions. During the 1950s there was a rise in retention within businesses, accompanied by a decline in the amount of income going in taxation and profits sent abroad. This may be seen in Table 12.2. There was also a slight rise in the proportion of income paid out in the form of interest and dividends. It is important to note that the percentages in this table are Central Statistical Office (C.S.O.) data, based on returns of both quoted and unquoted companies and obtained primarily from the Inland Revenue, as is the analysis of sources and uses of capital funds of industrial and commercial companies in Table 12.3. It will be seen from this table that un-distributed income, plus a small amount of capital transfers, provided the major source of funds for British companies during the mid-1960s. Bank lending and capital issues by quoted companies each provided one-ninth of total funds employed. Of the total funds employed, just over half was used in the replace-ment of existing plant, equipment and building, while one-ninth went into stock formation. The acquisition of subsidiaries in the United Kingdom in exchange

Table 12.2 Income Appropriation Account of Industrial
and Commercial Companies
(percentages of gross income)

Dividend and interest payments

Date	Ordinary and preference dividends	Other dividends and interest	Taxation and profits due abroad	Saving
Aug 1950-4	16.0	4.1	38.5	41.4
1958-9	17.7	5.7	30.1	6.5
1960-4	24.3	7.8	24.1	43.7
1965	26.9	9.7	17.8	45.6
1966	27.9	12.0	24.2	35.9
1967	25.4	12.3	26.6	35.7

Source: D.E.P., 'Statistics on Incomes, Prices, Employment and Production',
Table C1 (various years to 1969).

for cash, and overseas assets, represent a further eighth of funds employed. Fluctuations between years in the source and use of funds have been important in the provision of bank lending on the supply side. They have been equally important in inventory formation, and liquid assets in particular, on the 'use of funds' side of the balance sheet.

So far as individual industries are concerned, the Board of Trade analyses the accounts of quoted companies on a quarterly basis, in order to provide information relating to the appropriation of gross income in manufacturing industries, construction and a small number of service industries. Some important differences emerge when companies are classified according to industry. Depreciation plus reserves gives a fair approximation to cash flow, and this was high for companies in the chemical industry, construction, vehicles and transport and communications, taking an average for the years 1964-7. In contrast cash flow was low, compared with manufacturing industries as a whole, in tobacco, drink, clothing and retail distribution. In general, reserves appear to suffer compared with the gross pay-out ratio of dividends and interest. For example, reserves of companies in shipbuilding and marine engineering were drawn upon during this period in order to maintain an accustomed pay-out ratio. Industries with relatively high pay-out ratios were drink, tobacco, clothing and retail distribution, in addition to shipbuilding and marine engineering.

To some extent the use of reserves to maintain pay-out ratios reflects the activities of companies in seeking to keep dividends at levels which are com-

Table 12.3 Sources and Uses of Capital Funds of Industrial and Commercial Companies
(percentages of total)

	Sources of funds				Uses of funds					
Date	Undistributed income* and capital transfers (net)	Bank lending	Other loans and mortgages	Capital issues by quoted companies (net)	Gross fixed (domestic) capital formation	Increase in value of stocks and work in progress	Liquid assets	Cash Expenditure on acquiring subsidiaries in U.K.†	Overseas assets acquired	Residual
1963	74.1	13.9	2.3	9.7	53.5	9.4	15.0	4.6	4.8	12.7
1964	70.6	15.5	4.4	9.5	48.9	16.4	4.6	6.4	7.8	15.9
1965	72.8	12.3	5.3	9.6	52.8	13.1	2.0	6.4	6.1	19.6
1966	74.6	6.0	3.8	15.6	64.0	11.4	-0.4	7.9	4.9	12.2
1967	80.9	6.8	1.1	11.2	64.3	5.4	14.3	11.1	1.9	3.0
1968	76.0	11.8	2.1	10.1	52.5	13.4	1.7	6.7	3.9	21.8‡
Average (six years)	74.8	11.1	3.2	10.9	56.0	11.5	6.2	7.2	4.9	14.2

Source: C.S.O., 'Financial Statistics'.

* Before providing for depreciation, stock appreciation and additions to reserves.
† Including small allowance for cash purposes of unincorporated businesses as going concerns.
‡ Of which 1.5 per cent represents import deposits.

patible with the status of their share quotations. As stated in the chapter on company finance, the pay-out ratio may be vital to the share price of individual companies, especially in the warding-off of possible take-overs. Additionally, maintenance of a relatively high and stable pay-out ratio enables a firm to raise new capital more readily through rights issues. Important differences also exist between industries in the proportion of gross income going in tax payments. Provision for tax payments was relatively high, during the years 1964-7, in retail and wholesale distribution, drink and tobacco, metal goods and leather and clothing. It was relatively low in shipbuilding and marine engineering, transport and communications and vehicles. The tax position of individual industries also reflects their ability to earn profits and their tax allowance position with regard to initial allowance, cash grants and the old system of investment allowances. Comparisons between industries in this aspect of company finance is rendered more difficult because the Standard Industrial Classification allocates firms to industries on a principal products basis, emphasising physical characteristics of the products concerned. It will be recalled that many companies are multi-product firms, and too much emphasis on an industry viewpoint in this respect may be misleading.

2 THE STOCK EXCHANGES

(a) Their Raison d'être
The various stock exchanges provide a vital link between the financial requirements of companies and their source of funds. The stock exchanges provide both a market for the exchange of existing share and loan capital of quoted companies, and a market where new issues of share and loan capital may be floated. Considerable advantages accrue to a company by virtue of having its share and loan and capital quoted on one of the exchanges. Management always knows what value the market places on the particular company in question, and quotation makes it very much easier for a company to obtain additional capital from outside the company's own resources, should this be required for expansion purposes. Hence companies will frequently seek to 'go public' at some stage in their development; that is, they offer their shares to the public through the obtaining of a quotation on one of the exchanges. The council of the appropriate exchange will wish to see that a sufficiently wide market is created in those shares and loan stock for the price to be a fair valuation of the company's worth.

From the standpoint of the finance of industry, the existence of stock exchanges ensures that investors are able to buy and sell their holdings of industrial assets whenever they regard such purchases and sales as necessary and advantageous. The possibility of being able to realise assets in the form of cash has a great advantage to investors, whether they be individuals, industrial and commercial companies or financial intermediaries such as banks, insurance companies, and investment and unit trusts. Without this possibility of buying and selling securities, the finance of industrial companies on present scales could not have taken place. It is none the less worth restating that retained profits are still the major source of funds for company expansion, and that direct appeals to investors for the provision of new capital are a minor method of raising finance for expansion, as was seen in Table 12.3. Nevertheless such external finance is still of key importance, since it represents a large capital sum available at the time of issue. This contrasts with retentions, which at any moment of time may not be so large. Such an issue may facilitate a burst of growth which might otherwise have been constrained had retentions been the only source.

(b)   Their Organisation

Stock exchanges in the British Isles are dominated by the London Stock Exchange, both in the number of securities dealt in and the volume of transactions. Stock exchanges exist in twenty-one towns. The provincial stock exchanges have been unified into groups, following the establishment of the Federation of Stock Exchanges of Great Britain and Ireland in July 1965. The Federation comprises the stock exchanges of London, Belfast, Cork, Dublin, Midlands and Western, Northern, Scottish, and provincial brokers.

The London Stock Exchange is organised on the basis of a division of roles between stockbrokers and jobbers, corresponding roughly to a retail—wholesale distinction. Transactions, whether purchases or sales, will normally be made by the public through the offices of a broker, or firm of brokers, who receives set fees depending on the size of transaction for the work involved. Normally the broker will approach a jobber whose function it is to specialise in particular lines of stock. The jobber is said to 'carry a book' in a number of company securities. He may, for example, specialise in the securities of oil companies, property companies or investment trusts and the like. He will be prepared to buy and sell at stated prices, and in any approach made by a broker will quote two prices, a price which he is prepared to bid for the stock and a price at which he is prepared to offer stock for sale. The difference between the two prices is known as the 'jobber's turn', and out of this difference he meets the expenses incurred in running a book of stock. It should be emphasised that the jobber is operating on his account and *not* on behalf of a client, and hence his position differs from that of the broker. Occasionally, of course, the broker's client may be himself, but in the normal course of events he works on behalf of his customers.

The jobbing system of stock exchange operation is unique to the United Kingdom. The prime role of the jobber is to create a market in the securities in which he specialises. His resources must be correspondingly large, so that he will have securities in stock whenever he is approached by a broker, or else he will be able to obtain such stock by the end of the account period when all transactions must finally be settled by the transfer of cash and securities.

Since brokers and jobbers have to meet all liabilities arising out of transactions they are currently engaged in, they must carry considerable cash reserves. The risk of client's default can be spread through entering partnerships. This applies to partnerships of brokers as well as to partnerships of jobbers. Until mid-1969 firms of brokers and jobbers were not permitted limited liability. This is now allowed but directors' liability remains unlimited.

Membership of the various stock exchanges in the British Isles is indicated in Table 12.4. The bulk of stock exchange members are located in London, which has two-thirds of the total. In contrast, less than half the total number of firms of brokers and jobbers are located in London, and the London firms are on average twice as large as firms operating on the various provincial exchanges. Not only is the average size of firms greater in London than in the provinces, but there has been a considerable tendency towards amalgamations of firms of both brokers and jobbers since the end of the second world war. Whilst the number of members in firms of brokers on the London Stock Exchange was practically the same in 1968 as it had been in 1947, the number of firms almost halved. The movement towards larger firms of jobbers proceeded along rather different lines. High personal taxation and rising costs had the effect of reducing the number of jobbers, so that in 1968 their number was only one-third of that in 1947. During the same period the number of jobbing firms fell drastically from 230 to 36. By 1968 the average size of jobbing firms, measured in terms of partners, was just over double what it had been in 1947. In short, whilst the number of firms fell in both cases, the number of brokers remained constant whilst that of jobbers fell.

Table 12.4 Membership of Stock Exchanges, 1968

Exchange	Number of members (brokers and jobbers)	Numbers of firms	Average size of firm
London	2,001	234	8.6
Midlands and Western	207	51	4.1
Northern	341	84	4.1
Scottish	193	47	4.1
Provincial brokers	162	79	2.1
Total	2,904	495	5.9

Source: 'Midland Bank Review' (Nov 1968).

Table 12.5 Stock Exchange Transactions
(value of turnover, £m.)

| | | London Stock Exchange | | | Scottish Stock Exchange | |
| | | Company securities | | | Company securities | |
Date	Total	Loan and preference	Ordinary	Total	Loan and preference*	Ordinary
1965	20,486	480	3,478	235	27	157
1966	21,590	585	3,566	234	28	153
1967	35,957	787	6,804	358	37	243
1968	31,987	944	9,118	421	36	327

Source: Bank of England 'Quarterly Bulletins'.
*Includes small amount of non-company securities.

There are clear advantages to operating on a larger scale. Large transactions are less costly to put through than small ones. Such transactions enable them to carry the high cost of small deals. The large transactions come from what are known as 'the institutions' – insurance companies, investment and unit trusts, pension funds and similar institutions – nearly all of which act as financial intermediaries between individual investors and the stock market. These institutions in turn have come to expect a fair amount of service from the brokering firms in exchange for their custom. Brokers are often expected to perform valuations at regular intervals as well as tender investment advice. These functions have necessitated the use of computers as techniques of investment analysis have become more sophisticated. At the same time, clerical costs of handling customers' accounts have risen, as has the cost of putting out investment circulars and research publications. During the whole of these twenty years the process towards amalgamation has been an orderly one. The Companies Act of 1967 aided the process still further by altering the law relating to partnerships, by extending the number of partners permitted.

Failures have been exceedingly few, so that problems of control have been those concerned with conduct rather than finance. Control over the operation of the London Stock Exchange and the conduct of its members is vested in a council consisting of thirty-six members. There are a number of subcommittees, which cover amongst others such subjects as rules and disputes, property and finance of the Exchange, firms' accounts, commissions, quotations and official lists and publications.

(c) Company Securities

In terms of market activity, company securities dominate the London Stock Exchange. Of a total of 9,481 issues of securities of all types traded on the London Stock Exchange in 1968, 87 per cent were those of companies, 64 per cent being share capital and 23 per cent loan capital. Corresponding figures for 1958 were 76 per cent and 14 per cent respectively. A rather similar picture emerges in terms of the market value of company securities. In 1958 company securities represented just under half the total market value of securities traded on the London Stock Exchange. By 1968 the proportion had risen to three-quarters. In both cases the bulk of the market value of company securities was represented by ordinary capital. The percentage changes in value between 1958 and 1968 were especially marked. The market value of British Government stock rose by only 18 per cent, but the loan capital of companies rose by 260 per cent and that of share capital by over 400 per cent.

3 THE ROLE AND GROWTH OF THE INSTITUTIONS AS PROVIDERS OF LONG-TERM CAPITAL

During the 1960s there has been a good deal of discussion (in the financial press and elsewhere) of the growing importance of the institutions in the operation of the stock markets and in the provision of long-term capital for industry. As stated earlier, the terms 'the institutions' or 'institutional investors' are used to describe a group of financial intermediaries which take money from the public and invest it on their behalf, either by the purchase of existing quoted or unquoted securities or by subscribing to new issues of capital. The role of these institutional investors in the new-issue market will be considered in a later section of this chapter. For the present, attention will be focused on their holdings of company securities.

At the end of 1967 institutional holdings of the ordinary shares of United Kingdom registered and managed companies represented 28 per cent of their total market value. The institutional holdings are those of insurance companies, pension funds in the public and private sectors, and investment and unit trusts. Because insurance company holdings of securities are given at book value in the C.S.O.'s 'Financial Statistics' (whereas the holdings of the other institutions are given at market values), this percentage underestimates somewhat the true proportion of holdings by these institutions. Nevertheless they are considerable, and may have been increasing during the 1960s. Data for 1964, prior to the introduction of corporation tax, revealed a combined institutional holding of 25 per cent of ordinary shares at market value. In fixed-interest securities, institutional holdings predominate. The institutions held over 90 per cent of the total of company loan stock quoted on the London Stock Exchange. The actual figure may be somewhat lower than this, because some of the company loan stock is not quoted on the London Stock Exchange. It is possible that institutional holdings of loan stock have been declining as a proportion of the total during the 1960s, as companies have sought to raise additional capital from existing ordinary shareholders (which of course include persons) by means of convertible loan stock. In contrast, the proportion of preference stock held by the institutions has increased considerably, from just over 50 per cent at the end of 1964 to just under 90 per cent at the end of 1967. Under the corporation-tax regime introduced into the United Kingdom tax system in 1965, preference stock has become an attractive stock to the institutions, because receipts from that source represent 'franked income'; in other words, corporation tax has already been paid by the issuing company, and will not have to be paid again in the hands of the recipient institution.

The relative position of the institutions in terms of the ownership of shares of companies is of interest. Whereas the insurance companies and pension funds dominate the loan stock of companies, investment and unit trusts hold only minor amounts of such stock. The former hold a smaller proportion of preference stock. Combined holdings by insurance companies of preference shares represented 40 per cent of the total at market values at the end of 1967, compared with 30 per cent in the case of pension funds and 14 per cent in the case of investment trusts. All showed substantial increases from the end of 1964. The contrast is even more marked in the case of ordinary shares. Holdings at market values at the end of 1967 were: insurance companies, 8.3 per cent; pension funds, 9.6 per cent; investment trusts, 7.6 per cent; unit trusts, 2.3 per cent. In the case of investment trusts large amounts of the ordinary stock of non-United Kingdom registered and managed companies are also held, principally in North America, and the percentages of investment and unit-trust holdings here do not reflect their relative sizes as financial intermediaries.

Although institutional holdings of the shares of United Kingdom registered and managed companies appear to have been increasing as a proportion of their total capital outstanding during the second half of the 1960s, it is by no means clear that the proportion of all securities (British-owned and managed, foreign securities and government stock) quoted on the London Stock Exchange held by institutions has been increasing. Similar exercises relating to all securities quoted on the London Stock Exchange reveal a fall in institutional holdings during the same period, and the proportion of ordinary shares held by the institutions is also much lower.

It is in terms of dealings, however, that the institutions have become an especially important influence in the market since 1965. The introduction of long-term capital-gains tax for individuals and companies has so far made the former rather less willing to move into and out of the market than was previously the case. The personal investor is also discriminated against compared with these institutional investors, since he pays short-term capital-gains tax at the appropriate marginal income-tax rate, in most cases not less than 41¼ per cent (at tax rates prevailing in 1968), compared with the 30 per cent rate paid by these institutions. The increasing importance of the institutions could not fail to have an impact on the brokering firms, who have become rather more conscious of the requirements of such investors.

In order to woo the savings of individual investors, the institutions have been pointing to the cost advantages of investment through them. Because of the size of individual transactions, they are able to obtain better prices for the purchases and sales of securities. They are also able to use new and sophisticated investment decision techniques which have developed during the last decade or so, frequently involving the use of computers.

The total of institutional funds has been growing considerably during the last decade. Until the floating of the Unicorn (now Barclays-Unicorn) group of unit trusts in 1957, the post-war unit-trust movement had scarcely got under way. Since then total unit-trust funds have risen considerably much of them through the inflow of new money. The same is true of insurance companies and pension funds. Participation in the latter has come to form an important fringe benefit for employees of many companies. Substantial sums of money are available weekly for investment in existing company securities. The institutions which control the direction of flow of such funds are constantly seeking new outlets, either by investing in companies coming to the market for the first time, or in smaller quoted companies which had previously not had institutional shareholders.

4 THE EFFICIENCY OF THE STOCK EXCHANGE

The previous two sections of this chapter have dealt with the organisation of the stock exchanges and the role played by institutional investors. The present section deals with the efficiency of the machinery of the capital market. The efficiency of the stock exchanges may be judged on three grounds: first, the characteristics of the market; second, the basis on which the market operates; and third, the effect on resource allocation.

The Stock Exchange is a good market by all the normal criteria: large numbers of shares are exchanged daily, dealers in shares are in a competitive position, and no jobber or broker has a monopoly of a particular market. Good knowledge and excellent communications exist between jobbers, brokers and the general public. Shares within a given class of a company are indistinguishable from other shares of the same class. In this sense the product is homogeneous. In dealings in the shares of large companies with 'blue chip' status, where considerable numbers of shares change hands every day, no one deal will ordinarily affect the ruling price. The convention between jobbers and brokers is that the size of the deal is not usually mentioned until the transaction is complete, nor does the broker reveal whether he is a buyer or a seller. Hence individual deals are unlikely to affect the current price of a share. This does not deny that jobbers will adjust prices upwards or downwards according to whether the prevailing trend of business is towards increasing purchases or sales. Good communications enable shares to be marketed quickly; deals can be effected within seconds of a decision to buy or sell. Prevailing prices give shareholders a guide to what they would have to pay or receive if they were in the market for shares. The fact that shares can be bought and sold rapidly gives shareholders a feeling that they have not entered into irrevocable long-term contracts. They know that holdings can be switched or realised very quickly at or near the current market price. This has two effects: no individual feels himself tied to one particular company, and this enables companies to raise capital cheaply.

All the same the stock market has some shortcomings. Four of these will now be considered. They have one common feature, and that is imperfect knowledge. Perhaps the most important of those shortcomings is lack of day-to-day knowledge of company performance. Because companies usually publish balance sheets and interim statements only twice yearly, concrete evidence of company performance is usually only available twice yearly (when dividends are declared). In the meantime individual company prices can be influenced by rumour, speculation and estimate. Any radical change in company fortune can cause a substantial re-adjustment of share prices when the facts are revealed. Hence the stock market cannot discount company futures in a smooth and continuous fashion, but is inevitably confronted with positions where expectations may be out of line with reality, and a big adjustment of share prices follows. In recent years, however, companies have taken to giving information more frequently. Quarterly statements of profit performance are becoming less rare. This helps to avoid radical movements in particular shares. Such radical movements have a disturbing influence, for they cast doubt on the effectiveness of the market in summarising the performance of companies.

Another shortcoming is that some have more knowledge than others. On occasions this can lead to exploitation of inside knowledge by unscrupulous persons. For example, members of a company's management may know that a take-over is imminent, and some may feel tempted to exploit this knowledge by purchasing shares before the bid becomes public knowledge. The Council of the

Stock Exchange has a whole series of rules to prevent this sort of behaviour. Basically these rules are framed with a view to preventing persons in such a privileged position from taking advantage of their foreknowledge of the facts. However, there are instances which are beyond the reach of the rules. An example would be sales of shares in foreknowledge of an industrial dispute.

A third shortcoming of the stock market arises as a result of deals which involve the less widely held shares. These shares have a narrow market, and dealings are usually infrequent and in small numbers. They are subject to wide fluctuations in price even on relatively minor deals. Companies that only appear in the 'markings' (a record of deals taking place in all quoted securities), but not in the daily price changes of the major financial newspapers, are likely to be in this category. These are not 'blue chip' companies, and their market tends to be narrow. Current prices will only be an approximate guide to their realisation values.

A fourth shortcoming is similar in character. It concerns the effect of take-overs. In take-overs, a deliberate attempt is made to secure a sufficient number of ordinary shares to acquire control. A deal of such a size narrows the market. In consequence the share price is likely to rise above the pre-bid price. Where the take-over succeeds, there is always the question of how the correct price has been established in a narrow market. In Chapter 7 it was pointed out that success in such take-overs is ultimately a question of tactics and timing. A bid may succeed before opposition and other bidders can be mobilised. If so, control passes in a market which is exceptionally narrow, since there are only two contestants for the shareholders' favour. These are the raider and the defending company. When such situations arise, the market is less perfect than in normal dealings. This shortcoming has been recognised and even exploited by the Industrial Reorganisation Corporation, which has thwarted a number of bids and also intervened to ensure that particular bids succeed. This suggests that the authorities are not convinced that, left to itself, the stock market will always operate in the best interest of the community when take-over bids are occurring.

So far the efficiency of the Stock Exchange has been considered in terms of how good the market is, and its shortcomings have been outlined as divergences from perfection as a market organisation. Now another approach will be attempted. This is from the point of view of the individual shareholder. For him, 'the logic of the market' consists of alternatives foregone – in other words, opportunity costs. Any individual considering an investment has a whole range of alternatives in which he could place his money. The cost of his selected investment consists of opportunities foregone elsewhere. Stock market prices give precision to this choice. By pricing securities, the market is also assigning current yields. A glance at any of the major financial newspapers will show these yields calculated daily on a basis of dividends and earnings. Calculated this way, changes in the prices of shares will alter the current yields available on the shares. Such calculations are based on the last declared dividend or interest payment and the last earnings, as shown in the accounts. As these figures are usually made available only twice a year, current market prices are changing in relation to relatively fixed earnings and dividend figures. Effectively, therefore, rises in share prices depress yields, and falls in share prices raise yields. The market thus has a mechanism to adjust yields on all securities very quickly in the light of changing circumstances. Because the market is so good, these current figures are a fair indicator of the return to be expected on all the various types of securities dealt with on the exchanges. The individual contemplating any sort of investment, even if it does not involve the Stock Exchange, thus has a reference point to establish the opportunity cost of his particular investment. If he considers establishing his own business, the opportunity cost to him is immediately ascertainable. The market is good at establishing yields because of the facilities it provides for switching between various types of assets. Because purchases and sales can be effected quickly, the market may be represented as continually moving towards equilibrium. In other words the market is moving towards a situation where divergences in the yields on various shares have been narrowed to a level consistent with business expectations. Arbitrage between short- and long-term securities, between risky and safe ventures, between established companies and newcomers, and between all sections of the market, will ensure that the yields available on shares represent the current collective opinion of the market. A whole spectrum of yields is established by this process of arbritage. The advantages and disadvantages of every sort of security are weighed and assessed by the market, and appropriate yields determined. The potential investor is thus given guidance by the stock market in helping him towards an assessment of the opportunity cost of his particular venture. Arbitrage may take place on two levels, as between yields on industrial groups and as between individual companies within those groups. Data enabling such arbitrage to take place are given, for instance, in the 'Financial Times' in terms of yields of individual shares, and in terms of the industrial groupings of the F.T.-Actuaries share-price indices. In short, the stock market helps to guide the allocation of resources.

The third ground on which the Stock Exchange may be judged is in its direct effect on resource allocation. The argument in the preceding paragraph related to the way in which the stock market assigns yields to various types of securities. These are reference points which indirectly guide funds into the various investment possibilities. The stock market is, however, in a position to affect resource allocation directly, because the pricing of shares will affect both the amount of finance which companies can secure from shareholders and their liability to take-over. If resource allocation is to be aided by the stock market, the following circumstances should hold. One is that there should be a positive correlation between the quality of companies' financial results and share prices. (For if good results are not reflected in share prices, they will not safeguard companies from take-over.) Second, take-overs should be motivated largely by considerations of efficiency. Third, the pricing of shares should provide some insight into the likely future performance of companies.

Viewing these circumstances in relation to take-overs and mergers, the following considerations are relevant. Past results have an effect on share prices. Individual company profitability and valuation ratios are related, as are dividend payments and share prices. In addition, the past profitability achieved by companies affects their acquisition price in take-overs. It has also been pointed out that take-overs and mergers are not motivated entirely by considerations of efficiency. Ultimately, in a take-over situation tactical considerations at the time of the bidding may prevail. Successful companies are not necessarily earning profits which are above the average for the industry concerned. Companies that have large cash reserves are at an advantage in buying other companies. Large companies have the additional advantage of a choice between purchasing such companies for cash or offering their own, highly marketable securities in exchange.

The positive associations listed above are sufficiently strong to dispel any fear that the market might frustrate resource allocation. However, one problem remains, namely the predictive power of share prices. The prices of shares reflect two elements: one is past performance, and the other is expectations of future performance. Current share prices represent the collective opinion of buyers and sellers, and this opinion is influenced by both elements. The correlation between company profitability and valuation ratio suggests, however, that the market operates to some extent on a 'post hoc ergo propter hoc' basis. This means that prospects for the future are assessed to a significant extent by reference to past performance. The question arises whether faith in the past is a good guide to future performance. Stock Exchange prices should attract assets to the most efficient companies and ensure that these continue to make excellent use of these assets. Were it true that companies with above-average success and above-average share ratings would necessarily continue to achieve above-average results in future, then it could be stated that allocation would be actively improved by the Stock Market. Such a proposition cannot be proved empirically. There are a considerable number of studies which suggest that the stock market prices shares on a 'random-walk basis'. In terms of repeating past earnings growth, there appears to be no consistency between past results and future results. This has been described as 'higgledy-piggledy growth'. (7) Possible explanations for this phenomenon are as follows: fast changes in personnel and the quality of managers may occur so that results are not repeated; the erosive power of competition may narrow yields; and a random process such that good and bad luck falls on companies irrespective of the quality of their management.

It may also be important to note that differences in the statistical methods chosen would affect the reliability of these results. Different measures of company performance are used to show some greater degree of consistency. Investigators who have used measures of profitability and growth performance found an element of repetition of the standard of performance.

One other issue which may also have some bearing on higgledy-piggledy growth and the efficient operation of the stock market is the apparently very wide fluctuations in share prices exhibited over time. Any of the indices showing changes in the prices of 'blue chip' shares over the past ten years reveal a rising trend, but with wide fluctuations around that trend. If these wide fluctuations could be eliminated, it is reasonable to assert that the market would achieve greater standing amongst industry and the general public and also be more effective in activating savings. With less violent swings in the market, the casino-like activities of market operators, whereby fortunes may be made and lost within short periods of time, would be damped. Furthermore the small private investor may be less deterred from participating in direct share ownership if such hazards were reduced.

The reasons explaining the wide fluctuations in share prices about the trend probably lie with the nature of the market. Inevitably the market for industrial shares is greatly influenced by expectations of future business conditions. The way in which expectations are formed is a subject on which there is almost complete ignorance. There are obviously certain key signals such as the volume of company sales, the level of order books, prevailing prices and profits and the availability of finance which influence businessmen and the general public in their views as to the likely future. But the timing and nature of these influences is almost entirely unknown. Another feature is the cumulative nature of expectations. Expectations can be self-feeding: a given change may lead to an expectation that such a change will continue in the same direction. Thus in terms of the Stock Exchange, an upward movement of share prices may generate a belief amongst potential holders of shares that the future trend is upwards. Thus instead of a rise in prices choking off buyers, the opposite may happen. An increase in prices may be induced by an initial rise, in the belief that collective opinion has it that business conditions are now set fair. Consequently a rise may generate a further rise, and so on. If the Stock Exchange is susceptible to expectations, as inevitably it must be, it may be in the nature of the market that price movements will oscillate fairly widely from the trend. These oscillations represent the power of such a market to generate expectations, based on the cumulative effect of its own price movements. In jargon, this is sometimes called a destabilising effect. Instead of demand being reduced by increased prices, the opposite may happen. It is fairly plausible that such a mechanism does operate in the pricing of shares. All the world's stock markets exhibit a pattern of wide share-price fluctuations. All these markets inevitably suffer from a lack of objective knowledge about the trend of future events. Hunch and timing of purchases of shares play a crucial role. Because markets are so susceptible to hunch, share prices will fluctuate in response to aggregate changes in these hunches. When price changes have the power to generate expectations, the upward and downward movements of prices are going to be more violent than if expectations were completely determined by factors unrelated to the current state of the market.

The oscillatory-type price changes may provide another explanation of higgledy-piggledy growth. Destabilising price changes may have the effect of divorcing the current share rating of shares from future performance, in that expectations are currently overstated in terms of future realised performance. If this level of overestimation is not consistent in degree, a very low correlation between share rating and subsequent performance is extremely likely. The existence of higgledy-piggledy growth may therefore represent a statistical measure of the effects of expectation on share prices.

Altogether it is reasonable to assert, although very difficult to prove, that the stock market aids efficiency. It provides a wide and active market in shares, and also facilitates take-overs and mergers. These are the only fast means whereby assets committed in a business may be reallocated. The apparent lack of predictive power of the Stock Exchange pricing of companies appears at first sight, however, to be a considerable drawback to the market's claims to aid efficiency. However, on reflection this effect is hardly surprising. Competition, in effect, operates through narrowing disparities in yields on capital employed. Companies should not be expected to repeat dazzling performances. Rivals should be attracted by success to imitate their products and mode of operation. In addition, 'organisational slack' within companies may vary with their achieved results. Success may bring complacency; failure may bring the stimulus to improve results. An oscillatory type of pattern may result. Furthermore insight into the future is granted to very few. To expect the collective opinion of dealers in shares to provide an insight into the future is faith indeed in the majority. Consequently a final assessment of the Stock Exchange's contribution to efficiency turns on the quality of the market which it provides and the smoothness of the facilities which are provided to aid transactions. In these terms the market can claim to be efficient. The correlations mentioned above add force to these claims, in so far as they show that allocation is at least not frustrated by the pricing process.

5   THE NEW-ISSUE MARKET

The stock exchanges owe their importance to the fact that they exist principally to facilitate deals in existing capital. Nevertheless quoted companies are able to obtain further additions to capital by making offers to their existing share-holders or debenture holders. Further issues of loan or share capital to existing members of a company have tended to form the major proportion of all new issues of capital, as may be seen in Table 12.6, though their importance dropped considerably during the years 1965-7. Except for 1967, issues of ordinary shares by quoted companies have outweighed issues of fixed-interest securities during the last decade.

The principal City institutions involved in the flotation of new capital issues are the members of the Issuing Houses Association (I.H.A.). Within the ranks of the members of the I.H.A. are those belonging to the more exclusive Accepting House Committee. These are sometimes referred to as the merchant banks, banks which both accept deposits and bills of exchange as part of their everyday activities and are engaged in the business of foreign exchange. Additional

Table 12.6 Analysis of Capital Issues by Quoted U.K. Companies
on the U.K. Market by Method of Issue, 1959-68

(percentages of total value of gross issues)

Date	Public issues and offers for sale	Tenders	Placings	Issues to shareholders		
				Total	Ordinary shares	Preference shares and loan capital
1959	7.8	0.8	17.6	73.8	–	–
1960	7.5	1.1	15.4	76.0	–	–
1961	4.5	0.9	16.8	77.8	70.0	7.8
1962	14.8	2.0	24.2	59.0	46.0	13.0
1963	11.4	3.7	41.8	43.1	30.4	12.7
1964	5.4	1.6	45.4	47.5	33.5	14.0
1965	11.2	0.6	67.1	21.1	12.5	8.6
1966	22.8	0.3	50.1	26.8	16.3	10.5
1967	14.3	0.4	58.7	26.6	12.3	14.3
1968	4.5	1.5	26.2	76.8	51.9	15.9

Source: Calculated from data in Bank of England 'Quarterly Bulletins'.

functions include acceptance credits and advising on mergers and take-overs, as well as operating in the discount market and on the stock exchanges. Most are old-established names in the City of London. They consist of Arbuthnot Latham and Co.; Baring Bros and Co.; Wm. Brandt's Sons and Co.; Brown Shipley and Co.; Charterhouse Japhet and Thomasson; Antony Gibbs and Sons; Guinness Mahon and Co.; Hambros Bank; Hill, Samuel and Co.; Kleinwort Benson; Samuel Montagu and Co.; Morgan Grenfell and Co.; N. M. Rothschild and Sons; J. Henry Schroder Wagg and Co.; and S. G. Warburg and Co. These institutions give advice to both quoted companies and to those seeking a quotation for the first time, as to the method of issue most appropriate to the company concerned, the type of security which should be issued, the pricing of the securities issued and the timing of the issue. They also arrange for the fulfilment of the various legal formalities and the requirements of the appropriate stock exchange. Additionally such institutions will undertake the actual paper work involved in the receipt of money from the public, and will then issue the share or loan certificates. The London Stock Exchange is the most important organisation in new issues because 90 per cent of all United Kingdom quoted securities are quoted and subsequently dealt in on this exchange. Approaches to one or more of the issuing houses are normally made by the individual company's own stockbroker.

The data in Table 12.6 refer to methods of issue employed by companies already quoted on the United Kingdom capital market. Their relative importance may differ from that of companies first seeking a quotation, as may be seen from Table 12.7. The various methods of issue will be described briefly. In the

Table 12.7 Method of Issue by New Companies, 1959-63

Method of issue	Number of companies %	Estimated value (% of total value)
Public issues	7.3	24
Offers	31.1	36
Placings	43.0	19
Tenders	3.4	7
Introductions	13.0	14
Mixed	2.2	—
Total	100.0	100

Source: Data given in A. J. Merrett, M. Howe and G. D. Newbould, 'Equity Issues and the London Capital Market' (Longmans, 1967) Tables 4.3 and 4.6.

case of public issues a fixed number of shares are offered to the public at a stated price and the costs of the issue are met out of the proceeds. An offer for sale involves the sale of a large block of shares to an issuing house or a broker, who will then resell them in smaller amounts. A placing involves the acquisition of a large block of shares by an issuing house. The shares are subsequently sold to institutional investors, jobbers and private individuals. An offer for sale by tender is identical with an offer for sale, but instead of a single price subscribers are asked to bid for an allocation of shares at a variety of prices ranging from a stipulated minimum. Lastly, the Stock Exchange introduction is a method of creating a market in existing shares, and can be used only for a new company. There must be between fifty and a hundred ordinary shareholders, with no undue concentration of ownership.

It will be seen from Table 12.7 that during the five years 1959-63 a placing was the most widely used method of obtaining a Stock Exchange quotation, in terms of the number of companies using the method, but the offer for sale was the most important in terms of value, followed by the public issue. For quoted companies, a placing was the most important method used when rights issues to existing shareholders are excluded. Generally speaking, the placing method tends to be used for smaller companies.

There have also been considerable changes in the type of securities issued by quoted public companies during the last decade, as may be seen in Table 12.8. Between 1959 and 1962 issues of ordinary shares were the most popular form of raising new capital by all quoted companies, though the balance away from ordinary shares to loan stock had shifted in the case of non-financial companies in 1962. The movement towards the issue of loan capital was furthered, amongst other influences, by the 1965 Finance Act, and between 1965 and 1967 issues of ordinary shares were at a relatively low level. The year 1968, however, with booming stock market conditions, saw a return to the issue of ordinary shares.

Many of the smaller and a few of the larger issues are handled by broker firms without the aid of an issuing house. This can cut down the costs of securing a quotation or 'going public' to the small company. As pointed out in the previous section on the efficiency of the Stock Exchange, the Quotations Committee will wish to satisfy itself that a satisfactory market can be established in the company's shares. For the period 1959-63 it was found that the average size of a placing, the method mostly used by small companies, was just under £200,000, compared with £500,000 in the case of offers for sale, £900,000 for tenders and £1,300,000 for public issues. (2)

· Brokering firms and issuing houses may nurse small unquoted companies for a number of years before a decision is taken to bring the company to the market. The costs of going public are high for small companies. Whatever method of issue is used, the cost of issues of under £100,000 is around one-quarter of the

Table 12.8 Analysis of Capital Issues on the U.K. Market by
Quoted U.K. Public Companies, 1959-68
(percentages of total value)

Date				*Type of securities issued*		
	All companies			*Non-financial companies*		
	Ordinary shares	*Preference shares*	*Loan capital*	*Ordinary shares*	*Preference shares*	*Loan capital*
1959	65.0	2.0	33.0	55.2	0.8	44.0
1960	77.3	1.1	21.6	74.7	1.3	24.0
1961	76.2	−0.2	24.0	74.3	−0.3	26.0
1962	58.9	0.6	40.5	47.0	0.9	52.1
1963	42.8	2.3	54.9	34.5	3.1	62.4
1964	43.0	1.4	55.6	38.7	1.8	59.4
1965	19.2	−3.2	84.0	15.4	−3.5	88.1
1966	22.7	4.0	73.3	21.4	4.3	74.3
1967	15.4	−0.6	85.2	14.8	−0.5	85.7
1968	58.7	−1.6	42.9	61.9	−2.2	40.3

Source: Calculated from data in Bank of England 'Quarterly Bulletins'.

proceeds, so that a small company would end up with only £75,000 in cash. Costs diminish fairly rapidly as the size of issue increases. The cost of a placing tends to be rather lower than that of an offer for sale. The main ingredient of costs is the investigation into the company's affairs and standing carried out by the brokering firm or issuing house, and thus tends to be fixed whatever the size of the company. The costs of a public issue, for which a company needs to be fairly large, are considerably less than those of offers for sale or placings, and may amount to only about 5 per cent of receipts.

6   MERCHANT BANKS AND MERGERS

During the 1960s in particular the acceptance and issuing houses, sometimes referred to loosely as merchant bankers, have been seeking new outlets for their expertise. This has been found in giving advice to client companies on how to buy other companies and how to ward off unwelcome take-overs. With their expertise in assessing purchase price in the case of new issues, these institutions are in a unique position for advising on what price a predator company should offer for a prospective victim, or on the defence that such a victim might make.

What the merchant banking advisers bring to the merger and take-over business is ideas on techniques and presentation of a financial case, negotiating sense and, of course, ready access to capital.

In contrast to the position in continental Europe, where industrial associations and banks have frequently acted as advisers to both company and shareholders, the relationship in the United Kingdom has been less close where company organisation is concerned. During the 1960s the merchant banks have become company doctors, and this has involved a reorientation of their existing activities, with less emphasis than formerly on the provision of short-term credit facilities. This decade has seen the coming of specialists on company take-overs and defence within the ranks of merchant bankers, and men with professional qualifications have come to the fore. The banks themselves have moved away from the traditional partnership form of organisation to a company form, and have undergone considerable reorganisation on functional lines.

It is particularly in the follow-up field, after the completion of the merger or take-over, that the services of merchant banking advisers are important and have sometimes been lacking. To make a take-over or amalgamation really work along the most efficient lines may involve considerable reconstruction of the company both from a managerial and financial organisation standpoint. These are the kinds of activities which an issuing house will wish to satisfy itself on before agreeing to sponsor a company for market quotation. On the other hand it has been argued that during the 1960s the merchant banks have tended to concentrate rather too much on bringing spectacular new companies to the market and have been slow in 'after-sales service'.

The increasing number and size of take-overs and amalgamations has led to intervention by the Council of the Stock Exchange and the Issuing Houses Association and the establishment of various sets of rules regarding the conduct of bidding companies and their advisers in particular, as well as for the protection of shareholders of the company being bid for. A code of conduct for take-over bid situations was first issued by the Issuing Houses Associations in 1959, and was revised in 1963. The new 'City Code on Take-overs and Mergers' was prepared by a working party from various City institutions – the I.H.A., the Accepting Houses Committee, the Association of Investment Trust Companies, the British Insurance Association, the Committee of London Clearing Bankers, the Confederation of British Industries, the National Association of Pension Funds and the Stock Exchange – and it appeared in its present form in March 1968, subsequently to be revised in April 1969. The 1968 document coincided with the establishment of a Panel on Take-overs and Mergers, and the Director-General or his deputy is able to give rulings on points of interpretation of the Code whenever necessary. Disciplinary action will be taken by the Council of the Stock Exchange.

The Code deals with such matters as the approach by the bidding company, notification of the press, the manner in which such a bid should be considered by the vendor board, formal offers and documents supporting the offer, and dealings and changes in the situation of a company during a bid.

As shown in the chapters on the growth of the firm in Part I, the provision of long-term capital for industry is of considerable importance to company growth. The crucial phase in the life of companies may well come at the point when a decision has to be taken of whether to go public or remain as an unquoted company with inadequate access to outside funds. Going public inevitably involves some loss of control so far as the original owners are concerned, but the compensation is that a company's subsequent growth rate may be faster than it would otherwise have been. (3)

13 The Labour Market

1 INSTITUTIONS

It is convenient for economists to talk about the 'labour market'. This does not mean that human beings are bought and sold as in the days of the old slave trade, but it does imply that there is a market concerned with the supply and demand for man's efforts. The demand for labour is essentially a derived demand for a special factor of production. Unlike capital, however, labour is not homogeneous even in its untrained state. Human beings have different innate talents, no matter how well trained and developed those talents subsequently may be. Factors of production are organised to produce different commodities required by man, There is a considerable variety of occupations and a multiplicity of individual labour markets. The more a given occupation can be utilised on a wide variety of jobs, the greater the size of that particular labour market will be. Except where his talents are exceedingly scarce, the individual worker is, however, at a disadvantage in bargaining for his remuneration from a given employer, because the latter is in command of capital resources and has the knowledge of the market for his final output, which the individual worker lacks. As a result the labour market has become institutionalised, first by workers grouping together to form trade unions in order to improve the bargaining power of the individual worker, and second by employers banding together in the form of employers' associations to offset the bargaining power of the trade unions. This gives rise to a series of administratively determined prices or wage rates appertaining to a wide variety of occupations.

It is difficult to be precise about the extent to which individual industries or occupations are organised on the basis of collective bargaining between trade unions and employers' organisations. As opposed to the situation on the North American continent, labour is organised far less on an industrial basis in the United Kingdom and much more on an occupational basis. In this country workpeople were originally organised so as to protect those in individual trades or professions, and this has subsequently affected the whole structure of collective bargaining. Another major difficulty in assigning anything like accurate percentages to the degree of unionisation existing among individual industries lies in the existence of the large general unions, such as the Transport and General Workers' Union and the National Union of General and Municipal Workers, whose members extend into numerous industries and cover a wide variety of occupations. A rough indication of the position in the middle of the 1960s may be obtained from data in the 'Ministry of Labour Gazette' for November 1967. Coal-mining appears to be completely unionised and national and local government service to be between three-quarters and four-fifths unionised, with paper and printing about two-thirds. Transport and communications, metal manufacture, engineering, vehicles and metal goods had about half of their employees belonging to trade unions. Clothing, footwear and textiles, timber and furniture and professional and scientific services were only one-third unionised; and construction, agriculture and leather only about one-quarter. Little more or less than one-tenth of employees in food, drink and tobacco, chemicals, bricks, pottery, cement and glass, gas, water and electricity, and distribution and miscellaneous services belonged to unions. The degree of unionisation revealed for some of these industries (drink and tobacco, chemicals, cement and glass, and gas, water and electricity) may be inaccurate, because many of the workers in these trades belong to one of the general unions.

The size distribution of trade unions for 1967 is given in Table 13.1. There is heavy concentration of trade union membership amongst a relatively few very big unions, with the ten largest unions having over 250,000 members each and accounting for over half of the total trade union membership. In contrast, over

Table 13.1 Size Distribution of Trade Unions, 1967
(percentages)

Number of members	Number of unions	Total membership
250,000 and over	1.6	54.2
100,000 and under 250,000	1.8	15.4
50,000 ,, ,, 100,000	3.1	11.9
25,000 ,, ,, 50,000	3.2	6.5
10,000 ,, ,, 25,000	6.7	5.7
5,000 ,, ,, 10,000	5.2	2.0
1,000 ,, ,, 5,000	25.4	3.5
Under 1,000	53.0	0.8
Total	100.0	100.0
Numbers	555	9,967,000

Source: 'Employment and Productivity Gazette' (Nov 1968).

half the number of unions had fewer than 1,000 members, and their membership accounted for less than 1 per cent of the total membership of all unions. This size distribution of trade unions compares with that for enterprises and establishments in Chapter 10. Take-overs and amalgamations have reduced the total number of unions considerably during the last decade, from 685 in 1957 to 555 in 1967. Over half the decline in the number of unions has been amongst those with under 1,000 members, and this has naturally led to a greater degree of concentration of membership amongst the larger unions. Despite the amalgamation process, however, the individual employer may still be faced with a multiplicity of unions in the bargaining process, and this gives rise to considerable difficulties in the working-out of a mutually satisfactory wage structure for his company. The multiplicity of unions facing any one employer is not, however, simply a reflection of the total number of unions, but stems essentially from the occupationally orientated structure of unions. Unlike the amalgamation of firms, that of trade unions does not necessarily lead to a rationalisation of union organisation along industrial lines, and it appears to have made little difference to the extent of occurrence of demarcation disputes.

In some industries wage bargaining takes place not between individual employers and trade unions but between the unions or groups of unions and employers' federations. Unfortunately no readily accessible data appear to be available about the size distribution of employers' federations. The largest, however, is the Engineering Employers' Federation, and the manner in which bargaining takes place between it and the engineering unions is described in Chapter 15. It is frequently the case that wage bargains concluded between employers' federations and trade unions specify only certain key rates of pay, and further bargaining takes place on an individual employer basis and often on a workshop basis.

2   THE WAGE BARGAIN AND METHODS OF WAGE PAYMENT

The contract drawn up between the employers' federation and the trade unions involved in a given industry will contain not only details of certain key rates of pay for a number of occupations, but will also deal with hours of work and what have in recent years become known in the specialist labour economics literature as 'fringe benefits'. In union—employers' federation negotiations the former will have to take a decision on the 'bargain mix', that is the extent to which a straight increase in wage rates takes precedence over a reduction in hours, increased time off at holiday periods or, where applicable, the more difficult decision of pay now or at some future date in the form of increased pension rights. The latter are two of the most important of a growing range of fringe benefits. As real incomes rise, the latter come to take up an increasing importance in the package deal. With increasing state intervention in such fields, however, their importance may diminish so far as wage bargains in the private sector are concerned. In North America medical benefits are of importance as a form of fringe benefit. A deterioration in the British National Health Service could lead to their growth in this country. Such fringe benefits add an extra dimension to modern theories of wage bargaining and affect the optimisation process.

The nationally negotiated wage rate for certain key occupations mentioned above must be distinguished from earnings and from take-home pay after deduction of tax and social security payments, and the like. The chief division of methods of wage payment between time rates and incentive systems such as piece rates and individual and group bonuses has shown some alterations in trend during the last thirty years. Just before the war about 18 per cent of male manual workers were employed under some form of payment-by-results system, compared with 46 per cent of women workers. By 1947 the proportions were respectively 24 per cent for men and 39 per cent for women, and by the beginning of the 1960s they were 30 per cent and 44 per cent respectively. The attractiveness of payment-by-results systems to the individual firm tends to grow with the size of firm, and in part the growing size of firms since before the war has led to the increasing importance of this type of wage payment. As a firm grows in size, direct supervision of workers becomes increasingly difficult and costly, and a method of wage payment geared to the output of the individual worker or group of workers cuts down this constant need for supervision. To a limited extent the saving in costs to the firm by cutting down on direct supervision of workers is offset by additions to inspection costs of components and the final product. This fact emphasises the importance of introducing such schemes only where methods of production are really suited to them. Thus in many industries in the post-war period there has been a growing use of semi-skilled workpeople in the production of components. Product engineers have become increasingly aware of the need to design manufacturing systems which cut down the amount of skill required and increase the amount of capital required in the form of automatic cutting and stamping machinery, etc. Pay can then be linked to the rate at which the individual worker can operate the press, for example, as opposed to his skill in shaping a particular component. No official data appear to exist concerning the popularity of such incentive systems according to size of establishment, but private investigations show clearly that they do increase as the size of the establishment grows. A relatively low proportion of small establishments (employing under 100 workers), between 28 and 47 per cent, appear to make use of piece rates or individual bonuses, compared with much higher proportions in the case of medium and large-size establishments — 44 per cent and 62 per cent for piece rates and individual bonuses respectively. (1)

There is naturally considerable variation between different industries in the extent to which wage-incentive systems are used, but evidence collected by both the Ministry of Labour and the Prices and Incomes Board in 1961 and 1967 respectively indicates that such systems were not quite so widely used at the end of 1967 as they had been in 1961. Major declines in their use took place in coal-mining, shipbuilding and repair and tobacco, though smaller increases had taken place in their use in food processing, boots and shoes, papermaking and rubber manufacturing. Metal manufacture, rayon, paper manufacture, clothing, confectionery and rubber manufacture all had three-quarters or more of their manual workers operating under payment-by-results systems. At the other end of the scale, electricity, gas, coal-mining, chemicals and tobacco and food manufacture all had less than a third of their manual workers operating under such schemes. (2)

Apart from this important distinction between time-rate methods of payment and the various incentive methods, changes in wage rates of either type may be arrived at in a variety of ways. The proportion of wage increases arrived at via different methods is indicated in Table 13.2. During the period immediately following the Second World War, some 2 million workers had wage agreements which tied wage rates to rises or declines in the index of retail prices, in such a way that if prices rose by 3 per cent, for example, wage rates would also rise by 3 per cent. After the devaluation of sterling in 1949, the trade unions agreed to absorb half the increase in the cost of living which would follow devaluation. Soon afterwards, however, the outbreak of the Korean War accentuated tendencies towards rising prices, so that this agreement was not put to the test for long. During the 1960s the proportion of wage increases obtained through

Table 13.2 Method by which Wage-Rate Increases have been Achieved
(percentage of total by value)

Method	Average, 1946-60	Average, 1960-8
Sliding scale/cost of living	8.2	2.6
Arbitration	7.5	5.3
Direct negotiation	38.1	42.5
Wages Councils	19.1	15.4
Joint Industrial Councils	27.1	34.2
Total	100.0	100.0

Source: 'Ministry of Labour Gazette' and 'Employment and Productivity Gazette'.

the existence of cost-of-living agreements has declined considerably, though the rising cost-of-living argument has played an important role in direct negotiations for wage-rate increases. The importance of direct negotiations for wage-rate increases has grown somewhat during the 1960s as compared with the 1950s, as indeed has the proportion attributed to the operation of Joint Industrial Councils. These Joint Industrial Councils, consisting of representatives of employers' associations and trade unions, came into being at the end of the First World War, and during the 1960s there have been some two hundred of them in existence. In contrast with the Joint Industrial Councils, Wages Councils are statutory bodies, whose origins go back to the Trade Boards Act of 1909. Today they are governed by the Wages Councils Act of 1959. Such Councils consist of representatives of employers and workpeople, with the addition of not more than three independent members, i.e. persons not connected with either side of the industry. Wages Councils were introduced originally to give some formal recognition and representation to workers in trades which were ill organised from the workers' standpoint. As a source of wage determination their influence has diminished somewhat between the 1950s and 1960s, in contrast to that of the Joint Industrial Councils. Should direct negotiations fail, both parties to a dispute have the possibility of recourse to arbitration, but as will be seen from Table 13.2, wage increases coming about in this way have declined marginally as a proportion of all wage increases.

3 WAGE STRUCTURES

In the above discussion on the wage bargain reference was made to the concept of 'key rates of pay' for certain occupations. In modern discussions about wages, labour economists have moved away from the concept of the wage rate to that of the wage structure and movements within such structures. Wage-structure analysis is concerned essentially with explaining the system of wage differentials which exist between people doing different jobs either at the factory or work-shop level or on a national level. It is important at the outset of this discussion of wage structures to distinguish between the internal and the external wage structure. The former is essentially an intra-plant concept, and it relates to the structure of pay within a firm, a factory or any other association where the established set of wage differentials for different jobs is determined by the same authority. The latter, in contrast, is an inter-plant concept, and relates to the wage structure existing between firms, companies and plants. The main feature of an external wage structure is that the wage differences which arise between plants, firms, etc., are set not by the same but by different agencies. Nevertheless they have common links. The external wage structures frequently impinge on the internal wage structures of individual plants or firms, since these do not work in isolation from this whole set of outside influences.

In building up the pattern of an internal wage structure, economists make use of two important additional concepts, namely those of the 'job cluster' and the 'wage contour'. (3) A job cluster consists of a group of jobs linked in terms of techniques, production processes and social customs so that they have common wage-making characteristics. At the heart of such a cluster is a key job carrying a key wage rate and attached fringe benefits. Examples of such clusters are the toolroom of a workshop, the key job and key rate being the toolroom fitter. Other toolroom jobs, such as tool maker, setter, operator, etc., lie in a given relationship to this key job, and their rates of pay are in turn related to the fitters' rate of pay. A further example would be the manning crew of an open-hearth steel furnace, the key rate and key job probably being the chief melter, the other members of the crew such as first melter, charge machine operator, etc., down to unskilled members of the crew having closely related rates of pay. The internal pay structure of the engineering works or the steelworks as a whole will be built around a whole series of such job clusters. Changes in technology will clearly have an important, though usually gradual, impact on such job clusters.

The wage contour is a wider concept than that of the job cluster in that it looks to a linkage of common wage-determining units such as plants or companies. The plants or companies are linked together by having a similar range of products, and consequently similar sources of labour supply and common labour market organisation in the form of trade unions and employers' associations. As a result wage determination in each of the institutionally or economically linked plants or firms tends to follow a similar pattern. (4)

The wage contour has three dimensions. They are, first, the whole spectrum of job clusters to be found within the linkage of companies; second, the particular sector of industry to which these companies belong; and third, the geographical location of the companies concerned. Although it may appear at first sight as though the wage contour will correspond fairly closely with the wage settlement pattern of a particular industry, this is not necessarily the case. The wage structure of any single firm may fall within a number of wage contours. Firms within the food-processing industry will be linked together by a number of different wage settlements arrived at by various wage-negotiating bodies, but they will also be linked with wage settlements in some other industries. Part of the labour force of such firms consists of transport workers, whose wages and conditions of cmployment will be determined by the Transport and General Workers' Union in its negotiations with a wide range of other employers of transport workers, frequently conducted at least in part on a regional or local basis. This link will form part of just one contour. (5) (Regional influences are especially important in the widely spread geographical areas of North America. Pacific Coast links with firms in the United States may be more important to Canadian firms operating in British Columbia than links with similar industries in, say, Quebec Province. Studies of individual labour markets in the United States confirm this general observation.) (6)

Of those factors determining the internal wage structure of an individual firm, probably the most important are technological. The various types of payment-by-results systems outlined in the previous section are especially important in this connection. New runs of products will frequently involve a revision of the appropriate piece rate or bonus system in those plants where such methods of payment are common. The determination of such rates each time a new setting of machinery is made has tended to enhance the power of local shop stewards, who have been the major negotiators of the new rates with management representatives. Such frequently negotiated rates have been one of the chief factors lying behind the phenomenon of wage drift, the divergence of actual rates of pay from officially negotiated national wage rates. These frequently renegotiated rates tend to become embodied in a new and permanent wage structure so far as the individual firm is concerned, and they are used as the starting point in future negotiations for increased rates of pay at the plant level.

The frequent changing of wage rates at the plant level in response to changes either in technical conditions of production, such as the installation of new plant or machinery, or in response to changes in the type of product made, involving for example an alteration in the tool or jig, have given an incentive to management to employ job-evaluation techniques. The attitude of trade unions to job evaluation has often been one of scepticism, since it is thought that the timing of jobs for wage-incentive purposes may restrict existing wage differentials policy too narrowly. Such techniques are frequently considered to leave the unions with too little bargaining play. Nevertheless job-evaluation techniques have proved useful in removing certain inter-plant differentials in multi-plant firms and geographical differentials within an industry, the latter being especially important in North America. The connection between job evaluation and management techniques is becoming of increasing importance in the whole field of wage-fixing procedures, so that the determination of wage structures has become more systematic, with the outside market intervening mainly in the form of imposing general constraints on the whole process. The importance of correct procedures in the use of job evaluation for wage-rate determination was emphasised by the Prices and Incomes Board in its report 'Job Evaluation' (No. 83, Cmnd. 3772) in 1968. A major factor in the successful application of job evaluation to the determination of wage-rate structures is that it should be used as a process of continual assessment, and not as once-for-all solution to the problem of 'correct' wage determination.

4   EXTERNAL WAGE STRUCTURES

The following paragraphs examine in turn a number of wage structures external to the wage-determining unit, whether it be at factory or company level. Major sets of wage differentials occur as between types of occupations, between industries and between regions. Age and skill differentials also occur, but are perhaps of less importance than the three former sets of differentials.

Table 13.3 indicates some of the long-run changes which have taken place in the occupational wage structure of Great Britain since the beginning of the First World War. Taking the pay index of the unskilled worker as 100, the pre-tax pay of persons in the higher professional occupations has declined relative to that of other occupations; half the reduction in size of differential occurring during the quarter-century since the outbreak of the First World War and half in the quarter-century since the beginning of the Second World War. In contrast, the relative pay of the lower professional workers remained constant compared with that of the unskilled worker until after the Second World War. Again the relative position of managers and foremen improved between 1913-14 and 1935-6, though it declined again between 1935-6 and 1960 in the case of foremen. Indeed the whole half-century since 1914 saw a decline in the skill premium, the

Table 13.3 Occupational Differentials (Men)

	1913-14	*1935-6*	*1960*	*Percentage change 1913-14 to 1960*
Professional				
Higher	520.6	491.5	380.0	+520.1
Lower	246.0	238.8	158.3	+446.5
Managers	317.5	341.0	345.8	+825.0
Clerks	157.1	148.8	127.5	+588.9
Foremen	179.4	211.6	189.9	+798.2
Manual				
Skilled	157.1	151.1	148.8	+704.0
Semi-skilled	109.5	103.8	108.6	+749.2
Unskilled	100.0	100.0	100.0	+749.2

Source: Calculated from G. Routh, 'Occupation and Pay in Great Britain, 1906-60' (Cambridge U.P., 1965).

amount by which the wages of skilled workers stood above those of the un-skilled. This loss of position of skilled persons has been due to the erosion of differentials on account of flat-rate increases of pay during the two world wars. But it is also due to the changing supply and demand position with regard to trained workpeople in the labour force. The spread of education and the acquisition of skills has led to an increase in the supply of skilled labour relative to unskilled and untrained labour. At the same time there have been techno-logical changes which have both increased and decreased the demand for skilled workers. The introduction of typewriters during the inter-war years and of computers during the quarter-century since the end of the Second World War has seen the substitution of capital for labour in the clerical field. Despite large increases in productivity, the position of clerical occupations has declined relative to those of manual workers and in comparison with foremen and managers. Similar factors have led to a deterioration in the relative position of professional workers of all kinds compared with managerial and manual workers. Within the whole field of occupations of manual workers, the narrowing of the skill differential appears to have led to a decline in the supply of skilled workers. To some extent there has been a substitution of semi-skilled for skilled workers as technological changes have led to a de-skilling of some kinds of operations. In an age of rapid technical change, the one skilled manual occupation which appears to have moved in a direction counter to the general trend has been the skilled maintenance worker. Where a breakdown in complicated machinery can lead to a serious production loss, both the status and pay of skilled maintenance workers have improved.

The second set of major differentials external to the individual plant or firm is that existing between different industries. Table 13.4 indicates the state of differentials existing between average weekly earnings for men employed in different industries. Differentials between workers in respect of earnings in various industries have come about for a variety of reasons. High average earnings tend to be correlated with high productivity (output per worker employed), but the correlation is by no means perfect. High productivity tends to be associated with growing industries, and these are able to attract the labour they require for their expansion plans by offering higher wages. In practice, however, other factors, often of an institutional nature, upset the theoretical pattern which would emerge from the above considerations. Strong trade union pressure, for instance, may suffice to force up wage rates faster than the rise in productivity in the industry concerned. Increases in basic weekly wage rates, whilst moving in the same broad direction as productivity changes, have by no means been perfectly correlated on an industry basis during the decade of the 1960s. Thus whilst the chemical and allied industries have had one of the biggest rises in productivity during this period, they have also had one of the lowest

Table 13.4 Average Weekly Earnings of Men (21 Years and Over),
October 1967

Industry	£	s	Index (all industrie = 100)
1. Paper, printing and publishing	24	15	115.8
2. Vehicles	24	8	114.0
3. Metal manufacture	22	8	104.2
4. Chemicals and allied industries	22	5	104.1
5. Bricks, pottery, glass, cement	21	19	102.2
6. Shipbuilding and marine engineering	21	18	102.1
All manufacturing industries	21	18	102.1
7. Other manufacturing industries	21	17	102.0
8. Construction	21	14	101.5
9. Transport and communication	21	13	101.4
10. Engineering and electrical goods	21	8	100.0
All industries covered	21	8	100.0
11. Mining and quarrying (except coal)	21	5	99.0
12. Metal goods not elsewhere specified	21	1	98.5
13. Food, drink and tobacco	20	17	97.2
14. Timber, furniture, etc.	20	16	97.0
15. Gas, electricity and water	19	18	93.0
16. Textiles	19	11	91.5
17. Clothing and footwear	18	15	87.3
18. Leather, leather goods and fur	18	14	87.0
19. Certain miscellaneous services	18	5	85.0
20. Public administration	16	15	73.0

Source: 'Employment and Productivity Gazette' (July 1968).

increases in basic weekly rates. A comparison of inter-industry differentials in respect of average weekly earnings of male workers between mid-1948 and October 1967 reveals a widening of the range. Despite changes in the Standard Industrial Classification, some comparisons can be made for groups of trades. Taking the average for all industries covered as equal to 100, the highest and lowest industries in 1948 had indices of 113.6 and 81.1 respectively, compared with the position at the end of 1967 of 115.8 and 73.0. The three top industries in 1948 were also the three top industries in 1967, though their relative ranking had changed. In 1967 order they were paper, printing and publishing; vehicles; and metal manufacture. There was a considerable number of reversals of position in the middle-order industries, whereas industries with relatively low average earnings in 1948 tended to have low average earnings in 1967. For example,˙ public utilities, textiles and local government service were all low-paid industries in both 1948 and 1967. Industries with important changes in order were chemicals, moving from number 10 to 4, food, drink and tobacco from 18 to 13, metal goods from 4 to 12, and clothing from 11 to 17. Technical innovations during the two decades from 1948 to 1967 in the process industries of chemicals and allied trades, and in food, drink and tobacco, have led to rapid increases in productivity, especially in the former, and to a corresponding increase in their ability to pay much higher wages. Inter-industry differentials also conceal the operation of other differentials, such as age and sex. Many of the low-earnings industries are low-pay industries because they employ a relatively large proportion of women workers, and male pay tends to be high in comparison with that of women. Industries which employ a high proportion of women workers also tend to employ a large number of them on a part-time basis, thus further reducing the average level of pay in those industries. Hence the previous discussion of the relative position of industries was confined to adult male workers. Nevertheless it must be borne in mind that the relatively low pay of women workers in industries where these predominate tends to reduce the pay of male workers in those industries. Such is the position in textiles, clothing and footwear and leather goods.

The last major aspect of external wage structures is the regional dispersion of earnings. This is shown in Table 13.5. Figures of regional earnings have been published by the Ministry of Labour (now the Department of Employment and Productivity) only since 1960. Average hourly earnings and average weekly earnings of full-time male manual workers are consistently above the national average in the Midlands, the London and South-eastern region and in Wales, though the ranking of Wales has dropped since 1960, when its average earnings were the highest in the United Kingdom. In contrast, average earnings of male manual workers have remained consistently much lower than for the country as a whole in Northern Ireland and in the South-western region. It might be thought that such differences reflect the underlying industrial structure of the different regions, so that those regions where the share of employment in the region is concentrated on industries with higher than average earnings would be reflected in an above-average overall level of earnings for that region; and equally, those regions with an industrial structure biased towards low-paid industries would consequently have a below national average level of earnings. However, a recent Department of Employment and Productivity study indicates

Table 13.5 U.K. Average Hourly Earnings in Manufacturing
and Certain Other Industries, October 1966
(percentage of U.K. average)

Region	
London and South-east	104.6
Midlands	104.6
Wales	101.2
East and South	100.0
North	97.7
North-west	97.2
Scotland	96.3
Yorkshire and Humberside	93.9
South-west	93.6
Northern Ireland	85.7

Source: 'Abstract of Regional Statistics', no. 3 (1967).

that when due allowance is made for differences in industrial structure, substantial differentials in earnings still remain between them, even though their spread is somewhat narrowed.

5   WAGE STRUCTURES AND INCOMES POLICIES

Governmental concern at the post-war inflationary process has led during the 1960s to statutory interference in the wage-bargaining process and the setting-up of statutory bodies to control the rate of increase in incomes and prices. The overall success and failure of successive Governments to control the persistent rise in prices and incomes is dealt with in Part III of this book, and the present discussion will be confined to the impact of such policies on wage structures.

The first post-war regulatory body, the National Incomes Commission, was set up in 1961 to deal with wage and salary increases, and it had no power to concern itself with prices or dividends. During its short life it issued only four reports: an inquiry into the Scottish plumbers' and builders' wage agreements of 1962; into the wages and hours agreements in the electrical contracting section of heating, ventilating and domestic engineering of February–March 1963; and into a straight wage increase, following the breakdown of negotiations for a package deal concerning hours and rates, in the engineering industries agreed in November 1963. In each of these three cases the Commission was inquiring into agreements which had already been put into effect. In its only other case, into the remuneration of academic staff in universities, it acted as a board of inquiry into the determination of appropriate salary levels.

In each of the retrospective inquiries the Commission was concerned more with the overall impact of the agreements on pay in relation to productivity rather than in commenting on the pay structures of the industries concerned. Only in the case of pay in the universities did the Commission concern itself at all with the salary structure, where, in Chapter 12 of its report, it commented on the number of increments in the salary scale as well as recommending varying rates of increase in pay for different grades of university staff. (7) For example, para. 221 read: 'The result is that the scale we recommend gives larger proportionate increases over the corresponding points on the existing scale in the middle years than in the earlier or later years.' In general, however, increases at the lower end of the salary spectrum were roughly in line with those of the more senior university staff.

In 1965 the National Incomes Commission was abolished and replaced by the National Board for Prices and Incomes (henceforth referred to as the Prices and Incomes Board or P.I.B. for short), following a 'Declaration of Intent' on the part of the Government, trade unions and employers' organisations regarding the working of an incomes policy. Compared with the N.I.C., the P.I.B. has been exceedingly active. Indeed a major criticism is that it has been too active, churning out on average one report a fortnight, so that it has been unable to give proper attention to each individual case. It was only in the second phase of its operations, lasting from July 1966 to June 1967, when the Board had been converted from a Royal Commission to a statutory body established by Act of Parliament, that it began to operate on the basis of government-imposed rules. The various criteria under which the Board has interfered with the wage structures of individual industries have evolved gradually, and indeed have been in part due to promptings from the Board itself, which at times has appeared to force its own pace and criteria for wage-rate changes on government thinking and practice. Indeed, commenting on the fourth phase of incomes policy in its third annual report, (8) it pinpointed two exceptions to the ceiling of increases in earnings of 3½ per cent, namely 'marked contributions to increased output per man or a major revision of the pay structure', and considered the second of these to be 'an outcome of some of our individual reports'. (9)

This section of the present chapter considers the relationship between the overall requirement that increases in money incomes in the aggregate should be related to changes in productivity in the aggregate, with the application of such ideas on a micro and individual industry level. Does it follow from the overall relationship between price stability and increases in aggregate money incomes linked with aggregate increases in productivity that (a) the wage rate of the individual must be related to changes in his own productivity, and (b) that wage-rate increases in individual industries should be related to productivity changes in those industries? The P.I.B.'s thoughts on these matters will be examined in turn. Both may involve changes in wage structures, and the wage structures emerging from P.I.B. recommendations form a further example of external wage-rate structures.

Detailed examination of these two problems is preceded by a brief discussion of the objectives of incomes policy so far as wage structures are concerned. The Board itself has been somewhat confused in its discussions of objectives of incomes policy with regard to their application to individual industries, and it has been inconsistent in its interpretation of the criteria laid down for it in respect of permissible wage and salary increases. Indeed attacks on the P.I.B. have come about because it has frequently appeared that the Board has ignored or even attacked the various criteria under which it has been asked to operate. Thus it has claimed in the case of the pay of agricultural workers (Report No. 25) that it is almost impossible to separate out lower-paid workers, (10) and has attacked this criterion on the grounds that a narrowing of differentials resulting from an increase in pay of workers at the bottom end of a pay structure would lead to a loss of incentive to improve qualifications. None the less this has not subsequently hindered the Board from suggesting revisions of wage structures in such a way as to reduce the incentive to improve qualifications and to narrow differentials in favour of poorly qualified workers. (11)

A second instance of this flouting of criteria is the comparability issue, where the Board has mostly, but not always, taken an exceedingly narrow interpretation of the comparability of a group of workers falling 'seriously out of line with the level of remuneration for similar work'. The contrast between its treatment of workers in the General Accident Group of companies (Report No. 41), in the industrial civil service (Report No. 18), the armed forces (Report No. 10) and the Scottish teachers (Report No. 15) are cases in point. Indeed the impression received from reading report after report is that no comparisons can or should be made, whatever the White Papers on incomes policy may have to say on the matter. At the heart of the Board's utter disdain of comparability as an argument for equal pay for equal work lies its own particular interpretation of the inflationary process, which it appears to ascribe almost entirely to the pushfulness of trade unions.

Finally, even on direct issues, such as London allowances, the Board appears to have suffered from schizophrenia. Thus Report No. 91 on civil engineering pay stated 'There may well be a case for a premium-rate in London based on higher living costs, but it would be better for such a rate to be worked out and agreed on at a national level on the basis of factual evidence' (para. 107). Yet one month and only seven reports later there is the statement in Report No. 98

on university pay that 'The London allowance should be faded out' (para. 99). Nor did the Board's Special Inquiry No. 44, 'London Weighting in the Non-Industrial Civil Service', suggest that this compensation for higher living costs in the metropolis be abandoned.

The Board stated in its second general report (No. 40) in 1967 that its 'general approach to the whole problem of pay has been to try and loosen the relationship between pay within a factory or an industry and the pay thought to be paid elsewhere.' The Board has instead tried to substitute for this loosened relationship between internal and what is thought to be external pay, a closer relationship between internal pay and internal performance' (para. 47). Within the pay structure of the individual firm it has been argued that the pay of the individual worker should be subject to a much greater use of job evaluation, as explained in its report on that subject (No. 83). Job evaluation, it stated, 'is essentially concerned with relationships, not with absolutes. Whereas it provides data for developing pay structures by differentiating between job contents and conditions, it cannot determine what the associated pay level shall be' (para. 6). The application of job evaluation techniques to the rationalisation of wage structures has been suggested on many occasions by the P.I.B., for example in the building industry and to the determination of a wage structure for manual workers employed by local authorities, the National Health Service and in gas and water supply, but has been considered to be especially applicable to those industries where technical change has been most rapid.

Alongside job-evaluation techniques the Board has considered payment-by-results (P.B.R.) schemes as measures to raise productivity on an individual as well as on an industry basis, and it has frequently commented unfavourably on those schemes which it has found in existence. The use of merit money in order to encourage the efficiency of individual workers has also been widely canvassed by the Board in its reviews of wages structures, but it has not studied the implications of a wider use of such schemes in depth, nor their effectiveness in raising personal efficiency. It has admittedly asked for, but not received, such a reference up to the end of 1968. Indeed the fact that the widespread use of such a system leads to an infinitely complex wages structure for the individual company, and ipso facto for the industry, has been virtually ignored, as has the difficulty of obtaining an objective basis on which to measure merit in a wide range of industries. The Board's view as to what constitutes a rational wage and salary structure is set out in an annex to Appendix E of Report No. 68 into the pay of 'Other Engineering Firms and the Draughtsmen's and Allied Technicians' Association'. To quote: 'A rational salary structure should relate in a logical and equitable way the relative worth of different jobs. One technique which can contribute to this is job evaluation. The salary scales associated with the overall salary structure should reward such characteristics as skill, responsibility and qualifications. The salary structure itself should provide incentives to improve performance, establish the logical basis for salary negotiations, ensure fair treatment of each employee and provide a structure of promotion and the recognition of merit and long service.' (12) It is perhaps unfortunate that the latter part of this statement, relating to job opportunities or employment structure as opposed to wage structure, has so often been ignored or only briefly touched upon by the Board in its many reports. One of the few occasions when this important topic was commented upon was in the early report (No. 6) on the salaries of Midland Bank staff. Commenting on the bank's claim that it needed to raise salaries to recruit better staff, the Board wrote: 'the salary on recruitment and during the early years of service is only one of a number of factors which will be weighed by the type of person most sought after by the banks. Equally, if not more, important will be the career prospects offered and, in particular, the opportunities for early advancement to more responsible positions' (para. 39). The effect of diminishing promotion prospects on the attractiveness of university work was only briefly mentioned as a factor in Report No. 98, and no strong positive recommendation about improving promotion prospects was included in the Board's list of recommendations (para. 99).

The connection between individual firms and industries lies in discussions on productivity. The Board's reaction to firms or industries which have stated that they wish to raise pay because of difficulties in recruiting staff has been that they should *not* be allowed to attract more labour by offering more pay or even improved prospects, but that firms and industries should make better use of the labour they already have. Such, for example, was the Board's judgement on the various claims made to increase the pay of bus workers in a number of individual towns. The Board has played a useful role in asking firms or industries to consider whether their shortage of labour is indeed genuine, but it appears to have stuck too rigidly to this one view of the situation, in that it has all too rarely discussed either the long- or short-run labour demand forecasts submitted by the firms or industries in question or, in their absence, attempted to construct its own. Indeed it is a major criticism of the Board's approach that it has effectively jettisoned such important pieces of economic analysis as demand considerations in its preoccupation with productivity. It has tended to favour the substitution of a rigid employment structure, with little mobility of labour, for a rigid wage structure with mobility of labour taking place in response to improvements in pay and job opportunities as between firms and industries. Whilst it is true that many cases of a substitution of capital for labour will lead to an increase in output per person employed, and this will register in the form of increased productivity, not all necessary capital investment will be labour-saving in the sense that it can take place without some increase in the labour force. In many instances the concomitant of an increased capital—output ratio is an increase in the scale of operations involving an increase in the absolute number of workers employed, though this will eventually reduce the relative amount of labour used in a given production process. But in order to achieve such economies of scale and the desirable deepening of the capital structure, labour may have to be attracted from other firms or industries by improved pay and job prospects. Nevertheless the Board, along with the National Economic Development Council, (13) has rightly pointed out the shortcomings of managerial techniques for making capital investment decisions, and the fact that in a number of individual firms and industries capital equipment is not being used as economically as it might be because management has failed to reorganise its existing labour force so that it operates in a way most suited to the new equipment and techniques.

In discussing the various methods open to firms and industries to improve their productivity, the Board has also rightly had in mind the implications of the use of new and more capital on the wage structure of the firm or industry concerned. In particular it has pointed out in both its general reports and in reports on specific firms or industries 'that a policy of using pay as a lever for bringing manning practices up to date and for promoting productivity is possible only to the extent to which emphasis on traditional comparisons is reduced'. (17) In other words, those industries with a propensity to innovate, either in terms of new products or of new methods of producing old products at lower costs, may also need to be innovators so far as pay structure is concerned, working out new pay structures to correspond with the new types of jobs and new job opportunities which are coming to the fore, rather than trying to fit new wine into the old bottles of existing wage and job structures. Some firms with progressive managements, even in old-established industries, will bring in a completely new labour force, untainted with adhesion to established practices in the industry, to man plants using new techniques, just so that new wage structures may be introduced. In so far as productivity agreements at the individual plant or company level are concerned, it is difficult to decide whether the Board intends to encourage or discourage such agreements.

Encouragement to form genuine productivity agreements has come in the form of one of the incomes policy White Paper criteria. In its third general report, the Board pointed out that the operation of P.B.R. systems in one part of a plant or company might well lead to resentment on the part of other groups of workers within that plant or company, since the established wage structure had been upset. The Board's attitude to this problem is, however, ambivalent, since it goes on to argue (para. 43) that 'a shift of emphasis from national bargaining to plant bargaining may cause a decreased emphasis on "comparability" – i.e., pitching a claim in imitation of what has been conceded to somebody else — and an increased emphasis on "productivity" — i.e., pitching a claim in relation to what happens in the plant or enterprise in question'. If the comparability habit remains, but is transferred to a comparison of pay with productivity in such a way that 'payment related to productivity in a highly productive sector can be followed by payment unrelated to productivity in a less productive sector', the result *could* be inflationary. If part of the productivity gains of the highly productive sector are shared with the low-productivity sector in terms of lower prices, this need not follow.

Following this train of thought, the Board has consequently been reluctant to allow increases in pay related to increases in productivity, despite its emphasis on the latter and the various incomes policy White Papers. Thus in Report No. 91 on civil engineering pay, whilst admitting that productivity had in all probability risen rapidly in this industry, the Board stated (para. 152) that 'We cannot accept that past contributions to raising productivity in this industry form a sound basis for pay increases in the future'. But the Board is equally reluctant to allow pay increases until after productivity increases have been achieved. Thus in the second general report (No. 40), the Board wrote: 'There is one clear lesson which emerges from the Board's report on productivity agreements. It is that, while an increase in pay can legitimately take place concurrently with an increase in output, it cannot, consistently with stability in the economy, precede an increase in output' (para. 50). Workers may well ask, how then does anyone get an increase in pay based on contributions to increased productivity. The Board, unfortunately, fails to be precise about what it will, and what it will not, allow under the criterion of contributions to increased productivity, where workers have undertaken 'more exacting work' or a 'major change in working practices' and are in danger of being turned down by the Board because they have occurred in the recent past.

Finally, the whole object of the Board in the field of wage structures appears to be to impose what it calls a competitive solution. Thus in its third general report (No. 77), it wrote that if 'there were uniformly free competition between worker and worker and firm and firm, it would be difficult, in the absence of an excess of total demand, for workers to impose labour cost increases on manufacturers and for the latter in turn to pass these on to the consumer. It is the very absence in the practical world of such competition in some sectors which makes necessary a prices and incomes policy; and in the execution of such a policy we have endeavoured to ensure that our recommendations would produce results more closely in accord with those which might have obtained had restrictive arrangements or unilaterally determined prices not been present. It is the change in the practical world of the nature of the competitive process which in our view dictates the need for a prices and incomes policy' (para. 20). This statement appears to be concerned with an alteration in the bargaining positions of unions and management. In the absence of excess demand in the economy as a whole, it would equally be exceedingly difficult for firms to pass on to the consumer price increases based solely on increases in labour costs. The Board has swallowed the cost-push theory of inflation hook, line and sinker. Further, one is left wondering whether the economy is not being propelled back to the imaginary nineteenth-century world of perfect competition which existed in only a few industries and in the mind of a few welfare economists. In an age when so many comparisons are being made with the advanced Mecca of the United States from which all good things must flow, the P.I.B. is no exception to this view with its references to the state of affairs in the United States labour market and the superiority of American management techniques. Indeed it is as though the whole American concept of workable competition had never been heard of or discussed. And yet, after perusing so many P.I.B. reports, one is driven at times to the conclusion that we are back in the land of the labour theory of value. For the second general report stated, almost without quali-fication, that 'prices themselves are determined largely by wages' (para. 40). Supply and demand analysis would no longer seem to be a useful tool in the realm of labour economics, and is cast out by the back door, while the old labour theory of value enters revitalised through the front door in the guise of productivity!

6   SUMMARY AND CONCLUSIONS

This chapter has been concerned with outlining the problems involved in modern discussions of wage and salary determination at the level of the individual plant, company or industry, and with the tools now used by economists to analyse wage and salary structures. It has shown the movement away from a straight analysis of individual wage rates to a concentration on the wage–salary structure, and the problems posed for the implementation of an incomes policy by the interrelatedness of many wage and salary structures. The introduction of official control, in the form first of the National Incomes Commission and then the National Board for Prices and Incomes, has led to a great extension of our knowledge of the manner in which such structures have come into being, and the various methods used to preserve and change them. Many, though by no means all, of the P.I.B.'s reports have been illuminating first excursions into this relatively new field of study for British economists, and they have shown the need for more detailed and current statistical information on this important topic. If the P.I.B., by its at times apparently inconsistent judgements on a succession of wage and salary references, has earned itself some hostility, its existence has nevertheless led to a greater knowledge of wage structures and their attendant problems in relation to overall wage and salary movements. (15)

I.   M.P.M.E.

14 The Engineering Industries: I
Product and Competitive Structure

1 THE SCOPE AND SIGNIFICANCE OF THE INDUSTRIES

The industries to be studied in this and the following chapter consist of mechanical and electrical engineering, transport equipment, and the miscellaneous group of metal-using industries. The engineering industries have been chosen for special attention within the whole field of manufacturing activity because of their importance, first in terms of numbers employed, and secondly because they produce a large proportion of the total output of capital goods. The future rate of growth of the economy depends largely on the efficiency with which they produce such goods, not only for the home market but also for the country's customers overseas. Their importance has grown considerably during the last half-century. In 1911, 9 per cent of the occupied population obtained their livelihood from the engineering trades; by 1961 the proportion had grown to 18 per cent. During the same period the share of the occupied population employed in manufacturing industry had grown from just under one-quarter to just over one-third of the total, so that the share of engineering employment in manufacturing has risen from about two-fifths to about one-half.

This shift in manpower resources is part of the general shift in resources towards the production of capital goods. This reflected a rising demand for capital-intensive methods of production in a growing economy, and was also reflected in the composition of British exports. As overseas territories developed their economies away from a straight dependence on the production of primary commodities, they turned first to the manufacture of simple consumer goods in an attempt to diversify their economies. Consequently the British economy reacted to a relative loss of trade in consumer goods by moving to the production and export of capital goods. It is in the furtherance of trade in this direction that the future of the British economy lies. Such a shift has occurred not only in trade with the primary producing countries, but specialisation has developed between manufacturing countries in the production of capital goods themselves. Since about 1950 international trade has been moving more and more in this direction (see Chapter 24). Hence the importance of a study of the engineering industries.

The wide definition of the engineering industries used in this chapter follows that of the Organisation for Economic Co-operation and Development (O.E.C.D.). From the standpoint of industrial relations, such a wide definition makes good sense. The Confederation of Shipbuilding and Engineering Unions extends its activities into the fields of shipbuilding, vehicle manufacture and aircraft production. To quote the Department of Employment and Productivity's handbook 'Industrial Relations', the term 'engineering industry' covers a 'complex group of activities concerned with the manufacture, installation, maintenance and repair of goods made mainly of metal, and the fabrication of articles of plastic material. It includes work as diverse as founding and forging, scientific instrument making, aircraft and motor vehicle manufacture, constructional engineering, lamp and electronic valve manufacture.' (1)

Towards the end of the 1960s the engineering industries (excluding transport equipment) accounted for somewhat over one-quarter of the total number of employees in manufacturing, and if employees in transportation and equipment are included, for nearly one-half. The industries are amongst the country's major exporters: throughout the 1960s they contributed over two-fifths of the value of British exports. Thus the fortunes of the engineering trades can be seen to affect domestic prosperity and the balance of payments, even if no reference is made to the effects of engineering efficiency on other industries. Once those effects are taken into account, there cannot be many activities that can escape being affected by what happens in engineering.

2 THE STRUCTURE OF THE INDUSTRY

Turning to a consideration of the structure of the engineering industries themselves, comparable data are available, for 1961, analysing the size of establishments and the number of employees, classified according to different sizes of establishment. In that year there were over 18,000 establishments in the engineering industries, of which 58 per cent were in the mechanical engineering and electrical engineering and goods trades, a further 15 per cent in the manufacture and assembly of transport equipment, and a further 27 per cent were to be found in the production of metal goods.

Measured by employment rather than by the number of establishments, the structure of the industry was as follows. The largest group, mechanical and electrical engineering, was about equally important whether measured by employment (56 per cent) or number of establishments (58 per cent). But the transport equipment trades were twice as important by employment (30 per cent) as by number of establishments (15 per cent), while roughly the opposite held for the metal-goods trades (15 per cent by employment and 27 per cent by number of establishments). (2)

The size distribution of establishments according to numbers employed is shown in Table 14.1. It is apparent that very large establishments (2,000 employees and over) predominate in the transport equipment trades, where they accounted for over half the total employment in those trades in 1961. A quarter of total employment in the mechanical and electrical engineering trades was to be found in very large establishments. In contrast, only one-twentieth of employment in the metal-goods trades was concentrated in very large establishments. In these trades there was heavy predominance of employment in establishments of medium size (100 and under 500 employees). Medium-sized establishments also accounted for the largest proportion of employment in the mechanical and electrical engineering trades, though only slightly more so than the very large ones. Concentration of employment amongst very large establishments was greater for the engineering industries than for the manufacturing industry as a whole, 31 per cent of employees compared with 21 per cent. A correspondingly smaller proportion of employment was to be found in medium-size establishments in the engineering industries, 24 per cent compared with 31 per cent in all manufacturing industries.

The product structure of the engineering industries is complicated. The majority of firms are multi-product firms, manufacturing a variety of final or intermediate products. This is especially the case in the mechanical engineering trades. A greater degree of product specialisation exists in the electrical engineering trades, so that there are specialist cable-makers, transformer manufacturers, generating-plant manufacturers and so on. As a result trade associations tend to be built up round particular products. Where product specialisation does exist, there is none the less a variety of products of the same type. The major motor-vehicle manufacturers produce both commercial and passenger vehicles and a considerable number of models of each. Few shipyards are completely specialist, and will fulfil contracts to build dry cargo vessels or tankers or carry out repair work. To a large extent the engineering industries are unified by occupational considerations. Their workpeople are essentially workers in metal, though plastics may also play an important part, as in the electronic trades. Dies, presses, lathes, drills and multi-purpose machine-tools are major pieces of capital plant and equipment. Much of the output of the engineering trades is sold to other manufacturers in the engineering sector of the economy. (For every £100 of net output in 1963, £55 of input came from within the engineering industry.) Indeed, before the final product emerges from the engineering sector it may have passed through the hands of three or four different manufacturers.

The productive processes of the engineering industries mirror the type of products they sell. By the very materials in which it works, its output is largely of a durable nature, whether made as capital plant for the manufacturer or as

Table 14.1 Size Distribution of Establishments in the Engineering Industries, 1961

Size of establishment (employees)	Engineering and electrical goods				Transport equipment				Metal goods not elsewhere specified				Total			
	Establishments		Employees		Establishments		Employees		Establishments		Employees		Establishments		Employees	
	Number	%	Number ('000)	%	Number	%	Number ('000)	%	Number	%	Number ('000)	%	Number	%	Number ('000)	%
2,000 and over	131	1.2	509	25.6	110	4.1	570	54.5	9	0.2	26	5.1	250	1.4	1,105	31.2
1,000 and under 2,000	249	2.3	351	17.7	113	4.2	158	15.1	43	0.9	58	11.3	405	2.2	567	16.0
500 ,, ,, 1,000	426	4.0	298	15.0	171	6.4	121	11.6	125	2.5	86	16.7	722	3.9	505	14.2
100 ,, ,, 500	2,427	22.7	518	26.1	610	22.7	130	12.4	931	18.5	186	36.2	3,968	21.6	834	23.5
25 ,, ,, 100	5,166	48.4	268	13.5	1,114	41.5	57	5.4	2,655	52.7	136	26.5	8,935	48.5	461	13.0
11 ,, ,, 25	2,285	21.4	41	2.1	568	21.1	10	1.0	1,272	25.3	22	4.3	4,125	22.4	73	2.1
	10,684	100.0	1,985	100.0	2,686	100.0	1,046	100.0	5,035	100.1	514	100.1	18,405	100.0	3,545	100.0

Source: 'Ministry of Labour Gazette' (Apr 1962).

final products for the consumer. For many of its products the methods most commonly used are small-batch or unit production. This means that production may be of simple units to customers' orders, or it may take the form of the production of technically complex units, the fabrication of large capital plant in stages, or the production of small batches. At the other end of the scale are establishments using either large-batch or mass-production techniques. This may take the form of the production of components in large batches which are subsequently assembled diversely, for example electronic valves; the production of large batches on an assembly-line technique, as with cars or radio and television sets; or straightforward mass production of screws, nuts and bolts, razor blades and the like. Process production, which is common to trades in the chemical industry, is not normally found in the engineering trades except in the extrusion processes of wire manufacture.

On account of the variety of productive processes to be found in the engineering industries, the scope for technical economies of scale varies widely between trades. In the manufacture of telephone and telegraph apparatus there is much scope for technical economies of scale, and the largest plants employ 5,000 people and upwards. In motor-vehicle manufacture too, the largest plants employ 5,000 people and upwards. Both trades are using essentially mass-production assembly-line techniques, where large reductions in costs are available as the length of run of the product increases. On the other hand in both shipbuilding and aircraft production the largest units equally employ upwards of 5,000 workers. Very large size of plant is here explained by the complexity of trades required to assemble a bulky final product. In both instances assembly has to be done on the spot, with the workers moving from job to job and from one final product to the next. Similarly the largest plants in the manufacture of electrical machinery, which follows the type of assembly in aircraft and shipbuilding, employ upwards of 4,000 workers. For 34 trades in the whole spread of engineering industries, the largest plants are distributed as shown in Table 14.2.

Table 14.2 Distribution of Plant Size among Engineering Trades

Size of largest plant (number of workers)	*Number of trades*
5,000+	4
2,000+ to 4,000+	6
1,000+ to 1,500+	10
500+ to 750+	8
Under 500	6

Source: Calculated from Board of Trade Census of Production, 1963.

The trades coming under the general heading of 'manufacture of metal goods' tend to have the smallest size of largest plant, though they are joined by engineers' small tools (somewhat over 400 workers) and watches and clocks (somewhat over 200 workers) from trades within the mechanical engineering category.

Despite the prevalence of substantial technical economies of scale, numerous small firms have an important role to play in the engineering industries. Some of these small enterprises and establishments are branch factories of large companies or subsidiaries. The remaining independent enterprises and establishments owe their existence to the jobbing nature of much of the engineering industry. In many trades the amount of capital required to set up in business is still small enough to permit almost complete freedom of entry to prospective entrepreneurs. Small establishments employing fewer than 100 workpeople proliferate in the metal-goods trades. The 'little maister' of the Sheffield cutlery trade still survives despite considerable pressure on profit margins. He is not alone; repair work for capital plant and equipment accounts for the existence of many small firms in the mechanical and electrical engineering industries. Subcontracting accounts for another large slice of small firms, whilst others maintain their existence by becoming specialist component manufacturers. The remainder are just small and have often failed to grow through poor management, lack of capital or lack of ambition and technical ability. Such various reasons account for the 13,000 small establishments in the engineering industries (being 70 per cent of the total). Their direct impact on total employment and output of the engineering industries is small, but their influence is not limited to their direct contribution to outpur and employment. Without the efficient operation of many specialist firms and component manufacturers, assembly work in some of the giant establishments would soon come to a halt. This becomes apparent every time an 'unofficial' strike in one of those component firms affects production in larger firms which depend on those components.

Overall the engineering sector contains both expanding and declining divisions. In the years between 1954 and 1962 the engineering industries increased their labour force much faster than the economy as a whole, +16 per cent compared with +6 per cent, and their share rose from 12½ per cent of total employment to 14 per cent (excluding always 'metal goods, not elsewhere specified'). Subsequently the labour force in engineering industries continued to rise, and towards the end of the 1960s was almost one-fifth higher than in 1954. None the less its expansion relative to other civil employment appears to have come to a halt in the 1960s. That applies overall, but hides the continuing expansion of mechanical and electrical goods manufacture, and a continuing contraction of shipbuilding and marine engineering.

3   REGIONAL SPECIALISATION

The engineering industries affect nearly everyone in the country. But they do not employ everyone, nor are they equally distributed throughout the country. In the 1960s one-third of all engineering workers were to be found in the South-east, one-fifth in the West Midlands and one-eighth in the North-west. No other region employed more than one-tenth of all engineering workers. The regional distribution roughly reflected the concentration of the industrial population between the regions, though all regions except the South-east, the West Midlands and the North-west had a smaller proportion of their working population engaged in engineering industries than they would have had if engineering employment were distributed between the regions in proportion to their overall working population.

There was considerable specialisation on different branches of the engineering industries, whether by region or by trade. By region, the South-east was more specialised in engineering than any of the other regions, and by trade, mechanical engineering provided the largest amount of employment. Table 14.3 provides an index of regional specialisation in individual sectors of the engineering industries. It is derived in the following manner. Percentages of each region's employment in a single engineering industry are calculated for the total engineering sector employment in that region. A similar percentage is calculated for Great Britain. This latter distribution is taken as a base (equal to 100), indicating the proportion each of its engineering regions would have if all regions had a distribution similar to Great Britain. The specialisation index compares the actual regional distribution of engineering industries employment with that for Great Britain. Thus the actual percentage for employment in the South-west region in the aircraft industry in June 1966 was 21.1 per cent of its total employment in all engineering industries, compared with 6.2 per cent in aircraft for Great Britain, giving a specialisation index of 340.3 (with 6.2 per cent put equal to 100).

Comparing the percentage employment of each industry in each region with a regional percentage distribution for all engineering industries yields an almost identical specialisation index. Were the percentage shares of each industry's employment in each region taken alone, it would be found that the South-east region had either the largest or second-largest share of employment in eight of the nine industries shown, and that mechanical engineering was the most important in eight regions out of ten. In neither case is this a measure of the relative importance to a region of employment in a particular industry. The index of regional specialisation in Table 14.3 provides such a measure. There was heavy specialisation or dependence (index of 200 and over) in 14 per cent of the

Table 14.3 Regional Specialisation in Engineering Industries, June 1966

(G.B. = 100)

Industry	South-east	East Anglia	South-west	West Midlands	East Midlands	Yorks and Humberside	North-west	Northern	Scotland	Wales
Mechanical engineering	101.7	113.2	106.2	67.3	137.2	128.4	89.9	103.4	130.1	67.8
Electrical engineering	128.9	129.4	70.2	74.1	75.4	43.0	124.1	121.1	63.2	117.1
Marine engineering	75.0	..	175.0	..	..	..	125.0	366.7	366.7	..
Shipbuilding and repair	66.7	115.4	176.9	..	12.8	74.4	107.7	453.8	294.9	105.1
Motor vehicles	106.3	140.5	47.6	179.4	29.4	65.9	85.7	19.1	56.3	107.9
Aircraft	91.9	24.2	340.3	62.9	204.8	61.3	132.3	14.5	79.0	32.3
Railway rolling stock	68.4	..	147.4	15.8	200.0	200.0	178.9	110.5	115.8	147.4
Other transport	37.5	..	112.5	287.8	375.0	..	77.3	..	..	..
Metal goods	68.7	28.7	36.0	200.0		166.0		48.0	62.0	148.7

Source: Derived from data in 'Ministry of Labour Gazette' (Mar 1967).

N.B. .. = nil or original employment figure under 1,000.

total number of industries distributed regionally (77), moderate dependence (index 125-200) in a further 21 per cent, minimal dependence (index of under 50) in 17 per cent and low dependence (index 50-75) in 20 per cent of the total. Taking each industry in turn, shipbuilding is important on a relative basis to the Northern and Scottish regions, as is the associated marine engineering; mechanical engineering is important to the East Midlands, Scotland and Yorkshire and Humberside; electrical engineering to East Anglia, the South-east, the North-west and the Northern regions; motor vehicles to the West Midlands and East Anglia; aircraft to the South-west and East Midlands; railway equipment to the East Midlands, Yorkshire and Humberside and the North-west; other transport equipment to the East and West Midlands; and metal goods to the West Midlands, Yorkshire and Humberside and Wales.

Specialisation in particular branches of the engineering trades brings its own advantages and problems. Advantages are gained in a region having a labour force which possesses particular technical knowledge and skills. The establishment of one metal-working trade has in the past frequently led to the establishment of ancillary trades, creating a process of industrial expansion and the development of major engineering areas. Perhaps more than in most other sectors of the economy, this interchange of parts and components gives rise to the establishment of new trades, whose function is to serve the major industries on which a given region depends for its economic existence. Too much dependence on one major industry and its ancillary trades brings its own dangers to the economic health of a region. Should a structural decline in demand arise, that region will have unemployment problems of greater intensity than would be the case had it achieved a smaller degree of specialisation. Structural changes in demand have had a marked effect on the post-war fortunes of the shipbuilding and repair industry, and consequently on marine engineering. The Northern region and Scotland have been particularly affected. On the other hand increasing specialisation and division of labour in the West Midlands enabled the motor-vehicle industry to expand its output of cars and lorries, reduce costs and build up an important export trade during the 1950s.

Since almost all the engineering trades are producing goods of a capital nature, they are subject to those fluctuations in output and employment attendant on the course of the trade cycle. Such cyclical fluctuations may affect individual trades in a variety of ways. The demand for motor vehicles has depended on government reactions to various post-war booms, with their concurrent balance-of-payments difficulties. The use of interest rates and hire-purchase restrictions has affected the motor-vehicle industry in particular, and some regions more than others. Such restrictions have also affected those regions and towns with a relatively high proportion of their labour force engaged in that part of the electrical engineering goods trade producing consumer durables, such as washing machines, spin-driers, refrigerators and vacuum cleaners. In like fashion, specific towns and regions have been affected by the reactions of overseas Governments to their own balance-of-payment problems. The imposition of tariffs and quotas by these Governments has often been aimed specifically at cutting down such imports of 'non-essential' consumer durables.

4   THE NATURE OF COMPETITION

The economic structure of the engineering industries is almost as complicated as that of the economy as a whole. Trade agreements concerning restrictions on entry, market-sharing and price determination abound, as references to the Monopolies Commission and the Restrictive Practices Court bear out. One-third of all inquiries by the Monopolies Commission to June 1967 were concerned with references coming within the broad field of the engineering industries, whilst a fifth of all cases heard before the Restrictive Practices Court up to the end of 1966 were also within this sector of the economy. There is a large number of trade associations operating within the framework of the engineering industries. In 1967 there were 287 trade associations in the country, of which 93 were connected with some branch of the engineering industry. (3) They ranged from the extensive Engineering Employers' Federation to the Cable Makers' Association (which was investigated by the Monopoly Commission), the Water Tube Boiler Makers' Association (which was investigated by the Restrictive Practices Court), to small associations within the group of trades coming under the heading of 'metal industries not elsewhere specified', such as the Scythe, Sickle and Hook Manufacturers' Association or the British Radio Valve Manufacturers' Association (within mechanical engineering). The Monopolies and Restrictive Practices Commission in its inquiry into collective discrimination of June 1955 contacted some 94 associations within the engineering trades out of a total of 290 trade associations, of which number almost two-thirds (60) made statements describing practices within the reference made to the Commission out of 164 such statements. A rather higher proportion (64 per cent) of trade associations belonging to engineering industries described the operation of restrictive practices than did non-engineering trade associations (53 per cent).

Chapter 11 has already described how the Monopolies Commission makes use of concentration ratios in assisting examination of trades referred to it by the Board of Trade. A number of the engineering trades referred to the Commission have been so referred mainly because they have possessed high concentration ratios. Table 14.4 indicates the number of engineering industry trades which had sales or employment concentration ratios of given size in 1958. Concentration ratios in that year were generally higher for the engineering trades than for

Table 14.4 Concentration Ratios in Engineering Trades, 1958
(number of trades)

Concentration ratio (per cent)	Sales	Employment
90 and over	1	1
80 and under 90	2	2
70 ,, ,, 80	1	1
60 ,, ,, 70	3	1
50 ,, ,, 60	5	4
40 ,, ,, 50	4	5
30 ,, ,, 40	8	9
20 ,, ,, 30	4	3
10 ,, , 20	4	7
Under 10	2	1
Total	34	34

Source: Board of Trade Census of Production, 1958.

non-engineering trades, the median sales concentration ratio for engineering trades being 38.8 per cent and the upper quartile 55.0 per cent, compared with 28.0 per cent and 48.3 per cent for non-engineering trades. Alternatively, half the engineering trades had a sales concentration ratio of over 38.8 per cent compared with 28.0 per cent for half the non-engineering trades. From Table 14.4 it will be seen that 7 engineering industry trades had a high sales concentration ratio, of 60 per cent and over. These trades were locomotives and track equipment, railway carriages and wagons, ordnance and small arms – all enterprises in the public as well as private sector of the economy – motor and pedal cycles, watches and clocks, telephone and telegraph apparatus, and cans and boxes. Of these, only telephone and telegraph apparatus had been investigated by the Monopolies Commission up to mid-1967. Generally, high concentration ratios are more typical of electrical engineering and electrical-goods trades than they are of mechanical engineering trades. Because of the technical nature of their productive processes, electrical engineering and electrical-goods trades tend to have large technical economies of scale, leading frequently to large-scale enterprises as well as establishments.

Of thirty-four reports of the Monopolies Commission published by mid-1967, ten were into engineering-goods trades or products. The case against one of these (the supply of aluminium semi-manufactures) was found not to have been made out, and in three other cases the Commission found that, although the practices complained of had been proved or that monopoly conditions existed, the result was not against the public interest. Six of the inquiries involved electrical engineering or electrical goods, namely electric lamps, insulated electric wire and cables, electrical and allied machinery and plant, electronic valves and cathode-ray tubes, electrical equipment for road vehicles, and electric wiring harness for motor vehicles. Seven out of thirty-five cases heard by the Restrictive Practices Court to the end of 1966 were also concerned with the engineering trades. In five cases the defendants proved to the satisfaction of the Court that their agreements were not against the public interest. One of the two cases lost was the establishment of minimum prices under the Association Transformer Manufacturers' agreement. The evidence presented in this case, plus that collected by the Monopolies Commission on the six references mentioned above, enables a fairly accurate and comprehensive picture to be built up of competition in the electrical engineering and electrical-goods trades.

Products dealt with by the Monopolies Commission and the Restrictive Practices Court in the electrical engineering and electrical-goods trades have fallen into three classes: heavy electrical equipment, electronic and light electrical equipment, and electrical equipment for motor vehicles. Between them they form a large part of the total output of the electrical engineering trades and enter into a good deal of the remainder of electrical engineering products. In many instances trade associations play an important role in arranging and enforcing the observation of agreement between manufacturers. Agreements concerning prices have been a major feature of most agreements in this part of the engineering sector of the economy, with clauses relating to market-sharing generally taking a less prominent place.

The heavy end of the electrical engineering industry has different technological features and conditions of production from those existing in electronics and other forms of light electrical manufacture. A good deal of information about technical production conditions and pricing policy in the heavy electrical equipment trades can be gained from a study of the Monopolies Commission's report on 'The Supply and Exports of Electrical and Allied Machinery and Plant' (1957), and the case brought against the Associated Transformer Manufacturers' Association in the Restrictive Practices Court (1961). Trade associations are of considerable importance in the pricing policy of manufacturers of alternators and transformers. In this trade the Commission found that there were agreements to preserve common minimum prices below which members of particular associations would not quote, thus establishing a form of level tendering. Although the principal trade association, the British Electrical Appliance Manufacturers' Association (B.E.A.M.A.), was not strictly concerned with the commercial policy of its members, there existed 'trade' groups to which the major manufacturers were signatories. These were Associated Electrical Industries Ltd (through their subsidiaries British Thomson-Houston and Metropolitan-Vickers), English Electric Co. Ltd, General Electric Co. and C.A. Parsons Ltd. Because of the nature of the output in this field, few economies of scale are available on a technical level, though research and development economies are important. Alternators and transformers, being essentially very large capital-goods units, are most frequently built to consumers' specifications, and competition takes place as much through differences in design as through price variations. After the adverse judgement by the Restrictive Practices Court in 1961, agreements relating to the pricing of transformers have been abandoned. Although price competition has ostensibly been restored, non-price competition probably remains the most important element in the securing of orders. Despite the evidence to be found in the report of the Monopolies Commission and the findings of the Restrictive Practices Court, there is still room for considerable doubt regarding the suitability of price competition in the market for heavy electrical equipment, where firms are faced with essentially one major purchaser, namely the Central Electricity Generating Board (C.E.G.B.). (4)

The market for heavy electrical equipment is essentially an oligopoly situation, with a very small number of large producers of alternators, turbines and switchgear facing a monopsonist in the guise of the nationalised C.E.G.B. In the case of large transformers, where there are some twelve producers, the power of the C.E.G.B. to force price concessions is correspondingly greater. The remaining part of the market in heavy electrical equipment lies in the production of cables and wire. This trade was found by the Monopolies Commission (1952) to be dominated by the Cable Makers' Association (C.M.A., founded 1899) and the Covered Conductors' Association (C.C.A., founded 1928). There is considerable scope for technical economies of scale in the production of wire and cable, though covered conductors in particular have been subject to rapid technological development and have a large size range, thus cutting down the scope for such economies. Common prices, conditions of sale and exclusive buying rebates, and the operation of a quota system for sharing the market have been characteristics of these two associations. But they have also established a successful quality control in the face of falling standards, through price and quality cutting, in times of trade depression. In the output of submarine telephone and telegraph cables, land telephone cable and mains cable, one firm, British Insulated Callender's Cables Co. (B.I.C.C.), has tended to dominate. Countervailing power to the C.M.A. and the C.C.A. has been exercised by monopoly or near-monopoly buyers for all three products, namely Cable and Wireless Co., government departments and British European Airways (B.E.A.).

The light electrical engineering industries which were subjected to Monopolies Commission inquiries covered the output of electronic valves and cathode-ray tubes (1957) and electric lamps (1951 and 1968). In the case of electronic valves, the Commission found that common prices were established by the British Radio Valve Manufacturers' Association (1926) for retail sale at prices higher than those listed for first equipment. Apart from renting and relay companies, countervailing power is not strong, though different prices and discounts were allowed to various classes of customers classified according to minimum turnover levels. The Electric Lamp Manufacturers' Association (E.L.M.A.), whose members produced about 60 per cent of the total output of lamps in the United Kingdom in the late 1940s was established in 1933 to protect the interests of members at a time of severe economic depression. In a research-based industry, agreements include the pooling of patents, fixed retail prices and terms, exclusive dealing and an attack on non-signatories to the association's agreements by the withholding of lamp components. (5) The 1948 Lamp Agreement, which superseded the Phoebus Agreement of 1925 (ended during the 1939-45 war), was signed by major members of E.L.M.A. and Philips' Gloeilampenfabrieken N.V. of Holland. It provided for the sharing of international markets outside the United States through quota arrangements, and for local quotas based on the ratio of a member's sales to the sales of all members in a given territory. The common price and quota system, taken together, was intended to form the basis of a 'system of regulated competition' to ensure stability in the industry.

Another branch of the engineering industry, that of motor-vehicle components, accounts for large sales of electrical equipment. The Commission has made two investigations, first into the supply of electrical equipment for motor vehicles, and second into the supply of electric wiring harnesses for motor vehicles. In the case of electrical components, the Commission disclosed a dominance of the markets for such accessories by four firms, Chloride Electrical Storage Co., Champion Sparking Plug Co., Joseph Lucas Industries Ltd and S. Smith and Sons (England) Ltd. The only trade association of any importance in this field was the British Starter Battery Association. In 1960 Champion supplied 71 per cent of the market for sparking plugs; Chloride supplied 42 per cent of the market for batteries; Lucas supplied 79 per cent of ignition coils, 95 per cent of dynamos, 79 per cent of windscreen-wiper motors and 85 per cent of lamps; and Smiths supplied 76 per cent of heater devices and 65 per cent of instruments. In the initial supply market some countervailing power to these monopoly situations was supplied by the motor-vehicle assembly firms, but none existed in the replacement market. The supply of electric wiring harness for vehicles was effectively controlled by three firms: Rist's Wires and Cables Ltd, a wholly owned subsidiary of J. Lucas, supplied 51 per cent of the market in

1961-5, with Ward and Goldstone Ltd supplying 26 per cent and Ripaults Ltd 23 per cent. The Commission found (1966) that there was no evidence to suggest that Rist's was quoting uneconomic prices in order to drive its competitors out of business, and that adequate countervailing power existed from the motor-vehicle assembly firms.

The structure of the electrical-goods branch of the engineering industries has been considered in some detail because of the variety of competitive situations which it exhibits. Its products cover plant sold by a strong trade association, covering generating plant and equipment, to a nationalised industry with strong countervailing bargaining power. There are large manufacturers in motor-vehicle assembly, small enough in number to act as oligopsonists, facing monopoly sellers of components. Finally there are goods such as electric lamps, sold to the final consumer, who has no bargaining power with which to counteract conditions of sale imposed by strong trade associations. In all these respects the degree of competition exhibited by the various markets in electrical goods mirrors that existing in the engineering industries as a whole. The few large aircraft manufacturers face strong buyers at home, in the shape of British Overseas Airways Corporation (B.O.A.C.) and B.E.A., and suffer effective competition through the international market for aircraft. Motor-vehicle manufacturers form an oligopoly element in the home market, competing marginally on a price basis but largely on a 'quality' basis within a given price range, whilst being protected from the worst of foreign competition by tariff barriers. Here no countervailing power exists on the part of the individual consumer, each of whom must take his pick from amongst the products offered by a few giants. Mechanical engineering, like electrical engineering, is frequently supplying its products to corporate users, many of which are large. Restrictive practices do not appear to have been as widespread, or affected the final consumer so much, as in electrical goods. Furthermore the large corporate consumers possess adequate technical knowledge, and frequently sufficient bargaining power, to protect themselves.

5   MERGERS AND RATIONALISATION OF THE INDUSTRY'S PRODUCT STRUCTURE

(a)   Pre-1939

Most of the engineering trades suffered from the prolonged trade depression of the 1920s and 1930s. Their reaction was as protectionist as that of most industries. It included self-protection, such as the formation of trade associations and resort to restrictive practices, and 'rationalisation' through mergers and amalgamations. It also included protection conferred by the

Government, which would turn a blind eye to contraventions of common law rules in restraint of trade and gave tariff protection to the motor-car industry throughout and to practically all engineering trades in the 1930s. That this cut short an incipient movement in world trade towards an international exchange of manufactured goods for manufactured goods, and an international exchange of engineering products for engineering products in particular, may be a matter for retrospective regret — especially once the benefits of such exchange could be observed in the freer trading conditions of the 1950s and 1960s. At the time, however, when all the major countries became increasingly protectionist, industries everywhere sought protection of their home markets. Overseas competition was to be kept in check so that domestic self-protection could become effective.

If protection was the prime motive of 'rationalisation' in most of the engineering industries, that was not always the case in the expanding sectors. Even in those days there were growth industries. These included some of the major engineering trades, namely motor vehicles, electrical engineering and to a lesser extent aircraft. Their prime motive for 'rationalisation' would have been to take advantage of the economies of scale. But irrespective of whether rationalisation was due to protectionist or technical considerations, the reorganisation involved normally led to horizontal integration. In other words, firms at the same stage of production were brought under one management (amalgamation and mergers), or managements of separate firms would act in concert (trade associations and restrictive practices).

The self-defensive motive in the creation of mergers and amalgamations was a reaction to falling profits, and consisted in a rationalisation process aimed at closing down uneconomic units which could barely cover prime costs of production. This affected particularly the trades which were declining, such as shipbuilding and some branches of mechanical engineering (for example textile machinery). The establishment of trade associations during this period was aimed at maintaining prices through the sharing of (shrinking) markets and keeping out possible new entrants.

The other rationalisation motive was the existence of technical economies of scale in the expanding branches of the industry, especially in the manufacture and assembly of motor vehicles and in the electrical engineering trades. New production methods and the application of research to the development of new products, or improved models of the old, made a rapid achievement of greater size important. Mergers and amalgamations were believed to be one quick way to attain such a size, since plant and equipment could be organised on a more rational basis and such establishments within a company could specialise to a greater extent than before. Some of the main mergers and amalgamations were in the field of vehicle assembly and production. Probably the most significant was the Morris–Wolseley amalgamation in 1927, which incidentally marked the withdrawal of Vickers from the motor-car trade. (6) This was a rapid way of securing what was, at that time, a large, modern and integrated plant. In 1928 Humber, which was in financial difficulties, merged with the Hillman Motor Co. to form the basis of the Rootes Group. Acquisitions were also made by the motor-car manufacturers during this period to secure supplies of components. Whilst the history of mergers in the 1920s was dominated by the Morris acquisitions and amalgamations, that of the 1930s was dominated in turn by the Rootes Group. Rootes Bros entered the car-manufacturing industry proper in 1932 by acquiring the Humber, Hillman, Commer Group, followed in 1934 by Karrier Motors Ltd and in 1935 by Sunbeam Motor Car Co. and Clement-Talbot Ltd, all of which were rescued from bankruptcy. In general, the mergers of the 1920s and 1930s involved the purchase of old-established companies which had run into financial difficulties. Between 1922 and 1939 the number of car firms had fallen from 96 to 20. (7) Output, however, rose. There had been a movement towards fewer but more efficient firms.

The 1920s also saw the creation of Associated Electrical Industries Ltd, as a result of a merger between two former American companies, Metropolitan-Vickers Electrical Co. and British Thomson-Houston Co. (1928). 'Metro-Vick', originally the British Westinghouse Electrical and Manufacturing Co., established in 1899, was a British subsidiary of the American Westinghouse Electrical Manufacturing Co. This subsidiary was sold to the Metropolitan Carriage, Wagon and Finance Co. in 1917, which was in turn acquired by Vickers Ltd. The British Thomson-Houston Co. (B.T.H.) originated as the United Kingdom selling agent of the Thomson-Houston Electric Co., which in 1892 amalgamated with the Edison General Electric Co. to form the American General Electric Co. The merger which took place between the English Metropolitan-Vickers and the American B.T.H. Co. involved the sale of the American company, still under the wing of the (American) General Electric Co., to Metropolitan-Vickers by the issue of shares in Metropolitan-Vickers in exchange for B.T.H., the name of Metropolitan-Vickers being changed to that of a new holding company, Associated Electrical Industries Ltd. (8) Much more so than the car mergers referred to above, the Metro-Vick-B.T.H. merger appears to have been due to a strong body of opinion, current in the 1920s, that the growing competition from American and European combines, especially in the field of chemicals and electrical engineering, required the creation of equally large corporations in British industry in order to combat it. This motive also inspired the Imperial Chemical Industries (I.C.I.) merger in 1926.

One other example from the inter-war years of the growth of a company via acquisitions is Joseph Lucas (Industries) Ltd, a company straddling the motor-vehicle and electrical-goods industries. In the pre-war period Lucas acquired twelve companies which were competitors or potential competitors in its own line of business. (9) As in the case of the motor-car assembly firms, Lucas stated that its competitors were in financial difficulties following the collapse of the post 1914-18 war boom. Its two principal competitors – C.A. Vandevell Ltd and Rotax (Motor Accessories) Ltd – were thus acquired in 1926.

(b) Post-1945

(i) *Motor vehicles*. In the improved trading conditions following the Second World War there would seem to have been less need for protection. Moreover, as shown in Chapter 11, monopolies and restrictive practices came under public surveillance. Nevertheless the merger movement continued in a number of engineering industries, such as aircraft and shipbuilding. But the largest number and the longest series of mergers and take-overs occurred in the motor-vehicle and electrical engineering industries. At the end of the 1960s there was only one large, completely British-owned motor-vehicle firm left, and competition was assured only through the existence of American-owned firms operating in the United Kingdom and through imports of foreign-made vehicles. The merger movement in the motor-vehicle industry is the subject of the present subsection. Electrical engineering will be considered in subsection (ii) below. It will emerge that the merger movement in the motor-vehicle industry was of a somewhat defensive, if not altogether protectionist, nature, while that in electrical engineering was more motivated by economies of scale.

Both British- and American-owned vehicle-assembly firms have taken over motor-body manufacturers. The motive behind this move in the direction of vertical integration has been to secure direct control over supplies of components. This was the case with the British Motor Corporation's purchases of Fisher and Ludlow and of Pressed Steel, and also with Ford's purchase of Briggs Motor Bodies.

More in line with pre-1939 horizontal integration is the purchase of competitors. The aim is to reduce pressure on profit margins, and this is meant to be achieved through rationalisation of productive capacity once it is under one management. This motive predominated amongst the British-owned companies, though the above example of British Motor Corporation (B.M.C.) purchases of component producers shows that it was not exclusive.

The principal merger during the immediate post-war period was that between Austin Motor Co. and Morris Motors in 1952 to form B.M.C. The acquisition by B.M.C. of Jaguar in late 1965, and of Pressed Steel in early 1966, gave rise to a major capital reorganisation of B.M.C. to form British Motor Holdings (B.M.H.). Following this capital reorganisation, some consolidation of the company's body-production facilities was attempted. Thus, to quote the 1966 annual report, 'Pressed Steel Co. Ltd, Fisher and Ludlow Ltd, Nuffield Metal Products

Ltd, Morris Motors Ltd, bodies branch, have all been integrated into a single organisation named Pressed Steel Fisher Ltd. At the same time the engineering and domestic equipment activities of Fisher and Ludlow Ltd were separately reorganised under two new companies, namely Fisholow Products Ltd and Fisher-Bendix Ltd'. It was expected that this simplification would increase efficiency and improve the yield of these companies.

The Leyland Corporation entered the 1960s as a firm of commercial vehicle and bus makers. It leaves the 1960s at the head of the British motor-car industry, with interests in all its sectors from light passenger cars to heavy trucks. Early in the decade it entered the field of passenger-car production through the acquisition of Standard Triumph International. Subsequently it broadened its base in commercial vehicles through a merger with Associated Commercial Vehicles. But when B.M.C. acquired Jaguar, and so entered a specialised upper-income passenger-car market, Leyland would not be left out of any field covered by a British-owned rival. It countered through the acquisition of the Rover Company, which also specialises in the upper-income passenger-car market. In short, Leyland entered wherever B.M.C. was, whilst maintaining its lead in commercial vehicles.

Internally there was to be rationalisation in the combined Leyland and Rover group. Both the Leyland and Rover documents about the respective mergers referred to the concentration of manufacturing activities into larger units. As the Rover document stated, 'Competition continues to increase and as the industry's products became more and more sophisticated, the necessity to achieve increased efficiency and economies in engineering, tooling, production, buying, marketing and servicing becomes increasingly apparent. Moreover the industry is dependent on world-wide markets which today necessitate foreign assembly and manufacturing plants which can only reach their true potential when units are large.' The Leyland document stressed in turn the advantages to be derived from economies of scale in 'engineering, research and development, in group purchasing power, [and] in selection and training of personnel'.

The culmination of these post-war series of mergers and take-overs in the British motor-vehicle industry was the formation of the British-Leyland Motor Corporation in 1968. The stages in the formation of this company are shown in Fig. 14.1. This merger was assisted by the announcement, early in 1968, of a loan of £25 million by the Industrial Reorganisation Corporation (I.R.C.) to facilitate speedy rationalisation and development of the new giant company. One of the principal objectives in setting up the I.R.C. in December 1966 had been to promote take-overs and amalgamations which would cut out wasteful duplication of manufacturing and other facilities and permit the exploitation of economies of scale. These aims were to be realised in the motor-vehicle industry. Sales of just under £1 million for 1967-8 were thought to improve the relative

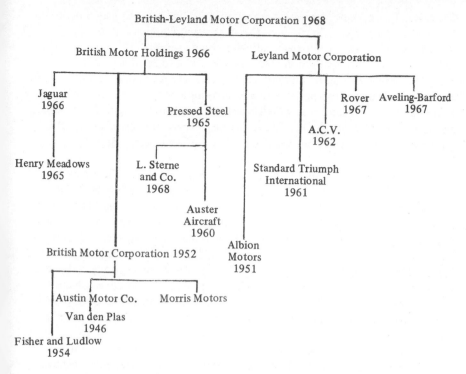

Fig. 14.1 The formation of British-Leyland Motor Corporation
Dates refer to time of merger or acquisition or
establishment of new company.

standing of British motor-vehicle manufacturers compared with the giant American firms of General Motors Corporation and Ford Motor Co. Sales of the new company, however, are still only one-eighth of those of General Motors, one-quarter of those of Ford, and less than half those of Chrysler. In terms of sales the new company is a little smaller than the German Volkswagenwerke and slightly larger than the Italian company Fiat, but almost twice the size of the French company Renault.

Since the amalgamation a good deal of reorganisation has taken place. The new company has seven divisions. They are the Austin Morris division, a specialist car division, the track and bus division, the Pressed Steel Fisher division, a construction division (which includes Aveling-Barford and Scammell Lorries Ltd) and lastly an overseas division to concentrate the overseas activities of the whole company. As part of the rationalisation process, the company sold

Fisher-Bendix, making domestic appliances, to Parkinson Cowan Ltd in July 1968, in exchange for securities in the purchasing company. A further step in this direction was the sale of the vending-machine interests of Fisholow Products to Guest, Keen and Nettlefolds Ltd towards the end of the year. In order to assist the reorganisation, £15 million of the £25 million I.R.C. loan was taken up in April 1968. In all, the post-war amalgamations amongst the British car manufacturers may be regarded as a defensive move against foreign, and especially American, competition in the home market, where the share of the British-owned car firms' sales had been falling as a proportion of total sales.

(ii) *Electrical engineering and electrical goods.* Some major post-war mergers and acquisitions in the electrical engineering trades are shown in Figs 14.2 and 14.3. The industry's product structure comprises several main divisions. They are the conventional capital-goods division, consisting chiefly of heavy electrical plant and equipment; domestic appliances such as cookers, space heaters, refrigerators and washing machines; electronic goods, which straddle the capital-goods and consumer-goods markets, based essentially on valves, transistors and cathode-ray tubes; and electrical equipment for motor vehicles. As noted in Chapter 10, technical economies of scale are of considerable significance in this sector of the engineering industries. Economies in research and development are also of importance. These factors in turn make for a large size of enterprise.

The major mergers and amalgamations in electrical engineering during the post-war period have finally resulted in the formation of an electrical engineering firm more comparable in size with the major American and European electrical firms. This was the formation in 1968 of the General Electric-English Electric Co. (G.E.-E.E. Co.). In terms of sales this newly formed company is larger than the German firms Siemens and A.E.G. Telefunken, though it is rather smaller than the Dutch firm Philips. The G.E.-E.E. Co. is roughly the size of the second and third United States electrical firms, Radio Corporation of America (R.C.A.) and Westinghouse, both in terms of sales and capital employed. The manner in which the G.E.-E.E. Co. was built up is illustrated in Fig. 14.2. The initial stage in the process was the take-over by the General Electric Co. of Associated Electrical Industries Ltd. The I.R.C. has also had a hand in some of the mergers and amalgamations leading to the creation of this new British giant electrical engineering firm. It assisted in the acquisition by the English Electric Co. of Elliott-Automation Ltd, for which it put up £15 million in June 1967. It also backed the G.E.C. take-over of A.E.I. in September 1967, though financial backing was not provided for this merger. The final G.E.C.-E.E. Co. merger was also supported by the I.R.C. £5 million of the earlier loan to English Electric was repaid and the terms of the remaining £10 million renegotiated.

In the events leading up to the G.E.C.-E.E. Co. merger, some reorganisation

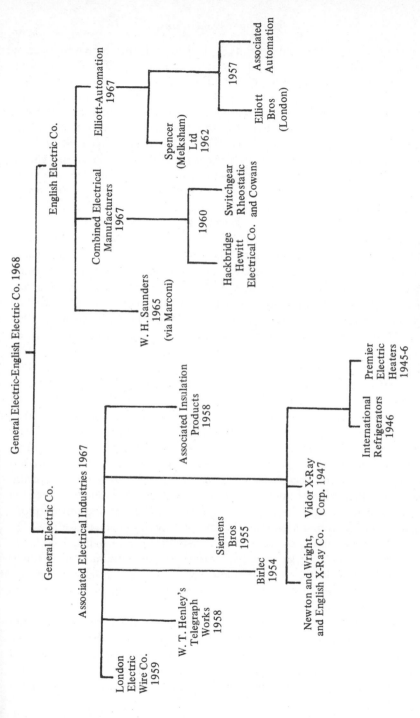

Fig. 14.2 The formation of General Electric-English Electric Co.

of capacity in switchgear and generating plant took place. There were sales by both G.E.C. and A.E.I. of assets in the turbo-generator field to C. A. Parsons. This company in turn merged its own interests in generating plant with the firm of A. Reyrolle, to form Reyrolle-Parsons in 1968. This new firm also merged with another electrical firm, Bruce Peebles, in March 1969, the I.R.C. offering a standby credit of up to £4 million to assist the operation. Such mergers have served to bring further rationalisation to the manufacture of generating plant. This concentration of turbo-generator capacity has strengthened the United Kingdom's ability to obtain major export contracts for such plant in the face of strong international competition. The reorganisation of transformer manufacturers was also prompted by the I.R.C., and involved deals between Reyrolle-Parsons and the A.E.I., English Electric and G.E.C. branches of G.E.-E.E. Co.

Mergers, acquisitions and important interconnections between three large companies supplying domestic appliances and radio and T.V. sets — Thorn Electrical Industries, E.M.I. and A.E.I. — are shown in Fig. 14.3. The formation of joint selling subsidiaries is indicated by arrows pointing away from the parent concerns to the subsidiaries. Arrows pointing to the parent concerns indicate acquisitions. Most of the joint concerns shown have been set up between 1957 and 1967. It would appear from Fig. 14.3 that a fair amount of rationalisation has proceeded without major mergers between these leading companies.

The electronics industry can be subdivided into two major sectors. One consists of telecommunications and computers, where capital costs are heavy and American competition severe. The other consists of radio, T.V. and domestic appliances. In the latter sector there is competition between British-owned firms and British subsidiaries of the Dutch Philips Lamp Co.; in the latter sector entry is still relatively easy, especially for small firms starting the manufacture of specialised components, for the amount of capital required is relatively small. New entrants to the electronics section of the industry have also come from the diversification of already existing firms in the electrical engineering industry into the production of electronic goods. Pressure on profit margins, resulting from a decline in the rate of growth of demand for new T.V. receivers, occurred during the early part of the 1960s, and this may have led to some 'overcrowding'. Perhaps this will ease with the introduction of colour television. The first half of the 1960s also saw a boom in demand for transistor radios, and its slackening-off during the second half of the decade has led to pressure on margins for this product.

There has been increasing competitive pressure in the telecommunications and capital-goods section of electronics, but the expansion of this section of the industry has been greater than in any other. The increasing importance of capital goods to the electronics industry may be seen from their rising share in the value of output of electronic goods. Between 1954 and 1964 the proportion of the

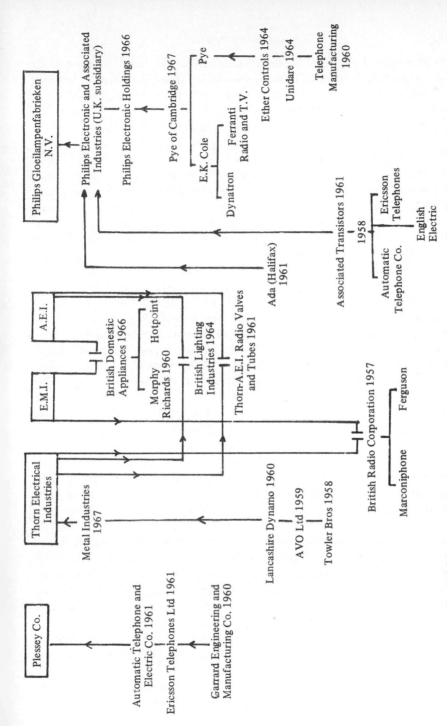

Fig. 14.3 *Important acquisitions, mergers and interconnections in radio, telecommunications and domestic appliances*

value of output of electronic goods going to defence fell from over one-quarter to about one-fifth, that of consumer products fell from nearly half to less than one-third, whilst that for capital equipment rose from less than one-fifth to over one-third; valves and transistors rose from 2 per cent to 6 per cent and components from 6 per cent to 8 per cent of the total. (10) The overall value of the output of electronic goods more than doubled during this decade.

In the home market, the telecommunications section of the electronics industry is dominated by the Telecommunication Engineering and Manufacturing Association. Total G.P.O. (a monopoly buyer) expenditure for the period 1963-8 has been almost wholly divided between a group of seven companies, G.E.C.-E.E. Co. (via the G.E.C. parent and A.E.I.), Standard Telephones and Cables (a subsidiary of the American International Telephone and Telegraph Corporation), Phoenix Telephone and Electric Works (owned by a consortium of the main telecommunications firms), Plessey Co., and its two subsidiaries, Automatic Telephone and Electric Co. and Ericsson Telephones, with Plessey and subsidiaries supplying about 40 per cent of the total. Overseas markets are rather different. They are less assured since there is no single buyer and there are more competitors. Price may become of greater importance in determining sales. As will be argued in Chapter 24, this applies to some export markets but not to all. The newer products tend to sell best in wealthy markets, which are quality-conscious rather than price-conscious. There may thus be a case for further amalgamations amongst British firms if this helps to reap economies of scale in research and development. At the time of writing, the question is not yet resolved in relation to this particular industry, but the subject is under investigation. (11)

The more immediate increases in demand for electronic goods, however, has been in the industrial equipment field. This kind of equipment may itself be considered under two headings — industrial process-control systems, and the demand for business computers sold as part of a broad range of office equipment. Competition in the case of the latter type of equipment has become exceedingly severe during the 1960s, especially from American companies such as Honeywell and International Business Machines (I.B.M.). This has already led to some rationalisation and reorganisation of the British firms in the industry, helped by government aid. International Computers and Tabulators took over Powers-Samas, and Ferranti sold its own computer business to I.C.T. in exchange for a 10 per cent holding of I.C.T.'s equity capital.

International Computer Holdings (a reorganised I.C.T.) is probably still the second-largest data-processing firm in the Western world following I.B.M., and the largest in Europe. In the mid-1960s it held around 8 per cent of the market for punched-card machines and around one-third of that for computers. The introduction of 'second-generation' transistorised computers led to a collapse of the punched-card market. It seems doubtful whether the British firms, and I.C.T. in particular, moved out of the tabulating market and into the computer market fast enough. By 1966-7 a third generation of large adaptable computers had come to the fore. From the cost of production standpoint, the movement away from tabulators to computers was a move from repeat orders to an 'one-off' type of production not conducive to the lowering of costs. With the 'third generation' of computers a good deal of success in competition now lies in the provision of 'software' (being the devising of systems which will extend the range of computer applications and the speed with which this may be accomplished).

Since there has been increased American, and especially I.B.M., competition in this field, companies which intend to stay in the market need to organise teams of specialists aiming at co-operation with their principal industrial customers. This particular field has been pioneered by Elliott-Automation. The Elliott philosophy has been to persuade firms to automate on a departmental basis, wherever use could be made of a computer, and to link these up at some future date. I.B.M. philosophy, in contrast, has been aimed at the installation of one large computer. So far as competition between British firms is concerned, it has been suggested (12) during 1965 that the main challenge to I.C.T. was likely to come from the English Electric Leo-Marconi series, but that English Electric's main difficulty lay in establishing itself as a powerful marketing force. The passing of Elliott-Automation into the English Electric fold in the middle of 1967, with its experience of preparing systems for industrial use, was a further and natural move in the British rationalisation process. This was needed all the more to meet American competition in continental Europe, coming about in part from the American General Electric Co.'s link with Machines Bull of France and the major domination of the continental European markets, in the mid-1960s by I.B.M.

Major new fields in the industrial application of computers have been in traffic-control systems for airlines and the handling of import and export cargoes in major docks, as well as payroll preparation (13) and the automatic control of steelworks (as instanced by an order to A.E.I. Automation at the end of 1964 by Dorman Long for its new universal plate mill at Lackenby). This latter was built under licence from the American G.E.C., and illustrates one facet of that company's move into the European market. In short, there were both offensive and defensive motives in the reorganisation of the electronics trades.

(iii) *Machine-tools.* Within the mechanical engineering sector of the engineering industries, the post-war period, especially from 1960 onwards, has seen mergers, acquisition and resultant rationalisation of the machine-tool trade. This rationalisation follows the report of the Machine Tool Advisory Council (M.T.A.C.)

subcommittee, which considered the implications for the United Kingdom of a report on the machine-tool industry in Western Europe. (14) This report recommended the rapid adoption of mass-production techniques in the machine-tool trades of Western Europe, and the standardisation of machine-tools so as to provide efficient machinery to user industries, at a price low enough to compete successfully with 'other mass producers of machine-tools'. Although the sub-committee of the M.T.A.C. did not agree with the conclusions of that report, the investigation did lead to some reorganisation of the trade. Despite the advantages of the large number of small firms in one-off type of production (15) such firms are unable to finance research and development on the scale required to market products of advanced design.

One of the principal factors militating against relatively long runs has been the highly cyclical nature of demand for the trade's products. Perhaps more than any other trade within a sector of manufacturing industry producing capital goods, the machine-tool trade suffers from fluctuations in demand from those trades which are themselves making capital goods or, in the case of motor vehicles, durable consumer goods.

The solution to the two main problems facing the trade during the first half of the 1960s lies in the realm of finance, and neither solution is available to small firms without considerable outside aid. The first involves production of machine-tools for stock. This implies a more standardised form of design and fewer models built to specific user requirements, and it also involves finance for stock holdings. Finance for the purpose of holding stocks has been provided by the Ministry of Technology. The second also involves the need for strong teams of designers and production engineers, so that machine-tools may be built for sale in the export field and for sale to home users who would otherwise buy imported machine-tools. Smaller firms are simply unable to pay salaries adequate to secure the qualified scientists and design engineers required to keep abreast of world competitors.

The need for stronger units in the machine-tool trade was stressed by the Minister of Technology in a statement to the House of Commons in 1965, and it was stated that the Machine Tool Trades Association would attempt to foster concentration and amalgamation. (16) Some strengthening of the trade has already taken place through a number of mergers and acquisitions, and also through greater attention in design being paid to consumer requirements for machine-tools of advanced type. During 1965 Charles Churchill Ltd, which celebrated its centenary in that year, was taken over by Tube Investments, the intention being to provide greater backing in the matter of finance and research and development. Only in the previous year Charles Churchill had itself pur-chased the gear-machine manufacturing section of David Brown Co. Inter-national Twist Drill was acquired in the early 1960s by Tap and Die

Corporation. The latter has since been taken over by Clarkson International.

One of the largest series of acquisitions, however, was that made by Staveley Industries Ltd, which bought Craven Bros Ltd of Manchester in 1965, Asquith Machine Tool Corporation in 1966 (against a rival bid from B. Elliott), Kendall and Gents, and the Watford-based United Kingdom subsidiary of the American firm Lapointe Machine Tool Co. (Mass.), also in 1966, and H. W. Kearns and Co. in 1967. The Staveley Industries document relating to the offer for Asquith referred to the growing complexity of machine-tools, expensive negotiations for selling machine-tools on a world-wide basis and the cost of essential research and development work. This was the purchase by a large firm, already spending considerable sums of money on research and development, of a company with a highly effective world-wide selling organisation, which Staveley Industries at the time lacked. With these acquisitions, Staveley Industries Ltd was approaching the size of Alfred Herbert Ltd, which had assets of £38 million in 1968-9. Not only is the latter company the largest machine-tool maker in the United Kingdom, but it is also probably the largest in Western Europe. It also ranks as one of the biggest machine-tool manufacturers in the world.

Towards the end of the last big take-over period in the machine-tool industry, seven large organisations began to emerge. (17) These are Alfred Herbert Ltd, Staveley Industries Ltd, the machine-tool division of John Brown Ltd, B. Elliott Ltd, the George Cohen 600 Group Ltd, Tube Investments Ltd and the American subsidiary, Cincinnati Milling Ltd. Between them these firms employ about half the industry's labour force and produce almost two-thirds of its output. Further mergers might serve to strengthen the industry's competitive power and aid rationalisation of its output.

(c)   The Effects on Labour

Since the purpose of many of the post-war mergers and amalgamations has been to rationalise the product structure of the trades where these have taken place, the efficient reorganisation of firms will inevitably involve some redundancies amongst workpeople. Such redundancies have been the subject of a number of studies, including some which have also involved unemployment resulting from technological change. (18) There have also been a number of international studies of the effects of redundancies, some of which have also been concerned with technological factors. (19)

Redundancies brought about by take-overs and mergers are not always the result of technological change. The reasons for the closure of particular plants following the take-over of a firm may be a complicated mixture of technological factors and some which are reorganisations in response to market forces. The latter occur when the acquisitor firm simply decides to rationalise the product structure of the combined firm by cutting out peripheral activities, or activities which are resulting in losses. Such market forces explain, in part, the closure of the A.E.I. works at Woolwich between 1968 and 1969, following the acquisition of A.E.I. by G.E.C. Here redundancies were on a large scale. Again, in electrical engineering, and also in south-east London, around 2,000 workers were affected by the closure of C. A. Parsons' Erith works during 1969-70.

Steps taken to modify the impact of redundancies caused either by technological change or market forces include advance warning to unions and workers of an impending lay-off and the introduction of severance pay under the Redundancy Payments Act, 1965, with payments graduated according to length of service. There has also been supplementation of unemployment benefit, with earnings-related benefits, during the first six months of unemployment. Further external measures include government retraining schemes under the Industrial Training Act, 1964. Separately from the Industrial Training Act, government training centres have been set up to deal with this problem, and these have expanded greatly during the last five years.

Apart from methods of easing the burden of unemployment by cash grants, and methods of facilitating the finding of new employment, firms have been urged to introduce methods of avoiding lay-offs from the company as opposed to particular plants, as far as possible by offering alternative employment in other works belonging to the company. In the case of older workers, some alleviation has been sought in early retirement. All these various measures serve to soften the harsh realities involved in creating more efficient firms by the closure of uneconomic units. Such measures apply not only to take-over or merger situations, but also to existing companies in the process of reorganisation.

15 The Engineering Industries: II Research and Development, Labour and Exports

1 RESEARCH AND DEVELOPMENT

Mergers and acquisitions may provide a framework for promoting greater efficiency, but technological and commercial opportunities must not only be available, they must also be used; and they can only be used by firms which devote much of their efforts to innovations. Where innovative and product competition is more important than price competition, each firm must make its own effort. In this respect the response of the various trades in the engineering industries vary, and the differences can be said to reflect the individual trades' views on whether their future lies in progress, with sales of high-quality new goods, or whether their future lies in repetitive sales of given goods in limited markets. As pointed out before, the former requires research and development (R. & D.) expenditure, and leads to average total-cost pricing, so that unit costs of R. & D. can be recouped. Repetitive sales of identical goods, on the other hand, require no new R. & D. expenditure, and cost cutting is possible only as experience shows how to use factors more effectively in traditional activities. The appropriate pricing policy is marginal prime-cost pricing. These implications should be borne in mind when reading the following survey of research and development in the engineering trades.

In the late 1960s there were just over 50,000 scientists and technologists working in Britain's engineering industries. They represented two-thirds of all scientists and technologists employed in manufacturing industry. Electrical engineering and electrical goods employed almost one-third of all scientists and technologists working in manufacturing industry, and were followed by the chemical industries with one-fifth of the total. In the engineering industries as a whole, as defined in the previous chapter, 5 per cent of all administrative, technical and clerical (A.T.C.) workers were scientists and technologists. Not only did the electrical-goods trades employ the largest number of scientists and technologists, but they represented a higher proportion of A.T.C. staff (10 per cent) than in the other engineering industries, and were equal to the chemical industries (also with 10 per cent). Electrical goods were followed by vehicles with 5 per cent, marine engineering with 4 per cent, mechanical engineering with

3 per cent, and metal goods came last with only 2 per cent. These percentages probably mask considerable variations between trades within the engineering industries, but the Department of Employment and Productivity furnishes no figures for individual trades.

Some further evidence on the proportion of workers engaged on R. & D. is provided in a monograph published by the Federation of British Industries in 1961, and analysed by the National Institute of Economic and Social Research. The evidence from this sample inquiry relating to manpower engaged in, and expenditure on R. & D. in manufacturing industry during 1959-60 confirms the findings of the previous paragraph. Of all qualified scientists and engineers (Q.S.E.) engaged on R. & D., 23 per cent were to be found in the chemical industry, 28 per cent were in electrical engineering and 15 per cent were in aircraft, thus leaving only 34 per cent spread between all other industries. The results of the inquiry were even more startling in respect of expenditure. The chemical industry accounted for 14 per cent of all expenditure on R. & D., electrical engineering for 22 per cent, aircraft for 36 per cent, and only 28 per cent was shared amongst all other industries. (1)

There were wide variations in the degree of use of Q.S.E. between the various trades. Aircraft employed the highest number with 2.18 Q.S.E. per 100 total employment (called the research ratio), followed by electrical engineering (1.42) and instruments (1.01). These all had higher research ratios than the average for all engineering industries (0.81) or than for manufacturing industry as a whole (0.66). Mechanical engineering, machine-tools, vehicles, other metal goods and shipbuilding were all below average. (2) It appears that during the 1950s many of these predominantly capital-goods trades were weak in the utilisation of Q.S.E. personnel engaged in R. & D. While some speeding-up of technological education has occurred during the 1960s, and management has become more accustomed to the use of Q.S.E. and better able to direct their employment in useful directions, the increase in the use of Q.S.E. has not proceeded far enough in the capital-goods trades. This is especially true of machine-tools and ship-building, and it reinforces the argument in section 5 (b) of the last chapter, concerning the need for amalgamations in the machine-tool trade in particular, in order to allow the spread of costly R. & D. departments of firms.

The truth of the argument concerning amalgamations and the spreading of R. & D. overheads is illustrated by the fact that in almost every engineering trade the large firms with 2,000 workers or more were employing a higher proportion of Q.S.E. on research and development than were those of medium or small size. It is again noticeable that no small firms (with under 300 workers) in the machine-tool trade employed any Q.S.E. on research and development, and the same applied to metal goods. Of small firms, those in electrical engineering and instruments came out best, employing five times as many and twice as many respectively as did small firms in the engineering industries as a whole.

Compared with the United States, the United Kingdom lags behind on almost every comparison of resources devoted to R. & D. on an industry basis, whether measured in terms of research expenditure or manpower. Data relating to research expenditure and to manpower for the United States and the United Kingdom are presented in Table 15.1. The totals for all engineering industries differ hardly at all from that for all manufacturing industries. There are, however, wide variations between different engineering industries in the extent to which the United States devotes a higher proportion of resources to R. & D. than the corresponding British industry. Even when due allowance is made for the number of employees, expenditure on R. & D. and the number of Q.S.E. in the United States are both at least two and a half times those in the United Kingdom. The divergence between the two countries is most striking in the case of vehicles. In the aircraft industry, where the size of British firms is large (2,000 workers and over), the divergences are not so great. But average research expenditure of large American firms compared with large British firms is much greater than in either of the other two measures on an employee basis.

All this goes to reinforce arguments that increases in the size of company arising from mergers and acquisitions are likely to lead to an increase in R. & D. expenditure per employee, at least for mergers between large firms. Again, despite all the statistical qualifications which have to be allowed for in such comparisons, there is a strong correlation between research expenditure and growth. For seventeen industries, a correlation coefficient between research expenditure and growth of +0.95 was found in the United Kingdom between 1935 and 1958, and of +0.76 in the United States. Furthermore the pattern of growth and R. & D. expenditure tended to be similar for both countries. Thus industries which had a high growth rate and a high R. & D. expenditure in the United States were the same as those in the United Kingdom. Similarly industries with a low growth rate and a low R. & D. expenditure in the United States were the same as those in the United Kingdom. This finding applies not only to all industries, but also to the engineering industries, with the possible exception of vehicles. (3)

If any conclusions can be drawn on relative growth performance and R. & D. expenditure, the British economy appears to have got much better value for money from R. & D. expenditure on vehicles than from aircraft. It also appears to have done better in electrical goods, with the exception of electronics, much better in machinery, and slightly better in instruments. Such conclusions should, however, be treated with extreme caution, since they take no account of differences in gestation periods between various trades, nor of the size of overseas markets for which they cater. The conclusions should be used as no more than a starting point for investigating the relationship between an industry's

K. M.P.M.E.

Table 15.1 Research Expenditure and Manpower in the U.S.A. and U.K. Engineering Industries 1958 and 1959
(ratios of U.S. to U.K. research)

Industry	Internal research expenditure		Q.S.E.	Expenditure per employee (U.S.A. co.÷U.K. co.)	Q.S.E. per employee (U.S.A. co.÷U.K. co.)	Average research expenditure per large firm (*) (U.S./U.K.)
	Including govt. expenditure	Excluding govt. expenditure				
Aircraft	4.4	4.4	6.2	1.7	2.1	1.3
Electronics	6.2	3.3	3.9	3.9	2.3	6.3
Other electrical	6.8	—				
Machinery	6.0	4.1	5.1	3.8	3.2	7.5
Vehicles	11.7	9.2	5.7	7.3	3.6	19.3
Instruments	7.3	6.1	6.6	2.8	2.5	3.5
Total	5.3	4.4	4.9	2.8	2.5	4.7
Total all industries	5.4	4.3	4.9	2.8	2.6	4.7

Source: C. Freeman, 'Research and Development: A Comparison between British and American Industry' in 'National Institute Economic Review', no. 20 (May 1962) Tables 1, 2, and 4.
* U.K., 2,000 employees and over; U.S.A., 5,000 and over.

growth performance and its R. & D. expenditure per head, and they should be used even more cautiously for policy recommendations.

The attitude of individual firms towards the presence or absence of R. & D. departments and the proportion of its annual budget which a firm is prepared to devote to expenditure on such departments is often taken as an indicator of its commercial attitude in general. Such considerations have been used as one of the criteria on which firms have been classified as 'thrusters' or 'sleepers' in the industrial world. (4) Government concern over the attitude of firms towards R. & D., and of firms in the engineering industries in particular, has been expressed in a number of ways. Development contracts have been awarded to firms by the Department of Scientific and Industrial Research (D.S.I.R.), and in 1964 the Government set up a new Ministry, the Ministry of Technology. The function of this Ministry was to keep under review the overall position with regard to R. & D. throughout British industry. Before the setting-up of the Ministry of Technology, most government contracts with industrial firms were concerned with defence projects. The use of government contracts to stimulate R. & D. for civilian use differs from those of defence projects, in that the Government was the sole purchaser of the final products which emerged from the contract. Negotiations to ensure that the Government gets a fair return on money invested in R. & D. for essentially civil projects present different problems from those conducted in the case of defence contracts. (5) Some progress in this direction was made by the Ministry of Technology in sponsoring pre-production order schemes, first announced in May 1966. In November 1967 the Ministry announced the award of an order for £1¼ million for the supply of a number of advanced types of machine-tools from A. Herbert Ltd. Other smaller orders to firms in the machine-tool trade had been made earlier in the year, but were worth only £485,500. Of these, the largest went to Churchill-Redman Ltd, a subsidiary of Tube Investments Ltd.

In announcing the awards, the Ministry stated that the resulting assessments would be made widely available to industry. The object of the awards and the method of publication of findings was intended to reduce the time-lag between the development of advanced equipment and its acceptance in industry on a scale which would justify fairly long production runs. On a much larger scale, the Ministry announced in late September 1967 a scheme to put £5 million into computer development, directed specifically towards 'softwear'. Again, the intention was that the results of such R. & D. would rapidly be made available to various industrial and commercial users, mainly through the offices of the National Computing Centre in Manchester. Such methods of speeding up the rate at which development of new products takes place could well be used in other sectors of the British engineering industries outside the two critical trades of machine-tools and computers. These methods could well become a regular feature of governmental policy for stimulating research into, and the rapid development of, new products throughout British industry.

2   THE LABOUR MARKET IN THE ENGINEERING INDUSTRIES

(a)   The Occupational Structure

No discussion of the engineering industries can be complete without considering the organisation of its workpeople and its manpower problems. Given the complex nature of the industries' product structure, their occupational structure must also be complex. Some introductory idea of the complexity of the occupational structure of the engineering industries may be obtained from the fact that the Department of Employment and Productivity distinguishes 33 separate occupational headings for production workers in these trades, and these headings are by no means narrowly defined. In consequence there are complexitites in labour organisation. Workpeople in the engineering industries in particular owe their loyalties to unions organised essentially on a craft basis. This has given rise to a number of problems in the field of wage bargaining and industrial relations. One outstanding example would be the inter-union disputes connected with the demarcation of jobs in the shipbuilding industry. Another example would be inter-union disputes relating to claims over loyalties of workpeople, which have been prevalent in, for example, the motor-vehicle industry.

The very broad definitions given by the Department of Employment and Productivity into (a) administrative, technical and clerical workers (A.T.C.), (b) skilled operatives, (c) mainly semi-skilled workers and (d) other workers varies between the major sectors of the engineering group of industries, as may be seen in Table 15.2. Differences between some of the broad divisions are considerable, with A.T.C. workers being especially low in shipbuilding and repair compared with engineering and electrical goods. Similarly differences arise in other categories of occupations. These major sectoral divisions of the engineering group of industries mask great divergences between different trades. Six of the 35 engineering trades distinguished by the Department of Employment and Productivity had an A.T.C. proportion of 35 per cent or over, the highest being in aircraft manufacture and repair, where the proportion was 40 per cent, and the lowest in cans and metal boxes with only 14 per cent. Similar extremes occur amongst the proportions of skilled workers in the engineering trades. These ranged from 56 per cent in shipbuilding and repair to 8 per cent in insulated wire and cables. One-quarter of the engineering trades had at least two-fifths of their workers in the skilled category, whilst one-seventh had under 15 per cent. Again, one-fifth of the trades had over two-fifths of their workers in

Table 15.2 Analysis of Employees according to Type of Worker, May 1966
(establishments with 11 employees and over)

(percentage of total employees)

Class of worker	Engineering and electrical goods	Shipbuilding and repair	Marine engineering	Vehicles	Metal goods
A.T.C.	31.8	15.0	22.7	27.0	20.6
Skilled	28.1	55.5	47.8	30.8	24.4
Semi-skilled	25.6	11.3	9.5	27.0	33.2
Others	14.5	18.2	20.0	15.2	21.8
Skilled workers only, by size of establishment (employees)					
500 and over	22.8	55.0	–	28.5	18.0
250-499	28.4	52.6	–	35.1	20.6
Under 250	39.8	58.5	–	49.9	30.5

Source: 'Ministry of Labour Gazette' (Jan. 1967) Table 34.

the semi-skilled category. There was also a tendency for large firms to employ a smaller proportion of A.T.C. workers than small and medium-size firms. This arises because of managerial economies.

Because of the possibility of breaking down engineering operations so that a lower degree of skill is required, those industries where production engineers have been particularly skilful in this respect will be found to employ relatively high proportions of semi-skilled workers. Thus manufacturers of metal goods, vehicles and electrical goods all have a relatively high proportion of semi-skilled workers. The engineering industries as a whole have tended to complain about the shortage of skilled workers during the inflationary periods of the 1950s and 1960s. Governments have consequently laid great stress on measures to increase the supply of skilled workers. The Industrial Training Act of 1964 was an attempt to persuade firms to devote a larger share of their financial resources to this end. An ingenious system of levies and grants is administered by industrial training boards for each industry. Levies have varied between 0.75 per cent and 2.5 per cent of individual industries' wages bills. Small firms have been consistent critics of this system, complaining that they require specialised training and not the general kind so often provided under the scheme. In the past, however, it has frequently been small firms which have benefited from labour trained by large firms.

It will also be seen from Table 15.2 that not only does the proportion of skilled workers vary as between sectors of the engineering industry, but it also varies according to the size of establishment. The Department of Employment and Productivity gives a breakdown for the major sectors of the engineering industries into small establishments (having less than 250 employees), medium-size establishments (250-499 employees) and large (500 employees and over). In general, the larger the size of establishment, the smaller the proportion of skilled workers employed. Small firms, especially in the engineering trades, tend to be specialist firms, engaging in activities where skill is at a premium, or else they engage heavily in repair work, where similar conditions apply. They owe their very existence to this ability to recruit and retain their skilled labour force, and often pay wage rates in excess of nationally negotiated minima. Only in shipbuilding and repair is there no significant difference between the proportions of skilled workers employed in different sizes of establishments. Again, many of the small establishments come within the category of single-establishment firms, and are frequently privately owned companies. They engage in 'one-off' jobs, very short runs or small-batch production, and are able to switch their capacity to a new job relatively easily. Many are manufacturers of special components, which are not suited to long-run production schedules. They are thus unable to break down the engineering processes involved to suit semi-skilled labour.

(b)   The System of Wage Bargaining

As may be inferred from the large number of occupations in the engineering industries, there is an equally large number of trade unions. In the mid-1960s some 35 in all were affiliated to a central organisation, the Confederation of Shipbuilding and Engineering Unions (referred to henceforth as the Confederation). The Confederation came into being in 1936, largely in order to achieve a compromise between the objective of the largest of its constituent unions, the Amalgamated Engineering Union (A.E.U.), to secure one union for the engineering industries as a whole, and the desire of the smaller unions to maintain their individual existences. In 1964 the Confederation had a total affiliated membership of 1.8 million workers, of which the A.E.U. had 770,000. Other large unions were the National Union of General and Municipal Workers (N.U.G.M.W.), with 180,000 members, the Transport and General Workers Union (T.G.W.U.), with 175,000 members, the Electrical Trades Union (E.T.U.), with 122,000 members, and the three sections of the United Society of Boilermakers, Shipwrights and Structural Workers (U.S.B.S.S.W.), with 120,000 members. These five unions accounted for practically three-quarters of the total affiliated membership.

It emerges from this account of the number of unions operating within the engineering industries that an individual employer might be faced with a labour force comprising members of a number of individual unions, each with its own interests. In the absence of some form of centralised bargaining in wage negotiations, the task of the individual employer in achieving a satisfactory settlement would be exceedingly difficult. Initial bargaining between unions and management is thus carried out between the Engineering Employers' Federation, founded in 1896 (henceforth referred to as the Federation), and the Confederation. The Federation is the largest of all employers' associations or other forms of trade association. In the mid-1960s it had a membership of around 4,500 firms, employing just under 1½ million manual workers and 600,000 staff workers. Thus the membership of unions affiliated to the Confederation represented about three-fifths of the total labour force of the engineering industries, excluding metal goods, some of which have non-affiliated unions. In turn, the non-staff employees of the firms belonging to the Federation represented just under half of the engineering industries' labour force, again excluding metal goods. Although most of the large employers belong to the Federation, there are a number of large non-federated firms. Examples of non-federated firms are the American-owned motor-vehicle firms Ford and Vauxhall, and the British-owned engineering firm Rubery Owen, which makes amongst other things vehicle components. During the 1950s most of the non-federated firms tended to apply wage increases broadly in line with those fixed in agreements between the Federation and the Confederation. Since the Conditions of Employment Act of 1959, it has been mandatory for non-federated firms to meet the terms of employment of the federated firms. Workers in the former must now be employed under conditions 'not less favourable' than those applying to workers in firms covered by national agreements.

Just as there are conflicting interests within the Confederation in arriving at agreements, because different unions represent pressures of various kinds, so there are sometimes conflicting interests amongst the various regional branches of the Federation. Within the Confederation, conflict of interest may arise between, for example, the A.E.U., whose members are mostly skilled fitters, turners and machinists, members of other craft unions with skilled workers, such as boilermakers, patternmakers, brass and metal mechanics, and unions such as the T.G.W.U. or the N.U.M.G.W., which are comprised essentially of unskilled workers. The craft unions will frequently attempt to maintain existing skill differentials in rates of pay, whilst the general unions will attempt to improve the pay and conditions of some of the lower-paid workers and thus narrow differentials.

Both the unions' and employers' organisations are organised on a regional basis, with district committees. In the mid-1960s the Confederation had a total of 49 district committees, to which the nationally affiliated unions belonged and on which they had representatives. A good deal of bargaining with the employers and the procedures for the settlement of disputes take place on a district basis. In turn, the Federation has 39 local associations of varying size and distribution. The local associations of the Federation do not always correspond with the district committees of the Confederation. Procedure for the settlement of disputes by discussion exists at the local level, and initial moves take place on this basis, but if settlement is not arranged at the local level, the dispute can be referred for discussion between the executive committees of the Federation and Confederation at the national level. The procedural agreement for the settlement of disputes starts with an important prologue: 'The Employers have the right to manage their establishments and the Trade Unions have the right to exercise their functions.' The agreement provides for the recognition and appointment of shop stewards, and for joint shop stewards' combine committees of an inter-union nature, usually with one shop steward to fifty members. These combine committees frequently carry out negotiations on a plant basis and sometimes on a district basis. But clashes may take place between these combine committees and district union representatives as to which of them is going to carry out a particular set of negotiations or discussions with management at a district level. Monthly meetings for the settlement of problems at a national level take place at York, the whole process being known in the industry as the 'York Conference', or 'Conference' for short.

Wage negotiations take place at both the national and local levels, the latter frequently on a plant or workshop basis. The national negotiations are conducted on an ad hoc basis at special conferences. The unions concerned write to the Federation requesting such a meeting, and briefly state their case for the wage claim. Such a wage claim may be of a general nature and can be made by any one or all unions in the Confederation. Normal practice is for national negotiations to be concerned only with major wage claims and conditions of work, such as a reduction in hours of the standard week and a number of allied matters. At such conferences only key wage rates are negotiated, usually time rates for fitters and unskilled workers, with variations being hammered out on a local basis. Again, equivalent adjustments for piece-rate workers will be negotiated on a similar basis, including minimum fall-back rates of pay for piece-rate workers. These are the rates shown in the Department of Employment and Productivity's handbook 'Time Rates and Hours of Work'.

There is no agreed procedure should negotiations break down at the national level, and the unions may take one of a number of actions should they decide to press their claim. They may seek conciliation, go to arbitration, or call a national strike or a work-to-rule. Equally, especially since 1961, the Government itself may intervene and refer the dispute, or even an agreed settlement, to the appropriate authority. In November 1963, for example, the Chancellor of the Exchequer referred the agreement of a series of claims to the National Incomes

Commission. Since the abolition of that body it may refer such a claim to the Prices and Incomes Board, and has in fact done so in 1967.

(c)   The Industry's Wage Structure

The preceding discussions of the occupational structure and system of wage bargaining in the engineering industries have shown that the engineering sector of the economy has no wages structure in the way in which this term is normally understood. True, the Conference lays down a series of bench-marks for the determination of wage rates throughout the engineering industries, but once this has been done, further bargaining takes place at the local or workshop level. In many ways it makes more sense to discuss earnings rather than wage rates, since it is to earnings that most workers look when making comparisons with their fellow workers in the same industry or in other industries. Rates in conjunction with hours worked determine earnings. The latter are also influenced by overtime rates of pay and other premia. Again, since only bench-marks are laid down at the Conference, there is considerable scope for regional and workshop variations from the nationally negotiated rates according to the degree of labour shortage experienced locally by the individual firm.

An analysis of the occupational structure of wages in the engineering sector is given in Table 15.3. It distinguishes the earnings of workers paid on a time-rate basis from those paid under various types of systems of payment by results. In the engineering industries as a whole, the proportion of manual workers paid according to one of the payment-by-results schemes is high. Within the major occupations given in Table 15.3, however, there are wide differences (not shown in the table). Over four-fifths of turners and machinemen (rated below fitters' rate) work under one of the payment-by-results schemes. This is the highest proportion of any one occupational class in the engineering trades. At the other extreme, rather less than one-fifth of toolroom fitters and turners and of the various classes of maintenance men work under such schemes. Just under one-half of semi-skilled workers operate under one of the payment-by-results systems, in contrast to labourers, where the proportion is just under one-quarter. Differences in earnings between labourers and semi-skilled workers are wide, no matter whether they are working on a time rate or incentive-system basis. Although skilled workers as a whole tend to earn more than semi-skilled, two grades of skilled workers earn no more than semi-skilled workers. In sum, the relationship between the earnings of major grades of engineering workers appears to conform to the following pattern. Semi-skilled workers earn 15 per cent more than labourers, 'ordinary' skilled workers 15 per cent more than semi-skilled, and highly skilled maintenance workers earn 10 per cent more than the 'ordinary' skilled workers. These are the rough occupational differences which the main craft unions of the engineering industries attempt to preserve, though,

Table 15.3 Occupational Wages Structure in Engineering:
Average Weekly Earnings of Adult Males, including Overtime, January 1967

Class of worker	Time workers	Payment-by-results workers
Average earnings of all workers covered	100.0	100.0
Fitters (skilled, other than toolroom and maintenance)	106.8	108.3
Turners and Machinemen		
(a) Rated at or above fitters' rate	106.9	107.0
(b) Rated below fitters' rate	91.8	92.9
Toolroom fitters and turners	120.4	113.3
Maintenance men (skilled)		
Skilled maintenance fitters	118.9	114.3
Skilled maintenance electricians	121.8	118.5
Other skilled maintenance classes	117.6	107.8
Patternmakers	113.5	102.3
Sheet-metal workers (skilled)	105.5	109.5
Moulders (loose pattern, skilled)	93.9	99.1
Platers, riveters and caulkers	106.2	102.2
All other adult skilled grades	108.5	107.5
All other adult semi-skilled grades	93.0	94.6
Labourers	78.2	77.3

	s	d	s	d
Average earnings for all workers	402	1	430	4.

Source: 'Occupational Earnings of Manual Workers', in 'Ministry of Labour Gazette', (May 1967) Tables 2 and 11.

as will be seen later, some narrowing of differentials has taken place during the last two decades. The pattern of earnings which has thus emerged relates principally to the external wage structure of the engineering industries. Internal wage structures of individual firms may differ widely from that shown in Table 15.3.

There are also considerable variations in earnings on an industry basis. Table 15.4 gives a breakdown of earnings for some of the major sectors of the engineering group of industries. There is a stark contrast between earnings in the aircraft and motor-vehicle industries, whatever the class of worker. The one exception to this is that labourers working under incentive schemes do particularly well in shipbuilding and repair. Regional differences, shown in Table 15.5, are more striking even than those between trades. To some extent the two are interconnected. Where a region has a high degree of specialisation in the motor-vehicle or aircraft industries, its earnings will tend to be higher than those for the United Kingdom as a whole. Table 14.2 should be compared with Table 15.5. In all cases the South-west region has lower average weekly earnings for the main sectors of the engineering industry than most other regions. But because

Table 15.4 Average Earnings of Adult Male Manual Workers,
including Overtime, January 1967.
(All engineering = 100)

Section of engineering	Skilled workers		Semi-skilled workers		Labourers	
	Time	P.B.R.	Time	P.B.R.	Time	P.B.R.
Mechanical engineering	96.6	97.5	95.8	94.9	98.3	96.3
Electrical engineering	97.9	97.9	95.1	96.2	97.3	100.6
Motor-vehicle manufacture	108.3	103.7	107.8	110.7	105.1	102.7
Aircraft manufacture and repair	109.1	107.9	103.3	101.3	108.7	104.7
Shipbuilding and repair	94.7	101.8	97.9	91.1	101.1	109.6
All engineering industries	s d	s d	s d	s d	s d	s d
Covered (excl. *shipbuilding)*	446 7	463 7	373 10	405 2	314 3	332 10

Source: 'Occupational Earnings of Manual Workers', in 'Ministry of Labour
Gazette', (May 1967) Table 6.

earnings are relatively high in the aircraft industry, and this industry is important in the South-west, average weekly earnings in 'vehicles' are higher than for other major sectors of the engineering industry. For each sector of the engineering group of industries, average weekly earnings were consistently above those for the United Kingdom as a whole only in London and the South-east. It will also be noticed that although average weekly earnings in Scotland tend to be below those for the United Kingdom as a whole for shipbuilding and marine engineering, vehicles and metal goods, they are higher than for any other region in the case of engineering and electrical goods.

So far this section has dealt mainly with the overall pattern of earnings for different sectors of the engineering group of industries, and the various regions and occupations. But as was noted at the outset, a large proportion of skilled and semi-skilled workers operate under incentive systems. It is here that bargaining at the individual firm and workshop level assumes considerable importance in establishing the internal wage structure, and eventually the earnings pattern at the national level. Since much of the work in mechanical engineering is based on batch production, there are frequent changes of run, and new piece rates or other forms of bonus payment have to be renegotiated, usually with the shop stewards. On this rests a great deal of their power and importance in the engineering industries. In the motor-vehicle industry their activities take a rather

Table 15.5 Average Weekly Earnings of Adult Male Workers in Major Sectors of the
Engineering Industries, 3rd Pay-Week, April 1967

(U.K. average = 100)

Region	Engineering and electrical goods	Shipbuilding and marine engineering	Vehicles	Metal goods	All manufacturing industries
London and South-east	101.4	100.1	101.8	102.8	105.3
Eastern and Southern	101.4	101.3	99.6	105.9	103.5
South-western	94.6	89.0	96.6	94.4	96.5
Midlands	102.4	102.9	104.2	99.5	101.9
Yorkshire and Humberside	94.9	100.6	85.0	101.0	93.7
North-western	96.1	104.4	93.6	95.0	96.3
Northern	100.1	103.9	91.7	99.8	98.8
Scotland	103.0	96.0	94.6	98.2	96.1
Wales	98.5	89.8	87.6	99.9	102.6
Northern Ireland	96.7*	—	90.1	77.9	86.5

Source: Calculated from 'Earnings and Hours in April 1967', in 'Ministry of Labour Gazette' (Aug 1967) Table 21.

* No separate figures are available for shipbuilding and marine engineering, and they are included in engineering and electrical goods.

different form of ensuring similarity of payment in different plants and work-shops within a firm. This is especially the case for semi-skilled workers, who form a relatively large proportion of manual workers in the motor-vehicle industry. For them there are no nationally agreed wage rates, and the motor-industry shop stewards are constantly engaged in bargaining on their behalf. (6) Because individual workshop bargaining takes place in a large part of the engineering industries, it is difficult to give a precise account of the typical factory wage structure. Indeed it is most doubtful whether there is a typical factory wage structure in the engineering industries. Furthermore factory agreements tend to be verbal rather than written, and can be discovered only by interviewing workers and management or by studying practices within a given firm. (7)

(d)   Overall Wage Movements and Productivity

Overall wage movements in relation to changes in productivity are of importance in influencing the competitive position of the engineering industries, especially in the face of international competition. Little is known about the cost structure of individual British industries. Census of Production data permit only a break-down of gross and net value-added figures, and no allowance can be calculated for income accruing to capital, tax paid and the like. Nevertheless some attempts to estimate the cost structure of individual industries have been made, using a variety of methods. No matter which method is used, and despite the statistical difficulties appertaining to each, it appears that wages and salaries account for around one-third of costs in the engineering industries as a whole, and that this element of cost is a good deal higher than for manufacturing industry as a whole. (8) Movements in wages and salaries can thus be of considerable importance in influencing the prices of engineering products.

General wage-rate changes in the engineering industry are shown in Table 15.6. Percentage changes in rates are given for fitters and unskilled labourers, since these are the key bargaining rates. During the post-war years skilled fitters' rates have risen on average by 5¾ per cent a year, with an additional rise of ½ per cent a year on account of reductions in hours worked with no loss of pay. Unskilled labourers' rates have also risen by 5¾ per cent a year, but the reduction in hours with no loss of pay has been worth an additional 1 per cent to them. Whilst the absolute differential between the rates paid to skilled fitters and unskilled labourers has increased during the post-war years, the percentage differential between them has remained roughly constant. In Table 15.6 the square brackets indicate the equivalent length of time since the last wage settlement where the new agreement was not of the straight wage-increase variety, or where the increase was postponed because of a wages freeze. Since 1945 there has been on average one wage change a year, counting reductions in hours

Table 15.6 Engineering Wages, 1946-68

Effective date of settlement	Amount of increase (per week)				Minimum time-rate after change				Percentage increase		Time in months since previous increase
	Skilled fitter		Labourer		Skilled fitter		Labourer		Skilled fitter	Labourer	
	s	d	s	d	s	d	s	d			
15 Apr 1946	6	-	6	-	102	-	86	-	6¼	7½	
6 Jan 1947					Reduction in labourers' hrs, 47 to 44				=6½+1½		[9]
					102	-	87	-			
4 Oct 1948	5	-	5	-	107	-	92	-	5	5½	33
13 Nov 1950	11	-	8	-	118	-	100	-	10¼	8¾	25
23 Nov 1951	11	-	11	-	129	-	111	-	9¼	11	12
10 Nov 1952	7	4	7	4	136	4	118	4	5¾	6½	12
5 Apr 1954	8	6	6	6	144	10	124	10	6¼	5½	17
14 Mar 1955	11	-	8	-	155	10	132	10	7½	6½	11
5 Mar 1956	12	6	9	6	168	4	142	4	8	7	12
27 Nov 1957	11	-	9	-	179	4	151	4	6½	6¼	20
6 Oct 1958	7	4	6	-	186	8	157	4	4	4	9
28 Mar 1960					Reduction in hrs, 44 to 42 = 4½%						[17]
26 Dec 1960	8	6	7	6	195	2	164	10	4½	4¾	26
9 July 1962	6	-	5	-	201	2	169	10	3	3	19
2 Dec 1963	10	6	9	6	211	8	179	4	5¼	5½	17
7 Dec 1964					Reduction in hrs, 42 to 41 = 2½%						[12]
5 July 1965					Reduction in hrs, 41 to 40 = 2½%						[7]
7 Mar 1966*	5	-	4	-	216	8	183	4	2½	2¼	27
3 July 1967*	5	-	4	-	221	8	187	4	2¼	2¼	[10]
1 Jan 1968†	—		—		257	8	217	4	—	—	—

Source: Ministry of Labour and Department of Employment and Productivity.
* Subject to wage freeze at stage 2.
† Consolidation of minimum earnings levels into minimum time rates.

worked with no loss of pay as equivalent to a wage increase. In most instances wage-rate changes have emerged as a result of negotiations, but a number have been obtained as a result of arbitration or courts of inquiry. The 1950 settlement, for example, went to the National Arbitration Tribunal, while the 1948, 1954 and 1957 increases were obtained as a result of investigations by courts of inquiry. (9) The agreement negotiated during November-December 1963, with pay increases to take effect from December 1963 and hours reductions from December 1964 and July 1965, was referred by the Government to the National Incomes Commission. The Commission condemned it as being contrary to the prevailing concept of a national incomes policy, and accordingly against the public interest. Nothing, however, was done to upset the negotiated terms of the agreement.

The wide extent of incentive systems of wage payment in the engineering industries has resulted in a high degree of wage drift, being the gap between weekly earnings and rates, with overtime excluded. Workshop bargaining has given rise to wage drift in a number of ways. 'Lieu payments' have been made to time-rate workers to give them increases comparable with those obtained by workers operating under incentive systems. It has been extended by the insistence on maintaining district rates and earnings differentials, even where there has been no justification for it in the state of the local labour market. Again, wage drift has been increased by methods employed in setting piece rates or individual bonuses. Errors in wage setting which have occurred when new runs of a product have been started have remained uncorrected, and the same has frequently been the case when new machinery has been introduced. Under conditions of inflation, these 'loose rates' have tended to be accepted by management, since such wage increases could always be passed on to the consumer in the form of higher prices. Skilled workers in particular have been able to exploit discontinuities in the production process, so as to create wage drift independent of changes in productivity. As the National Incomes Commission report on the engineering and shipbuilding agreements put it, the 'elimination of systems of payments by results would result in a significant diminution of those elements of wage drift which are not to be commended from an economic point of view'. (10)

In May 1967 the P.I.B. was asked to investigate the workings of the then current long-term engineering wage agreement, the package deal of December 1964 (referred to below as the Agreement). Two of the main ingredients of the package deal were, first, the conversion, from January 1968, of minimum earnings levels into new minimum rates of pay, which would be used in future to calculate overtime and night-shift premiums, holiday and guaranteed weekly payments; and second, changes in the minimum piecework standard and its components. Because the ingredients had not come into force at the time the reference was made, the Board decided to publish its findings in two reports. The first report (11) dealt mainly with the way in which the 1964 package deal had worked. The second report (12) dealt mainly with the effects of consolidation of minimum earnings levels into rates of pay.

The 1964 agreement involved the establishment of new minimum earnings levels. During the three-year period of the agreement, workers earning less than these levels would be brought up to them by a series of special increments at six-monthly intervals. The minimum earnings level was a new concept, designed to deal with the sense of grievance of workers who were obtaining only the consolidated time rates of pay in a situation where most workers were averaging more than these rates. (13) These new levels were based on the standard working week, and might be raised or lowered according to the number of hours worked.

292   Industrial Organisation

The establishment of such minimum earnings levels involved the gradual abolition of district minimum time rates. The second principal change was concerned with alterations in the minimum piecework standard and its components, so that workers of average ability could earn 15 per cent above the minimum time rates. As part of the package deal, the agreement provided for two small but equal general wage increases to be incorporated in the minimum earnings level. One of the main aims of the package deal was to simplify the national wages structure of the industry and to break the normal cycle of wage demands, by including a general pay rise with alterations in the overall structure of wages.

The findings of the two P.I.B. reports were to the effect that the agreement had failed in its attempt to restrict wage increases. It was found that earnings of skilled workers increased by 21 per cent between January 1965 and January 1968, and that those of unskilled workers had increased by 19 per cent during the same period. This amounted to twice as much as the agreement had provided for. Wage drift, consequential to plant bargaining, was blamed for most of this discrepancy. Although the nationally negotiated agreement had been honoured in the letter, there were many variations from it at the plant or workshop level. 'In general, where the Agreement conflicted with a plant's interests the conflict was resolved in favour of the plant. The conflicts were usually associated with differentials or the plant's conception of its labour supply and industrial relations needs.' (14)

The P.I.B. also concluded that from the long-run point of view the agreement had failed in the intention to keep increases in wages and improvements in conditions of work in line with increases in productivity in the industry. During the years 1960-7 output per operative hour increased on average by 2.9 per cent a year, whereas the average weekly earnings of male manual workers increased on average by twice as much. A similar relationship was thought to exist during the period of the agreement itself. During the 1960s the average rate of increase in weekly wage rates in almost all branches of the engineering industries had been in line with that achieved in all manufacturing industries. As a result labour costs per unit of output rose on average by 3 per cent a year.

So far as improvements in the future were concerned, the P.I.B. suggested that thought should be given by the Engineering Employers' Federation, and especially by the largest firms in the industry, to greater flexibility in negotiating arrangements. Such arrangements, it was suggested, should provide for the special needs of the large multi-plant firms, for small firms, for specific sectors of the industry, the development of company or plant agreements, and the establishment of minimum standards. Thus national negotiations would continue to be necessary on such matters as minimum rates of pay and hours of work, holidays, overtime and shift premia. Individual firms might, however, be encouraged to enter into formal factory agreements with the unions to replace what are now usually informal and fragmented arrangements and understandings.' (15) The problem of wage drift, however, remains.

3   THE INTERNATIONAL COMPETITIVE POSITION OF THE ENGINEER-
   ING INDUSTRIES

(a)   The Overall Position

During the late 1960s over two-fifths of British exports consisted of engineering products, including transport equipment, compared with just one-quarter immediately prior to the Second World War. This move towards a higher proportion of exports of durable goods resumed a trend which was discernible during the second half of the nineteenth century.

The principal markets for British exports of engineering products in the 1960s were the European Economic Community countries, which took one-sixth of the total, North America, with one-eighth, and the European Free Trade Association countries with one-ninth. The share of the two European groupings has been rising steadily during the 1960s. In contrast, that of North America has been declining. Since the beginning of the 1960s world trade between manufacturing countries has been expanding, and exports of machinery and transport equipment have shared in that expansion. Britain's share of world trade in manufactures has, however, been declining, as has her share of world trade in machinery and transport equipment.

Since world trade between the advanced industrial countries has been increasing rapidly in the more sophisticated type of capital goods, especially those coming within the engineering industries, it is important to examine the United Kingdom's position in such markets in more detail. Various studies (16) indicate that the international competitiveness of British exports has been declining. During the major part of the 1960s, whilst British exports doubled, those of her major competitors trebled in value. The National Institute of Economic and Social Research study, however, indicated that, with the exception of electrical equipment, the annual rate of growth of exports of engineering products had been declining during the latter half of the period studied (1960-6), though the decline was not peculiar to engineering goods alone. Nevertheless the Mechanical Engineering Economic Development Committee (E.D.C.) study indicated that for these years, while the mechanical engineering share of British exports remained constant, this share had tended to increase in many of her competitors. Again, while exports as a proportion of total deliveries of engineering products remained roughly constant for the United Kingdom between 1960 and 1966, this proportion rose in the case of nearly all other major European countries

British exports as a proportion of total deliveries declined between 1960 and 1967 in many individual engineering products. Continuous declines in the proportion exported were registered in tractors, industrial engines, mining machinery, pumps and industrial valves, water tube boilers, and shell boilers and plant. In contrast there were substantial increases in textile machinery, office machinery, packaging machinery, steel and non-ferrous rolling mills and plant, and in ancillary plant for such works. Despite a negative trade balance in the case of office machinery and metalworking machine-tools, all other mechanical engineering products had a positive trade balance before the 1967 devaluation.

The Mechanical Engineering Export Development Council regarded the slow growth of the home market as a major factor in the slow growth of exports of mechanical engineering products. Too many firms have geared their total deliveries to the home market rather than to the home and export markets combined. Examinations of fast-growing overseas markets by both the Mechanical Engineering E.D.C. and the National Institute suggest that substantial opportunities for export expansion have been lost. These investigations seem to support the view that Britain's international competitiveness in engineering products was declining in the 1960s.

(b) Reasons for Lack of Competitiveness

The reasons for Britain's lack of competitiveness in the world's engineering markets are complex, but three empirical studies are helpful in analysing the causes. The first consisted of a postal questionnaire sample of firms carried out by Political and Economic Planning (P.E.P.) towards the end of 1963, the object of which was to establish factual evidence from individual companies of what British exporters thought was wrong with British exports, and why they were not more successful. (17) By contrast, the second study was aimed at discovering what foreign consumers thought was wrong with British exports, and was carried out by the National Institute of Economic and Social Research (N.I.E.S.R.). (18) The Mechanical Engineering E.D.C. inquiry (19) was similar to the P.E.P. study, but aimed at covering a much larger proportion of mechanical engineering exports and considered in greater depth a more limited group of engineering industry exporters. This inquiry asked firms about changes in their export performances between 1960 and 1965 and, as in the P.E.P. study, what they considered to be important hindrances to exporting and what changes they would like to see to assist exporters. The inquiry was also concerned with export marketing, including selling methods, regularity of overseas visiting and after-sales service, market research and product design, and overseas trade, export insurance and finance.

The P.E.P. study found that most firms did not give lack of production facilities, lack of financial assistance or rising labour costs and prices as reasons for their failure to increase exports. Those firms which had increased their exports least complained particularly of increased competition in third markets, and tariffs and quotas. These findings were confirmed by the Mechanical Engineering E.D.C. inquiry. Table 15.7 analyses the answers of firms in the main engineering groups to the question of which were the two greatest hindrances to them in their search for export markets. It will be seen that the firms in the P.E.P. inquiry stated that they regarded tariff barriers and quotas as the most serious obstacle, and that this affected the engineering group of industries a little more than it did non-engineering industries. It also affected firms in the vehicles sector of the engineering industries particularly. In the case of firms in mechanical engineering, both inquiries found that price competition was slightly more important to firms than tariffs and quotas. (20) The diverse nature of export markets hampered the standardisation of products and the advantages to be obtained from long runs in one-sixth of all engineering firms, difficulties in

Table 15.7 Greatest Hindrances to Exports of Engineering Products, 1963-4
(percentages of answers)

Group	Number of firms in sample	Return on exports less than return on home sales	Difficulties in standardisation in export markets	Competition	Tariffs and quotas
Mechanical engineering	93	24	14	66	61
Electrical engineering and electronics	65	2	23	70	59
Shipbuilding	4	25	–	100	–
Vehicles	25	16	16	52	84
Metal goods	32	16	6	22	72
Group total	219	20	16	60	67
Non-engineering group	226	26	15	52	64

Source: Calculated from P.E.P., 'Firms and their Exports', in 'Planning' Nov (1964) Appendix 3, Table 5, p. 315. Answers given for the two greatest hindrances to exporting.

this respect being understandably greatest in the case of electrical engineering products, whose export markets differ widely in their standard voltages.

The N.I.E.S.R. study of the attitudes of buyers of British exports of machinery and transport equipment tended to confirm some of the findings of the P.E.P. inquiry. The general impression of centralised buyers in Eastern Europe was that British exporters were adversely affected by quoting too high an initial price in tenders compared with their competitors, though the final quoted price might be considerably lower. In design, German firms appeared to be ahead in chemical plant but not in textile machinery. On the other hand British industry appeared to be well ahead in the design of computers, an important product for centrally run economies. Except in the case of exports to Poland, delivery dates were not uncompetitive, and the Polish buyers also complained of lack of assistance given by smaller firms at the installation stage. Although credit facilities had improved, competitors occasionally gave longer repayment periods. After-sales service tended to be poor.

Many engineering products sell on design and ability to do a job, rather than on a straight price comparison. It might therefore be expected that price would not be such an important consideration in the exports of capital goods as in many other trades. In fact, the Mechanical Engineering E.D.C. inquiry, concluded that 'many mechanical engineering products were price-competitive before devaluation'. (21)

At the time of the 1967 devaluation, there were two contrasting views as to how devaluation might assist British exports. The first was that devaluation would enable British producers to quote lower prices in terms of foreign currency in major export markets. This would either assist by offsetting the effects of tariffs, so that the British product would be able to compete on more equal terms with the local product, or, where tariffs were already low or non-existent, it would give a clear-cut price advantage. The second view was that devaluation would act as a spur to British manufacturers to export a higher proportion of his output in those cases where he was able to maintain the price of the product in terms of foreign currency. This would be the case where the price elasticity of demand for the British product was low, and sold largely on a quality basis. The sterling price of exports would consequently be raised relative to price obtained in the British market. In this respect the passenger-car market is an interesting case. A clash of opinion was reported between British car firms and the British-based American subsidiaries, Ford and Vauxhall. Immediately following devaluation, it was reported (22) that Ford had decided not to make any price cuts in Europe, thus increasing its sterling equivalent of foreign currency earnings, stating that its policy was 'to price according to the market not to the pound'. In reaching its decision Ford stated that it feared the effects of an E.E.C. price war, especially from Fiat, Renault and Volkswagen. British

Motor Corporation and Leyland Motor Corporation, on the other hand, were cutting prices by between 4 per cent and 14 per cent in leading European markets in an attempt to increase sales.

The second factor to be considered is the pricing policy of firms' exports and the effects which devaluation might have on switching sales from the home to foreign markets. This concerns the methods used by firms' cost-accountants to arrive at rates of return on foreign and domestic sales respectively. The P.E.P. study provided some evidence to suggest that rates of return were worked out for individual markets on an average cost per unit basis including overheads. The lack of proper accounting procedures in calculating rates of return in home and overseas markets was also commented on by the Mechanical Engineering E.D.C. study. 'The fact that many companies quoted price competition as a major obstacle to exporting reflects (i) the world-wide dual pricing in capital goods; and (ii) the generally greater price sensitivity of less successful exporters. It is significant that the larger more successful exporters gave this factor only half the emphasis accorded to it by less successful exporters . . . many of whom manufacture less sophisticated products in which design differences are often small.' (23) Such questions will be dealt with more fully in Chapter 24. In sum, all three studies reached similar conclusions concerning the reasons for the lack of competitiveness of British exports of engineering products.

(c)   Suggestions for Improvements

All three studies mentioned above make broadly similar suggestions for improving the competitive position of British engineering exports. But the main contention is that although engineering products were frequently competitive from a technical point of view, their marketing problems tended to be neglected.

Frequently British firms lacked an export-orientated view such as existed during the nineteenth century amongst the exporters of cotton piece goods. These, however, were perfect substitutes and could be graded very accurately. Consequently the export side of the cotton trade could be entrusted to merchants who were commercially orientated, and who did not require a technical knowledge of the goods they were selling. Because these goods were such perfect substitutes, price competition of the old style existed and marginal-cost pricing was highly applicable to this trade. In the technologically sophisticated modern world it is far less easy to make use of the services of merchants and other selling intermediaries. Because of product differentiation, relatively few people understand the product being sold, and the producers themselves have to engage in much of the foreign travel which was formerly done on their behalf by selling agents. In contrast to the pricing policy applicable to standardised products, the appropriate pricing policy for sophisticated ones, with short-run production schedules, is average-cost pricing.

Attempts to change the attitudes of businessmen in these matters is particularly difficult, the problem being especially acute amongst small and medium-size firms. As the Mechanical Engineering E.D.C. study noted, in general the greater the growth of exports, the greater the growth of the company. The reverse may also be true. 'Sleepy' firms which lack a dynamic approach to selling will hardly be the most successful exporters. It is not, of course, true that all small firms are 'sleepy'. What matters is a desire on the part of management to see their firm grow. Suggestions for improvements here are that more status should be given to those managers in firms engaged in marketing and sales promotion compared with that given at present to, for example, production managers. This is a conclusion reached in many inquiries into British management. Sales-orientated firms tend to be successful both in home and overseas markets.

The Mechanical Engineering E.D.C. recommended that more companies should set up their own selling organisations abroad, and that medium and large firms in particular should increase the number of visits made abroad by senior export managers and other directors. Many of the complaints received from overseas customers related to after-sales service, which medium and small firms especially, cannot meet. An increased number of follow-up visits, resulting in an improved image for British management abroad, would assist sales in the future. In the field of market research, constant contact with the market is a prerequisite for success, and follow-up visits could be combined with visits to potential customers.

From the standpoint of outside agencies, most emphasis is placed on government assistance to exporters. Although the Government gives assistance through the Exports Credit Guarantee Department, and makes long-term loans, many customers have complained that British credit facilities are not as good as those of our major competitors. It has been suggested that what is chiefly required in this direction is an extension of credit facilities at present applicable to long- and medium-term loans to short-term export business. It is still true today, as it was in the 1930s, that it is much easier to get credit for up to three months or for twenty years without much difficulty. But medium-term finance for periods of between two and ten years is difficult to come by. The Mechanical Engineering E.D.C. was more specific, and suggested use of a scheme whereby the banks would make finance available on credit for up to two years at a fixed and favourable rate of interest. Such interest rates would be independent of changes in Bank Rate. Clearly much could still be done to assist exporters, and as much again could be done by exporters for themselves. (24)

16   The Chemical Industries

1   THE SCOPE AND SIGNIFICANCE OF THE CHEMICAL INDUSTRIES

The chemical industries are essentially process industries. They transform substances in a succession of continuous and regular actions. These processes
operate along two stages: the bringing together of substances under varying
conditions of temperature, pressure and mixture, and the separating-out of the
products of the reaction which has occurred as a result of the first stage. As
such, the chemical industries are in stark contrast to the fabrication type of
industries which have been encountered in the previous chapters on the engineering industries. The chemical industries have been chosen for this second
industrial study to illustrate some of the differences in economic organisation
which may arise owing to technical factors of production. Despite the differences which may be observed, many similarities will also be noticed.

In the United Kingdom the Standard Industrial Classification group III,
'Chemicals and Allied Industries', includes coke ovens and mineral-oil refining.
The Standard International Trade Classification, used by the O.E.C.D., is somewhat narrower than the United Kingdom definition, since it excludes mineral-oil
refining and coke ovens. Nevertheless a wide range of products are included
within the industry. The products are organic and inorganic chemicals; radio-
active materials; mineral tar and crude chemicals from coal, petroleum and
natural gas; dyestuffs; medicinal and pharmaceutical products; essential oils and
resins, perfume materials, soaps and polishes; manufactured fertilisers;
explosives; plastic materials; photographic film and chemicals; and insecticides
and disinfectants. Together, the chemical and allied industries in this country
provide employment for around half a million people, or about one-eighth of the
total employed in all engineering industries including transport equipment. The
industries are nevertheless of extreme importance in that they use new techniques, employ large amounts of capital per worker and tend to be heavy
spenders on research and development. The importance of the different branches
of the chemical industry is illustrated in Table 16.1. It will be apparent that the
industry is dominated by the branch entitled 'chemicals and dyes'. This, however, is an oversimplification of the position. Ethical drugs, which are those

Table 16.1 Branches of Chemicals and Allied Industries, June 1968
(percentage by type of employment)

Lubricating oils and greases	2.0	
Chemicals and dyes, of which*	47.4	
Inorganic chemicals		15.7
Organic chemicals		9.5
Gases and miscellaneous		15.7
Pigments		2.7
Ethical pharmaceuticals		3.8
Pharmaceutical and toilet preparations	16.3	
Explosives and fireworks	5.5	
Paint and printing inks	9.7	
Vegetable and animal oils, fats,		
soaps	7.5	
Synthetic resins and plastic materials	8.2	
Polishes, gelatines, adhesives, etc.	3.2	
Total	99.8	

Source: Department of Employment and Productivity Gazette, Sept. 1968.
* Estimated breakdown based on the Census of Production, 1958.

obtained on prescription from a medical practitioner, are included not under the heading of pharmaceuticals but under chemicals and dyes. Pharmaceuticals in this classification refer only to proprietary medicines. A rough idea of the general breakdown of the chemicals and dyes branch may be obtained from Census of Production data, though these relate to 1958. (1) Employment in the production of inorganic chemicals and gases and miscellaneous chemicals formed about one-third each of the total numbers employed under this heading, whilst organic chemicals formed a fifth, ethical pharmaceuticals one-twelfth and pigments one-twentieth.

2 THE STRUCTURE OF THE INDUSTRY

In 1961 the chemical and allied industries had just under 2,500 establishments with eleven employees and over, or about the same as in the manufacture and assembly of transport equipment within the engineering industries. The size distribution of establishments is shown in Table 16.2. It will be seen that employment is less heavily concentrated amongst a few very large establishments (with 2,000 employees and over) than was the case with the engineering industries. Medium-size establishments (100-499 employees) accounted for the largest grouping of employees, though small establishments (25-99 employees) predominated within size groupings just as in the case of the engineering industries. One of the features of a number of the chemical industries is that they tend to use a high proportion of capital to labour as compared with the position in many other sectors of the economy. They also employ a higher proportion of workers in research and administration than any branch of the engineering industries, with the exception of aircraft manufacture and possibly electronics. Because of the use of pipes and vessels in chemical plant, relationships between length and area as represented by volume are exceedingly important. Capacity to capital costs tends to be in the relation of 5:2.

Table 16.2 Size Distribution of Establishments in the
Chemical and Allied Industries, 1961

Size of establishment	Establishments		Employees	
Employees	Number	%	Number (,000)	%
2,000 and over	29	1.2	108	23.2
1,000 and under 2,000	56	2.3	74	15.8
500 ” ” 1,000	107	4.4	73	15.8
100 ” ” 500	685	28.0	146	31.3
25 ” ” 100	1,086	44.2	56	12.0
11 ” ” 25	488	19.9	9	1.9
Total	2,451	100.0	466	100.0

Source: 'Ministry of Labour Gazette' (Apr 1962).

Some idea of the importance of non-technical economies of scale in the various chemical trades may be obtained from the ratio of the average size of enterprise to the average size of establishment. Data for a number of trades are given for 1963 in Table 16.3. Large-scale establishments are clearly important in the manufacture of dyestuffs and explosives, indicating the existence of considerable technical economies of scale. Judging from the 1958 Census of Production data, they are somewhat less important in inorganic and organic chemical manufacture, the average size of establishment being 330 and 495 respectively. Non-technical economies of scale appear to be particularly important in the production of inorganic chemicals. In 1958, the ratio of the size of enterprise to the size of establishment was 2.15, in explosives and compressed gases. In the same year, the ratio of the size of enterprise to the size of establishment was 1.93 in fertilisers and pest control, and in vegetables and animal oils. In each case bulk purchasing of raw materials used in the production process is of importance, as well as the importance of size in helping to mobilise the amount of capital required to finance these large-scale technical operations. A further measure of size, which tends to reflect non-technical economies of scale, is net assets employed. Data for the chemical and engineering industries are presented in Table 16.4. There was much greater concentration of quoted

Table 16.3 Average Size of Establishment and Enterprise in
some Chemical Industries, 1963

Trade	Average size of Establishment Enterprise (number of employees)		Ratio Enterprise/ Establishment
Fertilisers and pest control	179	343	1.88
Pharmaceutical preparations	329	424	1.29
Toilet preparations	233	267	1.15
Dyestuffs	624	1,123	1.80
Explosives	542	1,058	1.94
Vegetable and animal oils	131	234	1.78
Soaps and detergents	370	485	1.31
Paint and printing ink	74	95	1.29
Gelatine and glues	50	60	1.20
Polishes	55	64	1.16

Source: Board of Trade Census of Production, 1963.

Table 16.4 Net Assets of Quoted Companies at end of 1963
(percentages)

Net assets (£ m.)	Chemicals and allied trades		Engineering industries		All manufacturing industries	
	Companies	Assets	Companies	Assets	Companies	Assets
25 and over	15.0	89.4	5.7	52.9	6.6	65.4
10 and under 25	5.0	2.8	8.9	18.8	7.5	13.0
5 ″ ″ 10	13.8	3.7	11.5	10.6	11.0	8.3
2½ ″ ″ 5	15.0	2.1	20.4	9.5	16.1	6.2
1 ″ ″ 2½	18.8	1.2	27.6	6.1	27.5	5.0
Under 1	32.5	0.7	25.9	2.1	31.3	2.2
Total	100.1	99.9	100.0	100.0	100.0	100.1

Source: Board of Trade, 'Company Assets, Income and Finance in 1963' (H.M.S.O., 1965).

companies measured by size of net assets amongst those with £25 million or more in the chemical and allied industries than was the case with all manufacturing industries and with engineering. From a financial point of view, firms in the chemical trades are large. The Board of Trade analysis of company assets and income also permits an identification of the individual companies concerned, in contrast to the analysis of size of enterprise in the Census of Production. The chemical industries are dominated by the giant Imperial Chemical Industries Ltd (I.C.I.) and by the Anglo-Dutch concern Unilever Ltd. Other large concerns with £25 million assets at the end of 1963 were British Oxygen, Boots Pure Drug, the Beecham Group, Albright and Wilson, Fisons, Glaxo, Laporte Industries, Goodlas Wall and Lead Industries and the American-controlled firm Monsanto. Between them these large concerns cover the whole spectrum of the chemical industries, and they include specialist leaders in a number of branches such as industrial gases, ethical pharmaceuticals and fertilisers. In comparison with the giant American chemical companies, however, the majority of British companies in the industry are small. Only Unilever and I.C.I. are well up amongst the leaders. Du Pont, Union Carbide, Procter and Gamble, Monsanto, Dow Chemical, Allied Chemical, Olin Mathiesen and American Cyanamid all have well over three times the sales of the next ranking British firms, British Oxygen and Albright and Wilson.

Even more so than is the case in the engineering group of industries, companies belonging to the chemical and allied industries tend to be multi-product firms, and exact classification of an enterprise to one trade in the Census of Production is exceedingly difficult. The extent of overlap may in many instances be gauged from the sales of products other than the principal one in the industry. For example, sales of principal products of the 'fertilisers and chemicals for pest control' industry sold by all establishments amounted to £120 million in 1963. One-sixth of this value of the fertilisers and pest-control chemicals was sold by firms not classified as belonging to this industry, and the industry itself sold other products valued at over one-fifth of the value of its principal products in addition to its principal products themselves.

The chemical industries contain fast-growing and slow-growing branches just as in the case of branches of the engineering industries. In general it may be considered that the growth of the industry is determined by the growth rate of the economy as a whole, in that a large proportion of its output consists of intermediate products. Output of the chemicals and allied industries sector of manufacturing has, however, grown faster than the rate of growth of output of all manufacturing industries. During the 1950s, for example, the annual average compound rate of growth of output was almost double that of industrial production, and the gap between the two has increased still further during the 1960s. The fast-growing components of this sector of industry have been plastic materials and organic chemicals, both with a rate of growth of output over twice that of the chemical industries as a whole, and the pharmaceutical industry, with a rate of growth one and a half times that of the chemical industries. Several branches of chemical production have had an average rate of growth. They include inorganic chemicals, fertilisers, paints and varnishes, and toilet preparations. In contrast, dyestuffs, vegetable and animal oils and fats, and soaps and detergents have all grown more slowly than 'chemical' output as a whole, or indeed industrial production.

3   REGIONAL SPECIALISATION

As in the case of the engineering industries, the distribution of employment in chemicals and allied industries simply reflects that of the distribution of the working population. Corrections similar to those made for the engineering industries give a better indication of the true association between the chemical industries and different regions. The results appear in Table 16.5. The chemical industries are much more heavily concentrated in certain regions of the country than was the case with the engineering industries. This is partly a reflection of the size of the industry, but it is also a reflection of locational factors. It will be seen that only the South-east and the North-west regions have the whole range of the chemical industries, and the number of blank spaces is a fair indication of extreme regional dependence and concentration. Again, only the large group of chemicals and dyes and the much smaller plastics industry are to be found in each of the regions.

The heaviest concentration appears in the case of explosives and fireworks, confined essentially, except for production in the East Midlands, to the Celtic fringe. Location away from main centres of population must, however, play some part in determining concentration of production in this industry. The importance of physical deposits of raw chemicals, access to port facilities to import these raw materials, supplies of fuel and plentiful amounts of water are more apparent in determining the degree of regional specialisation in the case of chemicals and dyes. The Northern region has a clear advantage in deposits of salt north of the river Tees, and these, coupled with good supplies of coal, led to the establishment of the I.C.I. works at Billingham. Again salt deposits have been of some importance in determining location in the North-west region, good port facilities at Liverpool for the import of vegetable oils and fats from Africa in particular. Unilever and Port Sunlight are practically synonymous, and the result is the high regional concentration index for vegetable and animal oils and fats for the North-west region. Polishes, etc., are heavily concentrated in the East Midlands and the South-east, partly reflecting their importance to the motor-

Table 16.5 Regional Specialisation in the Chemical and Allied Industries, June 1968
(Great Britain = 100)

Industry group	South-east	East Anglia	South-west	West Midlands	East Midlands	Yorks and Humberside	North-west	North	Scotland	Wales
Lubricants	136.8	–	–	–	–	–	121.1	–	–	–
Chemicals and dyes	70.0	103.9	107.6	83.5	35.6	129.1	126.8	158.0	96.3	62.8
Pharmaceutical and toilet preparations	187.8	–	–	–	275.0	71.6	48.6	27.7	35.8	48.6
Explosives	37.7	–	354.7	294.3	–	–	52.8	–	513.2	250.9
Paint and printing ink	144.9	116.9	96.6	192.1	–	–	71.9	74.2	70.0	–
Vegetable and animal oils, fats, soaps, detergents	58.0	–	–	–	111.6	75.3	227.5	59.4	59.4	–
Plastics	86.7	414.7	177.3	218.7	69.3	134.8	46.7	122.7	74.7	273.3
Polishes, gelatines, adhesives	189.3	–	–	–	332.1	–	39.3	–	–	–

Source: Derived from data in 'Employment and Productivity Gazette' (Mar 1969),
– = nil or original employment figure under 1,000.

vehicle industry, whilst the regional specialisation of plastics shows marked concentration on East Anglia and Wales, reflecting nearness to major markets and the influence of government location of industry policy.

4   COMPETITIVE STRUCTURE AND PRICING POLICY

The pricing policy adopted by companies in the chemical industries reflects the product structure of those industries and the position of individual companies within each trade. Tendencies towards restrictive practices and monopoly control of given markets may be approached via concentration ratios, as in the

Table 16.6 Concentration Ratios in Some Chemical Industries, 1951 and 1963 (percentages of employment/net output accounted for by a small number of enterprises)

	Number of		*Concentration ratios*			
Trade	*enterprises*		*Employment*		*Net output*	
	1951	*1963*	*1951*	*1963*	*1951*	*1963*
Fertilisers	3	5	75	70	73	71
Pharmaceutical preparations	3	4	19	30	23	26
Toilet preparations	3	5	41	35	35	41
Paint and varnish	3	4	20	29	19	37
Soaps	3	4	71	78	76	88
Polishes	3	4	33	67	41	67
Glues	3	4	41	69	39	64
Explosives	6	5	91	88	93	91
Dyes	4	6	89	96	89	96

Source: R. Evely and I.M.D. Little, 'Concentration in British Industry' (N.I.E.S.R., Cambridge, 1960) Appendix B, and Board of Trade Census of Production, 1963.

case of the engineering industries, in order to discover whether there is a prima facie case that any one trade is dominated by a small number of firms. Some concentration ratios, based on the 1963 Census of Production and relating to the largest enterprises, are given in Table 16.6, along with the corresponding concentration ratios for 1951. Unfortunately, because of changes in coverage not all trades in the chemical and allied industries group are comparable, and the Board of Trade 1963 census reports do not give employment or net output taken by fewer than the four largest enterprises. Nevertheless comparisons for some trades may be made. It appears that there is likely to have been some increase in concentration of employment and net output in pharmaceutical preparations and paint and varnish, but the increase in these two trades is not at all marked. In contrast, the increase in concentration in polishes and glues appears to have been fairly substantial, and *may* have lessened the degree of price competition. In a number of other cases, including explosives, dyes, soaps and fertilisers, the degree of concentration in both employment and net output was already very high in 1951, indicating the likelihood of limited competition.

In two instances the high degree of concentration of employment and net output amongst a few enterprises has been a factor leading to references to the Monopolies Commission. Thus chemical fertilisers and household detergents were investigated by the Commission, leading to reports issued in 1960 and 1966 respectively. Other trades to be referred to the Commission have been insulin and certain industrial and medical gases. In each case the reference has been concerned largely with restriction of supplies arising through the existence of economies of scale.

Three cases involving chemical trades have been before the Restrictive Practices Court up to the end of 1968. These were first the Phenol Producers' Association case (7 April 1960), where the Court found against the defendants over the existence of a fixed price for phenol (carbolic acid), which is used principally as a raw material in the plastic and pharmaceutical industries. The second and third cases involved the activities of the National Sulphuric Acid Association, which operates a buying pool and a system of common delivered prices (judgement given 12 July 1963 and 16 November 1966 respectively).

The P.I.B. has also dealt with a limited number of price references in the overall field of chemicals and allied industries. They are the prices of household and toilet soaps and soap powders (Report No. 4, October 1965), the price of compound fertilisers (Report No. 28, March 1967) and the prices of synthetic organic dyestuffs and organic pigments (Report No. 100, January 1969).

In addition there has been one special inquiry concerned with one trade coming within the orbit of the chemical industries, namely the ethical drug side of the pharmaceutical industry. This was the Sainsbury Report, 'Committee of Enquiry into the Relationship of the Pharmaceutical Industry with the National Health Service, 1965-67'. (2)

Whilst these various investigations and inquiries are revealing about the manner in which prices are determined in a broad range of chemical industries, it is clear that in the chemical industries, perhaps more so than in most other industries, competition does not take place solely via price manipulations, important though these may be at times. Competition takes place as much through product variations as it does through price. Attempts to differentiate one's product are of course well known in the final consumers' goods market, especially in the case of soap and detergents, toothpaste and synthetic fibres such as nylon and acrilan. But non-price competition is equally important within other kinds of markets. This attempt to introduce new products which are essentially a variant on already existing products is an important element of competition in the ethical drugs branch of the pharmaceutical industry, and is frequently accompanied by a complex system of patents. The length of life of a product in economic terms is the time which elapses before a new product is effectively displaced in the market by a near rival. During this period a company may earn quasi-rent on the product which it has pioneered, and will attempt to recoup research and development costs associated with that product, so far as it is able to distinguish between the costs of developing and producing individual products. In many instances in the chemical industry this will not in fact be possible, because so many products are by-products and produced under conditions of joint supply.

Where product innovation is rapid and the product structure complex, the traditional competition type of explanation of the manner in which firms determine prices is unilluminating. With rapid product obsolescence such as occurs in many of the newer non-basic chemical products, the traditional rules of competitive pricing no longer hold. In a situation of innovative competition, emphasis is placed on demand considerations. If a product has an innovational edge, this confers a degree of price freedom. There is no immediate rival for these products, and therefore price may now be set within wider limits, determined by such considerations as changes in consumers' incomes and producers' costs, potential new entrants and the prices of the product's nearest substitutes. In general, new products sell on quality rather than on price. Such products tend to be produced under conditions of increasing returns, whilst they are achieving market acceptance. In other words, the demand for new products tends to be income-elastic rather than price-elastic, whilst unit costs of production are likely to fall as output increases. In the stage where firms are developing new products and competing largely along these lines, an increase in output enables capital to be used more fully, so that overhead costs per unit of output will fall. All innovating trades, not only the chemical ones are likely to operate under such conditions. Examples include electronics and computers. All science-based industries, which tend to be heavily involved in innovation, will tend to adopt average-cost pricing rather than marginal-cost pricing.

As the product becomes well established and innovation largely exhausted, competition moves to the more conventional type. Emphasis is placed on price rather than product, and cost considerations become dominant. Output is now pushed to the point where decreasing returns set in. Thus competition has been so severe in sulphuric acid that it is not surprising to find that production takes place under the auspices of a cartel. Price elasticity of demand assumes much greater importance, and such innovation as takes place normally represents an attempt to produce the existing product in a cheaper way. Under cartel conditions the incentive to innovate necessarily remains weak. The cartel itself may attempt to widen markets so as to lower costs. Within a cartel, shared markets on some pro rata basis is the normal situation, but if pressure builds up on individual firms because industry demand falls off, the cartel will weaken and firms may break away. Barriers to new entrants for such basic products tend to remain fairly high because of the enormous capital cost of new basic chemical plant, and new firms which could possibly pose a threat to an existing home-based cartel will almost certainly be well-established leading international companies.

The defensive case for operation under cartel conditions is well illustrated by the evidence given of the activities of the National Sulphuric Acid Association when it appeared before the Restrictive Practices Court in respect of its operation of a buying pool for raw sulphur. In this instance the National Sulphuric Acid Association successfully argued before the Court that its buying pool was needed in order to counteract the selling power of an American corporation Sulexco, a cartel of mining companies formed for the purpose of exporting sulphur.

The complicated pricing position which may exist when by-products assume considerable importance is illustrated in the case of the Phenol Producers' Association before the Restrictive Practices Court in April 1960. In the face of a weak overall supply condition, the Phenol Producers' Association acted along the cartel lines outlined in the preceding paragraphs. Phenol, or carbolic acid, is an important raw material used in the plastic and pharmaceutical industries, so the situation was that of one chemical industry selling intermediate products to other producers within the chemical and allied group. Phenol is made either synthetically from benzene or extracted from coal-tar. The Association contended that the removal of the price restriction would lead to such a fall in revenue that tar would be diverted from distillation to produce phenol into its alternative use as a fuel. In this instance the defendants failed and the Court refused to uphold the price agreement.

In the older, well-established lines of chemical production, price leadership may assume considerable importance. Such a situation exists in synthetic organic dyestuffs, where it has been pointed out that 'dyestuffs producers with a predominant position in their home market can and do act as price leaders thereby protecting their home price structure'. (3) Indeed limited price competition appears to be the norm in each country's home market, but with producers practising price discrimination as between buyers, the stronger ones being able to obtain keener price quotations. The classic position of changes in pricing and output policy as new products become obsolete, however, is well described in The P.I.B. report (100) on dyestuffs and pigments prices, and it is worth quoting para. 27 of that report in full:

L. M.P.M.E.

27. The total market in dyestuffs and pigments is not affected by changes in price, but individual products are so affected. The dyestuffs and pigments sold in any market can be classified by their 'uniqueness'. All large producers will have certain products, patented or based on special know-how, which will be distinct from the products of other makers. These so-called 'speciality' products are usually more profitable so long as they retain their 'speciality' status. As time goes on other makers are often able to circumvent patents and imitate products; and sometimes the use for which the product was intended may decline. Speciality products therefore have a high expectancy of profit in their early lives, declining thereafter until they become 'bread and butter' items. It is estimated that around a third of the products sold fall within the 'speciality' class. It will usually pay makers to direct research into fields which are expected to yield the maximum of successful specialities and therefore of more profitable products. By offering a higher proportion of products with distinct properties a producer can hope to expand his market and raise average profitability. Even where he has discovered and launched a speciality product, however, he runs the risk that it will not meet the needs of the market and will be unprofitable. If he fails to discover enough new winners he will face a contracting market and declining profitability.

5   MERGERS AND ACQUISITIONS

Activity in mergers and take-overs since 1945 has been much less spectacular in the chemicals and allied industries sector of manufacturing than in the engineering industries sector. Many of the take-overs in chemicals have been of a defensive kind, with firms seeking to consolidate their position in existing markets. In a few instances forward integration has been a motive in take-over.

In contrast with the position in the engineering industries, (where the really large mergers and take-overs have taken place almost entirely since 1965) the major amalgamation in the chemical industries was in the pre-war years. Four major companies came together to form Imperial Chemical Industries in 1926. They were Brunner Mond and Co. Lt , United Alkali Co. Ltd, British Dyestuffs Corporation Ltd and Nobel Industries Ltd. Each of these companies had themselves taken over a large number of other companies before joining together. There have been several reorganisations of I.C.I. into different divisions, and several links established with other companies to deal with joint trading interests. The latest reorganisation process started in 1961. This date also marked the beginning of the most acute phase of aggressive marketing in Europe by the large American chemical corporations, going through an important price-cutting warfare in plastics, with prices ending at anything approaching one-half of what they had previously been. I.C.I. emerged from being what was essentially a technically orientated company, rather weak in marketing and administration, into an international company much more concerned with the relationship between progress in markets and its own investment policy. Administratively there has been a change from a presidential type of system of company organisation to a cabinet type. In the late 1960s the company has three major control groups controlling eight divisions: A, covering the dyestuffs division, Nobel division and also I.C.I. fibres; B, covering the heavy organic chemicals, Mond division and plastics division; and C, covering the agricultural division, paints division and pharmaceutical division. The distribution of sales between the different United Kingdom divisions and subsidiaries in 1968 indicates a considerable dependence on the textile industries, a relatively slow-growing sector of the British conomy, though this dependence is substantially less than it was in 1965. Indeed for some time I.C.I. has been in an uncomfort-able position with regard to the textile industry, having developed links with Carrington and Dewhurst Group Ltd, English Sewing Cotton Ltd, Klinger Manufacturing Co. Ltd, Lister and Co. Ltd, Northgate Group Ltd and Viyella International Ltd. The latter cut away from I.C.I. during 1967. In contrast, sales to agriculture have been growing rapidly and now take a much larger share of total sales than formerly. During the post-war years I.C.I.'s major acquisition has been Ilford Ltd, which it bought in 1967. This represents a return to former policies, since I.C.I. had sold its colour photography business to Ilford in 1958 in exchange for a 32 per cent holding of Ilford's equity.

Major acquisitions in the field of basic chemical production have been relatively few in the post-war years. Adequate data are not available, and thus the general principles involved have to be illustrated by a few individual cases. Perhaps the largest series of acquisitions has been that made by the Albright and Wilson Group, whose company structure is set out in Fig. 16.1. The most important and interesting of this company's acquisitions are those of Marchon Products in 1955 and Associated Chemical Companies in 1965. The former company was established in 1939, and its important subsidiary, Solway Chemicals Ltd, started the production of sulphuric acid from anhydrite, mined underneath the factory in Cumberland. The acquisition of Marchon Products was thus a form of backward integration, in that it secured an important alternative source of home-produced raw material to Albright and Wilson. The acquisition of Associated Chemical Companies was a mixture of horizontal integration, with the object of a reduction in competition in some fields of chemical production, and an important extension of capacity into areas of chemical production in which the parent company was not already active, such as chromium chemicals.

Another important series of acquisitions in the basic chemical production is that of Laporte Industries Ltd. Laporte Industries Ltd was set up as a holding company in 1953 to bring together the interests of Laporte Acids, originally acquired by the parent company as John Nicholson in 1948, Laporte Titanium,

Fig. 16.1. The Albright and Wilson Group 1968

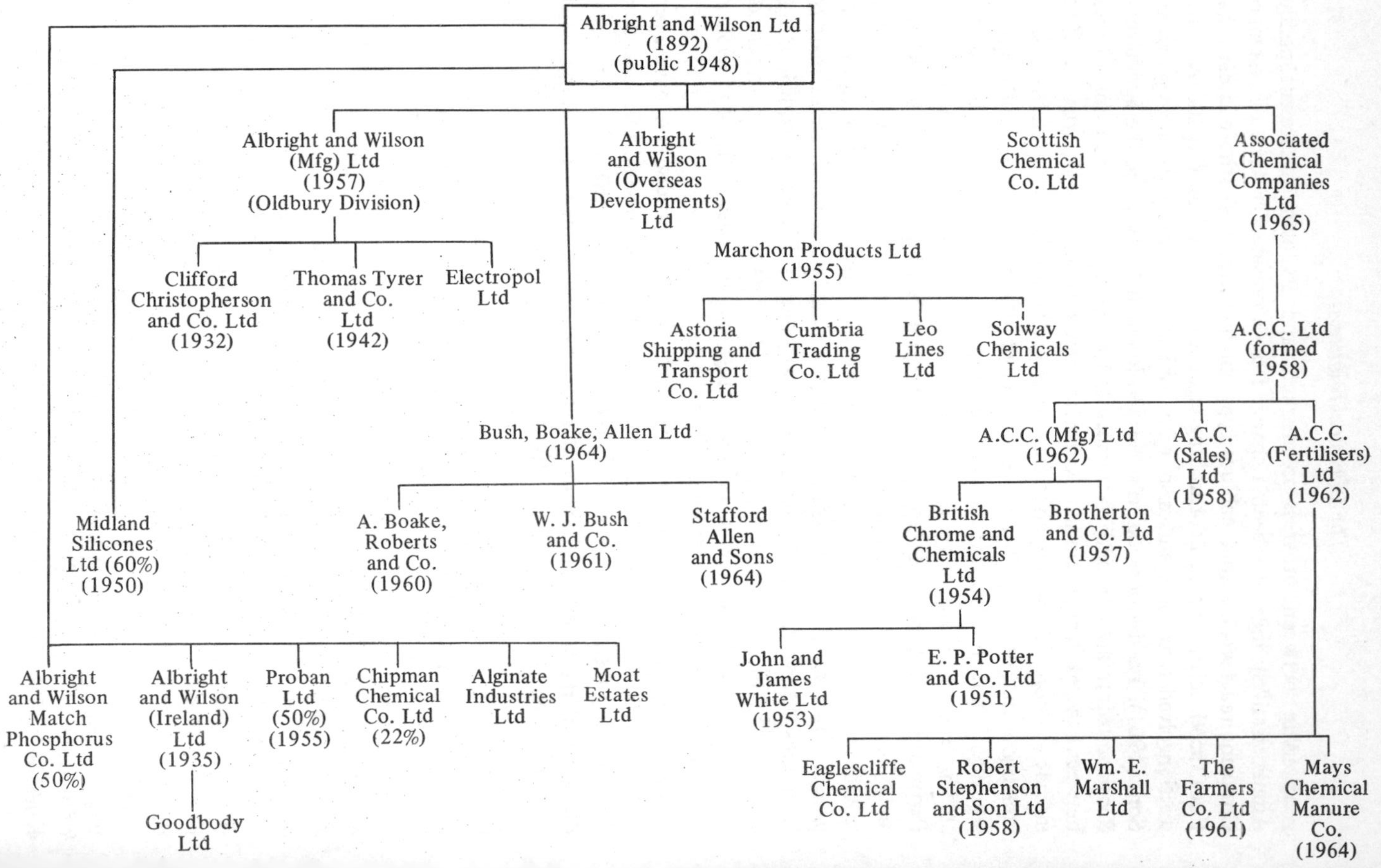

Albright and Wilson Ltd (1892) (public 1948)

Associated Chemical Companies Ltd (1965)

A.C.C. Ltd (formed 1958)

A.C.C. (Fertilisers) Ltd (1962)

A.C.C. (Sales) Ltd (1958)

A.C.C. (Mfg) Ltd (1962)

Brotherton and Co. Ltd (1957)

British Chrome and Chemicals Ltd (1954)

E. P. Potter and Co. Ltd (1951)

Mays Chemical Manure Co. (1964)

The Farmers Co. Ltd (1961)

Wm. E. Marshall Ltd

Robert Stephenson and Son Ltd (1958)

Eaglescliffe Chemical Co. Ltd

John and James White Ltd (1953)

Scottish Chemical Co. Ltd

Albright and Wilson (Overseas Developments) Ltd

Marchon Products Ltd (1955)

Astoria Shipping and Transport Co. Ltd

Cumbria Trading Co. Ltd

Leo Lines Ltd

Solway Chemicals Ltd

Albright and Wilson (Mfg) Ltd (1957) (Oldbury Division)

Clifford Christopherson and Co. Ltd (1932)

Thomas Tyrer and Co. Ltd (1942)

Electropol Ltd

Bush, Boake, Allen Ltd (1964)

A. Boake, Roberts and Co. (1960)

W. J. Bush and Co. (1961)

Stafford Allen and Sons (1964)

Moat Estates Ltd

Alginate Industries Ltd

Chipman Chemical Co. Ltd (22%)

Proban Ltd (50%) (1955)

Albright and Wilson (Ireland) Ltd (1935)

Goodbody Ltd

Midland Silicones Ltd (60%) (1950)

Albright and Wilson Match Phosphorus Co. Ltd (50%)

acquired in 1952, and A. W. Brooker, acquired in 1934. Acquisitions since the date of establishment of the holding company have been Cleckheaton Chemical Co. (acquired 1954), James Wilkinson and Sons (1959) and Sheffield Chemical Co. (1959), all now part of Laporte Acids. Important extensions of activities were involved in the acquisition of Fullers Earth Union (1954), and Howard and Sons (1961). The latter is associated with Bowmans Chemicals, the sole United Kingdom Manufacturer of lactic acid. A further group of acquisitions into the rare-earth and associated mining activities were Glebe Mines (1950), Fluorspar (1964), Cupola Mining and Milling Co. (1960) and Dales Chemicals (1964), which has mineral leases for fluorspar and barytes. An important producer of alum, Peter Spence and Sons Ltd, was acquired in 1960.

The paints section of the chemical industry has seen one large merger since the Second World War, namely that between Lewis Berger and Sons and Jenson and Nicholson to form Berger, Jenson and Nicholson in 1960.

One of the most important series of mergers and acquisitions within this group of industries has been in the pharmaceutical industry. The organisational structure of acquisitions of the Glaxo Group, formed in 1962, is shown in Fig. 16.2. The extension of activities as well as the elimination of duplication of products has been an important factor in this series of acquisitions. The main element in the formation of the group is the original company, Glaxo Laboratories, formed as a private company in 1935 and which later became public in 1947. The original stake in B.D.H. (British Drug Houses) in 1965 represented a form of forward integration within the wholesale trade, as in fact did some of the subsidiaries acquired with Edinburgh Pharmaceutical Industries in 1963. The purchase of Farley's Infant Foods was a natural move to consolidate an existing position in the field of baby foods, and represents further horizontal integration and an attempt to increase market shares in an area under attack from American competition (Heinz and Gerber).

6 NEW ENTRANTS AND PRODUCTS

The formation of new companies and the introduction of new products has been of considerable importance in the post-war history of the chemical industries. A detailed account of individual products and processes will not be attempted here, but some major developments are discussed. Perhaps the most important development in the whole of chemical industries has been that of petrochemicals, and especially their use as a base for the rapidly growing plastics industry. Other end-products based on hydrocarbons, the essential constituents of petroleum, are synthetic detergents, rubber and fertilisers. In the United Kingdom the production of petroleum-based organic chemicals rose over tenfold

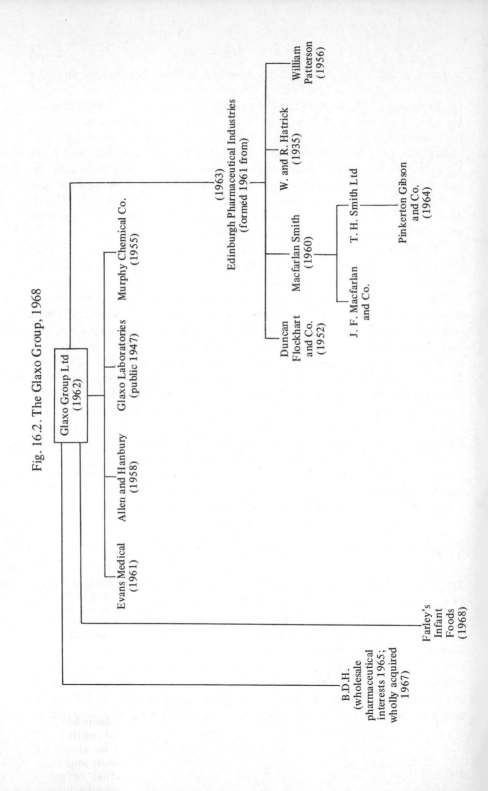

Fig. 16.2. The Glaxo Group, 1968

during the 1950s, and has almost trebled again during the 1960s. Development has been essentially capital-intensive, with the construction of large ethylene plants frequently being undertaken jointly by chemical and oil companies. This has made for a complex company structure. The amount of capital required to finance the new large plants which have come into being, especially during the latter part of the 1960s, has meant that entry into this field of chemical production has been confined essentially to the already existing large chemical and oil companies. Not only has there been considerable collaboration between such companies, but the necessity for physical proximity of petrochemical plant to the refineries has also made for close relationships. This close physical dependence is, however, being reduced gradually by the building of a network of pipelines. Thus Shell Chemical and I.C.I. have arranged pipeline links between the Stanlow refinery and Carrington and between Runcorn and Wilton.

The formation of petrochemical companies has involved not only collaboration between British oil and chemical companies, but also between British and American companies. Indeed a fair proportion of the capital needed to develop the petrochemicals industry in both the United Kingdom and in continental Europe has been supplied by American parent companies acting through European subsidiaries. More recently, however, much of the capital needed for such developments has come through the raising of Euro-dollar loans in the European money markets, and particularly in the United Kingdom.

At the centre of activities in the United Kingdom are the British Petroleum Chemical Co. and the Shell Chemical Co. British Petroleum's chemical interests are complex, and will be used to illustrate the manner in which the petrochemical industry operates on an international scale. These interests are illustrated in Fig. 16.3, which gives dates of founding and/or acquisition of the various subsidiaries, percentage of equity capital held and major products. By the end of 1967 British Petroleum stated that it had become the second-largest chemical group in the United Kingdom. (4) This fact underlines the growing importance of petrochemicals within the chemical industries as a whole. B.P.'s real interest in petrochemicals began shortly after the Second World War with the joint establishment by Distillers Company Ltd (D.C.L.) and B.P. of British Hydro-Carbon Chemicals. B.P.'s major acquisitions in chemical production have been during the second half of the 1960s. During 1965 it acquired the plastics interests of Mobil Chemicals, which gave it 'a share for the first time in the growing field of plastics fabrication and marketing'. The second and more significant acquisition was the chemical interests of D.C.L. in 1967, which put it in the forefront of chemical manufacturers. It will be seen from the capital composition of many of the subsidiaries in Fig. 16.3 that substantial co-operation exists between B.P. and various American oil and chemical interests. With the exception of a plastics plant at Stroud in Gloucestershire and a plant at

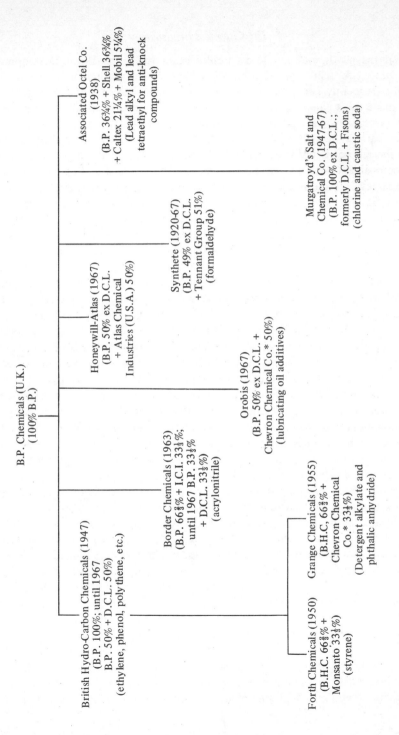

Fig. 16.3. Chemical interests of the British Petroleum Co. Ltd 1968

B.P. Chemicals (U.K.)
(100% B.P.)

Associated Octel Co.
(1938)
(B.P. 36¾% + Shell 36¾%
+ Caltex 21¼% + Mobil 5¼%)
(Lead alkyl and lead
tetraethyl for anti-knock
compounds)

Honeywill-Atlas (1967)
(B.P. 50% ex D.C.L.
+ Atlas Chemical
Industries (U.S.A.) 50%)

Synthete (1920-67)
(B.P. 49% ex D.C.L.
+ Tennant Group 51%)
(formaldehyde)

Murgatroyd's Salt and
Chemical Co. (1947-67)
(B.P. 100% ex D.C.L.;
formerly D.C.L. + Fisons)
(chlorine and caustic soda)

Orobis (1967)
(B.P. 50% ex D.C.L. +
Chevron Chemical Co.* 50%)
(lubricating oil additives)

British Hydro-Carbon Chemicals (1947)
(B.P. 100%; until 1967
B.P. 50% + D.C.L. 50%)
(ethylene, phenol, polythene, etc.)

Border Chemicals (1963)
(B.P. 66⅔% + I.C.I. 33⅓%;
until 1967 B.P. 33⅓%
+ D.C.L. 33⅓%)
(acrylonitrile)

Grange Chemicals (1955)
(B.H.C. 66⅔% +
Chevron Chemical
Co.* 33⅓%)
(Detergent alkylate and
phthalic anhydride)

Forth Chemicals (1950)
(B.H.C. 66⅔% +
Monsanto 33⅓%)
(styrene)

* Subsidiary of Standard Oil Co. (California).

Hull which manufactures phthalic anhydride, used in plastics and paint, and the largest acetic acid plant in Europe, also at Hull, nearly all the B.P. petrochemical plants are adjacent to the company's oil refineries, representing an important saving in transport costs of raw materials.

7 RESEARCH AND DEVELOPMENT

The previous chapter of this book has already discussed some of the major aspects of research and development in a broad sector of British industry, and the overall importance of research and development has been considered in Chapter 8. This section of the present chapter will consequently simply pinpoint one or two aspects of R. & D. of special importance to the chemical industries.

The principal facts relating to R. & D. in general chemicals and pharmaceuticals for 1959-60 may be summarised as follows. Q.S.E. per 100 persons employed was much higher amongst the specialist pharmaceutical firms (2.62) than it was amongst the general chemical firms (1.72), and both ratios were over twice as high as those for manufacturing industry as a whole. (5) Similar results also emerged in terms of internal expenditure on research and development per 100 employed. In relation to turnover, R. & D. expenditure in the chemical industries as a whole in the United Kingdom (3.0 per cent) lagged behind that of the United States (4.7 per cent) and West Germany (3.8 per cent). (6) Evidence suggests that Germany's concentration on R. & D. expenditure, as well as expenditure on plant and other fixed assets in the chemical industries, has yielded high returns in a much shorter time than Britain's concentration on R. & D. expenditure and on capital expenditure in the aircraft industries, where a long period must elapse before returns are shown. So far as exports and the balance of payments are concerned, short pay-off periods for reaping the benefits of a devotion of resources to R. & D. are important. The remainder of this section of the present chapter will discuss the importance of R. & D. in the pharmaceutical industry, one of the rapidly growing chemical industries, and its importance in the field of chemical process plant. The latter provides a link between the previous chapters on the engineering industries and the present chapter on the chemical industries.

(a) Pharmaceuticals
One of the most important facts of economic life regarding R. & D. expenditure is that it must be linked to a firm's profitability. But a straight comparison between the introduction of a profitable new drug and particular research expenditure is fraught with dangers and difficulties. Not only may a new drug emerge from research expenditure which was not originally intended

to produce just that drug, but the actual patenting and production of a given drug may depend to some extent on the research expenditure of entirely different companies. Without the research breakthrough of the other company, the present company's successful production and marketing of its own drug might never have seen the light of day. Again time-lags between a given research expenditure and particular drugs resulting from just that expenditure may be particularly long, with as much as eight years being suggested as a gestation period.

It is thus difficult to analyse the economic mechanisms which determine the size of research budgets of particular firms. Most evidence suggests that firms are usually unwilling to cut back on research expenditure, since this may result in the dispersal of a good research team. It is the actual processes lying behind decisions to expand a firm's research budget which are particularly difficult to disentangle. Individual companies are very reluctant to disclose this type of information, and the report of the Sainsbury Committee (7) was particularly unilluminating on this matter.

Two lines of criticism are frequently encountered in discussions of the importance of research expenditure. The first is that expenditure on pure research as opposed to expenditure on development is too great in Britain. The second is simply that Britain does not spend enough on research compared with other leading countries in the pharmaceutical industry, such as the United States, Switzerland and Japan. The Sainsbury Committee estimated (8) that on average during the years 1963-5 the distribution of total expenditure on research and development of thirty companies operating in Britain and having sales to the National Health Service of £1 million or more a year was as follows. Fundamental research accounted for 57 per cent of total expenditure, process development for 13 per cent, new forms of existing drugs 9 per cent, quality control 2 per cent, grants to universities, etc., 4 per cent, other research expenditure 8 per cent, and the remainder could not be allocated. Expenditure on fundamental research would appear to take a fairly high proportion of the total. The Sainsbury Committee therefore concluded that these claims were probably false and that expenditure on pure research was not neglected. (9) But it is difficult to know what standard of comparison should be made. How does this compare with the proportionate expenditure of other countries on fundamental research? Secondly, just what has been classified as fundamental research? Appearances suggest that total expenditure on R. & D. by the British firms during the mid-1960s was increasing at a declining rate compared with an increasing rate of expenditure by the other leading countries mentioned above, the result being that Britain's share in total R. & D. expenditure was declining. For an industry relying on the discovery of new drugs for maintaining its position in an internationally competitive market, this is a matter of some concern.

(b)   Chemical Process Plant (10)

The importance of design and manufacture of process plant to the oil and chemical industries in particular has been underlined by the early establishment of a process-plant working party under the auspices of the N.E.D.C. Investment in the chemical industry, including petrochemicals, accounted for over half the total investment in all process industries in the United Kingdom during 1963-7, and rather more than one-third of all investment in the process and allied industries, including gas pipelines and storage, petroleum distribution, food processing, and mechanical plant used in electricity generation. Exports amounted to one-sixth of total production of process plant. As a result of the high rate of growth of synthetic materials, based largely on organic chemicals derived from petroleum and natural gas, coupled with an increasing size of process plant, it has been estimated that investment in chemical plant, oil refineries and gas plant now accounts for about one-fifth of total annual investment in world manufacturing industry. Thus the importance of process-plant manufacturers both to the engineering and chemical industries is apparent. Potentialities in this field make it vital for the United Kingdom to improve its competitive position in a fast-growing sector of capital-goods demand and production.

Just as the consumers-goods market for pharmaceutical products is essentially one involving international firms, because of the large amounts of research and development expenditure required to keep abreast of one's competitors, so the manufacture of chemical process plant involves international firms competing in a capital-goods market. The development of these large international firms, specialising in the design and construction of process plant for the oil and chemical industries, is essentially a post-war phenomenon. As in pharmaceuticals, the chemical-plant contracting business is dominated by the large American concerns, such as the Kellog Corporation (a wholly owned subsidiary of the Pullman Corporation), Air Products and Chemicals Inc., Of the sixty-five principal specialist contractors, twenty-one are American, twelve German, nine British, eight Japanese, seven French, five Italian and three Dutch. American companies have also tended to obtain the lion's share of all export contracts, almost two-thirds of the total by value for 1960-6, followed by West Germany with one-tenth, Italy with one-eleventh and the United Kingdom with one-twelfth.

International contracts appear to be won on a combination of know-how and organisation. The former is naturally important in a contractor's ability to win orders, since such plant is ordered infrequently by individual customers and is clearly expected to put the customer in a competitive position vis-à-vis his rivals. Major operating economies may be achieved by installing plant with new designs.

A further consideration is maintenance costs, which can be exceedingly important, since a much larger proportion of labour in chemical plants, and especially petrochemical plants, is engaged on maintenance compared with labour engaged on direct production processes than is the case in the fabricating type of engineering industry. Most contractors make use of international know-how through licensing arrangements, and the British firms are no exception. Since the British contractors form such a compact group, it is worth listing them. They are: Constructors John Brown, Humphreys and Glasgow, Matthew Hall Engineering, Petrocarbon Developments (associated with Burmah Oil), Power-Gas Corporation (a subsidiary of Davy-Ashmore), Simon-Carves Chemical Engineering, Vickers-Zimmer, Geo. Wimpey and Co. and Woodall-Duckham, most of which belong to the British Chemical Engineering Contractors' Association founded in 1920. From an organisational standpoint there is a sharp contrast between that of the Japanese and Italian firms and those of Britain and the United States. Chemical engineering firms in the two former countries tend to be linked vertically with the major chemical firms and component manufacturers. American and British contractors, on the other hand tend not to be so linked and rely on close collaboration with their customers at the pilot-plant construction stage. The British exception is Petrocarbon Developments. The American oil and chemical firms in particular, tend to make considerable use of chemical engineering plant contractors and specialist component makers. This stands in contrast with the American car-assembly firms, which tend increasingly to manufacture a large proportion of their own components. From an organisational standpoint the National Institute inquiry stressed the importance of internal communication between chemists and chemical engineers in the customer chemical firms so that research on new processes was neither duplicated nor wasted because the chemists were ignorant of engineering factors in plant design. British firms were apparently no exception.

8 LABOUR MARKET ORGANISATION

(a) The Occupational Structures

The occupational structure of the chemical industries group is not so complex as in the engineering industries. From a physical standpoint the processes of the chemical industries have more in common than do the methods of fabrication in the engineering industries.

The chemical industries as a whole tend to employ a relatively high proportion of unskilled workers, and the importance of general unions in the pattern of negotiating machinery reflects this, as will be seen later. The group also employs a higher proportion of administrative, technical and clerical

(A.T.C.) staff than any other major group within the Standard Industrial Classification. In contrast, the proportions of both skilled and semi-skilled workers are particularly low. These overall proportions, however, mask considerable variations between different industries within the broad chemical industries group, as may be seen in Table 16.7. The proportion of A.T.C. workers is especially high in paint and printing ink. Although not strictly within the purview of this chapter, mineral-oil refining has been included in this table, since it seems likely that the pattern in this industry will be closely reflected in

Table 16.7 Analysis of Employees according to Type of Worker:
Chemical and Allied Industries, May 1966
(percentages of total employees)

Trade	Class of worker			
	A.T.C.	*Skilled*	*Semi-skilled*	*Others*
Mineral-oil refining	43.2	32.4	7.1	17.3
Lubricating oils and greases	45.4	15.4	6.7	32.5
Chemicals and dyes	38.5	19.3	16.0	26.2
Pharmaceutical and toilet preparations	41.2	9.4	19.9	29.5
Explosives and fireworks	20.1	14.3	30.2	35.5
Paint and printing ink	50.3	10.3	14.8	24.7
Vegetable and animal oils, fats, soaps, detergents	31.5	12.1	12.3	44.1
Synthetic resins and plastics materials	34.4	17.6	30.4	17.6
Polishes, gelatine, adhesives, etc.	35.1	20.2	15.6	29.1
Size of establishment, all trades (employees)				
500 and over	37.8	18.9	18.2	25.1
250 and under 500	39.3	16.6	18.3	25.8
11 " ," 250	36.9	12.2	16.8	34.1
Total	37.8*	16.8	17.8	27.6

Source: 'Ministry of Labour Gazette' (Jan 1967) Tables 34 and 37.
* Of which scientists and technologists 3.7 per cent.

petrochemicals. Here the proportion of skilled operatives is very high compared with other industries within the chemicals group. It will also be noted that the proportion of unskilled workers falls as the size of establishment increases, whilst the proportion of skilled operatives rises. But in contrast with the situation in the engineering industries, there is no significant difference in the proportions of A.T.C. workers between small, medium or large-size establishments.

(b)   The System of Wage Bargaining

Although the chemical industries group comprises a wide range of products and processes, there has long been a high degree of organisation of employers and workpeople. With the major exception of Imperial Chemical Industries Ltd, which engages in direct negotiations with its own employees on a strict company basis, the general system of wage bargaining is through the medium of Joint Industrial Councils (J.I.C.).

Throughout the chemical industries the principal labour organisations are unions consisting predominantly of unskilled workers. As has been seen above, this reflects the occupational distribution of the industries' labour force. These unions are the Transport and General Workers' Union, the National Union of General and Municipal Workers, the Union of Salt, Chemical and Industrial Workers, and the Union of Shop, Distributive and Allied Workers. Negotiations take place between representatives of these unions and the appropriate employers' organisations, occasionally with the addition of a specialist union. Until 1966 the major employers' association was the Association of Chemical and Allied Employers. In that year it merged with the Association of British Chemical Manufacturers to form the Chemical Industries Association. In contrast to the A.C. and A.E., the B.C.M. had not concerned itself with wages and labour problems. The C.I.A. is now the employers' main negotiating body.

There are five major Joint Industrial Councils in the chemical industries. The Chemical and Allied Industries J.I.C., constituted in 1936, deals with heavy chemicals, fertilisers and plastics. The function of this council is to negotiate basic rates of pay and conditions of work for both day and shift workers. The latter are particularly important in process industries, where continuous working is an important element making for the optimum use of expensive plant and so reducing operating costs. In addition to the main council there are three group councils dealing with matters peculiar to the three principal trade unions. A procedure exists whereby disputes not resolved after direct discussion between employers and unions at headquarters level are referred to the main or group councils. Other J.I.C.s are Drugs and Fine Chemicals; Gelatine and Glue, where the Amalgamated Society of Leather Workers is also involved in negotiations; Paint, Varnish and Lacquer; and finally Soap, Candle and Edible Fats Trades. A feature of the latter is that the negotiated national agreement classifies firms according to size and degree of mechanisation, and wage rates and conditions of work vary with each individual firm's classification. The wage structure of individual firms consists of a superstructure built on the basic rates negotiated by the J.I.C.s. This consists of a system of differentials, frequently involving bonuses based on job evaluation. A number of other payments, such as service and attendance payments, conditions money and lieu bonus payments, also exist.

It is thus not surprising to find that the chemical and allied industries are leaders in establishing productivity agreements based on plant bargaining. Of the five major productivity agreements referred to the P.I.B. in August 1966 and reported on in Report No. 36, 'Productivity Agreements', those concluded by I.C.I. and British Oxygen Co. Ltd come directly within the present scope of the chemical industries, and the Esso Petroleum Co. agreements are marginal. Other chemical agreements discussed in the report were those involving Petrochemicals, a subsidiary of Shell Chemicals, at Carrington, and four other oil-company agreements. Only three others fell outside these industries. These were all inspired in part at least by the original Esso productivity agreements in 1960. In most cases some forecasting was involved of the likely net gains in cost reduction and/or increased output likely to come about as the result of the agreements. The whole process of concluding productivity agreements in the chemical industry was taken an important stage further towards the end of 1967, when a guideline agreement was signed between the Chemical Industries Association and the twelve unions with whom they negotiate. The chemical industry's overall guidelines in respect of local productivity agreements and their relation to national minimum wage rates was commended in the Donovan Report on trade unions and employers' associations, and may provide a model which other industrial groups will follow.

(c)   Wage and Earnings Structure
In contrast with the position in the engineering industries, the proportion of workers in the chemical industries working under Payment-by-Result (P.B.R.) systems is relatively low, as may be seen from Table 16.8. Judging from the occupational earnings surveys of 1964 and 1967, the 1961 figures for adult male manual workers were either considerable underestimates of the position in the chemical industries, or else the proportion of male workers operating under P.B.R. systems has increased considerably during the 1960s. The proportions in 1964 and 1967 for all workers were 41.1 per cent and 43.3 per cent respectively, compared with only 22 per cent in 1961. According to the occupational earnings surveys there was no significant difference between the proportions of skilled and general workers operating under P.B.R. systems. The

Tables 16.8 Proportions of Workers operating under P.B.R. Systems
in the Chemical Industries, 1961
(percentage)

Industry	Men	Youths	Women	Girls	All
Mineral-oil refining	5	1	6	–	5
Lubricating oils, etc.	0	–	0	–	0
Chemicals and dyes	27	6	13	6	24
Pharmaceutical and toilet preparations	7	4	20	22	15
Explosives and fireworks	16	6	55	80	24
Paint and printing ink	22	14	17	–	20
Vegetable and animal oils, fats, soaps, detergents	15	5	14	8	14
Synthetic resins, plastics	27	13	18	–	26
Polishes, gelatine, adhesives, etc.	14	2	31	50	21
Total	22	6	20	24	21

Source: 'Payment by Results', in 'Ministry of Labour Gazette' (Sep 1961) Table 1.

very nature of process production makes the application of individual piece rates or bonuses or group bonuses impracticable, in that it is difficult to attribute output to particular individuals or groups of individuals. Thus it is hardly surprising to find that ordinary-type P.B.R. systems have been replaced by productivity bargaining at the whole plant level.

It is also easier to give a general account of the wages structure of the chemical industries. Key settlements, so far as craftsmen are concerned, are relatively easy to identify compared with the position for general workers. They tend to follow the pattern established in the engineering industries, and provide an example of wage contours and the influence of external wage structures. Thus separate rates are given for fitters, electricians and building craftsmen. The overall wage-earnings structure for the chemical industries is set out in Table 16.9. The importance of maintenance work in the process-plant industries is underlined by the high earnings of electricians and fitters, whether timeworkers or operating under one of the P.B.R. systems. Again, the relatively high earnings of general workers operating a continuous three-shift system underlines the importance of such working in cutting operating costs in the process industries. Indeed the physical nature of many of the chemical processes involved and the

Table 16.9 Occupational Analysis of Average Weekly Earnings,
including Overtime, for Adult Males
in Chemical Manufacture, January 1967
(average earnings for all workers covered = 100)

Class of worker	Time workers	Payment-by-results workers
General workers engaged in production		
Day workers	83.7	90.4
Continuous three-shift workers	108.8	100.9
Non-continuous three-shift workers	104.6	103.3
Two-shift workers	105.2	105.0
Others, including night workers	102.4	93.0
Craftsmen		
Fitters	111.5	109.9
Electricians	112.0	110.1
Other engineering craftsmen	111.8	102.9
Building craftsmen	100.7	102.5
	s *d*	*s* *d*
Average earnings for all workers	422 11	425 7

Source: 'Occupational Earnings of Manual Workers', in 'Ministry of Labour Gazette' (May 1967) Tables 4 and 11.

reaction cycle, make continuous shift working an essential ingredient of production.

Regional differences in the pattern of earnings are shown in Table 16.10. There is a considerable discrepancy between the position of workers in the South-west region according to whether they are operating on a time-rate or P.B.R. basis. Time workers appear to be either badly paid in the South-west compared with other regions, or to have far fewer opportunities to engage in overtime, whereas they are amongst the most highly paid when operating under P.B.R. systems. The most striking thing about Table 16.10 is the lack of consistency between the behaviour of regions. Rankings change widely according to whether workers are operating on a P.B.R. system or a time basis, or are general or craftsmen. Difference in the composition of the labour force in plant located in different regions appear to be far more important in determining earnings patterns than any characteristics of the regions themselves in terms of labour scarcity, etc.

(d) Overall Wage Movements and Productivity

Basic weekly wage rates in the chemical and allied industries have risen relatively slowly since the mid-1950s. In 1968 they were only 58 per cent above the

Table 16.10 Chemical Manufacture: Regional Analysis of Earnings, January 1967
(average weekly earnings, including overtime premium)
(Great Britain = 100)

Region	Time workers		Payments-by-results workers	
		Craftsmen	General workers	Craftsmen
London and South-east	97.6	101.0	102.7	106.2
East and South	98.1	99.0	89.7	90.9
South-west	82.6	–	106.3	106.7
Midlands	98.6	90.9	103.3	98.2
Yorks and Humberside	91.3	91.2	107.1	98.9
North-west	107.5	103.3	103.3	103.7
North	96.5	104.4	95.5	98.3
Scotland	99.7	121.4	93.2	87.6
Wales	106.5	92.9	–	–
	s d	*s d*	*s d*	*s d*
Great Britain	410 9	466 2	417 1	456 6

Source: 'Ministry of Labour Gazette' (May 1967) Tables 6 and 9.
– indicates that figure would reveal earnings in particular firms, or numbers too small.

Table 16.11 Average Weekly Earnings in the Chemical and
Allied Industries, 1963-8
(June 1963 = 100)

Date	Chemical manufacture			All manufacturing industries
	Fitters P.B.R.	General workers		
		Time	*P.B.R.*	
June 1963	100	100	100	100
Jan 1964	101.3	104.3	103.3	105.4
June 1964	108.4	110.7	108.1	108.0
Jan 1965	110.0	114.4	110.1	112.5
June 1965	112.3	115.0	116.1	116.6
Jan 1966	119.0	124.1	121.3	121.3
June 1966	121.3	128.2	122.3	120.8
Jan 1967	116.4	123.2	118.6	122.2
June 1967	122.5	124.6	122.5	126.6
Jan 1968	128.3	135.2	129.5	132.0
June 1968	133.3	133.0	133.0	136.7

Source: Ministry of Labour/D.E.P.

average for 1956, and only two industries, textiles with a 52 per cent increase and leather with a 57 per cent increase, had risen more slowly. The position with regard to average hourly rates has been no different. Earnings too appear to have risen less than the average for all manufacturing industries, as may be seen in Table 16.11. For firms affiliated to the Chemical Industries Association there has been no alteration in the wage-rate differential between day labourers and skilled fitters, electricians, etc., and during the 1960s the latter have consistently received an hourly wage rate one-quarter above that of the labourers' rate. This is also borne out by information available on earnings, where P.B.R. fitters have increased their earnings more or less pari passu with the increase shown by general workers employed on either a time or a P.B.R. basis.

Although not easy to measure accurately from published data, productivity in the chemical and allied industries appears to have been increasing rapidly during the 1960s. Changes in labour input in the form of numbers of employees are difficult to measure accurately because of changes in the scope of the figures issued by the Ministry of Labour/D.E.P. Productivity in the chemical industries has risen at about twice the rate of increase in output per man-hour worked in manufacturing as a whole. Gross fixed capital formation in the chemical industries, however, has been rising at only about the same rate per annum as in manufacturing as a whole. This increase in productivity has been achieved with only a small increase in the share of total capital formation going to the chemical industries, and it has resulted in a fall in the price of chemical products relative to the general level of prices.

9 THE INTERNATIONAL COMPETITIVE POSITION OF THE CHEMICAL INDUSTRIES

World production of the chemical industries is dominated by the United States. In the mid-1960s the United States produced over two-fifths of total world output of chemical products. No other country came anywhere near having much over one-tenth of world production, and the United States' main rivals in international trade in chemicals, West Germany, Japan and the United Kingdom, produced about one-twelfth of world output respectively. The United States is dominant on account of its huge market, and the high power of its scientific research and development, as well as through possessing abundant supplies of raw materials and cheap power.

It will be seen from Table 16.12 that the United States is somewhat less dominant in international trade than in terms of total world production. Compared with its two-fifths share of world production, its share in world exports in the mid-1960s was only just over one-fifth of the total, and it was

Table 16.12 Share in World Chemical Exports
(per cent)

Country	1937	1954	1965
United States	16	28	23
West Germany	36*	17	20
United Kingdom	17	16	12
France	11	9	10
Italy	2	3	6
Netherlands	n.a.	4	6
Switzerland	5	6	6
Belgium	6	5	4
Japan	3	2	5
Others	(4)	10	8
Total	100	100	100
Value of world exports (£m.)	164	1,280	3,740

Source: H. Tyszynski, 'World Trade in Manufactured Commodities', in 'Manchester School' (Sep 1951) and O.E.C.D., 'The Chemical Industry, 1965-1966' (Paris, 1967) Annex IV, Table 2.
* Includes East Germany

being challenged in this leadership by West Germany. E.E.C. countries combined, accounted for little short of half the total of world exports in chemicals. Whilst world exports of chemicals have been growing at an enormous rate since just before the Second World War, and have risen threefold in the decade from the mid-1950s to the mid-1960s, the United Kingdom's share of that total has been declining, with most of the decline coming since the mid-1950s. The United States' share has also been falling, whilst those of West Germany, Italy, the Netherlands and Japan have been rising sharply. The combined E.E.C. share rose substantially from 38 per cent in 1954 to 46 per cent in 1965.

A further measure of export performance is to consider the proportion of the industry's turnover exported. This is done for a number of leading exporters in Table 16.13. British performance on this basis is good, and the proportion of output exported has increased slightly during the first half of the 1960s, when pressure from competitors such as West Germany in international markets was particularly strong. Both West Germany and France have managed to increase the proportions of chemical turnover exports rather more than the United Kingdom. It should be noted that some small countries such as the Netherlands

Table 16.13 Chemical Exports as a Percentage of Chemical Turnover

Country	1954-6	1960	1964
United Kingdom	19.6	18.7	20.4
West Germany	22.5	24.8	28.2
France	13.8*	17.8	18.5
Italy	8.7*	10.1	11.0
United States	5.5	6.4	7.9
Japan	—	—	7.6

Source: O.E.C.D., 'The Chemical Industry'.
* 1956.

(45 per cent) and Switzerland (70 per cent) export much higher percentages of turnover than the larger countries. The position of West Germany in particular, and to a lesser extent the position of Italy in world chemical exports, has been assisted by an extension of intra-European trading following the formation of E.E.C., as is illustrated by Table 16.14. E.E.C. exporters supply well over half of the total E.E.C. import requirements. This has placed E.E.C. producers at an advantage compared with British firms. In a field where there are large economies of scale to be obtained from the operation of big modern plant, the advantage of a large home market as a base is critical. It is only during the latter part of the 1960s that British chemical firms have installed plant on such a scale that there exists a large spare capacity for export purposes. The figures of Table 16.13 may be expected to show a sizeable upward trend when data for the late 1960s become available. Unfortunately for the United Kingdom at the same

Table 16.14 Imports of Chemical Products Supplied by
Major Exporters, 1966

Exporters	Proportion of total chemical imports into		
	U.S.A.	E.E.C.	U.K.
United States	—	16.7	32.3
E.E.C.	28.2	57.2	40.5
United Kingdom	7.6	7.6	—
Switzerland	4.5	6.5	6.1
Japan	7.5	1.7	2.3

Source: O.E.C.D., 'Commodity Trade: Imports', series C (Jan-Dec 1966).

time as chemical exports have been rising rapidly, the same is true of imports, and the British trade balance in chemicals has remained almost stationary since 1958, in contrast to increasing positive balances shown by West Germany and the United States, and on a smaller scale by the Netherlands and Switzerland.

A study of British and West German exports performances by the Chemicals E.D.C. is illuminating. Germany is helped in its export performance by her membership of the European Economic Community. In the mid-1960s three-tenths of German exports of chemicals were going to other E.E.C. countries. But an important aspect of the growth of West Germany's chemical exports has been her penetration of the overseas sterling-area markets, where Britain's share in this area's total chemical imports slumped from supplying over half in 1954 to just under a third in 1965. In general the product structure of German chemical exports is orientated more towards those exports such as plastics and organics which are growing fastest in world trade than are British chemical exports. It is also the case that productivity as measured by turnover per person employed. (11) has risen slower in the United Kingdom during the last decade than in any other major West European chemical producer, though the West German position is not so greatly superior. Turnover per person employed in the United States was over two and a half times that of the United Kingdom, whilst Italy was half as much again and France and the Netherlands about a quarter as much again.

Finally one important aspect of international competition, especially in the chemical and allied industries, which a comparison of direct international trade figures tends to mask, is the presence of subsidiaries of the large international chemical corporations in countries outside the country of origin of the parent. Most of the leading American chemical corporations, such as Du Pont, Union Carbide, Monsanto, Dow Chemicals, Allied Chemical and Cyanamid, have subsidiaries based in Europe, which remit profits back to their parent organisations. American chemical companies during the latter part of the 1960s have been investing some $350 million a year in Europe, equivalent to almost one-tenth of their total capital expenditure. This has been directed in particular towards the rapidly growing petrochemicals and their organic derivatives. Although United States Government curbs on investment overseas could conceivably slow down this rate of investment, American firms have been turning more and more to the raising of Euro-dollar loans in order to finance these projects, and the trends established during the latter part of the decade of the 1960s seem likely to continue into the early 1970s. (12)

17 The Gas Industry

1 BACKGROUND

The three previous chapters have all been concerned with major sectors of private industry, where the rules concerning pricing and output are based on the predominantly commercial considerations of profit-making, the growth of the firm, or some similar objective. The avowed aim of the nationalised industries is different. Since nationalisation first became a reality during the second half of the 1940s, various Acts and White Papers governing the conduct of the nationalised industries have proclaimed that they should not be operated on purely commercial principles, but should take into account social as well as private costs. The present chapter aims to illustrate the principles involved in operating nationalised industries by a study of the gas industry.

There are a number of reasons why a study of the gas industry is appropriate in the present context. Many of the branches of the engineering and chemical industries are growing industries, subject to fairly rapid technological change, or are technologically advanced in an absolute sense. Of all the nationalised industries it is perhaps the gas industry which has been subject to most technological change during the 1960s. In addition it bears close comparison with the chemical industries studied in the previous chapter. Its present technology and production processes are essentially flow processes, and its principal function has been to convert a variety of raw materials by chemical methods into gas. Its modern plants closely resemble those of oil refineries and draw heavily on the chemical engineering industry for their design and construction.

As one of the original public utilities, the gas industry has long served an essentially domestic and commercial market in the provision of heating and lighting, the latter giving way to electricity around the time of the First World War. Alongside electricity, the industry early engaged the attention of economists in terms of its pricing and output policy. Monopoly of the traditional kind belongs to the gas industry largely in its control of the distribution and sale of gas. In contrast, it has both produced its own gas and bought gas from other producers who have surpluses, for example from the coke ovens of the steel industry. In terms of the provision of heating it is not a monopolist,

and has to compete with the other nationalised fuel industries, coal and electricity, as well as with the privately owned oil industry. As one of the group of
nationalised fuel industries it is constrained in its operations by whatever overall
policy is laid down by the Government of the day for the fuel sector of the
economy.

2   SOURCES OF SUPPLY

Changes in the sources of supply of gas output are shown in Table 17.1. This
table illustrates the rapid changes which have been taking place in the gas
industry, especially during the middle of the 1960s. From what was essentially a
coal-converting industry, with almost three-quarters of its output stemming from
that source in 1958, the industry of the late sixties is predominantly oil-based.
This change-over in source of raw material has meant heavy investment in new
gasification plant, the latest examples of which resemble oil refineries rather
than the old coke and gas works of the 1940s and 1950s. In addition, the
discoveries of deposits of natural gas, both on land and in the North Sea, have

Table 17.1 Sources of Gas Production, 1958-67
(percentages of total gas production)

Source	1958	1963	1967
Made at gasworks from			
Coal	65.8	50.9	23.9
Water	14.3	15.4	3.8
Oil	1.1	5.2	32.2
Producer gas, etc.	0.9	1.9	1.6
Total made	82.1	73.4	61.6
Bought from			
Coke ovens	16.4	14.2	9.1
Oil refineries	1.3	11.8	18.2
Natural gas producers*	0.2	0.6	11.1
Total bought	17.9	26.6	38.4
Total	100.0	100.0	100.0

Source: 'Annual Abstract of Statistics' (1968).
* Indigenous and imported.

created a third source of supply and are posing additional problems of adapta-
tion to technological change. Indeed the industry is now facing a second
revolution in its production techniques, within a few years of undergoing that
created by the change to oil. As a result of the exploitation of North Sea
deposits of natural gas, imports of oil used by the gas industry are expected to
fall dramatically. With the exploitation of natural gas, methods of storage
become of prime importance in total capital costs, as well as transmission costs
and those incurred in converting existing appliances for its use. The implications
of such changes for pricing and investment policy are considered later.

During the late 1960s the gas industry emerged as one engaging both in
manufacturing activity and as an important customer of the producers of natural
gas. Whereas the industry was still producing four-fifths of its total sales during
the late 1950s, a decade later the proportion of manufactured gas had fallen to
three-fifths whilst that bought in had doubled from one-fifth of the total to
two-fifths. Forecasts of changes in the sources of gas output between 1966-7 and
1972-3 are startling. While coal gas and oil gas each supplied 32 per cent of the
total in the former years, and natural gas only 8 per cent, it is anticipated that
supplies of coal gas will fall to 1 per cent, oil gas to 9 per cent, and that natural
gas will rise to 85 per cent by the latter dates.

To sum up the present 1968-69 supply position, it can be argued that the gas
industry consists of two separate industries existing side by side within the same
organisation, although the two industries have some measure of interdepen-
dence. On the one hand there is the old town-gas industry, with its own separate
distribution network, and on the other hand there is the new natural-gas
industry, also with its own distribution network. Physically the former is
manufactured, whilst the latter is drawn from wells. The main point of inter-
dependence lies in the manufacture by some town-gas oil reformers of substitute
natural gas.

3 ECONOMIES OF SCALE

The production of gas has been subject to considerable economies of scale,
leading to a long-run decline in marginal costs. Such economies arise both in the
manufacture of town gas from either coal or oil and in the distribution and
storage of natural gas, either in its gaseous or liquid form.

During the 1960s economies of scale have been confined principally to gas
manufacture. Here the economies to be obtained from large-scale production
have been considerable. Improvements have taken place in gasification plant
technology, especially in the case of oil-reforming plant. Indeed nearly all the
technical developments in gas production during this century have favoured

moves to larger-scale plant and the subsequent storage of the gas in large gasholders. As economies of scale in manufacturing plant have increased, the number of plants required to produce the industry's total output has fallen, even though consumption has risen, especially since the early 1960s. Between 1963-4 and 1967-8, for example, the number of manufacturing plants dropped from 272 to 192, whilst the number of employees in the industry remained constant and gas consumption rose from 2,979 million therms to 4,228 million therms. Economies of scale have also been achieved by the use of large gasholders, where a doubling of dimensions leads to a substantially greater increase in capacity. The use of large-scale manufacturing plants and gasholders has been aided by innovations in oil gas reformers, which have enabled gas to be produced under high pressure.

Initially the advantages to be gained from large-scale production could not be fully achieved because of the relatively small size of local markets. Gas had to be manufactured where it was consumed because of high transmission costs, and plants were located where distribution costs were lowest. Bringing coal to the gasworks provided a cost-minimising solution. The manufacture of gas in oil reformers enabled an important step forward to be made, since it is much easier to transmit gas for long distances under high pressure. Although the steel-tube producers were already used to providing pipelines capable of transmitting liquids under pressure for the oil companies, advances in steel technology enabled pipelines to be constructed capable of transmitting gas under these conditions. The possibility of establishing a gas grid was thus at hand. Local gas plants could now be converted from production to storage depots, and output concentrated in those places where raw-material costs were lowest. As a consequence the locational advantages swung away from a major emphasis on consumption centres to raw material centres. The laying-down of a national gas grid now involved relatively heavy investment in the transmission system as compared with expenditure on plant.

Economies of scale in the manufacturing process also acted as an aid to further research and development within the industry. Before the introduction of large-scale oil-reforming plant, the incentive to research and development within the industry itself was lacking, and it appears to have relied heavily on outside sources.

The discovery of natural gas in the North Sea has also led to a change in the type of economies of scale. In the case of town gas, the economies have been obtained mainly in production methods, coupled with some distribution economies. In contrast the economies of scale to be achieved in the case of natural gas relate to transmission and storage. Both operate in terms of the relationship between dimensions and volumes. The advantages appertaining to steel technology have already been mentioned, and the main form of investment during the early 1970s will be in pipelines, with recompression of the gas at intervals on the pipeline system. Technical problems of storage and economies to be achieved in that direction are important because of the diurnal and seasonal fluctuations in consumers' demand. This is a capacity problem which the gas industry has in common with two other nationalised industries, namely electricity and the railways. Storage may take place in aquifers (natural underground cavities), in their man-made equivalents such as disused salt-mines, or within the system itself via the use of line-pack and horizontal high-pressure cylinders. The new line-pack method of storage of natural gas in the mains means that the capacity of the mains has also effectively doubled, since natural gas has twice the calorific value of town gas. Liquid natural gas has also been stored in underground cavities, and much may be learned from the United States, where the problem has long been present. Each of these methods of storage has its own cost characteristics. The peak demands may also be met by the manufacture of substitute natural gas through the conversion of town-gas oil reformers, although the costs of doing so are high. Lastly there are important economies of scale arising in the ocean transportation of liquid natural gas in giant tankers, much of which at present comes from North Africa.

4 FUEL POLICY AND THE MARKET FOR GAS

During the second half of the 1960s the demand for gas rose sharply. From an increase of only 2 per cent in 1963/4, gas consumption rose to an average annual rate of increase of 10 per cent during the four years 1965-9. Gas Council forecasts estimated large increases of 27 per cent for 1969-70 and 21 per cent for 1970-1, with the rate of increase slackening to 14 per cent for 1971-2 and 10 per cent for 1972-3.

The demand for gas is affected largely by relative fuel costs. Increased consumption may take two forms. Existing consumers may simply increase their consumption of gas by using their appliances more intensively, or they may purchase new appliances. Or the prospects of movement in relative fuel prices in favour of gas may persuade users of other fuels to change over to gas. Prospects that the latter would materialise in the 1970s have been influenced chiefly by the discoveries of deposits of natural gas in the North Sea.

There have been some important changes in the pattern of consumers' demand during the 1960s, and further changes in the pattern of demand are forecast for the early 1970s. These changes are indicated in Table 17.2. It will be seen that large increases in the demand for gas during the latter half of the 1960s stemmed principally from domestic consumers, and that the proportion of industrial and commercial sales declined. Between 1964 and 1968 gas consump-

Table 17.2 Gas Sales and Forecasts, 1960-1 to 1972-3
(percentages of total sales)

Consumer	1960-1	1966-7	1972-3*
Domestic	48	60	51
Industrial	32	24	40
Commercial and other	20	16	9
Total	100	100	100

Source: Gas Council.

* Forecast.

tion by domestic consumers increased at an annual average rate of 14 per cent, compared with an annual average increase by industry of only 1 per cent and by commercial and other users of only 3 per cent. Increasing sales of space heaters, and more particularly central heating installations, have been of prime importance in explaining the increase in demand on the part of domestic consumers. Rising incomes have led to increased expenditure on central heating systems of all types, and sales here have been helped by a relatively high income elasticity of demand. This period has also seen a change in the image of gas from being a dirty fuel to that of a clean one. The spread of central heating installations has also led to research and development of compact household boilers on the part of the appliance manufacturers, and the introduction of small-bore piping has also helped to sell such installations. Gas has also tended to gain over solid fuel and oil in requiring no storage space for the fuel used.

In contrast to the rapid increase in domestic demand, industrial demand for gas-fired furnaces has been relatively slow to develop. Competition from oil-fired furnaces has been especially severe. However, the relative balance of fuel prices being likely to shift in favour of gas during the early 1970s has led to the formulation of forecasts of huge percentage increases in demand on the part of industry. Gas Council forecasts (1) indicate an 81 per cent increase for 1969-70 and a 43 per cent increase for 1970-1, falling to a 19 per cent increase for 1971-2 and 12 per cent for 1972-3. Industry's share of total gas consumption is consequently expected to increase from 24 per cent in 1966-7 to 40 per cent in 1972-3. Government forecasts in the 'Fuel Policy Blue Book' (2) were to the effect that natural gas was expected to meet about 15 per cent of the total demand for energy in Britain by 1975. This anticipation was based on a policy of introducing North Sea gas into the economy as rapidly as possible. Indeed it was suggested that proved North Sea gas reserves of 3,000 mn. cu. ft per day would be sufficient to support gas sales at least three times as great as they were in 1967. From an estimated life of fifteen years, North Sea gas reserves were later estimated to be of the order of twenty-five years at the same rate of exploitation. (3) By the mid 1970s the latest Government White Paper assumed that consumption might rise to a level of 4,000 mn. cu. ft per day, but that a major marketing effort would be required to use this volume of natural gas.

5 INVESTMENT POLICY AND FINANCIAL OBLIGATIONS

All industries use scarce resources which have alternative uses, and nationalised industries are no exception. In total the investment effort of the nationalised industries alone is equal to the volume of investment by the private sector of the economy. The impact which the nationalised sector has on potential economic performance is thus considerable. The initial criterion laid down for operating the nationalised industries was based on the formula that costs should be covered taking one year with another. This corresponds to a policy criterion of maintaining economic activity intact, but the policy target came to be 'growth with full employment' rather than just full employment.

In 1961 a White Paper (4) on the operation of the nationalised industries took the deliberate step of revising the previous criteria so as to make them more commercial. Each industry was set an overall target rate of return on capital, to be achieved over a five-year period. The intention of this change was to provide a financial incentive to improve performance, to lower the burden on the Exchequer by inducing the nationalised industries to generate a higher proportion of their own investment capital, and to provide a guide to their efficient working. Different target rates of return were set for different industries, according to their likely performance. Thus the gas industry was expected to achieve a 10.2 per cent gross return on net assets, whilst electricity in England and Wales was set a target of 12.4 per cent, both targets being for the financial years 1963-4 to 1967-8. The British Railways Board, on the other hand, was simply given the task of breaking even and reducing its deficit as soon as possible. An increased cash flow to meet current capital requirements, to be achieved by means of price adjustments, would throw the burden of the finance of new investment more fairly on the respective shoulders of the customers of each industry. Here the principle of operation was that those persons using given products or services should pay the capital costs of providing those products and services, rather than the provision of finance resting on the general body of taxpayers.

Although the 1961 procedure was a considerable step forward from the initial break-even criterion, it still suffered from a number of shortcomings. The fixing of just one target rate of return for the whole industry was basically too simple and summary to be an effective guide to managers within the nationalised industries, and indeed to Parliament, in assessing their efficiency. It was much easier for some industries to achieve their target rate of return than for others. Those, like electricity, with an element of monopoly power could more easily adjust prices upwards rather than cut costs so as to achieve their target. The nationalised air corporations, on the other hand, being subject to international fares agreements, could not so easily react by raising prices, but could only hope to reach their targets by cutting costs.

A further criticism of the single-rate criterion was that it gave managements in the nationalised industries no guidance on the rate of return to be expected on new investment. The marginal rate of return to be applied to new investment projects is not necessarily the same as the target rate. The normal assumption is that management ranks investment projects according to expected yield. On this basis, application of a 'cut-off' rate equivalent to the target rate would result in an overall return on these projects greater than the target rate if expectations were fulfilled. Thus if four investment projects (of equal size) in the gas industry were expected to, and did, yield 14 per cent, 12 per cent, 12 per cent and 10 per cent respectively, and the cut-off rate were equal to the target rate of 10 per cent, the overall rate of return would be 12 per cent and not 10 per cent. Effectively, therefore, no explicit guidance was given by the 1961 procedure to managers of the nationalised industries on the minimum rates of return expected on marginal investment.

A further development occurred in 1967 following the publication of a new White Paper on the nationalised industries. (5) Some of the shortcomings of the earlier procedure were recognised and economically more satisfactory arrangements were substituted. Nationalised industries were still subjected to an overall target rate of return, but this was to be more indicative of economic performance. A separate rate was set for each industry, varying according to its own particular circumstances. But the difference from 1961 so far as investment is concerned lies in the provision of common rules relating to new investment. A 'specific test rate' has to be applied by the management of nationalised industries to new capital projects.

Details of the common ground rules for investment are, first, the application of an 10 per cent test rate of return to new capital projects, 'risk being separately allowed for'. The application of this 10 per cent test rate may be waived on grounds of statutory obligation or social benefit. The calculation of yields on new projects had to be formulated in present value terms. Discounting procedures such as the discounted cash flow technique (D.F.C.) are now obligatory for all nationalised industries. Thus the gas industry makes use of D.C.F. techniques for all important capital investment projects, and uses computers for evaluation purposes.

The particular level of the 10 per cent test was derived from a moving average of rates of return achieved in the private sector during the preceding years, and represents an attempt to achieve comparability between the public and private sectors of the economy.

Second, the overall rates of return set for each individual industry reflect its particular circumstances, and are to be achieved over a number of years. Thus rates of return may be lower during the early years following the installation of new capital plant and equipment than during succeeding years. But an immediate low rate of return would not of itself be sufficient to stop investment from taking place. Thus the gas industry, in giving evidence to the Select Committee on Nationalised Industries, explained that the immediate returns on the heavy investment programme in distribution network arising from the exploitation of North Sea gas would fall below requirements. In particular, the witnesses representing the gas industry before the Committee were concerned about the burden of introduction costs, where a large part of the capital outlay would earn little money during the immediate future. (6)

The Gas Council was also concerned about the requirement to earn a specific rate of return on projects installed in the recent past. Because of the decision to exploit natural gas, these previous installations were in danger of becoming economically redundant. For example, heavy capital expenditure had been made on oil-refining plants during the mid-1960s, and the industry had hardly been able to recover these capital costs before the discovery of North Sea natural gas.

Planning and investment were also discussed by the P.I.B. in its report on gas prices. (7) The Board found that practices between the Area Boards varied in respect of the extent to which inflation was taken into account in the standard rate of discount. Some Boards, for example, assumed that the price of gas would rise sufficiently to cover increases in operating costs, but not in capital costs, so that the effective rate of discount would be less than the test rate. Thus the P.I.B. considered that Area Boards 'should adopt in their appraisals the assumptions which the Gas Council lays down regarding the changes in relative costs, and that they should ensure that their assumptions regarding costs, revenues and the rate of discount are consistent with one another'. (8)

6   PRICING POLICY AND TARIFF STRUCTURES

(a) The 1967 Criteria

The criteria used for assessing the viability of new capital projects and the efficiency of the industry as a whole cannot be isolated from considerations regarding pricing policy. Clearly, if target rates of return are to be realised, either price must be adjusted so that the industry's given target is met, or costs must be cut to achieve the same result. In assessing both the rate of return on particular projects and the pricing policy to be pursued, projects carried out principally on social grounds were to be omitted under the 1967 criteria. Such clashes between considerations of efficiency and the requirements of public interest would have to be resolved by the Minister concerned. This would be accomplished by ear-marking specific sums of money for goods and services deemed to be socially desirable.

So far as prices were concerned, the 1967 policy laid down that they were to be based on long-run marginal costs, and that the cross-subsidisation of activities should disappear. The connection between pricing and investment policy was discussed by the P.I.B. to the effect that 'The object which we recommend is not that of maximising net revenue (that is, profit) for this would entail a price inconsistent with the rapid absorption of natural gas. Broadly speaking, we think that the objective requires planning an investment programme which will meet at minimum cost the demand for gas corresponding to an appropriate pricing policy.' (9)

Setting prices tied to long-run marginal costs, it is argued, is a rational pricing policy in that it helps to secure an optimum allocation of resources in the economy. As is frequently the case with large firms, it is not always possible to allocate costs to specific goods or services. Where such unallocatable costs form a relatively large proportion of total costs, as happens with most of the national-ised industries, long-run marginal-cost pricing may fail to cover total costs. The traditional device used by public utilities has been a two-part tariff aimed at reconciling the two objectives. Thus a two-part tariff system of pricing has been used for many years by the gas industry. The flat-rate charge may be made to vary with some index related to capital costs of supplying the goods or services in question. The variable charge simply represents the volume of consumption. This is the system used in the gas industry. A variant, used by some Electricity Boards, is to charge a much higher price for the first x number of units and then a low price for the remainder of units consumed.

(b) Bulk-Supply Tariff

There are two major tariff structures to be considered in dealing with gas prices. They are the bulk-supply tariff (B.S.T.) charged by the Gas Council for supplying gas to the various Area Boards, and the retail tariffs charged by the Area Boards to their customers. The B.S.T. relates principally to charges for supplying natural gas to the Boards. In practice it sets a uniform rate for all Boards, even though the marginal costs of supplying gas to the different areas varies considerably, and may be expected to vary yet more widely as those areas most distant to the North Sea terminal points of Bacton and Easington are linked to the natural-gas grid. As the P.I.B. pointed out, (10) the policy of a uniform tariff implies a policy of cross-subsidisation, with the Area Boards nearest to the source of supply effectively subsidising those further away. It could thus be argued that the Gas Council's B.S.T. goes directly against the non-cross-subsidisation principles of the 1967 White Paper.

However, the question arises as to what constitutes long-run marginal costs in this context. It might be argued that the rapid expansion of the use of natural gas, thus enabling the Gas Council to recoup overhead costs more rapidly, requires considerable natural-gas sales in the more distant populated areas of the country such as Merseyside, the West Riding of Yorkshire, South Wales and the Clyde Valley. Since there are considerable economies of scale involved in the construction of pipelines and gas wells, building ahead will lead to some excess capacity initially. The Gas Council argues that as demand builds up it will need to install compressors and additional storage capacity. There is some justification in the Gas Council's arguments that consumers would not wish to see an immediate lowering of prices in those areas obtaining supplies of natural gas early, only to have prices raised again as additional distribution capacity was required, with the possibility of a reduction in the years still further ahead. Thus the 1967 White Paper argued as follows: 'New technological developments can greatly reduce the long-run marginal cost of providing some services, and it is right to have regard to these in pricing policy. But a gradual adjustment of prices in the light of reasonable expectations is generally preferable to sudden large changes occurring dicontinuously when major assets are replaced.' (11) Too rapid a fall in prices based on long-run marginal-cost considerations might stimulate demand to such an extent that a major result might be a series of short-run bottlenecks and shortages which could be met only by having recourse to obsolete plants, which are expensive to operate for short periods. Under the circumstances of falling long-run marginal costs, strict adherence to the suggested pricing principle would lead to considerable deficits, since average costs would lie above marginal costs and total receipts would be inadequate to cover total costs. The correct pricing policy would thus not be to make price proportionate to long-run marginal cost, but to long-run average cost. As the P.I.B. remarked, (12) 'A B.S.T. based purely on marginal costs would probably fail to meet the total revenue requirement of the Gas Council, so leaving a residual amount which has to be split between twelve Area Boards.'

(c) Retail Tariffs
Discussion of retail tariffs has also been related to long-run marginal costs as a base for pricing policy. Such discussion, however, has to recognise that there are effectively still two different gas industries existing side by side at the end of the 1960s, namely town gas and natural gas. Manufactured town gas and natural gas

drawn from wells are sold to customers through different networks. In order that a proper assessment can be made of the comparative costs of manufactured and natural gas, it is essential that the conversion costs of consumers from town gas to natural gas should be paid for by the latter. That is, the price at which natural gas sells should include not only the distribution costs from the coast but also an amount which will recompense the Area Boards for conversion costs so that the natural gas may be used. Such costs might be passed on to the consumer either in the form of a higher standing charge than would otherwise have been the case, or by raising the variable price per therm for gas consumed. It is thus possible to make out a case, as the P.I.B. has done in its second report on gas prices, for tariff differences according to whether town or natural gas is used. The P.I.B. did not, however, consider the monopoly position inherent in gas supply. The consumer is unable to make a rational choice between one type of gas and the other, since no choice is really available. The only choice the consumer has is between one branch of the gas industry and one of its rivals – electricity or oil.

The spread of the use of natural gas could also alter the balance between different aspects of costs, which in turn should be reflected in a revised tariff structure. For some time the Area Gas Boards have distinguished between commodity, capacity and customer costs, the former corresponding to manufacture costs, the second to investment in manufacturing plant and the latter being essentially distribution costs. Under the natural-gas regime, the first set of costs would disappear entirely, the equivalent of manufacturing costs now being borne by the producer companies. Capacity costs now become a form of distribution costs to Area Boards, costs which affect the B.S.T. initially but which must finally be passed on to the consumer. Customer costs assume greater importance for sales of natural gas because of conversion costs. Otherwise connection costs for the consumer should not be affected. The movement in costs is illustrated by the following data. Of total investment in the gas industry from 1963-4 to 1967-8, manufacture represented 42 per cent. This is expected to fall to only 7 per cent for 1968-9 to 1972-3. In contrast, investment in bulk transmission increases from 22 per cent to 45 per cent, and in distribution from 26 per cent to 38 per cent. (13)

The P.I.B. suggested (14) that 'the ideal tariff would be a compound of the B.S.T. and the additional costs of the Area Boards. As such it would include three separate types of charge: a standing charge on each individual consumer, different commodity charges at different times of the year and a capacity charge related to his consumption of gas at time of peak.' But although 'ideal', the Board admitted that such a tariff would be uneconomical to operate, and it concluded that a series of experiments to test consumer reaction to alternative tariff structures might be helpful. The P.I.B. favoured a greater degree of freedom for Area Boards to vary their pricing agreements with large industrial customers, and were anxious to see some relaxation of the non-discrimination rule which would enable them to do so.

7 WAGES STRUCTURE

Of the 121,000 employees in the gas industry in May 1968, 56 per cent were manual workers, 41 per cent were technical, clerical and administrative staff earning less than £1,650 a year, and the remaining 3 per cent were senior staff earning more than that amount. Wage negotiations in the gas industry are carried out largely through the medium of the National Joint Industrial Council (N.J.I.C.) for the Gas Industry, established in 1949. The parties represented are the Gas Council and the four principal trade unions, the National Union of General and Municipal Workers, the Transport and General Workers' Union, the National Union of Enginemen, Firemen, Mechanics and Electrical Workers, and the Confederation of Shipbuilding and Engineering Unions, with which latter there is a separate agreement in respect of craftsmen. The N.J.I.C. establishes rates of pay for labourers and fitters and determines conditions of service for these workers. This pattern is repeated at the local level by means of Area Joint Industrial Councils, which also determine local rates for other classes of workers. The rates so established are standard rates and not minimum rates, that is they are the rates which are actually paid, as opposed to the situation in the engineering industries. Three other negotiating bodies represent intermediate grades, gas staff workers and senior gas officers.

The wage structure of the gas industry is relatively complicated. Simplified versions are presented for manual workers only in Tables 17.3 and 17.4. The former gives an indication of the earnings disparities between day workers and shift workers, and approximates to the position indicated for shift workers and day workers in the chemical industry outlined in the preceding chapter. Only in the conurbations do shift workers have average weekly earnings below those of

Table 17.3 Wage Structure of the Gas Industry, 1967
(average weekly earnings of all manual workers = 100)

Area	Day workers	Shift workers	All workers
All manual workers	99.3	102.7	100.0
London Pay Area	106.4	110.4	107.4
Conurbations	100.7	98.5	100.3
Other areas	93.3	97.7	94.0

Source: Calculated from data in P.I.B. Report 29 (Supplement), Table 1(F).

Table 17.4 Average Weekly Earnings of Occupational Groups
(all manual workers = 100)

Occupation	Index	% of all manual workers
Labourers	87.3	12.3
Craftsmen's mates	98.8	3.8
Drivers (vehicles 2-5 tons)	100.1	4.7
Service layers	99.6	4.3
Mains layers	101.4	2.0
Retort-house stokers	95.7	4.7
Craftsmen, gas fitters	109.5	24.2
All others (including chargehands)	99.0	44.0
Total		100.0

Source: Calculated from data in P.I.B. Report 29 (Supplement), Table 2 (F)

day workers. There is considerable divergence between the earnings of day
workers in respect of the type of area where they are employed. The latter table
indicates the spread of earnings between occupational categories as well as the
importance of these categories within the overall employment pattern. The
average earnings of craftsmen and gas fitters tend to be just over one-quarter
above those of labourers.

The average earnings of manual workers are built up from a combination of
several items. The basic wage amounted to two-thirds of average earnings for
1967, and was supplemented by overtime amounting to another fifth. The
remaining eighth was made up mainly of a service increment, shift pay and
incentive pay. There are important regional differences in average weekly
earnings. The lowest are in the South-west region, being only 89.4 per cent of
the average for Great Britain. They were highest in the London and South-east
region, where they were 6 per cent above those for Great Britain. The Midland
and East and South regions were also both above the national average, all other
regions being below.

There have been two P.I.B. inquiries into the pay and conditions of workers
in the gas industry. The first inquiry (15) concerned manual workers, the second
staff workers. (16) The chief P.I.B. finding in respect of manual workers related
to the 'excessive' amount of overtime carried out, pay for which constituted
over one-fifth of total earnings. Total earnings themselves were not far from the
average for the economy as a whole. Weekly earnings increased on average by 5

per cent a year between 1963 and 1967, and outstripped the increase in overall productivity. An extension in coverage of incentive bonus schemes was suggested, though it was recognised that there were a number of things not amenable to such schemes. These related to working-time arrangements, inter-craft demarcations, reductions in manning schedules, the abolition of mates and reduced overtime working. Most of these items have been the subject of negotiations in other process industries for example in the Fawley productivity agreements in oil refining and in I.C.I. productivity agreements. (17)

In its second inquiry the P.I.B. abandoned attempts to measure increases in productivity of gas staff workers directly. Instead it concentrated essentially on improvements in the use of manpower, with more of the onus being thrown on the management side of the industry. Suggestions were made concerning, amongst other things, the extended use of job evaluation, organisation and methods programmes, work measurement and staff participation. Although comparability arguments were disallowed, productivity arguments in favour of increased pay were granted, and a pay increase along lines suggested by the Gas Council's offer was accepted. The report was of some importance in its attempt to assess some of the principles on which increases in pay might be achieved by workers whose output could not be measured directly. The Board also recommended that the agreement 'should include a clause in which management expresses its determination to press on with the development of modern techniques such as method study, work measurement and job evaluation, while at the same time the unions agree to continue to co-operate fully with the development and extension of such techniques wherever they are applicable'. (18)

8   COMPARISON WITH THE CHEMICAL INDUSTRIES

It may be useful at this stage to conclude by drawing some comparisons between the chemical and gas industries. The gas industry is probably unique amongst the nationalised industries in the speed of technological change it has had to contend with during the 1960s, changes which will continue into the early 1970s. In this it resembles the degree of change which has occurred in various branches of the chemical industry since the Second World War especially in the fields of petro-chemicals and plastics. Both these, together with the introduction of reforming processes for obtaining gas from oil and the discovery of deposits of natural gas in the North Sea, have acted as challenges to managements in both the private and public sectors of the economy.

Investment decisions in the two industries have been governed by the need to exploit innovations quickly, in the case of the private sector to meet foreign competition, and in the public sector to save the foreign exchange costs of imported oil. The criteria to be taken into account by the industries in the public sector have been moved gradually into line with those obtaining in major sectors of private industry, and the nationalised gas industry is no exception.

Problems of pricing policy arising from declining long-run marginal costs of particular products have been common to both industries, though the solutions have not always been identical. Nevertheless, in this aspect of business policy, as in investment decisions, the public and private sectors have been drawing more closely together, following the 1967 operating criteria for the nationalised industries. Finally, in facing manpower problems, both in cases of avoiding redundancy and in their establishment of deals to increase productivity, the chemical and gas industries have been to the fore in their respective sectors of the economy. (19)

Part III

INCOMES: A MACRO-ECONOMIC SURVEY

18 Factor Incomes and Factor Shares

Incomes are the earnings of factors of production in return for tasks performed by those factors. The economic function of those earnings is to enable factors to perform their tasks: human factors have to be fed, clad, housed, and what not, so that they can live and work. Material factors have to be kept in good repair, so as to aid rather than hinder the human factors' work. Were this book concerned with a static society, it would suffice to say that man must live to work and work to live, and that the material aids at hand must not be allowed to deteriorate. British society today, however, is a dynamic society where ways of living and methods of work change.

In an ever changing dynamic society it is not enough to keep factors going in their current tasks. It is necessary to direct and re-direct them into whatever activities society thinks today will be most valuable tomorrow. If it is expected now that in the days to come society will want more pilots rather than more motor mechanics, then relative personal incomes should make a pilot's life economically more attractive today than a motor mechanic's. For today – or, more precisely, 'in the current period' – young men must decide which of these, or other, occupations they will train for. Their willingness to be trained for one occupation rather than the other depends largely on how they see that pilots and motor mechanics live today and are currently rewarded. Since factors are valued at one point of time with a view to satisfaction at a later point of time, miscalculations and errors of judgement are bound to occur. This can lead to difficulties later on. Such problems arise in relation to all factor incomes, both for individuals and types of income. In the present macro-economic survey of factor incomes, it will be convenient to divide factor earnings into broad groups in order to see what economic forces promote or impede factors' relative rewards.

An analysis of what may happen to those broad groups cannot deal with individual problems. The following will not explain what pilots and motor mechanics do or should earn, let alone the economic fate of any individual. The latter nearly always diverges from the norm. The usefulness of macro-economic analysis to any individual is to discover how far, if at all, his individual experience diverges from the norm, so that he can either congratulate himself or try to take remedial action. Such divergences from the norm provide much of the material for micro-economic analysis. Here, however, the concern is with the common weal which is studied in macro-economics. It establishes the norm for broad categories of factor incomes within the national economy.

One possible approach is to divide factors of production into two main groups, live factors and material ones. The live factors are the labour and skill of human beings who are currently alive. Like all factors, they are means of production and are valued according to the contribution they make to economic activity. Unlike material factors, however, in any civilised society they are inseparable from those who own them. Since the purpose of all economic activity is the satisfaction of human wants, they are the ends as well as the means of economic activity. Their labour 'and skills are, however, valued according to their worth as factors. The material factors are simply means. They too are valued according to their contribution to economic activity, and their reward too accrues to their owners. In capitalist or socialist society all material factors have either a personal or a corporate owner.

Put briefly, all factors have an owner who reaps the reward, and everybody is the owner of at least one factor (being his or her own labour). Earnings are distributed according to ownership of factors of various worth. The minimum ownership is the ownership of labour. If that labour is made available, it is rewarded by a wage. The pure wage element in anybody's earnings is the current reward for the toil of self-owned labour currently performed. What may have happened in the past and what may happen in the future is of no importance or only of subsidiary importance in the determination of this purely economic wage.

At the other extreme are the earnings of material factors (which have never been alive) – or, more accurately, the earnings of the owners of such factors. Such earnings are a rent, and such rent is normally based on past valuations and frequently contractually extended into the future. Current human toil is either irrelevant or of subsidiary relevance.

These are extreme cases, and seldom will a factor earn a pure wage or a pure rent. Few people are paid while actually working; wages are normally received at the end of the day or week during which the work was performed. There is some time-lag between work and reward, so that strictly speaking there is some rent element in almost any wage; the payment is for toil which is no longer being exerted. Usually, however, the same toil will be exerted again, so that the rent element is significant only in the first and last pay period of the worker's active life. For all others (who have not just started their working life and are not about to retire) the wage is an intermittent payment for toil regularly performed within, say, a year. Matters may be different in times and places where employment is very irregular and where violent price fluctuations are liable to occur between pay-days. But the United Kingdom's post-war problems have not been of this nature. Time-lags of less than a year will be ignored in the following. Since time-lags between work and receipt of wages are almost invariably less than a year, and since everything that happens within a year can be taken as 'current', the rent element in wages will not be referred to again.

Pure rent is equally likely to be rare. Few if any can draw rents without at least a current effort of collecting it, but where the cost of administration is relatively small and not subject to frequent changes, the wage element in the earnings of owners of material factors can be ignored.

A substantial volume of earnings can thus be clearly classified as either wages or rent, but not all. There are instances where both the live and non-live contributions of a factor's earnings are of such importance that neither can be ignored. For instance, the reward for the labour of a factory manager or a teacher does not consist of the wage element alone, nor is the wage element so predominant that the rest can be ignored. The income of such a worker is known as a salary. A salary is the reward for current toil, like a wage, plus a reward for special skills and reputations acquired earlier in life which are often expected to be of continuing and increasing value to society. A salary thus includes an element of reward for past toil. Material aids owned by a salary-earner may also be of importance and add to the rent element of his earnings, but such material aids are subsidiary to the human factor. In short, salaries are a compound of wages and rent where the rent element consists largely of educational rent.

Finally there are profits. Like salaries, they are a compound of wages and rent. Unlike salaries, they are earned in organisational activities where the material factors may predominate. But whether the human or the material elements predominate is not the chief distinction between salaries and profits, nor is it one that must invariably apply. The chief criterion as to whether factor earnings should be classed as salaries or profits lies in the timing of the valuation of the factor's contribution to production. If wages are the current reward for current toil, and if rent is a current reward based on past valuations of a factor once created by God or man, then salaries are compounds of wages and rent, since they depend on both current and past valuations. To that extent salaries, like wages and rent, are certain whilst current tasks are performed (barring only employers' bankruptcy before pay-day or acts of God). Profits, however, are never certain at the time of toil. Profits are a reward for current toil which will be determined by the market after the toil is over. The reward may be positive and even large, but there is always the chance that it may be negative. In other words profits depend on future valuations and are always uncertain at the time of toil. Some entrepreneurs may work for fairly regular markets and escape much uncertainty, as may be the case with government contracts. If so the entrepreneur's reward becomes more like a salary than profit. Where, however, future valuations determine receipts for current effort, uncertainty is inescapable and the appropriate earnings will be called profits.

In the following there will be a macro-economic analysis of what determines wages, rent, salaries and profits in the British economy. As shown in Fig. 18.1, wages take a larger share of the national income than other factor earnings. Although subject to cyclical fluctuations, the share of wages in national income has not changed much from two-fifths of the total over the last hundred years. The diagram shows that this still applied in 1948-67, and it will have to be asked whether this was accidental or whether there were any reasons why society should value current effort in a near-constant ratio to total income. The diagram also shows some tendency for the share of wages in national income to fall from the 1950s onwards. It will have to be considered whether this is an accident, part of a cyclical movement, the result of government policy, or the beginning of a new trend.

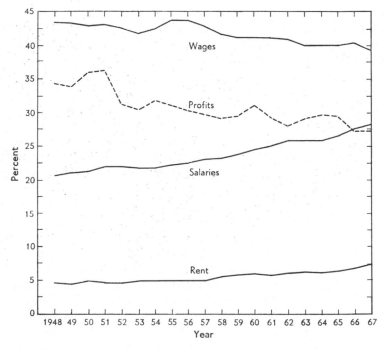

Fig. 18.1 Shares of national income represented by wages, salaries, profits and rent.

Derived from 'National Income Blue Books', *1966 and 1968, Tables 1 and 22.*
All items are expressed as percentages of national income. Profits include income from self-employment, gross trading profits of companies, gross trading surplus of public corporations, and gross trading surplus of other public enterprises.

Rent takes the smallest share of the national income, and a share that has fallen consistently throughout the present century until the 1950s. From the late 1950s onwards, however, there has been some rise in the share of rent in national income. Since rent is the least adjustable of all factor incomes, this may have been the result of a slowing-down in the rise of other factor incomes, changes in legislation relating to rent, or the beginning of a new trend.

More marked than the rise in rent was the rise in salaries, which became noticeable from the early 1950s onwards. This rise may have been a continuation of a trend noticeable throughout the present century. It may have been due to rising numbers of salary-earners and to greater demand for tasks performed by salary-earners. In either case it will have to be asked whether this is likely to be a continuing trend. It will be noted from the diagram that by 1967 the share of salaries for the first time exceeded the share of profits, and if the trends from the mid-1950s to 1967 continue, salaries will overtake wages in the not too distant future.

The share of profits emerges as the most volatile of factor shares. This accords with past experience. It also appears to be a declining share, though it is not yet clear whether this is part of a long cyclical movement or a new trend. Even if the marked fall in the share of profits in the early 1950s is ignored, profits appear to have been on a slightly downward trend from the early 1950s onwards.

It will also be noticed that, in the years from 1948 to 1967, wages and profits fluctuated more than salaries and rent. Since these two fluctuating factor earnings receded somewhat relatively to the more regular and growing salaries and rent, the impact of trade fluctuations on personal fortunes also receded. This may not have been of special importance in the 1950s and 1960s, when fluctuations were mild compared with past experience, but it may become important in the future. Whether this is to be entirely welcomed depends on the relative contribution to the economy's growth made by each of the various factors.

The following will not answer all these questions, but merely grope towards some of the answers. Special attention will be paid to whether changes in factor shares indicate relative scarcities of the various factors. In the later chapters of Part III there will be some consideration as to whether relative factor scarcities indicate growth or impediments to growth of the economy as a whole. Much of the argument will be in terms of a two-factor model, which has admitted imperfections. It is, however, necessary to simplify for the purpose of exposition. Moreover it is legitimate to the extent that factor earnings determined in the past are unalterable and, therefore, given, and to regard 'stability versus growth' arguments as arguments largely between those who exert current toil and those who bear uncertainty.

19 Wages

1 THE REWARD FOR CURRENT TOIL

A wage can be defined as the reward for current toil. Everyone who is in gainful employment receives a wage, but not everyone's earnings consist of a pure wage alone. Those with special skills have earnings which contain a rent element as well as a wage element; those with property rights have earnings where the rent element may predominate; and those who run the risk and uncertainty of what goods and services will be worth when exchanged, make profits or losses which may obscure any wage element in their earnings. Even those who are classed as wage-earners may receive more than pure wages; seniority increments or pay for special responsibilities contain a rent element, and special bonuses or profit-sharing schemes may give them a part of profit. Thus in practice classification of earnings is broad and in each category there is a mixture of the various types of income. The classification merely means that earnings are treated as wages if the pure wage element predominates.

The study of the determination of wages consists of analysis of what determines wage rates and what determines the aggregate payment to wage-earners. Wage rates will be considered in section 5 below. The concern of the first four sections, however, is mainly with the aggregate paid to wage-earners, which is usually referred to as the 'national wages bill'. This consists of the total paid to employees whose earnings are nearest to pure wages. Those employees are sometimes officially referred to as 'operatives'. (1)

Operatives are employees who, at work, move on shop or factory floors where they mind goods or machines. In their capacity as operatives they own no property which would yield them a rent. True, in their private capacities many operatives own houses, cars and other assets, but this does not affect their status at work. As employees, they contribute none of their savings or assets. They contribute their time and skill alone. Hence they run no monetary risk on behalf of their employers, and take no profits.

The operatives' training consists of secondary modern school education, augmented by apprenticeship and experience at work. Such training can reach high technical standards in relation to the current needs of production. It is, however, training largely relevant to the current needs of production and normally unrelated to the sort of skills wanted for long-term production planning, supervision and administration.

Longer-term tasks are performed by 'staff', who work in offices and are rewarded with salaries. (2) The managerial members of the salary-earning office staff must have more of the skills and foresight relevant to the longer-run activities than is expected of operatives. The skills of management are not necessarily higher than those of the operatives, but they are different; the judgements and errors of management have longer-run consequences. Besides the managerial members of the salary-earning office staff, there are members of staff who may need little or no foresight and may be technically less skilled than many operatives. For instance, a salary-earning typist may not even understand what she is typing and so is less skilled than a mechanic who understands what he is doing. Nevertheless a typist is a member of staff and not an operative; when she types a letter or account she does so as an arm of management. Her typing becomes of value later on in time, when the communication she has typed is read and acted upon. This contrasts with the operative's tasks, which have immediate effect. Hence the difference between the skills required of staff and operatives is not one of degree. It is one of kind. Staff is concerned with what is to happen. Operatives are concerned with what is currently happening. In so far as pay reflects the value of work performed, the pay of operatives reflects the value of current toil.

Earnings which reflect the value of current toil are received as reward for what, normally, are short-run activities. Such activities are often repetitive. After one hour's work there is another hour's work of exactly the same kind, and after completion of one task there is the same task to be performed again. In other words, where toil is repetitive it consists of repeat performances of identical short-run tasks. Even where the work is not altogether repetitive, it is normally work that can be performed equally well by any one of a number of operatives, so that there is a high degree of substitutability between operatives. In consequence, operatives can be employed for short periods, subject to no more than one week's notice either side. Such short-period employment is not incompatible with the nature of the tasks they perform.

Nowadays, however, the employment of operatives is seldom so casual as to extend only over the period required to fulfil one task — which would normally be even shorter than the one week mentioned. Usually employment is automatically renewed, week by week, without either side even mentioning anything about the renewal, and employment of operatives is expected to last for long periods of time. Termination of employment with just one week's notice still occurs, but is not normally expected and often comes as a shock. In Britain, where about two-thirds of the economically active population are wage-earning operatives, (3) it would cause intolerable confusion were employment changed after each task performed or even every week.

There are other reasons, besides the inconvenience to all concerned, that have made casual labour a rarity in modern Britain. The normal length of employment periods has lengthened beyond the time required for individual tasks, because labour is difficult to get. Labour has become a scarce factor and as such it is desirable to hold on to it. Matters are different in some other countries, where a substantial amount of potential labour is available for wage-paying employment. A large potential supply of labour is usually available where there is a substantial agricultural sector and remuneration is in kind. Such a sector is often referred to as a 'subsistence sector'. Where this subsistence sector is large, money-wage-paying employers can attract labour from the subsistence sector more or less at will, and employment can be casual and at wage rates not much above a subsistence level. (4) Similarly workers can return to the subsistence sector, if they want to or if they have to, and still survive. Twentieth-century Britain, however, has no subsistence sector for employers to draw on and for workers to return to. (5) The latter have become dependent on the money wages they earn, unless they are content with the dole. Thus neither side to an operative's employment could benefit from too much instability of employment.

There are variations on this theme. In prosperity, the scarcity of labour is enhanced; and since, in industrialised Britain, prosperity has more often risen than fallen, this tendency has been predominant. In depression, the worker's fear of losing his money wage is enhanced; and although in industrialised Britain depressions have been more rare than rising prosperity, depressions have often been sharp, and fears of recurrence of a deep depression like that of the 1930s have lingered on to the present day. In consequence, both parties to employment have become more reluctant to terminate it at short notice.

The tendency towards longer employment has also been reinforced by trade union vigilance, which precludes dismissals on personal grounds; by redundancy pay, introduced in 1965, which makes it costly to dismiss a worker of long standing with his firm, and so is a further incentive to prolong the employment of those already long in employment; and, last but not least, by any preference employers and employees may have for working with those they know.

Further variations on the theme could be thought of. Suffice it to say that, for all these reasons and more, individual operatives normally stay in the same employment for longer than the nature of their tasks dictates.

Nevertheless the nature of employment cannot be denied. It enables aggregate employment to respond fairly quickly to changes in aggregate demand, even if this is normally not fully reflected in the numbers of operatives employed. (6) Usually there is reluctance to force or face unemployment, and it is not always possible to offer or to take more jobs. It is, however, always possible to alter the number of hours worked or tasks performed, so that changes in aggregate demand can be reflected in a change in the national wages bill.

In brief, the nature of the operative's tasks allows short-period employment, but the scarcity of labour and labour's dependence on money wages encourages long-period employment. This leads to the next point; if effective demand for current toil is more volatile than potential supply of labour for such toil, the aggregate earnings of operatives are likely to reflect changes in aggregate demand. Whether effective demand is in fact more volatile than potential supply is the subject of the following section.

2   SUPPLY AND DEMAND

Let supply be considered first. The potential supply of labour for particular occupations can vary; where that is the case, the appropriate wages do not necessarily vary in the same direction as effective demand. The potential supply of labour for the economy as a whole, however, is never likely to vary as rapidly as effective demand can vary. Thus whatever may happen in particular occupations, changes in the aggregate effective demand for current toil are likely to be reflected in changes in the national wages bill in the same direction. The reasons are as follows:

The potential supply of labour for current toil of all sorts is the stock of labour of men and women of working age. The size of that stock is largely determined by the birth rate of fifteen to sixty-five years ago. Barring pestilence and war, the stock of labour is practically given from one week to the next, and it does not even vary markedly from one year to the next. (7)

Over the long period the stock of labour is not absolutely rigid. Between the census years of 1901 and 1961, the economically active population increased by about one and a half times. But this increase was less than that of the national income (at constant prices), which rose by about two and a half times. Moreover, while the increase in the working population was fairly regular, the changes in the national income were sometimes sharp and in both directions.

Not all the stock of labour is available for employment as operatives. Some are in salaried employment, some are self-employed and some are unemployable. If the proportion of operatives to the economically active population were constant, the preceding argument would require no modification. If the proportion of operatives to the economically active population falls, the preceding argument is strengthened; but if that proportion rises, the argument is weakened and may have to be adjusted or even abandoned. In what follows, the relevant changes in the British economy are examined in order to verify the argument.

In the census year of 1961, about two-thirds of the economically active population were wage-earning operatives. That is a smaller proportion than at the beginning of the present century, when about three-quarters of the economically active population were wage-earning operatives. This proportion had been even higher in the late nineteenth century. (8) Generally, as industrialisation of a country proceeds, there is a stage when the proportion of operatives in the labour force increases, and in Britain this stage lasted until the second half of the nineteenth century. But as industrialisation becomes more advanced, an increasing proportion of the labour force becomes employed in the more sophisticated activities of the professions and management. Throughout the twentieth century Britain has been at this advanced stage of development, so that a falling proportion of a growing labour force has been employed as wage-earning operatives. It has taken sixty years for the number of operatives to increase by one-tenth. (9)

(Details for the 1960s are not yet available, since the relevant information is not collected in between census years. It is thus unknown whether the British economy is still in that stage of an industrial employment structure, or whether it has entered a stage where the number of operatives is falling absolutely as well as relatively to the total of the economically active population. Although this is surmise, it is not impossible that this stage has already been reached, or will be reached during the remaining decades of the present century. The educational advance of our times enables increasing numbers of the new recruits to the economy to perform tasks of longer than immediate impact. As mentioned before, this is surmise. It is, however, also a warning to the reader of the present analysis of the second stage. That stage has been part of British economic experience during the last hundred years. But it may be passing or past by the time these pages are read.)

The slow increase in the number of operatives during the first six decades of the century, combined with a falling proportion of operatives in the economically active population, indicates a high degree of rigidity in the supply of operatives' labour. Since a rising proportion of the economically active population came to be employed in longer-term salaried tasks, the rigidity was even greater than may appear at first sight, for salaried employees usually refuse even to consider a change of occupation into a wage-earning activity. Once a worker is a salary-earner, he is effectively no longer part of the potential supply of labour for operatives' tasks.

Matters are different at an earlier stage of industrial development, when the proportion of operatives amongst the economically active population is increasing. Where that is the case, labour is attracted from other activities into operatives' activities. There is a net movement from other activities towards the short-run activities of industry and commerce. Those other activities provide a source of abundant labour for operatives' tasks, and thus the potential supply of operatives' labour may seem unlimited. (10) But that stage forms no significant part of twentieth-century British experience. (11)

For twentieth-century Britain to date, in times of peace, the potential supply or stock of labour must be regarded as given from year to year, let alone for shorter periods; and assuming an advanced stage of industrial development, the potential supply of operatives' tasks is likely to be even more rigid. There is no reason why effective demand should ever be equally rigid, and in twentieth-century Britain it has not been.

The demand for operatives' labour is more nearly a pure demand for current toil than the demand for any other type of labour. The demand for current toil rises as prosperity increases, so that employment and wages are pushed up, with the result that the national wages bill rises. As prosperity recedes, however, the effective demand for operatives' labour falls, with the result that either individual earnings fall or employment falls or both; but whether earnings fall or employment falls, the national wages bill falls.

Changes in the national wages bill thus reflect changes in aggregate effective demand. Any change in aggregate effective demand affects the demand for current toil and all wages. Since operatives' earnings are more nearly pure wages than any other earnings, the change in effective demand is more accurately reflected in operatives' wages than in any other earnings.

A change in aggregate effective demand roughly equals the change in the national income in money terms. The annual percentage change in national income from 1948 (compared with 1947) to 1967 (compared with 1966) averaged 6.8. The annual percentage changes in the national wages bill for the same years averageed 6.1. (12) In other words, the annual percentage change in the national wages bill was, on average, close to the annual average percentage change in effective demand.

3   THE SHARE OF WAGES IN NATIONAL INCOME

If aggregate pay for current toil moves roughly in line with current demand for goods and services, the share of wages in national income cannot change much. This will remain true unless there are major alterations in the proportion of the national income invested at home or abroad which affect the share of income available for current spending.

The share of wages in national income has in fact been fairly steady at around two-fifths of the total national income from the 1870s to the 1960s. There were annual variations, but the share has ranged between 37 and 42 per cent from 1870 to 1939 and between 39 and 44 per cent in the 1950s and 1960s. (13) The fluctuations in this share before 1939 were around a constant trend. The higher range of the post-war share is largely due to a change in statistical definitions (14) and coverage of wage-earners, (15) and if there was any trend away from near constancy, that trend was slightly downwards (see Fig. 18.1). At any rate, until the late 1960s the near constancy of the share of wages in national income has been maintained.

During those hundred years there have been changes in the share of national income devoted to capital formation. In the late nineteenth century and until 1913, the share of the national income devoted to net capital formation overseas increased. There has been British overseas investment since then, but this has been balanced by borrowing from overseas, so that net overseas investment can be said to have ceased (see Part IV). This has been more than balanced by an increase in home investment, which in the 1960s took more than twice the share of the national product than it used to take in the 1900s. (16) Britain appears to have saved between 15 and 20 per cent of her national product throughout those hundred years, and that share was higher in the post-war period than before. An increase in home investment does not, however, reduce current domestic demand as much as overseas investment. For overseas investment creates capital without a corresponding immediate increase in current domestic factor earnings, since at least the labour costs of construction or assembly are borne abroad, while home investment requires current payment to all factors engaged in domestic capital formation. Although domestic investment increased by more than net overseas investment decreased, the change in the investment pattern meant that the overall increase in investment has so far failed to restrain current demand as much as might otherwise have been expected. A further increase in the share of national income saved for capital formation may, however, do so. If so, the aggregate reward for current toil may cease to change in line with the national income.

For about a hundred years past, the share of wages in national income has been fairly steady. The reason given above is that changes in the national wages bill reflect changes in current effective demand more closely than do changes in other factor incomes. This may answer the question why there has been such steadiness of the share of wages in national income. It leaves unanswered the question how this steadiness has been maintained relatively to other factor incomes.

The mechanism of the steadiness of the share of wages in national income has been explained along the following lines. (17) The national income is divided into two sectors. One is a fluctuating sector, consisting of wages and profits which vary considerably with the trade cycle. The other is a stable sector, consisting of salaries and rents which are relatively unaffected by the cycle. (18) In years of increasing prosperity wages and profits both rise, thus leading to an increasing share of the fluctuating sector in the national income. But wages and profits do not increase to the same extent; wages tend to rise less than profits, so that the share of wages in the fluctuating sector falls. This compensation between shares, which themselves need not be steady, results in leaving wages with roughly the same share of the whole. In years of deepening recession wages and profits both fall, thus leading to a falling share of the fluctuating sector in the national income. But wages and profits do not fall to the same extent; wages tend to fall less than profits, so that the share of wages in the fluctuating sector rises. This compensation of shares again results in leaving wages with roughly the same share of the whole. In general, 'the share of wages in the fluctuating sector itself varies; but at the same time the share of this sector in the whole national income varies in the opposite direction, so as to compensate roughly the changes in the relations between wages and profits and leave wages a fairly steady share of the whole'. (19)

The 'why' and 'how' of past steadiness of the share of wages in national income does not enable a forecast of the future share to be made, but points to certain tendencies which could upset that steadiness. As long as rents and salaries can be regarded as 'stable' within national income, the relevant tendencies must be in the relationship between wages and profits.

Those tendencies have already been referred to but will now be considered together. Three tendencies, to be reconsidered, may lead to a fall in the share of wages in national income. Probably the most important of these is the one towards an increase in the share of national income saved for capital formation. In the past, the effects of this increase have not appreciably affected the share of wages in national income, since it came when there was also a shift from capital formation overseas to capital formation at home — and this shift increased the domestic wage content of capital formation. The effects of the shift cannot continue much longer and may already have ceased (since the balance-of-payments deficits of the 1960s implied net disinvestment overseas — see Part IV). Should the tendency towards relatively more capital formation persist, it will presumably be associated with some increase in the share of profits in national income. If salaries and rents are 'stable', a long-run trend towards higher profits may become sufficiently marked to outweigh the traditional cyclical compensation between the share of wages in the fluctuating sector and the share of the fluctuating sector in the total national income. If so the share of wages in national income may well fall. Since the traditional compensation between shares would continue, though to a less marked extent, such a fall in the share of labour is likely to be slight on a year-by-year basis, but could become noticeable over a long period.

In a fully employed economy an increase in the relative importance of investment activity would almost certainly lead to capital deepening. This means that capital employed becomes increasingly sophisticated. New technology is incorporated and methods changed. Capital widening, on the other hand, merely refers to duplication. Increasingly skilled labour is required when capital is deepened. This may accentuate another tendency towards a falling share of wages in national income, namely the tendency towards more employment of salaried staff, skilled in longer-run tasks, relatively to the employment of operatives with their responsibilities for current tasks. If so the share of wages may fall relatively to that of salaries.

From the increasing opportunities in alternative occupations follows the tendency for the number of operatives to decline relatively to the total economically active population. This could make a falling share of wages in national income compatible with rising wages for all individual operatives.

The enumeration of such tendencies implies no forecast that the share of wages in national income will fall or is even likely to fall. For there are other tendencies at work which, if unchecked, would raise that share. Three such tendencies will now be considered.

The first of those tendencies is the greater rise in incomes than in the size of the labour force. As mentioned before, the economically active population increased by only one and a half times between 1901 and 1961. Between these years the national income at constant prices increased by two and a half times, and by much more at current prices. (20) There was thus an excess demand for labour, which tended to push up the remuneration of labour and would have done so even in the absence of inflation.

This excess demand for labour, which operates in most years, raises the cost of labour and so encourages labour-saving investment. Since such investment is undertaken with a view to raising profits, it raises incomes and so ensures the continuance of the excess demand for labour. This effect cannot be evaded even through investing overseas, since overseas investment too is intended to raise home incomes. The effect could possibly be largely avoided through sole reliance on foreign capital for investment in Britain; although foreign investment in Britain creates some additional demand for British labour, it need not create any further additions to the income stream in Britain (provided all profits are repatriated and not even taxed here). Since such a course is impracticable, a continuous excess demand for labour must be assumed.

An additional tendency towards a rising share of labour may be operative in a slowly growing economy, where the nature of economic activity does not alter substantially from one year to the next. Where incomes rise, but the nature of economic activity is largely unchanged, more of current income is earned for repetitive tasks, whoever may perform them. The percentage of the wage element in all factor incomes rises, so that pure earnings fare relatively better than other earnings. Unchecked by other tendencies, the result would be a greater rise (or lesser fall) of the national wages bill than of national income.

The enumeration of such tendencies implies no forecast that the share of wages in national income will rise or is even likely to rise, just as the preceding enumeration of tendencies towards a falling share was no forecast. The six tendencies enumerated are merely concerned with the interplay of investment and incomes. If investment rises, the share of income derived from current toil falls; but investment also raises total income, and a general rise in incomes leads to a greater demand for current toil. The tendencies towards a falling share of wages in national income and the tendencies towards a rise in that share are not independent, but interact. Whatever the starting point in the sequence of events, more capital formation leads to higher incomes and so to higher wages, which encourages more capital formation and so on.

At first sight the case of the slowly growing economy appears to be an exception. However, even in this case investment and incomes interact. The only difference between this case and the case of a faster-growing economy is in the time it takes for the process to work itself out. As long as incomes rise, the tendency towards an increasing share of labour in national income is at work; but so is the tendency towards more investment which would lower the share of wages. The process is, however, slow, and this might explain some of the concern over the rise of wages in the slow-growth years of the 1960s – when in fact the share of wages in national income did not rise. (21)

In general, where investment and incomes interact, the tendencies towards a falling share of wages in national income interact with the tendencies towards a rising share. Unless one or the other of those tendencies predominates and the countervailing tendencies can be arrested, the share of wages in national income is unlikely to change much from year to year. If experience in the years from 1948 to 1967 is any guide, the largest increase in the share of wages in national income from one year to the next was 1.6 per cent of the total (in 1955), and the largest decrease 1.1 per cent (in 1967). (22) Moreover, irrespective of what happens to the share of wages in national income, the total national wages bill is *income*-determined. In consequence the standard of living of those engaged in current toil remains dependent on the growth of the national income relatively to their numbers.

4 THE SCARCITY OF LABOUR

Since wages are income-determined, today's national wages bill is already determined by recent national money income which provides the public's spending power of today. Attempts to alter the fate of operatives within the economy cannot succeed until a later date – when the national income will be different. There will be some change in the operatives' relative lot if the scarcity of the given stock of labour has been changed relatively to effective demand at the later date. Otherwise interventions by governments and trade unions affect the course of incomes rather than the distribution of incomes between wage-earning operatives and others.

Government and central bank action, through fiscal and monetary policies, has always exerted influence over the course of incomes. Indirectly such action has always affected the national wages bill, though this has not always been intended. Government can exert some limited influence over the stock of labour, through social legislation and control of migration. Social legislation affecting, say, the school-leaving age affects the potential supply of labour for the economy. Such legislation cannot, however, be frequently altered, so that the effects of such legislation on the growth rate of the stock of labour are once-and-for-all effects (which may be noticeable when such legislation is first put into effect, but not afterwards). Both in intention and effect, social legislation usually makes the stock of labour more stable. Measures to encourage emigration or to restrict immigration can, like social legislation, have once-and-for-all effects on the stock of labour, and they tend to be varied more frequently. In so far as measures relating to migration have been taken, however, the intention was usually to stabilise the stock of labour in the country. Thus the limited influence that the Government can exert over the stock of labour has normally been used to stabilise further what is already stable relatively to effective demand. It follows that government policy in relation to incomes and the national wages bill must be considered largely in the context of policies affecting aggregate effective demand.

The trade unions' duty to their members is to ensure that labour is treated as a scarce factor. Unable to alter the stock of labour, they endeavour to keep the price of labour as high as possible. Sometimes economic circumstances favour such action, but not always.

Modern trade unionism developed mainly in the late nineteenth and the early twentieth century. Since much of the thinking about trade unions still bears the hallmarks of those bygone days, some of the characteristics of those days must be considered before the position is assessed in relation to late twentieth-century circumstances.

The days when modern trade unionism developed were days when unemployment was seldom below 3 per cent of the labour force and usually much higher. (23) Those were also days when the number employed as operatives was increasing, but the proportion of the economically active population employed as operatives fell gradually from over four-fifths of the total in the 1870s to less than three-quarters in the 1920s. (24) Another feature of most of those days was that the money supply was regulated by the rules of the gold standard.

As shown in Section 3 above, whenever there is a recession in economic activity, wages and profits tend to fall or rise less than they otherwise would have done. This reflects a growing deficiency in effective demand relatively to the amount of labour and capital available. Another way of putting the same point is that labour and capital become more abundant relatively to effective demand. Since wages tend to fall less than profits (and a change in relative factor earnings reflects a change in the relative scarcity or abundance of factors), a recession implies not only greater abundance of both factors; it also implies a relatively greater abundance of capital than of labour. In consequence, relatively to each other, capital becomes 'the' abundant factor and labour 'the' scarce factor. This applies whether a recession be cyclical or of longer-term nature. When, over a longer period, the economy seldom or never attains full employment, there is a long-run deficiency in effective demand and general abundance of factors. Given a general abundance of factors, capital tends to be more abundant than labour. This point is of importance for a number of policy issues, some of which will be considered in Chapter 22. In the present context its importance lies in the relative bargaining power of capital and labour earlier this century. Although the general abundance of factors restrained all factor earnings, the relative scarcity of labour ensured that the earnings of labour would not fare worse than other factor earnings.

Such a situation is basically favourable to trade union organisation, though such organisation could not boast of much success if it only ensured what was to happen anyway. There were, however, countervailing tendencies at work, and the success of trade unions was that they did not let those countervailing tendencies spoil the relative strength of labour. There was a continuing increase in the working population which made labour more abundant. But the year-by-year increases were never large compared with the existing stock of labour, and were becoming less marked as population growth slowed down in the second half of the nineteenth century.

More important in this context was the influx of labour from the land. This had not entirely ceased by 1914. (25) It could weaken the position of wage-earning operatives in years when it was substantial, for it was an influx from activities which were not wholly remunerated with money. Agricultural remuneration was partly in a 'subsistence sector' (which means that remuneration is in kind, so that there is always poverty in money terms though not necessarily in real terms). There was thus 'surplus labour', (26) which was not yet in the money-wage-paying economy but could always be attracted into the towns through payment of wages somewhat above the subsistence level then prevailing in agriculture. Given the availability of surplus labour, and given the short-run nature of most operatives' tasks, it was possible for employers to satisfy some of their demand for labour through employment of casual labour at low wage rates. The task of the trade unions was to ensure that the effects of a potentially large influx of labour from the land did not lower the wage rates prevailing in the towns. This they endeavoured to achieve through collective bargaining of wage rates for given tasks, which prevented undercutting of money wages in the years when the potential influx became substantial. Theirs was a defence against a potential threat, which became less as the surplus labour from the land ceased to be substantial. It was a defence of the relative scarcity of labour in a world where factors were abundant.

During this period the money supply was regulated in conformity with the rules of the gold standard. The money supply responded to external pressures, but was unresponsive to internal pressures. (27) From the point of view of the labour market, the supply of money was given. Wage bargaining was therefore a struggle for a rising share of a given whole. (28) Neither side won, for the share of wages in national income remained fairly steady.

Circumstances have changed since the early days of trade unionism. Now there are days of full employment. Since 1942 the national unemployment rate exceeded 3 per cent only in 1947, and that was due to the severe weather conditions in the winter of that year. (29) The proportion of operatives in the labour force has continued to decline from three-quarters of the total in the 1920s to about two-thirds in the early 1960s. (30) The actual number of operatives increased until 1961, but it is uncertain whether this is still the case. Monetary policy has been divorced from gold since 1931, and at least one writer has called the present monetary system a 'labour standard'. (31)

In times of rising prosperity, wages and profits rise. This reflects an excess demand for labour and capital. Another way of putting the same point is that labour and capital become scarcer relatively to effective demand. Since wages tend to rise less than profits, rising prosperity not only implies greater scarcity of both factors; it also implies a relatively greater scarcity of capital than of labour. In consequence, relatively to each other, capital becomes 'the' scarce factor and labour 'the' abundant factor. This applies in cyclical boom and also when activity is at a high level for a long period of time. When, over a long period, the economy seldom or never lapses from full employment, there is a long-run excess demand and scarcity of factors. Given a general scarcity of factors, capital tends to be scarcer than labour. There is then a general tendency for factor earnings to rise, but the relative abundance of labour ensures that wages cannot rise ahead of other factor earnings.

As far as wage-earning operatives' labour is concerned, the relative abundance of labour is somewhat offset through the increasing opportunities the economy offers in salaried employment. Since those in salaried employment seldom return to wage-earning occupations, any move from wage-earning to salary-earning employments makes the scarcity of operatives' labour greater than the scarcity of all labour. To have effect on wage determination, however, such movements have to be sharp and swift in order to outweigh fluctuations in effective demand. This is so unlikely to happen that the movement from wage-earning to salary-earning employment will seldom, if ever, protect the earnings of wage-earners.

The money supply has become more flexible than it was in gold-standard days, though it would be an exaggeration to say that it has ever responded perfectly to increases in the national wages bill. Rather it has been kept sufficiently flexible so as not to endanger full employment, and the authorities may have erred on the side of keeping it too flexible. A rise in the national income of a fully employed economy creates an excess demand for factors, including labour, which can only be accommodated if the money supply increases in appropriate ratio.

The trade unions' task is to ensure that labour maintains its share of the national income. Since, however, labour is now relatively abundant, that could imply that the increments to wages may limp slightly behind profits. The importance of an adjustment of profits ahead of wages will be discussed in Chapter 22. Here let it suffice to say that some lag in wage increments may account for the slight tendency for the share of wages to fall, which has been observed in Fig. 18.1, though the share of profits also appears to have fallen somewhat. Since the fall in the share of wages is, however, within the traditional range of labour's share, a few more years' statistics will have to be studied before a firm assertion is possible.

However the labour situation has changed from one where labour was relatively scarce amongst abundant factors, to one where labour is relatively abundant amongst scarce factors. Eventually this may or may not weaken wage labour's position in the economy. So far, however, the struggle for shares has been vain in both situations, for in both situations the total paid for operatives' labour has been a function of the size of the national income.

5   WAGE RATES: THE MACRO-VIEW

The previous section of this chapter dealt with the role of trade unions under overall conditions of scarcity of factors of production. It was not concerned with the effects of changes in labour costs which may result from rising wage rates. This omission must now be repaired, especially since theories relating to cost-push inflation have influenced much public thinking and given rise to the 'incomes' policy of the 1960s.

The 'incomes' policy was based on a particular interpretation of the behaviour of trade unions under conditions of full employment. Trade unions were thought to engage in competitive bidding for higher wages in order to maintain their own individual shares of a slowly rising total real national product. It became apparent that between 1958 and 1967, real national product grew more slowly than in the previous ten years, and that Britain's economic growth fell behind that of most of the industrial world. An influential body of opinion attributed this to rising factor costs and pointed to a mere 3 per cent annual growth of industrial output per man, at a time when average weekly earnings rose at around 6 per cent a year compound. Since consumer prices were also rising at 3 per cent a year compound, this was attributed to the difference between the rise in wages and the rise in productivity. Not all of the rise in prices could have been due to the rise in weekly earnings, since some of the rise in consumer goods was attributable to rising import prices and other factor costs. Nevertheless much of government policy during that period was influenced by an interpretation of these facts as implying the existence of cost-induced inflation. Trade union pressure was seen as the major influence in higher wages, and these higher wages were passed on to the consumer by business enterprises in the form of higher prices. The postulated existence of cost-push inflation has almost been interpreted as a law, to the effect that a 2 per cent increase in average weekly earnings will automatically result in a 1 per cent increase in consumer prices.

The reflections of economists on these facts and relationships has led to the construction of a number of theoretical models of the economy aimed at isolating the causes of this persistent rise in money incomes and prices which has continued almost unabated since the end of the Second World War. Perhaps the most important of these models relate the rate of increase in money wage rates to the level of unemployment, or alternatively the rate of increase in prices to the degree of trade union pressure. All such models have been constructed so that they may be subjected to econometric testing.

One line of approach to these problems is to relate the rate of change of money wage rates and the level of unemployment. (32) The usual procedure has been to start by formulating a functional relationship between wage-rate increases and the level of demand as represented by the level of unemployment. Thus there is an equation of the type:

$$dW = a + bU^{-1}$$

where the rate of change in money wage rates dW depends on a constant factor a is inversely related to the level of unemployment U. The coefficient b indicates the size of this relationship. Graphically the functional relationship may be plotted as in Fig. 19.1.

The method used to estimate the strength of this relationship has been to fit regression lines by the 'least squares' technique and to test the size of the estimated coefficient b for significance by the use of appropriate statistical tests.

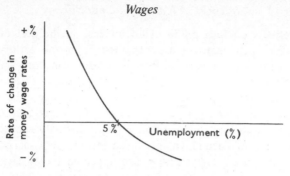

Fig. 19.1 Relationship between wage-rate changes and unemployment

Additional explanatory variables, such as the rate of change in retail prices and an index of productivity, have been added to the right-hand side of the equation in order to try and improve the goodness of fit of the regression line and its use in forecasting. From a practical point of view, the importance of this work has lain in the establishment of 'pay-off' matrices between the level of unemployment and the rise in money wage rates or prices. There might thus be the following imaginary matrix, relating consequential price increases to the level of unemployment and the rate of increase in productivity (output per man-hour).

Productivity and unemployment matrix for price increases

Percentage change in output per man-hour	Percentage level of unemployment			
	2	3	4	5
2	2½	2	1½	1
3	1⅔	1⅓	1	⅔
4	1¼	1	¾	½
5	1	⅘	⅗	⅖

In this matrix, it is assumed for simplicity that a 1 per cent increase in productivity reduces the price rise associated with different levels of unemployment by one-half. Thus with 3 per cent level of unemployment, the matrix suggests that prices would rise by 2 per cent if productivity increased by 2 per cent, or by only 1 per cent if productivity increased by 2 per cent, or by only 1 per cent if productivity were to rise by as much as 4 per cent. More complicated pay-off matrices can be constructed which would also take into account the subsequent effects on final prices of an increase in the cost of imports. The coefficients for such matrices are obtained from the estimated regression coefficients in the fitted equations. For the United Kingdom, estimates relating to the late 1950s and early 1960s indicate that a 1 per cent decrease in the level of unemployment would probably increase money wage rates by 3 per cent, and that this 3 per cent increase in money wage rates would lead to a 1 per cent increase in prices, so that in the absence of productivity changes a 1 per cent decline in the level of unemployment would tend to be associated with a 1 per cent increase in prices. The findings also appeared to indicate that it would require a 2 per cent increase in productivity to neutralise the effects of a 1 per cent price rise due to a 1 per cent decline in the unemployment rate.

An alternative approach is to view trade union power as an independent factor which may be used to force up wage rates and earnings, and consequently prices, almost irrespective of the level of unemployment. One author has used the degree of unionisation of the labour force as an index of trade union push-fulness. (33) If this is taken as an independent variable, uncorrelated with the state of demand for labour, it makes a statistically significant contribution to the explanation of wage-rate increases, not only at the aggregate level but also in terms of individual industries. (34) These findings suggest that, overall, a 1 per cent change in the degree of unionisation is associated with a 1½ per cent change in the annual percentage change in money wage rates. It is by no means proven, however, that the degree of trade union pushfulness is not associated with the level of economic activity as exemplified, for example, in the increase of unemployment levels (35) or the scarcity of factors (see section 4 above).

Allied to the concept of trade union pushfulness, though not essential to its impact on money wage rates and consequently prices, is the wages round or wage spiral. The classical exposition of this alleged phenomenon is to be found in the report by the Organisation for Economic Co-operation and Development on 'The Problem of Rising Prices'. (36) In spite of the evidence produced in this report, doubts have been cast on its applicability to British economic conditions in the 1950s and 1960s. The report's theory is that there is continuous leadership by certain industries or occupations, whose increased wages, either on an absolute basis of x − shillings per hour or week, or on a percentage basis, are seen to be copied by other industries or occupations which attempt to follow suit. British experience does not seem to provide much evidence for such a view. (37) Such a theory would imply that control over wage increases achieved by the leaders would then be reflected in smaller claims and increases obtained in those industries which are supposed to follow suit. This view consists of a straightforward theory of comparability, with wage claims being made in order to restore the status quo in respect of differentials calculated either on an absolute or percentage basis. It also implies the existence of a highly rigid wage structure, and it has been argued that the overall British wage structure is essentially of this type. (38) Analysis of the position in Britain (for example by the P.I.B.) has, however, failed to find such consistent leaders as would be required by such theories.

6 INCOMES POLICIES

During the 1960s incomes policy has been established in a more formal way than was the case in the 1940s or 1950s. The placing of incomes policy on a formal basis arose out of discussions of the Council on Prices, Productivity and Incomes, established towards the end of the 1950s. (39) The reports of 1958 and 1959 followed two quite different approaches in their line of argument. The first report stressed the importance of ensuring the movement of factors of production between industries, and in general adopted a demand approach to the interpretation of the rise in prices and money incomes since the end of the war. In contrast the third and fourth reports stressed the power of trade unions to initiate price increases through obtaining increased wages. The final chapter of the third report – 'A Policy for Money Incomes' – may be considered as the starting point for much of the interventionist approach to the direct control of personal money incomes at source during the 1960s.

The first major intervention towards influencing personal money incomes came in 1961: a nine-month pay-pause was announced by the then Chancellor of the Exchequer. This was followed by the first of a series of successive guideposts for incomes, a 'guiding light' of 2-2½ per cent, based on recent long-term trends in productivity. Simultaneously a National Incomes Commission (N.I.C.) was set up to review wage claims and settlements with set terms of reference. Its various reports have already been referred to in Chapter 13. From the macro point of view, the important aspect was that the N.I.C. quickly revised the 'guiding-light' of 2-2½ per cent upwards to 3-3½ per cent, a target which it was thought was more likely to be feasible in practice.

New attempts to instigate an incomes policy, accompanied by wage-freezes and money-income norms, came about with the change in government in 1964. The new attempts resulted from a tripartite agreement between the employers' organisations, the Trades Union Congress and the Government, and was set out in the form of a Declaration of Intent in December 1964. (40) Subsequently, to the end of 1968, incomes policy has gone through four different phases, based on two different models. The first model corresponds with the first phase of incomes policy for the years 1965-8, and saw incomes policy newly inaugurated on a voluntary basis. This phase also saw the replacement, in 1965, of the National Incomes Commission by a new body, the National Board for Prices and

Incomes (P.I.B.). The various criteria to govern wage increases under which the Board would operate were agreed on jointly by the Government, the Trades Union Congress and the Confederation of British Industries. Exceptions to the new norm, of 3 to 3½ per cent, had to be justified in terms of workers' contributions to productivity, relative manpower shortage, pay differences in comparable occupations and increased pay for lower-paid workers. Additionally there was introduced a set of specific criteria to be used in vetting price increases.

The second phase of incomes policy, lasting from July 1966 to June 1967, saw the inauguration of the second, compulsory model, coupled with deflation. It was also accompanied by the conversion of the Prices and Incomes Board from the status of a Royal Commission to a statutory board. During this period the Board was required to operate under rules which imposed a six-month freeze on all wage and price increases, subject to a very limited number of exceptions, these being rather wider during the subsequent six months of 'severe restraint'. The Prices and Incomes Act of 1966, which inaugurated this second phase of incomes policy, also provided for an 'early warning system' whereby unions were to give notice of impending wage claims. Part IV of this Act also gave the Government power to impose a statutory wage-freeze on prices and incomes and the right to impose penalties on law-breakers.

During the third phase lasting from July 1967 to March 1968, the Board was required to operate more or less under the same conditions as those which obtained during the operation of the voluntary incomes-policy model. But this time there was introduced a nil norm compared with the earlier norm of 3 to 3½ per cent. The Prices and Incomes Act of 1967, which reiterated the powers obtained by the Government in the 1966 Act, also gave the Government power to delay proposed wage and price increases for up to six months on reference to the P.I.B. The fourth phase from April 1968, lasting until well into 1969, reintroduced the initial 3-3½ per cent norm for pay increases, subject to two exceptions, namely the productivity case and major revisions of pay structures. The latter have already been discussed in Chapter 13. This phase was also accompanied by extended delaying powers of up to eleven months in the Prices and Incomes Act of 1968. This Act prolonged the Government's existing powers up to the end of 1969 and also added further to them, to the effect that the Government might (a) require a reduction of certain prices or charges until a recommendation was made by the P.I.B.; (b) delay Agricultural Wages Orders and the giving effect to Wages Councils' proposals, again subject to recommendations from the P.I.B.; and (c) control dividend and rent increases in both the public and private sector.

The outcome of this well-nigh medieval panoply of powers in search of 'just' factor prices does not appear to have been spectacularly successful, judged by the policy's performance to the end of 1968. A number of econometric-type investigations have been carried out with a view to testing the effectiveness of prices and incomes policies in reducing the rate of increase in prices and money incomes. One, carried out as a preliminary investigation on behalf of the P.I.B. itself, does not lend much credence to claims that the policy has been particularly effective. (41) The administrators of the incomes policy apparently claim no more than an annual 1 per cent reduction in the rise of income from employment during those years in which it has been in operation. An econometric study in the Caves Report, (42) using more sensitive quarterly series of prices and incomes, also throws doubts on the effectiveness of the policies, with the exception of the statutory freeze of 1966-7; the degree of effectiveness appears to depend in part on the precise statistical series used. For example, incomes policy appears to have had more predictable effects on weekly wage rates, but these may not be the most appropriate series to use when considering the impact of incomes from employment and labour costs on prices. Earnings series would be more relevant, but these do not exist for sufficiently short periods of time to be useful in quarterly analyses.

7   THE MICRO-ECONOMIC INCOMES POLICY IN PRACTICE

It is worth inquiring why 'incomes policy' is apparently not working. The answer covers a number of influences, which will include the ease of avoiding incomes policy, the susceptibility of the economy to international forces which are outside government control, and even the possibility that it may be to the advantage of the economy to frustrate the working of the policy. Incomes policy is easy to side-step. The small firm, far away from the public eye, may infringe the rules with comparative impunity. Men may be granted an increase in wages well above the norm. Alternatively, in order to disguise an outright infringement, their posts may be upgraded so that a higher rate of pay is 'justified'. Even the largest firm, which cannot act with such complete disregard for the rules, is in a position to flout them. What matters from the point of view of the whole economy is the aggregate pressure of demand on goods and services. A major force influencing this pressure is the effective demand of the wage-earning sector. This effective demand is determined not by officially negotiated wage rates, but by take-home pay. This is total earnings derived from employment. Any company has discretion to vary the hours of employment of its work force. Thus an indirect way of ensuring greater take-home pay, without officially increasing wage rates, is to raise the amount of overtime worked. Activity rates can be varied to secure greater total pay for the employees of a particular company, without any apparent violation of the incomes policy. The effect may be the same as if there had been a straightforward increase in wage rates.

Another point of importance to incomes policy is the extent to which external forces influence the economy. These forces are largely beyond the control of the Government and may frustrate the policy. The terms of trade are an example. Import and export prices are to a significant extent externally determined. Movements in the terms of trade may reinforce or weaken any inflationary pressure within the economy. The terms of trade show the relative position of unit import and export prices. If the terms of trade improve, the unit prices of imports decrease relative to unit prices of exports. In simplified terms, export prices increase and import prices decrease relative to each other. Such an improvement in relative prices may increase effective demand within the economy. Imports are now relatively cheaper, so real incomes may rise. Exports are now relatively more expensive and so greater revenue may be derived from export trade. The net effect may be an increase in inflationary pressure. A worsening of the terms of trade may also influence the level of effective demand of the economy. Unit exports prices are now relatively cheaper and unit import prices dearer. Exporters may derive less revenue from trading, and relatively dearer imports may mean that real incomes fall. This may induce cost-of-living wage claims and, depending on the nature of settlements, affect the level of home demand. This discussion of the effects of the terms of trade is deliberately highly simplified. The purpose has been to stress that internal economic policies are susceptible to external forces. With a high proportion of national income dependent on international trade, this cannot be ignored.

A further argument used to explain the apparent lack of success of incomes policy is that such a factor-price policy may actively harm the economy, and so that countervailing forces are generated which ensure it failure. In the private-enterprise sector of an economy, factors of production are attracted to and from current activities by the level of earnings. The normal signals to attract resources are relatively high wages, profit, salaries and rents. If these signals are outlawed, then allocation of resources may suffer. For example, employers anxious to secure additional men may not be permitted to pay premium wages. In this way they may be unable to compete to attract labour away from less good ventures, and so a net addition to the output of the economy may be lost. An incomes policy may therefore actively harm the economy by frustrating the movement of resources. But countervailing forces may ensure that this does not happen. As mentioned before, employers will either openly flout incomes policy or devise legitimate means to avoid it. The allocation mechanism may operate with such force that an incomes policy may merely be a legal charade, to which firms and unions pay lip-service and then ignore in practice.

The temptation to thwart incomes policy may also be reinforced by the problems firms and unions have in identifying their interests with those of the economy. Even if wage restraint is in the national interest, individual firms and unions are subject to a number of conflicting pressures. It may be to the advantage of individual economic units to violate incomes policy. Individual union members will secure higher pay, and firms may succeed in attracting the factors they require. There may therefore be a clash between the micro and macro aspects of this policy. Assuming that the policy is economically sound, the economy may benefit if the criteria are observed. But at the same time individual economic units will be tempted to take avoiding action, in the belief that they can secure a unilateral benefit. If only a few are successful, then they will secure an advantage. If a large proportion of the population manage to side-step the policy, then little or no benefit will accrue to individuals or the economy. For this sort of argument the soap-box analogy may be appropriate. One individual in a football crowd will secure an excellent view of the play if he stands on a soap-box. But once his neighbours see the advantage, they too will find something to stand on. Eventually the process will cumulate, until out of self-defence practically everyone will have a soap-box. The net result is the same as when the process started, except that now everyone is viewing from an unnecessarily elevated position.

The clash between the interests of individual economic units and those of the economy, as defined in terms of incomes policy, may be one of the reasons for the lack of success. The experience of the United Kingdom is similar to that of a number of European countries where such a factor-price policy has been adopted. (43) It would appear that, at the micro-level, individuals and economic units are not prepared to submerge their interests for those of the economy. Whether this is vital to the future of the British economy is difficult to determine. As indicated above, the case for an incomes policy is not completely established. In terms of the allocation of resources, such a policy may actually harm the economy. If so then its apparent failure is to be welcomed.

In defence of the incomes policy, it must be pointed out that there are two difficulties in assessing success or failure. Firstly, the results have to be judged on a hypothetical comparison; and secondly, the results have to be weighed, not in relation to the publicly avowed aims of the policy, but rather in terms of practical effect. A hypothetical comparison is involved because every exercise attempting to assess incomes policy is using as a yardstick what might have occurred in the absence of the policy. Thus a comparison is made of the trend of wages and prices during the period covered by the incomes policies, with a derived trend of what might have happened during the same period had no policy been implemented. This is a hypothetical comparison and subject to a whole number of reservations. Conclusions based on such comparisons must therefore be treated with considerable reserve. The second difficulty arises from the criterion of success or failure. Those who take an extreme view will maintain that every time a wage increase is granted in excess of the stipulated amount, the policy has failed. But from a more practical viewpoint, the appropriate yardstick will be the final effect. Thus even though incomes policy does not eliminate inflation, it may have some influence in slowing the rate of increase in prices. If, as a consequence, Britain has a slower relative rate of price inflation than her international trading rivals, some benefit may be gained. Over time, a small percentage difference in annual rates of inflation may aggregate into a notable competitive advantage for British goods. To this extent an apparently marginal impact on prices through incomes policy may become important. The practical aim of improving the competitive position of United Kingdom goods in world markets may be achieved.

A further point in defence of incomes policy lies with its potential long-term effects on the nature of wage bargaining. The explicit concern with the wages-productivity link may speed up the rate of diffusion of innovations in industry. Labour's concern to secure higher wages, and management's concern to retain labour and yet remain profitable, may have this effect. Productivity-based wage increases are a means whereby labour can officially secure wage rises above the guiding percentage. Productivity increases are the practical means whereby management can absorb wage increases. There is thus likely to be pressure from both sides of industry to improve output per man. One important means of achieving this is to adopt newer techniques of work and production methods. The gap between best and average techniques within industries should be narrowed under this incentive provided by incomes policy. This is likely to be a fairly long-term benefit simply because alteration and adoption of production functions usually involve considerable capital investment and time to absorb the change. Thus although incomes policy may appear a failure in terms of damping inflationary pressure, there may be beneficial side-effects. Wage negotiations are likely to become more explicitly concerned with trends of performance on both sides of industry, and this may provide a considerable impetus to the process of diffusion.

It is worth inquiring whether the results arising from the implementation of the incomes policy have been worth the amount of irritation caused. Was too much expected from an 'incomes policy' which meant detailed intervention in individual factor prices? It will be shown, in Chapter 22 below, that an incomes policy in the macro-economic sense implies monetary and fiscal policy. Nor does the factor-price policy, which went under the name of incomes policy, fit in well with the macro-economic forces which determine the share of wages in national income. There may be a case for reforming trade union organisation, actions and manner. The unions grew in order to ensure that labour be treated as scarce when factors were abundant. They must reform or be reformed at times of general scarcity of factors and relative abundance of wage labour. This is a long-term task. The 'incomes policy' of the 1960s was, at best, a stop-gap measure until the long-term implications of changes in relative factor scarcities have been fully considered.

20 Rent

1 RENT AS A RESTRAINT OF CHANGE

In some ways it might be best to consider salaries in the chapter following wages, for both are personal incomes from employment. However, as will be shown in Chapter 21, salaries contain a rent element, so that it is best to consider rent first.

The national income estimates define rent as the gross receipts from land and buildings, including the imputed rent of owner-occupied dwellings and farms, but excluding the imputed rent of owner-occupied trading properties (which are classed as trading incomes). (1) Defined this way, rent accounted for 5 per cent of the national income in the 1950s and 6 per cent in the first half of the 1960s. Earlier this century the share of rent in national income had been higher. Going back in time, it averaged 9 per cent in the inter-war years and 12½ per cent at the beginning of the century. (2)

Since those estimates include imputed rent of owner-occupied properties, rent 'received' exceeds rent payments actually made. Imputed rent is legal fiction; it is paid by an owner-occupier, in his capacity of occupier, to himself, in his capacity of owner. That these are fictitious payments did not prevent the tax authorities from levying income tax on such 'income' until as recently as 1963. Such tax demands are no longer being made, but the calculations continue on the same basis (and will presumably continue on the same basis as long as local rates are levied in given ratios to rentable values). Irrespective of taxation policy, the excess of rent 'received' over rent actually paid has become larger as the number of owner-occupiers has increased. At the beginning of the century only about one householder in ten and only about one farmer in ten was an owner-occupier. By the 1960s about one householder in two and about one farmer in three was an owner-occupier. (3) Thus if the official estimates of rent 'received' are taken to refer to the benefits from rent, and if rent payments actually made are regarded as the burden of rent, the benefits from rent (relatively to all incomes) have about halved in the course of the present century, while the burden of rent must have fallen much more.

The burden of rent consists of the actual payments made to preclude change.

A tenant wants somewhere to live and work. He is willing to pay for the use of another's property, as it is and where it is. Thus he escapes the inconvenience of a migrant's life without having to assume the responsibilities of ownership. The tenant's payments restrain the landlord from altering the present use of the preperty. Once the landlord accepts rent payments, he cannot develop the property for alternative uses, even if they were more profitable. Alternative uses will include the possibility of allowing the property to decay or letting to another tenant.

The benefits from rent consist of the income derived from letting the use of property, as it is and where it is. The landlord has no obligation beyond keeping the property intact. Thus for the duration of a rent contract the landlord escapes the worry of what else to do with his property. At times this particular escape from worry may cost the landlord dear in terms of alternative opportunities forgone, and the benefit of not having to worry about change becomes the burden of being unable to effect change. More will be said below as to why landlord or tenant may come to rue having entered into a rent agreement. Here let it suffice to say that rent is a restraint of change. That is its purpose. Its effect is to keep property as it is and where it is.

As shown above, the official definition of rent restricts the term to incomes and payments relating to the use of immovable property. Since the purpose and effect of rent is to preserve extant uses, the term is not strictly applicable where the relevant payment can affect supplies in one market at short notice. This excludes payments for the use of movable factors, such as a television set or a machine. There is a rent element in such payments in so far as a television set and a machine must be preserved, as they are, by both parties to the agreement, even if the preservation of quality may not be possible for long. Moreover changes in the relevant payment may lead to movement of the television set or machine from its present position. If the hirer does not pay the 'rent' for his television set, the set will be removed from him; but if a tenant does not pay the rent for a farm or dwelling, he can be removed from the property. In other words rent in the strictest sense of the term is the payment for the use of property as it is and where it is; while in the case of hire of durable factors other than land and buildings, the payment is for the use of the property as it is and where the hirer is. The latter payments include a rent element, but this is not the only element involved; at least there are transport costs if you hire a television set for use in your own home rather than just a television set wherever it may be. Such payments are best classed as a source of trading income rather than rent.

The same applies to all payments for the hire of anything for such a short period that there cannot be an effective restraint of change. The bridegroom's payment for the use of a morning coat on his wedding day constitutes hire rather than rent. So does payment for the use of a condemned property for selling Christmas cards before the demolition squads arrive in the New Year. Further excluded from rent are all payments made with a view to change of ownership, such as mortgage payments and hire-purchase payments. For the change in ownership is in itself a change.

Thus there is 'rent' only when repetitive payments are made and received for the use of immovable property (as it is and where it is) and such payments are an effective restraint of change. As mentioned before, the benefits and burdens derived from rent do not necessarily change in the same direction or at the same rate.

A definition of rent as a restraint of change has meaning only where change is contemplated or could be contemplated. This is normally the case in a multi-purpose economy, where almost any plot of land could be used for a variety of purposes. The same applies to most buildings. Where land can be used for a miscellany of agricultural purposes, for public buildings, private dwellings and factories; where a highly mobile population seeks frequent changes in accommodation so that the use of any particular dwelling could easily be transferred from this tenant to that; there rent may be a necessary restraint to allow time between sowing and reaping, between industrial input and industrial output, and for workers to dwell between moves. Such a situation is a far cry from the sort of economy envisaged by some of the classical economists (at least in their consideration relating to rent), where practically all land was used for the production of 'corn' and there were few or no alternative uses for land. Present-day Britain has a multi-purpose and mobile economy, so that rent cannot be entirely explained in terms of classical models which related to land as a factor with a single economic purpose. Where land use is given, restraint is irrelevant and rent should be nil. Some classical economists thought so too.

The classical economists thought of rent as an 'unearned increment' which accrued to the owners of land. In yet earlier times landlords may have earned a rent through special services in defence or the maintenance of law and order, which at least restrained destruction, but these functions increasingly became the responsibility of the central Government. The remaining services of landlords were to provide land, cottages and implements, pay the parson, act as local justices and the like, and these services may have been excessively rewarded through rent in classical times, and certainly were so in classical models. How relevant the classical view of rent is to modern Britain depends on how widespread ownership of single-economic-purpose land and buildings is. Wherever this applies, there is no case for rent in restraint of change since change is not contemplated anyway. In all such cases rent is unearned and should be nil.

In modern Britain single-economic-purpose land and buildings are normally owned by the National Trust or by the still growing number of owner-occupiers. Thus land and buildings administered by the National Trust are to be enjoyed, as they are and where they are, in perpetuity. The National Trust, as owner, desires no change and owes its support to the fact that change is not wanted by the general public, the user. More important are owner-occupied properties. Owner--occupied dwellings are meant to retain their present use for a lifetime and beyond. An owner-occupier may incur expenditure to maintain his property intact or to improve it, but he does not normally intend to alter his property's purpose of housing the family.

If purely economic considerations influenced individuals and business became prosperous enough, owner-occupied houses might become factories. But under present social circumstances owner-occupied houses are effectively single-economic-purpose units. Their owners contemplate no change, since they normally want owner-occupancy for its own sake. Because change is not contemplated, no payment is needed to restrain change. Where rent is thus unnecessary, the benefit of rent payments 'received' is unearned. Since no rent payments are actually made, the burden of rent is nil. In short an owner-occupier is deemed to 'receive' an unearned increment, but in fact this is nil.

The supply of National Trust properties and the supply of owner-occupied dwellings can be varied through purchases and sales. In the social climate of today, it can, on balance, only be added to. This means an increasing proportion of the country's land and buildings is once more becoming single-economic-purpose land and buildings. But where the owners and users of single-economic-purpose properties are identical, such as owner-occupiers of dwelling-houses, or where the owners and users have identical interests, as with National Trust properties, the total supply of such properties is beyond the influence of rent, simply because no payment is either made or received.

This does not apply where a property is used as a source of money income. The property's present use may or may not yield the highest possible return at today's prices, so that a change of use might be profitable. A payment in restraint of development towards more profitable uses is meaningful. That makes rent, as a restraint of change, relevant whenever owner and occupier are not identical and do not have identical interests. Landlords want incomes as such, and not tenants as such. They want tenants only when letting to tenants yields a higher return than they could get by selling the property or by letting it for other uses or to other tenants. Thus a landlord normally lets his property to a tenant only if, at the time the rent agreement is entered into, the agreed rent seems to offer the highest possible money income. The rent agreement fixes that money income over a number of years, during which time other prices will change and either landlord or tenant may come to rue the agreement.

In the remainder of this chapter rent will be considered only in relation to properties where owner and user are not identical. But it should be noted, in passing, that special complications arise in the case of owner-occupied farms.

The purpose of such farms is not only to provide a habitation but also to provide a money income. This makes such farms dual-purpose properties, in the sense that they have to satisfy the different aims of owner and occupier even where the owner is the occupier. Moreover, bearing in mind the variety of ways in which a farmer can work for his money income, it might be more correct to regard most farms as multi-purpose properties. Nowadays a field is not just an area of land where 'corn' is grown, but a source of alternative money incomes from ploughing or grazing or for use as a caravan site for tourists. Rent, as a restraint of encroachment of any of these purposes on any other, might be theoretically meaningful, but is impossible to calculate correctly. It is not surprising that no attempts are made to calculate farm rent in that way. But the way imputed rents of owner-occupied properties are calculated by the tax authorities cannot be accurate either. Such imputed rent is an estimate of the rent the farmer would have to pay if he were not the owner. In so far as such estimates assume that owner and occupier do not have identical interests, even if they are one and the same person, the theoretical reasoning behind such estimates is correct. But in so far as those estimates assume that farming is just farming, their theoretical basis is more appropriate to the single-purpose farming of classical models than to the multi-purpose farming of today. In the case of owner-occupied factory premises and shops, no attempt is made to calculate an imputed rent and all income from such properties is treated as trading income. On analytical grounds there is a case for treating all income derived from owner-occupied farms in the same way.

2 RENT AS AN 'UNEARNED' INCREMENT

(d) Rent in Times of Falling Prices Where property is used as a source of money income, and where owner and occupier are not identical, the relationship between owner and occupier is regulated by a rent contract. Such a contract is based on price relationships prevailing at the time the contract is entered into. The contract extends such valuation for as long as it is legally in force. At the time the contract is drawn up, both owner, and occupier consider the restraint worth the payment. The payment made by the occupier equals the payment received by the owner in money terms and in real terms. The burden of rent equals the benefit of rent and there is no 'unearned' increment.

An 'unearned' increment arises when other prices change while rents are fixed by long-term contracts or by law. When other prices fall and rents remain unchanged, the benefit to the landlord becomes greater in real terms than was foreseen at the time the contract was drawn up. The real burden on the tenant becomes correspondingly greater. Under these conditions, old rent contracts protect the landlord, for new rent contracts are based on valuations of the various alternative productive uses of the property now, and the money value of goods and services is less after a general fall in prices than before. The 'unearned' increment is the difference between the rent received under contracts drawn up before the fall in the general level of prices and the rent that would be received under contracts drawn up after the fall in the general level of prices. 'Unearned' is put in inverted commas to stress that the word has a technical meaning.

The basic condition for an accrual of an 'unearned' increment to the landlord is, then, a general fall in prices, coupled with a legal system which allows for the perpetuation of old rents through long-term contracts. Such conditions prevailed during the last quarter of the nineteenth century. Prices were falling at a time when it was lawful and customary to draw up rent contracts for a long period of time. From the landlord's point of view few other ways of investing money were as safe as houses, which in those days returned a steady money income and a rising real income. In consequence the supply of houses to let increased.

There would have been no gain in providing more and more house room to let, had the position not been tolerable for tenants. The position was tolerable for tenants, because in those days incomes were rising and prices were falling. The fall in prices was largely brought about by a fall in import prices, which in Britain meant lower food prices (with beneficial effects on all household budgets) and also lower raw-material prices (with beneficial effects on industrial costs and consequently on prices of manufactures). Thus even if a householder would find rent a constant money burden and a rising real burden, his standard of living would normally still rise as long as money incomes were rising and prices falling. In other words the general economic situation benefited landlords and compensated tenants. The landlords benefited from a rising real income derived from a constant monetary rent, and the majority of tenants could afford the rising real burden of rent, as long as other prices moved in their favour. No wonder, then, that by the turn of the century the vast majority of householders resided in rented properties, and that rent agreements were offered and accepted for long periods.

(b) Rent in Times of Moderately Rising Prices

The situation changed during the early years of the present century. The pre-1914 years of the century were years of rising import and retail prices, and even if the rise in prices was moderate compared with what was to occur in mid-century, it came after a long period of falling prices and so disappointed some expectations which had long been taken for granted. It disappointed land-lords since they could no longer derive rising real incomes from long-period rent contracts. Their 'unearned' income fell or even became negative. Prospective tenants were also disappointed, for new rent contracts took account of the rising price levels, so that higher rents were needed (to restrain change of use of properties) than had been available to previous tenants. Tenants under old rent contracts benefited in so far as an 'unearned' increment now accrued to them, but this led to no rise in their standards of living so long as other prices rose. The situation was still tolerable, since wages and salaries (4) rose roughly at the same rate as prices; but the condition for a mutually beneficial landlord—tenant relationship, of the late nineteenth-century variety, namely a fall in general prices, was no longer available. Property to let became a less suitable form of income, especially when it came to provide for a widow or unmarried daughter; and rent paid for property may have seemed a harsh burden on new tenants or even to old tenants who found it more difficult to make ends meet. It was in these days that the building society movement to finance owner-occupancy gathered momentum. But the phase of rising prices did not last long enough and was not intolerable enough to effect a major change in dwelling habits. In 1914 about 90 per cent of the 8½ million dwelling-houses then available were rented privately. (5)

(c)   Rent in Times of Falling Prices, Once Again

In the 1920s and until the mid-1930s, prices fell. Incomes moved less adversely but more irregularly. There was rent control, which had been introduced as a temporary measure during the First World War and, subject to a variety of changes, has been applied ever since. But rent control cannot have been very effective in those years, since persistently falling prices would make new rents nearly always lower than old rents, so that new and renewable rents could not have been raised in any case. In those days tenants were not so much repelled by high rents, or the fear of high rents, as attracted into subsidised council houses or into owner-occupancy.

These alternatives had been unknown or less widespread before 1914. But when council houses became available, increasing numbers of working-class tenants were attracted away from the private landlord, and the growth of the building society movement brought owner-occupancy within the reach of the middle-aged, middle-income earners. The increasing availability of mortgages allowed owner-occupancy to commence once the necessary deposit had been saved up (the deposit being a given percentage of the purchase price), and owner-occupancy became no longer confined to the rich who could afford to buy a house with one down-payment. Mortgages enabled owner-occupiers to pay the larger part of the purchase price after the commencement of owner-occupancy; but as long as deposits were a high percentage of the purchase price, this took a considerable time to save and meanwhile rented accommodation had to be used. Owner-occupancy was not yet for the young.

(d)   Rent in Times of Sharply Rising Prices.

In the mid-1930s prices began to rise again and continued to rise. This rise in prices has been much sharper than that of the 1900s and has already persisted for more than twice as long. The disappointment of landlords has been correspondingly greater and more persistent than in the 1900s, and would have occurred regardless of rent control. In the absence of rent control landlords could have escaped more easily from their contractual relationships with tenants, simply by offering shorter and shorter contracts each time one of the old contracts fell due for renewal. Eventually this would have led to such short contracts that tenancies would have become akin to the hire of hotel rooms rather than rent agreements in restraint of change. In times of rising prices, such restraint becomes increasingly irksome to landlords, who could always re-let at higher rents — which means that the landlords' 'unearned' increment becomes negative as long as old rent contracts last or are perpetuated by rent control.

When prices rise, any 'unearned' increment arising out of rent contracts accrues to the tenants. This benefit is assured when rent control prolongs the validity of current rent agreements, provided that prices continue to rise. Since prices in the 1960s were about four times what they were in the mid-1930s, it would take an unprecedented slump in prices to restore the landlord's expectations to what they were then, and an even sharper fall in prices would be needed to reverse the 'unearned' increment. But not all rent agreements are that old. Despite rent control, tenants move to other areas or into council houses or owner-occupancy or die, so that protection of tenants through rent control erodes with time. That time may seem long to landlords, especially if control does not extend current rent agreements over a fixed number of years but extends it over a fixed number of lives. For instance, at the present time control protects the tenant for his life and the life of a member of his family who has resided with him. This makes all protected tenants leaseholders for the length of two lives. But it does not follow that rent control must at all times benefit the tenant. For instance, the rise in the general price level between two arbitrarily chosen post-war years, say 1956 and 1966, was around 30 per cent. This was a substantial rise in prices; but if the past is any guide, it is not entirely impossible that such price movement may be offset by falling prices at some future date. Since the 1965 Rent Act is intended to control all rents, other than rents for luxury accommodation, it will turn out to be a 'tenants' charter' only if prices continue to rise. Should the general price movement ever again be in the opposite direction, it might become a 'landlords' charter'. Perhaps it was not possible, in 1965, to visualise any price movement but an upward one. But whoever should eventually be the beneficiary of the 1965 Act, by widening the net of rent control to include all rented properties below the luxury range (some of which had been decontrolled in 1957), it ensures that either the landlord or the tenant of each property will receive an 'unearned' increment. Given, however, expectation of the mid-1960s that the general price level will normally rise, the beneficiary will be the tenant. In other words the 'unearned'-increment element of rent is perpetuated whenever rent as a monetary restraint of change is replaced by legal restraint of changes.

(e)   The Escape from the Landlord

Even though rent control benefits the tenants, they may yet seek what alternatives are attainable, for, constant rents at a time of rising prices may help but do not guarantee a rising standard of living. This can be assured only when incomes rise much more than prices. On the whole the long rise in prices from the mid-1930s onwards has been accompanied by an even larger rise in incomes, and this in itself has assured a rising standard of living for the majority. Rent control gave additional benefits to tenants in privately owned dwellings.

But no one can be sure that his own incomes will always rise. In fact everybody expects a sharp drop in income on retirement. If he then still has to pay a fixed rent, however low, and prices continue to rise, the rent will then appear to him a rising burden, as it does to today's pensioners. The general rise in prices is no fault of the landlord's and entirely beyond his control. Yet a prudent tenant will wish to escape the private landlord before retirement, and can do so if he can afford to become an owner-occupier. This will be easier for most people when incomes rise more than the general price level.

Although the majority of the population has been in the fortunate position of having its incomes rising more than prices, not all could escape the landlord. Some were too old; building society mortgages must normally be repaid within twenty or twenty-five years, so that it can be difficult for anyone over the age of forty-five to start on house purchase with the help of a building society mortgage, simply because such repayment should be completed before retirement. Some were too young; until the mid-1960s it was almost invariably necessary to put down a deposit before commencement of house purchase with the aid of a building society, so that some money had to be provided first. This normally required saving (which takes time) or a bank overdraft, which is only given to those whose employment prospects are sound (which also takes time since the bank manager's confidence in a borrower depends on the latter's record).

No way has yet been found to help the old escape from the private landlord, except to a council house, where a public landlord replaces a private one and a politically determined rent a controlled one. But the fixed charge remains. Better escapes have been found for the young. The deposit requirements were gradually lowered. Twenty per cent was still needed in the 1950s, but only 10 per cent in the early 1960s. In the mid-1960s the Government not only intensified rent control but also gave guarantees to building societies which enabled the latter to grant 100 per cent mortgages. That measure may prove to be at least as important as the rent legislation. For house purchase can now commence on marriage, and there need no longer be a long wait in rented accommodation until the requisite deposit has been saved up.

Doomed by price movements and shunned by tenants, the private landlord's demise has been regulated rather than caused by rent control. It is by no means certain that, in the absence of government intervention, there would be more privately let dwellings available. All that is certain is that the combination of price movements, the increasing availability of alternatives to actual or prospective tenants, and rent control, taken together, have reduced the supply of private houses available for rent from over 7½ million in 1914 to a little over 5 million in 1963 (before the intensification of rent control). (6) But the rest of householders have not become homeless: in 1963 the total supply of houses was about double what it had been in 1914, but a quarter of households dwelled in local authority or other government-subsidised houses, and close on half were owner-occupiers. (7) Since most householders aspire to home ownership, some of the tenants of today are the owner-occupiers of tomorrow, but few owner-occupiers ever become tenants again. (8) Since home ownership is now possible on or soon after marriage, there is little scope for a return to late nineteenth-century dwelling habits unless both price movements and social habits revert to those then prevailing.

(f) Supply and Demand

The preliminary conclusion of this survey is that fixed rents and falling prices tend to increase the supply of properties to rent, while fixed rents and rising prices tend to reduce that supply. If personal incomes rise by more than prices (or fall less than prices), as has normally been the case during the last hundred years, the demand for house room to rent rises with the increase in the number of families as long as prices fall and no alternatives are available. If, however, incomes rise more than prices, and alternatives are available, the demand for rented accommodation falls relatively to the demand for all accommodation. Both supply and demand conditions point to the gradual disappearance of rented accommodation for long-term occupation. The law, however, has intervened. Through rent control, coupled with security of tenure for two lives, it has 'locked in' the existing landlords and repelled potential new ones. Moreover it has created an excess demand by tenants in receipt of an 'unearned increment'.

3   RENT AND CAPITAL VALUES

(a)   Rent Control and the Rate of Interest

Although rent control regulates, rather than causes, the demise of the private landlord, it still hurts those who were landlords when rent control was introduced or intensified and then could no longer escape being landlords. They are hurt through the effect of rent control on capital values. Once again it is important to distinguish between rent as an 'unearned' increment and rent as a restraint. The 'unearned' increment depends on a change in other prices after the rent contract has come into force, so that the 'unearned' increment is price-determined and not price-determining. The 'unearned' increment is a residual that accrues to either landlord or tenant. It ceases when the rent contract expires and has to be renegotiated in the light of the new price relationships. A freely negotiated new rent contract embodies the price of restraint of change. It is influenced by current prices and, in this sense, is price-determined like the 'unearned' increment. But it is not a residual arising out of other price changes. Rather it is one price amongst prices and therefore part of an interdependent price mechanism (where prices are generally determined by other prices and determine other prices). It is not difficult to see that rent of a trading property influences the costs of production on the land. Where dwelling-houses are concerned, there is no 'production' on the land, but the rent determines the landlord's return on his property and thus the capital value of such property. The restraint may be wrongly valued because of price changes or rent control, but none the less influences capital values.

The value of land and buildings depends on their various possible uses, which may be called the development possibilities of land and buildings. These development possibilities for a particular property vary with what part of it is taken into consideration. The land itself can be developed most easily for a large variety of purposes. Possible uses of buildings are more limited, at any rate once they are erected, and the least development possibilities are those of other fittings. For the time being, however, these complications will be ignored, and it will be assumed that land and buildings have considerable development potential.

There are various methods of estimating the capital value of anything bought for money. The most commonly used one equates capital value with the expected annual return $\times$ 100/rate of interest where 100/rate of interest gives the number of years' purchase, being the number of years needed for interest payments to equal the capital value. The capital value of land and buildings then equals the market rent $\times$ 100/rate of interest.

A more sophisticated valuation procedure involves summating the discounted future revenue flows. Thus the capital value of a property which is rented for

£100 per annum for ten years, when the prevailing rate of interest or discount is 10 per cent, is not £1,000 (as on the first method) but £614. This is the sum of the discounted annual rents over the ten years. The difference in capital value derived by the two methods reflects the influence of the discount factor. Effectively, the second procedure gives weight to the economic fact that time has a money value when there is a positive rate of interest. Thus £110 in year 2 is worth only £100 in year 1, because between year 1 and year 2 the initial £100 could have earned £10 of interest. Whenever the market rent rises between a purchase and a sale, there will be a capital gain, provided that the rate of interest or discount factor stays constant. When the rate of interest or discount rises, this can cause capital losses, but under normal circumstances capital gains occur when market rents rise.

Capital values are important in considering the effects of rent control. For rent control, applied to a particular use of land, has an effect on the capital value of that land or building in the same direction as a higher rate of interest. In other words such rent control has the same effect as a tax on the present owner, and it helps the tenant or the new owner (since the new owner will take the restriction of possible return into account before he agrees to buy). Any change in values, whether brought about by the market or by act of government, alters the relationship between effective demand and potential supply. If there is a general scarcity of dwelling units and, for whatever reason, an increase in paid rent is not allowed, then the authorities endeavour to enforce a rent which fits the situation of a larger supply. A lowering of capital values would attract buyers, but it does not increase the supply. A lowering of capital values would encourage new buildings only if new buildings could be erected at lower cost; but in the absence of new (and cheaper) methods of construction, lower building costs would require a prolonged squeeze or a lower demand, or both, in order to lessen pressure on building resources. If that is impossible, it becomes less attractive to let, and the supply of dwelling units to let is reduced simply because the replacement cost has become too high relatively to the possible return. When capital values are forced to a point below replacement costs, then there is a disequilibrium caused by an excess demand at current controlled rents.

The demand for house room does not change very much relatively to income. The proportion of consumer expenditure that goes into house room was about one-tenth in the 1930s and has been one-tenth in the very different conditions of the 1960s. If, then, lettable property becomes more difficult to get, the control may be evaded. Landlords may refuse to incur the cost of repairs, or may furnish accommodation in order to be subject to less severe rent control, and the like. Probably more important are escapes of tenants into council houses and owner-occupancy. The result of such escapes is to divert demand into additional demand for council houses and owner-occupied properties, leading to longer queues for council houses and higher prices offered for owner-occupied premises.

The last paragraph ignored the rate of interest, and this omission must now be repaired. An increase in the rate of interest has the same effect on the capital values of land and buildings as a fall in rent. Artificially low interest rates, as prevailed during and immediately after the Second World War, have the opposite effect. Hence in the 1940s rent control was still tolerable to the owners and the effect on supply was not too drastic, simply because the cost of borrowing for maintenance and replacement was not too prohibitive. But when interest rates rose in the 1950s, and stayed high throughout the 1950s and 1960s, matters became different. Capital values of land and buildings were depressed by the combined effects of rising interest rates and rent control. Although there was some dismantling of rent control in the 1950s, this was slow for political reasons. In any case the rent control was evaded through relatively more building of houses for owner-occupiers and less to let. The situation might yet have been different had cheaper building been allowed. But building regulations often insisted on largely traditional types of building, so that construction costs were kept up.

(b)   The Rent Act of 1965

The Rent Act of 1965 stiffened rent control. It was introduced at a time when its framers thought that interest rates could be lowered. In fact, however, interest rates were raised and kept high, and that in itself may account for the unexpected ineffectiveness of the Act in its first few years of operation. New buildings were costly and the supply of buildings seemed given. Tenants were cautious and often unwilling to appeal for a lowering of rents; and when they did, the rent could be raised as well as lowered. But the time may come when interest rates will fall again, and provided that rent control is not sharper in its effect than the fall in interest rates, the adverse effects on the supply of buildings might be avoided. It is not likely, however, that interest rates will fall markedly before prices fall. But should prices fall, rent control will become correspondingly less necessary.

The pre-1965 rent control helped the tenant by regulating the demise of the private landlord. Whether the 1965 Act will lead to the final disappearance of tenancies of dwelling-houses remains to be seen. Let just a few aspects of the Rent Act of 1965 be considered. It effectively covers all rents except those for luxury accommodation. Rent for non-luxury residential accommodation is fixed by a rent officer on the request of either the landlord or the tenant, or both, but if either landlord or tenant feel aggrieved they can appeal to a Rent Assessment Committee.

What can be taken into consideration by the committee has been decided by the Divisional Court of the Queen's Bench Division in April 1967. The decision is that the capital value of property is a useful guide to an economic rent, but not conclusive indication of a fair rent. In consequence a landlord who wants to be sure of what rent he will receive in return for his outlay should have the rent fixed before he purchases the property. Those who already own such property can have their expectations disappointed by rent control as well as by the general movement in prices.

The court also ruled that, in the assessment of rents, all circumstances have to be admitted but two. The two that are not admitted are the personal circumstances of either landlord or tenant, and the scarcity of rentable accommodation in particular parts of the country. The decision thus excludes the most relevant social considerations, for if the personal circumstances of the tenant are irrelevant, the intention to protect poor tenants may be frustrated. The decision equally excludes the most relevant economic considerations, for rent differs in different parts of the country just because prices in different parts of the country are different, so that varying restraints of change are needed. To ignore the restraint element of rent (which varies with scarcity) for fear of an 'unearned' increment, simply endeavours a transfer of that 'unearned' increment from the landlords of High Street to the tenants of High Street and from the tenants of similar properties in Slum Street to the landlords of Slum Street.

However, it would seem that a moderate policy of rent control can succeed in keeping the supply of rentable properties more nearly constant than would be the case in a free market, and so gives more security to the present occupier. Rent control stems the fall in supply of houses already let, though it also discourages additional supplies. It is meant to preserve the status quo and does. Because it preserves the status quo, it delays the general development of land and buildings. Where development potential is reduced, capital values are lowered towards the level of single-economic-purpose land.

4   LAND VALUES

If such is the intention of the authorities, then rent control must lead to the control of land values lest the rise in land values negate the intention of the rent controllers (which, after all, is to have houses to rent cheaply by the working classes, just as it was in the days of falling prices in the late nineteenth century when 'unearned' increments were rising because prices were falling).

In considering the control of land values it is necessary to distinguish between the elements of land that may be up for sale. The first element is its pure space value. It is there whatever may be paid for it. Land as land would be single-purpose property. Its rent (as restraint of change) is nil and any payment received is unearned. So why pay anything? Secondly, there is the use of land for a specific purpose. Paid rent in restraint of change must be positive, so that the capital value is positive. Exactly how high the capital value is, depends on the demand for the purpose for which the land is wanted, and the demand for the purpose is expressed through the price the purchaser is willing to pay. If prices of certain products rise, then there will be a rising demand for land on which such production can take place. If the demand for living in a particular area rises, the demand for land for dwelling units in that area will also rise. Control may then frustrate development and a free market would work better. Thirdly, the purpose for which the land is used depends on its site, and the purpose of the site may change without contribution by the owner of the land. That is particularly so when development is licensed by the authorities and land for different uses has widely different values. If so, should or should not the owner be allowed to benefit from a community decision? (9)

The above gives apparently contradictory advice by saying that the site value of land is nil and should not be paid for, but that the value of land for a particular purpose is positive and should be paid for. Matters are further complicated if the use can be changed only by a community decision, as is the case when only the authorities can decide whether agricultural land should be developed for building and when that decision raises the value of that land several times; or when the authorities decide whether there should be a motor road built, which relieves villages of through traffic and so raises the value of residential properties there, though it may hurt the cafés. Should the present owner reap the benefit (or loss) resulting from such a decision, or the community? In the immediate post-war period the law said that the community should benefit. There was a development charge of 100 per cent, which left the owner the site value of the land but no increment due to development value. Consequently the supply of land for sale dried up, and this form of taxation was abolished in the 1950s. But land values then rose sharply, and it seemed to the authorities that this was a form of profiteering. The idea gained ground that there should be a rising development charge. The reasoning was that as long as the present owner benefits, he will sell even if taxed, and as long as he is threatened by a rising charge he will sell now rather than later.

The problem is that the aggregate supply of land as such does not respond to price, but the supply of land for special purposes does. Control for one purpose alone diverts the use of land. For instance, rent control diverts a rise in rent from tenancies of rented houses to higher values of owner-occupied properties, and it diverts the supply of houses likewise. The difficulty is that the supply of land need not be paid for, but the supply of land for specific purposes has to be paid for. Now the increase in the supply of land for a specific purpose depends on a change in demand, and that means it depends on the market. But if rent control reduces the capital value of dwelling units, not as much land will be made available for residential building to let as otherwise would be the case. Should not the authorities intervene to purchase land for this and other neglected purposes and finance it out of profits from other developments?

The Land Commission, set up in 1967, tries to work along some such lines. Its purpose is to collect a betterment levy and to deal in land. The betterment levy is due when the property is sold in order to be used for a different purpose from the present one or when the property owner decides to develop his land in a way that alters the use of his land. The levy was first put at 40 per cent, but the Minister of Housing has authority to raise it to higher levels. The betterment levy is based on 'net development value' which equals the market value minus the base value (where the base value is either the price at which land was last bought or eleven times the existing use value, whichever is the higher, to which can be added expenditure on improvements or auxiliary rights), so that the higher the base value the less is the levy. This betterment levy is paid to the Land Commission and is intended to be one of the Commission's chief sources of income. Its other main source of income is to be derived from selling houses and other properties.

Only a 'material' development is chargeable. This means that a house must be enlarged at least 1,000 sq. ft before a levy is chargeable, or a factory has to be expanded by at least 10 per cent of cubic or floor area. The charge is levied on the person who realises the betterment value, that is, either the seller or the owner who wants to develop his own property. The Land Commission may take a long time to calculate what precisely the betterment value is when development takes place. To avoid uncertainty, developers may find it advantageous to sell such property to the Commission and then buy it back for a price which is sufficiently higher so as to give the Commission 40 per cent of the betterment value. In this way at least no further uncertainty arises. Whatever the case for or against such government interference with land values may be, it should be noted that it is the development value which is liable to tax and not the pure land value. Since the pure land value would be nil, that may be the only way of getting the revenue necessary for the Commission's activities.

If, however, the economic development of the country depends on continuous change in the use of factors of production, that does not exclude land and building. To tax such development is to tax the change of use of factors. The capital value of land is the capitalised restraint of change. Like rent control, the levy lowers the reward of restraint. Now rent, as a restraint of change, should preclude any but the most profitable uses of land or buildings. To lower the capitalised value of that restraint blunts the fineness of the price mechanism in selecting the most profitable use. From the point of view of the efficiency of the allocation of resources, this may be regrettable. A capitalised 'unearned' increment is created which is to benefit the Commission. If the Commission uses that unearned increment to keep land values down, costs of production in general will be kept down, since rent, as a restraint, influences production costs. Ultimately this will subsidise general economic activity at the expense of the most profitable use of land and buildings. As so often in economic policy, there is a choice between the most efficient allocation of resources (which helps a minority but facilitates the growth of the economy in the long run) and providing cheap access to existing resources (which helps the majority in the short run but delays long-term growth).

21 Salaries

1 THE SALARIAT

Salaries are personal incomes from employment under contract. In the census year of 1961 the share of salaries in national income was one-quarter of the total national income, and the proportion of salary-earners in the economically active population was also one-quarter. (1) The share of salaries in national income subsequently rose to above one-quarter, but no data are available for the number of salary-earners between census years (except for manufacturing industry).

Both the share of salaries in national income and the number of salary-earners have risen in the course of the present century. In the 1900s salaries accounted for less than one-sixth of the national income, (2) and the proportion of the economically active population in receipt of salaries was only one-tenth.

The greater rise in the proportion of salary-earners than of the share of salaries in national income might suggest that individual salary-earners have, on average, fallen somewhat behind in the general advance towards greater prosperity. But this is not comparing like with like. In the 1900s the salariat consisted of employed managers and administrators, male clerical workers, and foremen, inspectors and supervisors. These groups, taken together, may be regarded as the 'old salariat', whose numbers rose from 1.7 million in 1911 to 2.7 million in 1951, being 9 per cent and 12 per cent respectively of the total economically active population. By 1951, however, their numbers were slightly exceeded by the 'new salariat', consisting of professional men and women and of female clerks.

In 1911 most professional men were self-employed. Today very few are. Not only has the self-employed family doctor become a salaried general practitioner under the National Health Service, but the erosion of private family fortunes in war, depression and inflation, coupled with a progressive tax structure, has made it virtually impossible for, say, solicitors and business consultants to buy themselves into their professions. They must start in salaried status; and most of them stay there and want to stay there.

In 1911 there were only a few female clerks. In 1951 they numbered close on 1½ million, and in 1961 close on 2 million. Their rise is due to the emancipation of women during the first half of the century, which occurred just when automation was increasingly applied to the art of writing. In the 1900s most letters were written by hand and it saved no time to dictate a letter. Now it does. With the widespread use of shorthand and of mechanical aids such as typewriters and tape-recorders, much managerial time is saved thanks to the assistance of skilled female clerks. While the inclusion of professional men and women probably does not materially affect the average salary, female clerks are normally less well paid than male clerks. Since in 1961 female clerks accounted for about one-third of the total number of salary-earners, the average salary may have fallen as their numbers increased. If so the chief cause of the greater rise in the proportion of salary earners than of the share of salaries in national income, was the swelling of the ranks of salary-earners, especially at the lower end of the salary scale, rather than any alleged depression of the status of salary-earners as such.

The further increase in employment of female clerks between 1951 and 1961 has already been noted. The employment of male clerks also increased further, though to a lesser extent. Amongst the upper ranges of the old and new salariat, the function of managers, administrators and their professional advisers have now become so interwoven that they are best treated together. Taken together, their numbers did not change much between 1951 and 1961, though many more now describe themselves as professional men and fewer just as managers or administrators. This may reflect the higher educational background and skills required of today's managers as well as changes in definition. No details are available relating to the numbers of foremen, supervisors and inspectors in 1961, who would now class themselves as managers or operatives.

As mentioned before, the salariat has increased in numbers and has increased its share in national income. In 1951 its share of numbers and of income was over one-fifth of the total, and in 1961 around one-quarter. It is not known what happened to numbers between census years (except for manufacturing industry). It is known, however, that the share of salaries in national income remained fairly steady in the first half of the 1950s, but then rose continuously from 21 or 22 per cent in the mid-1950s to over 28 per cent by 1967.

2   THE DETERMINATION OF SALARIES

The steadiness of the national salary bill in national income in the first half of the 1950s, and its subsequent continuous rise, took place apparently irrespective of whether the national income itself advanced much or little in any one individual year. Yet what happens to salaries cannot be independent of the movement of income and prices.

Salaries are personal incomes, like wages. As such they may be expected to move with the national income, just as wages do. Yet while the share of wages in national income has remained fairly steady over the first two-thirds of the century, that of salaries has approximately doubled.

Salaries are personal incomes received under contract. The contract ensures that enough time can be devoted to employment in longer-run tasks. It also introduces an element of security, which, however, implies an element of restraint, just like a rent. Moreover any contract implies a bet whether other prices will rise during the period of validity of the contract; and if other prices rise while a salary contract is in force, the employer gets an 'unearned' increment.

Salaries are a compound of wages and rent. Yet while the share of wages in national income was steady and that of rent halved in the first two-thirds of the century, the share of salaries doubled. There must be aspects of the determination of salaries which either do not apply to the rewards of other labour, or do not apply to the determination of rent of material factors, or both.

Wage rates are largely determined through collective bargaining, where trade unions act on behalf of all their members. The result is that each worker's wage rate roughly equals the marginal social product of homogeneous labour anywhere in the country. An individual worker may raise his earnings through working overtime, but he cannot do so through the acquisition of special skills unless he can get himself upgraded. But unless he can get himself upgraded into the salariat, he will still be treated as homogeneous with workers of the same grade throughout the country. Since changes in the marginal social product of homogeneous labour cannot diverge much from changes in total incomes, the fate of wage labour depends roughly on what happens to the national income.

Divergences of private incomes from the national average depend on whether individual bargains are possible. In some salaried employments individual bargains are still possible, and that results in salaries which reflect the skill (and bargaining skill) of individual salary-earners and thus their marginal private product. There is no reason why this should change in direct ratio to changes in the national income.

Such individual bargains are, however, becoming rare, and nowadays they tend to be increasingly confined to the top positions in industry. Most salary-earners, like wage-earners, would not trust themselves to bargain individually, and if they did would often fare worse than they are doing now. Professional associations bargain on behalf of their members, and claim salary adjustments on the ground of better rewards received in equivalent posts in other occupations. In other words, there is a movement towards rewarding salary-earners in relation to their marginal social product rather than in relation to their marginal private product. But this has not yet gone as far as for manual labour.

Although salaries are frequently collectively negotiated, with professional associations taking the place of trade unions, there are usually wide scales within which the individual salary can be fixed. Considerable weight is given to differences in skill, responsibility and age; and while all this is not unknown in wage bargains, the range within which an individual salary can fall is normally wide (at least compared with the range possible for wage-earners). This means that there is still a range in which relative private marginal products matter, and at a time of widening educational opportunities, this benefits some salary-earners.

Nevertheless there are tendencies at work to narrow the scales. Particularly powerful professional bodies may secure equality of treatment for all members performing a particular task. Thus general practitioners under the National Health Service receive uniform pay and cannot vary their pay except by taking more patients on to their books. Their pay is substantially above that of manual workers. But like manual workers they are treated as a homogeneous factors. Any one general practitioner is treated as a perfect substitute for any other general practitioner, and additional earnings are possible only by an equivalent to overtime. The very success of the medical profession in bargaining for their general practitioners has also ensured that the general practitioners have a roughly fixed place on the national pay structure, and their future earnings prospects will depend largely on changes in the national income, just as do the earnings prospects of trade-unionised manual labour. That does not apply to all members of the medical profession, since there are substantial salary differences between specialists. Nevertheless any medical man who is not just content with being relatively high on the national pay scale, but is ambitious enough to wish to advance himself faster than the national average, must become a specialist (and so raise the national average through getting ahead of it).

Other professional bodies have not yet been so successful, but if recent discussions of the 'brain drain' are any guide, a narrowing of differentials may come into the salary structures of scientists, engineers and technologists. In Britain, education is largely free and nearly always subsidised. Engineers-to-be, and all other graduates-to-be, receive subsidies and grants whilst at school or university, so that each receives what may be termed a pre-salary. After graduation they enter employment, initially at relatively low salaries. In the course of their subsequent careers, however, their salaries can treble or even quadruple. (3) Matters are different in the United States. There is no pre-salary, and starting salaries tend to be about three times as high as in Britain; subsequently, however, they only double. (4) In consequence there is an outside demand facing British engineers and other graduates, with different effectiveness in relation to different age groups. (It is not suggested that the only outside demand is United States demand; but it is the largest, and for the purpose of exposition it is sufficient to deal with one outside demand.)

British undergraduates do not think of emigrating whilst they are undergraduates. To the best of the authors' knowledge, no other country pays pre-salaries. At that stage any outside demand for future graduates is ineffective.

Matters change after graduation. Emigration often offers opportunities for immediate sharp salary increments. The British home demand may be high and rising, but it is spread. As already mentioned, it is spread over time, through payment of pre-salaries. It is also spread over the whole tax-paying community which provides education and the pre-salaries. Were Britain a closed community, such a policy may seem the most providential there can be. Individual employers cannot possibly forecast the exact numbers of graduates they will wish to employ in future years, and many families could not afford to keep their children at school or university were there no pre-salaries. The British educational system thus ensures a larger supply of graduates than the country could otherwise hope to have. Whatever may happen to British demand for engineers and other graduates, supply is always more adequate than it otherwise would be; quite simply, new graduates have less scarcity value than if there were fewer of them. The supply, too, is spread and the supply curve shifted to the right. Nevertheless the total supply of graduates is inelastic from degree day to degree day, and if the universities' output cannot be markedly increased from one year to the next, the supply remains fairly inelastic over longer periods.

Where no pre-salaries are paid, matters are different. The supply of graduates would be just as inelastic, but the supply curve would be further to the left. (5) Without pre-salaries, the scarcity value of graduates would be that much greater; and this is reflected, for instance, in the disproportionately higher initial salaries paid in the United States (where there are no pre-salaries). In consequence there are special attractions for, say, British graduate engineers to emigrate to the United States, especially in the early stages of their careers. In fact most emigrants are between twenty-five and thirty-five years of age. (6)

A higher United States demand for engineers and other graduates of that age group, relatively to potential supply, would result from the concentration of United States demand on that age group (while the British demand is spread), even if no other causes were at work to accentuate it. Amongst those other causes is the greater R. & D. consciousness of United States than of British industry, so that the United States demand for graduates could be expected to be higher. In some years, but not all, United States industry grows faster than British, and this further accentuates the position. In all years these tendencies are reinforced by the Federal Government's wish that the United States should be best armed and that the first man on the moon (and elsewhere in space) should be an American, so that defence and Federal space programmes are superimposed on industrial R. & D. In other words the United States supply curve is relatively further to the left than the British, and the United States demand curve is further to the right. The result is a higher United States price for the services of graduates. (7)

The effects on Britain are not always easy to ascertain, since detailed emigration statistics are not collected. The most authoritative estimates available show, for the years from 1956 to 1961, that about one in six of Britain's engineering graduates emigrated, and about one in forty of the scientists. (8) Estimates relating to the emigration of doctors, between 1955 and 1961, suggest that one in four of the medical graduates sought his fortune abroad. In all cases the chief country of destination was the United States. (9)

The attractions of emigration to the United States wane with age. One reason is that emigration becomes more difficult as family commitments increase. Another reason, however, is that the prospects of self-advancement through emigration become less as the salary differentials narrow with age. To this may be added that the relative position of middle-aged and elderly persons in graduate employment is probably less favourable within United States society than in British society. Towards the end of his career an engineering graduate in the United States would earn between one and a half and two times as much as his counterpart in Britain, while average individual money incomes are about twice as high in the United States as in Britain. (10)

If the answer to the brain drain is higher salaries for young engineers and other graduates in Britain, without corresponding increases at the higher end of the scale, several results might ensue. If initial salaries were raised sufficiently to equal half of final salaries in accordance with the United States career structure, engineers and other young British graduates would be relatively more expensive than American ones because of their pre-salaries. Thus if the British career structure became like the American, British graduates might find themselves priced out of possible jobs in this country. There would be not so much of a brain drain, but rather an overflow of brains, and the number of emigrants might not be very different. It is, however, unlikely that there will ever be complete identity of career structures in the two countries, so that the most that can be expected is a move towards higher initial salaries in some graduate occupations. Others may prefer rising prospects.

Any move in the direction of higher initial salaries (relatively to final salaries) will make the relative position of engineers and other graduates more rigid within the British economy. That is already the case with general practitioners and has for long been the case with operatives. For the nearer a group gets towards uniformity of pay, the nearer is it to being a group of economically homogeneous factors. There is less encouragement given to individual skill and initiative, so that the group concerned becomes more rigid within society as a whole. Any narrowing of differentials in pay within a group is a move towards making that group rigid within society, and its pay becomes increasingly determined by movements in the national income as a whole.

The differentials there are, and the differentials which will remain, contain a rent element. Some differentials are solely based on seniority. They are often not necessary to keep a man in his occupation. For once he has reached his fifties or sixties, there is very little he can do well besides what he is already doing. In static or declining occupations (where there is little or no need of further recruitment), any differentials acquired through age could be narrowed or even eliminated without damage to the economy as a whole. Whether the younger men be paid more or the older ones less, that profession would have reached a static state in society and would no longer grow relatively to the rest of the economy. In such occupations an increment for seniority is an unnecessary 'unearned' increment, and since that occupation has now found its niche in economic society, special skills might be regarded as a disturbance. Such skills are now specific to particular types of occupation, and consequently mobility between activities is much reduced.

If, however, there is to be scope for advancement of the particular profession or occupation in society, the older and the particularly able should receive special rewards. For the older members taken by themselves, such increments would still be unearned, but this is not so for the profession as a whole. The profession recruits new graduates who might turn to any of a variety of occupations for which they are equally well trained.

Thanks to their training, the beginners are no longer homogeneous factors for the economy as a whole. The beginners are attracted into this or that occupation according to the pay received by the elderly members of the profession of a rank which appears within reach of all. Thus the first attraction towards becoming, say, an assistant lecturer in a university is not so much the pay of the vice-chancellor (since few can aspire that high), but the pay of an elderly lecturer. But this is not enough if the profession is not to stagnate. (Were it allowed to stagnate, the elderly lecturer would not have to be paid the increments he has received). There must be special rewards for teaching, administrative or research abilities, so that the most able can advance faster than the average advancement of the profession, and so raise the average advancement of the profession beyond the national average increase of incomes.

To ensure regular service in the profession, its members work under contract which precludes their leaving without adequate notice. Such a contract imposes a restraint of change. A university must pay the lecturer, and keep its laboratories and libraries in a state such that he can work there; in return it secures the services of the lecturer. A contract ensures such reciprocal restraint for a given period of time. In practice, however, these contracts work in a one-sided way. Few university teachers and other professional men would tie themselves in a way which does not allow them to better themselves through change of employment. They seldom accept a contractual obligation which they cannot terminate at three or six months' notice. In the past much longer contracts were customary. Professional men have secured a shortening of their contractual obligations which rent control has denied to landlords of land and buildings. If a professional man is the 'landlord' of his brain, the 'tenant' in the relevant contractural relationship is the employer. The employer is given no 'security of tenure' beyond short contractual periods. But the employer of professional men is not expected to hire and fire them at will. After a probationary period of a few years, salaried employees do not expect to be dismissed, save for unprofessional conduct or gross negligence in the performance of their duties. Any other dismissals would lead to an outcry. In short, in the relationship between professional men and their employers, the 'landlords' can change their 'tenants' whenever the latter do not pay enough, while the 'tenants' cannot escape their 'landlords'.

The result is a ratchet effect in the national salary structure. When prices and prospects fall, professional men stay in their posts and may suffer from delayed promotion rather than falling salaries. When prices and prospects rise, there is enhanced mobility from 'tenant' to 'tenant' so that 'tenants' in search of 'landlords' must be prepared to pay more. If the period of rising prices is accompanied by a widening of salary differentials, as has been the case in Britian since the mid-1950s, the opportunities for those who can bargain best improve disproportionately and so raise the share of salaries in national income. Even those who do not bargain well benefit from wider scales which ensure rising 'rents'.

Salaries do not, however, consist solely of the rent element. There is a wage element as well. That the share of salaries in national income doubled while that of land and buildings halved does not imply identity of gain and loss. The share of salaries was already slightly higher than that of rent (of land and buildings) at the beginning of the century. Nor is there any relationship between the fates of landlords of land and landlords of brain. It cannot therefore be ascertained how far the gain of salaries was due to higher rents received by the landlords of brain and how far they simply reflect movements in the national income (which are themselves influenced by the movement of salaries). It is, however, possible to make a very rough attempt to isolate the rent and wage elements of salaries earned in manufacturing industry. This is the task of the next section.

3   THE ADVANTAGE OF BEING A SALARY-EARNER

Details are available for the salaries and wages earned each year in manufacturing industry and also of the numbers who receive these salaries and wages. (11) Salary-earners in manufacturing industry are the administrative, managerial and clerical staff who work in offices. Wage-earners are operatives who work on factory floors. A works foreman who is attached to an office would be classed as a salary-earner, but a working foreman who moves about amongst his charges is a wage-earner.

The number of wage-earners in manufacturing industry rose from 6 million in 1950 to 6.3 million in the mid-1950s, but subsequently fell back to 6 million in the mid-1960s. It does not do much violence to the facts to regard the number of wage-earners in manufacturing industry as approximately constant in the 1950s and 1960s, so that changes in wage earnings must have been due to changes in demand for wage labour rather than to changes in supply.

The numbers of salary earners in manufacturing industry increased steadily and markedly from about 1¼ million in 1950 to 1½ million in 1955, to 1¾ million in 1960, and over 2 million by 1966. If, then, salary-earners of 1966 were of the same quality as salary-earners of 1950, one would expect a fall in the earnings of individual members of the industrial salariat relatively to those of individual industrial wage-earners. This happened only in the first half of the 1950s. If average industrial wage earnings in 1950 are taken as 100, the average industrial salary was 171. By 1955 the differential had narrowed; if average industrial wage earnings are again taken as 100, the average industrial salary was only 149. The number of industrial wage-earners had risen by only about 5 per cent and the number of industrial salary-earners by almost one-quarter. The narrowing of the differential may have been due to a relative rise in numbers which may have raised the relative scarcity of wage-earners in manufacturing industry.

Were this the full explanation, the narrowing of the differential between the average industrial salary and the average industrial wage would have continued. But it did not, despite the continuing increase in numbers of the industrial salariat at a time when the number of industrial wage-earners fell back to the 1950 level. Taking the average industrial wage earnings in any one year from 1955 to 1967 as equal to 100, the average industrial salary varied between 145 (in 1961) and 152 (in 1959), so that it is roughly correct to say that average industrial salary earnings were one-and-a-half times average industrial wage earnings (see Table 21.1).

The maintenance of this 1 : 1½ ratio, despite slightly falling numbers of industrial wage-earners and more rapidly rising numbers of industrial salary-earners, must have been due to demand conditions. The explanation is not far to seek. Much of the increase in the number of industrial salary-earners in the early 1950s was still the result of the increasing application of automation to the art of writing. While this depressed the average salary and continues to do so, the results of the post-war expansion of universities and other centres of higher learning began to show results in the 1950s. This highly trained personnel may

Table 21.1 Average Annual Earnings in Manufacturing
Industries

	Wages £	Salaries £
1950	303	508
1951	330	544
1952	360	576
1953	383	602
1954	408	635
1955	442	669
1956	477	703
1957	503	756
1958	525	790
1959	547	830
1960	590	868
1961	625	905
1962	640	939
1963	658	980
1964	715	1,039
1965	769	1,119
1966	817	1,180
1967	844	1,240

Derived from 'National Income Blue Books'.

enter employment at salaries below the average salary, but then climbs up the salary scale. By the time a substantial number of the technologically sophisticated salariat were on the climb, the average salary was continuously pushed upwards.

If such salaries rise, but salary-earners cannot perform their duties without the help of the more homogeneous wage labour, wages are carried along to avoid individual salary-earners losing that co-operation. In the years from 1950 to 1967, the 'lead' of salaries was normally somewhat over seven years. A glance at Table 21.1 will show this. Take the average industrial salary for any year between 1950 and 1967 and then look at the average industrial wage earnings seven or eight years later. In each case but one, the average industrial wage earnings have caught up with the average industrial salary within that time. The exception is 1963, when the lag was somewhat over eight years. An exceptionally hard winter caused much temporary unemployment amongst operatives and the consequent reduction in average earnings for the year. Nevertheless wages caught up with salaries in only a little more than the usual seven to eight years. In other words the salary-earners in manufacturing industry had a 'lead' of somewhat over seven years.

This seven to eight years' lead of salaries, and the 1 : 1½ ratio of industrial wage to salary earnings, occurred at a time when incomes and prices were rising. In times of falling incomes and prices, salary-earners might do relatively even better. They could invoke their contracts to delay or prevent dismissal or cuts in pay, but would need less assistance from more homogeneous labour. They could perform some of the assistants' tasks themselves. Thus neither the seven to eight years' lead nor the 1 : 1½ ratio should be regarded as inevitable, but merely as characteristics of the 1950s and 1960s. But while they lasted, the lead of salaries represented the difference between the income-determined wages of homogeneous labour and the 'rent' earned by 'landlords of brain'.

The total gain from being a salary-earner rather than a wage-earner in manufacturing industry, in the conditions of 1950-67, can be gauged from the following. If industrial salary-earners can earn about 50 per cent more than wage-earners in any year, and if salary-earners work on average forty-four years, while wage-earners work on average fifty years, then the difference can be calculated as follows. Take 100 as the 'wage earnings' and multiply by 50, representing the number of years worked. The total is 5,000. Then take 150 as the 'salary earnings' and multiply by 44, representing the number of years worked, and the total comes to 6,600. Since the ratio of 5,000 : 6,600 is the same as 1 : 1.32, it seems legitimate to regard 1 as the wage element of earnings over a lifetime and 0.32 as the rent element of average industrial salary earnings over a lifetime.

Alternatively, compare the difference between the 6,600 income units received by the average industrial salary-earner and the 5,000 income units received by the average industrial wage-earner. Then multiply this difference of 1,600 income units by the average industrial wage earnings, which in 1967 were £844. The total is £13,504, which is equivalent to eleven years' salary earnings or sixteen years' wage earnings. In 1967 such a sum might have bought between two and three semi-detached houses or about two dozen new mini-cars.

Individual industrial salary-earners may fare better or worse. An important factor can be the starting salary, where the difference between the initial salary paid to graduates of different finals grades attained at university or professional examinations, spread over a lifetime, may be worth as much as a semi-detached house. Capable men and women with poor university results may later overcome this handicap through accelerated promotion, but this applies only to a minority. Again choice of subject may matter. Engineers may be paid higher initial salaries than economists, since there is fear of a brain drain of engineers to America but not of economists. But the final salaries attained by economists may yet be higher than those of engineers, since economists may be better trained in the logic of choice between alternatives, and that matters in business. But whatever the details, the average salary-earner in industry secures substantially higher returns for fewer years' work in industry than the average wage-earner. It pays to be a landlord of brains beyond secondary modern school attainment.

It is a curious thought that while industrial salaries appear to pull industrial wages upwards, British industrial salaries are themselves pulled upwards by United States salaries. (Where should a British incomes policy start in an interdependent world?) That the industrial salary- and wage-earners' fate was relatively constant in 1950-67, with a fairly regular time-lag, does not necessarily imply such a fixed relationship for all times. Salary-earners are not necessarily to be regarded as wage-earners at a high level, just because they enjoy an educational rent which enables them to perform longer-term tasks. The educational rent gives them more security and higher incomes than wage-earners enjoy. There is, however, one more component in the salariat's position, and this is much greater uncertainty of the career structure for most of its members. In consequence there is a profit element in the earnings of the salariat's most successful members. But the uncertainty is within the range of the known salary structure, and the possible 'profits' are profits without risk of material capital. Limited uncertainty and absence of risk preclude the treatment of salaries as profits in the sense that the term will be used in Chapters 22 and 23 below. However, should salaries continue to rise beyond profits and salary-earners increasingly determine the course of economic events, these lines may have to be rewritten ere long. In the meantime the authors of this book remain earners of a compound of wages and rent. Whether there will also be 'profits' depends on whether the readers of this book recommend it to their friends.

22 Profits

1 THE REWARDS FOR TRANSFORMATION

Were wages and rent (of land and buildings) the only components of the national income, the national income would at best be stable and normally fall. This is because the national wages bill has for long been income-determined rather than income-determining, and the aggregate rent (of land and buildings) has reflected past values and so lagged behind, rather than led, the course of incomes. Hence these two kinds of factor earnings should be regarded as passive, being determined by current incomes and past prices respectively. Such earnings are part of national income, but that does not make them active determinants of the national income.

The same applies to salaries, being compounds of wages and rent. True, in times of rising prices 'landlords of brain' have frequently been able to anticipate the rise in general incomes, but such rise in their salaries could not have been sustained had not rising prices raised the money incomes of their employers. It remains true that an economy has the number of typists, teachers and doctors it can afford, and that the services of salary-earners aid, but do not create, an economy.

The creation of an economy is a task of transformation of factors of production into new forms and shapes. Although most of the physical tasks of transformation are effected by salary- and wage-earners, neither salary- nor wage-earners could on their own ensure that such tasks are performed. To enable transformation requires command over resources, which implies ownership. Individuals can exercise this through disposal of money or assets convertible into money, but not all money is so spent. While everyone who has money (or assets convertible into money) can use it so as to enable transformation, the bulk of incomes is spent on consumer goods which, as final goods, require little or no further transformation. Only a proportion of incomes is saved, and only a proportion of that is made available to entrepreneurs who know how to invest funds so as to enable further transformation.

Entrepreneurs take the responsibility in ordering transformation. Hence they run the risk of wasting the factors under their control and bear the uncertainty of what, if anything, their future reward will be. Their reward, if any, is profit.

Entrepreneurs can put only those factors at risk over which they have exclusive legal powers of disposition, be they exclusive rights to dispose over certain sums of money or the ownership of material factors. It follows that only those can run risk who have something to lose, and only factors that already exist can be put at risk. Factors are put at risk in an attempt to improve the allocation of resources. To affect this, they must be transformable. Coal can be transformed into heat and milk into cheese. In a society that uses money, the right to dispose over coal can be transformed into the right to dispose over cheese, so that coal can be 'transformed' into cheese. Since transformation always takes time and is performed with a view to future use, there is inherent uncertainty as to whether the end-product will or will not be more valuable than the original factors used up in its creation; and even if the end-product is more valuable, there is still uncertainty as to how much more valuable. Market conditions can change between input and output, so that the entrepreneur's reward can turn out to be greater or less than anticipated.

All production implies transformation and cannot take place unless transformable factors are available. But production does not depend on transformable factors alone. All production takes place on land, which is immutable, and all production requires human agency. The human factor cannot be 'transformed', since no civilised society today tolerates the ownership of one human being by another. Thus human labour cannot be put at risk, and this applies to all labour, including the entrepreneur's own labour. (Where the entrepreneur works under conditions of limited liability, that applies even to any part of his property which is not part of his business.) The human factor can only be hired for certain hours or tasks. True, there is always the risk that human labour may be inefficient, but it is not the human factor that is at risk here. Only the money that confers the transferable right to hire labour is at risk.

In the present context, risk refers to what the entrepreneur can lose, and uncertainty refers to what the entrepreneur can gain or lose. Profit is the net outcome of such gains, if any, and losses, if any. Uncertainty can be reduced through experience, and that will also minimise risk. Once risk and uncertainty are eliminated, there is no entrepreneurship and there can be no profit – even though valuable services may be performed. A number of activities which were once risk- and uncertainty-bearing are no longer so. Some of the chief examples are in professional services.

Amongst the problems created by nineteenth-century industrialisation and urbanisation was the 'uncertainty' of what medical services would be required in the towns. Amongst the problems solved by the twentieth century is a fair knowledge gained of what the requirements are. The organisation of the medical profession has changed accordingly. Earlier this century a doctor could establish himself only after he had bought his equipment and his practice. He had to put both material and money capital at risk, and he had to bear the uncertainty of what his patients might be able to pay him. Now, under the National Health Service, doctors are salaried, and what their patients can pay is the tax collectors' concern and not theirs. (In other professions the adjustment from entrepreneurial to salaried status has taken different forms and has not always gone so far. For instance, solicitors no longer have to buy themselves into chambers, but tend to be salaried until they become full partners of their firms. Although their firms charge the clients, charges are not normally related to the clients' individual abilities to pay, but are in accordance with standard fees laid down by the profession. Hence in fact, if not in name, solicitors are like salary-earners on piece rates. Altogether, most professional men no longer risk much that is transformable. They have ceased to be entrepreneurs, and their earnings have become salaries or akin to salaries.

Experience can eliminate risk and much uncertainty. This applies not only in the professions but also in important sections of manufacturing industry. True, in manufacturing industry risk and uncertainty can never be entirely eliminated, but they can be minimised and nearly eliminated in traditional industries which produce standardised goods by known processes. Firms in such industries re-create what has been before, and even an expansion of output is often a multiplication of the known. In such cases the incidence of accidents and technical breakdowns can be predicted with a fair degree of accuracy, and so can seasonal fluctuations in market demand. Predictable risks can be insured against through paying an appropriate premium to a specialist insurance company. Fluctuations in seasonal demand can be provided against through appropriate storage facilities (for, say, grain and Christmas decorations), and where storage is not practical because the goods are perishable, through production by one firm of a variety of goods demanded mainly at different seasons (such as, say, sausages and ice-cream). Enhanced knowledge of economic fluctuations and improved statistical forecasting can reduce risk and uncertainty over longer periods. Where that is possible, the entrepreneurial task of risk- and uncertainty-bearing becomes relatively less important, and the decisions by salaried managers become relatively more important. It can and does happen at times that some of the larger firms which afford the best statistical and accounting services are amongst the firms with profits relatively low and near the level of salaries, though this can be compensated through lesser fluctuations in profits. Regular earnings at or near the level of salaries are akin to a fixed-interest-bearing return on money capital, so that the entrepreneur approaches the status of a salaried money-lender.

A money-lender receives a return determined by prevailing interest rates, and that return is akin to a salary. Money-lenders may be banks which provide advances at prevailing interest rates in order to meet the day-to-day requirements of business, or they may be debenture holders who provide long-term finance for a fixed return. Entrepreneurs hold the firm's equity and share the profits. Where profits are regular, the return on equities becomes more like a return on debentures and the entrepreneur more like a money-lender.

The entrepreneur's task is to create, not just to re-create (which any money-lender could enable). Through bearing risk and uncertainty, the entrepreneur ventures into the new and unknown, and in that way he enables transformation into what had not been before. Now society does not always wish to venture the new. It may want more of the known. Or in times of stagnation it may be unable to venture the new and must concentrate its energies on preservation and replacement of the known. For instance, in the stagnant years of the mid-1960s public companies sought extra finance more through fixed-interest-bearing debenture issues than through inviting the public to take up new equity issues. The money they needed to finance further production was not primarily risk capital involving uncertainty-bearing, but money to carry on with whatever they were doing. Professional money-lenders' services were sought (whose 'salaries' were determined by prevailing interest rates), not *new* entrepreneurship. (1) Such tendencies were reinforced by the dividend restraint advised or imposed by successive government measures, culminating in 1968 in the limitation of dividends to previously prevailing levels. The effect was that for the duration of dividend limitation, entrepreneurship became more like money-lending. About that time, however, confidence in the growth prospects of the British economy returned, and this was evidenced by a marked revival of equity issues, (2) for new equity issues mean that further entrepreneurship is sought to venture the unknown.

What happened during dividend limitation and the revival of confidence illustrates in somewhat extreme fashion the normal difference between the rewards for old and new entrepreneurship. New entrepreneurship always involves much uncertainty. If successful, the new ways of transformation will be applied for some time – and then they will no longer be new. By then experience will have shown how to minimise risk and uncertainty, even if neither can be completely eliminated. To enable further production along such lines may require a money-lender, while the old entrepreneur receives a more regular return and also assumes the status of a money-lender. In the long run all entrepreneurs tend to become money-lenders. This tendency is seldom complete, unless industry becomes so set in its ways that it is incapable of further change. For normally entrepreneurs make their firms continue the search for new ways, if only to raise profits above the return received by a money-lender.

Any tendency for entrepreneurs to become money-lenders is likely to be marked if the economy has been successful in the past. Traditional activities then loom large in the economy, so that average profits are depressed towards the level of salaries. Such tendencies are reinforced if the economy passes through a phase of depression or even stagnation. During the long depression of the inter-war years, the economy worked below the level of full employment, even in boom years. Industry struggled to keep going and sought but few resources for new ventures, while those who still had funds to spare would often prefer a safe return from government securities or from established industries rather than bear uncertainty in a general atmosphere of pessimism. There were exceptions, such as the then expanding motor-car industry, but the exceptions were insufficient to outweigh the widespread longing for security.

In the relatively stagnant years of the mid-1960s industry did not have to struggle to stay in business, but it had to struggle to maintain its profit margins; and so, again, industry had relatively little to spare for new ventures. There was, however, no shortage of funds in search of uncertainty-bearing equity capital, as witnessed by the heavy over-subscriptions of most new equity issues. The position of the 1960s was one of acceleration of the normal trend for entre-preneurs to become money-lenders, reinforced by dividend limitation. In contrast to the inter-war years, however, the desire for new ventures was not swamped by the desire for security, so that the growth prospects of the economy at the end of the 1960s seem brighter than they were thirty or forty years earlier.

The prospects before the economy depend ultimately on the opportunities for enabling further transformation. As shown in Chapters 19-21, the other agents of production are rewarded with wages, rent and salaries; such rewards depend on current incomes and past prices, so that the sum total of what can be received in wages, rent and salaries is already unalterable. Profits alone remain alterable, since they alone are received after completion of any given production process. They are thr return for having enabled transformation.

Where risk and uncertainty are minimised, profits become a money-lender's reward, akin to a salary. In extreme cases, where risk and uncertainty are virtually eliminated, the only difference between such profits and salaries is that salaries must be paid while production is in process, while profits are only available after the production process has been completed and the goods or services have been sold. In practice a substantial part of profits will always be akin to salaries, simply because a substantial part of transformation must always be re-creation of what there was before and involves almost no uncertainty-bearing. Unfortunately it is not possible to estimate accurately what part of profits is derived from transformation that re-creates, and what part from trans-formation that creates the new. At best it might be guessed that, in times of full employment, a rise in total profits is likely to reflect additional transformation, and the maintenance of profits is likely to reflect re-creative transformation. If so the national income can be expected to rise when profits have risen, and any rise in the national income that is not preceded by a rise in profits must be ascribed to inflationary monetary policies.

2 PROFITS IN NATIONAL INCOME

Estimates of gross profits can be found in the 'National Income Blue Books', where they are recorded under gross trading profits of companies and gross trading surpluses of public corporations and of governmental trading bodies. The statistics do not (and cannot) distinguish between pure profits, as defined above, and the salary element contained in profits. What is shown are gross profits, which include both. The 'Blue Books' also show income from self-employment, which often contains a substantial profit element, though this was more important in the past than it is now. Any estimate of the share of gross profits in national income that includes income from self-employment is too high; but any estimate that excludes income from self-employment is too low.

For long-period comparison there is no choice: the data available for the years before 1914 do not distinguish between trading profits and income from self-employment. If income from self-employment is included, the share of profits in national income averaged slightly over one-third in 1948-66. Profits took about the same share of the national income in 1900-13, but less than three-tenths in the inter-war years. (3)

But this is not comparing like with like. As pointed out before, many who would have been self-employed before 1914 are now salaried, while others, still nominally self-employed, have earnings more akin to salaries than profits. On the other hand exclusion of income from self-employment also does some violence to the facts, since it means omitting the earnings of small shopkeepers, artists and other independent workers whose earnings can be uncertain and thus in the nature of profits. The case for excluding income from self-employment is somewhat strengthened, however, once it is realised that the largest group amongst the self-employed are independent retailers whose capital is largely provided by wholesalers (and the latter's earnings normally appear under company profits). Profits, excluding the income of the self-employed, took somewhat over one-eighth of the national income in the inter-war years and somewhat over one-fifth in the 1950s and 1960s. (The share of the self-employed fell from one-sixth of the national income of the inter-war years to one-ninth in the 1950s and 1960s.)

On either count, however, the share of profits was higher in the fully employed 1950s and 1960s than in the days of widespread unemployment between the wars. This is not surprising, for when the economy worked below a level of full employment, what was wanted was more of the known, and thus profits were depressed towards the level of salaries. In the fully employed economy of the 1950s and 1960s, however, further growth depended on more ingenious transformation and new creation, so that entrepreneurial uncertainty-bearing was more wanted and its reward greater.

Thus in the long run high profits coincide with prosperity and low profits with depression. Although the level of profits and the level of incomes are bound to interact, it does not suffice just to notice a coincidence. An attempt will be made to answer the question whether it is mory likely that high profits cause high incomes and low profits low incomes, or whether incomes are more likely to be the cause of profits.

The method adopted is as follows: A comparison is made of year-by-year changes in currently recorded profits with the year-by-year changes in the gross domestic product at constant prices. Profits can only be measured at the values at which they are recorded, but the national product as a whole can be measured at constant prices to indicate 'real' changes rather than purely monetary changes in the national product. Since the present problem is to compare changes in profits with changes in real prosperity, the right method is to compare changes in profits at current prices with changes in the gross domestic product at constant prices. The comparison shows whether a rise in profits is normally associated with a rise in real incomes, and similarly with falls. (4) (It should be noted that profits recorded in any one year relate to the financial years of a multitude of firms, ending at various dates during that year, so that part of the profits recorded in, say, 1967 were in fact earned in 1966. There is a lag between profits earned and profits recorded, but not between the national product earned and recorded.) If the change in recorded profits and the national product coincide, this means that profits have risen or fallen earlier than the national product.

Crude percentage changes are shown in Table 22.1. For pre-1948 data, national income estimates had to be used, but estimates for the gross domestic product at factor costs are available for subsequent years. For pre-1914 data, income from self-employment could not be separated from profits, though, as shown before, its inclusion is probably correct for those days. Subject to these statistical imperfections, the following results emerge.

There is a long-run tendency for the share of profits in national income to be higher in times of prosperity than in times of depression. This tendency is also evident in the short period, with the additional feature that the rise or fall in profits appears to precede the rise or fall in the national income (or product) at constant prices. In the years from 1901 (compared with 1900) to 1913 (compared with 1912), gross profits (including income from self-employment) rose in ten years, as compared with each preceding year, and fell three times. In

Table 22.1 Annual Percentage Changes over the Previous Year in National Product at Constant Prices and Profits at Current Prices, 1901-67

Year	National income	Gross trading profits and income from self-employment	Year	National income	Gross trading profits
1901	- 0.7	− 4.4	1936	+ 3.8	+12.6
1902	+ 0.8	+ 3.0	1937	+ 0.4	+11.6
1903	− 2.5	− 5.7	1938	− 0.1	− 5.8
1904	+ 0.5	+ 0.2		*Gross domestic*	
1905	+ 4.4	+ 7.1		*product at*	
1906	+ 5.5	+ 8.5		*factor cost*	
1907	+ 2.7	+ 3.8	1949	+ 3.1	+ 4.4
1908	− 3.3	− 9.4	1950	+ 3.2	+17.1
1909	+ 1.3	+ 2.3	1951	+ 3.6	+16.2
1910	+ 2.4	+ 3.6	1952	0 −	−12.7
1911	+ 2.7	+ 6.7	1953	+ 4.6	+ 8.0
1912	+ 2.8	+ 7.7	1954	+ 3.6	+12.6
1913	+ 2.4	+ 4.4	1955	+ 3.4	+ 9.1
		Gross	1956	+ 1.9	+ 2.5
		trading profits	1957	+ 1.9	+ 3.9
1922	+ 6.3	+64.4	1958	− 0.3	− 1.1
1923	+ 4.9	+ 7.9	1959	+ 3.5	+11.3
1924	+ 1.4	− 1.0	1960	+ 5.0	+15.1
1925	+ 1.6	− 4.7	1961	+ 3.7	− 1.6
1926	+ 0.1	− 9.6	1962	+ 0.9	+ 0.8
1927	+ 9.1	+14.9	1963	+ 4.2	+13.9
1928	+ 0.8	+ 3.5	1964	+ 5.8	+11.7
1929	+ 1.8	+ 4.5	1965	+ 2.9	+ 5.0
1930	− 1.1	− 4.5	1966	+ 2.0	− 4.4
1931	− 1.0	− 9.5	1967	+ 1.2	+ 4.4
1932	0 +	− 9.5			
1933	+ 6.7	+13.7			
1934	+ 3.3	+15.1			
1935	+ 4.5	+13.9			

Derived from A. R. Prest, 'National Income of the United Kingdom, 1870-1946', in 'The Economic Journal' March 1948, and 'National Income Blue Book', 1968, Table 14 (gross domestic product at 1958 factor cost) and Table 1 (gross trading profits of companies, gross trading surplus of public corporations, and gross trading surplus of other public enterprises).

the years when recorded profits rose, the national income (at constant prices) also rose. In the years when recorded profits fell, the national income (at constant prices) also fell. Since profits relate to returns on business activities in the various firms' financial years ending during the calendar year shown, much of the profits recorded for each year was earned before the calendar year for which they are recorded. As mentioned before, this means that when recorded profits rose or fell in the same years as the national income (at constant prices) rose or fell, profits must have risen or fallen before the national income rose or fell.

Between 1922 (compared with 1921) and 1938 (compared with 1937), gross trading profits (excluding income from self-employment) and the national income (at constant prices) rose together in ten years and fell together in three years. This leave four years, being 1924, 1925, 1926 and 1932. It will be noticed, however, that in 1924 the fall in profits was only slight and the rise in the national income markedly less than in the preceding year. In 1925 and 1926 profits continued to fall, while the national income rose only slightly in 1925 and was approximately constant in 1926. In 1932 profits continued to fall at the same rate as in 1931, while the national income remained approximately constant. These four 'exceptions' show that a fall in profits and a fall in the national income at constant prices are not necessarily concomitants, but that falling profits may instead be accompanied by stagnation (as in 1926 and 1932) or by decelerated growth of the national income (as in 1924 and 1925).

The coincidence of past changes in profits and national income at constant prices has been dealt with at some length, in order to provide a background for the evaluation of the importance of annual changes in the post-war years. Using 'National Income Blue Book' figures for gross trading profits and surpluses of enterprises (but excluding income from self-employment) at current prices, and the figures for the gross domestic product at factor costs and at constant prices, the following results emerge. Between 1949 (compared with 1948) and 1967 (compared with 1966), gross trading profits rose fourteen times, and on each occasion the gross national product at constant prices rose as well. Profits fell four times. On one of those four occasions (in 1958) the gross domestic product at constant prices also fell; on another occasion (in 1952) it remained approximately constant; and twice (in 1961 and 1966) there was a deceleration of the growth of the gross domestic product in the same year, the deceleration not becoming fully effective until the following year. The rise in profits in 1967 indicated that the economy would grow again in 1968, and it did.

The experience of the 1950s and 1960s thus accords with experience earlier this century. This can be summed up as follows. When profits rose, the national product at constant prices also rose. When profits fell, the national product at constant prices either rose more slowly than before or fell. Invariably the change in profits preceded the change in the national product at constant prices. The course of real incomes was thus predetermined by what had happened to profits.

If the comparison were made between changes in profits and changes in the national income or product at current prices, the effects would be somewhat blurred. For in inflationary times the national income at current prices rises more than the national income at constant prices, and vice versa in deflationary times. Nevertheless the importance of profits would still emerge.

3   THE RELATIVE SCARCITY AND ABUNDANCE OF CAPITAL

The greater volatility of profits than of the national income distinguishes profits from other factor earnings. Rent and salaries together constitute the 'stable sector' of the national income. (5) Wages fluctuate, but the share of wages in the fluctuating sector varies in the opposite direction from the share of the fluctuating sector in national income, so as to leave wages a fairly constant share of the whole. (6) Profits, however, vary in the same direction as the fluctuating sector. Thus in recession, profits fall more than wages and other incomes, and in boom, profits rise more than wages and other income, thus leaving profits always more unstable than the national income and also more unstable than the other fluctuating sector of the national income.

The relative fluctuations in wages and profits reflect changes in the relative scarcities of the factors which receive such earnings, namely, labour and capital. If wages rise relatively to profits (or profits fall more than wages), capital has become relatively more abundant than labour. If profits rise relatively to wages, capital has become relatively scarcer than labour.

4   THE ABUNDANCE OF CAPITAL

In depression, profits fall more than wages, which reflects an increasing abundance of capital relatively to labour. Capital is then 'the' abundant factor, while labour is 'the' scarce factor. That is true despite the unemployment of labour which prevails in depression. The reasons are as follows. As a depression deepens, the demand for all factors becomes less than before — which is another way of saying that all factors become more abundant than they were before. As a depression deepens, orders fall, so that some industrial capital immediately becomes idle. But labour is rarely dismissed until the idleness of capital has become marked and is believed to be persistent. In the meantime the employment of labour is maintained even if made less efficient through reduction in overtime or increase in 'work sharing' amongst employees. In other words a fall in the productivity of labour generally has preceded a fall in employment. The brunt of the cost of lower productivity is borne by profits. Generally both the employment and the aggregate earnings of labour tend to fluctuate less than those of capital, and in depression that reflects a greater increase in the abundance of capital than of labour.

The policy problem in depression is, then, to make factors scarcer. The classical remedy is to let prices fall so much that profits turn into losses, when not even minimal money-lenders' returns can be paid. Firms go bankrupt, and some capital is scrapped. The capital of the surviving firms becomes appropriately scarcer, its return rises, and it once more pays to enable transformation. The advantage of such crude reliance on the price mechanism is that the weakest entrepreneurs are weeded out and the revival in profits benefits only the relatively strong. The disadvantage is that it involves considerable waste of industrial capital and that re-employment of the remaining capital and of labour may be slow.

An alternative to price policy is an incomes policy. If it is possible, in depression, to clear the market by lowering prices to match the prevailing level of incomes, it is also possible to clear the market by raising incomes to match the prevailing level of prices. The rise in incomes should enable the re-employment of available industrial capital before it is discarded and before human unemployment has become intolerable. The chief problem is to use existing capital once again, rather than create new capital (though the latter is not necessarily excluded). Money-lending is needed rather than entrepreneurship proper, so that the remedies lie in the monetary and fiscal policies on the lines suggested by Keynesian and post-Keynesian economists. Those remedies include low interest rates and budget deficits. Low interest rates may encourage borrowing by managements of existing firms in order to make more use of existing capital than before. When much plant and equipment are idle, low interest rates may provide adequate money-lenders' salaries for 'entrepreneurs' whose chief tasks are to maintain employment and enable re-employment rather than new creation. Budget deficits can also help to facilitate re-employment; additional purchasing power is in the hands of the public, so that effective demand is raised and additional output can be absorbed. Although such remedies fail to weed out the weak (their very purpose being to preserve the usefulness of what there is), and although this failure may be inimical to future growth, these remedies are more humane and less wasteful of capital than reliance on the price mechanism.

The Keynesian and classical recommendations are alternative remedies for unemployment. They are relevant to an economy in depression or to an economy that, even in the long run, never quite reaches a level of full employment but fluctuates around an equilibrium level below full employment. The British economy of the inter-war years never attained full employment. Even in the comparatively prosperous years before 1914 the economy did not attain the degree of full employment which came to be experienced after 1945 – at any rate not since the early 1870s, and then only for a few years. (7) The Keynesian remedies work on capital, which is assumed to be the more abundant factor, and this assumption was correct at the time the Keynesian remedies were conceived and a fully employed economy just could not be visualised. (8) Even when full employment had become part of public policy, the first formulation of how to implement it still assumed a 3 per cent rate of unemployment. (9) Theoretical models and policy recommendations assumed a relative abundance of capital and a relative scarcity of labour, and while this was less marked in cyclical boom than in cyclical depression, in the long run the assumption seemed invariably right. But this is no longer the case.

5 THE SCARCITY OF CAPITAL

Since 1945 the economy has worked almost continuously at a level of full employment. The basic position has been one of prosperity and scarcity of all factors. It is thus pertinent to inquire what happens to the relative scarcity of factors in times of prosperity, be it cyclical or continuous. The clue is provided by the relative earnings of labour and capital in times of rising prosperity.

In prosperity, profits rise more than wages, which reflects an increasing scarcity of capital relatively to labour. Capital is then 'the' scarce factor, while labour is 'the' abundant factor. That is true even though there is not enough labour to perform all the tasks demanded of the economy. As prosperity rises, the demand for all factors rises, and all factors become scarcer than they were before. As orders increase and all employable labour is already employed, additional output can be achieved only through using capital more intensively or through using more capital. The problem is to prevent the scarcity of all factors, and since the supply of labour is largely given by the number of births between fifteen and sixty-five years ago, the escape from the scarcity of factors must be largely through further capitalisation. True, labour could often be more efficiently utilised than it is, either because restrictive labour practices hamper output or management is not as efficient as it should be. But without minimising the importance of better utilisation of labour, the solution of all labour impediments to production could only postpone the problems caused by the scarcity of factors; it could not circumvent those problems. In any case better utilisation of labour normally means better tools, and the provision of better tools is a problem of capital creation. An increase in output does depend on an appropriate increase in the productivity of labour, but such an increase is not so much a function of what the workpeople feel like doing as of the capital provided for them to work with.

The policy problem in prosperity is to circumvent the scarcity of factors. The policy weapons are the price mechanism or incomes policies or a combination of both. The price mechanism will be considered first.

6   THE SCARCITY OF FACTORS AND THE PRICE MECHANISM

Given a general scarcity of factors, factor prices will rise; and since this implies higher costs of production, product prices will rise as well. The rise in factor prices, as of any prices, is due to a rise in the effective demand for factors relatively to the potential supply of factors. As already mentioned, the potential supply of labour is in practice normally more rigidly limited than the potential supply of capital. If, then, labour and capital must be used in the same proportions, wages are liable to rise ahead of profits. Where this applies, a factor-price policy would concentrate foremost on stemming the rise of wages, and this is what was attempted during the wage restraint of 1949, the pay pause of 1961, and during the initial gropings for a more general 'incomes' policy in the mid-1960s. The validity of this interpretation, and the consequent usefulness of wages policy, hinge on the assumption that labour and capital must be used in the same proportions. This may be true in the very short run, but it seems incompatible with the long-run situation. The greater volatility of profits than of wages, the near constancy of the share of wages in national income, and the lead of profits towards a higher national product in real terms, all suggest that the labour—capital ratio varies.

Once enough time is allowed for the proportions of labour and capital to be varied – and judging from macro-economic data, that time is normally short enough to affect the overall position from one year to the next – there is no likelihood of a persistent lead of wages over other factor prices. The reason is that the demand for labour and the demand for capital are not demands for labour and capital as such, but both are part of a demand by those who can enable transformation for factors which can effect transformation. There is a demand for factors rather than a demand for specific factors. In the very short run, when factor proportions cannot be varied, that demand is for given amounts of labour and given amounts of capital; the moment, however, that factor proportions can be varied, the demand is simply one for factors. Enterprising firms do not normally take long to substitute capital for labour when they are faced with a general scarcity of factors, and they cannot, on balance, do much else if they wish to expand output. The result is that some of the additional demand for factors is diverted from labour to capital, so that the demand for capital rises relatively to that for labour.

When all factors are fully employed, additional capital formation requires resources to be commanded away from present activities. This implies higher rewards for factors in new capital formation than in present activities and so intensifies the scarcity of factors in present activities. There is a rise in factor rewards both in new capital formation and in present activities, so that there is a general rise in costs of production. In order to compensate themselves for higher costs of production, firms raise product prices. The rise in product prices hurts those who live on fixed incomes, but it does not hurt those whose wages are adjusted, nor those engaged in 'transformation'. The latter may even benefit because of the time-lags between input and output; goods currently sold have been produced with the aid of factors bought or hired at prices previously prevailing, and those prices were lower than current replacement costs. Firms, however, have to sell at prices which enable them to replace the factors used up in the process of production, and if replacement costs are above actual costs incurred, the difference should give the firms concerned an extra margin of profits. The extra margin of profits enables firms to continue production on the previous scale and/or to finance capital formation which may eventually counteract at least some of the increase in factor costs.

This does not always happen. Often competition or public opinion compels firms to sell at prices commensurate with factor costs actually incurred rather than with replacement costs. If so the benefit to the public is ephemeral. For the firms concerned are deprived of funds to invest in factor-saving innovations and may even have difficulties in maintaining the level of output. In the latter case prices rise, though the cause is enhanced scarcity of products rather than of factors. In so far as enhanced scarcity of products causes a rise in prices, it is possible to stem this rise through an appropriate curtailment of demand. Such a rise in product prices fulfils no lasting function, unless it leads to a rise in profits which alone can finance factor-saving innovation.

In short the price mechanism offers an escape from rising scarcity of factors. It is a humane escape and one not wasteful of capital, since factors remain employed until better employment is found for them. This escape is available if factor proportions can be varied towards a greater use of capital relatively to labour, and it implies some relative redistribution of the national income from wages to profits (through the greater rise in the latter). It may, however, be unacceptable to the tradition-bound. The tradition-bound may be owners of money capital who prefer a relatively safe money-lender's salary to uncertainty-bearing for themselves and do not like their competitors to be different. The tradition-bound may also be wage-earners who do not like to see the share of profits in national income rise while that of wages remains constant. But whoever the tradition-bound may be, they resent a change in factor proportions and so object to the price mechanism's escape from the scarcity of factors.

7 THE KEYNES–BEVERIDGE LEVEL OF FULL EMPLOYMENT

The alternative escapes are incomes policies, either of the Keynesian variety or of the variety attempted in the mid- and late 1960s. If prices are not to rise to meet the prevailing level of money incomes, money incomes must be restrained to restore equilibrium at the present level of prices or near the present level of prices. It follows that in times of prosperity incomes policies are prone to be restrictive. How restrictive they can become varies with the means chosen, and with the sort of equilibrium level the authorities have in mind.

In the first twenty post-war years the target appears to have been virtually complete full employment. Only unemployables were out of work for any length of time, so that there was general scarcity of factors. Before the 1960s there were no sustained attempts at tolerating a higher level of unemployment of labour, nor an appropriately higher amount of idle capital resources. The general scarcity of factors was accepted, and policy measures were directed at holding price increases in check rather than preventing them altogether. Wage restraint (1949) and the pay pause (1961) were thought of as ways of stemming the increase in labour costs, but as an alternative to wider unemployment rather than as its concomitant. Bank Rate changes and other monetary and fiscal measures were taken, from time to time, in response to deteriorations of the external payments position, but those measures were regarded as 'regulators' to counter cyclical booms, to be discarded as soon as possible. There does not appear to have been any conscious and sustained attempt at countering the long-term scarcity of factors by means of an incomes policy.

By the mid-1960s, however, an unemployment rate of around 2½ per cent became acceptable to the authorities. Since this is 2½ per cent of the insured working population (and insurance became general for all employees in 1948, and so includes the higher paid in more stable employment, while previously insurance was compulsory for only the lower paid, which in practice meant mainly wage-earners and a few salary-earners), this figure is roughly comparable with the 3 per cent suggested by Beveridge. (10) By the time of writing, a 2½ per cent unemployment rate was actually attained and even slightly exceeded in the recession years of the mid-1960s. There is as yet no sign that unemployment will fluctuate around this level rather than just down to this level in times of recession. However, should the Keynes–Beveridge level of unemployment be attained for any length of time, the scarcity of factors will be reduced. Firms will be able to expand output without so much new capital formation, since labour will be more readily available. When there is labour available in response to demand, there is more stability in methods of production and possibly even in prices.

The Keynes–Beveridge target level of unemployment, as visualised by its authors, was to be attained from a level of high unemployment. There was to be less unemployment. The target was stability with 'full employment', as then envisaged, in place of the abundance of factors which had caused such waste and misery. The means of attaining a high and stable level of employment were to be macro-economic incomes policies which were to operate on capital. In the mid-1960s the authorities once more accepted a level of unemployment similar to the Keynes—Beveridge one, but they started from a position of low unemployment. Once again the target was stability, but it had to be achieved through lowering effective demand to a level which would make the public content itself with what the economy could already produce. Among the means of lowering effective demand are macro-economic incomes policies which, in times of prosperity, are the Keynesian means in reverse. These operate on capital. When it was thought that these means would not suffice to restore stability, they were supplemented by attempts to influence the course of aggregate incomes through detailed regulation of personal incomes and prices charged by firms. Those attempts could be called a micro-economic incomes policy.

8   MACRO-ECONOMIC INCOMES POLICIES

The macro-economic policies will be discussed first. The chief instruments are Bank Rate policy and unbalanced budgets (though there are others as well). It is not difficult to see that these instruments must be used differently when there is excessive scarcity of factors than in times of excessive abundance of factors. But it is not enough simply to turn the policies upside-down. True, in times of excessive prosperity Bank Rate should be raised and budgets be in surplus, and to this extent there is a reversal of the recommendations one would make in depression. There are, however, some further complications.

The hoped-for effects of lower Bank Rate, in times of excessive abundance of factors, have already been referred to. For the sake of contrast with the following, they are briefly reconsidered here. One purpose of lowering Bank Rate is to lower market rates of interest and thus the cost of borrowing. The lower cost of borrowing raises the marginal efficiency of existing capital, so that more of it will be taken into employment. Unless and until the point of full employment is reached, capital remains abundant, and since those who can enable transformation normally prefer a low return to no return, money-lending is not discouraged. With borrowing encouraged and money-lending not discouraged, there can be an increase in activity along largely traditional lines.

When there is general scarcity of factors, prices tend to rise, and the rise in prices has a similar effect on the marginal efficiency of capital as a fall in interest rates. Expected money returns rise relatively to the cost of borrowing. A rise in interest rates may then be a way of restoring equilibrium. If so, interest-rate policy does not appear to have been used with this purpose as an overriding consideration. The increases in Bank Rate in the 1950s and 1960s were in response to external payments difficulties, and if such difficulties were thought to be associated with excessive price rises at home, the thought was not translated into action until after the situation had become acute.

Nor were interest-rate changes as sharp as is sometimes alleged;. Usually Bank Rate goes up by 1 per cent at a time, and even in times of 'crisis' it was not raised by more than 2 per cent at a time. Even those changes were not fully effective except for overseas transactions and such domestic transactions as are not allowable against income and corporation taxes (as, for instance, interest payment on hire-purchase debts). Interest payments on borrowing by firms from banks and building societies are, however, allowable against income and corporation taxes. (In the 1969 budget this tax concession was withdrawn for private borrowers from the banks, but continued for the other forms of borrowing mentioned.) Thus if the standard rate of income tax is 8s. 6d. in the £ (being 42½ per cent), and certain interest payments are allowed against income and corporation taxes, the effect of a 1 per cent increase in interest rates is not 1 per cent but only 0.575 per cent. Even an 8 per cent Bank Rate, which corresponds with market rates of up to 10 per cent, may mean an effective interest burden of only 5¾ per cent. The simultaneous operation of high interest rates and high direct taxation, with tax allowances for debtors, has therefore blunted the effects of monetary policy. Borrowing was not discouraged as much as might have been the case in the absence of tax allowances for interest payments. Lending was not encouraged as much, since lenders had to pay the same rate of tax but could not claim any tax allowances for interest received. In other words pressure on resources was not much reduced, and the enabling of further transformation was not as much encouraged, as might have been the case with more rigorous application of interest-rate policy. In addition, further complications arose from the effects of interest-rate changes on capital values.

The effect of changes in interest rates on capital values varies according to whether ownership is vested in the borrower or lender. But before these complications are discussed, the effect of a rise in interest rates on capital values will be considered in relation to pure money-lending, where no question of change in ownership arises.

A simplified case is as follows: the capital value of any material factor, or of a right to income, is the expected annual return times the number of years' purchase (where the number of years' purchase is the number of annual returns needed to pay for the factor or legal right). If the factor or right is purchased with borrowed money or could be purchased with borrowed money, the number of years' purchase equals 100 divided by the rate of interest. Thus if the expected return is £10 a year, and the rate of interest is 8 per cent, the capital value is £10 × 100/8 or £125. If the rate of interest rises to 10 per cent, the capital value falls to £100. Alternatively, assume interest rates to be constant, while an increase in taxation lowers the expected annual return from £10 to £8. Again the capital value falls from £125 to £100. Finally, assume that the expected annual return falls from £10 to £8 and the market rate of interest rises from 8 per cent to 10 per cent. The capital value then falls to £80 (being £8 × 100/10) (When discounting procedures are used to determine capital values, the arithmetic results are different from those illustrated but the ordinal effects are the same).

The simultaneous use of monetary and fiscal policies exacerbates the fall in capital values. Since capital values are potential realisation values, the loss must be borne by the present owners, in the event of sale after an increase in interest rates. For any potential purchaser takes the change in capital values into consideration before he makes an offer to buy.

Subject to only minor modifications, this applies to holdings of loan stock. The holders are money-lenders with a right to fixed-interest payments, but with no rights of ownership over tangible assets (which would involve the right to transform). Amongst the most important kinds of loan stock in the market are Consols, being units of the Consolidated National Debt. In the case of Consols the Government is the borrower, and since the Government pays no taxes, there are no complications arising out of tax allowances. Consols were issued at coupon interest rates prevailing at the time of issue, and these varied between 2½ and 4 per cent. The original purchaser of such stock of nominal value of, say, £100 could be certain of an annual income of £2 10s. or £4 in perpetuity or until he sold his holding. He did, however, incur some risk relating to capital value in case of sale, should the rate of interest change between purchase and sale. The risk involved could, however, be predicted through making some simple calculations on the lines sketched in the preceding paragraph. In the two extreme cases above, the holder had not bought the right to £100, but an annual income of £2 10s. or £4. With market rates of interest at around 7½ per cent, as in September 1968, 2½ per cent Consols sold for 33½ and 4 per cent Consols for about £52, representing effective rates of interest of 7.5 per cent and 7.7 per cent respectively. The difference was due to a technical factor: the purchaser of 4 per cent Consols acquired the right to the next interest payment due, but the purchaser of the 2½ per cent Consols had missed it. Other technical factors that may affect capital values of stock are stock shortages; in the case of dated stock, the proximity of the redemption date; in the case of loan stock issued by industrial and commercial companies, the market's confidence in the survival of the firm; and in all cases, expectations relating to changes in interest rates and the rate of inflation. Again, if discounting procedures were used, valuations would be different; but in practice markets seem to be guided by the simple procedure. Subject to such modifications, the rules set out in the preceding paragraph serve as a rough guide to the effects of interest-rate changes on money-lending. The money-lender has bought himself a 'salary', but incurs a fixed-odds risk relating to capital value.

Since the purpose of pure money-lending is to enable the continuance of present activities, and since present activities are inadequate to satisfy current effective demand at current prices, the old money-lender is penalised: either he must continue to accept what is now a low money income or he must sell at a capital loss. New lenders are, however, encouraged through higher interest rates. Old borrowers are benefited, since they pay what are now low interest rates, but new borrowing is discouraged. Less new borrowing and more funds available for pure money-lending combine to restore the traditional sector towards equilibrium. The rise in interest rates can stabilise money-lending and is thus an important weapon towards the attainment of a Keynes—Beveridge equilibrium (from above). But the rise in interest rates simply reflects and reveals an enhanced scarcity of factors. It is not the cause of such enhanced scarcity, nor, by itself, a remedy.

Remedies for the enhanced scarcity of factors rest with those who have or acquire ownership, for they alone can enable transformation. The acquisition of ownership does, however, normally require borrowing and lending, so that the price payable for the acquisition of ownership cannot be independent of what happens in the money market. Often borrowing is the prerequisite to the acquisition of ownership, and where this is so, higher interest rates are a disincentive to the acquisition of ownership. Since borrowing for the acquisition of ownership is usually borrowing for the acquisition of what already exists, the case is analogous to the market in loan stock. Such acquisition of ownership does not add to the supply of transformable factors and is discouraged by higher interest rates. Sometimes, however, lending is the prerequisite for the acquisition of ownership of assets that exist and assets that have yet to be created; where this is so, higher interest rates are an incentive to the acquisition of ownership. Capital values are kept down and returns are raised, so that higher interest rates can help to circumvent the scarcity of factors — even if interest-rate policy by itself cannot ensure such a result.

An example of acquisition of ownership by the borrower is house purchase assisted by a building society mortgage. Potential purchasers have to consider the interest payments. If interest rates rise, potential purchasers cannot offer as much to the present owners as they otherwise might have done. There is in effect a transfer of funds from present owners who sell their houses to building societies, which enable the purchase of existing houses. If this meant a transfer from individuals who cannot enable further house-building to societies which might do so, this would be a step towards reducing the scarcity of houses. That it is normally not an effective step in such direction is due to the following reasons.

Building societies are specialists in one form of money-lending. They lend (or, rather, re-lend what is lent to them) in order to enable borrowers to acquire ownership, but they do not seek ownership for themselves. What the societies lend has been lent to them, and lent to them by lenders whose chief concern is to keep money capital intact. For such lenders Consols would not be suitable, since the capital value of Consols varies inversely with the rate of interest. Rather than accept such risk, they are willing to accept some uncertainty of income. Building societies offer them an appropriate outlet for their funds, since interest payments offered by building societies normally vary in the same direction as Bank Rate. Lenders to building societies thus accept the uncertainty of their incomes resulting from Bank Rate changes, but they incur no risk of loss of money capital unless their society goes bankrupt. The societies can pay more to their lenders only if they charge more to their borrowers.

When borrowers have to pay more to their building societies, they have less to spend on other things, and that effect may be noticed at once. The impact may not be immediate where the period of repayment is varied to keep the annual sum to be repaid constant. Where the impact is immediate, it does not necessarily reduce the volume of transactions in the economy as a whole, since the lenders to the building societies have more to spend. But the higher interest payments also affect capital values of houses, and that effect becomes noticeable if and when a sale is contemplated. New borrowers take the higher rate of interest into account when making their offers, so that the new owners pay less in capital and more in interest than they would otherwise have done. The reduction in purchasing power affects the vendor, while increased sums flow towards the building societies. Were the building societies primarily engaged in house-building, the effect would be an increase in the supply of houses. But mid-twentieth-century British building societies were first and foremost specialist money-lenders, not builders, so that the transfer is from those who have sold houses and those who are still paying off their mortgages to lenders whose chief concern is the preservation of money capital. To that extent a rise in mortgage interest rates may be a move towards equilibrium between borrowing and lending in one section of the money market, but it would be sheer accident if it stabilised the house market and reduced the scarcity of houses in relation to effective demand.

A rise in interest rates is intended to limit borrowing for all purposes, but there is no reason why the demand for the acquisition of house ownership should be proportionately discouraged. In fact the tax system ensures that this will not be so. Interest payments to building societies can be set off against income for tax purposes, but standard rate of income tax is deducted from the lenders' receipts. Although higher interest rates encourage lending (assuming constant tax rates), borrowing is not correspondingly discouraged. Purchasers still offer more for houses than they could do in the absence of tax allowances for interest payments, and requests for mortgages from building societies exceed what building societies can lend. Such situations occurred frequently in the 1950s and 1960s.

Hence even if higher interest rates effectively reduced the demand for houses, the excess demand for houses in relation to the finance available for house purchase may well be raised. If so the result is a narrower market with an accelerated rise in prices. Thus even if the general rise in prices did not carry house prices along, and even if rent control did not further push up the price of houses with vacant possession, a tax system that favours acquisition of owner-ship by borrowers somewhat perverts the effects of an increase in interest rates. The reason is that an increase in interest rates should reduce borrowers' chances of acquiring ownership and raise the return on lending. If the tax system discriminates between borrowers and lenders, and does so in favour of borrowers, then the effectiveness of the interest-rate weapon is blunted or even perverted, and Bank Rate has to be all the higher or other restrictive measures have to be more severe if the economy is to be deflated towards a Keynes–Beveridge level of 'full' employment.

In the case of Consols the borrower parts with no rights. The lender acquires a fixed money income and so avoids any uncertainty as to money income, and he assumes only strictly defined risks in relation to capital. In the case of mid-twentieth-century building society lending, the borrower usually acquires ownership over existing assets, while the lender contracts out of risk relating to his money capital and accepts only strictly defined uncertainty regarding his money income. If attention is confined to those two sections of the money market alone, it could be argued that a ruthless application of interest-rate policy (with sharper changes than those of the 1950s and 1960s, and without offsetting tax concessions) could effectively lead towards a Keynes–Beveridge equilibrium. Where the borrower creates no assets but just retains or acquires ownership over existing assets, and where the lender does not assume the entre-preneurial functions of 100 per cent risk-bearing and unlimited uncertainty-bearing, high interest rates may restrict the acquisition of ownership by borrowers (who are in no position to enable the creation of the assets they acquire). Overall, this may make relevant assets more abundant relatively to effective demand, though this does not necessarily follow in individual sections of the market. The target of policy is to regulate overall effective demand so as not to exceed available supplies of capital assets. But there is no creation or destruction of capital assets.

Unable or unwilling to drive interest-rate policy so far as to stabilise the economy by this means alone, the authorities frequently tried to deflate the economy through budgeting for surpluses of tax receipts over expenditure. The theory was that the Government would withdraw more purchasing power from the economy than it puts in, and this would have general deflationary consequences. But the policy has been frustrated by the existence of a large National Debt. Whenever the Government accumulates a surplus of revenue over expenditure, it must normally use such funds to retire a portion of the National Debt. Such a course is not only prescribed by an eighteenth-century statute (The National Debt Redemption Act, — which, however, could be amended or repealed),but is also mere prudence for any debtor who does not wish his credit to be impaired. Impairment of confidence in a government's credit would be reflected in a fall in the value of the money it issues, and that would aggravate the inflation which the budget surplus is intended to cure.

The simplest way of retiring a portion of the National Debt is for the authorities (or their agents) to buy government bills and bonds in the market. Since this is liable to drive up the capital value of such bills and bonds, it somewhat counteracts one of the intended effects of a rise in Bank Rate. Moreover it increases the cash reserves of the holders of the National Debt, and the principal holders are banks and other financial institutions. To ensure that this does not increase bank lending, the authorities then have to enjoin the joint-stock banks not to increase their advances beyond specified limits.

Bank advances are used for all sorts of purposes, but most are given to borrowers who wish to acquire or preserve existing assets. The borrowers may be private individuals who want to buy cars (which already exist) or houses (which already exist) and seek temporary financial assistance; or they may be large corporations seeking temporary finance pending a share issue in the market; or they may be firms of all sizes that seek temporary finance to meet their day-to-day expenses, which can include purchases of raw-material stock and wage payments which are necessary to carry on the business. The last-mentioned group is of special importance, and their dependence on bank advances varies with the time which must elapse between input and output. For that category of borrowers, bank advances provide much of the short-term finance needed to carry on with traditional activities. Already handicapped by high interest rates (unless the increased cost of borrowing can be passed on either in the form of higher prices of the output or of lower payments for inputs), a limitation of advances available to past levels precludes all prospect of expansion for traditional activities that depend on such finance.

Traditional activities were not so severely restricted because they were able to find alternative finance. Some firms found an escape in overdraft facilities provided by overseas banks and by non-bank financial institutions. More important in the mid-1960s was the reduction in the stamp duty on bills of exchange, and this reduced the cost differential between financing the purchase of materials out of bank overdrafts and through bills of exchange. Firms could use more of their existing overdraft facilities to defray their other current expenses.

Whatever the details, all attempts at restricting aggregate effective demand are measures which ultimately amount to a capital levy on the owner of existing capital, coupled with an increased current burden on the borrowers who seek to employ profitably whatever assets they already own. Ruthlessly applied, these policies could depress the economy towards a Keynes–Beveridge level of unemployment and beyond.

Unfortunately nobody could possibly know in good time when exactly the Keynes–Beveridge level was reached, and once the authorities have overshot the mark, the pre-war type of economy might be restored — which is just what Keynes, Beveridge and many others strove to avoid. There would not even be wage stability, for with unemployment beyond the Keynes–Beveridge level, all factors would be abundant and labour relatively scarce. Even though wage demands might then be less in absolute terms, they would be relatively more burdensome to meet. To offset relatively dear labour would require cheap money and budget deficits on the lines advocated by Keynes. But the overriding policy problem of the 1950s and 1960s was the value of sterling, and that would have ruled out low interest rates and deliberate budget deficits. It is thus by no means regrettable that the authorities did not overshoot the mark. One might argue that they should not have blunted their policies and tolerated or even encouraged escapes, since less severe measures might have sufficed had they not shied too much from the consequences of the measures they took. But whatever the details, there is no point in limiting the scope of traditional activities unless there are other activities to take their place.

An economy can always replace existing activities by new ones, provided that new means of production are created (which includes making better use of existing means of production). The new means of production will be owned by public authorities, private business enterprises or individuals. In so far as the creation of new means of production can be influenced by general economic policy, such policy must be directed at making such ownership profitable. The appropriate policy measures do not stabilise values of what there is, but encourage the creation of new values. The target of policy is not the limitation of effective demand but the extension of potential supplies. Any measure which operates on effective demand influences potential supply, and vice versa. When there is general abundance of factors, there is no problem of potential supplies and policy measures should be assessed with special reference to their impact on effective demand. In times of general scarcity of factors, however, there is no deficiency in effective demand, so that the principal criterion in the assessment of policy should be the effect on potential supplies.

Additional means of production have to be created, and this involves expenditure of money captial. Additional means of production must be owned by someone, so that their creation implies additional ownership. Such ownership is acquired through provision of money capital. The money capital provided is 100 per cent at risk, and future income is uncertain and may be much delayed. 100 per cent risk-taking and uncertainty-bearing are the functions of entrepreneurship.

Only where the additional means of production are largely replacements of what there was before, and involve but little change in the borrowing firm's established methods, is it likely that firms can find new outside finance without parting with ownership. If so, the firm concerned may be able to obtain its money capital through the issue of fixed-interest-bearing loan stock and the lender acquires no rights of ownership. Normally, however, the creation of new means of production implies at least some improvement over the old ones and so implies some risk; hence this means of finance is normally only available to the largest firms, whose overall methods will not be appreciably affected. Smaller firms, and all firms venturing the new, will find cautious money-lenders uninterested. They have to seek money-lenders willing to assume the burdens and benefits of entrepreneurship. Nor will most firms be reluctant to do so, for should expansion prove to be a chimera, the owners bear the consequences and the traditional sector of the firm may even continue its activities unaffected. In other words firms shift uncertainty on to shareholders.

If venturesome firms are short of capital, they can seek it in the market by selling shares in the equity of the firm. Such shareholdings entitle the holder to vote at shareholders' meetings on how transformation is to be effected; and because the holder's subscription has enabled transformation, he is entitled to his share of the dividend. The smaller firms are, however, unable to go to the market for subscriptions to their equity, while some of the large firms may have enough monetary reserves to make resort to the market unnecessary. They may rely entirely on self-finance and increase the assets attributable to the equity that way. Whichever route is taken towards the increase of the firm's equity, it represents an increase in what is put at risk and an increase in uncertainty-bearing – which in turn might mean an increase in the worth of ownership.

However many shareholders in the equity there are, each firm has only one owner, being all the holders of the equity acting in unison and bound by majority decisions. The shareholders are rewarded or penalised according to the share in the equity they hold, for to that extent they are deemed to have enabled transformation, and to that extent they bear uncertainty. The shareholders do not, however, actually effect transformation, which is performed by wage- and salary-earning employees of the firm. Only to the extent to which a shareholder commands or carries a majority at a shareholders' meeting can he influence the way transformation is actually effected. Since those who enable transformation are lenders and those who effect transformation act on behalf of the borrower (being the firm), the effectiveness of interest-rate policy on industrial activity varies with the relative importance of shareholders and management in decision-taking.

If the firm borrows, but the lender acquires ownership or a stake in ownership, the borrower's decisions on what activities to expand or curtail can often be almost independent of considerations relating to the rate of interest. That is something which concerns the owner rather than the management, and where management has to concern itself with such matters, its views may conflict with those of the owners. Such conflict may not be apparent when factors are generally abundant, for then the problem of decision is primarily one of how much use to make of existing factors. When factors are generally scarce and becoming scarcer, however, such conflict becomes more apparent; where factors are scarce and becoming scarcer, the owner's profits depend largely on how far factor-saving innovations are applied, but the management's peace of mind may be greater if existing factors can be used as before. If interest rates rise, and this rise reflects the enhanced scarcity of capital, such conflict of views may be all the greater.

It is not suggested that management is always against change. Qualities of individual managers apart, what is good for the profits of a firm is good for the managers' salaries and for the managers' prestige. Nor is it suggested that owners or part-owners normally push their point of view so far as to compel management to follow their will. Nowadays shareholders do not often sway management at shareholders' meetings. If discontented, they find it easier to sell their holdings and purchase elsewhere rather than have the unpleasantness of an argument with technical experts. The consequence is that the lender's point of view is often mute, and the effect of changes in monetary policy on business decisions is not always what it should be from the lender's point of view.

Were shareholders more vociferous, monetary policy would be more likely to assist with the circumvention of the scarcity of factors. Once again it may be useful to draw a distinction between the situation of general abundance of factors and one of general scarcity of factors. Where factors are generally abundant, any investment in industry is subject to greater risks and uncertainties than straightforward money-lending to government or building societies. The mere addition to industrial assets undermines the value of existing assets. That applies especially to any capital-saving installations, but it even applies to reinvestment which merely replaces what there was before. Any lender, then, runs risks and uncertainties, and adds to the risks and uncertainties borne by previous lenders. He must therefore be attracted through higher rewards than those available on Consols. To attract money capital into industry, then, requires to keep the yield on Consols relatively low, in order to produce the appropriate 'yield gap'.

Where factors are generally scarce, prices rise. The rise in prices adds to the marginal efficiency of existing capital, and the rise in prices continues until contained by an appropriate increase in potential supplies (which normally presupposes investment in additional industrial assets). The rise in prices reduces both the risk of investment of money capital and the uncertainty of the yield. If the rise in prices continues for a long time and is expected to continue, the risk of lending for investment in industrial assets may be regarded as negative – in the sense that it may be regarded as insurance for maintaining the real value of capital intact. Moreover the uncertainty of future income may turn into a greater certainty of real income than could be obtained from any fixed-interest-bearing security.

All this should attract money capital into equity lending and does. High interest rates can assist further, for the capital value of existing assets is kept down, and this attracts more buyers for assets that are 'cheap' relatively to other current values. The tendency is reinforced by a lesser rise in the price of capital goods than in the general price level – though it is impossible to say how far this is the result of interest-rate policy and how far the consequence of a greater rise in productivity in the capital-goods sector. Whatever the reason, capital goods and titles to capital goods are both relatively cheap and relatively certain to rise in money value.

The near certainty of the rise in capital values is also ensured by the time-lag between input and output. The rise in prices raises the marginal efficiency of existing capital and so encourages more money-lending for the purpose of creating additional capital. Any additional capital created does not become effective immediately but only later, so that the marginal *effectiveness* of capital does not rise until after the marginal efficiency of capital has risen. Marginal effectiveness of capital is the actual yield which is achieved by capital. This contrasts with the marginal efficiency of capital, which is the planned or prospective yield when managers are at the decision-making stage. The rise in the marginal efficiency of existing capital continues until it is balanced by the enhanced marginal effectiveness of the newly created capital. If the rise in prices continues in the meantime, the marginal efficiency of capital rises further and continues to exceed the marginal effectiveness of capital. As long as prices rise more than interest rates, the equity money-lender is almost in a position where he cannot lose, unless he is abnormally reckless or foolish.

When such conditions prevail, a money-lender who takes up Consols continues to risk his money capital, and a money-lender to building societies remains uncertain of the purchasing power of his income; but the equity lender appears relatively immune from risk and uncertainty. Consequently the yield gap of the days of abundant capital is reversed – and it is still widely referred to as 'the reverse yield gap', though it is the only possible one once markets have become aware of widespread scarcity of factors and their consequences. In the days of abundant factors the yield gap meant that risky equities yielded a higher return than the safer gilt-edged securities. In days of factor scarcity, the position is reversed.

The reverse yield gap reflects the attractions of the equity market to numerous money-lenders whose prime concern is the maintenance of the real value of their money capital and the near certainty of a future income of at least constant purchasing power. Pension funds, insurance companies and private individuals mindful of their future widows' old age, all are attracted into the equity market which was not really designed for them.

One purpose of the market in equity shares is to attract or repel funds to and from individual firms. True, much of the market has always been in secondhand shares, so that ownership has changed hands more often than it has been increased; but since the value of secondhand shares is an indication of the value of the equity, the market has always served as a rough guide to the terms at which firms could raise further money capital in the market, which is the counterpart to the terms at which it could offer new ownership. Old and new owners of the equity alike bear risk and uncertainty. Theoretically, the owners of the equity still bear risk and uncertainty; but with prices rising more than interest rates can rise, equity shares have come to be regarded as hedges against inflation, with risk and uncertainty normally less burdensome than available in any other outlet for money-lenders.

In consequence, many who in the past would have ensured their own or their clients' futures through the purchase of Consols or building society shares, have diverted their demand to equities. This has several consequences: the price of Consols falls or fails to rise with other prices, so that the Government must keep interest rates high; building societies are in perpetual difficulties as to where to find the funds needed to continue with their activities; and last but not least, the equity market is flooded with an excess demand for transfers of ownership. The velocity of circulation of equity ownership may be increased, but the number of assets which can be owned does not increase proportionately, if at all. True, the rise in equity values enables firms to raise further money capital at more favourable terms to themselves. That such new issues were inadequate to counter the excess demand for equities is suggested by the larger rise in equity share prices than in general prices.

As it is, the equity market has become a money-lenders' market, where regularity of dividend payments often counts for more than the prospects of future profits. Firms that pass a dividend, for whatever reason, often find themselves penalised through low valuation and difficulties in obtaining further funds from the market, so that short-term dividend considerations often have to take priority over the long-term growth prospects. Nothing else can be expected as long as important holders of industrial equity seek in the equity market the security their forebears found in Consols. Such equity holders seldom attend shareholders' meeting, and if they do, they tend to be mute. The result is that management is left in undisputed control, and management must normally identify itself with the borrowing firm rather than with the firm's lending owners. The opportunities offered by the combination of rising prices and high interest rates may often go unheeded.

Whatever the details, the result has been a greater increase in the velocity of circulation of ownership than in the volume of 'ownable' assets. The problem will remain unsolved until those willing to bear risk and uncertainty resume a greater say in the decision-making processes of firms. For all the many attempts to work through the borrower have more or less failed. For instance, several varieties of tax concessions have been tried to encourage industrial investment, in the form of investment and capital allowances; but since these were given to borrowing firms and not to the lenders whose ownership was affected, the results have often been disappointing. To give similar tax concessions to lenders would probably not be feasible on political and administrative grounds, nor is there a strong case for tax concessions to lenders where circumstances already make the lender's position too safe. Escapes must rather be sought on other lines, which would rid the equity market of excessive pressure from those who seek security, and also in ways which would increase the number of equity shares to be held by a narrower market.

The security-minded could probably be hived off, were it possible for the Government to issue a form of Consols where the return varies with the cost-of-living index. More complex still would be a solution to the problems of the equity market proper. There would have to be more issues as firms expand, so that the number of titles to ownership expands in line with the assets to be owned. Otherwise existing titles just rise in money value and the spread of ownership is made more difficult. Moreover it would be necessary to increase the ownership especially of those with a direct interest in the firms concerned, possibly on the lines of issuing employee shares, as already practised by a number of firms. The more widespread use of payment through 'entitlement to capital assets' has now been recommended by the National Board for Prices and Incomes. (11) Although recommended in a micro-economic context, this recommendation could lead to important macro-economic results. It would give a stake in ownership to those who effect transformation and so could lead to a greater sense of direct responsibility amongst all engaged in industry. At best it would show how transformation must be enabled before it can be effected, and that a rise in industrial rewards is a function of the rise in profits. At worst it might just swell the ranks of money-lenders who want security of capital or income. The recommendation shows no sure way towards overcoming the scarcity of factors, but points to one possibility. There may be other ways. Whatever way may eventually be found, it must lead to the creation, or re-creation, of a class of money-lenders with an interest in entrepreneurship. For in times of general scarcity of factors, the alternative to restraint is an increase in potential supplies, and this normally depends on an increase in ownable assets.

23 Income and Growth

1 THE RELATIVE SCARCITY OF FACTORS RECONSIDERED

The preceding four chapters considered the distribution of incomes as a reflection of the relative scarcity of factors. A rise in profits indicated the economy's reward for growth and reflected a rising scarcity of capital for growth. The national wages bill reflected the scarcity of labour for current activities. Rent reflected the unalterable past. Salaries were defined as a compound of wages and rent, so that they could be considered as a mixture of present and past, though the salary-earner's ability to anticipate future growth also implied a profit element. Ignoring the unalterable past, it was possible to present much of the argument in terms of a two-factor model, where the two factors were labour and capital and the appropriate factor rewards were wages and profit; and where wages represented the reward for current ways of carrying on economic activities, and profits the reward for the venturesome.

If so, a growth economy must be profit-conscious. Past experience shows that a rise in profits, relatively to other factor incomes, leads to a rise in real incomes and tends to be followed by a rise in other factor rewards. This was so in the earlier twentieth-century days of general abundance of factors; and should such a situation of abundance recur, knowledge of the Keynesian remedies should enable the authorities to revive profits and growth along traditional lines. The same applied in the 1950s and 1960s; but those were days of a general scarcity of factors, when Keynesian prescriptions were used to restrain demand but could not help towards a circumvention of the scarcity of factors. Growth along traditional lines was limited by the scarcity of factors, and while there was substantial growth along venturesome new lines, the United Kingdom's growth performance did not rival that of her major competitors. There must have been special problems, peculiar to the British economy of the 1950s and 1960s, which made it more difficult to circumvent the scarcity of factors in the United Kingdom than in most rival economies. Those problems may have been structural or organisational or both.

Some of the structural problems will be dealt with first. It is not possible to deal with all aspects of those problems. The argument will be confined to those aspects of the problems which emerge from the preceding discussion and require further elaboration. It will be useful to consider three stages of possible development (which does not imply that there cannot be others). The first stage is one where labour is an abundant factor. That stage has been no part of British mid-twentieth-century experience. It will be elaborated solely because it is instructive for the purpose of comparison. The second stage is where labour is relatively scarce, but all factors are still abundant. This second stage was part of British experience from at least the 1870s to the 1930s. The third stage is the stage of general scarcity of factors, as experienced in the 1950s and 1960s.

Labour is an abundant factor whenever there is a substantial volume of human activity that receives no monetary reward. There are some such activities in all societies, and this will continue until mother is paid for cooking the dinner. In twentieth-century British society, however, such activities are confined to services rendered within the narrowest circle of family and friends. Outside this narrow circle, labour services can be obtained only in return for money wages. Since everything that commands a monetary reward has some scarcity value, labour cannot be absolutely abundant in modern Britain (though it can be relatively abundant). Matters are different elsewhere. In many other countries substantial volumes of activity take place in traditional farming and military sectors, where the reward is given in food, clothing, shelter and suchlike, and the monetary reward is negligible or nil. For argument's sake, let only the extreme case be considered, where the monetary reward in the 'subsistence sector' is nil and all 'wages' are paid in kind. In societies that neither want nor seek change of any sort, the subsistence sector is all-embracing; labour receives no monetary reward and in this sense is absolutely abundant. In practice there are few societies, if any, that are so completely 'underdeveloped' (just as at the other extreme there can be no society that is completely 'developed' as long as family relationships remain beyond economic considerations).

The moment some labour is rewarded with money, the society concerned has an economic sector in the sense that values are measurable and are determined on economic grounds. Whether this sector be primitive and poor or sophisticated and wealthy, initially it does not comprise the whole of an underdeveloped country's society. There is, beyond the economic sector, an 'unlimited supply of labour' (1) which the economy can attract. The attraction appears to be a money wage which affords a standard of living slightly higher than that available in the subsistence sector. (2) Labour can be attracted on those terms, and if it is no longer needed in the economic sector, it can often return to the subsistence sector. The wage rate paid to each worker per unit of time is thus largely given. Where employers can vary the supply of labour at will, the wage rate is for all practical purposes constant.

Where the wage rate is constant, the total wages bill varies with the volume of employment in the economic sector. An increase in demand for the economic sector's wares leads to an increase in the volume of employment and in the total wages bill, and vice versa when demand falls. Hence an increase in demand facing the economic sector leads to an increase in total earnings of wage-earners, and a fall in such demand leads to a fall in total earnings of wage-earners, leaving the wage rate unchanged in either case. Since the wages bill rises only in proportion to output, any increase in demand (which is not accompanied by a corresponding increase in potential supplies) leads to a rise in prices and so to an increase in profits. A rise in profits, without a proportionate rise in wages, implies an increase in accumulation of money capital. This can be the source of further growth.

Growth is assisted by a disproportionate accumulation of money capital; but it is not assured, since the accumulated money capital may not find a suitable outlet and may be squandered. All that is asserted is that there are special growth opportunities which may or may not be taken. If they are taken, an underdeveloped country can advance with relative rapidity and so create 'islands of development'. (3) In those 'islands', scarcity of certain kinds of labour may emerge and so lead to relatively high rewards for such labour, while the bulk of the country's actual or potential labour force remains abundant at the accepted wage. Special problems can arise when relatively high labour costs slow down the growth of the 'island economies' and opportunities in other activities are only slowly recognised. A dual economy may persist for a time, and this may be a long time. Once opportunities for further development in the money-wage-paying economic sector are taken, such further development can still proceed with constant wage rates and disproportionate accumulation of money capital, until all labour is employed exclusively for money.

What happens in underdeveloped or dual economies cannot explain events in an advanced industrial country. Such extreme cases are nevertheless instructive even for an advanced country, subject to appropriate modifications. For in all countries there are agricultural sectors where at least part of the farm workers' remuneration is paid in kind and only some of it in money. Such dual remuneration means that the scarcity of farm labourers is not fully reflected in their money wages. Although no longer perfectly abundant, such labour is not perfectly scarce (in the sense that scarcity should be reflected in the appropriate monetary reward). Even where a farm labourer's standard of living is the same as an industrial worker's in real terms, in money terms the farm worker fares worse. Since a wage paid entirely in money gives more freedom of choice than one paid partly in kind, a money wage is often preferred (even if it does not buy more goods). In consequence any growth in the money-wage-paying sector will tend to attract labour from the land.

Such tendencies are reinforced when an increase in agricultural productivity repels labour from the land. An increase in agricultural productivity has been a feature of the economic development of the advanced countries throughout the 1950s and 1960s, with the result that a larger agricultural output is produced with a smaller labour force. Former agricultural labour moved to the towns, and this meant that semi-abundant labour became available to manufacturing industries. The effect was most marked in countries where that transfer involved relatively large numbers and where agricultural labour's remuneration was largely in kind. In Britain, however, the agricultural sector was already small, so that the number of workers involved was relatively small. Moreover the proportion of farm workers' wages payable in money is higher in Britain than in most countries. While the combination of industrial growth and falling agricultural employment enabled some advanced industrial countries to reap the fruits of the final stages of underdevelopment (in the form of a somewhat slower rise in wages relatively to profits than would otherwise have been possible), this avenue towards a higher rate of capital accumulation was not open to the British economy.

Agriculture need not be the only possible source of abundant or semi-abundant labour. That agriculture is often the main source of such labour is due to its pay structure rather than to any other characteristics of agricultural activity. Wherever there is a substantial volume of labour paid wholly or partly in kind, there is a potential source of abundant or semi-abundant labour for manufacturing industry or other money-wage-paying activities. In twentieth-century Britain the chief source of such labour has been female labour. This did not effectively keep labour costs down because of a variety of special circumstances. The economic emancipation of women was not a gradual process, but became effective during the three jolts caused by the two great wars and the 1929 depression. Although widely ready for economic emancipation before 1914, these three jolts threw women from domestic activities (which were wholly or partly remunerated in kind) into factories and offices. (4) That may have eased some of the problems of war economics and aggravated some of the problems of the 1929 depression. But those were once-and-for-all events. There was no continuous increase in the availablity of such labour for the money-wage-paying sector. Moreover much female employment was in new occupations not normally coveted by men, (5) while (predominantly male) trade unions saw to it that the employment of women did not undermine men's wages. The concatenation of those circumstances meant that the economic emancipation of women did not make the British labour market revert to a state appropriate to a still developing economy.

Another possible source of additional labour for manufacturing industry could be service trades. International experience has shown that national economic growth tends to be associated with an even larger rate of growth of manufacturing. (6) In the mid-1960s, there was a widespread feeling that the British growth rate was inadequate, and if international experience was any guide, an increase in employment in manufacturing might be a remedy. The Government accepted this point of view, and in 1966 introduced a selective employment tax which taxed employment in the service trades and was coupled with a subsidy for employment in manufacturing. In its original form this kind of tax discrimination was applied for two years only (since the subsidy was abolished except for industrial employment in the specially favoured development areas), so that there was not enough time to see whether tax discrimination would lead to the desired redeployment of labour. Even if it did, and even if it helped to overcome some shortage of labour in this or that manufacturing firm, it could do little to keep labour costs down. For the numbers in service employment who were partly remunerated in kind must have been small. While it is not denied that the redeployment of labour may be affected by tax incentives and tax penalties, an additional supply of labour that keeps labour costs down must come from activities where remuneration is wholly or partly in kind. Only such labour is abundant or semi-abundant.

British male labour in manufacturing industry has been 'scarce' for at least a hundred years, in the sense that such labour could only be hired in return for a money wage. Where labour is remunerated by a money wage only, that wage is a reflection of the scarcity of labour. There was always risk that the scarcity of industrial labour would be undermined through an influx of labour from the land or from domestic service or through female employment. But those threats were not of sufficient impact to be effective. In any event they were resisted by trade unions who would not tolerate cuts in their members' wage rates, even in depression, although this often meant unemployment for more of their members. Had the trade unions tolerated cuts in wage rates in the face of an influx of labour or in depression, there might have been less unemployment. But there would also have been abundant or semi-abundant labour, and the remuneration of all workers would have fallen towards subsistence level. Unemployment was part of the price that had to be paid to maintain the scarcity of labour. Thus before the Second World War the scarcity of male industrial labour was not incompatible with general abundance of factors and unemployment of labour. In fact it would have been undermined had there been less unemployment.

Once there is scarcity of labour, the national wages bill rises with the demand for labour, and the demand for labour varies with the national income (which in turn depends largely on the course of profits in the immediate past). When the demand for labour rises, wage rates and employment rise; and when the demand for labour falls, wage rates cannot rise and employment falls. Wage rates become variable, and the national wages bill becomes a near constant. This does not deny the possibility of some cyclical variations in the share of wages in national income, but over the last hundred years the share of wages in national income has never been far from two-fifths of the total.

If the national wages bill rises roughly in proportion to the total national income, the share of the total that is available for capital accumulation is less than would be the case in an economy at an earlier stage of economic development (when the national wages bill does not rise in proportion to the national income). In the late nineteenth and early twentieth centuries this relative scarcity of labour in Britain encouraged investment overseas, where there were countries at earlier stages of economic development and where the abundance of other factors enabled faster capital accumulation than at home. As will be shown in more detail in Part IV, the fruits of overseas investment brought British consumers an increasing quantity and variety of goods, so that British standards of living could rise despite a slower rate of growth of British manufacturing industry than had been experienced earlier in the nineteenth century or was to be experienced after the Second World War. Overseas investment provided an outlet for abundant British capital, and the resulting rise in standards of living made some unemployment tolerable, at least until 1914.

But these were problems of the past. The present problem is one of general scarcity of factors, where capital is even scarcer than labour. But the scarcity of labour continues and so does the constancy or near constancy of the share of labour in national income. As before, this makes capital accumulation somewhat more difficult than in countries at an earlier stage of development. Now, however, the escape of using capital abroad rather than at home is no longer available, for the simple reason that net capital investment abroad requires abundant capital at home. The British economy is fully developed, in the sense that there are no abundant factors anywhere, and at earlier stages of development such abundance or semi-abundance of factors enabled a disproportionate rise of profits and thus of capital accumulation which could finance further growth. But in a fully developed economy further capital accumulation is limited because of the scarcity of labour and the rise in the national wages bill in almost direct proportion to the national income. If this problem cannot be overcome, there is the possibility that the economy will stagnate. The relatively slow rate of growth of the British economy in the 1950s and 1960s may be a warning that even highly skilled manpower and sophisticated machinery do not suffice to keep an economy moving. There is still a need to overcome the scarcity of factors, and nobody can do that without a prior increase in capital accumulation.

This problem of the British economy is one of the most challenging that has ever faced economists. No economy has ever been in this position before, at least not in modern times. It is one where Britain 'leads'. For all economies aspire to the highest possible stage of development, so that all economies might one day be faced with the same problem. Britain, however, cannot wait until others solve that problem in one way or the other. She has to solve it herself, and soon.

Since the problem is one that has only become acute in the 1950s and 1960s, it is not surprising that it took time to diagnose and even less surprising that no perfect remedy has yet been found. When new problems arise, and they have to be dealt with at once, the remedies for past ills are tried again, simply because no others are yet available. The present authors regret that they can offer no perfect remedies either. They can only point to some of the treatments that have been tried or suggested and add a few comments.

The initial approach to any new problem is liable to be negative. If insufficient capital accumulation impedes growth, and if a constant share of wages in national income leaves relatively less for capital accumulation than is the case in countries at an earlier stage of development, the initial response may be an attempt to apply past remedies. Restrict the rise of wages, the argument runs, so that consumption is restricted and more resources are available for growth. It is sometimes, tactfully, omitted that there is an intermediate stage requiring capital accumulation which is a precondition for further growth. The difficulties with this approach that have been experienced seem unavoidable once it is realised that it implies treating labour as if abundant or semi-abundant labour were available. It is an approach based on confusion between relative and absolute factor scarcities. If all factors are scarce and capital scarcer than labour, then labour is relatively abundant. But it is not absolutely abundant, and thus there is no reason why the share of labour should not continue to rise in direct ratio to the increase in national income. Force may be used, but it will be resented and quite possibly be of no avail since the abundance of labour cannot be restored by decree. Nor would it help to use or misuse monetary policy to restore an equilibrium level below the Keynes–Beveridge level, since this would only create a situation where labour is relatively scarce, and even lesser wage increases than are now customary would be relatively more burdensome. Nor should it be forgotten that, in the seventy or more years before the Second World War, when factors were generally abundant and labour relatively scarce, trade union action could ensure that male labour in industrial employment was treated as if it had been absolutely scarce. This is always possible for any factor which can be hired only for money and can refuse a nil return (as labour can and capital cannot).

The negative approach can be no more than a stop-gap measure. Whatever its merits in the short run may be, in the long run it would only restore a lower stage of development than the United Kingdom has attained. A more positive approach has been suggested along neo-Keynesian lines. (7) Economic growth is associated with an even greater rate of growth of manufacturing, (8) and 'a higher rate of growth of manufacturing output breeds higher rates of productivity growth, but not enough to obviate the need for a faster rate of growth of employment'. (9) If a mature economy were defined as one where real income per head has reached broadly the same levels in agriculture and mining, manufacturing and the service trades, (10) so that there is no incentive to move from one sector to another, it follows that special measures are needed to redeploy labour from services into manufacturing. The reasoning hinges on the assumption that labour is 'the' scarce factor.

This approach has the merit that it suggests a positive way of redeploying the labour force towards the sector capable of greatest growth and capable of carrying the rest of the economy along. It is an analysis in real terms and suggests a solution. But the means towards the solution are another problem. As mentioned before a transfer of labour from service trades into manufacturing does not by itself solve the problem of how manufacturing industry is to finance expansion, unless there is spare capacity. At the time the above theory was put forward (in 1966), the British economy was in recession and there was spare capacity. Fortunately, however, recessions do not last for ever, and the problem of creating additional capacity for expansion became acute again two years later.

The present approach is somewhat different. The definition of a mature economy as one where real incomes per head in the different sectors are identical is not incompatible with he definition used here, which defines a mature or developed economy as one where factors are rewarded entirely with money. The present argument shares the view that future economic growth in the United Kingdom will depend largely on the growth of the manufacturing sector. The argument in favour of a redeployment of the labour force is accepted as a short-run solution, though for a long-run solution more emphasis is put here on the importance of capital accumulation. The reason for this difference in emphasis is that labour is regarded as one scarce factor and not as *the* scarce factor, and that the relative scarcity of capital is regarded as greater.

So far no solution has been suggested. It may even be said that the present argument endeavours to combine two apparently incompatible ends. On the one hand it is suggested that the scarcity of labour does not admit of any long-term solution that would lower the share of wages in national income. On the other hand it is argued that a steady share of wages in national income may restrict the possible growth of profits and thus of capital accumulation and real investment, while a growth of profits is a precondition for growth of the economy.

The charge is admitted. Somewhat feebly, it may be said in defence that even a steady share of wages in national income does not eliminate profits. It only restricts their possible growth. If, however, the rate of growth of the economy is to be accelerated, the rate of growth of profits must be accelerated first. It cannot be accelerated at the expense of wages. Since the argument is conducted in terms of a two-factor model, there is an apparent impasse.

To solve it, the argument returns to the initial assertion that wages are a reward for current human toil, and profits a reward for bearing the uncertainty of future returns. If the return for current toil restricts the reward for uncertainty-bearing, measures should be taken to raise the reward for uncertainty-bearing relatively to the reward for current toil. There should be a positive increase in future returns relatively to current ones. Can this be done, given the scarcity of labour?

It can be done, provided it is realised that scarcity of labour is reflected in wages. The scarcity of labour ensures that the reward of labour will be a near constant relatively to national income, and the even greater scarcity of capital necessitates higher profits. There is no escape from either of those two income requirements. This leads to an impasse only if wage-earners and profit-earners must always be different people. If, however, labour can be rewarded partly in wages and partly in 'entitlement to capital assets', as suggested by the National Board on Prices and Incomes, (11) the impasse might be avoided. If it is true that current toil is overpaid in the sense that such payments lead to consumption in excess of what the economy can currently produce; and if it is true that the share of current labour in national income is roughly given and a near constant; then additional rewards for labour could be increasingly paid in the form of entitlements to capital and so both maintain the share of labour in national income and increase capital accumulation.

In the mid-nineteenth century limited liability was invented, and this enabled the thrifty middle-income groups to participate in the finance of industry and commerce. This gave the middle-income groups a stake in industry and led to a responsible attitude on the part of those groups towards the economic needs of the country. Since then there has been a marked rise in working-class prosperity, but no corresponding rise in opportunities for the working classes to buy a stake in industry. If wage-earners are rewarded entirely in money for the present, they will think only of the present. If they received wage increases at least partly in money for the future, they would become more conscious of their long-term interest — which, after all, is that profits should rise so that wages can rise. This is a long-term solution which may take time to be effective. But it is one that combines the social advantages of integration of the working classes into a forward-looking society with the need for rising capital accumulation and the constant share of the reward for current toil in national income. 'Money for the future' is not a retrograde step in economic development. But to reduce the reward for current toil below its accustomed share in national income could be a retrograde step towards a stage of development with abundance of factors.

2   INFLATION

Should it remain impossible to defer the effectiveness of some currently earned money claims towards a future date, the choice becomes one between inflation and unemployment. The latter would revive the economic situation of the past. Whatever consequences might result from the return of old times, a faster growth rate would not be one of them. For growth implies more and better utilisation of factors, not less utilisation of factors. The growth rate in the unemployment days of the present century was in fact less than in the 1950s and 1960s. The problem of the 1950s and 1960s was not the absence of growth but the restraint on growth imposed by a higher stage of economic development than had been attained elsewhere.

What growth there was, was associated with inflation. Unemployment was rejected; and although there were attempts at integrating the working classes into a profit-conscious society (through schemes for profit-sharing, the issue of employee shares and the like), there has as yet been no attempt at paying wage increments partly or wholly in 'entitlement to capital assets'. Where unemployment is not acceptable and money for the future not available, growth is likely to be accompanied by inflation for the following reasons.

Venturesome management, backed by entrepreneurship, normally endeavours to expand and to improve. There are always some such firms. If faced with a general scarcity of factors, expansion of any activity involves a rise in factor rewards in order to attract factors. This tends to be followed by rising factor rewards elsewhere, since other firms seek to maintain their activities and to retain their factors. The purpose of paying higher factor rewards in the growth sector is to effect further transformation, and the resulting increase in output should more than compensate for the increase in costs. In other activities, however, the purpose of paying higher factor rewards is simply to maintain output, so that more is paid for the same work as was done before for less pay.

Were the increase in factor costs confined to the growth sector, the inflationary effects would be ephemeral and probably minor. The reason is that the increase in factor costs would eventually be compensated for by increased and improved output. Moreover public knowledge that more or improved goods are forthcoming may put a damper on price increases that are possible in the meantime. The increase in factor costs in the sector that just wishes to maintain output is another matter. That sector is on the defensive, and pays more for the same work just to keep going. Since no additional output is forthcoming from the defensive sector, there is no compensation for the increase in factor costs save in price increases. Since no additional output is expected by the public, there is no strong consumer resistance to price increases.

In other words growth is associated with inflation. The inflation is started in the growth sector, but it is most felt in the traditional sector. Given a general scarcity of factors, this leads to a curious result: if the growth sector is small and its rate of growth slow, and the traditional sector is large and on the defensive, the inflation will be more marked than if the growth sector is large or its rate of growth high and the traditional sector is small and willing to contract. For, given general scarcity of factors, any growth anywhere, however small, raises costs elsewhere; while growth itself, however marked, has fewer inflationary effects in the growth sector itself. This may well help to explain why countries with a high rate of growth often experience less inflation than countries with a lower growth rate. International comparisons are, however, difficult because they involve comparisons of countries at different stages of development. It may be better to look for evidence in British experience of the 1950s and 1960s.

Experience in the 1960s supports the above argument, but experience in the 1950s does not. The evidence of the 1960s is as follows: the years with relatively fast growth were 1960, 1961, 1963 and 1964, when the gross domestic product at constant prices rose by more than 3 per cent. In those years the retail price level rose by 3 per cent or less. The slow-growing years were 1962, 1965 and 1966, when the gross domestic product at constant prices rose by less than 3 per cent and the retail price level rose by more than 4 per cent. (12)

This experience points to the possibility of the above assertions, but it provides no proof. The retail price index is influenced by import prices, and import prices depend on what happens in supplying countries as well as on what happens in the United Kingdom. The aggregate data of the growth of the gross domestic product do not reveal whether growth was widely based or confined to narrow sectors. On the other hand it can be argued that the retail price index reflects domestic events more than international ones, that even import prices are not independent of what happens in the United Kingdom, and that British economic growth in the 1960s was largely due to exertions in specialised fields rather than to all-round advance. Thus while the weakness of the statistical evidence for the 1960s is admitted, it does not disprove the assertions.

What appears more damaging at first sight is the absence of such a relationship between prices and growth in the 1950s. Both the 1950s and 1960s have been described as decades of general scarcity of factors, so that whatever does not apply to both decades may be regarded as unconnected with the general scarcity of factors. On the other hand, it will be recalled from Chapter 22 above that the reverse yield gap did not become permanent until 1959, and this too is a feature of the general scarcity of factors; and in Part IV below, it will be shown that the import of manufactures did not begin to rise disproportionately until 1960, and such imports are another feature of a general scarcity of factors in the home economy. Thus there are at least three features of a general scarcity of factors that did not become noticeable until around 1959 or 1960: the reverse yield gap, the disproportionate rise in the imports of manufactures, and the inverse relationship between growth and the rise in prices. This may suggest that the British economy was approaching the stage of full development in the 1950s, but this did not become absolute until around 1959 or 1960. Since then the problems of the British economy have been similar to those of the 1950s, but more severe.

On this interpretation, a fully developed economy is likely to have less cost inflation if growth is widespread and rapid, and more cost inflation if growth is retarded. It is not denied that cost inflation could always be choked off if the authorities cut off the money supply and if they allowed fewer escapes from the impact of their credit policies. It is asserted, however, that more drastic monetary policies than have been pursued could all too easily have led the economy back to an earlier stage of development, and that it was a lesser error to let inflation continue. There must, however, be plenty of discussion of positive alternatives so that they can soon be applied.

The first issue in a discussion of alternatives is to diagnose the problem; and if the preceding is correct, the basic economic problem of the 1960s was the absolute scarcity of factors. The second issue to be considered is the means of escape. If the argument in Chapter 22 is correct, the escape lies through the creation of more ownable assets and a climate of opinion that encourages the acquisition of the ownership of such assets. If the argument of the present chapter is correct, there is need for more working-class acquisition of ownership of such assets, since this allows both the maintenance of the share of wages in national income (which is fairly steady whenever labour is scarce) and an increase in capital accumulation and profit earning (which has to go on rising as long as capital is even scarcer than labour).

The solution of the problem is harder if the aggressive growth sector and the defensive traditional sector are entirely separate and different. It is somewhat easier if there is a growth sector and a traditional sector in each firm. For argument's sake the two sectors have been treated as separate, and it will be convenient to continue to do so a little longer.

Suppose the growth sector pays wage increments partly or wholly in 'entitlements to capital assets' (or 'future money' or whatever the most acceptable designation of such payment may be). The labour force would then have a direct interest in maximising their firms' receipts, which are the source of wages anyway, though the link would become clearer to all concerned. There would be no cut in wages, but a deferment of the benefit of the increment towards the time when the firm has experienced growth. The greater the growth of the firm, the greater would be the eventual money-income increment received by its employees. Both sides of industry would benefit: the employers would benefit since capital accumulation would be less restrained through increased labour costs; and the workers would benefit through acquisition of a share in the benefits of capital formation.

Difficulties would arise in the traditional sector. If wage increments are paid in the form of entitlements to capital assets, but there is no increase in those assets, the only clear result would be a dilution of the firm's equity. This objection can be overstated, however, since higher factor costs and constant output would in any case lower the value of the equity. Moreover firms that fall too much behind in the growth race are likely to go out of business or be suitable targets for a take-over.

In reality there cannot be many firms where all is growth or where all is tradition. In most firms there are growth sectors and traditional ones. The importance of one sector relatively to the other varies, but as long as there is some element of growth, the suggestion put forward for the growth sector is applicable.

Since a firm's growth can always be measured, there would be no new difficulties in job evaluation. There would, however, be problems in deciding on the proportion of wage increments to be paid in the new way. The proper ratio would vary from firm to firm and would vary with the proportion of growth activities to traditional ones.

Whatever the details used to ensure identity of interests of all sections of the working community, in one way or another the scarcity of factors may be overcome: either ownable assets will have to be increased, with or without the participation of the labour force; or an unemployment level higher than the Keynes–Beveridge level will reappear, and the British economy will become a less developed one.

Part IV

OVERSEAS TRADE

24 Merchandise Trade

1 ECONOMIC GROWTH AND OVERSEAS TRADE

An economy can grow when either more or better factors become available for employment, so that an increase in demand can be met. More factors can become available through an increase in the working population or capital widening. Growth of the working population may have provided a major impetus towards an acceleration of eighteenth- and nineteenth-century British economic growth; but given twentieth-century population trends and prospects, this can no longer be relied upon. Despite a marked increase in female employment, the twentieth-century growth of the economically active population has been at a slow rate, (1) and this is almost certain to continue in the 1970s. (2) The argument of Chapters 22 and 23 was that capital widening is inappropriate to a fully employed economy, as the British economy was in the 1950s and 1960s. Instead, the British economy's growth depended upon the availability of better factors.

More education and research could be an escape route in the long period, but they depend on the availability of capital. The principal domestic escape route from slow growth thus lies through capital deepening. In a fully employed economy only better capital can. make all factors go further. Were the British economy a closed economy, the argument would stop here. In an open economy, however, access to better factors may also be obtained through increased participation in overseas trade. This implies increased specialisation, so that each participating country can make its factors go further. The economies of specialisation mean that each country's factors are used more efficiently. They are 'better'.

The following example may help to indicate how a country can gain from increased participation in international trade. All the temperate-zone food eaten in Britain could be produced from British soil. Continuous investment in British agriculture could raise domestically produced food supplies to such levels that the population could eat about as well as now, and without the need to import. Relatively more people would work on the land and fewer in manufacturing industry. If the population of this country wanted nothing beside temperate-zone food, such a course might be recommended. But people want more than just food. The cost of producing all food at home would thus have to be measured in terms of industrial goods foregone. For more than a hundred years this cost has been considered excessive. Instead of producing all food at home, this country has imported a substantial proportion of her food and paid for it out of the proceeds from exports of manufactures or services. By concentrating on manufactures and services, this country has been able to purchase at least as much food as could have been home-produced. Since she could produce more manufactures and services than were needed to pay for such food imports, she has gained from trade – the gain being the additional manufactures and services available at home as well as the greater variety (and possibly quantity) of food available for consumption in this country.

International specialisation makes it possible to 'produce' more with given factors. The result is the same as if there had been an increase in the supply of factors. As each country specialises more, each utilises its factors to better advantage, so that increasing specialisation has the same result as any capital deepening which improves the quality of factors. As trade expands, each country gains access to more factors and improves the quality of its own factors, without there being necessarily any change in the various countries' factor endowments. In other words participation in international trade is an alternative to domestic capital widening or an increase in the economically active population or both; and increasing participation in international trade is also an alternative to domestic capital deepening or an improvement in general education or a combination of both. In either event the domestic scarcity of factors may be circumvented. This is always advantageous when there is full employment and, by implication, general scarcity of factors within the country, though this does not necessarily follow when there is widespread unemployment and factors are already abundant. In short, the growth of international trade is factor-saving. This makes it particularly beneficial when it takes place between growing and fully employed economies. Special problems arise, however, if national growth rates differ.

When the British economy grows at the same rate as overseas economies there is improved utilisation of factors all round, and the scarcity of factors need not lead to any balance-of-payments difficulties. Matters are more complex when growth rates differ, as they usually do. Some of the problems involved will be discussed at some length in the subsequent considerations relating to export prospects and overseas investment. Here two simplified models must suffice. One is relevant to the United Kingdom's economic position in the world at the beginning of the present century, and the other to the United Kingdom in the 1960s.

At the beginning of the present century the British economy was ahead of most of the world, but development was proceeding at a faster rate elsewhere. Because Britain was ahead, she could, with relative ease, pay for more imports than she needed. The balance-of-payments surplus was used to invest in overseas development, be it to supply more and cheaper products for the British market, or to raise overseas purchasing power to buy more British goods. The more successful British overseas investment was in cheapening imports or raising overseas purchasing power, the greater would the balance-of-payments surplus become and enable yet further overseas investment. At the beginning of the century British-centred world economic growth must have seemed self-perpetuating.

By the 1960s the British economy was one of several advanced ones. A few other economies had advanced further, and those few were the economies that also advanced fastest in the 1950s and 1960s. In other words a few overseas economies had learned to use their factors to better advantage than the British economy did, and those economies also continued to improve the overall utilisation of their factors at a faster rate than the British. Relatively to those economies, the British economy fell somewhat behind. In order to catch up with those few economies, the British economy needed either more capital deepening at home or more participation in the international division of economic activity. As shown in Chapters 22 and 23, domestic capital deepening had not yet gone far enough by the end of the 1960s; and it will be shown below that, although there was increased participation in the international division of activity, there was not enough of it. It may, however, be mentioned here that increased participation in international trade is easiest for those who are ahead, and since no country can be ahead of all others in all activities, this requires increasing specialisation, which in turn normally requires some capital deepening. As it was, some other economies improved the use of their factors more than the British economy did in the 1950s and 1960s, so that the British economy's relative position deteriorated, and the former export surplus waned and vanished by the mid-1960s.

The preceding is a simplification, but it may be sufficient to highlight one important twentieth-century change in the British economy's international position. At the beginning of the century the British economy grew slowly at home, and that slow growth left factors abundant. In those days, however, the slow domestic growth could be compensated by increased activities of British factors overseas. In the 1960s the British economy still grew relatively slowly at home, but this was caused by difficulties experienced in overcoming the scarcity of factors within the economy. Such difficulties cannot be evaded through shunting factors overseas, but only by making factors go further.

It does not follow that overseas trade can be ignored, nor that British economic growth must depend solely on domestic innovations. At any one point of time the international division of economic activity offers an escape from the scarcity of domestic factors and so may raise standards of living. This escape can be relied upon as long as there are no external payments difficulties. But payments difficulties are likely to arise whenever an economy has for some time lagged behind rival economies in increased participation in international economic activities, so that the lagging country may find it more difficult to intensify participation in the international division of activities. Applied to the British economy of the late 1960s, there seem to be two possible avenues of escape. One can be derived from the above simplified model relating to the 1960s, and the other from the simplified model relating to the 1900s.

The model of the 1960s calls for an escape from the scarcity of factors via capital deepening at home. This requires money capital and skills and a multitude of other factors which are scarce. Capital deepening of all activities would be impracticable. Success is more likely if the economy concentrates on a few efforts, with a view to obtaining a comparative advantage in a few activities. This may involve concentration on a few industries, or even concentration on a few activities within industries. The following example may illustrate this point. The British aircraft industry is, overall, as advanced as any country's aircraft industry, and it has displayed a comparative advantage in engines over parts. Consequently it can pay to sell engines from the United Kingdom to the United States, and import some completed planes from the United States. (3) As long as the British aircraft industry has a comparative advantage in some aircraft engines, and the United States aircraft industry in some airframes, both countries' airlines can fly better aeroplanes if the British industry produces more engines and the American one more airframes. Thus capital deepening by itself is not enough. It should be capital deepening where a comparative advantage can be obtained. Both countries could produce aeroplanes wholly by themselves. If they do, neither will advance as fast as possible. There must be wider markets as well, in order to make full use of any comparative advantages which may emerge. In short, the model of the 1960s points to an escape through concentration on fewer activities for wider markets.

The model of the 1900s suggests a different escape route from external payments difficulties. It depends on an acceleration of growth in economies which are still less advanced than the British economy, as long as they do not actually catch up with the British economy. In this case any increase in British output can be used for more trade of the traditional kind. That would be a return to the trading pattern of the early years of the century, when the growth of British overseas trade meant an increasing exchange of manufactures for primary products.

The two escape routes are not mutually exclusive. In practice both may have to be taken, since there is much trade of both kinds. Such considerations will be dealt with at greater length in later sections.

2   THE PURPOSE OF IMPORTS

All trade is reciprocal trade. Yet much discussion of a country's international performance tends to be conducted as if it were entirely a matter of export successes or failures. The reason is probably that such discussion tends to be in terms of money values, so that exports are treated as revenue and imports as costs. Exports raise domestic money values because producers are paid from overseas, with the result that there is more money in the country. Since they are paid for sending goods abroad, there is no corresponding increase in the supply of goods and services at home. Hence exports inflate home demand and deflate home supplies. There is, however, no point in exporting for exporting's sake. The point of exporting is that the proceeds of exports can be spent on imports. Imports can be purchased immediately, or the export proceeds can be used to add to the country's foreign exchange reserves or to its overseas investment, and either course assures that it will be possible to import in future. Whenever export proceeds are used to buy imports, there are more goods and services in the country, and the country's real income rises. The purpose of importing is to translate a rise in money incomes (earned by the export trades) into a rise in real incomes.

Imports, however, destroy domestic money incomes. (4) Purchasing power has to be withdrawn from the home economy in order to pay overseas producers. The net balance between imports and exports determines whether the immediate result of trade has been a rise in real incomes, when imports exceed exports, or whether it has been a rise in money incomes, when exports exceed imports. If there is to be no imbalance between changes in money incomes and changes in real incomes, the best result will be attained when an increase in exports leads to an increase in imports, and vice versa.

Accepting the case for increased participation in international trade, there is the question of the commodity composition of the additional trade. The answer must vary with circumstances. In general the export effort should concentrate on goods which, with available factors, can be produced at comparatively lower costs in this country than overseas; while imports should consist of goods which, with available factors, would be produced at comparatively higher costs in this country than overseas. Thus in the early nineteenth century British industrial activities could grow at the rate they did only because land-intensive raw materials for industry could be imported; and when domestic food production proved inadequate to feed the people, free trade in food helped to solve the problem. In those days the British labour force was more highly skilled than the rest of the world's, and the accumulation of capital had advanced more in Britain than elsewhere. Hence capital and labour were relatively more abundant in Britain than elsewhere; but land was not. The relative scarcity of land might have put a limit on the possible expansion of the British economy, had it not been possible to circumvent it through specialisation on capital- and labour-intensive industries, coupled with the importation of land-intensive raw materials and food. In return Britain exported goods which required relatively more capital and labour in their production, and she even exported labour (through net emigration) and capital (through overseas investment).

This situation continued until 1914; but even before 1914 further specialisation was possible between capital- and labour-intensive activities. In Britain capital accumulation had proceeded further than elsewhere, so that capital was relatively abundant and labour relatively scarce. It was then possible, and economically desirable, to concentrate on capital-intensive activities, such as advanced manufacturing and international finance, and to import the products of the more labour-intensive activities. Since primary production is normally more labour-intensive than manufacturing or finance, the old trade pattern continued: the United Kingdom imported food and raw materials in return for her manufactures and services. (5)

The same held for the inter-war years, though for somewhat different reasons. True, Britain was still one of the most highly capitalised countries in the world, and on this ground alone a trade pattern akin to the traditional one might have been expected. But this was no longer the sole reason. Protection and unemployment also ensured that the composition of trade did not change much. Protection froze the trade pattern, especially since it restricted imports from foreign countries more than from Empire countries – and foreign countries included some of the most advanced industrial countries, while the exports of the (then) Empire were largely primary products. The prolonged period of unemployment also froze the trade pattern. As shown in Part III, when there is unemployment all factors are abundant, and capital more so than labour. Because international trade allows for better utilisation particularly of the relatively abundant factor, the United Kingdom continued to be a net exporter of capital-intensive goods and a net importer of labour-intensive ones.

In the late 1940s, and even in much of the 1950s, it may have seemed as if the old trade pattern would re-emerge. A major cause may have been that trade with Sterling Area countries was much freer than trade with foreign currency countries, and Sterling Area exports were mainly primary products. During the 1950s, however, there was general liberalisation of trade, and by the end of the decade it became apparent that there had been some underlying changes in the United Kingdom's position in the world. Two of these changes warrant special mention in the present context. One was a change in the outside world, and the other a change within the British economy. They must now be considered.

In relation to the world as a whole, it is no longer true that the British economy is the most capitalised. Others have caught up and have added relatively more to their respective capital stocks than the British economy. In relation to other industrial countries, the British economy has ceased to be the most capital-intensive, and this has implications for about half of the United Kingdom's overseas trade. At the same time the British economy has been fully employed throughout the post-war period to date (excluding only a few weeks during the exceptionally cold winters of 1947 and 1963). Once more the relevant point from Part III must be recalled: when there is full employment, all factors are scarce and capital is scarcer than labour. In short, both in relation to half of her trading partners and on the grounds of her own economic situation, the United Kingdom has become a country where capital is relatively scarce. Since the purpose of international trade is to overcome problems created by relative factor scarcities, this purpose is now best served by allowing imports of some goods which are relatively capital-intensive as well as the traditional labour-saving imports. Given that the change in the purpose of imports from mere labour saving to labour and capital saving (with emphasis on the latter) is a new development, and given that this change was frustrated by quantitative trade controls until the late 1950s, it was somewhat drastic and caused some consternation when it eventually became apparent in the 1960s. It may have added to the balance-of-payments difficulties of the 1960s, but a reimposition of quantitative trade controls would have provided no more than temporary relief to the balance of payments. For imports save British factors, and when factor saving (of whatever kind) is restricted, the British economy grinds to a halt. It does so because a fully employed economy requires factor saving if it is to grow, and imports save factors. In the circumstances of the 1960s capital was especially scarce, and one way to relieve the scarcity of factors was through increased imports, and especially capital-intensive imports.

3   THE COMPOSITION OF BRITISH IMPORTS

The most capital-intensive imports tend to be manufactured goods. Although there are exceptions, it is probably a legitimate assumption in a comparison of imports of all manufactures with total imports. On this assumption, the only sure result of import restrictions on manufactures would be an aggravation of the domestic scarcity of factors. This might be welcome in an economy which suffers from unemployment, but not in a fully employed economy. But before it can be concluded that such import restrictions should not be imposed, even on balance-of-payments grounds, it must be asked whether the demand for imported raw materials (6) and imported food (7) is at all likely to slow down sufficiently to allow the country to spend more of its export earnings on imported manufactures. For in the long run the volume of imports the country can afford depends on its export performance. This sets the limit to total imports in the long run, even if borrowing or drawing on exchange reserves allows for some additional imports in the short run. Export problems will be discussed below, from section 4 onwards. Here the question is not export performance but how, with any given volume of exports, imports are likely to be distributed between food, raw materials and manufactures.

Imports of *raw materials* will be considered first. They are least likely to be disturbed by import restrictions, for it has long been recognised that import restrictions of raw materials would hurt British industry as much as the suppliers. If the past is any guide, the growth of imports of raw materials tends to be associated with the growth of industrial activity in the country. When the rate of employment rises, imports of raw materials will normally rise more than total imports, and when the employment rate is low, the share of raw materials in total imports tends to be low. For a long time before the mid-1960s such a statement could be made almost without qualification. The rise in the imports of manufactures during the 1960s slightly complicates matters, but it qualifies rather than contradicts the above assertion. It will be convenient to consider first the position prior to the mid-1960s, and then the qualifications necessary for the second half of the decade.

Between 1907 and 1965 (8) there were forty-six years of peace-time trading. (9) In twenty-six of these years the employment rate was 95 per cent or higher; (10) and the share of raw materials (11) in the value of total imports varied between 29 and 43 per cent, being usually about one-third. In twenty of those years the employment rate was 91½ per cent or less, and in only two of these years did the share of raw materials in total imports exceed 30 per cent; usually it was between 25 and 29 per cent.

During the first half of the 1960s the share of raw materials in total imports fell from 35 per cent (in 1959) to 30 per cent (in 1964 and 1965), and then fell further to 28 per cent (in 1966) and 27 per cent (in 1967 and 1968). As just stated, in the past a raw-material share of less than 29 per cent would have been associated with an employment rate of 91½ per cent or less. Such a low employment rate would have meant a deep depression. In fact there was no deep depression in 1966-8. Nevertheless there was some fall in the employment rate: it fell from close on 99 per cent (in the early months of 1966) to about 97½ per cent (in mid-1967) and was to remain below 98 per cent throughout 1967 and 1968. (12) Thus it remained true, to 1968, that a raw-material share below 29 per cent was associated with a fall in the employment rate. But it was no longer true, in the 1960s, that this would mean a deep depression. Nevertheless, by the standards of the 1960s there was a fall below the customary rate of employment. It still meant that the rate of unemployment almost doubled.

The preceding implies no forecast. If, in 1907-68, a minimum 29 per cent raw-material share in total imports was associated with a high level of employment by the standards of the time, this will remain true only if other imports do not rise independently. The share of manufactures in total imports rose from 26 per cent in 1958 and 28 per cent in 1959 to 44 per cent in 1967 and 48 per cent in 1968. Should this continue, the share of raw materials may continue to decline. Nevertheless, on the whole raw-material imports are imports for British employment and largely unimpeded by trade controls; while other imports may also assist the British economy, but are primarily for British consumption (in the sense that they need little further processing after importation and before use by the final buyer). Hence some association will continue between the raw-material share in total imports and the rate of employment. It cannot be firmly forecast, however, whether the crucial share will be 29 per cent, as in the past, or whether it will be at some other percentage. If a forecast is nevertheless to be hazarded, it is that any change in that crucial share is likely to be in a downward direction. This point will become clearer after the consideration of structural changes in the British economy, below.

Whatever the crucial share in years to come, the level of economic activity has been, and will continue to be, a major determinant of what happens to the share of raw materials in total imports. In the past years of the century, price movements did not disturb this relationship and may at times have supported it. Perhaps it should be mentioned in this context that there are not enough domestic substitutes available for imported raw materials to keep the wheels of industry turning, and often none at all. Hence domestic raw-material prices cannot often diverge much from prices of imported raw materials. Now if prices of imported raw materials move favourably and there is already full employment, demand is unlikely to rise; and if activity is below the level of full employment, a favourable movement in raw-material prices may raise both demand for such materials and activity. An unfavourable movement in raw-material prices may cause a decline in activity, but this does not appear to have happened for a long time (and certainly not in the post-war years).

The United Kingdom has for some time now been able to ignore the fear of reduced activity through unfavourable movements in prices of imported raw materials, for two main reasons. One is that British incomes have been running sufficiently high to enable firms or their customers to absorb any increases in such prices. The other reason is that the possibility of such price increases is lessened, partly because of structural changes in British industry and partly because of increases in productivity. At the beginning of the century the textile

industry provided more industrial employment than any other industry; in the
1960s the engineering industries have become the principal employers of
industrial labour, and the import content of the output of the modern engineering industries is only about one-third of that of the textile industry in the
past. (13) Moreover firms in competitive industries must use raw materials as
sparingly as possible, if they are to avoid a cost disadvantage; and as experience
in any particular production process is gained, it usually becomes possible to use
materials less wastefully. This year's output of a unit of any particular product
should normally require a lesser raw-material input than last year's. In short,
structural changes and competitive raw-material saving should together make the
British economy less and less dependent on imported raw materials as time goes
by. These tendencies have been further accentuated through achievements in the
production of manufactured substitutes for natural raw materials — as, for
instance, in the substitution of man-made fibres for natural ones. These
manufactured substitutes are often home-produced. The result is that even the
textile industry is now much freer from worry about import prices than it used
to be.

The net result of these various tendencies has been a marked deceleration of
the growth of raw-material imports relatively to national output. Early this
century imports absorbed about one-third of national expenditure, and in
prosperous years raw materials would account for about one-third of total
imports. In the 1960s only one-sixth of national expenditure went on imports,
and less than one-third of that on raw materials. This is a reduction of expenditure on imported raw materials from nearly 2s. 3d. in every pound spent in the
1900s, to less than 1s. in the 1960s. The reduction would appear larger if only
raw materials known at the beginning of the century were included. For
instance, mineral fuels, then hardly known, accounted for about one-third of
imported raw materials in the 1960s. (They are included under 'raw materials',
although the official trade returns now class them separately because they are
raw materials from the point of view of industrialists, householders and
motorists.) Even with the inclusion of mineral fuels, the rise in raw-material
imports has been at only about half the rate of the rise of incomes during the
first two-thirds of the century. Nevertheless the share of raw materials in total
imports is still linked to the state of prosperity. In other words there has been a
secular decline in the marginal propensity to import, and other imports have not
taken the place of the saved raw materials.

Other imports, and especially *manufactures*, might have taken the place of
some of the saved raw materials had there not been increasing protection during
the first half of the century. As it was, the share of manufactures in total
imports was a fairly constant quarter of the whole during the free-trade years of
the century, before the First World War; during the era of moderate protection

in the 1920s; during the protectionist 1930s; during the even more protectionist late 1940s; and in the years of trade liberalisation in the 1950s. This share would rise or fall in individual years, but would not diverge for long. Before the 1960s it always came back to one-quarter. But in the course of the 1960s it rose from about one-quarter to about one-half. Since this followed the final abolition of quantitative import controls on manufactures towards the end of the 1950s, some commentators have taken the view that trade liberalisation has gone too far and that a reimposition of quantitative import controls would have eased some of the balance-of-payments difficulties of the 1960s. It might have done, in so far as it could have eliminated one-quarter of the imports of the late 1960s; but it would also have frozen the import structure to meet the requirements of the past, and might therefore have done no more than defer some of the problems of the 1960s to the 1970s. Whether this would or would not have been so will be discussed later in this section. But first there must be some more explanation as to why the share of manufactures used to be steady before the 1960s, and of the influences which determine the share of food.

Ignoring for the moment the unprecedently high and rising share of manufactures in total imports in the 1960s, the former long-term constancy of the share of manufactures may be explained as follows. Years of high activity were years of high raw-material imports, so that the share of other imports was kept down. At the same time years of high activity were also years of high incomes and thus years of more spending on manufactures, whether home-produced or imported. Since personal incomes tended to rise before an increased domestic output became available (simply because most factors had to be paid during the process of production and only the rewards of capital were deferred until afterwards), an increase in imports was likely whenever personal incomes rose. These additional imports were abandoned when activity slackened; and since imports of raw materials also slackened, the share of manufactures in total imports could be maintained.

In other words the demand for imported manufactures varied with incomes, and so was income-elastic rather than price-elastic. The main reason why income changes rather than price changes determined imports of manufactures appears to have been the following. The British economy is a highly diversified industrial economy, and there cannot be many manufactured products which could not be produced within this economy. Moreover, until there was absolute scarcity of factors, output of almost any product could always be raised without proportionate inflation. In consequence the prices manufactures could bear in the home market were normally set by home producers. Exceptions occurred in the days of post-war shortages of, say, steel, when home producers did not raise prices in accordance with the market scarcities then prevailing, while foreign producers did. But that was the result of official intervention or the fear of official intervention, and such behaviour is unlikely to occur in many industries over any length of peace-time trading. Occasionally it was alleged that foreign producers sold at unduly low prices, but such allegations were made more often than substantiated. It could not pay a foreign producer to sell in this country, at, say, 10 per cent below the prevailing British price, unless he could divert from other markets quantities equivalent to 10 per cent of his British sales and do so without undue loss. This could be done when other markets were depressed. But depressions are seldom localised for long, so that British incomes would also be affected and all manufacturers have to lower their prices in order to maintain their sales. If past experience is any guide, prices of imported manufactures and prices of domestically produced manufactures are unlikely to diverge by much and for long. Nor have they. (14)

Before turning to the increase in the share of manufactures in total imports in the 1960s, *food* will be considered. The main point is that as long as imports of raw materials and manufactures are functions of what happens to domestic incomes and activity, food becomes the variable item amongst British imports.

Imported food tends to be cheaper than home-produced food. This has been true for a long time, and it is still true, even if the difference is not apparent from the prices payable in shops. The difference is hidden, since the agricultural support scheme, in force since 1947, leaves market prices to be determined largely by import prices. Domestic farmers are protected through a system of deficiency payments; the Government spends some of the taxpayers' money on compensating farmers for the difference between a target price and achieved market prices (where the target price is negotiated between the Ministry of Agriculture and the National Farmers' Union on the basis of domestic costs, and the market price largely determined by import prices).

At no time in the twentieth century has all the food eaten in this country been produced in this country. Nor could it have been produced within the country without major structural changes. Home producers could never have complete control over the price, since they could not satisfy all of domestic demand, while overseas producers might have done. Thus food imports are not only the variable amongst British imports but are also differently determined. Their volume is not determined in the same way as that of other imports; it is not so much a function of British incomes and activity as a function of overseas prices.

The implications are twofold. Since the availability of cheap food is a chief determinant of anybody's current standard of living, the British standard of living is largely influenced by the British balance of payments: for balance-of-payments success or failure determines how much of the variable item can be afforded at world prices. The second implication is that the British balance of payments is particularly susceptible to changes in overseas food prices. The British economy determines the prices of manufactures and raw materials in the

British market, and does so in accordance with domestic incomes; but it lets itself be guided by world markets for its food prices. (15) It is sometimes over-looked that British balance-of-payments difficulties are almost invariably preceded by sharp changes in world food prices. The balance-of-payments difficulties of the mid-1960s were no exception. Import prices of food rose by 9 per cent between 1962 and 1964. (16) The subsequent efforts to improve the balance of payments were not just problems of high finance; what was involved was whether it would be possible to afford as much food, at world prices, as before. In other words it was a question of the standard of living, and especially a question of the standard of living of the poorer sections of the community (who spend relatively more on food).

If food is the variable amongst British imports, food imports are dependent on the long-term balance-of-payments position. It does not follow that there are special variations in volumes of food imports during a trade cycle. On the contrary; given long-term balance-of-payments success, there are likely to be fewer cyclical variations in food imports than in other imports. Thus in depression, low incomes and low activity will keep down the imports of manufactures and raw materials. The share of food imports in total imports is then likely to rise (irrespective of what may happen to absolute amounts). If there are quality differentials between home and imported foods, and these quality differentials are reflected in price, the marginal propensity to consume the cheaper imported food may rise as incomes fall or fail to rise at the accustomed rate. (This holds even under the deficiency payments scheme of price support, since it does not normally interfere with quality differentials.) In times of prosperity the opposite is likely. High incomes and high activity will raise imports of manufactures and raw materials. At the same time the marginal propensity to consume high-quality food is likely to rise; and home-produced food is often fresher and so of higher quality than imported food. Partly because of the rise of other trade and partly because of the shift in demand, the share of food in total imports is likely to fall as prosperity rises. Thus the variability of food imports in relation to total incomes and total imports is compatible with relative stability in the volume of food imported – provided balance-of-payments difficulties are ephemeral.

Long-run balance-of-payments trends are, however, reflected in the proportion of food imported. Nineteenth- and early twentieth-century industrial and financial successes allowed the United Kingdom to import half of her food requirements in the years before 1914, being two-fifths of total imports in prosperous years, when the share of raw materials in total imports was high. In the inter-war years this country still imported half of her food, being then half of her total imports, in a period of long-drawn-out depression and low share of raw materials in total imports. By the 1960s only two-fifths of food was imported. In 1960 this accounted for one-third of total imports. It then fell, and, by 1968, was slightly below one-quarter. The share of food in total imports had not been as low as one-quarter at any time between the abolition of the Corn Laws (1846) and 1967. (17)

Throughout, two tendencies appear to have influenced the share of food in total imports. One is the cyclical tendency for the share of food to fall, relatively to that of raw materials, in times of prosperity. By historic standards, even the mid-1960s were years of high activity. Hence the somewhat greater fall in the share of food than in the share of raw materials was in accordance with expectations. (The fall of both was due to the rising share of manufactures, which was a new development and will be considered towards the end of this section.) The other tendency appears to be a secular fall in the share of food in total imports.

This secular tendency is sometimes difficult to discern. Sometimes it was counter to the cyclical tendency, and sometimes it was accentuated by special developments, such as the rising share of manufactures in the 1960s. Consequently all comparisons of different periods during the present century must allow for special developments. Nevertheless it may be of some use to compare the relatively prosperous years before 1914 with the prosperous years of the early 1960s. This shows a fall in the share of food in total imports from about two-fifths to about one-third. If it is legitimate to compare the deeply depressed inter-war years with the mildly recessed mid-1960s, the fall was from one-half to one-quarter. Whatever the value of any particular comparison, it is impossible to obliterate the impression of a secular fall of the share of food in total imports. This fall is even larger in relation to national expenditure. As mentioned before, in the course of this century the proportion of national expenditure on all imports fell from one-third to one-sixth.

The chief reason for the fall in the share of food in total imports (and the share of total imports in national expenditure) was the balance of payments. Cheap food imports depended on balance-of-payments success, and balance-of-payments success depended on the United Kingdom's comparative advantage in manufacturing and finance. This comparative advantage remains. But as will be shown in later sections, it is no longer a comparative advantage in almost all manufactures and all financial activities over all of the outside world. By now the comparative advantages over some of the outside world is confined to certain manufactures and certain financial activities. Although a comparative advantage in fewer goods and services is compatible with any balance-of-payments result, it can be favourable once the necessary structural adjustments are made. Whatever the future may hold, a balance-of-payments surplus of the size of the 1913 one (at constant prices) is far off. Even in the 1920s and the 1950s, when the balance of payments was normally in surplus, the surpluses never matched the 1913 one (at constant prices). The reduced surpluses limited the possible rise in imports. Given that food is the variable amongst British imports, the balance of payments no longer allowed for as much reliance on imported food as had been possible earlier this century. Domestic food production had to be raised by one protectionist device or another. Cheap food prices in the shops could be maintained only through subsidising domestic farmers at the taxpayers' expense. The poor still benefited, but they benefited indirectly from a policy of domestic redistribution of incomes (in favour of farmers) rather than from the country's industrial and financial supremacy.

Although the balance of payments was the main reason why reliance on cheap imported food had to become less, it was not the sole reason. There were changes in the quantity and quality of food demanded. The twentieth-century increase in population has been less than the nineteenth-century increase, so that there was less increase in the amount demanded. At the same time real incomes continued to rise, and this led to a shift in demand towards higher-quality foods, be they fresher home-produced foods or imported foods cleanly packed by domestic distributors. In either event there was some reduction in the import cost of food expenditure, although there was no reduction in consumers' expenditure on food. (18) There were changes not only in demand but also in potential supply. The efficiency of British agriculture has increased over the century, and by the 1960s much of it had become highly sophisticated and capital-intensive. At the same time many of the overseas suppliers sold more of their food in their own home markets, and so had less available for export to this and other countries. Moreover temperate-zone food production anywhere in the world has become increasingly capital-intensive, and so has to compete more and more with manufacturing industries for factors. In consequence there was a move towards assimilation of agricultural factor prices to industrial factor prices, and product prices could not fail to be affected. In short the United Kingdom cannot afford to rely as much on imported food as in the past, but she neither wants nor needs to raise expenditure on imported food as much as in the past; and even if she did, she might meet increasing difficulties in obtaining it. The latter difficulties could be overcome only through further development of comparative advantages in other activities, which would benefit the balance of payments. The argument thus reverts to the balance of payments.

As long as food is the variable amongst British imports, an important element in the British standard of living depends on the comparative advantage of British manufactures and finance over imported food. Yet while exports rose throughout the 1960s, and so would have allowed for a rise in the British standard of living through more imports of cheap food (in terms of manufactures), imports of *manufactures* have risen more than other imports. As mentioned before, in the course of the 1960s they rose from one-quarter of the total to one-half. Is this a cause for regret?

It is not. It would be cause for regret only if the sole way towards higher standards of living were via cheap food. That this path was successfully trodden before 1914 does not mean it is the only way for the 1970s. The rise in imports of manufactures might also be a cause for regret if full employment became endangered, and imports might endanger domestic employment were they largely imports of labour-intensive manufactures (in terms of British factor scarcities). This was not the case in the 1960s. The unemployment rates of the mid-1960s may have been higher than those experienced earlier in the post-war period, and they may have approached the Keynes–Beveridge level. Historically, however, any unemployment rate of less than 5 per cent reflects a high level of activity. Even the highest national unemployment rates of the mid-1960s were nowhere as high as 5 per cent. (19) Moreover the increases in imports of manufactures in the 1960s were notably in sophisticated machine-tools and engineering products. These did not so much endanger the employment of British labour as help to overcome the scarcity of British capital. If the country is to export more and prosper, it must overcome the scarcity of capital largely through factor-saving innovations. This can, however, be aided by imports of capital-intensive goods. There should not be investment to replace those imports, but investment to pay for them.

In the past, imports of food were imports for consumption, and imports of raw materials were imports for employment. Before the 1960s, imports of manufactures largely reflected the state of domestic incomes. On the basis of this import structure rested much of the prosperity of the 1900s. This import structure survived the 1913 world by almost half a century, but it ceased to be so important as a basis of domestic prosperity. In consequence such imports became less necessary and the proportion of national expenditure on imports halved over the first two-thirds of the century. This was no cause for self-congratulation on balance-of-payments grounds. For it reflected the relatively slow growth of the British economy during that half-century, and it was part of the cause. Politics, traditional trading ties, imperfect economic foresight, and the like, all combined to prevent the British economy from specialising as much on some capital-intensive trades as might have been technically feasible and from buying the remainder abroad. If imports of specialised manufactures should continue to rise, one of the impediments in the way of faster British economic growth will be overcome.

For in a mature economy, where all factors are scarce, the purpose of imports includes circumvention of the scarcity of factors. This requires more specialisation between manufacturers the world over. The British import structure must adjust itself to the new need. There will still be food imports for consumption. There will still be imports of raw materials for traditional employment. But both must recede somewhat, as manufactures for more profitable employment also come into the country. The imports of manufactures have thus ceased to be a mere reflection of domestic incomes. Much of the new imports of manufactures are imports for employment. To that extent they have come to resemble imports of raw materials. But they are imports for different kinds of employment. Changes in the volume of raw-material imports are associated with changes in the level of employment; and if there is already full employment, such imports are unlikely to rise disproportionately to total imports. Changes in the new imports of manufactures are more likely to be associated with changes in the quality of employment; and if there is already full employment, activity can grow only if factors are more effectively deployed. Since this normally requires more capital goods, a fully employed economy's demand for more capital goods can in part be met from abroad. If there is free trade between industrial countries, this will lead to increasing specialisation in different capital goods. Although there was not complete freedom of trade between the United Kingdom and the major industrial countries, trade became freer. The result was more specialisation and an increasing international 'division of capital'.

The traditional international division of labour still persists and remains important. Thus towards the end of the 1960s about one-quarter of imports were still imports of cheap food for mass consumption. About another quarter were imports of raw materials (including mineral fuels) to maintain traditional employment in manufacturing. If pre-1960 experience is any guide, another quarter consisted of the sort of manufactures which reflect changes in domestic incomes. The new development of the 1960s was the importation of manufactures for employment. Such imports reflected the growing international division of capital, and this affected the import trade as well as the export trade. In this international division of capital, the chief criterion is not cheapness but quality. If the United Kingdom can import (as well as export) high-quality tools for industry, domestic production becomes more profitable and exports more attractive to overseas customers. The prime overseas trade precept for the British economy is no longer 'buy cheap', but 'sell quality'. Hence the import structure had to change.

4   THE NATURE OF BRITISH EXPORTS

The United Kingdom still needs imported raw materials to work with, and imported food to have a well-fed population. She now also wants imported manufactures in order to prosper. In the mid-1960s, all that absorbed about one-sixth of national expenditure. (20) It was paid for out of the proceeds of the exports of merchandise, services and borrowing. Services will be considered in Chapter 25 below, and borrowing will be referred to in Chapter 26. Here only exports of merchandise will be considered. Although exports of merchandise have seldom paid for all of the United Kingdom's imports, they make the principal contribution towards paying for them.

About nine-tenths of the exports of merchandise in the 1960s were manufactures. Other commodity groups contributed about 3 per cent each. They were food, raw materials and mineral fuels (which include the once important coal trade). In short the United Kingdom pays for her imports mainly with exports of manufactures. Over the first two post-war decades the most successful amongst those exports were products of innovating industries. Examples are the products of the engineering industries (such as aircraft engines, telecommunications apparatus and office machinery) and of the chemical industries (especially synthetic plastics). (21)

Most success with these new products was achieved in trade with other industrial countries. The reason was that Africa and India could not afford to spend so much on, say, aviation as North America and Western Europe. At first sight it may seem surprising that growing markets could be found for such goods in North America and Western Europe, which after all could produce such goods for themselves. The surprise wanes once it is realised that North America and Western Europe too have prospered over most of the first two post-war decades. In varying degrees they too have approached general scarcity of factors, which normally implies greater scarcity of capital than of other factors. The industrial world as a whole has an increasing interest in the international division of capital; and the British economy, the most mature of the major advanced economies, has probably a greater interest in it than most. Nevertheless the United Kingdom participated less in this international division of capital than most industrial countries. Why this was so will become apparent later in this chapter and in the following two chapters.

More participation in the international division of capital requires more concentration on capital-intensive activities, in the sense that increased output depends more on additional input of capital than of labour. In the sections on imports it was simply accepted that manufacturing is usually more capital-intensive than primary production, and modern manufacturing more capital-intensive than traditional. Over long periods and broad product groups this was probably true in most of the first two-thirds of the century. It must be stressed that these definitions apply at the margin. Applied to export problems, what matters is whether additional export production requires a greater input of capital than of labour. It will be recalled from Part III that in a mature economy, where all factors are scarce, only further applications of capital can circumvent the scarcity of all factors, and that only new capital can save both capital and labour. Further problems arise as to when exactly activity becomes more capital-intensive, and there are problems as to what should be included under the term 'capital'. These problems will now be dealt with.

A capital-intensive activity may be defined as one where net output is high *and* rising, and one where overhead costs have not yet been recouped. If total output rises (and price does not fall correspondingly), total receipts become greater relatively to overhead costs, so that overhead costs fall per unit of output. In other words the capital–input ratio has been raised effectively, so that the capital–output ratio can now fall. As long as it is possible to produce more at lower unit cost, the particular activity can be said to be in a state of increasing returns on capital employed. In some industries, and nowadays especially in some of the major branches of the engineering and chemical trades, products can become obsolescent relatively sooner than in other industries. In industries with a large number of products which are prone to rapid product obsolescence, there is an almost continuous need for injections of capital. Such industries never seem to get out of the increasing returns (on capital) stage. They bear much uncertainty because of the overall emphasis on new products. If markets are brought to 'criticality' quickly, the benefit is reaped in declining average costs and rising profits. Overseas tariffs, however, tax the exporters' profits and so limit the profitability of exports. If profits rise less, the effort of selling abroad has fewer rewards. This is of special importance to the new industries. Fewer exports mean a smaller output and a lesser fall in average costs. The growth potential of the new industries is thus particularly susceptible to the adverse effects of overseas tariffs.

If overseas tariffs or low overseas incomes restrict the size of the market, sales may be inadequate for proper utilisation and recoupment of capital. The industries concerned may be unable to survive without government support. Government support, however, means taxation, and therefore lower net profits for other industries which have to pay the taxes but may themselves face similar problems.

Thus the opportunities offered by increasing returns may be enhanced by free access to wider markets, and especially to prosperous markets. The new industries' case for free trade rests upon their need to recoup capital quickly. They need rapidly increasing returns. Consequently they seek the widest possible markets. There are such industries in each industrial country. Normally they are amongst the growth industries within each industrial economy, and they also tend to be amongst the most successful in exports to other industrial countries. Overseas tariffs thus limit not only the export prospects of the new industries, but also restrain national economic growth. British experience in the 1950s and 1960s was no exception.

Increasing returns are not solely confined to material capital. They can also accrue to 'brains'. Brains are in part a gift of God and in part trained by man. The training takes time and normally requires a substantial capital input, though the material capital input may have taken place many years ago. The training of scientists, technologists and economists takes time and involves considerable capital outlays on colleges, laboratories and libraries. Such training entitles the recipient to an educational rent, so that he earns a salary and not a mere wage. This educational rent is the reward for skills acquired in the past and applied at present, so that the salary-earner should be capable of using factors more intelligently than the average wage-earner. In other words he should be an innovator, or at least receptive to innovation. Without disrespect to any salary-earner, he should be a piece of 'walking capital'. If so, his educational rent is justified. In the present context the use of brains should encourage factor-saving activity and therefore an innovating one. Usually this factor saving implies the installation of material capital equipment, whether at the university the 'walking capital' attended in years gone by or at the plant where he is working now. Walking capital is most successful if the market for his ideas is wide, whether these be ideas embodied in a patent or his firm's products. His potential salary as well as his firm's profits benefit from increasing returns and thus from widening markets. This gives the salariat an interest in a successful export trade.

In the following, the term 'capital-intensive' is used to denote that an increase in output depends more on the additional application of material and walking capital than on additions of pure labour. Throughout it should be borne in mind that this is of relevance only to marginal changes. These are the relevant changes in the present context, since they determine (or reflect) whether any particular activity grows. Any activities which do not imply innovation are called 'labour-intensive'.

The capital-intensive industries (as here defined) are the industries most likely to reap increasing returns on capital employed (as here defined). The reason is that they are likely to have widening markets, so that capital is spread over a larger output. They are likely to have widening markets because their goods may be new (as a result of product innovation) or less costly (as a result of process innovation) or both. Markets widen if the new goods are in response to a latent demand but have not been marketed for long. Once the goods are accepted, demand is likely to rise. This allows for an increase in output. If the goods initially require a greater increase in capital input than in labour input (so as to give them an innovational edge or alter the production function or both), the widening market leads to increasing returns on new capital employed.

The products of capital-intensive industries tend to be amongst the most sophisticated of the day, being the products of innovative ingenuity and the best material aids. Because such products are generally produced under conditions of increasing returns on capital employed, they are relatively expensive; marginal-cost pricing is precluded, since overheads on material capital could not be covered, nor the salaries of walking capital (whose educational rent could be regarded as a contribution to the 'overhead costs' of becoming walking capital). Such products must be priced at average costs. Since average costs are in excess of marginal costs as long as there are increasing returns, the products are in a sense 'expensive'. In consequence such products are most saleable where incomes are high, and where markets are as keen on technological achievements as they are in this country. These markets are in Western Europe, North America and Australasia. When they increase their purchases of British goods, they look for the products of capital-intensive ingenuity, and they are willing to pay the appropriately high price.

The world outside Western Europe, North America and Australasia has different requirements. The less developed countries do not so much aspire to the new as to the known. They do not buy the latest aircraft which they could neither afford nor fly. They rather want clothing, furnishings, the older models of motor-cars, and the tools and machines for the less capital-intensive activities. It so happens that about half of the United Kingdom's exports go to countries whose wants are mainly of this nature. Their share in the British export trade has been declining for some time, partly because of greater British export successes elsewhere and partly because overseas development itself converts more and more of overseas demand from the known to the new. But as long as such countries take about half of British exports, their requirements cannot be ignored. The new industries have relatively little to offer to such customers. The latter's wants will often be better met by industries that have passed out of the increasing returns (on capital) stage.

It does not follow that one set of industries should do all the exporting to advanced countries and another set of industries should do all the exporting to less developed countries. This division of products into increasing and decreasing returns sectors does not correspond to the traditional definition of industries. Nowadays industries are multi-product, so that it is no longer possible to classify all their activities under a single heading of increasing or decreasing returns. The overall cost structure of an industry represents a weighted average of all the component activities. This overall cost structure reveals little about the relevant decision-making process with respect to individual products. Individual activities must be distinguished. The following example may illustrate this point. A new model of a motor-car cannot be produced without the installation of new capital which is different from the capital used before. In other words there must be capital deepening. Part of the motor-car industry is then in the stage of increasing returns (on capital employed) until a certain output of the new model is reached. That is when, with the existing labour force, the firm's capital is fully utilised. Afterwards the model concerned becomes an old model, for diminishing returns set in and output can be increased only by the employment of more labour or through capital widening. To take labour first, there is a limit to the amount of labour that can be employed with existing capital; but the range may be wide, since spare capacity can often be reduced, shift working introduced and the like. During the stage when output can be increased through the employment of more labour relatively to capital, the industry is becoming more labour-intensive. The possibility of capital widening somewhat complicates the argument, but does not upset it. Capital widening is a repetition of known processes with known factor proportions. It does not involve uncertainty-bearing in the way capital deepening does. In contrast to capital deepening, which is a venture into the unknown, capital widening repeats the known. To produce more units of a model of a motor-car which the market is used to, involves the repetition of human toil; and a reduction of unit costs may involve the employment of more labour or of more efficient labour relatively to capital. The production of a known model is, at the margin, a labour-intensive activity; it is becoming more labour-intensive as experience with the capital structure is gained and the capital structure is increasingly taken as given.

In terms of factor utilisation within the British economy, most of the old-established industries are in the category of labour-intensive industries. Given the general scarcity of factors in the British economy, the question arises whether the persistence of such industries helps or hinders the prospects for export growth. The chief domestic case for their retention is that they can make do with existing capital. The new industries may be the industries which can help most with the saving of capital, the scarcest of factors. But they must incur the cost of capital deepening before the new capital can save aggregate capital and other factors. This takes time. Moreover, if the new capital is to pay, markets must widen. Until the prospects for wider markets in the industrial world are further improved, the labour-intensive industries must remain important. In the international context the British labour-intensive industries may be capital-intensive from the point of view of importing countries, since the establishment of such industries within their national economies would involve a great deal of capital deepening. Thus as long as there are technically less developed countries overseas, there will be a demand for the products of British labour-intensive industries.

The last point indicates that the British labour-intensive industries are labour-intensive only from the point of view of production possibilities within the British economy (or within other advanced economies). Large parts of the world cannot produce what the British labour-intensive industries produce; and they could not hope to produce the same kind of goods unless they went in for substantial capital deepening within their countries. From their point of view, British labour-intensive industries can be capital-intensive. This continues unless and until capital deepening in their countries has gone far enough to make their domestic industries as capital-intensive as their rival British industries. By that time the United Kingdom will cease to find export markets for the goods concerned. The process can be accelerated by overseas protection, as the British cotton textile industry has found out to its cost.

Whatever the details, British exports must always come from capital-intensive industries (as seen by the importing country). Goods which are labour-intensive in the United Kingdom are liable to be amongst the first to become capital-intensive abroad. They then cease to be exported, at least in their former quantities. Goods which are capital-intensive in an advanced country, such as the United Kingdom, are also likely to be amongst the most capital-intensive overseas. In order to sell well abroad, British goods must always be more capital-intensive than similar goods produced in the importing country concerned.

If so, it follows that an underemployed British economy, which has abundance of factors, can always raise exports through producing more labour-intensive and known goods for sale in technically less advanced countries. A fully employed British economy, faced with general scarcity of factors, cannot easily produce more known goods, so that its export success must depend increasingly on the production of new goods for sale in economically advanced countries.

5   THE DESTINATION OF BRITISH EXPORTS

The nature of exports determines their possible destination. This statement is also true in reverse: the ease and difficulty of access to the markets of various countries determines the overall nature of the export trade.

The history of the British cotton textile trade provides an example. In the early nineteenth century, British cotton textiles were capital-intensive from the whole world's point of view. In the 1820s half of British cotton textile exports went to continental Europe, then the richest part of the world outside the United Kingdom; one-tenth were sold in the United States; and only one-twentieth in the Far East. By the 1880s only one-twelfth of British cotton textile exports went to Europe, only one-fiftieth to the United States and one-half to the Far East. (22) By the mid-twentieth century, protection and development in the Far East had restricted those markets for British cotton textiles, and the United Kingdom actually became a net importer of cotton textiles from the Far East. There were no further substantial markets left where British cotton textiles were something 'new'. British cotton textile exports, such as they still are, are fairly thinly spread over the world. But where British cotton textiles left off, the British man-made fibre textile trade appears to be repeating the earlier stages of the pattern; they sell best in North America, Australasia and Western Europe. In general those trades sell best in those areas for the simple reason that those markets are rich enough to afford new goods as well as known ones.

The rich markets can be further subdivided. The old Dominions and Europe form one group, and the United States one by itself. The post-war pattern of destination of the more successful exports was often as follows. Success tended to come first in Europe and the old Dominions, only later in the United States and later still elsewhere. That is how it was in motor-cars, aircraft engines, plastics and several other commodities. In many instances this is visible in the export statistics. In other instances, however, exports become invisible; overseas producers may acquire the appropriate patents for their markets, and the balance-of-payments credit comes in the form of royalty receipts rather than in the form of visible exports. (It may be added that, when such exports become invisible, the British industry concerned may take longer to get out of the increasing returns stage, because British capital is utilised less at home.)

The reason why the old Dominions and Europe tend to be the first successful export markets is as follows. The economies most like the United Kingdom's are in Europe, and the economies most built in the United Kingdom's image are in the old Dominions. Those economies are comparable with the United Kingdom's. If British manufacturers try to market a new and capital-intensive good, they will normally seek for openings in the home market and in markets most like the home market. For in such markets the article concerned is most likely to be both new and within the reach of potential customers' pockets. To sell the same article in the United States often requires perfection before it can appear as capital-intensive and new in the richest market in the world. That stage can be presumed to be near the peak of success, when experience has been gained and sales are large enough to allow for lower prices (of a good still produced under increasing returns on capital employed). The peak of success is achieved when no further capital deepening is possible, when the product is as good and as cheap as it is ever likely to be. Then the time is ripe for capital widening. Capital widening usually means standardisation and cheapening of the product for mass consumption, by cutting out some of the trimmings and selling at a price equal to marginal cost. Then and only then is the product likely to be within the reach of the relatively poor, at home or overseas.

To sum up: Europe and the old Dominions are the British exporters' trial grounds. Sales in the United States are the peak of success. Sales elsewhere provide this country's bread and butter. If the past is any guide, this is the normal pattern of events. But history does not only consist of success stories. Often there was lack of success. Was it because, when sales to the trial grounds are impeded, there are just fewer success stories to be told?

6 DIVISION OF EXPORT INTERESTS

If British exports to the old Dominions, Western Europe and the United States are lumped together as 'exports to economically advanced countries', exports to advanced countries accounted for somewhat under half of total British exports in the early 1950s, and for somewhat over half in the late 1960s. For the 1950s and 1960s taken together, it can be said that about half of British exports went to advanced countries, and, with some liberty of language, 'the growing half'. The advanced countries have economies which to varying degrees are competitive with the British economy (in the sense that most of what they produce is, or could be, produced in the United Kingdom, and most of what is produced in the United Kingdom is, or could be, produced in those economies).

The other 'half' of British exports went to complementary economies (in the sense that their exports consisted predominantly of goods which cannot be produced in the United Kingdom, or cannot be produced in the United Kingdom in adequate quantities; and in the sense that their economies cannot or would not produce what the United Kingdom produces – at least not for many years to come). Such trade accounted for over half of British exports in the early 1950s and for less than half towards the end of the 1960s. Taking the 1950s and 1960s together, such trade constituted the 'declining half' of British exports.

Given a near 50:50 division of British export interests, and given consistently low growth rates in the complementary economies and consistently high ones in the competitive economies, British economic growth should be at about half the rate of the growth of competitive economies and about three-quarters the rate of the growth of the world economy. This assumes that British economic growth was export-led; and this assumption is valid in the absence of special British population growth and in the absence of inventions and innovations which could only be applied in the United Kingdom.

Although the fortunes of individual countries and trades varied, world economic progress was most concentrated where it had already reached the highest levels; (23) and the most marked growth of world trade was in trade in manufactures between advanced industrial countries. The British economy adjusted itself to this situation through greater increase in trade with competitive countries than with all countries. Since this adjustment benefited only half of the United Kingdom's export interests, the rate of growth of total British exports was at about half the rate of growth of world exports of manufactures. In the absence of special causes of growth, the British economy's growth rate is export-determined. If so, the British economy would just about maintain its competitive position within the industrial world if its growth rate was at about half the rate of the industrial world's. This was achieved. (24) By implication, the growth rate was at approximately three-quarters of the world's rate, and as far as this can be estimated, this too was achieved. (25)

It may be thought that the United Kingdom's competitive efficiency in the world economy should have increased rather than just been maintained, at a time when trade in manufactures grew more than other trade — which should suit an industrial country. But that requires a consistent policy, designed to assist industries which produce what sells best in other industrial countries (as could be pursued in the United States, France, Western Germany and other countries whose main exporting interests lie in the markets of other industrial countries). An alternative policy would be to work against the trend and try to capture larger shares of markets in complementary economies (as was done by Japan both before and after the Second World War). If it is clear where the majority of exporting interests lie, a consistent policy can be pursued. The United Kingdom, however, turned hither and thither, since nobody could state for certain where her majority interests lay. In the course of the 1960s a consensus appears to have emerged that the future lies more with exports to industrial countries than with exports to more complementary economies. This view came to prevail as trade with advanced countries became the 'larger half' of trade. But it takes time to translate new attitudes into policies (even if there were no political complications), and even more time before such policies can show results. Whether this new attitude is in the United Kingdom's long-term interest depends on whether trends in the world economy continue along the lines of the 1950s and 1960s. These trends in turn will continue to be in the whole industrial world's interest, as long as high levels of activity can be maintained — so that path-breaking innovations must be in capital deepening and factor saving, and their full utilisation requires widening markets.

On the assumption that world economic developments in the 1950s and 1960s are a guide to British export policies in the 1970s, it will be possible to pursue a clearer policy towards exports. This involves changes in former attitudes towards trade and trading partners, as well as towards trade policies. The alternative trade policies, and some of their implications, will be discussed in sections 7 and 8 below.

7　EXPORT POLICIES: THE OLD RECIPE

Until the 1950s, it seemed reasonable to assume that the United Kingdom's overseas trading interests lay chiefly in the exchange of manufactures for primary products. Even towards the end of the 1960s, such interests constituted nearly half of the country's export interests, albeit the declining 'half'. But even if this aspect of the United Kingdom's overseas trading interests should recede further in relative importance, it must remain significant. The purpose of the present section is to examine what sort of policies could, or should, be pursued with reference to this 'declining half' of exports.

It is always possible to expand business at home or abroad through selling a known product more cheaply than before, or through selling a new product for which there is demand but no perfect substitute. Since the problem of this section is trade with countries whose exports are largely primary products and whose demand for British goods is largely a demand for known goods, the relevant recommendation is to sell known goods at lower prices than before, or at least at lower prices than others charge. The industries which produce known goods are normally in the labour-intensive stage of development (as defined in section 4 of this chapter), and price tends to equal marginal prime costs. Should one firm, in an industry concerned, find ways of lowering prime costs, it will lower price correspondingly. Other firms in the same industry must either follow suit or go out of business. Price must be kept as low as is compatible with staying in business, because there is competition between firms for patronage in given markets. Income effects are incidental; customers' real incomes rise when the goods they used to buy are now cheaper, and this may raise their demand for the cheapened products. But price considerations are the primary considerations; the size of one firm's market can expand by more than the rise in real income, even if the demand for the product is fairly inelastic, since the demand for one firm's products is always more elastic than the demand for the whole industry's products.

In export markets the following further considerations apply. If there is an established industry in the importing country which rivals the exporting industry concerned, and the exporters reduce prices, the established industry suffers. British cotton textiles once did that to the Indian industry. The latter have since returned the compliment. If there is no established industry, or the established industry is bankrupted, the exports become beneficial to the importing country's consumers who would otherwise have to go without the goods concerned. The benefit to consumers in the importing country is the greater, the cheaper British exports are.

In international markets there is usually competition from other industrial countries or from a local industry that has managed to survive outsiders' competition. Under such circumstances an exporting country's share of the market depends on continuous price vigilance; price must always be kept below a level which would let too many rivals in. The continuous need for cheapening is even greater than in a competitive home market, since cost reductions by any rival firm anywhere in the world might have adverse effects. Since the concern is with exports of known goods, and known goods are normally produced by labour-intensive industries; firms in such industries must continuously try to keep wages as low as possible.

Government policies to further the exports of labour-intensive industries must take such considerations into account. But they must also take into account whether the domestic economy suffers from unemployment or whether it is fully employed. First, assume that there is unemployment at home, so that there is general abundance of factors and capital is more abundant than labour. Where capital is relatively abundant, it should be cheap, and a cheap money policy is appropriate. A cheap money policy encourages the widening of capital and so enables more exports without restriction of the home market. Such export success is achieved at a price: more of the same goods are available, so that unit prices of exports are likely to fall. Success can then be sustained only when overseas demand is highly elastic within the relevant price range, so that quantities exported increase proportionately more than unit prices fall. Such a policy seemed appropriate in the 1930s, but was frustrated by overseas and home events. Overseas, trade barriers rose and rising trade barriers normally restrict trade to 'essentials', for which demand tends to be rather inelastic. At home, wages could not be reduced sufficiently to make the policy work. Nor is it at all certain whether any feasible reduction in wages could have succeeded in the face of high and rising trade barriers.

Now assume that there is full employment at home, so that all factors are scarce and capital is becoming scarcer than labour. Cheap money would encourage waste of the scarcer factor. In any case, where capital is already fully employed, capital widening puts additional pressure on already scarce capital resources, and so raises the cost of capital (for any particular purpose) without appropriate increase in returns. Moreover capital widening does not by itself encourage greater overseas sales efforts at falling unit prices, and when the home market prospers, potential exporters may shun such tasks.

The only way to ensure capital widening for export from a fully employed economy is to restrict the home market by means of high interest rates and other deflationary restraints. The total volume of capital in the economy may then be constant, and yet more of the available capital is devoted to export production. The result is the same as if there had been capital widening for the export sector.

If an established industry previously sold a high proportion of its output at home and the restriction of the home market is severe, there can be beneficial price effects in export markets — at least for a time. For the established producers normally work under conditions of increasing costs, so that the reduction of output lowers unit costs. With lower prices, exports may rise until the rise in exports equals the fall in home sales. By that time the initial beneficial price effect is offset, since total output and unit costs are once more what they were before. To maintain the gain in export markets, home sales must continuously be restricted by more than the quantitative increase in exports. The result could be that the home economy becomes depressed and underemployed — by which time a cheap money policy might once more be resorted to.

The old recipe for encouraging the export of known goods ultimately works best when the economy operates below the level of full employment. Below this level capital is the more abundant factor (than labour) and capital widening is both feasible and desirable. Capital widening can take the form of duplication of efforts by existing firms, or it can take the form of duplication of the efforts of existing firms by newcomers to the industry. The latter ensure that costs will always be kept low, so that price can be kept low. Since falling prices are required, firms can maintain their profits only through expansion of output.

The argument rules out the expansion of the home market relatively to overseas markets. Hence there must be greater expansion of overseas markets than in the home market; and if no more new countries can be opened up, this result depends on greater growth of overseas incomes than of home incomes (which requires an appropriate domestic deflation, or at least less inflation at home than overseas). As long as overseas incomes rise more than home incomes, the continuous 'fall' in price becomes tolerable; it can start from a relatively high level (in relation to domestic prices) and can even rise, as long as it rises less than overseas prices in general. If, however, overseas incomes do not rise enough, expansion of one firm's sales is at the expense of other firms. If these other firms are located in an importing country, they will seek protection and often get it. The excluded exporters may try to expand in third markets instead; but when more has to be sold in unprotected or less protected markets, the fall in price there may become too large to make exporting attractive. Preferential tariff arrangements with third countries might help, though ultimately they only shunt the problem on to others, who in turn may intensify protection in their own markets.

Thus there are two main conditions for furthering the success of exports of known goods. They are firstly to have an economy that works below the level of full employment; and secondly that the home market should always grow less than the export market. The chief means towards those ends are all the various deflationary devices known to restrict the home market. The chief effect is cheap selling. This effect may be further ensured through competitive organisation of production and competitive organisation of overseas selling. The latter is usually best done by specialist merchants rather than by the producing firms themselves.

The purpose of this analysis is not to advocate or denounce a particular policy or combination of policies. It is merely concerned with the question of what sort of policies suit certain circumstances. Nevertheless it may be mentioned that, of the policies discussed in this section, only competition may have widespread approval. Falling prices are sometimes popular, as long as they are falling prices of what others produce; but the implied effects on incomes and employment are amongst the taboos of the mid-twentieth century. Such taboos may have to be broken if there are no alternatives. Hence the next task must be to inquire whether there are alternative ways of raising exports — irrespective of whether such alternatives are more compatible with present-day attitudes towards incomes and employment, or whether they would cause even greater difficulties. As will be shown in section 8 below, the answer is not necessarily easy and clear-cut.

8   EXPORT POLICIES: THE NEW RECIPE

The feasibility of alternative export policies depends largely on the availability of new goods which are marketable overseas. As shown before, new goods are goods which are not yet ready for standardisation and mass production, so that an increase in output is associated with a decrease in unit costs. Those who produce the new goods do not compete so much with established firms in established markets as the producers of known goods do. The reason is that there are no perfect substitutes for new goods. Producers of new goods do not so much compete for shares in established markets, but they try to create new markets. In order to do so they must tap incomes, and especially rising incomes. Their prime selling considerations must be based on what happens to incomes in the markets where they wish to sell. When incomes rise, new goods tend to be more marketable than when incomes are stable, let alone when incomes are falling. Price considerations are important, but they are of secondary importance to incomes. As a rule of thumb, price should be set within the following limits: price can rise as long as it does not rise proportionately more than customers' incomes are rising, and as long as it is not entirely out of line with the price of the nearest substitute available in the importer's home market (or even in the exporter's home market, since buyers tend to resent discrimination).

Exporters of new goods do not so much supplant what the importing countries can produce for themselves, as supplement what the importing countries can produce for themselves. That requires increasing international specialisation. As specialisation increases, decreasing costs become more likely. Once specialisation is complete, this particular benefit to producers ceases, and the considerations relating to trade in known goods apply.

Thus the case for more trade in new goods applies as long as specialisation becomes more widespread and ceases when this process is complete. Trade in new goods is inherently more ephemeral than trade in known goods. It is no less important for that; one reason is that it helps producers to reach a higher output at lower unit costs, which implies long-term beneficial money income effects for the producers and long-term beneficial real income effects for their customers; the other reason is that, in manufacturing, no technical limit to further specialisation can be foreseen. Only political events may bring this to a premature halt.

Even if the relevant political decisions are initially favourable, it does not follow that it will invariably be possible to have more trade in new goods. Assume unemployment at home which, to repeat the point once more, implies that capital is becoming more abundant than labour. More trade in specialities may then have disadvantages. Additional use of domestic resources could produce close substitutes, and their higher cost may be regarded as a lesser evil than unemployment. A cheap money policy would not help, since it is not conducive to more selective use of capital and encourages capital widening rather than capital deepening. As shown in the preceding section, this encourages price competition and leads to situations where governments find it difficult to resist claims for protection. In short, the case for more trade in new goods hardly arises when there is widespread unemployment. The case rests on the assumption of full employment at home and in all other countries which are expected to participate in further international specialisation.

Once there is full employment, the case for freer trade between industrial countries commands attention. It rests on further specialisation between those countries, and its success depends on the pursuance of appropriate domestic economic policies (and not only on the lowering of tariffs, however important that is).

Since full employment implies a general scarcity of factors, and sustained full employment an increasing scarcity of capital relatively to labour and other factors, the first requirement is a dear money policy, in order to encourage the more selective use of capital. This normally discourages capital widening. Since it does not discourage capital deepening so much, if at all, there is relatively more room for 'new' industries in the economy.

Dear money can ensure that the home economy makes relatively more factors available for new activities. It cannot ensure markets for industrial products. To ensure export success, the products must be of high quality, and they must be so priced that they can attract some of the rising overseas incomes. The rule suggested earlier in this section is that price should not exceed the price of the closest substitute by a larger percentage than the rise in incomes in the importing country. At the same time the industries concerned are usually in the increasing returns on capital stage, so that expansion of sales anywhere would lead to falling unit costs. Add to these points the fact that the authorities can exert some influence over the home market, but none in overseas markets, the following conclusion emerges. If the new industries are not to price themselves out of export markets, the authorities should encourage the home market for new goods.

At first sight there may seem to be a conflict between the recommendation of dear money and the recommendation that the home market should be encouraged. Admittedly there might be such a conflict in an underemployed economy, if lower interest rates would allow for a larger aggregate demand. In a fully employed economy that could apply only in the short run, if at all. In an underemployed economy the relevant point is that high interest rates discourage existing activities. In a fully employed economy such activities should be discouraged, so as to release factors for the new industries. Since factors employed in new industries normally create more value than factors employed in the old activities, the additional value created adds to aggregate demand. Aggregate demand is not necessarily reduced and may even be raised. For thanks to the employment of available factors in more intelligent ways, there can be more additional real value and more aggregate demand without inflation.

It so happens that the new industries are also the industries which tend to do best in international trade. The new industries are also prone to rapid product obsolescence (which is a major reason why some of them never get to the stage of being known industries). This implies that capital has to be paid for quickly, if it is to be paid for at all. An 8 per cent Bank Rate corresponds to a market rate of 10 per cent, which allows for ten years' purchase. Most of the industries prone to rapid product obsolescence have not got ten years in which to pay for capital, so that in their case high interest rates may not be an important impediment to expansion. (If tax allowances are taken into account, the argument becomes even stronger.) Thus high interest rates can redistribute economic activities in favour of new activities, without loss of aggregate demand at home (though with some loss of purely inflationary demand for more known products); and given the nature of the development of world trade in the 1950s and 1960s, such redistribution can only benefit the overall export performance. What often hurt the new industries was not the rising structure of interest rates, but some of the other paraphernalia of controls which imposed quantitative restraints on domestic growth, such as ceilings on lending and restrictions on plant expansion; or the fiscal restraints which would sometimes treat new goods as luxuries and subject them to penal indirect taxation; or the restraints on profits and wages, in so far as they were applied indiscriminately between known and new activities.

Since not all products of a particular industry (in the wider sense) are new goods, it is sometimes considered necessary to follow the old recipe as well as the new. For instance, if old models of motor-cars should be taxed more, in order to restrain home demand in accordance with the old recipe, and new models of motor-cars should be taxed less, in order to encourage home demand in accordance with the new recipe for export success, the implementation of such a policy might lead to an outcry. If the old and the new models must be taxed alike, for political reasons, the producers of the new models may have to be compensated through, say, investment allowances or other discrimination in favour of new activities. Were the authorities content to rely on monetary controls alone, rather than accompany changes in interest rates with a 'package' of fiscal and physical controls, such complications would not arise. For interest-rate policy alone would discourage demand for old models and encourage the supply of new ones. If the authorities cannot resist 'package' control, they should at least avoid special restraints on demand for new goods and special restrictions on the production of new goods — provided export success is the sole aim of policy.

As stated before, prices of exported new goods should not exceed the prices of the closest substitutes in the importing countries by more than the percentage rise of incomes in the importing countries. This can be abbreviated into: export prices of new goods must not 'rise' by more than overseas incomes. If there is concern about the prices of new goods, then the home market should be encouraged to keep unit costs down. That is the more important, the smaller the home market still is. Since the new industries work under conditions of decreasing unit costs, the expansion of export sales may actually be encouraged through the expansion of home sales. Should that raise incomes at home, there is no problem: the prices of the new industries must not 'rise' more than world incomes and, in the case of the new industries, the rise in home incomes raises home demand and so helps to keep prices *down*.

To sum up so far: the new recipe for raising exports requires, above all, full employment and possibly some inflation in the home economy, in order to ensure the greater scarcity of capital than of other factors. High interest rates can encourage a more selective use of capital, and this allows for relatively more production of new goods. A domestic boom does not hurt export prospects of new goods; on the contrary, it helps in so far as it leads towards lower unit costs.

Producers of new goods are less interested in protection of the domestic market than in unimpeded access to world markets. Rather than clamour for tariffs, they urge the dismantling of trade barriers elsewhere. Where demand is income-elastic rather than price-elastic, as tends to be the case with new goods, what can happen to price is given by what happens to overseas incomes. Exporters cannot charge much more than what is charged for the nearest substitute in overseas markets; nor will they want to charge much less, unless they are interested in charity rather than commerce. If there are overseas tariffs, the consumers in the protected markets will not pay much more than what they pay for the nearest substitute. Exporters to such markets must pay the tariff duty or go without the market. The position is as if overseas incomes had grown less, so that exporters get less profits and their growth prospects are impaired.

Where exporters of new goods have free access, they supplement rather than supplant local production. The less restraint there is on new trades, the less direct is the competition between different producers in world markets as well as in the home market. The fear of monopolistic practices is, however, unfounded in the new trades, at least as long as they are new and producers need quick sales to pay for capital, and as long as newer products can always replace the new products of yesteryear. The fear of monopoly rests on firmer foundations where tariffs, cartels and restrictive practices of all sorts ensure for capital and other factors in known trades returns which are as high as if they were engaged in new trades. Such protection retards progress by putting a premium on the known — with the result that fewer resources are available to venture the new. But those engaged on production of what is new in the world economy seldom seek protection in their home markets. Even if they got it, it would be useless. For product obsolescence ensures that capital in new trades cannot be effectively protected. In other words there can be no monopolistic exploitation by new trades. It does not follow that the new trades must be organised like the known ones.

As just argued, where there is specialisation there is no direct competition in production. Nor can there be competitive selling through merchants where scientific expertise of the product is likely to be confined to the producers, and where the market is so specialised that it can hardly be understood except by producers of similar (though not identical) goods. Selling must often be done by the firms' own directors, or by other technical specialists, who may or may not have the business acumen of merchants. Often an escape is found through specialist firms acting not only on their own behalf, but on behalf of others in the trade. For instance, in the machine-tool trade much of the importing and exporting of machine-tools is done by 'factors' who are merchants as well as producers. It takes time, however, before a new generation of salesmen can be trained who are equally at home in science, commerce and foreign languages. Not all of the new trades have managed to get equally far in meeting these requirements. This may be as important in determining sales as quality, novelty, price and whatever else one may think of. Hence salesmanship is not excluded from the need for increasingly capital-intensive methods, be it through material aids or more education of salesmen.

In many ways the new recipe for export success via new trades has more attractive implications than export success via the known ones. Full employment and rising incomes at home may seem preferable to running the home economy below capacity and below world growth rates just in order to ensure cheap selling. It does not follow that the new recipe leads to a world without problems, as will become apparent in section 10 below, which will consider the adjustment problems of the British economy to a changed world surrounding. At most, the new recipe suggests a way towards greater export success than that achieved in the 1950s and 1960s. This does not minimise the successes that were recorded. All that is implied is that there may be more export successes to come.

All the same, even if the new recipe seems preferable, only half of British exports go to countries where the new trades can do well, even if this is the larger and expanding 'half'. The other half of exports cannot be ignored, even if it was the 'declining half' in the 1950s and 1960s. Nor will that declining 'half' necessarily continue to decline. Although the opportunities for the international division of capital may seem limitless, the new trades of today are the known trades of tomorrow. Although it may seem difficult to visualise a mass market for many of the products of science-based industries, ultimately some of the new trades of today will become known trades of tomorrow. At the same time the mass market can be satisfied only after experience has been gained in the home market and the overseas trial grounds; and if the home market is restricted and access to the overseas trial grounds impeded by tariffs, there are not only fewer new goods to sell today but also fewer known goods to sell tomorrow.

Although trade in known goods keeps an economy going, it does so at a declining rate. For it depends on lesser growth at home than abroad, and therefore restrains total economic growth at home. Slow domestic growth is then almost inevitable, unless the known trades are continuously supplemented and replenished by trades in new goods of yesterday and today. The trades in new goods are the trades which also further domestic economic growth. In short, if the interests of the known trades cannot be ignored, those of the new trades cannot be ignored either.

Neither the known trades nor the new trades can be ignored in the sort of economy the United Kingdom had in the 1950s and 1960s. Since the known and new trades often have different interests, policy measures intended to improve the export performance of one set of those trades often hindered the chances of the other.

Had there been widespread unemployment, there would have been no such conflict of interests. The problem would have been how to produce more known goods; the domestic policy means could have been low interest rates and low wages; and it would have made sense to follow the rule: produce cheap and sell cheap goods to those poorer than yourself, at home or abroad.

In times of full employment, as in the 1950s and 1960s, matters are more complex. It is impossible to produce more known goods by tried methods. Attempts to sell more known goods to the masses abroad require restraint of growth of domestic incomes. In order to achieve this, the authorities tried high interest rates and restraint of personal incomes. The high interest rates impeded the growth of current activities, but to the extent to which restraint of wages was successful, the industries concerned were compensated and encouraged to continue with traditional labour-intensive methods of production. That countered the redeployment of labour into more capital-intensive activities which the high interest rates should have encouraged. High interest rates are meant to discourage existing activities but release factors for new ones. New goods are produced under conditions of increasing returns (or decreasing unit costs), so that such goods cannot be priced at marginal costs (if total costs are to be covered); and in this sense such goods can never be 'cheap'. They must be sold to the rich, at home or abroad. The rule becomes: produce with ingenuity and sell to those who can afford the best. If this is not to lead to undue social strain, more must become richer at home as well as abroad.

Much of British economic policy in the 1950s and 1960s was determined by balance-of-payments considerations and intended to raise exports. Given, however, the 50 : 50 division of British export interests during those two decades, whatever policy was tried was foredoomed to be at best half a success.

9   THE PATTERN OF WORLD TRADE

(a)   Pre-1950
The special export problems of the 1950s and 1960s arose from the 50 : 50 division of British export interests. These problems may recede; by the end of the 1960s the British export trade was more adjusted to the trading requirements of the rapidly growing industrial countries than at the beginning of the 1950s. By the 1970s it may be possible to pursue clear-cut policies, in the interest of the majority of exporters. Given the world economic trends of the 1950s and 1960s, the majority interest should be in trade with other industrial countries. This is no forecast. It is also possible that trade with the less advanced countries will accelerate more than trade with the industrial world, so that an earlier trade pattern might re-emerge, and such a development would also allow for more consistent policies.

While the world trade pattern of the future can only be guessed, it is possible to indicate the sort of problems the British economy faces when the world trade pattern changes. One possible method is to compare some aspects of the British and world trade patterns in the past, with the patterns which emerged in the 1950s and 1960s. In those two decades the pattern of world trade changed from what it had been for at least seventy years before. (26) In the seventy years before 1950, and possibly for longer, the development of world trade could be regarded as largely a function of the growth of world manufacturing activity; and the growth of world trade largely took the form of a growing exchange of manufactures for primary products. (27)

As a rough generalisation for the seventy years before 1950, it can be said that any 1 per cent change in the volume of world production of manufactures (or 'manufacturing') was associated with a 0.8 per cent change in the volume of trade of manufactures and also in the volume of trade in primary products. (28) Growth rates in individual years diverged from the trend, but over long periods the relationship between the growth of manufacturing and the growth of trade seemed constant. (There were a few years, in the 1900s and the 1920s, when trade in manufactures grew more and seemed to break away from the constant relationship with manufacturing, but this was not maintained.)

Since manufacturing grew at a faster rate than international trade in manufactures, the potential supply of manufactures for trade (or any other purpose) grew more than the effective demand for internationally traded manufactures. Consequently it became relatively easier to satisfy the demand for traded manufactures, and values of internationally traded manufactures would tend to move less favourably than domestic values of manufactures. (29) Manufacturers would regard international trade in manufactures as a second-best trade, and the literature of the time often referred to such trade as a trade in surpluses.

Manufacturing also grew more than trade in primary products, which indicates that manufacturing became less and less dependent on international trade in primary products. Hence demand for internationally traded primary products grew less than income in industrial areas. One result was that primary products too tended to become 'cheap'.

When all international trades were in 'cheap' goods, international trade was beneficial to consumers but eyed askance by producers. Imports seemed a threat to domestic values. Producers clamoured for protection, and governments did not always deny them. From the 1880s onwards, one industrial country after another reverted to protection. The more protection was given, the more were domestic values raised in each protected market (behind tariffs), and the lower were the prices foreign suppliers could hope to receive in such markets (since the foreign suppliers had to pay those tariffs or sell less). Increased protection accentuated whatever tendencies there were for international trades to become 'cheap' trades, and pleas for protection could never be assuaged.

The United Kingdom, alone amongst the major powers, resisted protection until the inter-war years. Free trade put her in a special position (or was made possible by her predominant position). One of its results was that British development reflected the development of world trade: British manufacturing, exports of manufactures and imports of primary products grew at almost exactly the same rate until the great depression of the 1930s. (At a time when world manufacturing grew more than world trade, this implied that British manufacturing would grow less than world manufacturing.) The situation had changed by the 1930s. Although the growth of British manufacturing and imports of primary products continued at the same rate, exports of manufactures lagged somewhat behind. In the 1930s a 1 per cent change in British manufacturing or imports of primary products was associated with a 0.9 per cent change in the exports of manufactures. (30)

One implication is that before the 1930s international demand for British manufactures grew at about the same rate as domestic demand for British manufactures. There were divergences in individual years. Over the years, however, manufactures are produced only if there is a demand for them. Identical growth rates, over the years, of output and export of manufactures were possible only as long as domestic and overseas demand for British manufactures grew at the same rate. Where that applies, manufacturers are inclined to view the world as one market. Only when export growth falls behind domestic growth will manufacturers fear international trade as a drag on values and prefer a protected home market to international opportunities. This did not happen to British manufacturers until the 1930s.

Before 1914 the British economy underwent a stage of economic development which was largely development of known goods at home which were still new goods in many parts of the world. Because development was largely in known goods, equilibrium was below the level of full employment and factors were abundant (see Chapter 22). Production was cheap and prices at or near marginal cost. British goods were cheap. Because they were new in many parts of the world, British exports of manufactures were sought after and their values could not be undermined by foreign competition.

As long as the United Kingdom was ahead of others, it cost her relatively less effort to obtain goods internationally than it cost her rival economies. She could accumulate export surpluses and use those surpluses for overseas investment. The income from overseas investment paid for some imports, so that at any one point of time imports were cheaper for the country than for the individual importers. For importers had to pay current market prices, but these often included payments to British owners of overseas securities. Only when war and depression had reduced income from overseas investment did the United Kingdom embrace protection, half-heartedly in the 1920s and whole-heartedly in the 1930s.

The United Kingdom's return to protection did not alter the old pattern of world trade, but reinforced it. For it contributed to a situation where trade could not grow as much as production. The old pattern continued until the 1950s, when world trade in manufactures came to grow more than manufacturing. But before 1950 any such tendencies were frustrated by protection, depression, war, or price movements.

As mentioned at the beginning of this section, the old pattern of the world economy was one where, by volumes, the growth of trade lagged behind the growth of manufacturing, and the lag of trade was at a constant rate (over long periods, whatever may have happened in individual years). Moreover the lag was roughly the same for manufactures and primary products, so that the volumes of the two main branches of trade grew in roughly constant ratio to each other. Such constancy in relative movements of volumes could persist only as long as relative price movements discouraged any divergence. This was the case, since any tendencies for trade in manufactures to grow faster led to a deterioration in the terms of trade of manufactures over primary products (as happened in the 1900s and in the early 1920s). Similarly, any 'undue' expansion of trade in primary products would turn the terms of trade against primary products (as happened in the late 1920s and early 1930s). The result was that, by value, the share of manufactures in world trade tended to fluctuate around a constant share of two-fifths of the total. (31)

Values in trade would correct divergences in volumes of traded manufactures and primary products. The growth of volumes remained linked to, and lagged behind, the growth of manufacturing activity which was the determinant of world development of trade, and that increase in world trade reflected mainly manufacturers' increased demand for raw materials. Although there were exchanges of primary products for primary products, and to a lesser extent of manufactures for manufactures, these were of subsidiary importance, and they seem to have played little or no part in determining changes in the structure and growth of trade. Before 1950 world trade could be regarded as largely an exchange of manufactures for primary products, and that exchange was geared to the requirements of manufacturing. In short, manufacturing led and trade followed.

If two-fifths of world trade was in manufactures and a similar proportion of British exports went to industrialised countries, and if three-fifths of world trade was in primary products and a similar proportion of British exports went to primary producing countries, the structure of British exports reflected the structure of world trade. If British manufacturing grew at the same rate as British exports, while world manufacturing grew more than world trade, British manufacturing growth was more directly related to trade than that of the whole industrial world. The growth of British manufacturing was not unconnected with that of world manufacturing, but the link was indirect and via the primary producing world. Any change in world manufacturing would raise the world demand for primary products and consequently primary producers' incomes; this in turn would affect the demand for British exports and thus the growth of British manufacturing. If British manufacturing during the first half of the present century often lagged behind changes in world manufacturing, that was not necessarily a disadvantage. Change is not always beneficial. It can be negative as well as positive; and less change is advantageous when the world economy moves into depression. It is disadvantageous only in times of rising prosperity.

During the first four decades of the century, when the economy was never fully employed (in times of peace) and often heavily depressed, the lag in 'growth' could be welcomed as stabilising. Even around 1950, when the only twentieth-century experience of full employment was in war and reconstruction years, a stabilising export trade structure seemed welcome. Other industrial countries might go into deep depression, but would cut their imports of raw materials later than their imports of manufactures. Full employment in the United Kingdom could be more easily assured if links with other industrial countries were indirect via the primary producing world, rather than direct.

So it may have seemed in 1950. The British export trade reflected the structure of world trade as it had been for so long. Of all the major economies, the United Kingdom's could be regarded as the one best adjusted to the world economy as a whole. It could have been argued that the best possible policies would be policies which preserved the traditional export structure.

(b)   The 1950s and 1960s

What happened after 1950 was that the pattern of world trade changed rapidly, but the pattern of British exports changed more slowly. In 1950 trade in manufactures was about two-fifths of world trade, which was the traditional share of manufactures in world trade. Subsequently trade in manufactures grew more than total world trade, and by the late 1960s the relative shares of manufactures and primary products had been reversed, with manufactures accounting for three-fifths of the total. Much of the additional trade in manufactures was trade between industrial countries. The growth of trade in manufactures was no longer a growing exchange of manufactures for primary products, but became a growing exchange of manufactured specialities for other manufactured specialities. The terms of trade moved in favour of manufactures (in most years), so that price movements supported this development. This contrasts with pre-1950 experience, when a greater growth of trade of manufactures than of primary products would have been associated with a movement of the terms of trade against manufactures.

The growth of trade in manufactures, coupled with a movement of the terms of trade in favour of manufactures, is perhaps the most significant of all the changes that occurred in the world economy during the 1950s and 1960s. For had trade in manufactures grown in the same relation to manufacturing as in the past, world trade in the mid-1960s would have been less than two-thirds of what it was, and world trade in manufactures less than one-half of what it was. It is impossible to be more precise, since no one can tell by how much manufacturing activity would have been retarded. (32)

Trade in manufactures grew more than manufacturing and trade in primary products. A 1 per cent growth in the volume of manufacturing came to be associated with a 1.4 per cent growth in the volume of world trade in manufactures and a 1 per cent growth of world trade in primary products. The basic pattern of world development of manufacturing, trade in manufactures and trade in primary products has thus changed from the traditional ratios of 1 : 0.8 : 0.8 to new ratios of 1 : 1.4 : 1. Although these relative growth rates varied from year to year, the ratios shown are representative of the changed growth rates of world manufacturing and world trade. (33) Trade in manufactures led world economic development, and this carried along both manufacturing and trade in primary products.

Since international trade in manufactures grew more than manufacturing, the effective demand for internationally traded manufactures grew more than the potential supply for all purposes. Relatively more manufactures were made available for trade, and that could be sustained only as long as values in international markets moved more favourably than in domestic markets. This in turn depended on increasing industrial specialisation between countries – which alone made it possible for industrialists to benefit from comparative advantages. (34) In other words international trade in manufactures was no longer a second-best trade in surpluses, but a sought-after trade in specialities.

For most countries, and in most years, international prices moved more favourably than domestic prices. (35) In those countries there was enhanced scarcity of manufactures for trade and a corresponding upward movement in values of internationally traded manufactures. For many industrialists the export trades came to be amongst their best trades, so that they devoted more of their activities to meet international demand. As more manufactures were attracted into the export trades, domestic demand could not always be satisfied at prevailing prices. Domestic prices had to follow the movement of international prices; and since rising exports raised domestic incomes, the domestic markets could absorb higher prices. In short, exports led and raised domestic incomes, and a rise in domestic values followed.

International trade in manufactures, far from being a drag on domestic values as it had been before 1950, became a cause of rising values and an impetus to increased activity. Exports raised values – or at least maintained them. For domestic values are automatically 'protected' if exports grow relatively more than production. Imports gave consumers a wider choice of high-class goods, and were less feared by producers than used to be the case in the past. Such development was possible because there was a high level of employment in each of the major industrial countries, so that each country could best raise its income through specialisation in goods rather than through multiplication of known activities. That could be maintained only through the increased liberalisation of trade which characterised the 1950s and 1960s.

The growth of exports of manufactures carried other activities along.

Manufacturing increased and trade in primary products increased at the same rate. This happened despite the fact that tendencies towards raw-material saving by established industries did not abate. It was offset by the demand for raw materials of new industries and by increased industrialisation throughout the world. Industries tend to be more wasteful of raw materials during the early stages of their development than later on, and this applies to new industries in established industrial areas and to older industries when they get established in new areas. Much of world industrialisation would not have been possible without additional imports of raw materials. The same can apply to food when urbanisation increases. Countries with growing industries had to take more liberal attitudes towards imports of primary products, if they were not to frustrate their industrialisation.

As the demand for internationally traded primary products grew in direct proportion to the increase in manufacturing, there was a simultaneous improvement in the fortunes of primary product importing interests and of the manufacturing world as a whole. As prices of manufactures rose, prices of most primary product exports also rose. The export prices of primary products rose because of the increase in manufacturing, not because of the increase in trade in manufactures. Export prices of manufactures rose more, and this gave an appearance of deterioration of the terms of trade of primary products. If unit prices of exports of all manufactures and all primary products are taken into account, the terms of trade moved in favour of manufactures. But much of the increase in trade in manufactures, and much of the rise in export prices of manufactures, occurred in trade amongst industrial countries and in commodities of little interest to primary producers. Much of the increase in trade amongst industrial countries was due to the reduction or elimination of tariffs, and that gave exporters higher export prices since the importing countries no longer taxed those goods as much as before. Moreover the greater profitability of exports allowed for more specialisation amongst manufacturers, and this led to more trade in producer goods or components of final goods. In short the movement of the international terms of trade during most of the 1950s and 1960s is best described as one favouring exports of manufactures, rather than as one against other interests. As mentioned before, primary product prices also rose in most years, and if they rose later and less than export prices of manufactures, they were still raised by the increase in manufacturing – which in turn had its values raised by the greater increase in trade in manufactures. Thus even if the terms of trade favoured manufacturers, internationally traded primary products too ceased to be 'cheap' (relatively to values in the industrial world).

When there are no 'cheap' international trades, the purpose of trade is to improve the quality of the goods which are available in each country. Imports increase choice and exports raise producers' profits. Both consuming and

producing interests benefit from the increase in trade. They urge their governments to negotiate the removal of trade barriers in other countries, and they are
more willing to sacrifice national protection in order to achieve this end.
Industrialists were amongst the more ardent supporters of the removal of
quantitative trade controls in the 1950s, of the universal tariff reductions
negotiated under the General Agreement on Tariffs and Trade throughout the
post-war period to date, and of the various regional free-trade schemes of the
late 1950s and the 1960s.

These changes in the world's trade pattern affected the British economy. Its
specially close links with the primary producing world became less of an
advantage than it had been in the past. Its near-perfect adjustment, in around
1950, to the pre-1950 pattern of world trade caused new problems of
adjustment — especially since the relevant pattern of the United Kingdom's own
development did not change so much as the world pattern. As shown before,
pre-1950 world economic development was led by the growth of manufacturing,
and trade lagged behind; while post-1950 world economic development was led
by trade in manufactures, which carried along both manufacturing and trade in
primary products. Outside the United Kingdom a producers' world had become
a traders' world.

There was not so much change in the United Kingdom. Before the 1930s
British manufacturing, exports of manufactures and imports of primary products
had all tended to grow at the same rate over time, so that production and trade
had been of equal importance in British development. In the 1930s the export
trade of manufactures lagged somewhat behind the growth of manufacturing,
but manufacturing and the import trade in primary products still grew at the
same rate. In the 1950s and 1960s the pre-1930 position was restored: manufacturing and all trade once more grew at the same rate. There was once again equal
emphasis on production and trade, and this was a restoration of the traditional
pattern of British development, after a temporary lapse in the 1930s.

This balance between the growth of manufacturing and the growth of trade
distinguished the British pattern of development from that of the rest of the
world. Unchanged herself, the United Kingdom faced a changing world.
Compared with the producers' world of the past, the British economy appeared
to be one where traders were unusually important. Compared with the traders'
world of the 1950s and 1960s, the British economy seemed less trade-orientated
than the world's. The difference between basic patterns of development may
help to explain some of the differences in attitudes towards problems of trade
liberalisation in this country and elsewhere, and some of the decisions and
opportunities taken and missed.

On the whole the pattern of British development required less trade liberalisation than the world pattern of the 1950s and 1960s; and the lesser participation

in trade liberalisation left the British pattern unchanged. In the late 1940s the United Kingdom was in the vanguard of the movement towards the liberalisation of European trade from quantitative controls. By the late 1960s hers was the only major economy still restricted by exchange control after twenty-five years of peace. Although a participant in universal tariff reductions under the General Agreement on Tariffs and Trade, and thus a beneficiary from freer access to overseas markets, she failed to increase the size of her unrestricted market as much as her major competitors did. Her home market did not grow as much as the home markets of the United States and continental European countries. Preferential tariff treatment in the Commonwealth became less important and was sometimes withdrawn altogether. The United Kingdom first refused, and then was refused, entry into the European Economic Community, which gave each member free access to larger markets than their own. Although the United Kingdom gained free trade in industrial goods in the European Free Trade Association, her partners' economies, taken together, do not quite double the size of her own home market, though her participation multiplied the area of free access for each of her partners. The pattern of her development had made her less keen for an enlargement of her free market than others were in the 1950s; and because some opportunities for freer trade were missed and withheld, the pattern of her development in the 1960s was still the traditional one.

The cause or result (or both) of the unchanged pattern of her own development is that British industrialists once more view the world as their market, as they had done before the lapse of trade in manufactures in the 1930s. But the outside world has not become a preferred market. An identity of long-run rates of growth of manufacturing and exports of manufactures, by itself, would indicate that domestic prices and export prices of manufactures move in the same direction. This happened even though, on the whole, export prices rose somewhat less than domestic prices. As far as exports of known goods to less advanced countries were concerned, it was only to be expected that international competition would keep prices down. Exports of new goods to advanced countries were not so much subject to price competition as to quality competition. They had to be sold at prices prevailing in the various importing countries. Since such exports were specialities, they should have been particularly profitable. Often they were. But with price given in the various importing countries, any tariff duties in the importing countries had to be defrayed by the exporters. Thus, given that price movements in the less advanced countries could not be as favourable as price movements in the home market; and given that the benefit of price movements in the advanced markets could not be fully reaped because of tariffs; and given that British exporters did not enjoy the same tariff reductions as some of their competitors; it is more notable that the United Kingdom's pattern of development did not revert to that of a producer's economy (as in the 1930s) than that her pattern failed to become that of a trader's economy (as the economies of other industrial countries became in the 1950s and 1960s).

Rising overseas incomes offset the effects of tariffs; and tariffs were falling, even if they were falling less for British exports than for some other countries' exports. In consequence British exports could grow, though less than those from competitive economies which benefited from more tariff reductions. The result was an adjustment in the British pattern of development from the producers' economy of the 1930s to a 'balanced' economy; while other countries, which had producers' economies for longer and to a more marked degree, were becoming traders' economies.

Whether this is to be welcomed or deplored depends on whether stability or growth is the most desired end. The traditional balance of the British pattern of development is more stable than either a producer's or trader's pattern. The relatively stable British pattern rested on equal export links with industrial and primary producing interests. Since exports raise domestic incomes and are therefore a source of growth, a 50 : 50 division of export interests would lead to British growth about half-way between the growth rate of the industrial countries and the growth rate of the primary producing countries. Trade and production were both stabilised in relation to the world and in relation to each other.

This stable pattern of development could not immunise the British economy from overseas trade fluctuations, but it could ameliorate the effects on the British economy of trade depressions originating in another industrial country. When an industrial country goes into depression, it curtails its imports simply because its national income falls. Imports may be further curtailed if the Government of the depressed country raises tariffs or introduces other protectionist devices. An industrial country that goes into depression will normally curtail its imports of manufactures more than its imports of primary products. If the depressed country is an important country, the British economy is bound to suffer some of the repercussions of that country's depression. These repercussions, will, however, be less if the United Kingdom's trade links are indirect via the primary producing world than if they are direct. If they are direct, a sharp fall in exports of manufactures is likely. If they are indirect through British exports to primary producing countries and primary product exports to the depressed industrial country, British exports still suffer, but probably to a lesser extent. If so, the repercussions of depressions in other industrial countries are likely to be less severe the more indirect the British trading connection with such countries is. In the days when industrial countries were just rivals and would not co-operate, and when full employment was rare and depressions deep, the United Kingdom probably did best by developing her direct trading ties mainly with other primary producing countries.

If a pattern of development ameliorates the repercussions of overseas fluctuations, it does so whether the overseas world goes into depression (which is negative growth) or whether the overseas world enjoys a period of rising prosperity (which is positive growth). If overseas growth is largely in industrial countries, and the United Kingdom's trading ties more with primary producing countries, the repercussions of the overseas industrial boom are also ameliorated. This is what happened in the 1950s and 1960s. Only because the overseas industrial boom was so persistent was there a gradual adjustment, British exports to primary producing areas becoming the lesser 'half' while exports to the most prosperous industrial countries became the larger 'half'. By the end of the 1960s British exports went to industrial countries and primary producing countries roughly in proportion to their aggregate contributions to world trade. British exports still reflected what happened in the world as a whole, the country's growth rate was roughly equal to the average of the growth rates of the industrial world and the primary producing world; and the pattern of development of trade and production was still stable. Should overseas development continue along the lines of the 1950s and 1960s, trade with industrial countries will become increasingly important and the link with the industrial world more direct. If so, the growth rate should accelerate. It should accelerate even faster if the pattern of British development can become a trader's one.

The British pattern of development is more likely to become a trader's pattern if British exporters can gain the same ease of access to wider markets as are enjoyed by their competitors. Only then can British industrialists hope to reap the same economies of scale in the world's widening markets. If so, the pattern of British economic development will become less stable.

The destabilising effects of more direct commercial links with other industrial countries apply not only overall. There will have to be further structural alterations within the British economy. For with general scarcity of factors, more trade with other industrial countries means specialisation on fewer, but higher-quality, goods. This involves problems ranging from firms' investment decisions to issues relating to industrial location, and from educational policies to the question of which governments are most likely to co-operate with the British Government. For nothing less is involved than whether the British economy should have stable development and reflect the world, or whether it should grow as fast as possible and become a province in the Atlantic Economy. (36) The decision must be made on political grounds. Whichever way it goes, it will be reflected in export performance.

25 Invisible Trade

1 INVISIBLE TRADE AND THE BALANCE OF PAYMENTS ON CURRENT ACCOUNT

A country must pay for its imports, and the principal way of doing so is the exportation of merchandise. But this is not the only means. Income from overseas investment, commissions earned on financial services, transport services and other invisible earnings may compensate or more than compensate for a deficit on merchandise trade.

In the United Kingdom's case, the balance of merchandise trade has usually been in deficit for as long as there are records. Going back in time, there were surpluses on the balance of merchandise trade in 1958 and 1956 and then none until as far back as 1822. Nevertheless the balance of payments has normally been in surplus. Between 1815 and 1914 the balance of payments was in surplus in all years but three. After 1918 there were balance-of-payments deficits in 1919 and 1926, due to special post-war problems and the General Strike respectively, but until 1930 there were surpluses in all other years. In the 1930s and 1940s, however, deficits became the rule and the surpluses of 1930, 1935 and 1948 were the exceptions. In the 1950s the balance of payments seemed restored to its traditional surplus position, though there were misgivings whether the surplus was big enough to retire war debts and restore the United Kingdom's traditional role as an overseas investor. There were two exceptions, 1951 and 1955, but the former was attributed to the Korean War and the latter to ephemeral cyclical factors. The country entered the 1960s with confidence, only to be rudely shaken by a balance-of-payments deficit in 1960, to be followed by only meagre surpluses in some years and marked deficits in others – which finally led to the devaluation of sterling towards the end of 1967. (1)

The balance-of-payments weakness of the 1940s was a by-product of war and reconstruction problems and can be disregarded in an analysis of peace-time economics. The 1930s and 1960s however, must be explained. The 1930s were lean years for all, but amongst the hardest hit by the slump were primary producers and those whose business it was to finance and convey goods in international trade. Much of the United Kingdom's overseas investment was located in primary producing countries and reduced by bankruptcies and low returns. The volume of world trade in the 1930s never recovered the levels attained in the late 1920s, so that demand for shipping space was below capacity and freight rates were adversely affected. Less trade also meant less merchanting, banking, insurance and brokerage and corresponding loss of commissions. These losses lowered the United Kingdom's invisible earnings. Although the fall in world trade had even more adverse effects on the United Kingdom's merchandise trade than on her invisible trade when imports and exports are looked at in isolation, the balance of merchandise trade deteriorated less, and for a time even improved. Yet even when the deficit on the balance of merchandise trade was less, the surplus on the balance of invisible trade no longer sufficed to compensate, let alone over-compensate, for the deficit on the balance of merchandise trade.

Invisibles could not cover the balance-of-payments deficits of the 1930s but softened them: the average balance of payments of the 1930s was a deficit of £25 million a year, (2) and the average surplus on invisible trade somewhat over £230 million. Had there been no net invisible earnings, the average annual balance-of-payments deficit would have been about ten times larger than it was – and since the exchange reserves could not have stood the strain, there would have had to be further cuts in imports with adverse effects on industrial activity (see Chapter 24, section 3).

The position of the balance of payments on current account in 1960-6 has some similarities with that in the 1930s (3) but only some. The first similarity is that each of those two decades started with a fall in the invisible surplus of about £100 million; (4) that there was a recovery on both occasions; and yet the average annual invisible surplus of 1960-6 remained about £100 million below that of 1953-9, just as the average annual invisible surplus of 1930-8 had been about £100 million below that of 1921-9. (5) The second similarity is that the reduced invisible surplus still softened the deficit on the balance of payments on current account: instead of averaging somewhat over £80 million a year, as it did in 1960-6, it would have been about three times as large – and since the exchange reserves could not have stood the strain, there would have been need of much more severe deflationary measures to reduce activity and the demand for imports. But here the similarities end.

The drop in invisible earnings in the 1930s was one of the consequences of the depression then prevailing in world trade. But 1960-6 were years of trade expansion. There were setbacks, but these took the form of slower than accustomed growth rather than of actual decline. British trade too expanded, and in those years was valued at 14 per cent more than in 1953-9. But imports and exports of merchandise grew at the same rate, and since imports were larger than exports, the merchandise trade gap widened by over £130 million. The combined result of the larger deficit on merchandise trade and the £100 million drop in net invisible earnings turned the balance of payments on current account from surplus into deficit: the annual average surplus of 1953-9 was slightly over £150 million and the annual average deficit of 1960-6 was over £80 million.

It may seem curious that net invisible earnings should have fallen at a time of trade expansion. Income from overseas investment should benefit from an expansion of world trade and did. The financial services of the City of London should be in greater demand and were. Transport services should benefit, and although on balance they did not, there was no marked deterioration either. There was some increase in net travel expenditure abroad, but this was not of sufficient importance to account for the difference. The difference was largely due to an increase of, on average, £230 million a year of net government expenditure overseas. All other items on the invisible balance, taken together, would have compensated for the deterioration in the balance of merchandise trade. Had it not been for the increased cost of the British Government's overseas commitments, the annual average balance of payments of 1960-6 would have shown a surplus of around £150 million, as in 1953-9. Had there been no net overseas expenditure by the Government in either period, the balance of payments on current account would, on average, have shown surpluses of near £300 million a year in 1953-9 and again in 1960-6.

2 POLITICAL AND COMMERCIAL BALANCE ON CURRENT ACCOUNT

Current government expenditure overseas consists of military expenditure, cash grants to developing countries, diplomatic expenditure and contributions towards the administrative expenses of international agencies. None of that expenditure is incurred for purely economic reasons, but all of it has to be defrayed by the economy. When British Government expenditure overseas exceeds the expenditure of overseas governments in the United Kingdom, the British balance of payments has to bear an invisible burden on behalf of the British polity.

Net government expenditure overseas is not new. Only its scale is. Even in the years between the wars, government expenditure overseas was often in deficit, but this never accounted for as much as half of the balance-of-payments deficits occurring then. Since the end of the Second World War, net government expenditure overseas has varied with political commitments, the expenditure overseas governments incurred in the United Kingdom to finance military bases and diplomatic missions, and the rise of overseas prices which substantially raised the costs of the United Kingdom's political commitments overseas. It should be noted that this political burden on the balance of payments was scaled down to £54 million in 1952, only to rise each year ever since. It exceeded £100 million by 1954, £200 million by 1958, £300 million by 1961, £400 million by 1964 and amounted to £460 million in 1966. Were no foreign exchange problems involved, a rise in any one particular item of government expenditure by about £400 million within fifteen years would present no major problem. But the additional £400 million were spent abroad and gave overseas residents additional potential claims on the British gold and foreign exchange reserves. (Not all of that was actually claimed in gold or foreign exchange, since the recipients could use the money to buy British goods or accumulate sterling reserves.) All the same, there was an increase in the supply of sterling in international markets, without a corresponding increase in the demand for sterling. The correct comparison of those particular £400 million is not with the gross national product which, in the relevant years, rose from under £15,000 million to over £30,000 million, but with the gold and foreign exchange reserves which never quite reached £1,200 million at the end of any of the relevant years. A politically unencumbered balance of payments on current account could have added about £300 million a year to the gold and foreign exchange reserves or added that much to the United Kingdom's overseas assets.

The £300 million are an approximate annual average. The balance of payments would have been stronger in some years and weaker in others. But 1951 would have been the last major deficit year. There would have been a slight deficit of £17 million in 1955 and none thereafter. Even 1960, 1964 and 1967 would have shown small surpluses of £17 million, £33 million and £49 million respectively.

To point to certain economic consequences of political causes implies no comment on whatever may have motivated the political decisions which had those particular economic consequences. Nevertheless it is legitimate for economists to point to the political origins of the balance-of-payments weakness of the 1960s especially since so much comment at home and abroad has attributed it to this or that alleged weakness of the British economy. A fair comment would be that, although the commercial balance of payments has been in regular surplus since 1952 (subject to only one minor exception), that surplus has failed to rise in step with the rising cost of political commitments overseas.

It failed by only a short length: the shortfall of the balance of payments on current account in 1960-6 below that of 1953-9 averaged £230 million a year, so that the task is to raise exports (of either merchandise or invisibles) by that much more than imports (of either merchandise or invisibles). Given the values of merchandise and invisible trade in the mid-1960s, that would require a 3 per cent increase in exports and stable imports; or, if imports must rise to maintain the level of activity, a correspondingly larger increase in exports. Whether such increase is more likely to come in the balance of merchandise trade than in the balance of invisible trade or vice versa, cannot be forecast. Past experience may, however, offer some guide towards the relative contributions the two constituent balances are likely to make.

3 LESSONS FROM THE PAST

In the following brief commentary on past events, the political part of the balance of invisible trade will be ignored. The invisible balance will be treated as a commercial balance of invisible trade and not as a commercial-cum-political balance of invisible transactions. This is the correct procedure, since net government expenditure overseas may be influenced by economic considerations but can never be determined by them, so that such expenditure must be taken as a given burden, uninfluenced or largely uninfluenced by the interplay of economic relationships. To avoid confusion, the balance of payments on current account will be referred to as the current commercial balance, (6) and the balance of invisible trade, net of government transactions, as the commercial invisible balance.

The first question is whether the balance of merchandise trade and the commercial invisible balance are more likely to move in the same direction (and so strengthen or weaken the current commercial balance simultaneously) or whether they are more likely to move in opposite directions (so that the greater strength of one can somewhat offset or even outweigh the enhanced weakness of the other).

Year by year, from 1953 (compared with 1952) to 1966 (compared with 1965), the two balances usually, though not always, moved in the same direction. But improvements in the balance of merchandise trade averaged sums more than twice as large as the average improvements in the commercial invisible balance, and deteriorations in the balance of merchandise trade averaged nearly four times the sums involved in deteriorations of the commercial invisible balance. The net change from 1953-9 to 1960-6 was a deterioration in the annual average deficit on the balance of merchandise trade from close on £120 million to over £260 million, and an improvement in the annual average surplus on the commercial invisible balance from over £420 million to over £550 million, thus leaving the total current commercial balance only slightly weakened.

Thus between 1953 and 1966 the annual movement in the two balances was largely in the same direction, but the long-term movement was in opposite directions. These apparently conflicting results were the outcome of the greater volatility of the negative balance of merchandise trade, especially in a downward direction (which means that deteriorations in the balance of merchandise trade from one year to the next were, on average, larger than improvements from one year to the next), and the greater stability in the commercial invisible balance, especially in a downward direction (which means that improvements in the commercial invisible balance were, on average, larger than deteriorations).

Which of those two movements is likely to predominate? The more distant past may point to what is possible. From the 1830s to the 1900s, the annual average balance of merchandise trade was in larger deficit each decade than in each preceding decade, and the annual average commercial invisible balance was in larger surplus each decade than in each preceding decade. The two balances had a trend which moved in opposite directions, and this was true of each decade and of the majority of individual years. This regular movement of the two balances in opposite directions ceased during the last ten years before the First World War. Between 1904 and 1913 both balances improved over the decade and in most individual years: the balance of merchandise trade deficit was reduced and the surplus on the commercial invisible balance continued to improve.

1904-13 were years of an exceptional overseas investment boom. Returns on overseas investment were relatively favourable and this encouraged further export of capital for overseas investment. More overseas investment meant more demand for the sort of capital goods Britain could supply, and this strengthened the balance of merchandise trade. The goods had to be financed, shipped and insured; and once put to productive use overseas, further added to income from overseas investment. This strengthened the balance of commercial invisible trade. Special circumstances improved both balances, but those special circumstances were cut short by war and were never to return to date.

The 1920s saw a return to the traditional relative movement of the two balances: the balance of merchandise trade tended to deteriorate and the commercial invisible balance to improve. Comparison with the past is of limited value because of the intervention of the First World War and subsequent monetary disorders; but for what it is worth, it may be mentioned that the annual average balance of merchandise trade of the 1920s showed a larger deficit than in 1904-13 and the balance of commercial invisible trade a larger surplus. (This comparison takes no account of price changes, but there is no way of calculating invisible earnings at constant prices. Since the concern is with current balances, and not with volumes of transactions, current prices are more relevant anyway.)

The next break came with the great depression from 1929 to 1931. Both balances deteriorated sharply, and this was more marked for invisibles than for merchandise trade. Although both balances subsequently improved, their annual averages for the 1930s remained below those of the 1920s, and this weakness was more marked in invisibles.

The balance of merchandise trade recovered first, mainly as a result of the return to protection, and for some years it showed smaller deficits than in the late 1920s. But this was not maintained. As the recovery from the depth of depression gathered momentum by the mid-1930s, imports began to grow more than exports and the balance of merchandise trade was as much in deficit as in the late 1920s. One cause was that any growth of total British trade will raise both imports and exports; and since the sum of imports is larger than the sum of exports of merchandise, the merchandise trade gap is liable to widen in recovery. Another cause was that the recovery was a recovery under protection which favours the growth of traditional activities; even then, the traditional activities had a relatively higher import content than the newer industries.

Protection was no help to invisibles. Their recovery had to wait until general recovery was in progress. But the recovery was never complete: bankruptcies affecting British overseas investment income had taken their toll, and an age of economic nationalism does not favour the growth of international service trades. Even in 1937, the best year of the 1930s, the surplus on the commercial invisible balance was approximately the same as in 1921, the worst year of the 1920s.

In short, protection at first helped the merchandise balance but not the invisible balance and later on hindered both. Recovery helped the invisible balance but caused the merchandise balance to deteriorate.

1904-13 and the 1930s were exceptional periods. The former was one of an unusually marked overseas investment boom; the latter was one of unusually marked depression, followed by incomplete recovery under economic nationalism. Those were the only periods on record when both balances moved in the same direction as compared with the preceding decade. Even in the later 1930s the usual tendency for the two balances to move in opposite directions tended to reassert itself.

In so far as history is any guide, the long-term movement of the two balances in opposite directions from 1953-9 to 1960-6 seems a better indication of what is likely to happen than the frequent year-by-year changes in the same direction from 1953 to 1966. It does not follow that exact or near compensation is likely. There was none before 1930, when the commercial invisible balance normally improved more than the merchandise trade balance deteriorated. There was none during the recovery phase of the 1930s, when the commercial invisible balance improved less than the merchandise trade balance deteriorated. The near compensation from 1953-9 to 1960-6 should be regarded as accidental and as a warning that over-compensation can no longer be relied upon.

To say that the trends of the two balances are historically more likely to move in opposite directions, implies no forecast. There were exceptions in the past. Even if the unusual conditions which caused those exceptions may not recur, other changes in the nature of trade may cause another 'exception'. For instance, in the past a reciprocal trade expansion would increase the deficit on the balance of merchandise trade; but the expansion of trade would also raise invisible earnings and improve the commercial invisible balance. Should future developments in merchandise trade lead to greater growth of exports than of imports, the expansion of trade should raise invisible earnings. Whether it would also raise the commercial invisible balance will depend on how the various constituent items on that balance will be affected.

4   INVISIBLE TRADES IN DEFICIT

There is a large variety of invisible trades, so that some grouping is necessary. It may then happen that whatever is said relating to the prospects of a particular group is inapplicable to any particular constituent item, just as much as what was said above relating to the invisible balance as a whole does not apply to each of the groups. For instance, 'travel' and 'private transfers' are normally in deficit, though the commercial invisible balance as a whole has been in surplus for as long as there are records. Transport services have made no major net contribution to the invisible balance for some years, though they were important in the past. The regular commercial invisible surplus is due to services other than transport and to income from overseas investment. These groups will be briefly considered in ascending order of the net contribution they have made to the commercial invisible balance in the 1950s and 1960s.

Travel is the most negative of the groups mentioned. Its annual average deficit in 1953-9 was over £10 million, and in 1960-6 this had risen to nearly £60 million. This rise was the combined result of the relaxation of exchange control and rising prosperity.

A growth of trade raises prosperity and so enables more private travel. It also encourages more business travel. In consequence the travel balance is likely to deteriorate when trade is good, just at the time when the balance of merchandise trade is historically most likely to deteriorate. In a way this makes the travel balance 'worse' than the political balance, which at least is independent of what happens to the balance of merchandise trade.

The travel balance is, however, one of the most easily controlled items on the balance of payments. The reintroduction, in 1966, of tight control of personal and business expenditure outside the Sterling Area effected some savings. Since the travel balance includes the cost of inland transport, paid for in foreign exchange (but not the cost of sea and air passages, which are included under the estimate for transport services), and since average distances covered by British travellers abroad are always likely to be longer than the average distances covered by overseas visitors in Britain, a favourable travel balance is difficult to achieve. There would have to be more overseas visitors to the United Kingdom than British travellers abroad, or overseas visitors would have to spend disproportionately more in hotels and shops just to compensate for the shorter inland routes covered. Further improvements and expansion of the British tourist services would help, but this takes time, takes factors away from other employments and does not necessarily bring more tourists if the sun shines brighter in Italy.

Private transfers are not of major importance in the balance of payments. There is a deficit when emigrants take more money out of the country than immigrants bring in, when residents send more expensive gifts by parcel post to their friends and relatives abroad than they receive in return, and when the incidence of disasters is such that more relief funds are sent abroad than received. Like travel, such transfers are subject to exchange control. Unlike travel, they do not necessarily rise with prosperity. They resemble government transactions overseas in so far as they are often determined by non-economic considerations. But on balance they are not very important.

5   THE TRANSPORT BALANCE

International transport services consist of shipping and civil aviation. Both freight and passenger services are important, with freight more important for shipping and passenger services more important for civil aviation.

For balance-of-payments purposes, imports and exports of merchandise are valued f.o.b. (free on board) and the freight charges are assumed to be the importer's liability. Thus credits are freight payments made for the export of goods carried in British ships (but not freight payments made for exports carried in foreign ships, since these are regarded as transactions between overseas residents); and debits are freight payments for imports carried in foreign ships (but not freight payments for imports carried in British ships, since such payments are regarded as internal transactions). The same applies to air freight. Because goods are valued f.o.b., the cost of inland transport is deemed to be part of the value of goods entered on the balance of merchandise trade.

Other credits are freight on cross-trades, disbursements by foreign ships and aircraft in British ports and receipts from sale of passenger tickets abroad for use on British ships or aircraft. Other debits are disbursements by British ships and aircraft abroad and payments made in Britain for passenger tickets valid on foreign ships and aircraft. (The sale of rail or bus tickets is not included here, but under travel expenditure.)

The net earnings from transport services, as estimated for balance-of-payments purposes, give no indication of the profitability of British shipping and aviation. They relate only to the net balance of such transport services rendered or received as involve foreign exchange earnings and liabilities. This net balance was not substantial in the years from 1953 to 1966.

Shipping services showed, on average, a small surplus of less than £20 million a year in 1953-9 and a deficit of less than £20 million a year in 1960-6. Civil aviation showed a negligible surplus in the earlier period and one of over £20 million in the latter.

Historically, this is a disappointment. Early in the nineteenth century net shipping earnings had been the largest single positive item on the balance of payments, and by themselves approximately compensated for the deficit on merchandise trade. Although overtaken by income from overseas investment as early as the 1830s, net shipping earnings continued to grow, though not quite as fast as the merchandise trade deficit. In the years just before the First World War, net shipping earnings by themselves covered about two-thirds of the merchandise trade deficit. In the 1920s, net shipping earnings were still worth nearly one-half of the merchandise trade deficit, and in the 1930s, one-quarter. After the Second World War there appeared to be a revival, and in 1952 net shipping earnings reached their post-war peak with a surplus of £130 million. This was actually larger than the merchandise trade deficit in that year.

The revival did not last. The surplus fell year by year until it turned into a small deficit in 1955. During the following ten years half the years showed small surpluses and the other half small deficits.

Over the present century net shipping earnings have suffered from depression, competition from civil aviation, economic nationalism and changes in the nature of trade. But there was no deep depression in the fifteen years after 1952. Some of the ill effects of the inter-war depression on British shipbuilding may still linger and affect the tonnage available, but shipbuilding abroad and other industries at home have forgotten those days. The explanation seems out of date. Competition from civil aviation has been important in passenger services but not yet in freight, and even in the case of passenger services there was loss of growth of earnings rather than actual loss. This explanation seems premature. Economic nationalism is not without importance even these days. Overseas preference for consigning in ships sailing under the exporting countries' flags is still widespread, and although this is sometimes in part compensated through larger disbursements by foreign ships in British ports, there is no compensation at all if it means by-passing the British entrepôt trades. But the worst effect of economic nationalism in the past was that it restricted the volume of world trade. Although the post-1952 world was not without its trade restrictions, these restrictions were on the wane and did not prevent a marked expansion of world trade including British trade.

The trade expansion was marked, but did not lead to a corresponding increase of British net shipping earnings. That was due to a variety of causes. Amongst the most important of those causes were that average trade routes became shorter, traded goods lighter (per unit of value), and British exports were more affected by those changes than British imports. The difference between effects on exports and imports is of special importance in the present context, since British ships carried over half of British exports and foreign ships over half of British imports.

The mid-twentieth-century trade expansion was largely, though not exclusively, an intensification of trade in the North Atlantic area. It was thus in marked contrast to what had happened in the nineteenth century. In the nineteenth century the expansion of world trade was at first an expansion of trade between industrial Britain and primary producing countries further and further away, and later an expansion of trade of an increasing number of industrial countries with primary producing countries further and further away, so that the trading world became larger and trade routes lengthened. In the mid-twentieth century, trade expansion was more marked amongst the industrial countries, most of which are in the North Atlantic area, so that it was a trade expansion between nearby countries rather than distant ones. The trading world did not become smaller, but rather more concentrated. In consequence the average length of trade routes shortened.

In British trade this change was more marked in exports than in imports, and especially so in the 1960s. It is not yet possible to discern the full effects on net shipping earnings since the shorter sea routes are often the more profitable ones. All that can be said is that such changes in trade alter the number and nature of vessels required. Since British ships are, on average, more suitable for the more valuable cargoes, (7) it is not impossible that such advantage can compensate for shorter average routes.

Probably more important was the change in weight of world trade. The intra-North Atlantic trade of the mid-twentieth century grew especially in manufactures. Normally manufactures weigh less and take up less shipping space than primary products of the same value. Amongst manufactures, the more sophisticated and valuable did relatively best, and that again raised the value per ton in trade – which, for the present purpose, means it lowered the tonnage per unit of value. In short, trade became lighter (per unit of value). British exports too became lighter, but imports did not.

For British exports, lighter trade is no new development. In the mid-1960s (8) the tonnage of British exports was less than half of what it had been in 1929, though the value (at constant 1958 prices) had risen by more than half. (9) Hence exports of the mid-1960s weighed, on average, only about one-quarter of what they used to weigh in 1929. (10) The trend towards lighter exports continued in the 1960s: between 1960 and 1966 exports became 15 per cent lighter. (11)

The tonnage of British imports of the mid-1960s was somewhat over two and a half times that of 1929, though the value (at constant 1958 prices) was only somewhat over one and a half times that of 1929. (12) That made British imports, in the mid-1960s, somewhat over one and two thirds times heavier than in 1929. (13) The trend towards heavier imports continued in the 1960s: between 1960 and 1966 imports became 5 per cent heavier. (14)

Heavier imports and lighter exports create a gap between the tonnage required for imports and exports. This problem arose in the 1930s and has been aggravated since. In 1929 the ratio of the weight of imports to that of exports had been approximately 3 : 4. By 1938 it was about 4 : 3. By 1950 imports weighed twice as much as exports; by 1957 three times; by 1961, four times; and by the mid-1960s, 4.8 times. (15)

The causes of this widening and unfavourable tonnage gap lay in changes in the nature of trade. Most important was the change in the balance of the fuel trades from the export of coal to the import of mineral oils. The decline in the coal trade made exports lighter. In 1929 the weight of coal exports alone exceeded the weight of total imports. By 1938 the weight of coal exports was still over half of the weight of imports. By 1950 it was one quarter; by 1957 under one-tenth; by 1964 under one-twentieth; and by 1966 under one-fortieth.

In the days when the coal export trade flourished, the carrying ships could be used to bring back, say, grain. The balance of payments benefited from freights received for exports in British ships, and since those ships could be used to carry imports, there was no burden on the balance of payments through appropriate freight payments to foreign ships. Any surplus shipping space available could be used to earn additional foreign exchange in cross-trades (which means they would pick up cargoes, wherever available, to take to any destination).

While the export trade in coal declined, the import trade in mineral oils expanded. In relation to total imports, mineral oils accounted for less than one-twelfth of the weight of imports in 1929; one-sixth in 1938; one-third in 1951; one-half in 1960; and about 60 per cent in 1966. Compared with the weight of exports, imported mineral oils weighed one-tenth of the total export tonnage in 1929; one-quarter in 1938; were almost equal to it in the early 1950s and exceeded it in 1954; were double the weight of all exports in 1961; and weighed nearly three times as much in 1966. The tankers carrying mineral oils cannot carry other imports as well, and they are not suitable for the carriage of most British exports. British tankers would have sufficed to supply the home market in the mid-1960s but not in the cross-trades as well. (16)

In the absence of the fuel trades, an unfavourable tonnage gap would have been of longer standing, but would have narrowed in the post-war period. In

1929 the weight of imports, other than mineral oils, was over three times the weight of exports, other than coal. In the 1930s that gap actually widened when raw-material imports revived more than exports of manufactures, and in 1938 the tonnage ratio of non-fuel imports to non-fuel exports was 4.8 : 1. But that was not reattained in the 1950s and 1960s. Even the 1938 ratio has not been exceeded since 1949, when it was 3.7 : 1. Since 1950 it has been regularly below 3 : 1, averaging slightly less than 2½ : 1. (17)

It is thus by no means certain that the tonnage gap between all imports and all exports will continue to widen. The coal trade has not got much further to fall. Imports of mineral oils may continue to rise, though the rate of the rise may become less. Motorisation and industrial conversions from coal to oil were amongst the characteristics of the 1950s and 1960s. While neither will come to an end, the rate of increase may slacken and substitutes may become available. Battery-driven cars are no longer impossible and may become important in the 1970s. Even more important would be industrial conversions to natural gas as a major source of power for industry and possibly even as an export. (18)

Whatever the future may hold, while the tonnage gap widens and widens unfavourably, it acts like an invitation to foreign ships to come, and so has adverse effects on British shipping earnings. The 'invitation' to foreign ships will be considered first with reference to two extreme assumptions. At one extreme it is assumed that, at any one point of time, all British exports are carried in British ships. Even were all those ships suitable for carrying grain or oil or whatever else the imports are, there would not be enough space in those ships to bring the required volume of imports. Some imports would have to be carried in foreign ships, and those ships would compete for cargoes for their return journeys. There would be a built-in tendency towards a rising share of foreign ships in British export trade.

Next, assume the other extreme position where, at any one point of time, all British imports are carried in British ships. There would not be enough cargoes for the return journeys and, given the flag preferences of many nearby countries, it would be increasingly difficult to find them elsewhere. Some imports would be left for foreign ships to carry, even if all ships engaged in the carriage of British exports were suitable for the carriage of mineral oils and other imports. There would be a built-in tendency towards a rising share of foreign ships in British import trade. Such problems may be aggravated by foreign flag preferences, but they are inherent in a widening unfavourable tonnage gap. Although neither of the extreme positions applies, tendencies in the direction indicated are at work as long as the tonnage gap widens.

Given the tonnage gap, it is not surprising that British ships carry a larger proportion of British exports than of imports, and given a rising tonnage gap, it is not surprising that the share of British shipping in British trade fell in both directions. The fall was more marked and occurred earlier in imports than in exports. British ships carried about two-thirds of British trade either way in 1929 and again at the beginning of the 1950s. The share of British ships in British import tonnage then fell to one-half by the end of the 1950s and to 44 per cent by the mid-1960s. The share of British ships in British export tonnage also fell, but to a lesser extent. It was around 60 per cent at the end of the 1930s, and still over one half by the mid-1960s. (19) Foreign ships had accepted the 'invitation' into both trades. Between 1960 and 1966 the imports carried in foreign ships increased by nearly as much as the increase in total imports, and the exports carried in foreign ships increased by more than the increase in total exports.

A widening tonnage gap militates against the share of British ships in British trade. Given constant freight rates, it indicates adverse effects on the growth of British shipping and gross earnings, but it only warns of a probable deterioration in net payments. As mentioned before, more directly relevant for balance-of-payments purposes is the gap between the tonnage of imports carried in foreign ships and of exports carried in British ships. The latter gap is the true 'payments tonnage gap'. Given constant freight rates, a widening of the payments tonnage gap shows that the net payments position has worsened.

The payments tonnage ratio and the total tonnage ratio coincide if British ships carry half of imports and half of exports. The payments tonnage ratio rises more than the total tonnage ratio if the share of foreign ships in imports rises or the share of British ships in exports falls or both. Both happened in the 1960s, so that the payments tonnage ratio can be presumed to have worsened more than the total tonnage ratio. In 1965 the ratio of import tonnage carried in foreign ships to export tonnage carried in British ships was 5.5 : 1. (20) The payments tonnage gap was thus wider than the total tonnage gap of 4.8 : 1 mentioned before.

It does not follow that total freight payments on imports carried in foreign ships were over five times the total freight payments charged on exports in British ships. They were in fact less than one and a half times higher. (21) It follows that average freight charges per ton exported in British ships were nearly four times as high as the average freight charges on imports in foreign ships. (22) This is a crude estimate, applicable only to 1965.

That average freight rates per ton on exports in British ships were substantially higher than average freight rates per ton on imports in foreign ships, was largely due to differences in the nature of the trades. Exported manufactures may be lighter than imported primary products, but they are more difficult to handle, and although they normally take up less shipping space per unit of value, they normally take up more shipping space in relation to weight. (23) As long as exports continue to become lighter relatively to imports, average freights per ton of exports are likely to rise relatively to those on imports, and such a tendency in average freights can offset the payments effects of a widening payments tonnage gap. In recent years, however, this was not enough: with relevant export freight rates not quite four times as high as relevant import freight rates, but relevant import tonnage five and a half times larger than relevant export tonnage, the freight balance was in deficit.

The shipping balance as a whole was in near balance, largely because the freight deficit on British trade was more than offset by the surpluses earned from freight on cross-trades. If the tonnage gap in British trade has been discussed at some length and nothing at all has been said about the cross-trades, this does not mean the latter are unimportant. In 1952 they contributed over £300 million to the balance of payments, and in the mid-1960s around £400 million – while the freight balance deteriorated from a surplus of £20 million in 1952 to a deficit of around £80 million in the mid-1960s. (24) Nor is it unimportant that the growing foreign tonnage in British trade reduced the deficit arising from larger disbursements of British ships abroad than of foreign ships in the United Kingdom. The reason for concentrating on the tonnage gap in British trade is that it emerges as a major cause of the disappointing contribution of net shipping earnings to the balance of payments of the 1950s and 1960s. (25)

Until the late 1950s, the transport balance was largely a shipping balance. In 1959, however, *civil aviation* for the first time contributed more to the balance of payments than shipping and then continued in surplus, while shipping was frequently in deficit. So far the gains of civil aviation have been largely in passenger services. Air freight transport is still in its infancy, though growing.

There are not yet as many airports as seaports, and the difficulties in waiting for entry are greater and more costly for aircraft than for ships. That necessitates licensing of air routes and landing rights, and such licensing is normally on a nationally reciprocal basis per number of flights. The United Kingdom's chance of raising her net earnings from civil aviation then depends on making the best possible use of the number of flights available. Larger aircraft might help, in so far as they raise the number of foreign passengers carried in British aircraft relatively to the number of British passengers carried in foreign aircraft. In air freight earnings, it helps if British aircraft carry exports which can bear higher freights than the imports carried in foreign aircraft. There does not appear to be any immediate risk of a widening unfavourable tonnage gap, as occurred in shipping.

Ultimately the demand for all transport services depends on what happens to merchandise trade. Any growth of merchandise trade should help gross earnings of all forms of transport. The net contribution of transport services to the balance of payments, however, does not just depend on what happens to the value of imports and exports, but even more on what happens to the relative weight of imports and exports.

6   INVISIBLE TRADES IN SURPLUS

Sections 1 and 3 above have shown that, in the past, the commercial invisible balance often improved when the balance of merchandise trade deteriorated, and that this happened again from 1953-9 to 1960-6. But travel, private transfers and shipping, taken together, deteriorated by about £90 million and civil aviation improved by only £20 million. The major improvements came in services, other than transport, which improved by £80 million, and income from overseas investment, which improved by £120 million. Both 'other services' and income from overseas investment tend to do best in times of growing trade, and given an excess of imports over exports of merchandise to start with, growing trade tends to be associated with a deterioration in the balance of merchandise trade.

Other services consists of a miscellany of items, and those items do not necessarily behave in the same way. There are services which depend on past British effort, such as royalties on books, films and patents. There are services which depend on the state of trade elsewhere rather than on the state of British trade: examples are services rendered to overseas residents by British engineers, accountants and antique dealers. In the present context, however, the most important 'other services' are the services rendered to overseas residents by the City of London and other marketing centres; and 'City services' are currently rendered and flourish with the growth of world trade as well as with the growth of British trade.

The net contribution of all 'other services' to the balance of payments rose from over £125 million in 1953 to over £275 million in 1966. The annual average for 1953-9 came to under £180 million and that for 1960-6 to about £260 million. Details relating to constituent items are available from 1964 onwards and show that about half of these contributions came from City services. (26) This puts the net contribution of City services at around £130 million, which, however, underestimates the contribution those services make to the balance of payments. The reasons are as follows.

City services consist of insurance, brokerage, merchanting and banking. Merchanting includes services rendered to importers and exporters, and the appropriate commissions charged are part of the value of imports and exports as recorded on the balance of merchandise trade. Imports represent foreign exchange liabilities. But in so far as the value of imports includes the cost of British merchants' commissions, the foreign exchange liability arising from imports is correspondingly offset. Commissions on imports are thus treated as credits on the invisible balance. Exports represent foreign exchange earnings. But in so far as the value of exports includes the cost of British merchants' commissions, the foreign exchange receipts from exports are correspondingly less. Commissions on exports are thus treated as debits on the invisible balance. Such procedure may be the only practical one of compiling the balance of payments estimates, but it treats important City services as a balancing item rather than as services in their own right.

City spokesmen seem to treat all commissions on imports as part of the City's contribution to the balance of payments, and make no deduction for commissions on exports. (27) This is legitimate on the assumption that commissions on exports are, in effect, internal transactions. On this basis the contribution of City services came to over £190 million a year in the mid-1960s. Roughly comparable estimates are available for 1956 and 1961, when those earnings were estimated at £125 million and £150 million respectively. (28) This suggests a steady rise in those earnings. Much of this was due to the abolition of exchange control for overseas residents at the end of 1958, which in effect reopened the City for many of its traditional and new services to the outside world. But not enough data are available to quantify such an assertion.

It could be argued that City services made an even greater contribution to the balance of payments than the above estimates suggest. In the absence of British merchants' services to exporters, exports would have been less or British exporters would have had to pay commissions to foreign merchants. In either case the balance of payments would have been more adverse. Again, it is impossible to quantify such an assertion. All that can be said is that all available estimates of the contribution of City services to the balance of payments assume merchandise trade as given, and do not allow for the effects of the availability of such services on the volume of merchandise trade.

Moreover it is not just the City of today that contributes to the balance of payments. The City enabled overseas investment in the past, and the income from overseas investment contributes even more to the balance of payments of today than all services taken together.

Income from overseas investment is a return on past British effort which has enabled current overseas activities. It shares this characteristic with royalties, but much larger sums are involved. The annual average net receipts were £240 million in 1953-9 and nearly £360 million in 1960-6. There were, however, substantial annual variations, depending on the state of trade overseas, and these variations can be unfavourable as well as favourable. Thus falls in income from overseas investment contributed to the weakness of the balance of payments in 1955, 1960 and 1966. But there were increases in all other years from 1953 to 1965, and the long-term movement was upwards: from £220 million in 1953 to nearly £450 million in 1965. (29)

In money terms, those £450 million were an all-time peak. As shown above, the annual average of such income in 1960-6 was one and a half times that of 1953-9, and this meant a somewhat larger growth rate than for 'other services' and more than three times the growth rate of exports of merchandise. The annual average net earnings from overseas investment exceeded the deficit on merchandise trade by nearly £130 million in 1953-9 and by £110 million in 1960-6. Only in four of the fourteen years did net income from overseas investment by itself fail to cover the deficit on merchandise trade. (The four years were 1953, 1955, 1960 and 1964.)

For all that, net income from overseas investment made a lesser contribution to the balance of payments of the 1950s and 1960s than at any time between the end of the Napoleonic Wars and the outbreak of the Second World War. The purpose of overseas investment is to get imports or the means of paying for imports; and the contribution which net income from overseas investment makes to the balance of payments is best measured by the proportion of imports it pays for. That proportion was consistently below one-tenth in the years under review. (The annual average came to a fraction above 7 per cent in 1953-9, and to a fraction below 8 per cent in 1960-6.) In the inter-war years net income from overseas investment had paid for about one-fifth of imports, and in the early years of the century for about one-quarter. To find years in the nineteenth century with a contribution of less than one-fifth, it is necessary to go back to the first half of the 1880s; it was over one-tenth for as far back as 1816 and may have been so for longer. (30)

Given the good growth rating of income from overseas investment, and given its (historically) low contribution to the balance of payments of the 1950s and 1960s, it may be tempting to conclude that efforts should be concentrated on raising income from overseas investment. But as mentioned before, income from overseas investment is not a return on current effort in Britain; it is a return on past British effort. Like all investment, it requires abstinence for the sake of a future return.

The abstinence needed in the present context is abstinence from importing. If the value of imports of goods and services is kept below the value of exports of goods and services, there is a surplus on the balance of payments on current account. This surplus is sometimes referred to as the 'export of capital' or as the 'import of securities'. It is an export of capital because it creates claims on future overseas production. The claims on future overseas production are held in the form of money or titles to such production, so that there is a corresponding import of securities.

Capital exports (or imports of securities) can be used to augment the exchange reserves, to retire debt owing to overseas residents or to acquire ownership of overseas assets which yield profits, dividends and interest. If the balance-of-payments surplus is invested in the augmentation of exchange reserves, future claims on overseas production equal that surplus but no more. If the surplus is used to reduce overseas claims on the British economy or to increase British claims on overseas economies, net income from overseas investment will rise in future years. But before that happens, there must have been a surplus on the balance of payments on current account; and before that happens on a noticeable scale, that surplus must have been substantial and sustained over a number of years.

It does not follow that the creation of overseas investment exactly equals the surplus on the balance of payments on current account. Were this so, the surplus on current account would be exactly balanced by the export of capital on the balance of payments on long-term capital account (where such capital exports appear as liabilities, since they create claims in overseas countries on British-owned securities and the appropriate assets are acquired or created overseas even if British-owned). All the surplus on current account shows is how much overseas investment is possible without effect on the exchange reserves. If British overseas investment exceeds the surplus on the balance of payments on current account, the exchange reserves are weakened through the appropriate accommodating monetary movement. If British overseas investment falls short of the balance of payments on current account, the exchange reserves rise.

The balance of payments on current account thus shows how much a country can afford to invest overseas. The balance of payments on long-term capital account shows how much it actually invests. What the country can afford to invest overseas is a credit on current account; and what it actually invests overseas is a balancing debit on long-term capital account. Any discrepancy between what the country can afford to invest overseas and what it does invest overseas, is balanced through monetary movements. The annual average position in the 1950s and 1960s was as follows.

As mentioned before, the annual average of the commercial balance of payments on current account was near £300 million both in 1953-9 and 1960-6. In 1953-9 current government expenditure overseas took half of this, so that about £150 million was available for net overseas investment or the augmentation of the exchange reserves. Commercial investment overseas averaged somewhat over £130 million a year, so that there would still have been something left to augment the exchange reserves, had not government investment overseas taken over £45 million a year. Government investment overseas is the net balance of settlement of inter-governmental debts and subscriptions to international organisations, so that it must be taken as given. Nevertheless the combined commercial and governmental overseas investment in 1953-9 was somewhat in excess of what the country could afford without weakening the British contribution to the Sterling Area's gold and foreign exchange reserves.

In 1960-6, when current government expenditure overseas averaged £80 million more a year than the commercial surplus on current account, there should have been net investment from overseas in the United Kingdom rather than net British overseas investment. But that happened only in 1961. In the other years there was net British overseas investment. True, commercial net overseas investment was only slightly over £65 million a year, or approximately half of what it had been in 1953-9, but government overseas investment exceeded £90 million a year, or double what it had been in 1953-9. To avoid a weakening in the exchange reserves, investment from overseas in the United Kingdom should have been larger; or British commercial overseas investment should have been less; or government net investment overseas should have been less rather than more. As it was, the United Kingdom's contribution to the Sterling Area's gold and foreign exchange reserves was weakened. In so far as this added to the need to borrow from abroad to support the exchange reserves, any benefits of increased income from overseas investment will be offset by increased repayment of debt (though the offset will not be exact). However beneficial current overseas investment may be to the balance of invisible trade of the future, it is a way of strengthening the future balance of payments which can be afforded only when the current balance of payments is in surplus.

7   OVERSEAS INVESTMENT: PAST AND PRESENT

A country that can produce commercial balance-of-payments surpluses of around £300 million a year can afford overseas investment, if it so wishes. There is a choice between spending such surpluses on political activities overseas or augmenting the exchange reserves or adding to net overseas investment. Normally the choice will be a combination between those three possibilities. If political commitments ran rather ahead of commercial possibilities in much of the 1950s and 1960s, that was part of the winding-up of empire and cannot be repeated. Given that there will be a choice, the question is whether overseas investment is likely to become as important in the future as it was in the nineteenth century and until 1939, whether its role will be permanently reduced to that of the 1950s and 1960s, or whether an intermediate position will emerge.

The growth of income from overseas investment in the 1950s and 1960s indicates that this item on balance of payments can more than keep pace with the growing demand for imports and that it has done so better than most other 'exports'. Whether its former importance to the balance of payments can be restored, depends on whether conditions are conducive to the net outflow of capital from the United Kingdom. This alone can create the source of further income from overseas investment. The conditions are that the United Kingdom must have capital to spare and others the ability to absorb it into their economies; that the products of overseas investment are available for sale in the United Kingdom or countries with convertible currencies; and that the financial framework allows overseas investment to take place without undue disturbance of the balance of payments on capital account.

All those conditions were met at the turn of the century. The position at that time will be briefly surveyed before an attempt is made to appraise future prospects.

In the late nineteenth and early twentieth-century heydays of British capital exports, the British economy had been at the then most advanced state for some time and was as capital-intensive as then feasible; while abroad there were economies which, though less advanced, were becoming more capital-intensive at a relatively more rapid rate. At home, further progress meant more known goods; the fruits of past technological achievements were spread to wider and wider sections of the population, which become better clad, had more coal for more grates and generally more of known goods. Domestic investment went largely into known activities, where uncertainty is normally less than in new ones – and where uncertainty is less, profit per unit produced tends to be less and domestic industrial growth tends to be less.

Since the ratio of capital to labour is normally less in known activities than in new ones, the domestic economy became more labour-intensive (36) (see Chapter 24, section 4) rather than more capital-intensive. Although capital continued to accumulate, this was not accompanied by an equivalent increase in the demand for capital for home investment. Hence capital became increasingly abundant. The increasing abundance of capital implied an increasing abundance of all factors (37) (see Chapters 22 and 23), so that wages as well as profits were kept low and there was some unemployment. (It should be noted that low factor prices and unemployment both sprang from the abundance of capital and not from each other.)

The result was a low-profit, low-wage and low-price economy at home. Yet it achieved rising standards of living and could afford the additional clothing, or whatever else the home economy produced more of, largely because of falling import prices until 1900 (which helped the poor) and rising income from overseas investment until 1914 (which helped the rich). Both benefits derived from British overseas investment which had assisted with development elsewhere.

Although the United Kingdom was most advanced, some other countries were advancing faster. The more rapidly advancing overseas economies were less capital-intensive than the British economy but were becoming more capital-intensive. Traditional British activities, such as, say, railway and port construction, were new and uncertain from the point of view of those countries, and earned appropriate rewards there. Since those countries were becoming more capital-intensive, capital was scarce; and where capital is scarce, all factors are scarce and factor rewards high. Amongst the developing countries of the nineteenth century were first the United States (31) and later the old Dominions. They developed as high-profit, high-wage and high-price economies, relatively to Britain's. The difference still persists, though it may not persist for ever.

High incomes for overseas producers and falling prices for the British were compatible because of the way British capital was invested overseas. British investment was not so much in direct ownership of American or Dominion productive assets, but largely in the creation of the means of communications. Railways, ports and financial services were the chief targets of British investors. British investment did not so much help to create the goods, but helped to make them more accessible. Lower transport costs and better financial services allowed for both higher incomes in the producing countries and lower prices in the principal consuming country.

Those who provided the finance for British overseas investment wanted a return in sterling. This was best assured when the borrowing countries could sell freely whatever they produced, in order to earn enough sterling to repay. As long as overseas products could be sold to Britain (or to third countries which, in turn, could sell to Britain), there was enough sterling available to enable repayment. The continuing attraction of overseas investment thus depended on the growth of British imports. There was a growing demand for imports as long as domestic industrial expansion depended on an appropriate increase in overseas-produced raw materials and as long as a growing population could be increasingly fed from abroad.

The growing demand for imports was allowed to be effective through British free trade. Free trade attracts goods but it repels factors. For goods can be sold without let or hindrance, so that factor rewards in traditional activities are kept in check through the availability of goods from abroad. British free trade was not reciprocated. For whatever reason, the developing countries of those days all had tariffs, so that production in their territories was protected from free competition. Protection repels goods but attracts factors. Since the growth industries of the then developing countries were traditional British industries, British factors were both repelled from Britain and attracted elsewhere. Commercial policy thus accentuated the tendency for British capital (and other factors) to move from the most capital-intensive economy of those days to the economies which were then becoming more capital-intensive.

All that was possible, without damage to the British balance of payments, because the finance for capital exports was provided largely by means of portfolio investment. Loans to colonial governments and other overseas agencies were issued in London. There the money capital was kept, until the borrower drew on it for the purchase of goods and services. Those goods and services were almost invariably British. When a borrower drew on a loan, there was an export of British money capital and thus a liability on the British balance of payments on long-term capital account. That burden on the balance of payments on long-term capital account arose only when goods and services were purchased. The purchase of British goods and services led to a corresponding increase in the export of merchandise or services, and such exports are credits on the balances of payments on current account. In other words the export of capital was balanced by an export of merchandise or services, and in consequence any current weakening of the balance of payments on long-term capital account was offset by a corresponding strengthening of the balance of payments on current account. Later on, when interest was received, income from overseas investment rose correspondingly, and the British balance of payments on current account was strengthened. Later still, when capital was repaid, the British balance of payments on long-term capital account was strengthened. Altogether it was possible to finance British overseas investment without detriment to the immediate British balance of payments and to the ultimate benefit of the British balance of payments.

Technically it is still possible to finance overseas investment by means of portfolio investment, and about one-third of British-owned assets overseas are still financed that way. (32) But for reasons to be discussed below, most additions to British-owned assets overseas now come through direct investment in firms operating overseas. Technically, unilateral free trade could be restored any day, were there a consensus that the profitability of overseas investment is an overriding consideration. There is no such consensus. Altogether there is no lack of City institutions to facilitate overseas investment of any kind, nor is there lack of knowledge of what legal framework would be most helpful. The obstacles to an early restoration of overseas investment to its former importance are not institutional or legal. They are economic. The British economy's role in the world has changed.

Superficially, there may be some resemblance between the state of the British economy at the turn of the century and in the 1960s. At both times the British economy seemed as fully developed as possible, given the state of technological knowledge and the availability of factors. Around 1900, the escape into a higher growth rate lay through further employment of British factors in overseas activities, in order to spread abroad what was already fully developed at home.

In the 1960s, however, the chief limitation to British economic growth was not lack of further opportunities at home but lack of factors that could use all the opportunities which presented themselves. The limitation was a scarcity of factors which made it impossible to catch up with others, let alone lead in the utilisation of new opportunities save in a few specialised fields. Britain is no longer ahead of all other countries, and any attempt to catch up with the even more advanced countries will keep factors scarce for some time to come. The escape into a higher growth rate thus does not lie so much in spreading the employment of British factors across the globe, but in making them go further at home. This means capital deepening, continuous scarcity of factors, full employment at home and relatively fewer factors to spare for overseas investment.

If there was a choice between, on the one hand, spreading the economy to the poor at home or abroad and, on the other hand, deepening the economy, that choice has been made. Amongst the growth industries of the 1960s were electronics and computers, plastics and pharmaceuticals, aircraft and natural gas. All of those industries were hungry for capital. They were not particularly hungry from imported raw materials. Their growth was far more independent of imported materials than, say, nineteenth-century cotton. The growth of the newer industries of the 1960s provides less of a guarantee that overseas investment will pay on a substantial scale than did the growth of past industries.

The choice has been made, perhaps tardily and even unwillingly. The country entered the 1960s with plans to spread known goods to those who had less of them – if need be, through more social services at home and more aid abroad. It leaves the 1960s with most of those schemes shelved, with pride in its aircraft rather than in subsidised school meals. Inevitably this implies a choice in favour of home investment rather than overseas investment, whenever a choice has to be made.

To spread an economy to the poor, at home or abroad, depends first and foremost on the success of overseas investment. This alone makes the country's techniques known abroad and cheapens overseas supplies. It is not yet sufficiently widely appreciated that the choice in favour of capital deepening means overseas investment must become relatively less important than home investment, and that all attempts to make our goods cheap and wages low are that much more difficult, if not altogether doomed.

Any domestic growth that seeks to circumvent the scarcity of factors makes domestically employed factors more valuable. There is a tendency towards a high-profit, high-wage and high-price economy that seeks to sell dear at home and abroad, rather than buy cheap at home and abroad. The transition was not completed in the 1960s, and it was often obstructed by the attempts to restore the cheap economy at a time when income from overseas investment made only about one-third of the contribution it made before 1914. Should the tendencies towards domestic capital deepening continue, only the most profitable overseas investments will continue to be attractive. Those will be in countries which are doing even better than Britain. In the 1950s and 1960s those were the most advanced industrial countries.

Relatively more of available money capital is wanted at home to deepen real capital at home. The forces of repulsion no longer operate as much as they did earlier this century. What of the forces that attract British capital into overseas activities?

Most of the world is still less advanced than the United Kingdom. But in much of the 1950s and 1960s most of the less advanced countries also had lesser growth rates than the United Kingdom. One reason was that world exports of primary products grew less than world exports of manufactures, so that the less advanced countries, which depend relatively more on the export of primary products, had less export-led growth than the industrial countries. By implication, the less advanced countries' ability to pay interest and repay capital was not as certain as that of the more advanced countries.

Although the primary producing countries have, on the whole, advanced less than the industrial countries, they have not stood still either. Their internal development often implied increased urbanisation, and that means that more of the food they produce for the market is sold to markets in their own towns and relatively less is available for export. Matters are different in countries where agriculture is a highly mechanised industry. That is the case of agriculture in the advanced industrial countries, where it often enjoys protection and is subsidised by national exchequers. Such agriculture does not need British capital.

In the past, overseas investment brought cheaper raw materials — which are relatively less needed now — and it brought cheaper food — which will be more difficult to get.

There may still be gain in overseas investment in such countries, as long as there is a country that is more advanced than others and seeks to spread those benefits to the poor at home and abroad. The country that is most likely to benefit from such a 'cheap economy', for the rest of this century, is the United States and not Britain. American ways of investing abroad are beyond the scope of this book, but the investment of United States dollars via the City of London is relevant in the present context. In the mid-1960s there were over $10,000 million in the London Euro-dollar market, (40) which is a market where American and other owners of United States dollars deposit dollars with London banks whence they are re-lent to borrowers anywhere. Such investment of American funds through London earns the City commissions and to that extent benefits the British balance of payments. For accounting purposes, the benefit appears under 'other services' and not under income from overseas investment.

So far, however, the chief destination of Euro-dollars lent via London has been Europe (including Britain). Euro-dollars provided no exception to the general tendency of international capital to flow towards the world's most developed areas. This is not surprising, since the net flow of capital tends to be from capital-intensive economies to those that are becoming most markedly more capital-intensive; and it so happened that, in the 1950s and 1960s, the countries that were becoming most markedly more capital-intensive were the countries that had already achieved a high level of development. (34)

The sort of activities that most attracted foreign capital into each country were activities in the various growth sectors. If perhaps over one-eighth of the capital in the manufacturing sector of the British economy is foreign-owned; if that proportion is substantially higher in the countries of the European Economic Community; and if that proportion is not altogether negligible even in the United States; (35) this is the outcome of increased and increasing specialisation amongst the industrial countries. Each is somewhat further advanced in certain specialities than any other, and each has to overcome the scarcity of factors. It pays to make use of the international division of capital by letting innovations be applied by those who first made a commercial success of them, rather than to duplicate the necessary expenditure on research and development. It pays the innovator to reap the rewards of uncertainty-bearing in several countries rather than just one. As long as the industrial world remains divided by tariffs, there are two main ways to overcome tariffs and other obstacles to trade in new goods. One is to sell the new process to established firms elsewhere and earn royalties of right; any such royalties received raise income from 'other services'. The other way is to buy or set up branch factories behind each tariff wall; any profit, interest or dividend remitted to the parent firm raises income from overseas investment.

From the individual firm's point of view, the chief purpose of such overseas investment is to reap the profits of uncertainty-bearing as many times as possible. During the early stages of production the article is perfected until it is ready for mass production in whatever way is most suitable for each market. Until the mass-production stage is reached, profits of overseas branch firms are likely to be ploughed back locally. It may be some years before the parent country's income from overseas investment is favourably affected.

Given the present stage of development of the British economy and other European economies, the process normally stops at this point for the British and other Europeans. Given the even more advanced stage of development of the United States economy, there may be one further stage. It may pay American firms to produce in the United Kingdom, not just for British consumption but even for American consumption. For instance, traditional American products, such as motor-cars, may be produced in the United Kingdom even for American consumption, as long as British factors are cheaper than American factors. This is part of the process of building a 'cheap economy' in the United States. This cannot go on for ever, but it can go on until British factor prices have caught up with American factor prices (a process which itself is speeded up as American demand puts additional pressure on British factor supplies). While the process continues, the British balance of payments benefits: first on capital account, when Americans set up or purchase British factories; and then on merchandise trade account, when the American branch factories start to export. (Later on, however, there is a burden on the British balance of payments, in so far as American firms repatriate profits and dividends.)

It will have been noticed that the form of overseas investment referred to is the purchase or setting-up of branch factories or firms. This kind of investment is known as direct investment, since the investor acquires direct ownership and control over overseas assets. Most overseas investment in Britain is of this nature, and so is most new British overseas investment, which by the 1960s had become twice as large as portfolio investment overseas.

When there is a direct overseas investment by a British firm, there is a corresponding liability on the British balance of payments on long-term capital account. The extent of the liability is what it costs to set up a branch factory or firm, or the purchase price if the investment takes the form of acquisition of an overseas company. If British materials are needed to set up an overseas subsidiary, there is an offsetting increase in the export of merchandise which creates a credit on the balance of payments on current account. According to the most detailed estimate available (36) the average effect of any additional £100 of direct investment overseas includes additional exports of merchandise of £9. On this basis, the additional burden on the balance of payments on long-term capital account is insufficiently offset on the balance of payments on current account to allow for such smooth overseas investment as was possible at the beginning of the century. There are yet future benefits in the form of increased income from overseas investment, but it takes some years before these benefits materialise. Since the purpose of direct investment overseas is to establish British ownership overseas, there is no long-term benefit to the balance of payments on long-term capital account simply because there is no repayment on capital.

Direct investment is thus altogether different from portfolio investment, both in its purpose and its balance-of-payments effects. Portfolio investment was suitable to make supplies more accessible to the investing country and therefore cheaper; it was safe in countries under English law or similar law; it was often in fixed-interest-bearing securities which are attractive to hold when the domestic price level is falling, or at least stable. Direct investment, however, is resorted to in order to make British know-how accessible to other countries, and there is no reason why this should be cheap; it takes place in countries with all sorts of laws; and its return, in money terms, is always uncertain.

The world has its ports and railways. The nineteenth century achieved that. The British demand for imported raw materials is relatively less (though absolutely more) than in the past; and the increase in the availability of overseas food supplies is less certain than in the past, and also relatively less necessary, as population expands less and incomes rise. The overseas world has moved away from English law, and British prices have been rising for a considerable period of time. That makes portfolio investment less secure and, in so far as it is fixed-interest-bearing, less attractive. The need now is for the international division of capital, which can be made more effective through reciprocal direct investment. But the direct investment that a country can export must be more nearly balanced by the direct investment she imports, if adverse balance-of-payments effects are to be avoided.

To sum up, invisible trade has traditionally balanced the deficit on the merchandise trade. But its chief constituents have behaved in different ways. The transport balance of the 1950s and 1960s was disappointing, possibly for temporary reasons. Services, other than transport, have done well and will continue to do so as long as world trade expands and as long as some items, formerly income from overseas investment, are transferred to commissions. Income from overseas investment has done well, and yet could not contribute as much to the balance of payments as at any time between 1816 and 1939. It will not become unimportant. But it will have to be more evenly balanced between the export and import of capital for as long as the United Kingdom's interest lies in participation in the international division of capital and the restoration of the cheap economy remains an unattainable dream.

26   Sterling

1   GOLD AND THE 'CHEAP ECONOMY'

Every economic situation has its monetary counterpart. The twentieth-century changes in the United Kingdom's economic structure and place in the world economy required appropriate changes in monetary policy. It was, however, not always possible to foresee what sort of monetary policy would be needed; and even when this was understood, it was by no means easy to find ways of implementing it. From the 1920s to the 1960s there were difficulties in monetary adjustment to new situations, with the result that adjustments in production and trade were hampered and delayed. The gold standard may have suited the circumstances prevailing before 1914; but the attempt to restore it in the altered circumstances of the 1920s ended in failure. A managed currency system began to be evolved in the 1930s, only to give rise to difficulties in the different circumstances of the 1960s.

It would be beyond the scope of this book even to attempt a full account of the complex relationship between monetary and 'real' changes. It must suffice to indicate some of the ways in which monetary policy can foster or frustrate the growth of production and trade. In Part III this was done with reference to the domestic scarcity of factors. The present chapter is concerned with monetary policy in relation to overseas trade. The discussion proceeds in historic sequence, starting with the situation at the beginning of the twentieth century.

In those days monetary policy was the concern of the Bank of England alone. The single aim of policy was the maintenance of the gold standard. Subject to that, the responsibility of the Bank was confined to the regulation of credit on sound banking principles. Above all, the Bank would check any expansion which might undermine confidence in credit and, incidentally, threaten the convertibility of the currency and thus of the gold standard itself.

The Government considered itself in politics and not in business. It took no part in the framing of monetary policy, except when new legislation was in question, and it took no responsibility for prices, incomes, employment and the state of trade or any other aspect of economic affairs beyond what was needed to provide a framework for the smooth running of free trade. In short, the only central economic control was monetary control, and that was concerned only with money.

A self-centred monetary system suited the circumstances of the time. However unintentionally, it ensured that all goods were cheap. Credit control limited the domestic money supply and thus the possibility of a domestic rise in prices. If credit control limited some opportunities for domestic economic growth, that was compensated by overseas investment which ensured cheap supplies. Cheap raw materials kept industrial costs down, and cheap food kept the cost of housekeeping down. As mentioned in Chapter 24, imported food is traditionally a major variable in the British standard of living. It was brought to Britain through the services of financiers and helped especially the lower income groups towards an adequate diet. One of the results was a community of interests between City financiers and the urban working class, and this is a piece of social cement not lightly to be discarded. Even to the present day the staunchest defenders of the primacy of a strong currency over all other policy considerations include political representatives of the urban working class.

Whatever the position today, at a time when a major sector of the British economy operated overseas, and even in countries where the Queen's writ did not run but British money was acceptable, the only controls which could be equally effective throughout the British economy at home and overseas were monetary controls. As already mentioned, the monetary controls would regulate credit at home and also regulate the flow of capital between the home and overseas sectors of the economy. The controls were not used for the sake of accumulating excessive hoards of gold. In the 1900s and to 1913, the Bank of England's gold reserves varied between £30 million and £40 million. Those were 'low' reserves compared with the £1,000 million now widely considered the minimum necessary to assure the exchange rate, even when full allowance is made for the fall in the gold parity and the rise in prices since then; and the reserves were also low compared with those of other central banks at the time. High reserves are only needed by the weak and by those who do not understand banking. Britain's position was strong, since there was universal confidence that the Bank of England's outpayments would be matched by at least equivalent inpayments. The art of central banking, as then practised by the Bank of England, kept British capital in profitable circulation throughout the world. At a time when the British economy was the most advanced economy, but other economies were developing faster, British capital could be kept in circulation abroad by keeping interest rates at home higher than they need have been in the absence of capital exports, and yet lower than they were in the principal developing countries of the time. This helped to ensure Britain's long-term creditor position. Since the problem was how to repel British capital (and not how to attract foreign capital), a change in British monetary policy would directly affect the bulk of the capital flow. A rise in interest rates would delay the export of capital or even encourage speedier repatriation; a fall in interest rates would repel capital all the faster.

Although capital was often repelled from Britain, it does not follow that British industry was deprived of capital. At home there was abundance of factors. Moreover in the 1890s and the 1900s there were substantial balance-of-payments surpluses, but these were exceeded by income from overseas investment. The balance-of-payments surpluses indicate fairly accurately the export of capital, since a country's net capital exports equal its balance-of-payments surplus plus or minus a change in the exchange reserves (and the gold reserves were too low to change much). If, however, income from overseas investment exceeds the export of capital, the country's current money income is still higher than if there were no overseas activities, and there are thus more funds available for domestic activities than would otherwise be the case. Where such conditions prevail, the capital-exporting country reinvests some of its overseas profits and does not deprive itself of net savings. Only in the last few years before the First World War (as also before the 1890s), did the balance-of-payments surplus exceed income from overseas investment, so that domestic savings were made available for net capital creation overseas. Thus in the first decade of the present century there was a tendency towards an inflow of profits and dividends earned overseas, and not all of this was reinvested overseas; only in the last few years were there tendencies towards a net outflow. The cheap economy works best when capital is kept overseas, so as to prevent domestic inflation and ensure cheap imports. That was the 'real' counterpart of the gold standard system of those days, even if the monetary authorities' thought was on the monetary aspect alone.

There was no need for the monetary authorities to consider the real counterpart of their policies, as long as safeguarding the gold reserves produced just that result. As already implied, the usual problem was to prevent an undue accumulation of idle gold reserves and to encourage profitable overseas investment instead (which ensured future inpayments). There were, however, disturbances which were associated with sudden changes in direction of the international terms of trade of manufactures over primary products. In those days such movements in the terms of trade usually took the form of an unexpected rise in primary product prices in terms of manufactures. Uncontrolled, such a change in the terms of trade might have attracted more capital abroad, but that would have led to two kinds of disturbances which the authorities counteracted. One disturbance was to the balance of payments. The worsening of the terms of trade weakened the balance of payments, and the authorities could not therefore take it so much for granted that inpayments would exceed outpayments. To counteract such tendencies, Bank Rate was raised. The other disturbance was that overseas supplies ceased to be cheap, and that threatened the very basis of the British economy of those days. The increase in Bank Rate counteracted this as well, even if this effect was incidental to a policy change made on balance-of-payments grounds. These points will be dealt with in the following paragraphs.

Since an increase in Bank Rate would lead to a general rise in interest rates in Britain, one effect was that British money capital earned more at home and so was attracted to stay at home or even to return home. The tendency towards deficit in the balance of merchandise trade could thus be countered by an induced tendency for capital to stay in Britain, so that the aggregate balance of payments showed less of a deficit or more of a surplus than it otherwise would have done.

Internally, however, the rise in Bank Rate would raise the cost of borrowing for existing activities and capital widening, and so depress the general level of activity. The attraction (or non-repulsion) of capital did not necessarily have compensating effects, for much of overseas investment was in fixed-interest-bearing stock, and when capital stayed at home, Consols would often seem a more suitable alternative to overseas investment than industrial capital. If there was compensation for the harm that crisis Bank Rates did to industrial activity, this was more in the price effects of higher interest rates than in the availability of money capital.

A rise in Bank Rate would immediately affect the discount rate for bills and so affect the finance of trade. A rise in interest rates lowers values of existing capital and makes new capital formation more expensive. Capital includes circulating capital, being the stock-in-trade of business enterprises, and in so far as it includes food and raw materials, it includes items which are of major importance amongst Britain's imports. Since imported stock-in-trade was largely purchased through bills of exchange and higher interest rates would lower the value of bills of exchange, merchants would find it more expensive to replenish their stocks. They would offer lower prices to their overseas suppliers or replenish their stocks more slowly (which would make overseas suppliers more inclined to accept lower prices rather than have stocks left on their hands). Britain's predominance as buyer of primary products would make it almost certain that primary producers accepted the lower offers. The cost of imports was reduced; the balance of payments improved; and the cheap economy, as well as the gold standard itself, was once more assured.

When raw-material prices fell, industry was somewhat compensated for the higher cost of borrowing, and this compensation cut depressions short. (This does not deny that domestic depressions could be accentuated, and possibly even caused, by higher interest rates.) Since there would be time-lags between the adverse effects on the level of domestic activity and the favourable effects on raw-material prices, and since compensation could never be perfect, a rise in

Bank Rate would raise unemployment before it cut the depression short. More unemployment meant more poverty, but poverty was alleviated by the fall in food prices.

In this way, and quite unintentionally, the pre-1914 Bank Rate mechanism acted somewhat like a crude welfare state without the means test. An increase in Bank Rate would alleviate the lot of each of the poor – even if it temporarily increased their number. Moreover the purpose of Bank Rate changes was to safeguard the currency, and in the long run the strong currency safeguarded cheap food for the workers, cheap raw materials for industry and low prices of home-produced goods as well as of imports.

All that cheapness depended on sterling. Because of the importance of British capital exports, sterling was in circulation throughout the trading world. Because free-trade Britain provided a ready market for goods moving in world trade (often thanks to overseas investment), there was as safe a return as there could be for British investors. Sterling was in circulation and would come home with interest. Sterling was as good as gold. It was on gold. Or more accurately, gold was on sterling.

In a purely historical account of what happened before 1914, it would not matter whether gold was on sterling or sterling on gold. They were synonymous, since the value of the pound sterling was fixed in terms of gold, and both were freely interchangeable and acceptable at home and overseas. In an analytical account, however, and in an explanation of some of the disappointments of the 1920s and 1960s, it is of importance whether the pre-1914 monetary standard was based on gold or on sterling.

This chapter started with the assertion that every economic situation has its monetary counterpart. It is equally valid to say that every monetary situation has its 'real' counterpart. All attempts to restore one without the other are likely to end in disappointment.

The 'real' counterpart of the pre-1914 gold standard was the cheap economy. It was workable because the monetary mechanism had a 'real' base in the substantial volume of British overseas investment. It worked through the regulation of the flow of funds between the British economy at home and the British economy overseas. The chief instrument of control was Bank Rate. This was an efficacious instrument of control, because it regulated the flow of funds in accordance with monetary requirements, and at the same time it regulated import prices in accordance with 'real' requirements. The effect on import prices came about through the impact of Bank Rate changes on the value of trade bills – at a time when a well-organised bill market was chiefly concerned with trade bills payable in sterling.

In the 1920s an attempt was made to put sterling back on gold. It failed, because gold was no longer on sterling. In the 1960s strenuous efforts were made to keep product and factor prices down, and so re-create a cheap economy. Again there was failure, because in the 1960s the monetary system was geared to other ends. Both policies were dreams, inspired by different aspects of the pre-1914 state of affairs, and both were followed by rude awakenings (in 1931 and 1967 respectively). (1)

2 OVERVALUATION

The primacy of sterling over gold was revealed when the gold standard was suspended at the outbreak of war in 1914. For when Britain borrowed, she borrowed in sterling. That was unusual prestige for a currency, since international loans are normally in gold or the lender's currency. At the same time the suspension of the gold peg meant that the various currencies of the world were no longer at fixed exchange rates, but fluctuated relatively to each other. Exchange-rate fluctuations enhanced the risks of international trade, and the costs of covering those risks in the exchange markets could be prohibitively expensive. That did not matter so much during the war, when commercial considerations were suspended, but was irksome during the post-war period of reconstruction. A return to an orderly foreign exchange market was sought. It was attempted through the re-establishment of the gold standard in 1925. The return to gold was at the old sterling—gold parity.

That parity was an overvaluation in relation to gold, which once more became the base of domestic credit. There would have to be deflation to enforce the gold parity. It was thought, however, that deflation would keep British prices low so that British exports would be at an advantage in international markets. There would be an export surplus which would lay the foundations of a revival of the pre-1914 type of economy. An export-led revival would eventually take care of the unemployed. There were also political considerations. War debts to the United States were to be repaid at their full value. Whatever the merits of such arguments, few subsequent commentators had a good word for the decision to return to gold at the old parity. The attempted restoration of the gold standard ended in failure, for reasons the policy-makers of 1925 had either not understood or to which they had attached insufficient weight.

The critics attacked the decision largely on the ground of the domestic consequences of overvaluation. They rightly pointed out that overvaluation meant credit restraint and denied all hope of relief for the serious unemployment problems of the time. They paid less attention to the international implications which alone make the decision comprehensible. Without wishing to rake up old controversies as to whether honour demanded the repayment of war debts at their full value (or whether this object could have been achieved through revaluing the debts rather than the currency), it may not be irrelevant to point to the greater difficulties the United Kingdom had in securing American supplies during the early stages of the Second World War, when she could no longer borrow from the United States in sterling. The critics of the 1920s may not have thought that the United Kingdom might ever have to borrow in a currency·other than sterling, and later critics may have overlooked this point.

The contemporary critics may also not have thought of the possibility that the United Kingdom might ever have to face sustained balance-of-payments difficulties. To them, this must have seemed a by-product of war and exceptional labour unrest, scarcely to be contemplated as a permanent problem. If the authorities thought too much of the gold reserves, they deserve at least more sympathy from their critics after the balance-of-payments experiences of the 1930s and 1960s than they got from their contemporaries.

As far as the balance of payments was concerned, the policy of 1925 was at least not a complete failure. The balance of payments stayed in surplus (2) as long as sterling was overvalued in relation to the dollar. Only when the world depression led to an even greater overvaluation of the dollar (and other currencies tied to gold), did the balance of payments of the United Kingdom turn into deficit. (For then overseas customers could not afford to buy so many goods, including British goods.) (3)

If the 1925 policy was not an immediate failure on balance-of-payments grounds, it cannot be rated a success either. For the country's external and domestic economic performances were intertwined. The level of employment had been low since the collapse of the post-war boom in 1921, and the decision of 1925 denied all prospects of early relief. In consequence sterling's home base was weakened. The low level of activity at home limited the demand for the products of overseas investment, and this denied the need for an export surplus as the foundation of overseas investment. Hence sterling's overseas base was weakened. For reasons to be explained below, Bank Rate control could no longer be as effective as it had been in regulating the flow of British funds between the two bases of sterling. These points must be discussed at length. First, however, attention must be drawn to the emergence of the exchange-rate problem for the pound sterling.

Before 1914 there could be no exchange-rate problem for sterling. Gold was on sterling, so that other currencies were valued in relation to sterling. By 1925, however, the dollar had emerged as a currency of equal stature to sterling's. Gold, as an international medium of exchange, was not so much on sterling as on the dollar – the more so since the United States had resumed gold payments earlier and without much difficulty. If gold was to be both on sterling and the dollar, the return of sterling to gold should have been at a parity that correctly reflected the sterling–dollar parity. A two-centre world monetary system might then have been workable. Since, however, both currencies were returned to gold at the old parity, this implied an undervaluation of the dollar in terms of sterling and an overvaluation of sterling in terms of the dollar. The dollar had become an internationally more desired currency, so that on this ground alone the exchange rate should have been moved in favour of the dollar.

As far as the sterling–dollar exchange rate was concerned, it would not have mattered whether the dollar should have been returned to gold at a higher parity or sterling at a lower parity. There were, however, domestic implications as well. Under a gold standard system, the base of the money supply is in ratio to the central bank's gold reserves. The money supply is adequate if there is a high level of employment. During most of the 1920s the level of employment was unprecedentedly high in the United States and unprecedentedly low in the United Kingdom. In other words the money supply was adequate in the United States until 1929, and the dollar was correctly valued for the needs of its home base, while sterling was overvalued in relation to domestic needs as well as in relation to the dollar.

To maintain the overvalued sterling exchange parity required deflation in the United Kingdom. This restricted the possibilities of expansion of the home economy. Any hopes of compensation through expansion of overseas investment and cheap imports were disappointed through the effects of overvaluation on the profitability of overseas investment and through changes in the bill market. These points must be dealt with in turn, starting with the effects of overvaluation on overseas investment.

At first sight overvaluation may seem to encourage overseas investment. Overvaluation makes it cheaper for British investors to acquire claims over overseas assets, so that new overseas investment should be encouraged. The reverse side of such a situation is, however, that it becomes dearer to borrow from the country with the overvalued currency. Since there was abundance of factors in the United Kingdom in the 1920s, capital should have been available at relatively low rates of interest. Had this been the case, there might have been an upsurge of overseas investment as there had been in the last few years before 1914. But interest rates were kept high for the sake of the exchange rate, so that borrowing in London became expensive (for those seeking loans at home or overseas).

Moreover not all overseas investment is new investment. In the 1920s as in the 1890s and the 1900s, income from overseas investment exceeded overseas investment, so that on balance overseas investment was re-investment rather than new investment. As far as old overseas investment is concerned, the effects of overvaluation are likely to be entirely adverse. If sterling was overvalued by 10 per cent (which was the figure widely quoted at the time), income from overseas investment in non-sterling countries would have to yield 10 per cent more than before overvaluation, just to give the same sterling return as before. Overseas enterprises, which had to make fixed-interest sterling payments, became correspondingly less profitable and were pushed that much nearer to bankruptcy, while equity dividends just became worth that much less in sterling, to the disappointment of British lenders who were also pushed that much nearer to bankruptcy.

The preceding considerations apply to overseas investment in foreign currency areas. In countries that kept their currencies tied to sterling, the impediment to successful growth of overseas investment was not the exchange rate itself but the deflation which was enforced to maintain the exchange rate. The deflation limited the growth of all sterling economies. In the United Kingdom this implied a limitation of demand for the products of overseas investment and therefore of its profitability. Roughly speaking, overvaluation limited the prospects for overseas investment in the Americas, and deflation limited it in the Empire. Above all, deflation to maintain overvaluation restricted sterling's home base.

Bank Rate was still the chief instrument of control. Historically, it may not have been unduly high, but it was high for an economy afflicted by unprecedented unemployment problems. As shown in Part III, an underemployed economy has an abundance of factors, and especially of capital. In such circumstances borrowing for both domestic and overseas purposes should be encouraged, in order to raise effective demand and reduce the abundance of factors. Thus Bank Rate should have been lowered in the 1920s in order to raise the demand for available British factors. Instead it was kept high in order to support overseas demand for British money.

Overseas holdings of sterling could be in cash, sterling bills or sterling bonds. Usually Treasury bills predominated in such holdings. As a by-product of war and post-war finance, Treasury bills had replaced trade bills as the chief short-term securities in the money market. Substantial overseas holdings had emerged as another by-product of war and post-war finance. While the gold standard had been suspended, overseas countries could not convert their sterling earnings into gold; and when the gold standard was restored, they often did not. They had discovered that the holding of securities, such as Treasury bills, was profitable: Treasury bills earned interest, while gold did not, and Treasury bills were readily marketable and could be converted into foreign exchange at any time. A reserve currency system emerged: overseas countries held some of their reserves in sterling (and dollars) instead of gold. This was encouraged by high interest rates.

Overseas demand for British securities could be influenced by Bank Rate policy. Nevertheless substantial overseas holdings of British bills blunted the efficacy of Bank Rate as an instrument of control. Overseas owners would be responsive to British interest rates, but they would also be responsive to what happened in their own countries. The problem of monetary control was no longer the pre-1914 one of regulating the flow of British money capital between the home economy and overseas. Instead it had become a problem of how to attract overseas demand for British money. In other words sterling control had given way to the control of sterling.

Substantial overseas ownership of British bills arose from the evolution of the reserve currency system. This made it more difficult to control the flow of funds by means of British Bank Rate alone. The reasons are as follows. The increase in overseas ownership of British bills had been made possible by a change in the character of the bill market. Once primarily a market in trade bills, it had become primarily a market in finance bills. It will be recalled from section 1 above that the 'real' counterpart of the pre-1914 gold standard had been the cheap economy, and that the efficacy of Bank Rate as an instrument of 'real' control had derived from its impact on the trade bill and consequent effect on import prices. When the pre-1914 cheap economy had been threatened by an adverse movement in the terms of trade, a rise in Bank Rate could effectively counter such a threat. After 1925, import prices fell, but until 1929 they did not fall markedly more than export prices. Had it been possible in 1925 to improve the terms of trade by 10 per cent or more, it might have been possible to clear the home market at the level of incomes then prevailing. This did not happen, and might have been difficult in any event, given the magnitude of the domestic unemployment prevailing and the reduced opportunities for overseas investment. It could not happen at a time when trade bills were less used to finance imports than in the past, and when the bill market was swamped by Treasury bills. In consequence Bank Rate was blunted as an instrument of 'real' control as well as of monetary control.

Moreover, given the sort of difficulties that faced the British and overseas economies in the 1920s, Bank Rate had become rather irrelevant. As an instrument of control it had worked best in the 1890s and 1900s, when crises were associated with a movement in the terms of trade against the United Kingdom. In such circumstances an increase in Bank Rate would depress import prices. This would have welfare effects at home, and would be tolerable to overseas producers, in so far as it enabled them to maintain output; while a fall in Bank Rate would allow for a recovery in import prices and encourage an expansion of overseas production, aided by British capital exports. These conditions were not given in the 1920s.

There had been no sharp movement in the terms of trade immediately before 1925. In the later 1920s import prices were falling, but so were export prices. Both may have been accentuated by British deflation. The fall in British prices was largely due to the low level of domestic activity. The fall in overseas primary product prices was the result of overproduction. While Europe had been at war, overseas primary production increased; when Europe recovered, overseas primary production was not cut back. The result was a slide in world primary product prices from the mid-1920s to the mid-1930s. Even the lowest possible British Bank Rate would almost certainly have failed to raise overseas primary product prices and production, and it could not have made overseas investment more profitable when world primary production capacity was already excessive. The problem was no longer how to cope with temporary price movements against the United Kingdom and how to encourage long-term overseas expansion, but how to cope with falling prices and excess supplies. True, had Bank Rate been lower, there would have been less deficiency in domestic demand, and that might have helped to stem the fall in overseas prices and helped with the problems created by excess supplies. But it would also have let the British terms of trade deteriorate, which would have aggravated domestic problems, and it would also have made it more difficult for overseas countries to accumulate exchange reserves, which would have countered the benefits of lower Bank Rate. The basic problems of the 1920s were just not of a nature to be solved through Bank Rate policy. In so far as interest-rate policy could have helped, that would have required more international co-operation than was possible in those days.

Blunted and irrelevant to the problems of the inter-war years, Bank Rate was abandoned as an instrument of policy in 1932. Subsequently it was kept at the lowest possible level for twenty years, save for a few days at the outbreak of the Second World War. A cheap money era was to follow the cheap economy and the attempt at its restoration. By 1932, however, the gold standard itself had been abandoned. To sum up, the restoration of sterling to gold failed because the overseas investment base was weakened and was further weakened by overvaluation; because the instrument of control was blunted and irrelevant to the problems of the time; and because overvaluation weakened the home base for overseas investment, while the attendant deflation denied alternative domestic development. In fairness, it should be added that the attempted return to gold did not cause the basic British economic problem of the time; unemployment had been high before 1925 and continued at a high rate after the abandonment of gold. The attempted return to gold failed to solve that problem and aggravated it. What had happened was that gold was no longer on sterling, and because the contemporaries did not see it that way, they chased the shadow of departed gold and failed to seek alternatives. (4)

3 DEPRECIATION

The attempt to reach gold was abandoned in 1931. By then the whole world was in deepening depression. In 1929 world production and trade began to fall, and by 1932 both were at about two-thirds of their 1929 levels. World production was not to regain its 1929 level until the mid-1930s and world trade not until after the Second World War. Such depression in world economic activity implies that currencies in general were becoming increasingly overvalued. As stated before, a currency is correctly valued only if it fulfils both of the following requirements. One is that there is domestic full employment (without inflation), and the other is that the balance of payments is in equlibrium (without change in the currency area's gold reserves).

Leaving aside the balance-of-payments aspect until later, a world trend towards falling activity implies general overvaluation of currencies in relation to domestic needs. During the depression the dollar became overvalued, and the same applied to most currencies. Overvaluation was no longer a problem of the pound sterling alone. It continued to be a general currency problem throughout the 1930s, when unemployment remained high. But the main problem was not overvaluation of one currency in terms of another, but overvaluation of most currencies in terms of gold. For even when the international gold standard was abandoned, countries still regulated domestic credit in relation to their gold reserves, even if less rigidly than before.

The general overvaluation of currencies did not ease the problems of sterling. On the contrary, overseas overvaluation led to difficulties for the export trades. As far as the United Kingdom was concerned, the 1929 slump was export-led, and it had adverse effects on the domestic employment situation and on the balance of payments.

As mentioned before, import prices fell during the second half of the 1920s, but as long as import prices fell no more than export prices, the terms of trade were not changed. From 1929 onwards, the fall in import and export prices accelerated, and the fall in import prices accelerated markedly more than that of export prices. The United Kingdom's terms of trade improved sharply, but this gave her no more than a relatively improved position amongst general world impoverishment. Even this relative improvement was not altogether beneficial, for the greater impoverisation overseas had adverse effects on the export trades. Unemployment rose in the export trades, and since home conditions did not improve, there were no alternative opportunities for the abandoned factors of production. Instead the reduced employment in the export trades lowered effective home demand, with adverse effects on the domestic trades. In general, the rate of unemployment doubled: in 1929 one worker in ten had been unwanted; two years later the figure was one in five. Since the prime function of any currency is to enable a high level of economic activity, sterling fulfilled its proper role even less during the slump than before the slump. Already over-valued before 1929, it became even more overvalued after 1929.

Since the slump was export-led, there were adverse effects on the balance of trade. Conditions were worsening faster overseas than at home, so that exports fell faster than imports. There was no relief from invisible earnings; with the falling level in industrial activity and trade, income from overseas investment was adversely affected, and so were shipping earnings and City earnings. The balance of payments deteriorated from a surplus of over £100 million in 1929 to a deficit of over £100 million in 1931.

One year's deficit would not have driven sterling off the attempt to reach gold, had it not aggravated the gold payments difficulties the Bank of England had experienced for some time. A feature of the monetary scene of the 1920s had been the evolution of a reserve currency system, whereby other countries' central banks held some of their exchange reserves in sterling. After the return of the French franc to gold, however, the Bank of France began to convert its foreign exchange holdings into gold, and from 1928 onwards pressure on sterling became marked. Intensified deflation enabled the Bank of England to resist this pressure and maintain its gold reserves intact until 1930. When the British balance of payments deteriorated, that was no longer possible. The Bank of England had to abandon gold payments.

When sterling was divorced from gold in 1931, no new exchange parity was fixed. The pound sterling was left to float to find its level in the market. It immediately depreciated against gold by about 30 per cent. Since gold continued to be the base of domestic credit until the Second World War, the depreciation made domestic credit expansion possible. Credit expansion was further eased through increases in the fiduciary issue and by 'cheap money'.

Cheap money meant that Bank Rate was kept inactive at 2 per cent, but that did not make all money 'cheap'. The joint-stock banks have consistently given advances at Bank Rate plus 1 or 1½ per cent, subject to the assumption that Bank Rate is never less than 4 per cent. In consequence any day-to-day finance of business that depended on bank advances still carried at least a 5 per cent interest burden, and that was a high burden in times of trade depression. Cheap money was available only to the Government and to financial institutions that were independent of bank advances. The Government, however, still pursued a cautious fiscal policy, and although there was some increase in public works, this was on a moderate scale. Deliberate budget deficits and substantial central government borrowing for economic purposes remained subjects for academic discussion rather than for practical policy. It was left to local authorities and building societies to take up the easier credit. There was a housing boom, which can be regarded as the most beneficial economic achievement of the 1930s. The cheap economy of the past had fed and clad the masses more adequately than ever before; cheap money was to house them properly. This was one of the great levelling-up activities of British economic history, and the first that did not depend on growing net overseas investment activity (which had ceased). It helped towards recovery from the 1929 slump, but it did not suffice to cure the basic unemployment problem of the inter-war years.

The domestic depreciation of the currency in relation to gold provided a base for easier credit, but business response was insufficient to achieve full employment. Even in 1937, the best year of the 1930s, the unemployment rate was still slightly higher than it had been in 1929. In short, the depreciation helped towards recovery, but despite rising gold reserves it did not go far enough. That it did not go far enough does not make it unimportant: the United Kingdom, the first major country to be forced off gold, was the first to recover from the slump. The recovery, however, was only a recovery to the level of activity of the 1920s. The currency continued to be overvalued in relation to domestic needs.

Externally, however, the depreciation did not even lead to partial recovery. The balance of payments stayed in deficit. Currency uncertainties continued to hamper the flow of trade, at a time when world impoverisation and protection already restricted its volume.

International trade flourishes most when there are no exchange risks, or the exchange risks are sufficiently small that they can be covered in the forward exchange market. Otherwise currencies have to be hoarded (in the form of exchange reserves) before there can be trade, and the uncertainty about exchange rates can make such currency hoarding unduly risky unless it be hoarding of gold. In the years following 1931 there was a six- to sevenfold increase in the sterling value of the gold reserves, and towards the end of the period the reserves were about twenty times what they had been before 1914. Yet, as shown before, this was not enough for domestic purposes, and it was not enough for external purposes either. For with a floating exchange rate, overseas trade remained unduly risky (and possibly more so for exporters who were paid in overseas currencies, than for importers of food and raw materials who could still normally pay in sterling).

Sterling's freedom to float led to exchange rates varying from $3.20 to over $5. Immediately after the abandonment of the gold peg, sterling depreciated sharply in foreign exchange markets. There was uncertainty about the authorities' intentions, and there were further conversions of overseas sterling holdings into gold. The latter became necessary for some overseas central banks which held sterling, but were obliged by law to hold their reserves in gold or currencies convertible into gold; when sterling ceased to be convertible, it no longer fulfilled this requirement. In consequence one of the weaknesses of sterling before 1931 continued for a time after 1931.

In 1932 sterling began to recover; but this recovery endangered the domestic depreciation. By then it had also become clear that erratic day-to-day fluctuations in the exchange rate were injurious to trade. To combat these fluctuations, the authorities set up an Exchange Equalisation Account. The Account was to even out day-to-day fluctuations, but was not meant to interfere in long-term movements in the exchange rate. No new exchange rate was fixed, but the exchange rate became managed.

To start with, the Exchange Equalisation Account was endowed with sterling securities and no gold, so that it could only exert downward pressure on sterling through selling sterling for gold. Later on it could have exerted upward pressure on sterling through the accumulation of idle sterling balances, though it did not do so. As mentioned before, there was a substantial increase in the gold reserves; gold losses towards the end of the 1930s were due to renewed depression and fear of war rather than to any actions of the Account.

Since the foreign exchange market is one market, it was possible to influence the exchange value of sterling by operating on just one foreign currency. The Account operated on the dollar (by buying dollars for sterling and converting dollars into gold). This somewhat accentuated the already severe deflationary strains from which the United States was then suffering. In 1933, however, the dollar was taken off gold, and in 1934 a new gold parity for the dollar was fixed, at $35 a fine ounce — a parity which has been left unchanged ever since. In those days it meant that the dollar was devalued by more than sterling had depreciated, so that the exchange rate of sterling came to be above the pre-1931 dollar parity.

At the same time the United States authorities set up an Exchange Equalisation Fund, charged with the task of keeping the value of the dollar at the desired level. Fund and Account then operated on the French franc. The French franc was taken off gold in 1936, and an exchange equalisation fund was set up by the French authorities. The risk of a major currency trial of strength was avoided through the Tripartite Monetary Agreement of that year, in which the three Governments agreed to give each other twenty-four hours' notice of major changes in currency policies, and so restored at least minimal exchange stability.

Subsequently sterling was allowed to drift downwards, to a level slightly below the pre-1931 dollar parity. The chief cause of further depreciation was conversion of sterling holdings by overseas Sterling Area countries, which after 1937 suffered from a renewed fall in primary product prices. There was no formal devaluation of sterling, since no new exchange rate was fixed, until the outbreak of war in 1939. Then sterling was devalued by 16 per cent below the pre-1931 parity. That was a deliberate undervaluation in relation to the dollar, taken in anticipation of a greater impairment of British than of United States commercial efficiency during the war.

In the 1930s competitive depreciations and devaluations of currencies were resorted to in order to relieve the depression that afflicted British industry and its competitors alike, and from which they could not extricate themselves as long as their currencies were overvalued in relation to gold (which was still the ultimate base of domestic credit). In the process, however, each country that acted first, aggravated the problems of others, be it through the monetary action described above or be it through adverse effects on other countries' export trades. For industry in a country with a depreciated currency could undercut industries of countries that had not (or not yet) depreciated, and that added to the deflationary problems in the latter countries. They in turn would not tolerate such effects and answered with monetary measures or intensified protection or both.

The depreciation of 1931 and after did not lead to a substantial realignment of the sterling–dollar parity, save for a few months between the British and United States depreciations when no clear rate emerged. Nor was there any reason to suppose that sterling was overvalued relatively to the dollar, at a time when the depression was worse in the United States than in the United Kingdom.

The balance of payments stayed in deficit. As mentioned before, this was largely because the British economy was less depressed than others, so that imports recovered before exports. There is no reason to suppose that a different exchange rate would necessarily have led to a more favourable balance of payments. This point must now be dealt with.

One condition for an improvement in the balance of payments after depreciation is that the economy can 'absorb' additional production without inflation. This condition applied at a time of widespread unemployment and idle capital. It could even be argued that, had depreciation gone further, more might have been produced and more goods would have been available for consumption at home and abroad. If so, the depreciation did not go far enough, and any effects of further domestic depreciation on the dollar parity of sterling would have been incidental. The absorption condition is, however, not the only one.

A second condition is that additional British goods must be acceptable abroad or fewer overseas goods acceptable in Britain. Acceptability abroad will be dealt with first. One point has already been made: the United States and France did not for long 'accept' a lower exchange rate for sterling. But even without their exchange-rate changes there would have been difficulties.

After depreciation, British exporters could sell at lower foreign currency prices and yet receive the same return in sterling. Alternatively they could maintain foreign currency prices and receive a higher return in sterling. The former possibility should attract customers; the latter should enhance sales efforts. In the circumstances of the 1930s, when there was widespread unemployment, increased production would raise supplies, mainly of known goods. Since known goods sell on price, a fall in foreign currency prices would be required. Depreciation helped British exporters to charge less in foreign currencies, but this did not necessarily make British goods more acceptable overseas.

Because international trade is competitive trade, it is sometimes assumed that lower prices, in terms of foreign currencies, always raise overseas demand. Whether this is so depends on the overseas price elasticity of demand being greater than 1. (Elasticities should be measured by comparing alternative situations. In the present context, the implication, is that these elasticities must become greater from one point of time to the next.) At first sight this condition seemed to be satisfied. With recovery from the slump came an expansion of world activity and trade. Incomes rose again and markets should have widened. Since the rise in activity took place while there was still substantial unemployment the world over, the rise in activity was largely in known goods and services, and such goods and services tend to be particularly susceptible to price competition (see Chapter 24 sections 4-7). If domestic activity grows by more than international trade, international price competition is liable to become fierce (see Chapter 24, section 9). On these grounds, overseas price elasticities of demand should have risen, and the fall in the exchange rate should have helped the export trades. This was frustrated, however, by a variety of circumstances and policies, which either reduced the demand for British goods or intensified price competition with British exports.

The basic restraint was still the widespread overvaluation of currencies (in relation to domestic needs), which limited overseas customers' ability to buy any goods, irrespective of their origin. In order to ensure that demand be diverted to their own national producers, governments raised tariffs or imposed quotas on imports, so that overseas customers' demand was diverted from British (and other imported) goods. International demand became more confined to 'essentials' for which the price elasticity of demand tends to be low. Overseas price elasticities of demand thus became less and not greater. If overseas governments let their currencies depreciate or devalued them, there was some relief for overseas incomes. While this might have been of some help to British exporters, it also meant lower foreign exchange prices for foreign goods and thus more international price competition. In short, overseas customers either could not or were not allowed to buy more British goods, while intensified international price competition made exports less profitable than sales in the (protected) home market. All the circumstances and policies of the time militated against an improved export performance.

Had imports been cut back more than they were, there might still have been favourable balance-of-payments results, despite the restraints on the expansion of exports. If there had been a sufficient price elasticity of demand for imports, the economy would have 'accepted' fewer imports. True, imports had been cut by protection. But this took the form of one sharp cut in imports, especially from industrial countries. Once the immediate effect of protection was over, the British demand for imports was more confined to 'essentials' and therefore less price-elastic. This precluded an improvement in the balance of payments (through price restraint of imports) when the recovery came. Without protection, the balance of payments might have been more adverse. All that is asserted here is that, in the absence of a rising price elasticity of demand for imports, the depreciation did not lead to an improvement in the balance of payments (through making imports less acceptable). In so far as the depreciation was a cause of recovery, it ensured a rise in imports.

Nor were overseas suppliers willing to abandon the British market. The United Kingdom was the world's leading importer of primary products, and losses in this market could not easily have been compensated elsewhere, even under more favourable trading conditions. Rather than face an irreplaceable loss in their principal market, they would accept British prices rather than a depreciation of sterling in terms of their currencies. They would let their own exchange rates depreciate as much as sterling depreciated or more; or they would devalue their currencies in terms of sterling, so as to maintain or lower the parities of their currencies with sterling.

Many primary producing countries had no independent exchange reserves of their own. Their currencies used to be linked to gold via sterling. After the divorce of the sterling exchange rate from gold, they had to choose between gold and sterling. Many chose sterling. They included countries with Commonwealth ties, but this was not decisive: Canada stayed outside this new sterling system and several foreign countries participated. All the members of the 'Sterling Area' had substantial trading ties with the United Kingdom but often the decisive consideration was that the United Kingdom was their chief creditor (since it is easier to repay debts and obtain further loans if there is no exchange problem in repayments). In any case they found it easier to build up exchange reserves in sterling than in gold or in any other currency.

In order to build up their exchange reserves in sterling, those countries had to earmark some of their export earnings for the accumulation of sterling reserves. Such export earnings were then held in the form of sterling securities and not spent on British exports, so that deflationary pressures in the United Kingdom were further intensified. There were, however, some compensating advantages for Britain: in so far as these sterling reserves were held in Treasury bills and other British Government securities, there was an excess demand for such bills and other securities which helped to keep interest rates in Britain down. That may have helped the British domestic economy, but it did not help to keep the value of sterling low in terms of overseas Sterling Area currencies. For in order to buy these securities, they first had to earn sterling (or foreign exchange which could be converted into sterling), and this created a continuous excess demand for sterling. To that extent it somewhat countered the attempt to keep the value of sterling low.

The demand for a currency to hold is in addition to the demand for that currency for trading purposes. In this sense a reserve currency may be overvalued in relation to the currencies dependent upon it, at least for as long as the dependent currency countries wish to accumulate further reserves. This applies regardless of the parity of the reserve currency in terms of gold or dollars. The other currencies in the area want a parity which facilitates the accumulation of the reserve currency. If the countries concerned export mainly highly graded primary products (which are subject to intense price competition), they will normally undervalue their currencies in terms of the reserve currency. Only when the reserve currency country is heavily in debt towards the area can other area countries afford not to undervalue their currencies relatively to the reserve currency. That happened after the Second World War, though it was not until the devaluation of 1967 that the majority of Sterling Area countries would not follow sterling downwards. But before this and other post-war currency problems are considered, it may be mentioned that the reserve currency system enabled the United Kingdom to borrow in sterling from the Sterling Area during the Second World War and after.

Such implications for defence and other emergencies should be placed alongside the other aspects of currency policy in the 1930s. The salient features of those other aspects, as shown above, were: the depreciation enabled recovery from the slump, but did not suffice to let the economy approach full employment; the depreciation failed to improve the balance of payments because there was overvaluation of other currencies, so that many countries could neither accept a lower exchange rate for sterling nor a sufficient increase in British exports to balance the United Kingdom's external payments through increased exports; nor did the British economy accept a sufficient reduction in imports to balance external payments that way. (5)

4   1949

(a)   The Decision to Devalue

Before 1914, when gold was on sterling, Britain could buy cheap. In the 1920s, when gold had left sterling, she sought to buy cheap. In the 1930s, when the sterling exchange rate was divorced from gold, attempts were made to raise domestic values through depreciation, while the drop in the exchange rate avoided a proportionate rise in prices against overseas customers. After 1945, gold was almost forgotten; the domestic credit structure was managed independently of the state of the gold reserves, and save for a brief and unsuccessful experiment in 1947, the free convertibility of sterling into gold or other currencies was not attempted until the late 1950s. Nevertheless a hankering after the cheap economy lingered. At the time, the overriding fear of economists and politicians was an export-led post-war slump of the 1921 or 1929 variety. It was widely believed that such a slump could be avoided, or at least ameliorated, through charging low prices in foreign currency. Britain was to sell cheap.

If this was to be done, and the home economy not be depressed by low values, the exchange rate could not be kept too high. The misjudgement of 1925 was to be avoided. It was, however, impossible to repeat the 1931 experiment of letting the exchange rate float, and it was also impossible to repeat the nationally managed exchange-rate system of 1932-8. For the International Monetary Fund had been set up with a view to avoiding the uncertainties caused by floating exchange rates and the harm done by past competitive depreciations (whereby countries used to 'export' unemployment). Countries had to fix their exchange rates, and in return for their subscriptions to the Fund would get accommodation for temporary balance-of-payments difficulties. The Fund's resources were, however, inadequate to cope with chronic balance-of-payments disequilibria, so that countries in chronic balance-of-payments difficulties would have to seek approval of the Fund for an alteration in the exchange rate. In 1949 the United Kingdom appeared to be in chronic balance-of-payments deficit. With depreciation ruled out, the only way to lower the exchange rate was to devalue to a lower fixed exchange rate.

In the following, there will be some discussion whether the statistics were right, whether the outside world was willing to accept the 1949 devaluation and whether the British economy could absorb it. Before this is done, however, it may be useful to consider why the 1949 devaluation was a devaluation of sterling relatively to the dollar, and why devaluation was resorted to in that particular year.

Under International Monetary Fund rules, exchange rates have to be fixed either in terms of gold or in terms of a currency with a fixed gold parity. In practice the United States dollar was linked directly to gold, while other countries have chosen parities in terms of the United States dollar. This was silent recognition of the fact that gold had moved to the dollar, in the sense that gold had become a substitute for the dollar (just as, before 1914, it had been a substitute for sterling).

Relatively to the United States economy, the British economy had suffered more from the war, so that the United States had relatively much to sell that was attractive and the United Kingdom relatively little. Could not the difference be compensated through lower prices (expressed in foreign exchange)? The British task of reconstruction was not yet complete and was viewed as a task of restoring productive capacity in order to create more known goods. The balance of payments seemed in chronic deficit because invisible earnings made a lesser contribution than in times past, because war debts had to be repaid, and because the competitive position of British industries had been impaired by war. The gap would have to be filled through more exports of merchandise, and in times of reconstruction that would largely be more known merchandise produced in traditional ways. Since known goods should always be sold as cheaply as possible and overseas customers were to be favoured over domestic ones, was a lowering of the exchange rate not *the* answer?

The timing too may have seemed right. 1949 saw a slight recession in the United States, and it was widely feared that this was the beginning of the expected post-war slump. A recession would release factors for employment in export industries, and it would also lead to fiercer international price competition. Through giving British exporters a price advantage, they would suffer less and employment in the export trades would be protected. Moreover there was no fear of retaliation by the United States. The United States economy was so preponderant that the possibility of a counter-devaluation of the dollar was probably not even considered, though this did not apply to other currencies. Nor was there any risk of a protectionist reaction in other ways. The United States was bent on lowering tariffs, took a leading part in convening and reconvening negotiators to the General Agreement on Tariffs and Trade, and made substantial concessions in the resulting trade agreements. Other industrial countries, including the United Kingdom, had such tight trade controls that changes in regulation could only be towards freer trade. Primary producing countries in the Eastern Hemisphere had accumulated substantial sterling credits during the war, so that they had no problems of accumulating sterling balances. If the Sterling Area countries amongst them would devalue with sterling, at least they would not devalue more. In short, intensified price competition was expected as a result of recession and trade liberalisation, and it was thought that other countries would not offset the British devaluation by greater devaluations of their currencies.

The authorities thought that the United Kingdom's trade problems could be solved by charging less overseas (in foreign exchange) and making exports more profitable (in sterling) – and devaluation would do just that. A 30½ per cent devaluation was resorted to, establishing an exchange rate of £1 = $2.80. Apparently the authorities believed that a rate of approximately £1 = $3 was indicated to offset the United Kingdom's diminished competitive position relatively to the United States, and to be in line with the rates at which sterling then exchanged in 'free' markets. A somewhat lower rate was chosen to make it clear to the market that this was a final step and not just a tentative one. (6) It was realised that some of the anticipated benefits would be lost once higher import prices had affected domestic factor costs, but it was hoped that this would not offset more than half of the devaluation.

It seems curious that the authorities should have let themselves be guided by the 'free' market rate. Had there been a floating exchange rate for the pound sterling, a free market rate might have emerged which could have been a guide to an equilibrium exchange rate. Sterling was, however, subject to exchange control, and the 'free' market was concerned with transactions amongst non-residents beyond the reach of the exchange control. Sterling owned by non-residents was not to become freely convertible until 1958, so that sterling holdings were worth less to their owners than an equivalent amount of dollars. Hence 'free' sterling stood at a discount below the official rate of exchange. Such a discount could be eliminated only through making sterling more con-vertible and not through devaluation. It was not eliminated through devaluation, for it was an indication of the cost of inconvertibility to the owners of such sterling. It was no guide to an equilibrium exchange rate.

Whatever the choice of rate, the whole case for devaluation in 1949 must be re-examined with the wisdom of hindsight. In the following it will be shown that some of the arguments which carried the day in 1949 no longer convince. In fairness, however, it must be pointed out that the authorities had no experience in choosing a rate for an exchange-controlled currency (which may excuse the way the new rate was chosen); that they could not know that the best balance-of-payments data then available were inaccurate; and that they could not forsee that, after 1950, world trade would develop in ways that were to make an expanding world demand more income-elastic rather than price-elastic. The authorities knew that the British economy was then fully employed and unable to absorb a lower exchange rate without a rise in factor prices, but they feared an export-led slump and could not know the unemployment rate would remain below the Keynes—Beveridge level of 3 per cent for many years to come.

No more need be said about the way the new exchange rate was chosen. Only brief comments will be made on the accuracy of the balance-of-payments statistics then available, before the discussion turns to the acceptability of the devaluation overseas and the ability of the British economy to absorb it at home. At the time of the 1949 devaluation the authorities had before them estimates which purported to show a British balance-of-payments deficit each year from 1946 to the middle of 1949, amounting in total to over £1,000 million, and the deficit seemed to be increasing again in 1949. They must have been under the impression that there was a chronic deficit which, under International Monetary Fund rules, called for a devaluation. Subsequently the statistics were revised, and it is now 'known' that the deficit in those years amounted to less than £500 million and that the balances of payments of 1948 and 1949 were near balance. (7) Even if due allowance is made for the payments difficulties some overseas Sterling Area countries then experienced, one wonders whether the authorities would have decided to devalue so much, if at all, had the revised statistics been at their disposal.

(b)   Acceptability of the 1949 Devaluation
The new exchange rate, however arrived at, was better received abroad than the rates that emerged after the depreciation of 1931. As already mentioned, the United States accepted the 1949 exchange rate for sterling. Most Sterling Area countries devalued with sterling, but none by more. Most European countries devalued with sterling, but none by more (at least immediately) and most by less. Generally, in 1931 most other currencies were left to depreciate or devalued by as much as sterling depreciated or more; in 1949 they were devalued as much as sterling or less. Moreover there was no long-drawn-out process of competitive depreciations and devaluations such as there had been in the 1930s. Most of the 1949 realignments of exchange rates were made within a few days of the devaluation of sterling. As far as technical acceptance of the 1949 devaluation was concerned, it was a success.

The success of any economic measure does not, however, depend on its technical acceptance alone. The 1949 devaluation was intended to improve the balance of payments of a fully employed economy. To do so it would have to be acceptable in trade and be absorbed by the home economy. Its acceptance in trade will be examined first, with reference to the reactions of primary producing countries, industrial countries and the home economy. The problems of absorption will be dealt with afterwards, in subsections (c) and (d) below.

Primary producing countries were initially more favourably disposed to let the British devaluation succeed than they had been towards the depreciation of 1931. They showed this in greater willingness to raise prices against the United Kingdom. In 1949 the British market was less dominant than it had been eighteen years earlier, and there was no lack of alternative outlets in a post-war world still hungry for primary products. Moreover many overseas primary producing countries had accumulated sterling reserves during the war and did not want to accumulate more. They felt no need to undervalue their currencies in relation to sterling just to facilitate the accumulation of sterling reserves. The result was that British import prices were more affected than had been the case after 1931. It is not clear, however, how much of the rise in import prices in 1950 and 1951 was due to the devaluation, and how much to the general rise in world prices that was accentuated by the Korean War.

For overseas Sterling Area countries, and for other countries which had accumulated sterling, the devaluation meant a loss. They had accumulated sterling whilst supplying some of the United Kingdom's requirements during the war and the early reconstruction period, and now found the dollar value of their sterling holdings reduced. This meant a loss of exchange reserves for external trade. Moreover, in so far as Sterling Area countries regulated their domestic money supply by their sterling holdings, there could be domestic deflationary consequences. The latter were not of immediate consequence, since sterling holdings were in excess of domestic monetary requirements, but were to become of importance in the 1950s. The external loss too was deferred, for two reasons. One was a renewed rise in world primary product prices in 1950 and 1951. The other was that if those countries satisfied their import requirements through purchases from the United Kingdom, and British exporters quoted devalued sterling prices, there was no loss. Their ability to buy elsewhere was, however, reduced as their sterling exchange reserves were worth fewer dollars. In consequence they would buy more from the United Kingdom than they otherwise might have done.

As long as British export prices did not catch up with dollar prices, devaluation conferred a certain amount of protection to British exports to Sterling Area countries and other countries that had accumulated sterling balances. Since those countries then took over half of British exports, and since their demand for British goods was largely a demand for known goods which became increasingly available as reconstruction proceeded, devaluation may have protected some of the achievements of early post-war reconstruction. If so, the benefit did not last.

For the rise in world primary product prices came to a halt in 1951 and was subsequently reversed. Overseas Sterling Area countries found their exchange earnings reduced and tried to stave off domestic retrenchment through drawings on their sterling balances. Exceptionally large withdrawals by major holders could then cause payments difficulties for the whole Area. Examples are the withdrawals by Australia in 1952 and India in 1957. On both occasions the loss of the Area's gold reserves occasioned by those withdrawals caused the British authorities to deflate the home economy, even though the British balance of payments was in surplus and there were no exceptional domestic inflationary tendencies. After the Indian withdrawal of sterling balances, in excess of her monetary requirements, there were no major balances outstanding beyond those needed for monetary purposes, and monetary stringency returned to the overseas Sterling Area. From then onwards British exports to the Sterling Area have grown but slowly.

Until the return of monetary stringency in overseas Sterling Area countries at various dates in the 1950s, the Sterling Area had been the most rapidly expanding market for British exports. It had been so throughout most of the first half of the century, and it could not have been foreseen in 1949 that this would not continue. If devaluation accelerated the growth of trade with the overseas Sterling Area more than trade with other countries, this may have seemed a development in accordance with past trends. That it had simply accelerated war-debt repayment (partly through default and partly through diversion of overseas Sterling Area demand towards the United Kingdom) did not become apparent until after the war debts had been paid off and the growth of exports to the overseas Sterling Area decelerated.

In the meantime the additional demand for British goods from the overseas Sterling Area put additional pressure on the already fully employed British economy and so accentuated inflationary pressures within the British economy. Since, however, British export prices did not regain their 1949 parity with United States export prices (see Table 26.1), some price advantage remained. This made it relatively easier for British exporters to sell traditional goods, for which the market was most favourable in many Sterling Area countries. When, however, war-debt repayment (accelerated by devaluation) came to an end towards the end of the 1950s, British exporters were that much less ready to meet the different requirements of the more rapidly growing markets in the North Atlantic area, for European and North American demand grew most for new goods (see Chapter 24, sections 5, 8 and 10).

As already mentioned, the additional fillip which devaluation gave to exports to the overseas Sterling Area ceased when the overseas Sterling Area had spent its excess sterling balances by the end of the 1950s. By then, the earlier British partial default (through devaluation) on those countries' exchange reserves became a disadvantage to British exporters. By the 1960s, the overseas Sterling Area could afford to purchase only about one-third of British exports. It may not seem far-fetched to suggest that the 1949 devaluation bunched British exports to the overseas Sterling Area into the early and mid-1950s and thinned them out afterwards.

The remainder of British exports goes largely, though not exclusively, to industrial countries. Amongst the latter, the North Atlantic countries are the chief markets.

At the time of the 1949 devaluation, Europe was still war-shattered. Reconstruction had proceeded further in the United Kingdom than on the Continent. Almost anything British industry could produce was wanted on the Continent, and the chief limitation to exports was the Continent's inability to pay. If the British were willing to restrict home demand and sell at lower prices in terms of continental currencies, they could have more orders. So it seemed in 1949; and initial experience in 1950 seemed to bear out such expectations. The boom of 1950-1, however, was characterised by a sharp rise in food and raw-material prices. Most continental countries had to earmark their limited foreign exchange earnings for the purchase of expensive food and raw materials, and less was left for manufactures irrespective of price. Subsequently intra-European trade controls were relaxed, and quantitative controls disappeared entirely by the end of the 1950s. By then, however, the tasks of post-war reconstruction were nearly complete, and Europe's new economies emerged as capital-intensive with demand for high-quality goods rather than mere quantity. In the circumstances trade barriers were harmful, because they reduced the exporters' profits. But the world's trade barriers were falling, and this helped – though in the 1960s the European Economic Community's trade barriers became increasingly discriminatory, and that hindered. It is futile, however, to counter the remaining trade barriers by selling at lower foreign currency prices, since this only further reduces the exporters' profits in foreign exchange and does not necessarily increase sales of capital-intensive goods (see Chapter 24, section 4).

As far as exports to the United States are concerned, it is doubtful whether lower dollar prices for known goods ever helped substantially. The United States market of the mid-twentieth century is particularly impressed by orginality in techniques and designs, so that the income elasticity of its demand matters more to most British exporters than the price elasticity of its demand. While it is not impossible that the United States will increasingly raise her standards of living through cheap imports, that was not (or not yet) an overriding consideration during the 1950s and 1960s. In short, neither United States demand at any relevant time nor European demand since the late 1950s grew in a way that made the undervaluation of sterling of much help in attracting an enlarged share of such demand.

Since there were no lasting benefits to the export trades, the devaluation could have led to a lasting improvement to the balance of payments only if it effectively curtailed imports. The matter was not put to the test at the time, for quantitative controls continued. There was food rationing until the mid-1950s, so that food imports were under control irrespective of the exchange rate. Imports of manufactures were held in check through quantitative controls on imports from foreign currency areas. These controls applied to imports from the dollar area, principally the United States and Canada. Imports from Western Europe were treated more liberally, but were not free from control. The quantitative import controls did not entirely disappear until 1958. This leaves imports of raw materials. A cut in imports of raw materials is, however, normally associated with a fall in the level of employment (see Chapter 24, section 3), and this would not have been tolerated. In short, imports were either not cut or were controlled by other means for so long after the 1949 devaluation that no immediate effect can be discerned.

By the time quantitative controls of food consumption and imports of manufactures had finally disappeared, the situation had changed so as to make a low exchange rate less relevant to the control of imports. The capital-intensive sector of the British economy had become more important than it had been in 1949. In the 1960s the capital-intensive sector was to be the chief determinant of changes in the demand for imports and the ability to supply exports. The demand of that sector and the demand facing it both tend to be more susceptible to income changes than to price changes. Whether the growth of that sector has been held down by excessive devaluation of sterling forms the major part of the considerations of subsection (c) below.

Before the question of the absorption of the 1949 devaluation is considered, it may be useful to sum up how it was accepted. Technically it was a success: there was no dollar devaluation, and although other currencies were devalued with sterling, they were not devalued by more than sterling. The trade effects were more complex. The overseas Sterling Area accepted more British goods as long as it had surplus funds, but this effect ceased as war-debt repayments came to an end. The 1949 devaluation appears to have been irrelevant to exports destined for the United States, and from the late 1950s onwards also for Europe. Last but not least, the home economy did not 'accept' lower raw-material imports. In the 1950s other imports were still subject to alternative controls, and in the 1960s the economy did not accept lower imports of manufactures.

(c) Structural Absorption of the 1949 Devaluation

A devaluation may improve a country's balance-of-payments performance if it does not divert the economy from a more profitable path. This condition is satisfied whenever there is widespread unemployment and the currency is over-valued. At such times devaluation or depreciation are ways of cutting domestic factor incomes in real terms, so that a drop in the exchange rate can be regarded as an alternative to a reduction in money wages and other factor incomes. Consequently the economy can produce more cheaply; and since factors are abundant, the economy can produce more without risk of rising factor prices. If the economy can produce more and cheaper, it should be able to sell more abroad as well as at home. Since it should be able to produce cheaper, it should be able to sell at lower unit prices in terms of foreign currency. That should give it a competitive advantage over foreign rivals. In other words the economy should be able to absorb devaluation without an offsetting rise in factor prices. Otherwise the rise in domestic factor prices offsets the fall in the exchange rate, and the price advantage of devaluation is lost.

The domestic conditions for lowering the value of the money unit were given in 1931, and it was feared in 1949 that such conditions might recur if not forestalled. The balance-of-payments effects of the 1931 depreciation, however, were frustrated because the trade effects were unacceptable to other countries. The latter wished to maintain their markets and to relieve their own depressions. They did not want 'cheap' goods from the United Kingdom or anywhere else. In 1949 the outside world wanted more goods. The United Kingdom, however, could not supply more goods. It does not follow that there were no domestic consequences. For a time at least, individual British producers could either sell more abroad at lower prices expressed in terms of overseas currencies, or they could take a larger sterling profit from overseas sales, or they could combine the two possibilities by selling somewhat cheaper and taking some more profit. The effects on the structure of the British economy can be theoretically analysed. The effects on British factor prices can be shown statistically. The former effects will be dealt with in the present subsection; the latter will be considered in subsection (d) below. Before these effects are examined at length, it may be useful to commment briefly on whether devaluation was the only way of ensuring full employment in the circumstances prevailing in 1949.

As mentioned before, the situation in 1949 was misinterpreted as the beginning of 'the post-war slump'. One way of ensuring full employment would be to produce cheap. Since money wages, salaries and rents were rigid in a downward direction, devaluation would be a practical alternative way of cutting British factor costs. It was not the only way. In times of slump, attempts should be made to clear the market either by lowering prices to match the prevailing level of incomes or by raising money incomes to match the prevailing level of prices. Had there been a major slump in 1949, it would not have been impossible to raise money incomes. The gold reserve restraints on the domestic note issue and credit creation had finally disappeared during the war. Under the war-time and post-war policy of suppressed inflation, factors had been paid as before but spending was limited by rationing and other controls, so that there was ample potential purchasing power hanging over the market. That purchasing power was gradually being released, so that there was no risk of shortage of effective demand. Thus, given the rigidity of British factor prices in a downward direction, there would have been alternative ways of countering a slump, had the slight and ephemeral recession in the United States developed into a major world slump. It is not suggested that the decision to devalue was taken solely with a view to avoidance of an imaginary slump, but the spectre of past overvaluation haunted many minds, so that the point is by no means irrelevant.

As it happened, full employment was maintained and could probably have been maintained without devaluation. Nevertheless devaluation made more work, and since the economy was already fully employed, too much of it. The error of overvaluation was avoided. Instead there was undervaluation.

As shown in subsection (b), for about a decade devaluation raised overseas demand for British goods beyond what it otherwise would have been. That raised the demand for the services of British factors. British firms tried to satisfy such overseas demand when it gave them higher profits in sterling. To sell cheaper to overseas customers and yet make more profits in home currency, without even changing one's ways, that is the dream of all devaluers. The dream can come true when there are unemployed factors at home, so that the additional demand can be satisfied without undue strain on domestic resources (provided, of course, that devaluation is accepted by other countries). When domestic factors are fully employed, however, additional supplies for export can be made available only through commanding factors away from other employment; and that can be done only by attracting factors through higher rewards than they earn in their present employments. The sole exception can be capital employed in existing activities, which receives a higher reward in sterling whenever the sterling equivalent of export earnings rises.

The more general the increase in overseas demand, the wider spread are the profits earned in existing activities, and the more will other factors be commanded away from alternative employments. As shown in subsection (b), overseas demand was not evenly increased after devaluation, and that led to differences in the degree of cost inflation induced in various industries. It is impossible to go into detail, but the following observations may indicate the problem.

Where the character of overseas demand emphasised price elasticity rather than income elasticity of demand, devaluation enabled established British exporters to secure a larger share of the market than they would have done otherwise. This was of special importance in Sterling Area trade, until the Area had exhausted its war-time credits, and also in Europe, before Europe had fully recovered from the war. In both cases a special fillip was given to British exports to countries which, on the whole, were not (or not yet) in a position to produce for themselves what the United Kingdom already produced. On balance this meant a special impetus to British industries, as they then were. (Existing industries are labour-intensive, in the sense defined in section 4 of Chapter 24, since expansion along existing lines means that the labour–capital ratio is constant or rising.) Industries earned more profits in sterling without changing their ways. In order to maintain output, they had to retain factors; to expand output, they had to attract factors from other occupations. They were able to pay higher interest rates, higher rents and higher wages. The established export trades could produce and sell 'cheap' abroad and yet make more money in sterling. That gave then an extended lease of life and delayed the transfer of factors to newer activities. In short, devaluation underwrote the status quo of Britain's industrial structure.

In the pre-1950 world that might have been welcomed. Even in the 1950s there was still much known demand to be satisfied. At the time it may have seemed advantageous that the boom of the 1950s could proceed largely along familiar paths and so avoid much uncertainty and structural redeployment. But it also meant rising factor prices, which are especially harmful to the labour-intensive industries. For (according to the definitions used here) labour-intensive industries comprise diminishing returns activities, and any rise in costs makes returns diminish that much faster. Devaluation can create an excess demand for known goods, but cannot create the goods. If the economy is fully employed, devaluation can only divert known goods from the home market to export markets, and such diversion cannot go on for ever unless the home market is increasingly restricted. Where the home market cannot be permanently denied — and it is no function of any economic policy to deny the home market indefinitely — the initial rise in overseas demand becomes increasingly offset by rising costs so that the excess overseas demand dwindles. Thus not only overseas demand conditions, but domestic cost conditions as well, may cause a continuous decline of the share of British exports to just those markets where devaluation was initially most successful. This points to the ephemeral nature of the export advantages that a fully employed economy can derive from devaluation. Of special importance in Sterling Area trade, this is perhaps the chief domestic reason why trade with the Sterling Area has ceased to expand at the former rate. This point should be considered alongside the exhaustion of war debts to the Sterling Area, considered in subsection (b) above. These two points do not provide a full explanation of what happened to trade with the Sterling Area, since the rise of trade with third countries also played its part (through attracting British exports elsewhere and rival goods into the Sterling Area). Nevertheless much Sterling Area trade was bound to decline in importance as the effectiveness of devaluation waned.

While undervaluation helped trade in labour-intensive products less and less as time went by, it handicapped the trade in capital-intensive products, and this handicap was diminishing only slowly. The handicap arose largely because of the effects of undervaluation on domestic factor costs and incomes. Let factor costs be considered first. Because more factors were kept in the labour-intensive industries than otherwise would have been the case, the capital-intensive industries too had to pay higher factor prices to retain or attract factors, and this raised their costs. Since the capital-intensive industries comprise increasing returns activities, any rise in their costs delays their returns. To offset such a rise in costs, the industries concerned need all the longer production runs to be profitable. It helps if overseas tariffs fall and the market can widen internationally. It may help even more if the domestic market is allowed to expand. That will be so when firms sell most of their output in the home market — and the majority of them do. Moreover the home market is widely considered as more certain than overseas markets, since it is immune from exchange risks and the rise in tariff barriers which is always possible abroad. The home market has its uncertainties due to economic fluctuations in one economy and the actions of one government, but the export market is faced with different fluctuations in two hundred economies and the actions of two hundred governments. Thus in the absence of an expanding home market the risk of investment is accentuated, so that less investment will be ventured in the production of new goods. If so, then a larger home market is a precondition for the reduction of unit costs of increasing returns activities. In such cases rising domestic incomes are the best guarantee that the product can quickly reach a price low enough to be comparable with that of the nearest substitute produced abroad. Only when the price is down to such a level can exports expand and imports become less attractive.

Much of the possible rise in domestic demand was, however, denied. Frequent resort to squeezes and freezes may have played its part, but the most persistent cause was the devaluation itself. It gave a boost to labour-intensive activities, for it devalued British factors and so raised the profits from their employment. Consequently traditional activities paid better than they otherwise would have done. As shown before, traditional activities are labour-intensive, since any expansion of such activities maintains or raises the ratio of labour to capital employed. Moreover growth along traditional lines tends to raise real incomes proportionately with input, while growth along capital-intensive lines can raise real incomes more than proportionately in relation to input. The encouragement devaluation gave to labour-intensive activities diverted the economy from a more profitable path.

Since the economy was fully employed, the labour-intensive activities kept and attracted more factors than they otherwise would have done. This raised factor prices, especially those of the factors most important to traditional activities. While factor prices in capital-intensive activities also rose, they rose less than otherwise would have been the case. In a way this may seem equilibrating and suggests that, by the time the devaluation had worked through the system, the capital-intensive activities would be at an advantage. Note, however, that this is only the same advantage as the one they originally could have had. In the meantime there are years of an unnecessarily low growth rate. In the meantime the greater rise in factor prices in the labour-intensive activities gives a misleading impression of rising opportunities there, and so attracts too many factors into such activities.

In short, devaluation of the currency of a fully employed economy first boosts the profitability of existing activities, and subsequently attracts too many factors into such activities. The result is slower growth and less rise in real incomes than would have been possible with a less undervalued currency. The lesser rise in real incomes denies the rise in the home demand necessary for capital-intensive expansion.

Thus while it remains true that the restriction of home incomes can lower costs and make more goods available from labour-intensive activities, different measures are needed to secure such results from capital-intensive ones. The capital-intensive activities want rising domestic incomes to enable production at lower unit costs and therefore sales at lower prices. But the relative rise of incomes was distorted by the excessive devaluation, and the aggregate growth of incomes retarded. The result was slower redeployment from the labour-intensive to the capital-intensive industries, and consequently a slower domestic growth rate and a slower growth of exports than would have been possible with less, or no, devaluation.

It may be asked whether lower prices, larger sales and, therefore, longer production runs could not be achieved through lowering prices in overseas markets simply through devaluation. In this connection it will be recalled that the price attainable for a capital-intensive good in another industrial country tends to be the price of the nearest substitute produced in that country plus or minus quality differential minus whatever tariff is levied by the importing country. If British costs are higher than costs in other industrial countries, devaluation can help to get British prices within the range set by overseas substitutes, but it does so once and for all. The result may be an increase in overseas orders without certainty that the market will continue to widen. Without such certainty, additional investment is not so promising of rising profits as if the market were continuously widening (as, for instance, through rising incomes at home or abroad). The additional orders will then be excess orders in relation to capacity, with the result that delivery dates will be delayed. Often a delay in delivery dates is more costly to the purchaser than a higher price would have been; he may have assembled other factors to work with the imported good, and all these factors are wasted if the imported good does not arrive in time. The result is ill-will. If, however, British costs are not higher than in other industrial countries, it is futile to sell at prices below those prevailing abroad. The market for such goods depends on quality and the state of overseas incomes much more than on price (up to the limit stated).

In short, there was delay in industrial adjustment. Undoubtedly there were many causes at work to delay adjustment in this industry or that, but one cause that affected all industries was the undervaluation of the currency which had put a premium on the status quo. The delay in domestic adjustment did not even curtail the demand for imports. In the 1950s the greater reliance on labour-intensive activities meant greater reliance on activities which depend relatively more on imported raw materials. By the 1960s when other industrial countries had advanced further, domestic growth depended more on imported machinery than might have been the case with less delay in the 1950s.

Devaluation of the money unit is a form of protection from change. In times of deepening depression, when values (of everything other than money) are low and falling, money is overvalued. To devalue the money unit then raises other values and so stems the depression. More than devaluation may be needed to restore prosperity, but at least it prevents the depression from getting worse. In times of rising prosperity, devaluation again stems change, though in times of prosperity it stems change for the better. When values are high and rising, the money unit is not overvalued. If it is incorrectly valued, it can only be under-valued. Devaluation then protects existing activities, as it does at all times. Because it does that, it also delays the search for new activities which would make factors go further. For if values of existing activities are rising without effort, it becomes less necessary for individual producers to seek new ways which involve effort in thought and development. No more than undervaluation is needed to retard growth.

This effect must not be ignored. It must not be exaggerated either. At a time when domestic credit was no longer determined by the state of the Bank of England's gold and foreign exchange reserves, not all values were immediately affected. In Britain, however, where import prices of food and raw materials are basic prices, factor costs were bound to be affected. (That did not apply in 1931, when overseas suppliers did not 'accept' the new exchange rate for sterling, but in 1949 many of them 'accepted' all or part of it.) Given the effect of a lower exchange rate on factor costs, the devaluation eventually percolated through the whole economy. Subsection (d) will show that this was a long-drawn-out process. Here one would like to quantify by how much the 1949 devaluation delayed British economic growth. Unfortunately no precise estimate is possible, and it must suffice to point to some of the qualitative effects of undervaluation on the country's economic structure.

Devaluation delays. In the two years before the 1949 devaluation, the United Kingdom's economic growth rate was close to 4 per cent a year; (8) in the two years after devaluation it was about 3½ per cent, and for the 1950s about 3 per cent compound. If too much should not be read into a comparison of what happened in two years of post-war reconstruction and the peace-time years to follow, it should be noted that the British growth rate slowed down at a time when that of her major rivals accelerated. Most of her major rivals had either not devalued or devalued by less, so that they had not subsidised existing activities or not subsidised them so much. That subsidy is not a free gift but comes at the expense of growth. To labour the point once more, the subsidy that devaluation confers on existing activities encourages growth with present production functions, and if there is already full employment, such expansion is possible only with a scramble for factors and corresponding increases in factor prices. There is, however, no disproportionate rise in output relatively to input. The latter depends on innovation. But if existing activities are subsidised through undervaluation, individual firms see less need to alter their ways. They innovate less. By how much less is difficult to say. If, for argument's sake, the pre-devaluation growth rate of 4 per cent is taken as the potential growth rate of the British economy, and the post-devaluation growth rate was only 3 per cent, the real loss was a 1 per cent addition to the national product a year. Put this way, the loss was slight and hardly susceptible to proof. Once it is realised, however, that an economy which grows at 4 per cent a year doubles its output within eighteen years, while one that grows at 3 per cent takes twenty-five years to double its output, the difference is by no means slight. It means a delay of 'seven' years (out of twenty-five). The 'seven' are put under inverted commas since it should be regarded as illustrative rather than as factual.

This purely illustrative 'seven years' delay' is, however, roughly in line with the observable facts of the 1950s. Much of the industrial world's growth in those years took the form of a boom in consumer durables. Amongst its features were motorisation and the mechanisation of household chores. All that came somewhat later in the United Kingdom than in comparable economies elsewhere in Europe. Eventually it did come, and by the 1960s the British public had caught up in motorisation and some domestic mechanisation (such as washing machines), though not in all (for example domestic central heating). Differences in tastes, production possibilities and taxation policies can account for this or that delay, but not for all. The only common feature of the overall delay was the undervaluation of the currency which had reduced the urge to innovate. Fewer innovations were applied than would have been technologically possible, and this delayed people in their homes and on the way to work, whilst at work their labour was devalued and so was the contribution of other factors. Factors were 'cheap'. What is too cheap tends to be used wastefully. Managements were faced with wrong values, and that delayed their search for ways of circumventing the scarcity of factors. That might not have mattered too much had Britain not been the first country to encounter general scarcity of factors in or around 1960. As it was, the delays of the 1950s added to the difficulties of the 1960s.

Devaluation delays but does not destroy. If the effect was a slowing-down of the growth rate by perhaps 1 per cent a year, the annual overall loss was not in ratio of 4 : 3 but only in ratio of 104 : 103; and since undervaluation does not destroy but preserves the status quo, it ensured preservation of 100 units of what there was before against the loss of one unit of new goods that might have been created. Moreover, if there was loss of one unit of new goods a year, and if that meant some delay in the modernisation of life in the 1950s and into the 1960s, that was a delay in the consumer durable-goods boom of those years — and that boom is probably largely over. It does not follow that there will be equal tardiness in grasping the new opportunities of coming decades (though this point must be left for further discussion until section 5 below). Some delay in economic growth may be regretted, but it must be set against everything else that constitutes a standard of living. Most people in the United Kingdom continued to be at least as well fed, clad and housed as people in comparable walks of life elsewhere in Europe, so that there was no impairment of the economic achievements of the past. They may have got some of the modern amenities of life somewhat later, but probably kept more of the traditional ones.

They could lead a quieter life, since the economic progress of the 1950s could proceed along preconceived lines with fewer of the worries and uncertainties associated with new ventures. Above all, there was security of employment in familiar occupations.

Were the British economy a closed economy, undervaluation might be commended as giving protection to whatever there is, and the additional security might be prized more highly than additional growth. Were the British economy still faced with a pre-1950 external pattern of trade, there would be no clash between the search for more domestic security and balance-of-payments considerations. As it was, the balance-of-payments disadvantages of undervaluation were slow to reveal themselves. At first there was the advantage that the problem of war debts (though not of post-war debts) was got out of the way within a dozen years. Exports could grow along more familiar lines, as long as there were overseas countries hungry for traditional British goods and sated with British money. Only when that ceased did the structural delays become a disadvantage. Undervaluation had encouraged those delays and so encouraged familiar ways at home and reliance on familiar markets abroad.

The United Kingdom was not the only country to devalue in 1949, but amongst industrial countries she devalued most. Hence she delayed most. If the British economy was less prepared to meet the international demand of the 1960s than were some rival economies, and if this eventually undermined sterling in the 1960s, the cause was not overvaluation of the currency. The chief monetary cause was that sterling had been undervalued as long ago as 1949. The devaluation of 1967 will be discussed in section 5 below. Before that is done, however, there must be a brief review of how British factors reacted to being undervalued.

(d)   Factor-Price Absorption of the 1949 Devaluation
In times past, it might have been legitimate to think of the economy as a vast draper's emporium, always able to please and attract custom through giving longer lengths of cloth for the same money. The analogy is appropriate to an economy that specialises in the transformation of raw materials into intermediate goods, to be made up by the customers. An example of such intermediate goods would be cotton piece goods. The draper could please, if he got his materials cheaper or if he was willing to devalue his cloth and his labour. Nowadays, however, this analogy is no longer so applicable to Britain. Specialisation has penetrated the market for final goods, so that a better analogy would be a tailor's shop that sells on quality and style. Attempts to sell more quantity, where quality is demanded, are as if your tailor tried to please you by cutting a suit that is too large for you. He will have devalued his cloth and his labour, and he will have less cloth and more work. But will his balance of payments with you

improve?

Your tailor may yet lose your custom if he raises his costs more than other tailors do. That may happen to him if he sets up shop on the assumption that factors of production are cheap and this assumption is falsified by events. He will be at a disadvantage compared with a competitor who started off with a less distorted production function. Moreover the assumption that factors are cheap will make him plan with a view to sales in the mass market of today rather than in the quality market (which may become the mass market of tomorrow). Hence his activities will be more labour-intensive than his rivals'. He is then particularly vulnerable to a rise in labour costs, even if capital is scarcer than labour.

Since the 1949 devaluation was primarily a devaluation of sterling relatively to the dollar, it implied a cheapening of British factors relatively to United States factors. One would expect a devaluation of sterling relatively to the dollar to encourage more labour-intensive development in Britain than in the United States, with the result that the demand for labour relatively to the demand for capital would rise more in Britain than in the United States. Given the scarcity of factors, this would raise labour costs more relatively to capital costs in Britain than in the United States. This is borne out by Table 26.1, which compares the rises of wages, prices of capital goods and export prices in the two countries.

Wages will be considered first. Wages in either of the two countries in 1949 are taken as 100. Then take the percentage increase in wages in each of the two countries over the 1949 level, and see whether there has been an excess rise of British wages over United States wages. For instance, with wages in 1949 equal to 100, British wages in 1959 were 188 and United States wages 163, thus giving an excess rise of British over United States wages of 15 per cent. (9)

A 15 per cent excess rise of British over United States wages was still within the limits foreseen by the 1949 devaluers, who devalued as much as they did because they foresaw a 'loss' of perhaps half of the devaluation through rising

Notes to Table 26.1

Derived from London and Cambridge Economic Service, 'Key Statistics of the British Economy, 1960-1966'; Central Statistical Office, 'National Income Blue Books' and 'Monthly Digest of Statistics'; U.S. Department of Commerce, 'Survey of Current Business': International Monetary Fund, 'International Financial Statistics'.

Labour costs: U.K. — average weekly earnings of male labour in manufacturing industries; U.S. — average weekly gross earnings per production worker in all manufacturing establishments. Capital costs: U.K. — price indices derived from 'National Income Blue Book' data relating to gross fixed capital formation at current and constant prices; U.S. — price indices derived from 'Survey of Current Business' data relating to fixed investment at current and constant prices.

Table 26.1 Indices of Relative Rise of British and United States Labour Costs, Capital Costs and Export Prices, 1949-67

	United Kingdom	United States	United Kingdom excess
Labour Costs			
1949	100	100	–
1959	188	163	115
1960	205	163	126
1961	216	170	127
1962	222	176	126
1963	231	181	128
1964	249	187	133
1965	266	195	136
1966	282	203	139
1967	295	208	142
Capital Costs			
1949	100	100	–
1959	147	137	107
1960	148	138	107
1961	151	139	109
1962	156	140	110
1963	159	142	112
1964	162	144	112
1965	168	148	114
1966	174	150	116
1967	176	155	114
Export Prices			
1949	100	100	–
1959	139	111	125
1960	141	112	126
1961	141	114	124
1962	142	113	126
1963	147	113	130
1964	150	114	132
1965	153	117	131
1966	158	121	131
1967	161	124	130

factor costs. The 1949 devaluation was one of 30½ per cent – or, in terms of indices, from 100 to 69.5. Hence British wages would have to rise by 44 per cent to restore the 1949 parity between British and United States wages – that is, from an index of 69.5 back to an index of 100.

As already mentioned, this was not the case in 1959. Subsequently, however, there was a greater excess rise of British over United States wages (compared with 1949). In 1960 to 1963 the excess rise of British wages (over the 1949 wage parity) fluctuated between 26 and 28 per cent, rose to 33 per cent in 1964, and reached 42 per cent in 1967. Given that the percentage rises are only approximately accurate, it may be said that the 1949 wage parity was approximately restored by 1967. Those who regard relative wage costs as one of the chief causes of cost differentials between products from the two countries, may argue that the 1949 devaluation had eroded in this respect. If the 1949 wage parity was the wage parity of a devaluation year, does it or does it not follow that the restoration of that parity indicates the need for renewed devaluation in 1967?

Those who think that it follows, implicitly assume that sterling had been overvalued in 1949; that labour costs are a true reflection of all costs; and that there are never any disturbances in the United States economy. In fact, labour costs are only about two-fifths of all costs. If labour costs are closely correlated with general price movements, the reason is that the price of labour is one price amongst many, and in an economy where labour is a scarce factor, changes in national wages costs tend to be determined by trends in aggregate money incomes. Moreover the most marked excess rise of British wages over United States wages occurred in the early 1960s, at a time of relative stagnation in the United States. A greater rise in British than in United States labour costs can reflect weaknesses in the United States economy as well as greater wage increases in the United Kingdom.

Even if, as far as the cost of labour is concerned, the 1949 devaluation was exhausted by 1967, this was not so with capital goods. In neither of the two countries did the cost of capital goods rise as much as the cost of labour, probably because it reflects the increase in productivity in both countries. Here, however, the concern is with relative price movements. In Table 26.1 the cost of gross fixed capital formation in either country in 1949 is taken as 100. Price indices for 1967 show the British index as 176 and the United States one as 155, thus giving a British excess rise in the cost of capital formation of 14 per cent. The excess was still within the limits of the rise in factor prices anticipated at the time of the 1949 devaluation. Moreover it was only about one-third of the increase that would have restored the 1949 capital-cost parity (10). It suggests nothing anywhere near exhaustion of the 1949 devaluation. Since the cost of gross capital formation includes labour costs, the true excess rise of the cost of capital goods was almost certainly less than the indices in Table 26.1 suggest.

True, the excess rise of British capital-goods prices widened in the 1960s. It had reached 10 per cent in 1952 and did not vary much from this figure until 1959. In 1959 and 1960 it was down to 7 per cent, but it then rose to a peak of 16 per cent in 1966. In 1967 it fell back to 14 per cent. As far as relative costs of capital goods are concerned, there seems no overwhelming evidence to suggest that the 1949 devaluation had been exhausted and that further devaluation was required – unless the restoration of the 1949 capital-goods cost parity is in any way regarded as desirable. If so, the 14.3 per cent devaluation of 1967 restored that parity.

Since changes in factor costs affect product prices, there should also be a comparison of the relative movements in British and United States prices in markets where the two countries compete on equal terms. This is so in export markets, even though preferential trading arrangements and tied aid may somewhat distort the picture. Such arrangements probably benefited the United Kingdom more in 1949 than in the 1960s, and their erosion may have checked the rise in British export prices (since the purpose of preferential arrangements is to enable exporters to receive higher prices). Whatever the details, within two or three years of the devaluation British export prices had risen by about one-quarter more than United States export prices, and this differential remained fairly steady until 1962. It then rose to about one-third. This was still well below the 44 per cent rise required to restore the 1949 export-price parity.

Admittedly, all this is derived from aggregate data, but devaluation is an aggregate measure. The case for taking this measure again, in 1967, is perhaps least unconvincing in relation to wages. Since, however, wages have not risen disproportionately in relation to national income, the case remains unproven. It has even been suggested (11) that the undervaluation of sterling imposed in 1949 led to a tendency for wages to rise until a correct wage parity would be restored, and that the authorities have ever since vainly tried to stem the forces they themselves have unleashed. Since changes in wage costs reflect the marginal change in reward for current effort more truly than other factor earnings, there is much force in such an argument, which implies that further devaluation was bound to accentuate tendencies towards a rise in factor costs. It must, however, also be considered why this effect of devaluation should have been more marked for wages than for capital costs in 1949-67, and whether this was a peculiarity of those years or an inevitable effect of undervaluation of the currency.

At first sight the greater relative rise in wage costs than in capital costs seems puzzling. On reflection, however, it fits in with the approach to the subject suggested throughout Parts III and IV of this book, and with section (c) above. The 1949 devaluation had given a boost to the status quo in activity, with the result that British economic progress became more labour-intensive and less capital-intensive than it otherwise would have been. In consequence there was a disproportionate increase in the demand for British labour and a less than proportionate increase in the demand for British capital.

No evidence has ever been produced that in 1949 British labour was less skilled than United States labour, though it has often been asserted that United States technology was superior to British. To overcome this technological gap would have required a greater rise in the rewards to British capital than in the rewards to British labour. The devaluation undervalued British labour most. That, however, was not a corrective for the technological gap, since it made British labour too cheap. Because British labour had been excessively undervalued, and the economy was fully employed, there had to be an equilibrating price movement. The equilibrating price movement had to raise labour costs most, since labour had been devalued most. The combined effect of the undervaluation of labour and rising labour costs delayed recognition of the approaching absolute scarcity of factors (which, as shown in Chapter 23, became apparent around 1960). Hence it obscured the need for more capital-intensive development. For even if labour costs rose most, labour was still 'cheap' and labour-intensive development encouraged, even if to a diminishing degree.

Thus the 1949 devaluation diverted the British economy from a more profitable path. It did so, in the first place, through undervaluing all British factors, which encouraged more traditional labour-intensive development than would otherwise have been the case; it therefore delayed change. Secondly, it did so through undervaluing factors which were already fully employed, so that there had to be an equilibrating rise in factor prices. Thirdly, it did so through undervaluing British labour more than British capital, so that the equilibrating price movement raised labour costs relatively more than capital costs; and this rise in labour costs increasingly impeded the labour-intensive development which the devaluation had originally encouraged.

With capital-intensive development delayed by an undervalued currency, and labour-intensive development increasingly impeded by the equilibrating factor-price movements, the British economy entered the 1960s less well placed to meet the international demand for new goods than some of its rivals were.

Throughout the 1960s to 1967, persistent attempts were made to stem the increasing weakness of sterling. These attempts paid insufficient attention to raising the rewards for new enterprise. Instead they concentrated on limiting the rise in factor prices, especially of wages. They dealt with symptoms. They ignored the fundamental undervaluation. Perhaps it was too late by then to correct the misvaluation of 1949. Nevertheless the fall of sterling in 1967 cannot be attributed to overvaluation, but must be taken as a penalty for the delays in modernisation caused by persistent undervaluation.

Thus the misvaluation of 1949 brought its penalty just as the misvaluation of

1925 did. On both occasions the ultimate penalty was a fall in the exchange rate of sterling. If the same penalty had to be paid for the two misvaluations, they were yet misvaluations in opposite directions. The damage wrought by the over-valuation of the 1920s was largely quantitive and domestic, while that wrought by the 1949 undervaluation was qualitative and injurious to the balance of payments rather than to the domestic situation.

It will be recalled that, in the 1920s, the traditional industries were depressed and there was mass unemployment; but even in those days there were growth industries, such as the motor-car industry. Overall, the quality of national output was not impeded. There just was not enough of it. Overvaluation may not have been the only cause of the quantitative inadequacies of the 1920s, but it was an all-pervasive one that led the home economy into a vicious circle where there were never enough goods produced for the 'emporium' and there was never enough money to pay for all of those that were. Externally, however, the United Kingdom remained solvent as long as the major overseas countries did not impoverish themselves through overvaluations of their currencies. When eventually they did, in 1929 and after, the external balance of payments turned into deficit.

The experience of the 1920s has been reiterated for the sake of contrast. 1925 brought an overvaluation at a time of widespread unemployment, 1949 an undervaluation at a time of full employment. The undervaluation gave the traditional industries an extended lease of life, so that there were not enough factors available for growth industries. British factors were undervalued, and labour probably more so than capital. At any one point of time this encouraged labour-intensive activities over capital-intensive ones, since labour seemed relatively cheap. Over time, however, this caused a greater equilibrating rise in wages than in the price of capital goods. There was a new vicious circle, where labour was always too cheap and wages were always rising too fast. 'Tailors' planned their production as if labour were cheaper than it turned out to be when their plans were put into effect, and they planned for markets where customers were assumed to be poorer than they eventually turned out to be. If so, produc-tion would be too labour-intensive and quality would lag behind market require-ments. In short, not only were labour relations impaired, but so were production and market opportunities.

British capital goods too were undervalued, but, given the technological gap, they were undervalued to a lesser extent. The equilibrating upward price movement of capital goods was appropriately less than that for labour. That, however, reflects a lesser rise in pressure on capital resources than on the stock of labour; and this indicates a lesser rise in capital-intensive than in labour-intensive activities. This in turn suggests greater emphasis on quantity than on quality.

T   M.P.M.E.

Undervaluation thus has the desired effects on factor prices if, and only if, there is unemployment. If that is the case, labour is relatively scarce (see Chapters 19, 22 and 23), and a move towards equilibrium requires greater pressure on the stock of labour than on capital resources. That was not the case between 1949 and 1967. With full employment, all factors are scarce and capital relatively scarcer than labour, so that a move towards equilibrium in prices and production necessitates more use of capital. A greater marginal value of a unit of capital than of a unit of labour is a characteristic of a fully employed growth economy. The equilibrating factor-price movement which followed the 1949 devaluation had the opposite effect.

In short, a fully employed economy needs more capital-intensive activities to circumvent the absolute scarcity of factors and to grow. Undervaluation of the currency, however, encourages quantitative growth which cannot easily be accelerated once the economy is fully employed. Since quantitative growth is more labour-intensive than qualitative growth, undervaluation of the currency distorts the relative marginal values of labour and capital from the relationship required by a growth economy. This point is re-inforced if, through currency devaluation, labour becomes relatively more devalued than capital so that the subsequent equilibrating price movement raises wages more than prices of capital goods.

There are limitations to the preceding analysis of the factor-price absorption of the 1949 devaluation. The cost comparison is with the United States alone and not with other countries which have become more important since 1949. Nevertheless the procedure seems justified; in the years from 1949 to 1967 the dollar was the basic currency, since all other International Monetary Fund currencies were valued in terms of dollars.

An implied limitation of the preceding is that it ignored the effects on the United States. If Sterling was undervalued relatively to the dollar, the dollar was overvalued relatively to sterling. If the undervaluation of sterling made British economic development more labour-intensive relatively to United States economic development, it may also have encouraged more capital-intensive development in the United States. The same would apply to British economic development in comparison with economic development in countries that had less undervalued currencies (relatively to the dollar). A full examination of this point would require an exhaustive study of the relative movements of factor prices throughout the industrial world. Here it must suffice to say that, if the undervaluation of sterling somewhat decelerated British economic growth, it may also have been a contributory cause of the acceleration of economic growth elsewhere.

Another limitation of the preceding discussion is that it is purely macro-economic analysis. The experience of this industry or that may have been different. Currency policy is, however, macro-economic policy and must be judged according to its overall effects. The overall effect of a lowering of the value of the currency is to encourage labour-intensive activities (as defined in Chapter 24 section 4). In other words it encourages quantitative expansion. That was overdue in 1931. In 1949 and after, matters were different because there was full employment. Quantitative expansion was limited by the availability of factors. The only road towards faster growth was through qualitative improvements, but undervaluation of the currency is no help towards that. In the circumstances of 1949-67, it hindered.

Generally, it is always difficult to find a 'correct' exchange rate through administrative decision, and it may be wellnigh impossible within a few years of a major war. If it is fixed too high, as in 1925, the result is unemployment. If it is fixed too low, as in 1949, the result is delayed growth. In either case there are adverse balance-of-payments effects. If the exchange rate is too high, exports suffer because not enough is produced. If the exchange rate is too low, exports suffer because not enough of the right quality is produced to attract overseas demand. The 1949 devaluation was an answer to the problems of the 1920s and 1930s. Through its qualitative effects, however, it delayed the qualitative improvements the economy was technologically capable of. Hence the extraordinary phenomenon of Europe's technologically most advanced country being faced with increasing external payments problems.

None of this contradicts the findings of the preceding chapters, which depicted the road to 1967 as strewn with too few innovations and too many restrictive practices, with too much loss of invisible earnings and too much rise in invisible spending and the like. All that was important, but none of it as insidious as the undervaluation of the currency. In short, 1949 bred 1967. (12)

5   1967

(a)   Undervaluation and Devaluation

A full assessment of the implications of '1967' must await the passage of more time. At the time of writing, only eighteen months have gone by since the devaluation of November 1967, so that only a preliminary sketch is possible. It will start with some general remarks on the position of currencies in the late 1960s, to be followed by preliminary comments on the acceptability of the devaluation and the authorities' attempts 'to make devaluation work'.

Amongst the lessons of the past is that a currency's domestic and international problems tend to interact, so that they should never be viewed in isolation. Thus if a country has full employment at home, it can never have an overvalued currency, though it may have a misvalued currency. In the United

Kingdom the Keynes–Beveridge level of unemployment was seldom approached in the years from 1949 to 1967 (and exceeded only during a spell of unusually cold weather in 1963), so that sterling was not overvalued at any time during that period. Some other industrial countries had more unemployment during various phases in the 1950s and 1960s, so that they then had overvalued currencies. Towards the end of the 1960s high unemployment had ceased in all the major industrial countries, so that none of the major currencies was overvalued. Since full employment was accompanied by some rise in the general price level in each of those countries, there was some undervaluation of all the major currencies.

When all currencies are undervalued, they are not likely to be undervalued to the same extent. The one which is most undervalued discourages its economic growth most and impairs the balance of payments most. With full employment, purely quantitative growth can be but slow; with undervaluation, qualitative improvements are discouraged (or at least not encouraged). Hence a bundle of representative exports does not improve so much in quality as the state of technological knowledge would permit. The international purchasing power of such a bundle from the country with the most devalued currency is then likely to rise less than representative bundles from rival economies. It follows that, the greater the degree of undervaluation and the longer it persists, the more will there be a tendency towards a worsening in the balance of payments.

The currency which is least undervalued also loses purchasing power at home and abroad, as long as it is undervalued. Relatively to other currencies, however, it loses purchasing power least. Its representative bundle of exports thus becomes relatively more attractive abroad. As long as undervaluation is greater elsewhere, it still has a higher growth rate than others and a tendancy towards a growing surplus in external payments.

At such times the country with the most undervalued currency may have to face a twofold problem. One is to accept an exchange rate which takes account of the present degree of undervaluation relatively to other currencies. The other is to find ways of preventing further undervaluation, if devaluation is not to breed further devaluation. For an exchange rate which reflects the greater undervaluation must be lower than the previous one, and under an international system of fixed exchange rates, this can only be attained through devaluation. But devaluation, unaccompanied by other changes, only reflects and accentuates the undervaluation. Left to itself, devaluation of an already undervalued currency can only lead to experiences akin to those of sterling after 1949.

Whether the second problem will be faced, depends on the aims of economic policy. If the sole aim of policy is the maintenance of the current level of employment, that can always be assisted by undervaluation. If the pattern of world economic activity and trade is assumed to be given, excessive devaluation and undervaluation may be voluntarily resorted to. This kind of argument may have appealed in 1949. It was rather irrelevant in 1967.

By 1967 the target of policy was no longer full employment alone. It had become full employment with faster growth. Sterling was already undervalued, so that further undervaluation was not needed to maintain full employment. Sterling was already one of the most undervalued currencies, and further under-valuation could only be inimical to long-term growth prospects. Devaluation was resisted as long as possible. If that resistance was finally broken in 1967, it was because overseas countries would no longer support an exchange rate that had been undermined by persistent undervaluation.

These points indicate a basic difference between the 1949 and 1967 devalua-tions. In 1949 the authorities deliberately sought undervaluation. In 1967 they had to acknowledge its effects.

If the 1967 devaluation is not to breed further devaluation (through retarded growth), the various possible sources of undervaluation have to be brought under control. Since devaluation by itself only accentuates undervaluation, alternative measures have to be all the more drastic. There is no reason, however, to let those alternative measures go so far as to endanger full employment. Balance-of-payments considerations dictate a lessening of undervaluation to ensure an assortment of exports with greater overseas appeal, and domestic growth considerations point the same way. But at a time when all the major currencies are undervalued, some growth can be sacrificed to greater security of employ-ment. In these days of rapid technological change, some other economies have achieved full employment and maintained higher growth rates than the British one. The same can be done in the United Kingdom, if the second problem is faced.

(b)   An Agreed Devaluation

In 1967 the British authorities did not so much decide to devalue as to acknowledge the effects of persistent undervaluation. Matters were beginning to come to a head with an exceptionally large balance-of-payments deficit in 1964, but it was hoped that a traditional dose of deflationary measures and external borrowing would avoid the need to devalue. The possible efficacy of some of those deflationary measures will be discussed in subsection (c) below. There was external borrowing from overseas central banks, so that balance-of-payments deficits would not show in the published figures of the exchange reserves. The purpose was financial window-dressing. The borrowed funds could not be used to raise the potential supply of British-made goods relatively to the supply of British-made money. In other words overseas funds, lent for financial purposes, could hide some of the symptoms of undervaluation, but they could not be used to cope with the domestic source of undervaluation. What was needed was an additional supply of capital goods. What was obtained was an additional supply of money capital. Yet an international system of fixed exchange rates depends on flows of funds which finance transfers of real capital, and not just on flows of funds. As it was, the United Kingdom borrowed paper to hide a crack rather than cement to fill it.

The crack widened again in 1967 when the balance of payments on current account became once more as adverse as it had been three years earlier. 'The tailor's shop' was not bankrupt, but had lost some value relatively to rival establishments'. When this was acknowledged, the British authorities did not spring a surprise. There were consultations amongst central bankers and governments, relating to the timing of the devaluation and the rate they would accept without feeling forced to realign their currencies. The 1967 devaluation was the first devaluation to be agreed amongst the major currency countries before it was put into effect. The 'tailor' was to have his 'sale'; there were to be no rival 'sales' in Monetary High Street; and some more paper was made available to hide the crack until it could be filled in.

Because the 1967 devaluation was an agreed devaluation, it was limited geographically and in amount. In 1931 practically all currencies followed the downward path of sterling; in 1949 nearly all Western European and Sterling Area currencies were devalued at the same time as sterling; but in 1967 only a minority of lesser currencies followed – and even the majority of Sterling Area countries did not. Those that followed, either have economies closely linked to the United Kingdom's or intended to devalue anyway and took this as an opportune moment.

The agreed percentage devaluation was 14.3 per cent. It is believed that the other major currency countries were willing to accept any devaluation up to 15 per cent, and a 14.3 per cent devaluation brought the exchange rate down to a round figure of $2.40. That was about half the rate of the depreciation of 1931 or the devaluation of 1949, when competing economies were expected to lower their exchange rates. (It has also been suggested that the choice of rate may have been influenced by the investment dollar rate, which at that time was around $2.40. The investment dollar rate is the rate at which United Kingdom residents can buy dollars for investment purposes. That, however, was no guide to an equilibrium rate. There was exchange control for United Kingdom residents, so that investment dollars would stand at a premium as convertible currency. When exchange control was tightened after devaluation, the investment dollar premium rose.)

As an agreed devaluation, the 1967 one was a technical success at the time. Later on, there were some technical complications. Thus before the devaluation the Bank of England had supported the sterling exchange rate through forward sales of dollars, and since it did not have the dollars, it had to buy them. As long as these operations continued, sales and purchases of dollars were about equal and the value of the dollar was not affected. After the devaluation in November 1967, these operations ceased. The last forward sales commitments of dollars matured in February 1968, and since no further purchases were made, there was an excess supply of dollars which was no longer counteracted by an appropriate excess demand. This shook the international monetary system. Since support operations for currencies often take the form of three months' commitments, a series of three-monthly crises followed, affecting sometimes one currency most and sometimes another. Even eighteen months after the 1967 devaluation, some of those technical repercussions still reverberated. It cannot yet be forecast whether, when and how they will cease.

This is but one example of the technical problems that follow even an agreed devaluation. If the currency is relatively unimportant, such problems may be minor. Sterling is no longer as important as it was before 1914 or even in 1949. But next only to the dollar, it is still the world's most widely used currency. Its parity can be altered by agreement, and the change localised and minimised; but its parity cannot be changed without repercussions throughout the trading world and over some time.

(c)   The First Eighteen Months After

The first eighteen months after the 1967 devaluation divide themselves into three phases. First there were four months of somewhat utopian euphoria, then eight months of reliance on fiscal correctives, and finally the beginnings of a search for new monetary policies.

The euphoria was of two kinds. There was that of the general public which behaved as if Christmas had come to stay. In anticipation of rising prices and factor earnings, there was unprecedented spending on consumer goods. Four months later this was arrested (but not reversed) by a sharp increase in indirect taxation. Somewhat different was the euphoria of those who had hoped for an improvement in the balance of payments, once British goods became cheaper in terms of foreign currencies. They pinned their hopes on considerations along the following lines.

If overseas price elasticities of demand for British goods were high, British exporters could sell more by charging lower foreign currency prices and yet maintain (or even raise) their sterling receipts. The Kennedy Round of tariff negotiations (under the General Agreement on Tariffs and Trade) had been brought to a successful conclusion earlier in 1967, and since tariff reductions normally allow for more trade in 'inessentials', intensified price competition was to be expected. Moreover the European Free Trade Association had completed the dismantling of tariffs on industrial goods, so that the same result could be expected all the more within that area. If price elasticities should disappoint, exporters could charge the former foreign currency prices and earn more profits in sterling. That would encourage them to intensify their export efforts. There would not necessarily be such a rise in factor prices as to frustrate the devaluation, since unemployment had been rising for some time before the devaluation, In short, either the elasticity conditions for a successful devaluation would be given, and the devaluation be as acceptable to the trading world as to the bankers who had agreed on it; or the absorption conditions would be given; and on the most favourable reading of the situation, the devaluation would be accepted and absorbed.

Past experience suggests that it is not enough to have just some of those conditions satisfied. The 1931 depreciation was not accepted and the 1949 devaluation could not be absorbed, so that neither had been a panacea for the British balance of payments. While it is too early to pass final judgement on the 1967 devaluation, initial experience suggests that it was not fully accepted in trade and could not be absorbed.

It was not fully accepted because it was largely irrelevant to much of the export trades. The importance of the Kennedy Round and of free trade within the European Free Trade Association are not denied. The Kennedy Round had led to substantial tariff concessions by the advanced industrial countries, and not too much had been asked of the less developed countries. The concessions were largely on commodities and in countries where income elasticities of demand are more important than price elasticities. The sort of goods most affected are those that sell best whenever quality improves. In other words they are capital-intensive goods (as defined in Chapter 24, section 4). Tariff concessions on capital-intensive goods matter primarily because they enable exporters to take untaxed profits (and not so much because they enable exporters to charge less, for that would only deprive them of profits and their country of foreign exchange). The same applies to much of free trade within the European Free Trade Association.

Price elasticities matter more in the non-industrial world. But primary producing countries, like anybody else, can accept more British goods only if they can pay for them. The most important primary producing markets for British goods are the overseas Sterling Area countries. It will be recalled that the 1949 devaluation had led to an increase in British exports to the overseas Sterling Area, but the special conditions of those days cannot be re-created. Then, most overseas sterling countries had more sterling reserves than they needed for monetary purposes, and the devaluation diverted some of their spending to the United Kingdom. In 1967 the overseas Sterling Area countries had few sterling reserves beyond their monetary requirements. What reserves they had, were reduced in value by the devaluation. Although the high rates of interest they could earn on their sterling holdings would compensate them within about two years, in the meantime their reserves were curtailed. While most overseas Sterling Area countries no longer relied as exclusively on sterling as they used to do, their sterling reserves still formed the major part of their exchange reserves and backing for their national currencies. In consequence, devaluation caused some monetary difficulties in those countries. Until these difficulties are overcome, the countries concerned cannot afford to import as much as they otherwise could have done. If devaluation gave British exporters a competitive price advantage in overseas Sterling Area markets, it also made those markets smaller than they need have been.

Irrelevant to much of the trade with advanced industrial countries and, at least initially, injurious to Sterling Area trade, devaluation could not lead to quick and easy export successes in the major overseas markets. The rest of the world, however important from various points of view, could not provide comparable markets for British goods.

Whatever the details, 1968 saw a 6½ per cent increase in the dollar value of British exports. That in itself was a substantial increase, and it looks even more impressive in comparison with 1967, when the dollar value of British exports fell by 2 per cent. It does not look so impressive in comparison with 1965 and 1966; in both of those years the dollar value of British exports had risen by 7 per cent. In short, the growth of exports in 1968 was markedly greater than in devaluation year but no greater than in the last two pre-devaluation years. More revealing may be a comparison of the growth of British exports with the growth of exports from all industrial countries. In 1968 the dollar value of exports from all industrial countries rose by 13 per cent, so that the British export performance was half of the industrial world's (in terms of growth rates). In 1965 and 1966 the dollar value of exports from all industrial countries had risen by 10 per cent and 11 per cent respectively, so that the British export performance in those two pre-devaluation years had been about two-thirds of the industrial world's. (13)

The overall export performance in any one year provides no conclusive evidence of the effects of the 1967 devaluation. Any number of special circumstances, at home or abroad, may have distorted the overall result. Above all, the decision to trade has to be taken before trade takes place, and the time-lag involved may be considerable. Much of 1968 trade had been decided upon in 1967 or even earlier, while some of the 1968 decisions could not affect trade until 1969 or later. Moreover there can be special delays. For instance, much 1967 trade was delayed by a prolonged dock strike, and orders for British goods may have been delayed by overseas buyers who anticipated devaluation. These two examples suggest that some 1968 trade was specially delayed 1967 trade, so that the change in export performance was less drastic than annual trade returns suggest. It is, however, just as possible that the 1968 export statistics understate the underlying trend. Some delayed trade diversions may yet come. In traditional trades, established commercial connections may be valued for their own sake, and only the lure of substantial and sustained price differentials may lead to their eventual severance. Should some such disruptive success follow the 1967 devaluation, it will take time. Commercial loyalty is probably not so relevant to the new trades – nor is devaluation.

The export trade statistics for 1968 may have understated the underlying trend of British exports, but no adjustment of the British statistics can hide a worsening of relative performance. The statistics may also have overstated the rate of growth of the industrial world's exports. There may be delayed trade anywhere. In 1967 the industrial world's exports grew by only 5 per cent, and the acceleration to 13 per cent in 1968 may have been swollen by some delayed trade. The average for 1967 and 1968 was somewhat less than the average for 1965 and 1966. If the growth of British exports in 1968 could be compared with the industrial world's average for 1967 and 1968, the British relative performance would appear about the same as in the last two pre-devaluation years. In short, the most favourable interpretation of the statistics would suggest that the United Kingdom's 1968 export performance was no worse, relatively to the industrial world's, than it had been in the last two pre-devaluation years; but on any straight reading of the statistics it was worse. Whichever way the statistics are viewed, they suggest no devaluation 'benefits' for British exports. (14)

If exports responded 'perversely' or not at all, imports did likewise. They rose by value, as expected, since import prices (in sterling) had been raised by the devaluation, and other countries were less willing to adjust their prices to British prices than they had been in 1949, let alone 1931. The outside world accepted the British 1967 devaluation, or at least a substantial part of it, by letting British importers pay more. Had the British economy also accepted the implications, there would have been a fall in the volume of imports or at least a slowing-down of the rise in the volume of imports. In fact the volume of imports continued to rise, and it rose somewhat faster after devaluation than before. (15) Thus imports responded as 'perversely' as exports.

The response of trade was 'perverse' only on the assumption that sterling was overvalued before devaluation. It is true that there was some rise in unemployment during the second half of 1966 and in 1967, and that the rise in unemployment started after the intensification of deflationary measures in mid-1966. But this was a false alarm. Not only did the rise in unemployment merely approach the Keynes–Beveridge level, but it had begun to recede before devaluation. Moreover at least some of the increase was due to the introduction of redundancy pay in 1965, which enabled dismissed workers to take more time over finding a suitable job rather than take the first one available. The British economy has thus effectively remained a fully employed economy throughout the 1960s. As shown before, a fully employed economy cannot have an over-valued currency.

The 1967 devaluation of sterling was a devaluation of an already undervalued currency. It intensified the undervaluation, and therefore encouraged existing activities relatively to new ones. More than before, expansion would be attempted without adequate factor saving. One result was an intensified scramble for factors, which reinforced all tendencies towards a rise in factor prices. For devaluation is meant to inflate existing activities, but in the British economy of the 1960s practically all factors were already employed. At the same time any advanced industrial country's demand for imports tends to be more income-elastic than price-elastic. This has been true of the British economy for longer than of most economies, and there was no reason to suppose that this would be any different in 1967. The combined effect of devaluation, full employment and the high income elasticity of demand for imports led to dis-equilibrium in prices and production and to disequilibrium in money supply.

With full employment, a high rate of economic growth depends on factor saving. Devaluation, however, encourages growth without factor saving. Once again a situation was created where devaluation had made factors too cheap to make factor saving attractive, while the resultant scramble for factors raised factor prices so much as to make the continuance of existing activities more difficult. In short, factors were too cheap and factor prices rising too fast. After 1949 this had been particularly marked for labour. The same point cannot yet be proved for the aftermath of 1967, though it is probable: with full employment, labour is the relatively more abundant factor and therefore more vulnerable; and compared with the world's leading economy of the day, the United States, there was still a technological gap rather than an educational one. It is thus probable, though not yet certain, that the 1967 devaluation under-valued labour even more than capital; it is certain that it undervalued all British factors. Whatever the details, there was renewed disequilibrium in prices and production.

The disequilibrium in prices and production was accompanied by dis-equilibrium in money supply. Devaluation raised money incomes (in sterling) of all engaged in export activities. This result follows from a lowering of the exchange parity, as long as volumes of exports do not actually fall. The scramble for factors may spread this new money rapidly throughout the economy. But whether it is spread or not, somewhere in the economy there is more sterling. This means an increase in purchasing power in the hands of the public, and in the present context it does not matter which members of the public. In times of unemployment this result is wanted: devaluation lowers factor costs and the additional purchasing power is needed to provide the means of buying more goods. In 1967, however, there was full employment. When exporters got a higher sterling return for their overseas sales, there was an increase in money supply (since more sterling was given in return for foreign exchange). Since there were no abundant factors, so that there could be no corresponding increase in domestic output, the immediate result was purely inflationary.

The new purchasing power could be used for more domestic capital formation or for more current spending. New capital formation always seems attractive in a growth economy, and since it normally leads to an increase in output, the inflationary consequences may eventually be offset. In the months immediately after devaluation, however, when more profits could be earned without changing one's ways, there was rather less incentive to invest in factor-saving innovations. Instead, more was spent on current consumption (including business consumption), and since there was no increase in the supply of domestic goods, there was an increased demand for imports. Generally, a fully employed economy is likely to spend somewhat more on imports after devaluation than before devaluation. This happened in 1968, when the beneficiaries of the 1967 devaluation included overseas suppliers.

So far the new monetary disequilibrium has been viewed from the point of view of the British economy alone. It remains to consider whether the devaluation is likely to have accentuated or relieved the undervaluation of sterling relatively to other currencies. In the United Kingdom more profits could be made (in sterling) from exporting what had been exported before, produced in the way it had been produced before. Exporters thus received a 'rent' for having been there, rather than genuine additions to profits to reward their enterprise. Since the equilibrating rise in factor prices takes time, factors had become 'cheaper' relatively to profits (as swollen by 'devaluation rent'). That made the excess money supply even larger than the previous paragraph suggests. For there was not only that much more money in circulation, but the proportion of money supply needed to finance current output was also less. The incentive to resort to factor saving was correspondingly less. In countries that had not devalued in 1967, there was no change in the incentive to resort to factor-saving innovations. In so far as the increased British demand for imports exerted any influence, the pressure on overseas resources was increased, and that may even have encouraged some overseas factor saving. Even if this last point can be ignored, on the ground that the additional British demand for imports probably exerted little additional pressure in any one overseas economy, the relative effect on British and overseas factor saving cannot be ignored. That relative effect could only be adverse. For producers, in receipt of 'devaluation rent', would make more money without more ingenuity, and this could not fail to make firms plan their production along more traditional lines than they would otherwise have done. But producers abroad, who had received no such 'rent', would not delay their modernisation.

In short, devaluation had increased the supply of sterling relatively to the supply of foreign currency, and this made it relatively easier to earn sterling than other currencies. This obscured the basic British economic problem, which is that the British economy stands in greater need of factor saving than economies that have not yet reached the state of maturity where all factors are scarce. Left to itself, the 1967 devaluation would not just have acknowledged past under-valuation; it would have been a source of further undervaluation, further delays and yet further devaluation.

As pointed out in Chapter 23, the challenge that faced the British economy in the 1960s was to find a solution to the problem of scarcity of all factors. That was an entirely new problem which took time to diagnose, let alone solve. The 1967 devaluation was an acknowledgement that the problem had not yet been solved. Its solution will require more than just monetary policy; but its solution can be impeded by monetary policies that discourage change.

In some ways the authorities appear to have recognised this throughout. After all, they had resisted devaluation as long as they could. Moreover, when devalua-tion was announced, it was accompanied by an increase in Bank Rate from 5½ per cent to 8 per cent and an intensification of a number of other deflationary devices. Measures along those lines had not prevented devaluation, but they were an attempt to counter some of the inflationary implications of devaluation and thus to stem yet further undervaluation. Yet all those measures combined could not be expected to counter all of the 14.3 per cent drop in the exchange rate. Hence the euphoria, mentioned at the beginning of this section, in the expectation of more money to come.

The general public's euphoria was cut short by the budget of March 1968. That was an important budget in more senses than one. It imposed a sharp increase in taxes and shifted the relative burden of taxation more towards indirect taxes. In the present context, however, its chief significance lies in the recognition that the chief source of the weakness of sterling lay at home. It endeavoured, by fiscal means, to reduce the volume of purchasing power in the hands of the public. In a way, the 1968 budget was the culmination of attempts to deal with the country's economic problems by means of price policy.

The sharp increase in indirect taxation was meant to raise product prices against home consumers, in the hope that this would divert goods into export markets. The 1968 budget thus supplemented the 1967 devaluation, which had been intended to raise prices against home consumers whilst devaluing their earnings. At the same time the budget complemented the micro-economic 'incomes policy' which was intended to restrain the rise in factor prices.

The purpose of these various price policies was to raise product prices against home consumers (devaluation and the 1968 budget), and to lower or restrain factor prices (devaluation and the micro-economic incomes policy), so that the result would be a rise in product prices relatively to factor prices. The public should have to pay more and afford less. With production cheapened and consumption more expensive, more goods should be sold abroad.

The idea that any surplus of British production over and above home consumption can always be sold abroad, provided prices are low enough, is more appropriate to the pre-1950 pattern of world trade than to the post-1950 one. Leaving aside this point, there were still difficulties in creating the required export surplus through raising product prices relatively to factor prices. The reason was that these policies attacked various symptoms of the situation and ignored some of the implications of devaluation. Thus while it is true that the devaluation initially undervalued domestic factors, it also added to the money supply and so set off equilibrating forces to raise factor prices. The micro-economic incomes policy thus endeavoured to support the initial disequilibrium created by devaluation and counter the equilibrating consequences. There was still an increase in money supply, and even a successful micro-economic incomes policy can do no more than stop the spread of the increased money supply to factors.

Similarly the rise in product prices was a symptom rather than a cause of an excessive supply of money. To raise product prices even faster only accentuated the disequilibrium between product and factor prices, which had been a feature of the economic scene since 1949 and was accentuated in 1967. Moreover the increase in taxation could not, by itself, reduce the money supply. It only diverted some of it from the general public to the Government. The Government did not destroy the money but used it to retire portions of the National Debt or to borrow less. Hence more funds were in the hands of debt-holders or potential debt-holders. If that was not to enlarge credit for other purposes, the authorities had to resort to tighter credit control — which is monetary policy.

In November 1968 the authorities effectively admitted that devaluation and other price policies had failed to improve the balance of payments. Emphasis shifted to monetary policies, with directives to the joint-stock banks to cut advances to pre-devaluation levels and with the introduction of a temporary import-deposit scheme. The directives to the banks were Treasury orders (though conveyed through the Bank of England) to effect quantitative retrenchment to specified historic levels of lending. Whether this was a once-and-for-all measure to counter some of the monetary implications of devaluation, or whether such negative quantitative controls will become a permanent feature of British monetary policy, remains to be seen. Whatever the answer, it will have more important consequences than a temporary import-deposit scheme may have. In the present context, however, the latter is not to be ignored, since it provided a useful lesson in where the source of balance-of-payments weakness lay and how to cope with it.

Originally intended as another way of curbing imports, the import-deposit scheme turned out to be a supplementary measure of credit control. The use of money for financing imports was to be made less attractive than the use of money for other purposes. Importers of industrial goods were required to deposit half of the value of imports with H.M. Customs, for a period of six months and free of interest. During the first few months of the operation of the scheme, the majority of importers did not appear to find undue difficulties in obtaining the requisite finance in the market, so that there was no drastic and immediate effect on the volume of imports. Nevertheless the measure was not unimportant, since it effectively tied up loanable funds.

The scheme was introduced for one year only. If not renewed, the last deposits would be made in November 1969, and funds thus tied up until May 1970. That meant eighteen months of additional credit restraint. Since the British demand for imports depends more on the state of domestic activity and incomes than on prices, policies to restrain imports should have direct impact on activity and incomes. The volume of credit influences both activity and incomes. Hence credit control is a more effective way of controlling imports than devaluation or other price policies. At a time when the authorities considered restraint of imports overriding, they introduced a measure which would reduce the available supply of loanable funds whenever imports rose. It seems unnecessary, however, to tie credit control to a rise in imports which is already taking place. Almost any kind of effective credit control would serve the same purpose, and it could be used to forestall a rise in imports rather than penalise current importers.

In all this there lies hope as well as warning. There is hope that the 1967 devaluation has provided the shock which led to re-examination of central control of the economy, and that it is now realised that the external and domestic values of the currency cannot be viewed in isolation but are different aspects of the same problem. In a fully employed economy, undervaluation is a source of domestic and external disequilibrium, and the two problems demand an identical solution. There is, however, also a warning. Historically, a cut in British imports has been associated with a rise in unemployment. Excessive credit restraint could lead to a return to such conditions. Since an under-employed and poorer British economy would depend relatively more on activities with a high import content, the result would not even include an improved balance of payments. Only the cause would differ: it would be overvaluation and no longer undervaluation.

In short, any misvalued currency causes balance-of-payments difficulties. If the misvaluation is an undervaluation, it may eventually lead to devaluation. If devaluation is to be avoided, a corrective credit squeeze may have to be severe, and there is risk of going too far. The problem is somewhat eased for a mature economy. One reason is that credit restraint squeezes out traditional activities and the newer ones normally have a lower factor input per unit of output. Another reason is that undervaluation supports traditional activities which tend to have a high import content, while the newer ones have a higher input of domestic skills. The growth of the new activities can then offset the adverse income effects of a credit squeeze and yet reduce the import content per unit of national output. In consequence, growth can accelerate *and* the balance of payments can improve.

Policy should be directed towards this target. Needless to say, it will always be difficult to achieve exact balance. Some undervaluation may have to be tolerated in order to avoid the evil effects of overvaluation on the level of employment. Since the fear of overvaluation is not confined to the United Kingdom, a moderate undervaluation of sterling need not have adverse balance-of-payments effects. At a time when all currencies are undervalued, any undervaluation of sterling should be kept in line with the undervaluations of other major currencies, and cease to go beyond it. If this can now be achieved, the age of sterling devaluations should be over.

6   BANK RATE RESTORED

The idea that credit control is the proper instrument to safeguard the currency would have sounded familiar in the early days of the century. The idea that this should be done by the Treasury laying down a maximum for the volume of bank advances would have sounded strange. It would have sounded strange even in the 1950s and the 1960s, before 1968. True, there had been an increasing tendency for the authorities to interest themselves in the volume of bank advances, and Bank Rate changes alone were no longer trusted to bring about the requisite results. In the 1930s and 1940s, when Bank Rate changes were suspended, other measures had to be used; and in the 1950s and 1960s, when Bank Rate changes were restored, it was used as part of a 'package' of (usually) deflationary measures rather than by itself. But whatever credit policies were pursued, they concentrated on the joint-stock banks' cash base (16) and left it to the banks themselves to readjust the credit structure in accordance with prudent banking principles. Even when the 'package' accompanying a Bank Rate change included instructions relating to the criteria on which further bank advances would be granted, these tended to be roughly in line with the criteria bank managers themselves would apply after a change in interest rates. Thus although the banks and the public had become used to increasing official concern in the volume of advances, official intervention still operated largely on the cash base, and the banks were left to decide how to conduct banking business on an altered cash base. If direct control of the volume of bank advances was resorted to in 1968, this may have been due to the special post-devaluation problems referred to in the previous section. It may also be interpreted as a sign of the ineffectiveness of the more traditional monetary policies that had failed to avert devaluation.

Only the future can tell which interpretation is correct. A detailed examination of the various possibilities would require a specialist volume. The following will be no more than an indication whether Bank Rate alone could once more become as efficacious as it had formerly been. Section 7 below will consider some implications of changes in the use of sterling as a reserve currency.

The return to monetary policy does not date from 1968 but from 1951, when Bank Rate was restored as a flexible instrument of policy. But what was restored in 1951 was not the razor-edged instrument of pre-1914 days, but an instrument even more blunted than it had been in the 1920s. As shown in Chapter 22, the higher rates of income tax prevailing since the Second World War, coupled with tax allowances for interest payments, made changes in Bank Rate much less effective than they otherwise might have been. Should the 1968 budget presage a shift in the tax burden from direct to indirect taxation (even when tax rates fall), and should the abolition of tax allowances on interest payable on personal bank advances in the 1969 budget presage a general abolition of tax allowances on interest payments, Bank Rate changes will become much more efficacious.

Tax allowances on interest payments were not the only reason why Bank Rate had been blunted. As shown in section 2 above, Bank Rate had already been blunted in the 1920s, when the bill market had become primarily a market in Treasury bills, and Bank Rate had become a means of shunting financial funds from centre to centre rather than a means of affecting import prices. That held for the 1950s as much as for the 1920s.

Since then, commercial bills have become more important. Difficulties in obtaining increased bank advances from the joint-stock banks led to a minor revival in the use of commercial bills to finance trade in the late 1950s; the reduction of stamp duty on commercial bills in 1961, from an ad valorem rate to 2d., gave an incentive to the use of commercial bills; and a gradual reduction in the supply of Treasury bills in the 1960s forced banks and discount houses to seek more commercial bills. Between 1960 and 1967, the supply of commercial bills in the discount market increased fourfold, while that of Treasury bills fell; and amongst the joint-stock banks' assets of bills discounted, the proportion of commercial bills rose from about one-sixth to about two-thirds. (17) In general, any reduction in the supply of Treasury bills, and any difficulties in obtaining bank advances for the finance of trade, raise the importance of the commercial bill market. In the past, the impact of Bank Rate on the commercial bill market had substantial effects on the value of stock-in-trade and thus on import prices.

It would seem that the restoration of the commercial bill market was an essential prerequisite for a restoration of Bank Rate as an instrument of policy with balance-of-trade effects. If so, Bank Rate could become more efficacious in the 1970s than it has been for a long time.

It does not follow that Bank Rate can ever again be as powerful as it had been before 1914. Nor does it follow that it will (or should) be used in the same way as before 1914.

Bank Rate cannot be so powerful as it once was, partly because the United Kingdom is no longer so predominant in the world's import trade as she used to be, and partly because primary products are no longer so predominant amongst the United Kingdom's imports. But even if the United Kingdom is no longer the world's chief importing country, she is still the principal importer of a number of primary products, and one of the principal importers of nearly all of them. Hence British Bank Rate action can still have a major impact on primary product prices, especially if British importers finance trade through commercial bills rather than out of bank advances. All the same, interest-rate changes elsewhere have come to matter more in relation to primary product prices than they would have done in the early years of the century. Consequently British Bank Rate changes are now more likely to have the expected effect on import prices if they are in the same direction as interest changes in the other major importing countries.

In the 1960s imports of primary products rose, but the share of primary products in total imports fell. That weakened the possible impact of Bank Rate changes on import prices in general, since primary product prices tend to be more susceptible to interest-rate changes than modern manufactured products. All the same, imports of primary products will continue to be important. If only half of import prices respond to Bank Rate changes, that is not insignificant.

The possible impact of Bank Rate changes on import prices does not depend on changes in British trade alone. Equally relevant are commercial policies and structural changes overseas. Supplying countries may raise their reserve prices through commercial policies, such as commodity control, or on account of structural changes in their economies. Thus commodity control may limit the range of possible fluctuations of their export prices. Such schemes are in force for few commodities and not always effective. Should commodity control become more widespread and more effective, the possible impact of British Bank Rate changes on import prices would become less. It would, however, also be less necessary. The function of Bank Rate changes has never been to enforce any particular level of prices. Rather it has been to counter sharp changes in import prices which disturbed the balance of payments. If the exporting countries could minimise price fluctuations, by means of commodity control or otherwise, one of the chief needs for British Bank Rate changes would disappear.

It does not follow that all overseas policies and changes will make Bank Rate changes less important. For example, the gradual disappearance of 'abundant labour' from temperate-zone agriculture may have the opposite effect. If temperate-zone agriculture now has to compete for factors with manufacturing industries, factor prices in temperate-zone agriculture may become as rigid in a downward direction as they are in industrial activities. Since factor prices and product prices tend to move in the same direction, there is less risk of sharp falls in prices of temperate-zone agricultural products; but while abundant labour is disappearing from such agriculture in country after country, there is still the possibility of occasional sharp upward movements of temperate-zone agricultural prices (in terms of manufactures). If the past is any guide, Bank Rate policy is most effective when it counters upward movements in import prices.

It did so in the years before 1914. Then, however, the sole aim of monetary policy was to safeguard the currency. The cheap economy was the real counterpart of the strong currency, but it was not the direct object of monetary policy. With the strong currency as its sole object, the monetary policy-makers were oblivious of the connection between import price movements and the balance of payments. In consequence, Bank Rate was used as a post hoc corrective rather than as an ex ante means of control. It is still so used.

If Bank Rate is used as a post hoc corrective, it will not be used until after a disturbance in the terms of trade has percolated throughout the market and weakened the balance of payments. Since the origin of disturbances consisted of a sharp deterioration of the terms of trade and were followed by more gentle and gradual improvements, the appropriate Bank Rate changes consisted of sharp increases and more gradual reductions. Since the disturbances were always unexpected, Bank Rate action never occurred until the original price disturbance had already caused a monetary disturbance. Two policy habits formed: one was that Bank Rate would rise sharply and come down gradually; and the other was that Bank Rate followed the market and did not lead it. When Bank Rate changes were restored in 1951, these policy habits were also restored.

Despite increased knowledge of the various economic relationships involved, it would still be difficult to use Bank Rate as an ex ante means of control. Even if domestic implications of Bank Rate changes could be ignored, and even if the Bank Rate weapon were all-powerful, there would still be difficulties in knowing all relevant price movements in time and in interpreting them correctly. Effective Bank Rate action in time might have averted or ameliorated some of the balance-of-payments difficulties of the 1950s and 1960s. But even if the instrument had been less blunted, such a statement can be made only with hindsight. Until there is further knowledge of what causes sharp changes in the terms of trade and forecasting techniques are further improved, Bank Rate will remain a post hoc corrective. If the subject is nevertheless pursued further, the reasons are that the revival of the commercial bill market should make more effective Bank Rate action possible, and that overseas structural changes increase the need for an instrument that stabilises import prices of temperate-zone agricultural products. If Bank Rate can stabilise food prices, some vestige of the cheap economy can yet be preserved. If not, there will have to be a revised food policy.

The argument will proceed entirely in terms of food. In the past, imported food was the main variable in the British standard of living. If the quality of manufactured exports now rivals the price of imported food as determinant of the British standard of living, this still leaves imported food as one of the major variables. Not all food is imported, but all is priced as if it were imported. (If domestic costs exceed costs of imports, domestic producers are compensated through deficiency payments, financed out of general tax revenue.) The course of world food prices thus affects the standard of living; it also affects the balance of payments.

The course of world food prices (18) from the mid-1930s onwards has been roughly as follows. After the great depression of 1929, world food prices fell until 1935. They recovered slightly in 1936, and then rose sharply (by 9 per cent) in 1937. At that time the rise in 1937 was regarded as no more than recovery from depression levels. Bank Rate action would have been ruled out on other grounds, and in any case food prices fell again in the following year. War and post-war shortages led to rising food prices until 1948, while the 1949 devaluation raised them further against the United Kingdom. From 1950 to 1951 they rose by 11 per cent, which was then attributed to the Korean War. In any event Bank Rate action was not taken until the end of 1951, when prices were already falling. The next sharp rise in food prices occurred in 1954, when they rose by 8 per cent. This did not affect the United Kingdom as much as the world as a whole, and British import prices of food (including beverages and tobacco) rose by only 4 per cent from 1953 to 1955. In any event no Bank Rate action was taken until 1955, when the rise in world prices was already over. The next rise in world food prices occurred in 1957, with a mere 2 per cent, while British import prices of food remained steady. In that year Bank Rate was increased sharply for different reasons, and this may have contributed to the 8 per cent fall in world food prices in the following year – 4 per cent for the United Kingdom. Afterwards world food prices continued to fall until 1962, but the fall was at a diminishing rate and finally reversed itself into a rise in 1962. In 1963 world food prices rose by no less than 14 per cent. As far as British imports were concerned, the rise was less marked, but it was still 9 per cent. Moreover, taking the price movement from 1961 to 1964, there was a 15 per cent rise in British food import prices. Subject to minor variations, they continued at around that higher level, and at the time of the 1967 devaluation they were 16 per cent above the 1961 level. These aggregate data hide a sharper and more persistent rise of temperate-zone food prices than of tropical ones. The latter fell back after their initial rise in the early 1960s, but the former did not. Although this price movement weakened the balance of trade, any Bank Rate action taken during those years appears to have been taken on other grounds. True, there was a 7 per cent 'crisis rate' in 1961, and this may have delayed the upswing in world food prices; but it was lowered to 6 per cent in the same year, and lowered again in stages until it was 4 per cent in January 1963. It was not raised again until February 1964, when it became 5 per cent, to be followed by another 7 per cent 'crisis rate' in November of that year. In short, Bank Rate was lowered just at the time when world food prices were rising.

It may well be that, when Bank Rate changes are under consideration, no one gives a moment's thought to the price of food. If so, this is another policy habit inherited from the past. It would not have been inappropriate before 1914, when the Bank Rate corrective for monetary problems would incidentally correct the price movements which had led to monetary difficulties. It would have been suitable in the bill market conditions of the 1920s and 1950s, when Bank Rate changes would affect Treasury bills rather than commercial bills, and the balance-of-payments effects would show in monetary movements rather than on the balance of trade. In the early 1960s the revival of the commercial bill market was still only on the way and far from complete, and this may account for the use of Bank Rate in disregard of an unusually sharp and adverse overseas price movement. Many other considerations may have carried the day, and the price of food may not even have been considered.

Yet sharp upward movements in food prices preceded the balance-of-payments difficulties of 1937, 1951 and 1964-7. They weakened the balance of payments through higher import prices. They raised the most basic of all prices, which none can escape, with adverse effects on savings (of wage- and salary-earners, if they did not secure compensating increments, or of their employers if they did). That sort of situation might have been dealt with through an increase in Bank Rate. That was not done in 1937 and 1950-1, while Bank Rate was actually lowered at a time when food import prices were rising in 1962-4. It does not follow that a Bank Rate increase would have been suitable in 1962-4, even if attention is confined to imports.

For a peculiarity of the movement of the terms of trade in the early 1960s was that it was not one movement of the terms of trady of manufactures over all primary products, but consisted of three separate movements. The terms of trade over temperate-zone foodstuffs deteriorated sharply and there was no reversal of that change. The terms of trade over tropical-zone agricultural foodstuffs first deteriorated and then improved. The terms of trade over basic materials did not begin to deteriorate until two years after the deterioration over food. In other words it is not suggested that even an earlier revival of the commercial bill market, and therefore greater effectiveness of Bank Rate over import prices, would have provided an easy solution for the price movements of 1962-4 which contributed to the balance-of-payments difficulties of the mid-1960s. Should such situations recur, it may be that different interest-rate policies would be appropriate for different commodity groups.

Whatever the details, given the revival of the commercial bill base on which Bank Rate can operate so as to influence import prices; and given the special need to watch out for sudden sharp increases in prices of temperate-zone agricultural products (which are the sort of price movements Bank Rate used to correct in the past); Bank Rate should become more effective and more needed. Even if it cannot become as powerful as it once was, it should provide the authorities with a means of monetary control with direct impact over a substantial part of the cost of imports; and even if it is not yet possible to use Bank Rate policy as an ex ante means of control, it should at least become possible to use Bank Rate before overseas price movements have weakened the balance of payments. These are considerations relating to the future use of Bank Rate which should strengthen the monetary system. But while the ground was being prepared, and commercial bills became more widely used to finance, say, stock-in-trade, bank advances which had formerly been used for such purposes became available for other uses. Thus any long-run strengthening of the monetary system was bought at the expense of some short-run inflation of advances unless countered by an appropriate restraint of the growth of advances.

Perhaps it was unfortunate that Bank Rate could not be restored as a more powerful instrument of policy, before the balance-of-payments difficulties of the mid-1960s came to a head; and perhaps it was unfortunate that the temporary 'inflation' of advances for other purposes had not ceased by that time. But let regrets be left to historians. As far as economic lessons are concerned, this particular concatenation of events is unlikely to recur.

7   STERLING AS A RESERVE CURRENCY

If the supply of bank advances was swollen in the 1960s because of transitional problems arising out of the restoration of Bank Rate as a more powerful instrument of policy, changes in the overseas Sterling Area system also contributed to a relaxation of pressure on the possible supply of bank advances. In the 1930s and 1940s, overseas Sterling Area countries had been accumulating sterling balances, with the result that British domestic bank credit was somewhat deflated. In the 1950s and 1960s, most overseas Sterling Area countries no longer added to their sterling reserves, so that this particular restraint on British domestic credit had ceased. The reasons will emerge from the following discussion of why and how overseas sterling reserves were built up, and of the prospect for changes in those holdings.

Overseas Sterling Area countries are countries which find it convenient to hold a substantial part of their exchange reserves in sterling. Those reserves are used as backing for domestic note issues, and they guarantee the exchange value of the national currencies concerned. Such reserves are acquired in intra-area transactions or in transactions with other currency areas. In the latter case, gold and foreign exchange earnings are handed to the Exchange Equalisation Account of the Bank of England in exchange for sterling. In either case, sterling is deposited, by the overseas central bank concerned, with a British bank (be it the Bank of England or another bank). Sterling Area central banks have always had the right to convert their sterling holdings into gold or foreign exchange, though they may sometimes have exercised restraint in the interest of the Area as a whole. In the 1950s these reserves were still swollen by war debts, so that overseas Sterling Area countries could sometimes meet national payments difficulties through heavy withdrawals from their reserves (which implied either purchase of British goods, with payment out of the reserves; or conversion of such sterling, by the Exchange Equalisation Account, into gold or foreign exchange. That had adverse effects on the Sterling Area's joint gold and foreign exchange reserves, for example in 1952 and 1957.) (19) By the end of the 1950s, however, none of the major overseas Sterling Area countries had reserves in excess of monetary requirements, so that the prospect of large-scale withdrawals had ceased.

The prospect for substantial increases had ceased as well. Even if the overseas Sterling Area earned major surpluses, there is no compulsion to keep such earnings in sterling rather than in gold or dollars. When the exchange rate of sterling is under suspicion, overseas countries are unlikely to add to their sterling reserves. The exchange rate of sterling was under suspicion in the 1960s because the balance of payments of the United Kingdom was adverse; and when a country has an adverse balance of payments, it is a net borrower and not a net lender. This last point is of special relevance in the present context, since most overseas Sterling Area countries rely heavily on capital imports. Although the borrowing country has to repay, whatever the currency system, loans from other currency areas can only be repaid out of export proceeds; but loans from the reserve currency country can be repaid either out of export proceeds or out of the proceeds of domestic development (as long as sterling remains a perfect substitute for their national currency). The situation towards the end of the 1960s was that the United Kingdom was the principal creditor of the overseas Sterling Area countries, but that they had to look increasingly elsewhere for new loans. One implication is that the borrowing countries are unlikely to sever their existing links with sterling but may forge new ones in other directions. Eventually they may change their currency link, as Canada did when the United States became her principal creditor in the 1920s. Even then they will want some sterling as collateral for their outstanding debts to the United Kingdom. On this ground, there should be no major increase in sterling reserves held in the immediate future, and no major diminution either.

In the 1960s there were fluctuations in the amount of sterling held by some oil-producing countries, where the amount of sterling held is determined by oil revenues rather than by monetary considerations. But those were fluctuations in trade rather than fluctuations arising out of the reserve currency system. Political considerations may also have played a part in changing reserves from one currency to another, but probably led to a reshuffling of holdings rather than a change in aggregate holdings.

This leaves currency fears as the major possible source of disturbance. As mentioned before, devaluation meant default on the overseas Sterling Area countries' sterling reserves, though in 1967 interest rates on sterling securities were high enough to compensate the overseas holders within about two years (in so far as the reserves were held in interest-yielding securities — about nine-tenths were). Nevertheless, once a currency becomes prone to devaluation, confidence is not easily restored. Private overseas holders of sterling had for some time before devaluation, switched into and out of sterling according to the current balance-of-payments performance of the United Kingdom. But this did not affect overseas Sterling Area central banks until after devaluation. Then it did; and although there was no danger that they would withdraw all of their sterling holdings, any withdrawals were claims on the Sterling Area's joint gold and foreign exchange reserves (which are the Bank of England's reserves).

The overseas Sterling Area central banks' fears had to be allayed. This was done in the 'Basle facility' (20) of September 1968, whereby the United Kingdom received a stand-by credit from the major non-sterling central banks, to be used in the event of heavy withdrawals of sterling by Sterling Area holders. Moreover the United Kingdom guaranteed that nine-tenths of overseas Sterling Area countries' official reserves would maintain their dollar value. The arrangement is such that the first one-tenth of a sterling country's official reserves are not covered — which roughly corresponds to the proportion held in cash for day-to-day trading purposes. The true reserves, being the remaining nine-tenths, are so guaranteed. The guarantee applies only to countries which do not lower the proportion of sterling in their foreign exchange holdings below the level at the time negotiations for the facility began.

Since the official sterling reserves of overseas Sterling Area countries have become devaluation-proof, the probability is that there will be no major changes in such sterling holdings for some time to come. By implication this means that the reserve currency system is unlikely to have a major impact on the domestic credit structure, unless the way these reserves are held is fundamentally changed.

As mentioned before, in the 1960s about one-tenth of the official sterling reserve holdings were held in cash. The remainder was held in Treasury bills and long-dated British Government stock, including some government-guaranteed stock. Before the 1960s the bulk of those holdings were in Treasury bills, but the gradual reduction of the supply of Treasury bills in the 1960s forced official overseas holders of sterling to seek British Government bonds rather than bills. Thus while the sterling reserves were built up and in the 1950s, the bulk of those holdings was in Treasury bills; while at the end of the 1960s, when the total of those reserves appears to be stabilised, there were more official overseas holdings of long-dated bonds.

Treasury bills are amongst the British joint-stock banks' liquid assets. If they are acquired by overseas holders, they are not available for the British banking system. But if they are available, they broaden the liquid assets at the banks' disposal. True, the banks have to pay for the bills, but the Government spends the money, so that the appropriate sums are soon redeposited with the banks and their cash reserves restored. The following simplified example may help to show what happens next when the bills are available for the British banking system and when they are not. Suppose the banks' distribution of assets into liquid assets, investments and advances is in ratio of $30 : 20 : 50$ or $1 : \frac{2}{3} : 1\frac{2}{3}$. (It is not suggested that these ratios were ever actually just like that. The liquid assets ratio may normally be somewhat lower, and the proportion of investments was higher in the 1950s and lower in the 1960s. But they are not impossible ratios and may serve to illustrate the point.) Given such ratios, an increase in the joint-stock banks' Treasury bill holdings, by any given amount, would induce the joint-stock banks to increase their advances by $1\frac{2}{3}$ times that much. Similarly a reduction in the supply of Treasury Bills for the British joint-stock banks would lead to reductions in advances in some such ratio. In other words, while the overseas Sterling Area's reserve holdings were increasing and largely took the form of holdings of Treasury bills, there was some deflationary effect on the volume of bank advances available from the British joint-stock banks. That was of some importance in the 1930s, (21) and may have exerted some restraint on bank advances in the 1950s. That restraint became less with the reduction in the supply of Treasury bills in the course of the 1960s.

If overseas holders of sterling take up long-dated British Government stock instead, there is no such restraint. Although the banking system will normally absorb all the Treasury bills on offer, that does not apply to long-dated government stock. Moreover, although a liquid to long-term assets ratio of approximately $3 : 7$ is normally adhered to, there appears to be no rule relating to a proper ratio between investments and advances. If overseas holdings of long-dated government stock ever deprived the British banking system of any such stock it would like to hold — and joint-stock bank 'investments' consist exclusively of long-dated government and government-guaranteed stock — the reduction in investments might allow for an equivalent increase in advances. Since, however, the banks are not deprived of any investments they would otherwise hold, there is no actual incentive to raise advances. All that happened was that there is no longer a restraint on advances through overseas holdings of Treasury bills.

In itself, this may have been a minor point. But this restraint on advances ceased just at a time when the need for advances was lessened (through increased availability of commercial bills for the short-term finance of business), and it also came at a time when devaluation would have inflationary effects on the domestic economy. The end of this particular restraint may have come at an inconvenient time, when the authorities wished to restrain bank advances for a variety of different reasons. Again the monetary difficulties of the mid-1960s were aggravated; but again these were special circumstances which are not likely to recur.

8   ONE CURRENCY

There would have been less need, if any, to worry about the reserve currency role of sterling, had sterling not been persistently misvalued for over half a century. The *overvaluation* of the 1920s, and to a lesser extent of the 1930s, caused a deficiency in demand for goods and services. This hurt traditional domestic activities and so limited quantitative growth below what it could have been. It also limited the demand for imports, so that there were adverse effects on overseas incomes with detrimental consequences for British exports. The overvaluation of sterling was, however, only one of many influences on world incomes and the balance of payments of the United Kingdom did not turn into deficit until all the major currencies became overvalued during the great depression. The *undervaluation* of sterling, in the 1950s and 1960s, allowed quantitative growth to the limit of the availability of factors. In this respect the undervaluation was a lesser error than the overvaluations of the past, but it went too far. It helped existing activities, and so obscured the need for factor saving, which alone would have allowed for more qualitative growth. The net result was that the British economy advanced at a fast walking pace in a motorised world. The British economy was not short of effective demand. On the contrary, there was an excess supply of money which made it easier to maintain full employ-ment in existing activities. Others got ahead in offering attractive new goods. Imports increased ahead of exports. As sterling became one of the most undervalued currencies, the balance of payments weakened.

The lesson to be derived from the twentieth-century history of sterling is that sterling is *one* currency. It must be correctly valued in relation to the needs of the British economy. If sterling is undervalued in relation to those needs, there are structural effects which weaken the balance of payments. Sterling has its overseas roles as well as its domestic one, but the overseas roles reflect whether the British economy widens or narrows its sphere of overseas operations, and this in turn reflects the balance of payments. In a world of competitive industrial economies, the effects of undervaluation on the domestic economic structure affect the country's competitive position in the world, and thus the balance of payments. The relative value of currencies thus depends on the relative degrees of misvaluation of the various currencies in relation to their various domestic needs.

Sterling is first and foremost the currency of the United Kingdom. The way it fulfils this role determines world confidence in its value. After 1967 this became increasingly recognised, and policy was adjusted accordingly. What was needed was to eliminate excessive undervaluation. The solution of this basic domestic monetary problem is a prerequisite of both faster domestic economic growth and a stronger balance of payments.

27 Problems of a Mature Economy

Whenever an economic problem is solved, new ones arise. Around 1950 there was a widespread consensus that the unemployment of the past must not recur. Economists had shown ways of preventing mass unemployment. Their precepts were applied and this particular problem was solved. Around 1970 there are new problems. The economy has done well, but it could have done better. Moreover other industrial economies did better, and eventually this came to be reflected in the balance of payments. There seemed to be a vicious circle: delayed growth weakened the balance of payments, and measures to improve the balance of payments caused further delays.

The balance of payments was weakened for other reasons as well. There were heavy political commitments overseas. Without them, there might have been only few and minor deficits. The balance of payments was weakened further by the change in the fuel balance, which upset the shipping balance. Were the United Kingdom still an exporter of coal rather than an importer of fuel oils, overseas political commitments might have been met without any balance-of-payments deficits. It seems tempting to say that an empire was exchanged for the motor-car when it was not possible to have both. The temptation must be resisted as a superficial explanation of the course of events in the 1950s and 1960s. These disturbances to the invisible balance brought matters to a head earlier than might otherwise have been the case, but they were not the cause of the relatively slower growth rate of the British economy than of other industrial economies.

The fundamental reason why the growth rate of the British economy fell behind that of its major competitors was that it had become the most stable of industrial economies. To some extent this was the result of the British pattern of development, with its equal emphasis on production and trade, and this was both cause and effect of a 50 : 50 division of export interests. This pattern had emerged in response to past needs and has much to be commended. It made the British economy less susceptible to outside fluctuations, and this was advantageous in times of world depression. But subsequently it also restrained growth in times of rising world prosperity.

This pattern of development has been extended by economic policies. Public opinion insisted on remedies for past maladjustments, and governments responded. Past fluctuations in employment were to be avoided, and remedial measures were taken on the assumption that past patterns of development would persist. Amongst the many measures taken, the most all-pervading and effective was the undervaluation of the currency. Undervaluation is meant to facilitate the continuance of existing activities and the use of factors as they were used before. It worked; and because it worked, it obscured the need for factor saving which alone can ensure growth in a fully employed economy.

This might not have mattered had there been abundant factors, as there had been in the British economy in the past and as there still was, to a diminishing degree, until some time around 1960. Around that time the United Kingdom's economic problems had become the problems of a mature economy.

A mature economy cannot increase output by existing methods, simply because there are no spare factors. The problems arising from maturity were only gradually recognised. The British economy is the first industrial economy to face such problems, so that there are no precedents to guide analysis. The symptoms appeared only one by one, and while each, by itself, could have been ue to other causes, together they point to the emergence of new problems. Moreover the symptoms had to persist for some time before they could be recognised as indicators of new problems rather than as exceptions.

An economy with absolute scarcity of factors cannot grow without further specialisation. This in turn requires more use of sophisticated capital which alone can save factors. The costs involved can be more easily met if markets widen at home and abroad, so that much depends on the possibilities of an international division of capital throughout the widest possible trading area. Specialisation and capitalisation also require an appropriate change in factor shares in national income. There must be more emphasis on profits, which are the chief source of finance for industrial expansion and which provide the funds for higher earnings of other factors. A rising share of profits in national income must be reconciled with the maintenance of other factor shares, and if this is impossible with present methods of factor remuneration, those methods themselves require reconsideration.

As problems are recognised, solutions become possible. The various parts of this book should have shown that these problems are increasingly recognised and remedies are being applied. If this could not be done quickly enough to avoid some of the difficulties of the 1960s, the chief reason was that it took time to recognise the problems involved. Before the present generation of economists accepts too much blame for not having found all 'the answers' to every problem, perhaps it should be recalled that unemployment problems had persisted from at least the 1870s, and that they had become intolerable before they were correctly diagnosed, in the 1930s, and remedies applied only after the Second World War.

If the public insisted on overdoses for the ills of the forebears, new problems were inevitably tackled with less vigour. It may even be claimed that the new problems would not have arisen so soon, had old complaints not been dealt with, and perhaps dealt with too successfully. As it was, the old remedies delayed somewhat the solution of new complaints. Devaluation delayed; the traditional trade pattern delayed; restrictive practices delayed; old systems of wage payments delayed — to mention but a few examples.

Despite all these delays, the patient's health would show. Monetary problems are under review and the monetary system in process of reform; the attitude towards external trade problems has undergone a fundamental change; restrictive trade practices are being brought under control; and industrial relations are under review. These are responses at the centre. They would not suffice were there not awareness of present needs in the various industries. The growth of new basic fabrication activities in the engineering industries provides an example — even if the statistics sometimes obscure the fundamental growth through inclusion of the more out-of-date sectors in their classification of activities. The growth of processing activities in the chemical trade provides another example; and the development of the gas industry from an antiquated producer to a modern distributor of a superior product provides yet another. New ideas are needed, and should be widely discussed, relating to all aspects of industrial organisation at a time when 'the firm' may have become bigger than the industries in which it operates, and when the new industrial competition has become increasingly more important relatively to the price competition in traditional activities. The new industrial competition is innovative competition. It implies that growing firms must try to have new goods to sell if they want to accumulate funds for further growth. But such markets are uncertain, so that they also want old goods to sell in established markets, so as to ensure against possible failure in the new ones. Production of the old goods is normally under conditions of decreasing returns and price at marginal cost. Production of the new goods is under conditions of increasing returns and price at average costs. The former must be 'cheap' and the latter of high quality.

The quality market is open to those who are ahead of others in at least one line of activities. Then only can they hope to attract markets by the quality of their products rather than struggle for shares in existing markets for old products. They must have access to potential markets through the widest possible area of free trade. But they must also be ready for the market, through appropriate R. & D.

In an economy with abundant factors, any kind of R. & D. might do — though the existence of abundant factors also limits the need for R. & D. of all kinds. In a mature economy R. & D. is more important, but not any kind of R. & D. It must be factor-saving and, given the general scarcity of factors, it must be capital-saving, for only capital can save both capital and labour. Factor saving is of importance at any stage in the chain of production, but is likely to be most valuable at an early stage. If it occurs at such an early stage, it induces changes in production functions at later stages. In those later stages it has the effect of a process innovation. Since, however, a change in the production function usually leads to an improved product, there are likely to be induced product innovations at all the later stages of production. If the innovation is at the final stage in the chain of production, it will only induce similar innovations at the same stage of production. There will be only one new product. But if the innovation is applied at an earlier stage, there is likely to be a multitude of new products. Induced innovations at the same stage of production may be part of the traditional competitive process. Innovations which induce further innovations are the basis of 'industrial revolutions'. In the present-day world, the presence or absence of such industrial revolutions can be gauged from a study of the development of the basic fabrication or transformation industries, of which the engineering and chemical trades are the chief examples.

Industrial change is costly. It can be made profitable more rapidly if markets widen. The widening of markets is so often a prerequisite of successful innovations, that the growth of economies (through innovations) becomes largely a function of access to world markets. Given the nature of overseas economies, this requires access to all industrial markets which alone offer scope for industrial specialisation. Of special importance are the 'trial grounds'. It should not be forgotten that, of the trial grounds, the most important for British industry is the home market. Wider markets are, however, of no avail if home producers do not respond to their challenge. If there are cartels to prevent change in production functions, trade unions opposed to change in the employment structure and 'incomes policies' which may ossify it even further, there can only be less change. The widening markets of the world are left to others, and the home market expands less.

Of the major remedies needed to accelerate the rate of growth of the British economy, only the tariff problem depends for its solution on international action. Most, if not all, of the other solutions depend on action within the country. The insidious effects of undervaluation can be remedied through monetary reform (where international co-operation helps but the remedies must be found by the British monetary authorities). Attitudes towards mergers, monopolies and restrictive practices are matters for domestic legislation and administrative action. The ultimate need is for realisation of the benefits of change, right on the factory floor, where workers must get a share in the proceeds of quality goods and managements provide the means. The quality economy must take the place of the cheap economy. There is no need to throw overboard the past achievement of full employment. In fact the quality economy is the logical sequel to the earlier solution of the quantitative employment problem. All this is in train.

Notes

CHAPTER 2

1. R. Marris, 'The Economic Theory of Managerial Capitalism' (Macmillan, 1964).
2. J. Downie, 'The Competitive Process' (Duckworth, 1958).
3. Ibid.
4. Ibid.; A. Singh and G. Whittington with H. T. Burley, 'Growth, Profitability and Valuation' (Cambridge U.P., 1968).
5. I. M. D. Little and A. C. Rayner, 'Higgledy Piggledy Growth Again' (Blackwell, 1966).
6. P. E. Hart, 'Studies in Profit, Business Saving and Investment in the United Kingdom, 1920-62', vol. ii (Allen & Unwin, 1968): G. J. Stigler, 'Capital and Rates of Return in Manufacturing Industries' (Princeton U.P., 1963).

CHAPTER 3

1. G. Pratten and R. M. Dean in collaboration with A. Silberston, 'The Economies of Large-scale Production in British Industry' (Cambridge U.P., 1965).
2. D. Paige and G. Bombach, 'A Comparison of National Output and Productivity of the United Kingdom and the United States' (O.E.C.D., Paris, 1959).
3. J. M. Samuels and D. J. Smythe, 'Profits, Variability of Profits and Firm Size', in 'Economica' (May 1968); Singh and Whittington, 'Growth, Profitability and Valuation'.
4. James Bates, 'The Financing of Small Business' (Sweet & Maxwell, 1964).
5. 'Patterns of Company Finance', in 'Economic Trends' no. 169 (Nov 1967).
6. Federal Trade Commission – Securities and Exchange Commission, 'Quarterly Financial Report' (4th quarter, 1963).
7. Samuels and Smythe, in 'Economica' (May 1968); Singh and Whittington, 'Growth, Profitability and Valuation'.
8. N. R. Collins and L. E. Preston, 'The Size Structure of Industrial Firms', in 'American Economic Review' (Dec 1961); P. E. Hart, 'The Size and Growth of Firms', in 'Economica' (Feb 1962); P. E. Hart and S. Prais, 'The Analysis of Business Concentration', in 'Journal of the Royal Statistical Society', series A, cxix(2) (1956); P. Sargant Florence, 'New Measures of Growth of Firms', in 'Economic Journal' (Mar 1957); S. Hymer and P. Pashigian, 'Firm Size and Rate of Growth', in 'Journal of Political Economy' (Dec 1962); H. F. Lydall, 'The Growth of Manufacturing Firms', in 'Bulletin of the Oxford University Institute of Statistics' (May 1959); H. Simon and C. Bonini, 'The Size Distribution of Firms', in 'American Economic Review' (Sep 1958).
9. There is also the possibility of the 'regression bias effect'. If closing size is used in classifying firms, then this may generate a spurious correlation. This may occur because companies which are now large may have grown rapidly during the period to achieve their present size.

10. See Downie, 'The Competitive Process'.
11. Little and Rayner, 'Higgledy Piggledy Growth Again'.
12. R. Gibrat, 'Les Inégalités Économiques' (Paris, 1931).
13. See Y. Ijuri and H. Simon, 'Business Firm Size and Growth', in 'American Economic Review' (Mar 1964); J. Steindl, 'Random Processes and the Growth of Firms' (Griffin, 1965).
14. Singh and Whittington, 'Growth, Profitability and Valuation'.
15. Ibid.
16. See ibid., and M. J. Barron, 'The Effect of the Size of the Firm on Profitability', in 'Business Ratios' (spring 1967).
17. Singh and Whittington, 'Growth, Profitability and Valuation'.

CHAPTER 4

1. See F. W. Paish, 'Finance for Industry' (Pitman, 1953).
2. B. Tew and R. F. Henderson, 'Studies in Company Finance' (N.I.E.S.R., Cambridge, 1959).
3. Ibid.
4. Details are published in 'Economic Trends', the 'Board of Trade Bulletin' and the 'Bank of England Quarterly Bulletin'.
5. Bates, 'The Financing of Small Business'.
6. The marginal as opposed to the average propensity to save of small and large companies, is, however, much the same, at around 0.85; i.e. in terms of unit change in the profit rate and the ratio of saving to assets, small and large companies appear similar. See J. Bates and R. F. Henderson, 'The Determinants of Corporate Saving in Small Private Companies, United Kingdom, 1954-56', in Hart, 'Studies in Profit, Business Saving and Investment in the United Kingdom, 1920-62' vol. ii'.
7. J. Bates, 'Hire Purchase in Small Manufacturing Business', in 'Bankers' Magazine' (Sep-Oct 1957).
8. Bates, 'The Financing of Small Business'.
9. J. R. Meyer and E. Kuh, 'The Investment Decision' (Harvard U.P., 1957).
10. Ibid.
11. Singh and Whittington, 'Growth, Profitability and Valuation'.
12. J. F. Weston, 'The Scope and Methodology of Finance' (Prentice-Hall, 1966).
13. Tew and Henderson, 'Studies in Company Finance'.
14. Singh and Whittington, 'Growth, Profitability and Valuation'.
15. Ibid.; see also T. Barna, 'Investment and Growth Policies in British Industrial Firms' (Cambridge U.P., 1962).
16. Singh and Whittington, 'Growth, Profitability and Valuation'.
17. Ibid.
18. P. Sargant Florence, 'Ownership, Control and Success of Large Companies' (Sweet & Maxwell, 1961).
19. Marris, 'The Economic Theory of Managerial Capitalism'.
20. Ibid.; see also, for more complex definitions, D. Prusman and G. Murphy, 'Gearing in British Quoted Companies', in 'Business Ratios' (winter 1968).
21. Tew and Henderson, 'Studies in Company Finance'.
22. Singh and Whittington, 'Growth, Profitability and Valuation'.
23. Tew and Henderson, 'Studies in Company Finance'.
24. E. A. G. Robinson, 'Monopoly' (Cambridge U.P., 1959) p. 190.
25. Singh and Whittington, 'Growth, Profitability and Valuation'.
26. Ibid.
27. Tew and Henderson, 'Studies in Company Finance'.

28. Singh and Whittington, 'Growth, Profitability and Valuation'.

29. R. E. Caves, 'Market Organisation, Performance and Public Policy', in 'Britain's Economic Prospects' (Brookings Institution, Washington; Allen & Unwin, 1968).

30. For a discussion of factoring, see W. Minchinton, 'Finance of Exports', in 'District Bank Review' (Dec 1963) and 'Finance Problems of the Smaller Company: An Institute of Directors Guide to the City' (1967).

CHAPTER 5

1. Harold Quinton, 'Financing Growth Industries in an Inflated Economy: Standards, Theory and Practice, in Long Range Planning in an Expanding Economy' (American Management Association, General Management Series, no. 179) p. 29.

2. Bates, 'The Financing of Small Business'.

3. F. Modigliani and M. H. Miller, 'The Cost of Capital, Corporation Finance and the Theory of Investment', in 'American Economic Review' (June 1958).

4. See G. R. Fisher, 'Some Factors Influencing Share Prices', in 'Economic Journal' (Mar 1961); M. G. Scott, 'Relative Share Prices and Yields', in 'Oxford Economic Papers' (Oct 1962); Modigliani and Miller, in 'American Economic Review' (June 1958); Myron J. Gordon, 'Dividends, Earnings and Stock Prices', in 'Review of Economics and Statistics' (Feb 1959) and 'Investment, Financing and Valuation of the Corporation' (Irwin, Homewood, Ill., 1962); J. Lintner, ' Dividend Earnings, Leverage, Stock Prices and the Supply of Capital to Corporations', in 'Review of Economics and Statistics' (Aug 1962).

5. Singh and Whittington, 'Growth, Profitability and Valuation'.

6. See chapter 4 of A. Robichek and S. C. Myers, 'Optimal Financing Decisions' (Foundations of Finance Series, Prentice-Hall, 1965).

7. I. Friend and M. Puckett, 'Dividends and Stock Prices', in 'American Economic Review' (Sep 1964).

8. Ibid.

9. Ibid.

10. See Lynch, Merrill, Pierce Fenner and Smith, 'Annual Report' (1959).

11. A rights issue should not be confused with a scrip or bonus issue. In a scrip issue, shareholders are allocated *free* shares in proportion to their holdings. There is no expectation that the old rate of dividend per share will be maintained on the increased number of shares, as no funds have been subscribed. Scrip issues are used to make shares less 'weighty' in cost per share, and also to bring issued capital in line with the present size of companies.

12. Singh and Whittington, 'Growth, Profitability and Valuation'.

13. Ibid.

14. See P. Sargant Florence, 'Size of Companies and Other Factors in Dividend Policy', in 'Journal of the Royal Statistical Society', series A, cxxii (1) (1959).

15. Ibid.

16. F. W. Paish, 'Company Profits and their Distribution since the War', in 'District Bank Review' (June 1955).

17. Tew and Henderson, 'Studies in Company Finance', p. 28.

18. We are most grateful to the Economist Intelligence Unit for this information.

19. R. K. Jaedicke and R. T. Sprouse, 'Accounting Flows: Income Funds and Cash' (Prentice-Hall, 1966).

20. The close company which is owned or controlled by five or fewer shareholders is somewhat different. If net trading income is above £1500, a distribution of 60 per cent is normally required for tax purposes.

21. J. Lintner, 'The Distribution of Income of Corporations amongst Dividends, Retained Earnings and Taxes', in 'American Economic Association, Papers and Proceedings' (May 1956).

22. M. Howe, 'Variations on the Full Cost Theme', in 'Manchester School' (Jan 1964).

23. Florence, in 'Journal of the Royal Statistical Society', series A, cxxii(1) (1959).

24. Hart, 'Studies in Profit, Business Saving and Investment in the United Kingdom, 1920-62', ii.

25. Singh and Whittington, 'Growth, Profitability and Valuation'.

26. Ibid. p. 32.

27. R. L. McAlpine agrees with the view of Lintner, in 'A.E.A. Papers and Proceedings' (May 1956); see Hart, 'Studies in Profit, Business Saving and Investment in the United Kingdom, 1920-62', vol. ii.

28. 2½ per cent on undistributed profits and 27 per cent on distributed.

29. See 'The Finance of Quoted Companies', in 'Economic Trends', no. 102 (Apr 1962).

30. See National Income and Expenditure 1968. Note; these definitions differ widely from those used in Table 12.2, Part II.

31. Meyer and Kuh, 'The Investment Decision', p. 204.

32. Singh and Whittington, 'Growth, Profitability and Valuation'.

33. Ibid.

CHAPTER 6

1. Barna, 'Investment and Growth Policies in British Industrial Firms'; J. E. S. Parker, 'Profitability and Growth of British Industrial Firms', in 'Manchester School' (May 1964); R. Marris, 'Incomes Policy and the Rate of Profit in Industry', in 'Proceedings of the Manchester Statistical Society' (Dec 1964); Singh and Whittington, 'Growth, Profitability and Valuation'.

2. Barna, 'Investment and Growth Policies in British Industrial Firms'.

3. See Singh and Whittington, 'Growth, Profitability and Valuation'.

4. Ibid.

5. G. U. Yule and M. G. Kendall, 'An Introduction to the Theory of Statistics' (Griffin, 1940); W. E. G. Salter, 'Productivity and Technical Change' (Cambridge U.P., 1966).

6. I. M. D. Little, 'Higgledy Piggledy Growth', in 'Bulletin of the Oxford University Institute of Statistics' (Nov 1962).

7. Little and Rayner, 'Higgledy Piggledy Growth Again'.

8. Ibid., p. 31.

9. Singh and Whittington, 'Growth, Profitability and Valuation'.

10. R. M. Cyert and J. G. March, 'Organisational Factors in the Theory of Oligopoly', in 'Quarterly Journal of Economics' (Feb 1956).

11. Barna, 'Investment and Growth Policies in British Industrial Firms'.

12. Singh and Whittington, 'Growth, Profitability and Valuation'.

13. Ibid.

14. Ibid.

15. Ibid.

16. A. S. Mackintosh, 'The Development of Firms' (Cambridge U.P., 1963); data processed by Marris, in 'Proceedings of the Manchester Statistical Society' (Dec 1964).

17. E. T Penrose, 'Theory of the Growth of the Firm' (Blackwell, 1959) p.185.

18. 'Non-quoted Companies and their Finance', in 'Economic Trends', no. 136 (1965).

19. M. H. Cooper and J. E. S. Parker, 'Profitability Ratios and Foreign-owned Subsidiaries', in 'Business Ratios' (autumn 1967).

20. Ibid.

21. See J. H. Dunning, 'The Role of U.S. Subsidiaries in Britain and their U.K. Competitors', in 'Business Ratios' (autumn 1966).

22. M. H. Cooper and J. E. S. Parker, 'Measurement and Interpretation of Profitability in the Pharmaceutical Industry', in 'Oxford Economic Papers' (Nov 1968).

23. Caves, 'Britain's Economic Prospects', p. 296.
24. Barna, 'Investment and Growth Policies in British Industrial Firms'.
25. Singh and Whittington, 'Growth, Profitability and Valuation'.
26. Ibid., p. 183.

CHAPTER 7

1. Tew and Henderson, 'Studies in Company Finance'.
2. 'Economic Trends', no. 114 (1963).
3. J. F. Weston, 'The Role of Mergers in the Growth of Large Firms' (University of California Press, Berkeley, 1953).
4. See R. W. Moon, 'Business Mergers and Take-over Bids' (Gee, 1960).
5. J. Bates and J. R. Parkinson, 'Business Economics' (Blackwell, 1963).
6. Singh and Whittington, 'Growth, Profitability and Valuation'.
7. J. Kitching, 'Assessing the Effects of Mergers', in 'Harvard Business Review' (Nov-Dec 1967).
8. Examples of conglomerate companies are Slater Walker, Unilever, and Rank Organisation.
9. Downie, 'The Competitive Process'.
10. Tew and Henderson, 'Studies in Company Finance'.
11. H. Rose and G. D. Newbould, 'The 1967 Take-over Boom', in 'Moorgate and Wall Street' (autumn 1967).
12. 'Economic Trends', no. 114 (Apr 1963).
13. Until 1967 the majority of them claimed exemption from filing their accounts with the Registrar of Companies. The 1967 Companies Act withdrew this privilege.
14. Little and Rayner, 'Higgledy Piggledy Growth Again', p. 94.
15. Singh and Whittington, 'Growth, Profitability and Valuation'.
16. Ibid.
17. Ibid.
18. Rose and Newbould, in 'Moorgate and Wall Street' (autumn 1967).
19. P. Lesley Cook and R. Cohen (eds), 'The Effects of Mergers' (Allen & Unwin, 1958)
20. Ibid.
21. G. D. McCarthy, 'Acquisitions and Mergers' (Ronald Press, New York, 1963).
22. Department of Economic Affairs, 'The National Plan', Cmnd. 2764 (H.M.S.O., 1965) para. 37.
23. A. Hopkins, 'How to Find a Partner', in 'Financial Times', 10 Mar 1967.
24. See 'Economic Trends', nos. 114 (Apr 1963) and 145 (Nov 1965).
25. 'Reorganisation of the Cotton Industry', Cmnd. 744 (H.M.S.O., 1959).

CHAPTER 8

1. J. Schumpeter, 'Business Cycles' (McGraw-Hill, 1939) and 'Theory of Economic Development' (McGraw-Hill, 1936).
2. E. Mansfield, 'Technical Change and the Rate of Imitation', in 'Econometrica' (Oct 1961).
3. C. Freeman, 'The Plastics Industry: A Comparative Study of Research and Innovation' in 'National Institute Economic and Social Review' (Nov 1963).
4. J. Schmookler, 'Invention and Economic Growth' (Harvard U.P., 1966) p. 44.
5. J. Schmookler, 'Technological Change and Economic Theory', in 'American Economic Review, Papers and Proceedings' (May 1965).

6. J. Schmookler, 'Inventors, Past and Present', in 'Review of Economics and Statistics' (Aug 1957).

7. R. E. Johnston, 'Technical Progress and Innovation', in 'Oxford Economic Papers' (July 1966)

8. W. Paul Strassman, 'Risks and Technological Innovation' (Cornell U.P., Ithaca, N.Y., 1959).

9. E. Mansfield, 'Entry, Gibrat's Law, Innovation and the Growth of Firms', in 'American Economic Review' (Dec 1962) and 'The Rate of Return from Industrial R. and D.', in 'American Economic Review' (May 1965).

10. Schmookler, 'Invention and Economic Growth'.

11. F. M. Scherer, 'Corporate Inventive Output: Profits and Growth', in 'Journal of Political Economy' (Apr 1965).

12. F. M. Scherer, 'Firm Size, Market Structure, Opportunity and Output of Patented Inventions', in 'American Economic Review' (Dec 1965).

13. E. Mansfield, 'Industrial Research and Development Expenditure: Determinants, Prospects and Relation to Size of Firm and Inventive Output', in 'Journal of Political Economy' (Aug 1964).

14. Schmookler, 'Invention and Economic Growth', p. 93.

15. Ibid.

16. Ibid.

17. Ibid., p. 184.

18. 'Science, Economic Growth and Government Policy' (O.E.C.D., Paris, 1963).

19. Scherer, in 'American Economic Review' (Dec 1965).

20. Ibid.

21. B. Williams, 'Technology, Investment and Growth' (Chapman & Hall, 1967).

22. E. Mansfield, 'The Size of Firm, Market Structure and Innovation', in 'Journal of Political Economy' (Dec 1963).

23. J. Enos, 'Rate and Direction of Inventive Activity' (Princeton U.P., 1962).

24. Ibid.

25. E. Mansfield, 'Economics of Technological Change' (Norton, New York, 1968).

26. H. Villard, 'Competition, Oligopoly and Research', in 'Journal of Political Economy' (Dec 1958).

27. Scherer, in 'American Economic Review' (Dec 1965).

28. D. Hamberg, 'Size of Firm, Oligopoly and Research: The Evidence', in 'Canadian Journal of Political Science' (Feb 1964); Scherer, in 'American Economic Review' (Dec 1965); J. Schmookler, 'Bigness, Fewness and Research', in 'Journal of Political Economy' (Dec 1959); J. Worley, 'Industrial Research under New Competition', in 'Journal of Political Economy' (Apr 1961); Mansfield, in 'Journal of Political Economy' (Aug 1964).

29. J. Markham, 'Market Structure, Business Conduct and Innovation', in 'American Economic Review, Papers and Proceedings' (May 1965).

30. Ibid.

31. Mansfield, in 'Journal of Political Economy' (Dec 1963).

32. Ibid.

33. C. Carter and B. Williams, 'Industry and Technical Progress' (Oxford U.P., 1957).

34. Figures quoted in Mansfield, 'Economics of Technological Change'.

35. J. Duckworth (Managing Director, N.R.D.C.) in 'Financial Times', 13 Mar 1969.

36. M. H. Cooper, 'Patents and Innovations', in G. Teeling-Smith (ed.), 'Innovation and the Balance of Payments: The Experience in the Pharmaceutical Industry' (Office of Health Economics, 1967) p. 38.

37. Hamberg, in 'Canadian Journal of Political Science' (Feb 1964).

38. Ibid.

39. Hart, 'Studies in Profit, Business Saving and Investment in the United Kingdom, 1920-62', vol. ii.

40. Villard, in 'Journal of Political Economy' (Dec 1958).

41. See Marris, 'The Economic Theory of Managerial Capitalism'.

42. J. R. Minasian, 'The Economics of Research and Development', in 'The Rate and Direction of Inventive Activity' (National Bureau of Economic Research, New York, 1962).

43. Schmookler, 'Invention and Economic Growth'.

44. D. Mueller, 'Patents, R. and D. and Measurement of Inventive Activity', in 'Journal of Industrial Economics' (Nov 1966).

45. Caves, 'Britain's Economic Prospects'.

46. R. Nelson, M. Peck and E. Kalachek, 'Technology, Economic Growth and Public Policy' (Brookings Institution, Washington, 1967).

47. D. Hamberg, 'Invention in the Industrial Research Laboratory', in 'Journal of Political Economy' (Apr 1963).

48. Carter and Williams, 'Industry and Technical Progress'.

49. Ibid.

50. Williams, 'Technology, Investment and Growth'.

51. Villard, in 'Journal of Political Economy' (Dec 1958).

52. J. Jewkes, D. Sawers and R. Stillerman, 'The Sources of Invention', 2nd ed. (Macmillan, 1969).

53. Schmookler, in 'Review of Economic Statistics' (Aug 1957).

54. Cooper, in Teeling-Smith (ed.), 'Innovation and Balance of Payments: The Experience in the Pharmaceutical Industry'.

55. Minasian, in 'The Rate and Direction of Inventive Activity'; E. Mansfield, 'The Speed of Response of Firms to New Techniques', in 'Quarterly Journal of Economics' (May 1963).

56. Scherer, in 'American Economic Review' (Dec 1965).

57. Mansfield, in 'Journal of Political Economy' (Aug 1964) and 'Industrial Research and Technological Innovation' (Norton, New York, 1968).

58. E. F. Denison, 'Why Growth Rates Differ' (Brookings Institution, Washington, 1967) p. 288.

59. Salter, 'Productivity and Technical Change'.

60. Mansfield, in 'Econometrica' (Oct 1961).

61. Salter, 'Productivity and Technical Change'.

62. Denison, 'Why Growth Rates Differ'.

63. Nelson, Peck and Kalachek, 'Technology, Economic Growth and Public Policy'.

64. E. M. Rogers, 'Diffusion of Innovations' (Macmillan, New York, 1962).

65. Mansfield, 'Industrial Research and Technological Innovation'.

66. Mansfield, in 'Quarterly Journal of Economics' (May 1963).

67. Mansfield, 'Industrial Research and Technological Innovation'.

68. Ibid.

69. Schmookler, 'Invention and Economic Growth'.

70. For an exposition of the 'learning by doing' hypothesis, see K. J. Arrow, 'Economic Implication of Learning by Doing', in 'Review of Economic Studies' (June 1962).

71. A. Phillips, 'Concentration, Scale and Technological Change in Selected Manufacturing Industries, 1899-1936', in 'Journal of Industrial Economics' (June 1956).

72. Scherer, in 'Journal of Political Economy' (Apr 1965).

73. Carter and Williams, 'Industry and Technical Progress'.

74. Johnston, in 'Oxford Economic Papers' (July 1966).

75. Mansfield, in 'American Economic Review' (May 1965).

76. J. Duckworth of N.R.D.C., quoted in the 'Financial Times', 13 Mar 1969.

77. C. Freeman and R. Evely, 'Industrial Research in Manufacturing Industry, 1959-60' (Federation of British Industries, 1961).

78. C. Carter and B. Williams, 'Investment in Innovation' (Oxford U.P., 1958).

79. Williams, 'Technology, Investment and Growth'; Freeman and Evely, 'Industrial Research in Manufacturing Industry, 1959-60'; J. H. Dunning and C. J. Thomas, 'Change and Development in the British Economy' (Hutchinson, 1961).

80. Williams, 'Technology, Investment and Growth'.

81. Findings quoted in Mansfield, 'Industrial Research and Technological Innovation'.

82. Scherer, in 'Journal of Political Economy' (Apr 1965).

83. Mansfield, 'Industrial Research and Technological Innovation'.

84. Ibid.

85. Ibid.

86. Carter and Williams, 'Investment in Innovation'.

87. D. C. Corner and A. Williams, 'The Sensitivity of Businesses to Initial and Investment Allowances', in 'Economica' (Feb 1965).

88. Schumpeter, 'Business Cycles' and 'Theory of Economic Development'.

89. Nelson, Peck and Kalachek, 'Technology, Economic Growth and Public Policy'.

90. Caves, 'Britain's Economic Prospects'.

91. Ibid.

92. Ibid.

93. Hamberg, in 'Journal of Political Economy' (Apr 1963).

CHAPTER 9

1. P. D. Henderson, in R. Turvey (ed.), 'Public Enterprise' (Penguin Books, 1968).

2. See Weston, 'The Scope and Methodology of Finance'.

3. See, for example, any edition of 'Business Ratios'.

4. M. Tamari, 'Financial Ratios as a Means of Forecasting Bankruptcy', in 'Bank of Israel Bulletin', no. 21 (Apr 1964).

5. K. E. Boulding, 'Reconstruction of Economics' (Wiley, 1950) p. 24.

6. H. Simon, 'Decision Making in Economics' in 'American Economic Review' (June 1959).

7. See F. Katona, 'Psychological Analysis of Economic Behavior' (McGraw-Hill, 1951).

8. Singh and Whittington, 'Growth, Profitability and Valuation'.

9. Political and Economic Planning, 'Thrusters and Sleepers' (Allen & Unwin, 1965).

10. S. Ashton, 'Investment Planning by Private Enterprise', in 'Lloyds Bank Review' (Oct 1962) p. 23.

11. 'Investment Appraisal' (National Economic Development Office, 1965).

12. See, for example, G. P. E. Clarkson, 'Managerial Economics' (Penguin Books, 1968); J. F. Weston and E. E. Brigham, 'Managerial Finance' (Holt, Rinehart & Winston, 1962).

13. Present value = $\sum\limits_{i=1}^{i=n} \dfrac{A_1}{(1+x)^i}$

Marginal efficiency of capital is the solution r to

$$C = \sum_{i=1}^{i=n} \frac{A_1}{(1+v)^i}$$

where

C = initial capital outlay;
A_1 = net cash flow at the end of year i, where project has a life of n years;
r = firm's cost of capital.

See A. J. Merrett and A. Sykes, 'Finance and Analysis of Capital Projects' (Longmans, 1963).

14. Ibid.

15. J. M. Samuels, 'An Empirical Study of the Cost of Equity Capital', in 'Business Ratios' (summer, 1968); A. J. Merrett and A. Sykes, 'The Return on Equities and Fixed Interest Securities, 1919-1966', in 'District Bank Review' (Sep 1967).

16. 'Nationalised Industries: A Review of Economic and Financial Objectives', Cmnd. 3437 (H.M.S.O., Nov 1967).

17. See, for example, Clarkson, 'Managerial Economics'.

18. Penrose, 'Theory of the Growth of the Firm'.

19. Cyert and March, in 'Quarterly Journal of Economics' (Feb 1956).

20. Dunning and Thomas, 'Change and Development in the British Economy'.

21. See, for example, 'Financial Times', 26 Oct 1968.

22. Carter and Williams, 'Industry and Technical Progress', p. 134.

23. Derived from a series of interviews conducted by members of the University of Exeter Economics Department with major companies in the U.K. pharmaceutical industry. Also see Committee of Enquiry into the relationship of the Pharmaceutical Industry with the National Health Service 1965-67, Cmnd. 3410, 1967, Annex F.

24. Carter and Williams, 'Industry and Technical Progress'.

25. In Williams, 'Technology, Investment and Growth'.

26. Ibid., p. 147.

27. See Caves, 'Britain's Economic Prospects'.

28. G. Hutton, 'We Too Can Prosper' (Allen & Unwin, 1953); L. Rostas, 'Comparative Productivity in British and American Industry' (N.I.E.S.R., Cambridge, 1948); M. Frankel, 'British and American Productivity: A Comparison and Interpretation', Bureau of Economic and Business Research, Bulletin Series, no. 81 (University of Illinois, Urbana, 1957); Paige and Bombach, 'A Comparison of National Output and Productivity of the United Kingdom and the United States'.

29. See J. H. Dunning, 'The Role of American Investment in the British Economy' (Political and Economic Planning, 1969).

30. J. H. Dunning, 'U.S. Subsidiaries in Britain and their U.K. Competitors', in 'Business Ratios' (autumn, 1966).

31. Cooper and Parker, in 'Business Ratios' (autumn, 1967).

32. Ministry of Labour, 'Electronics', Manpower Studies, no. 5 (H.M.S.O., 1967).

33. Department of Employment and Productivity, 'Company Manpower Planning', Manpower Papers, no. 1 (new series) (H.M.S.O., 1968).

CHAPTER 10

1. E. A. G. Robinson, 'The Structure of Competitive Industry' (Cambridge U.P., 1932); P. S. Florence, 'The Logic of Industrial Organisation' (Kegan Paul, 1933); J. Steindl, 'Small and Big Business' (Blackwell, 1945); J. S. Bain, 'Barriers to New Competition' (Cambridge, Mass., 1958) and 'Industrial Organisation' (Wiley, New York, 1959); G. J. Stigler, 'The Economies of Scale', in 'Journal of Law and Economics', i (1958).

2. Penrose, 'Theory of the Growth of the Firm'; Marris, 'Managerial Capitalism'.

3. The various cross-section studies made during the period 1940-50 are summarised by Caleb A. Smith in N.B.E.R., 'Business Concentration and Price Policy', Special Conference Series No. 5 (Princeton, U.P., 1955).

4. For the use to which economists put this type of data, see R. Turvey, 'On Investment Choices in Electricity Generation', in 'Oxford Economic Papers', xv (Nov 1963).

5. See, however, M. Chisholm, 'Economies of Scale in Road Goods Transport?', in 'Oxford Economic Papers', xi (Oct 1959); A. A. Walters, 'Economies of Scale in Road Haulage: A Comment', in 'Oxford Economic Papers', xiii (Feb 1961); and A. J. Harrison, 'Economies of Scale and the Structure of the Road Haulage Industry', in 'Oxford Economic Papers', xv (Nov 1963).

6. This method has been introduced by Stigler, in 'Journal of Law and Economics', i (1958).

7. Rostas, 'Comparative Productivity in British and American Industry'.

8. G. Maxcy and A. Silberston, 'The Motor Industry' (Allen & Unwin, 1959).

9. Bain, 'Barriers to New Competition', pp. 245-7, 262.

10. Stigler, in 'Journal of Law and Economics', i (1958).

11. J. G. McLean and R. W. Haigh, 'The Growth of Integrated Oil Companies' (Harvard Business School, Boston, 1954).

12. Pratten and Dean, 'The Economies of Large-Scale Production in British Industry'.

13. Bain, 'Barriers to New Competition', pp. 233-5.

14. P. M. Frankel and W. L. Newton, 'The Location of Refineries', in 'Institute of Petroleum Review', xv (July 1961).

15. The Benson Report (British Iron and Steel Federation, 'The Steel Industry: The Stage 1 Report of the Development Co-ordinating Committee', (July 1966) states that out of 285 works engaged in producing mainly common steel in 1965, 21 were fully integrated works, whereas 216 were re-rollers and other specialised works.

16. Quoted by Pratten and Dean, 'The Economies of Large-Scale Production in British Industry'.

17. R. Evely and I. M. D. Little, 'Concentration in British Industry' (N.I.E.S.R., Cambridge, 1960).

18. Ibid.

19. W. G. Shepherd, 'A Comparison of Industrial Concentration in the United States and in Britain', in 'Review of Economics and Statistics', xliii (Feb 1961) pp. 70-5.

20. J. S. Bain, 'International Differences in Industrial Structure' (Yale U.P., New Haven, 1966) pp. 76-81.

21. Florence, 'The Logic of Industrial Organisation', pp. 130-5, and G. Rosenbluth in N.B.E.R., 'Business Concentration and Price Policy', pp. 70-7.

22. Evely and Little, 'Concentration in British Industry'.

23. Suggested further reading:

Books

J. S. Bain, 'Barriers to New Competition' (Harvard U.P., Cambridge, Mass., 1958).

——, 'International Differences in Industrial Structure' (Yale U.P., New Haven, 1966).

R. Evely and I. M. D. Little, 'Concentration in British Industry' (N.I.E.S.R., Cambridge, 1960).

E. Mansfield, (ed.), 'Monopoly Power and Economic Performance' (Norton, New York, 1964).

E. S. Mason, 'Economic Concentration and the Monopoly Problem' (Harvard U.P., Cambridge, Mass., 1959) esp. Part I.

N. B. E. R., 'Business Concentration and Price Policy', Special Conference Series no. 5 (Princeton, U.P., 1955).

R. L. Nelson, 'Concentration in the Manufacturing Industries of the U.S.' (Yale U.P., New Haven, 1963).

C. Pratten and R. M. Dean, 'The Economies of Large-Scale Production in British Industry' (Cambridge U.P., 1965).

Articles

N. R. Collins and L. E. Preston, 'The Size Structure of Industrial Firms', in 'American Economic Review' (Dec 1961).

P. E. Hart, 'Business Concentration in the United Kingdom', in 'Journal of the Royal Statistical Society', cxxiii(2) (1960).

—— and S. Prais, 'Measuring Business Concentration', in 'Bulletin of the Oxford University Institute of Statistics', xix(3) (1957).

H. Leak and A. Maizels, 'The Structure of British Industry', in 'Journal of the Royal Statistical Society', cxiii(1-2) (1945), a pioneering classic.

B. P. Pasigian, 'Market Concentration in the United States and Great Britain', in 'Journal of Law and Economics', xi (Oct 1968).

G. J. Stigler, 'The Economies of Scale', in 'Journal of Law and Economics', i (Oct 1958).

W. G. Shepherd, 'A Comparison of Industrial Concentration in the United States and Britain', in 'Review of Economics and Statistics', xliii(1) (Feb 1961).

CHAPTER 11

1. Evely and Little, 'Concentration in British Industry'
2. Ibid.
3. See the arguments used by Leyland Motor Corporation and Rover Motor Co. in merger discussions (Chapter 15).
4. Especially in A. R. Burns, 'The Decline of Competition' (McGraw-Hill, New York, 1936).
5. Monopolies and Restrictive Practices Commission, 'Collective Discrimination', Cmnd. 9504 (H.M.S.O., June 1955) para. 40.
6. In legal terms the issue is referred to as the problem of 'justiciability'. For an excellent discussion of this problem, see G. Marshall on 'Justiciability', in A. G. Guest (ed.), 'Oxford Essays in Jurisprudence' (Oxford U.P., 1961), and R. R. Summers, 'Justiciability', in 'Modern Law Review', xxxvi (1963). See also I. A. Macdonald, 'The Restrictive Practices Court: A Lawyer's View', in 'Oxford Economic Papers', xvii (Nov 1965).
7. Law Reports 1, Restrictive Practices, p. 103.
8. The exact wording of para. 21 of the Act is given in C. Brock, 'The Control of Restrictive Practices from 1956' (McGraw-Hill, 1966) Appendix B, pp. 173-4, and in R. O. Wilberforce, A. Campbell and N. P. M. Ellis, 'Restrictive Trade Practices and Monopolies', 2nd ed. (Sweet & Maxwell, 1966) para. 1103, pp. 484-5.
9. The 'Financial Times' ran a centre-page article on 26 Nov 1962, entitled 'Has Leniency Crept in This Year?'.
10. T. Wilson, 'Restrictive Practices', chap. 4 in J. P. Miller (ed.), 'Competition, Cartels and their Regulation' (North-Holland, Amsterdam, 1962). See section ii, esp. pp. 119-120.
11. Law Reports 1, Restrictive Practices, pp. 285, 431.
12. Law Reports 2, Restrictive Practices, pp. 1, 43.
13. For an application of this to the pharmaceutical industry, see M. H. Cooper, 'Prices and Profits in the Pharmaceutical Industry' (Pergamon Press, 1966).
14. Law Reports 1, Restrictive Practices, pp. 285, 334.
15. J. B. Heath, 'Restrictive Practices and After', in 'Manchester School', xxix (May 1961).
16. For a good account of this case, see A. Hunter, 'Competition and the Law' (Allen & Unwin, 1966) pp. 175-180.
17. Section 5 of the Restrictive Practices Act, 1968, introduced the registration of information agreements.
18. By Heath, in 'Manchester School', xxix (May 1961).
19. Suggested further reading:
R. O. Wilberforce, A. Campbell and N. P. M. Ellis, 'Restrictive Trade Practices and Monopolies', 2nd ed. (Sweet & Maxwell, 1966).
This is the standard legal work on the subject and contains summaries of reports of the Monopolies Commission and of cases before the Restrictive Practices Court.
G. C. Allen, 'Monopoly and Restrictive Practices' (Allen & Unwin, 1968).
Board of Trade, 'Mergers: A Guide to Board of Trade Practices' (H.M.S.O., 1969).
C. Brock, 'The Control of Restrictive Practices from 1956' (McGraw-Hill, 1966).
A. Hunter, 'Competition and the Law' (Allen & Unwin, 1966).
—— (ed.), 'Monopoly and Competition: Selected Readings' (Penguin Books, 1969).
'Oxford Economic Papers', xvii 3 (Nov 1965). Whole issue devoted to the Restrictive Practices Court.
C. K. Rowley, 'Mergers and Public Policy in Great Britain', in 'Journal of Law and Economics', xi (Apr 1968).
—— 'The Monopolies Commission and the Rate of Return on Capital', in 'Economic Journal', lxxix (Mar 1969).

R. B. Stevens and B. S. Yamey, 'The Restrictive Practices Court: The Judicial Process and Economic Policy' (Weidenfeld & Nicolson, 1965).

T. Wilson, 'Restrictive Practices', chap 4 in J. P. Miller, 'Competition, Cartels and their Regulation' (North-Holland, Amsterdam, 1962).

CHAPTER 12

1. Little and Rayner, 'Higgledy Piggledy Growth Again'.

2. A. J. Merrett, M. Howe, and G. D. Newbould, 'Equity Issues and the London Capital Market' (Longmans, 1967) Table 4.6.

3. Suggested further reading:

W. J. Baumol, 'The Stock Market and Economic Efficiency' (Fordham U.P., New York, 1965).

J. Dundas Hamilton, 'Stockbroking Today' (Macmillan, 1968).

I. M. D. Little and A. C. Rayner, 'Higgledy Piggledy Growth Again' (Blackwell, 1966).

A. J. Merrett, M. Howe and G. D. Newbould, 'Equity Issues and the London Capital Market' (Longmans, 1967).

G. K. Young, 'Merchant Banking' (Weidenfeld & Nicolson, 1966).

CHAPTER 13

1. See D. C. Corner, 'Financial Incentives in the Smaller Business', Occasional Papers in Social and Economic Administration, No. 5 (Edutext, 1967) p. 11.

2. Prices and Incomes Board, Report No. 65, 'Payment by Results Systems', Cmnd. 3627 (H.M.S.O., May 1968).

3. See J. T. Dunlop, 'The Task of Contemporary Wage Theory', chap. 5 in G. W. Taylor and F. C. Pierson (eds), 'New Concepts in Wage Determination' (McGraw-Hill, New York, 1957).

4. J. Stieber, 'The Steel Industry Wage Structure' (Harvard U.P., Cambridge, Mass., 1959).

5. H. M. Levinson, 'Determining Forces in Collective Wage Bargaining' (Wiley, New York, 1966) esp. chaps 2 and 3.

6. Ibid.

7. 'Employment and Productivity Gazette' (Mar 1969) pp. 232-4.

8. Report No. 77, Cmnd. 3715 (H.M.S.O., July 1968).

9. Ibid., para. 2.

10. 'We do not think, at any rate for the purpose of settling pay, there can be laid down a "standard" need at some particular figure in pounds, shillings and pence to divide the lowest-paid from the rest' Cmnd. 3199 (para. 8).

11. Report No. 98, 'University Pay', Cmnd. 3866 (H.M.S.O., Dec 1968).

12. Ibid., 20.

13. 'Investment Appraisal' (N.E.D.C., 1965).

14. 'First General Report', No. 19, Cmnd. 3087 (H.M.S.O., July 1966).

15. Suggested further reading:

J. T. Dunlop, 'The Task of Contemporary Wage Theory'; E. R. Livernash, 'The Internal Wage Structure'; A. M. Ross, 'The External Wage Structure'; all three are chapters in G. W. Taylor and F. C. Pierson (eds), 'New Concepts in Wage Determination' (McGraw-Hill, New York, 1957).

E. M. Hugh-Jones (ed.), 'Wage-Structure in Theory and Practice' (North-Holland, Amsterdam, 1966).

J. L. Meij (ed.), 'Internal Wage Structure' (North-Holland, Amsterdam, 1963).

National Board for Prices and Incomes, General Reports:
   No. 19, Apr 1965-July 1966, Cmnd. 3087 (H.M.S.O., July 1966);
   No. 40, July 1966-Aug 1967, Cmnd. 3394 (H.M.S.O., Aug 1967);
   No. 77, Aug 1967-July 1968, Cmnd. 3715 (H.M.S.O., July 1968).
D. J. Robertson, 'Factory Wage Structures and National Agreements' (Cambridge U.P., 1960).
G. Routh, 'Occupation and Pay in Great Britain, 1906-60' (Cambridge U.P., 1965).

CHAPTER 14

1. Ministry of Labour/Department of Employment and Productivity, 'Industrial Relations' (H.M.S.O., 1961).

2. Ibid.

3. Ministry of Labour, 'Directory of Employers' Associations, Trade Unions and Joint Organisations' (H.M.S.O., 1967).

4 See G. B. Richardson, 'The Pricing of Heavy Electrical Equipment', in 'Bulletin of the Oxford University Institute of Statistics', xxviii (May 1966).

5. In 1967 the principal members of the E.L.M.A. consisted of A.E.I., G.E.C., Philips N.V., Siemens, Crompton Parkinson (a subsidiary of the Hawker Siddeley Group), British Electric Lamps and Aurora Lamps. It excluded the major independent, Thorn Electrical Industries, and Erco, of which it owned 51 per cent of the capital.

6. See G. Maxcy, 'The Motor Industry', chap 4 in Cook and Cohen, 'The Effects of Mergers'.

7. S. Pollard, 'The Development of the British Economy, 1914-1950' (Edward Arnold, 1962).

8. This account is based on G. Walker, 'The Development and Organisation of the Associated Electrical Industries Ltd', in R. S. Edwards and H. Townsend, 'Business Enterprise' (Macmillan, 1958) pp. 303-16.

9. Monopolies Commission, 'Supply of Electrical Equipment for Mechanically Propelled Road Vehicles' (H.M.S.O., 1964) pp. 24-7.

10. Electronics E. D. C., 'Statistics of the Electronics Industry' (H.M.S.O., June 1967) Table 35, p. 95.

11. Late in 1969 the I.R.C. submitted a confidential report to the Government on the structure of the telecommunications industry and its relations with the G.P.O.

12. P. Coldstream, 'The Price of a Place in the Computer Market', in 'Financial Times' (7 July 1965).

13. For instance, the £200,000 I.B.M. 360-30 ordered for the Mersey Docks and Harbour Board in 1965.

14. Seymour Melman, 'Productivity of Operations in the Machine Tool Industry in Western Europe', European Productivity Agency Project No. 420 (1959).

15. 200 out of 350, accounting for only 10 per cent of output in 1959.

16. 'H.C. Parl. Deb.', 5th series, vol. 714, 14 June 1965, cols 31-40.

17. See 'Machine Tools: A Special Report', in 'The Times' (23 June 1969).

18. D. Wedderburn, 'White Collar Redundancy', University of Cambridge Department of Applied Economics, Occasional Paper No. 1 (Cambridge U.P., 1964) and 'Redundancy and the Railwaymen, University of Cambridge Department of Applied Economics, Occasional Paper No. 4 (Cambridge U.P., 1965); R. R. Thomas, 'An Exercise in Redeployment' Pergamon Press, 1969).

19. O.E.C.D., 'Geographical and Occupational Mobility of Workers in the Aircraft and Electronics Industries', Regional Trade Union Seminar (Paris, 1967) and 'Study of Redundancy Practices in the U.K. and the U.S.A.' (Paris, 1966).

CHAPTER 15

1. F.B.I., 'Industrial Research in Manufacturing Industry, 1959-60' (1961) Table C, p. 35.

2. Ibid., Table 3.

3. See C. Freeman, 'Research and Development: A Comparison between British and American Industry', in 'National Institute Economic Review', no. 20 (May 1962).

4. See P.E.P., 'Thrusters and Sleepers', chap 7, and Carter and Williams, 'Industry and Technical Progress', esp. chap 6.

5. P.E.P., 'Thrusters and Sleepers', chap 13.

6. H. A. Turner, G. Clack and G. Roberts, 'Labour Relations in the Motor Industry' (Allen & Unwin, 1967) pp. 205 ff.

7. An interesting insight into the way in which the internal wage structure of an individual firm is built up may be obtained from Lisl Klein, 'Multiproducts Ltd' (H.M.S.O., 1964).

8. J. Bates, Chap 10 in P. E. Hart, 'Studies in Profits, Business Saving and Investment in the United Kingdom, 1920-62, i (Allen & Unwin, 1965) Tables 10.7 and 10.10.

9. For a detailed examination of the 1957 dispute, see H. A. Clegg and R. Adams, 'The Employer's Challenge' (Blackwell, 1957).

10. National Incomes Commission, Report No. 4, 'Agreements of November-December 1963 in the Engineering and Shipbuilding Industries', Cmnd. 2583 (H.M.S.O., Feb 1965) para. 250.

11. P.I.B., 'Pay and Conditions of Service of Engineering Workers (First Report)', No. 49, Cmnd. 3495 (H.M.S.O., Dec 1967).

12. 'Second Report', No. 104, Cmnd. 3931 (H.M.S.O., 1969).

13. A. Marsh, 'Industrial Relations in Engineering' (Pergamon Press, 1965) pp. 206-7 and Appendix C.

14. P.I.B. Report No. 104, para. 69.

15. Ibid. para. 90.

16. R. L. Major, 'Note on Britain's Share in World Trade in Manufactures, 1954-1966', in 'National Institute Economic Review' (May 1968); Mechanical Engineering E.D.C., 'Market—the World' (July 1968).

17. P.E.P., 'Firms and their Exports', in 'Planning', xxx, 483 (Nov 1964).

18. G. F. Ray, 'Export Competitiveness: British Experience in Eastern Europe', in 'National Institute Economic Review' (May 1966).

19. Mechanical Engineering E.D.C., 'Market—the World'.

20. Cf. Table 15.7 with Table 28 of the Mechanical Engineering E.D.C. study.

21. Mechanical Engineering E.D.C., 'Market—the World'.

22. In 'The Observer', 10 Dec 1967.

23. Mechanical Engineering E.D.C., 'Market—the World'.

24. Suggested further reading for Chapters 14 and 15:
The position of a number of individual engineering industries is examined for the 1950s in D. Burn (ed.), 'The Structure of British Industry', 2 vols (N.I.E.S.R., Cambridge, 1958).
Official reports and publications:
'Shipbuilding Inquiry Committee, 1965-1966', Cmnd. 2937 (H.M.S.O. Mar 1966) (The Geddes Report).
'Report of the Committee of Inquiry into the Aircraft Industry' Cmnd. 2853 (H.M.S.O., Dec 1965) (The Plowden Report).
National Incomes Commission, 'Agreements of November-December 1963 in the Engineering and Shipbuilding Industries', Cmnd. 2583 (H.M.S.O., Feb 1965).
Ministry of Labour, 'Manpower Studies No. 2: The Metal Industries' (H.M.S.O., 1965).
National Board for Prices and Incomes, 'Pay and Conditions of Service of Engineering Workers (First Report)', No. 49, Cmnd. 3495 (H.M.S.O., Dec 1967), and 'Second Report', No. 104, Cmnd. 3931 (H.M.S.O., 1969).

Other publications:

K. Hartley, 'The Mergers in the U.K. Aircraft Industry, 1957-60', in 'Journal of the Royal Aeronautical Society', lxix 660 (Dec 1965).

A. Marsh, 'Industrial Relations in Engineering' (Pergamon Press, 1965).

G. Maxcy and A. Silberston, 'The Motor Industry' (Allen & Unwin, 1959).

J. R. Parkinson, 'The Economics of Shipbuilding in the U.K.' (Cambridge U.P., 1960).

A. Silberston, 'The Motor Industry, 1955-64', in 'Bulletin of the Oxford University Institute of Economics and Statistics', xxvii (Nov 1965).

D. J. Robertson, 'Factory Wage Structures and National Agreements' (Cambridge U.P., 1960).

G. Turner, 'The Car Makers' (Penguin Books, 1964).

H. A. Turner, G. Clack and G. Roberts, 'Labour Relations in the Motor Industry' (Allen & Unwin, 1967).

CHAPTER 16

1. Full results of the 1963 Census of Production were still not available for this group even in early 1969.

2. Cmnd. 3410 (H.M.S.O., 1967). See esp. chap. 5.

3. P.I.B. Report No. 100 'Synthetic Organic Dyestuffs and Organic Pigments Prices', Cmnd. 3895 (H.M.S.O., Jan 1969).

4. 'Annual Report and Accounts' (1967) p. 8.

5. F.B.I., 'Industrial Research in Manufacturing Industry', Table 2, p. 66.

6. International Statistical Year, 'The Overall Level and Structure of R. and D. efforts in O.E.C.D. Member Countries' (O.E.C.D., Paris, 1967) and 'The Chemical Industry, 1966-1967' (O.E.C.D., Paris, 1968) p. 136.

7. 'Report of the Committee of Enquiry into the Relationship of the Pharmaceutical Industry with the National Health Service 1965-1967', Cmnd. 3410 (H.M.S.O., Sep 1967).

8. Ibid., para. 184.

9. But cf. with the estimates in the Association of the British Pharmaceutical Industry survey for 1964 of £10 million spent on R. & D., with 25 per cent of this on fundamental research. Quoted in Cooper, 'Prices and Profits in the Pharmaceutical Industry', p. 168.

10. This subsection draws heavily on C. Freeman and others, 'Chemical Process Plant: Innovation and the World Markets', in 'National Institute Economic Review' (Aug 1968).

11. See Midland Bank, 'The Chemical Industry in Some European Countries' (autumn 1967).

12. Suggested further reading:

D. W. F. Hardie and J. D. Pratt, 'A History of the Modern British Chemical Industry' (Pergamon Press, 1966).

M. H. Cooper, 'Prices and Profits in the Pharmaceutical Industry' (Pergamon Press, 1966).

C. Freeman and others 'Chemical Process Plant: Innovation and the World Market', in 'National Institute Economic Review' (Aug 1968).

——, 'The Plastics Industry: A Comparative Study of Research and Innovation', in 'National Institute Economic Review' (Nov 1963).

'Report of the Committee of Enquiry into the Relationship of the Pharmaceutical Industry with the National Health Service, 1965-1967', Cmnd. 3410 (H.M.S.O., Sep 1967) (The Sainsbury Committee).

Midland Bank, 'The Chemical Industry in Some European Countries' (1967).

G. Teeling-Smith (ed.), 'Innovation and the Balance of Payments: The Experience in the Pharmaceutical Industry' (Office of Health Economics, 1967).

P.I.B. Report No. 105, 'Pay of General Workers and Craftsmen in Imperial Chemical Industries Ltd', Cmnd. 3941 (H.M.S.O., Feb 1969).

Chemicals E.D.C., 'Exports of Chemicals' (H.M.S.O., June 1967) and 'Imports of Chemicals' (H.M.S.O., Dec 1966).

CHAPTER 17

1. 'Investment in Natural Gas' (H.M.S.O., May 1968).
2. Cmnd. 3438 (H.M.S.O., Nov 1967).
3. 'Exploitation of North Sea Gas', Cmnd. 3996 (H.M.S.O., Apr 1969).
4. 'The Financial Obligations of the Nationalised Industries', Cmnd. 1337 (H.M.S.O., 1961).
5. 'Nationalised Industries: A Review of Economic and Financial Objectives', Cmnd. 3437 (H.M.S.O., Nov 1967).
6. 'Ministerial Control of the Nationalised Industries', Sub-committee A, vol. ii, Minutes of Evidence H.C. 371-11, para. 862 (H.M.S.O., July 1968).
7. P.I.B., Gas Prices (Second Report)', No. 102, Cmnd. 3294 (H.M.S.O., Feb 1969).
8. Ibid., para. 190.
9. Ibid., para. 20.
10. Ibid., chap. 4.
11. Ibid., para. 21.
12. Ibid., para. 62.
13. Ibid., Table 1, para. 17.
14. Ibid., para. 69.
15. P.I.B. Report No. 29, 'Pay and Conditions of Manual Workers in Local Authorities, the National Health Service, Gas and Water Supply', Cmnd. 3230 (H.M.S.O., May 1967).
16. P.I.B. Report No. 86, 'Pay of Staff Workers in the Gas Industry', Cmnd. 3795 (H.M.S.O., Oct 1968).
17. See the P.I.B. report 'Productivity Agreements', Cmnd. 3311 (H.M.S.O., June 1967).
18. Ibid., para. 75.
19. Official references for suggested further reading:
'The Financial Obligations of the Nationalised Industries', Cmnd. 1337 (H.M.S.O., 1961).
'Nationalised Industries: A Review of Economic and Financial Objectives', Cmnd. 3437 (H.M.S.O., Nov 1967).
'Fuel Policy', Cmnd. 3438 (H.M.S.O., Nov 1967).
Gas Council, 'Investment in Natural Gas' (H.M.S.O., May 1968).
'Ministerial Control of the Nationalised Industries', Sub-committee A, vol. ii, H.C. 371-11 (H.M.S.O., July 1968) (The Mikardo Report).
P.I.B., 'Pay and Conditions of Manual Workers in Local Authorities, the National Health Service, Gas and Water Supply', Report No. 29, Cmnd. 3230 (H.M.S.O., May 1967).
P.I.B., 'Pay of Staff Workers in the Gas Industry', Report No. 86, Cmnd. 3795 (H.M.S.O., Oct 1968).
P.I.B., 'Gas Prices (Second Report)', Report No. 102, Cmnd. 3294 (H.M.S.O., Feb 1969).
'Exploitation of North Sea Gas', Cmnd. 3996 (H.M.S.O., Apr 1969).

CHAPTER 19

1. See, for instance, Censuses of Production.
2. For instance, a works foreman who has an office is a member of staff; a working foreman who moves around the factory floor is an operative. Cf. Hilda Kahn 'The Distinction between Wages and Salaries', in 'Scottish Journal of Political Economy' (June 1956).
3. Derived from General Register Office, 'Census 1961, Great Britain' Summary Tables.
4. W. Arthur Lewis, 'Economic Development with Unlimited Supplies of Labour', in 'Manchester School' (May 1954).
5. R. C. O. Matthews, 'Why Has Britain Had Full Employment since the War', in 'Economic Journal' (Sep 1968).

6. W. Arthur Lewis and F. V. Meyer, 'The Effects of an Overseas Slump on the British Economy', in 'Manchester School' (Sep 1949); and fluctuations calculated from London and Cambridge Economic Service, 'Key Statistics of the British Economy, 1900-1966.

7. The potential supply of labour, or stock of labour, is the total amount of labour at the economy's disposal. Not all of that labour is used. What is actually used is the effective supply of labour. The effective supply of labour is more flexible than the potential supply of labour. The effective supply of labour can vary in the short period, since employment alters because everyone can vary hours and the intensity of their work. The effective supply is the supply the economy has actually commanded. It will vary in response to changes in values. In the determination of changes in values, however, the sort of supply that matters is the supply the economy could command, which is the potential supply. The interaction between a change (or lack of change) in potential supply and a change (or lack of change) in effective demand determines whether price will change. The price of labour is no exception. If the effective demand for current toil rises in the short period, in which the potential supply of labour must be regarded as given, the national wages bill is likely to rise. Similarly a fall in the effective demand for current toil can occur suddenly, or at least more sharply than the potential supply of labour can change, and is thus likely to lead to a fall in the national wages bill.

8. Derived from Census data; A. R. Prest, 'National Income of the United Kingdom, 1870-1946', in 'Economic Journal' (Mar 1948) Table II; E. H. Phelps Brown and P. E. Hart, 'The Share of Wages in National Income', in 'Economic Journal' (June 1952) Table 1; and 'National Income and Expenditure Blue Books'.

9. Derived from Census data.

10. Lewis, in 'Manchester School' (May 1954).

11. Matthews, in 'Economic Journal' (Sep 1968) p. 565, considers that unlimited labour was of some importance up to 1914, but it cannot have been of major importance even then.

12. Derived from 'National Income and Expenditure Blue Book, 1968', Tables 1 and 22.

13. Phelps Brown and Hart, in 'Economic Journal' (June 1952) and 'National Income and Expenditure Blue Books' (Tables 1 and 22 in the 1968 Blue Book).

14. On the question of definitions, the pre-1948 national income estimates relate to gross national product rather than income. National income estimates are used for the post-war period since wages are paid out of income.

15. Shop assistants, policemen and firemen have been classed as wage-earners since 1952.

16. Calculated at constant prices from London and Cambridge Economic Service, 'Key Statistics of the British Economy, 1960-1966', Table B.

17. By Phelps Brown and Hart, in 'Economic Journal' (June 1952).

18. Ibid., p. 264.

19. Ibid., p. 266.

20. London and Cambridge Economic Service, 'Key Statistics of the British Economy, 1900-1966', Tables A and B.

21. Derived from 'National Income and Expenditure Blue Book, 1968'.

22. Ibid.

23. B. R. Mitchell and Phyllis Deane, 'Abstract of British Historical Statistics' (Cambridge U.P., 1962) pp. 64-5.

24. Phelps Brown and Hart, in 'Economic Journal' (June 1952) Table 1, col 6.

25. Matthews, in 'Economic Journal' (Sep 1968).

26. Lewis, in 'Manchester School' (May 1954).

27. J. R. Hicks, 'Economic Foundations of Wages Policy', in 'Economic Journal' (Sep 1955).

28. C. W. Guillebaud, 'Wage Determination and Wages Policy' (Nisbet, 1967) esp. p. 13.

29. London and Cambridge Economic Service, 'Key Statistics of the British Economy, 1900-1966', Table E.

30. Phelps Brown and Hart, in 'Economic Journal' (June 1952), and Census data.

31. Hicks, in 'Economic Journal' (Sep 1955) p. 391.

32. A. W. Phillips, 'The Relationship between Unemployment and the Rate of Change of Money Wage Rates in the United Kingdom, 1861-1957', in 'Economica', xxv (Nov 1958); and R. G. Lipsey, 'The Relation between Unemployment and the Rate of Change in Money Wage Rates in the United Kingdom, 1862-1957: A Further Analysis', in 'Economica', xxvii (Feb 1960).

33. A. G. Hines, 'Trade Unions and Wage Inflation in the United Kingdom, 1893-1961', in 'Review of Economic Studies', xxxi (Oct 1964).

34. A. G. Hines, 'Wage Inflation in the United Kingdom, 1948-62: A Disaggregated Study', in 'Economic Journal', lxxix (Mar 1969).

35. Phillips, in 'Economica', xxv (Nov 1958), and Lipsey, ibid., xxvii (Feb 1960).

36. C(61), 12 May 1961, pp. 53-5.

37. See K. G. J. C. Knowles and O. O. Thorne, 'Wages Rounds, 1948-59', in 'Bulletin of the Oxford Institute of Statistics', xxiii 1 (Feb 1961); and K. G. J. C. Knowles and D. Robinson, 'Wage Rounds and Wage Policy', in 'Bulletin of the Oxford University Institute of Statistics', xxiv (May 1962).

38. L. A. Dicks-Mireaux and J. R. Shepherd, 'The Wage Structure and Some Implications for Incomes Policy', in 'National Institute Economic Review', no. 22 (Nov 1962).

39. Under the chairmanship first of Lord Cohen, and then of Lord Heyworth.

40. 'Joint Statement of Intent on Productivity, Prices and Incomes', in 'H.C., Parl. Deb.', 5th series, vol 704, 16 Dec 1964, cols. 385-8.

41. P.I.B., 'Third General Report, August 1967 to July 1968', Report No. 77, Cmnd. 3715 (H.M.S.O., July 1968) Appendix A.

42. Caves, 'Britain's Economic Prospects'; see chap. iii, 'Incomes Policy', by D. C. Smith.

43. F. Paish and J. Hennessy, 'Policy for Incomes', Hobart Papers (Institute of Economic Affairs, 1967).

CHAPTER 20

1. For a detailed definition of rent, see 'National Income Blue Book, 1968', item 19, p. 99.

2. Derived from ibid., Table 1; and London and Cambridge Economic Service, 'Key Statistics of the British Economy, 1900-1966', Table A.

3. Figures derived from Department of Agricultural Economics, University of Exeter. Note that these are national averages which are subject to wide regional variations.

4. 'Income from employment' as shown in London and Cambridge Economic Service, 'Key Statistics of the British Economy, 1900-1966', Table A.

5. A. J. Merrett and Allen Sykes, 'Housing, Finance and Development' (Longmans, 1965) p. 1.

6. Ibid., p. 27.

7. Adela A. Nevitt, 'Housing, Taxation and Subsidies' (Nelson, 1966) esp. p. 9.

8. L. Needleman, 'The Economics of Housing' (Staples Press, 1965) esp. p. 145.

9. See also A. C. L. Day, 'The Land Boom and the Community' in 'Westminster Bank Review' (May 1964).

CHAPTER 21

1. Data in this section are taken or derived from Central Statistical Office, 'National Income and Expenditure of the United Kingdom, 1967'; Prest, in 'Economic Journal' (Mar 1948); Guy Routh, 'Occupation and Pay in Great Britain, 1906-1960' (Cambridge U.P., 1965); and General Register Office, 'Census 1961, Great Britain', Summary Tables.

2. Salaries are the major part of the 'intermediate incomes' shown in Prest, 'Economic Journal' (Mar 1948).

3. Committee on Manpower Resources and Technology, 'The Brain Drain', Cmnd. 3417 (H.M.S.O., 1967, paras 74-5).

4. Ibid.

5. This is an elaboration of an idea first propounded by Brinley Thomas, 'The International Circulation of Human Capital', in 'Minerva' (summer 1967) p. 419.

6. 'The Brain Drain', para. 19.

7. Thomas, in 'Minerva' (summer 1967).

8. Ibid., Table III.

9. Ibid., pp. 485-6.

10. 'The Brain Drain', para. 159; Thomas, in 'Minerva' (summer 1967) p. 504.

11. 'National Income and Expenditure, 1967', Table 18. The figures for the number of salary-earners do not include directors in receipt of fees, but the salaries earned include a rough estimate of such fees. The difference is almost certainly not large enough to affect the argument of the section.

CHAPTER 22

1. This does not deny that uncertainty is involved in every business decision, including a 'no change' decision. There is always risk of loss. But even in the most recessed years of the 1960s, such risk was low by historical standards. Moreover, under any normal conditions there is usually a greater element of uncertainty involved when companies are venturing into new markets, new methods of production and new modes of competition. These sorts of ventures distinguish the entrepreneurial function from the purely money-lending one.

2. They were about as large in the first half of 1968 as in the whole of 1967. Cf. Lex, 'Capital Gains and the Level of Share Prices', in 'Financial Times', 22 July 1968, p. 1.

3. See London and Cambridge Economic Service, 'Key Statistics of the British Economy, 1900-1966', Table A, and work cited under Table 22.1.

4. If the percentage change in the *share* of profits in gross domestic product at current prices is compared with the percentage change in the national income at constant prices, a similar pattern is revealed.

5. See Phelps Brown and Hart, in 'Economic Journal' (June 1952).

6. See also Chapter 19 above.

7. Mitchell and Deane, 'Abstract of British Historical Statistics', pp. 64-5.

8. J. M. Keynes, 'General Theory of Employment, Interest, and Money' (Macmillan, 1936).

9. Sir W. Beveridge, 'Full Employment in a Free Society' (Allen & Unwin, 1944).

10. Ibid.

11. National Board for Prices and Incomes, Report No. 77, 'Third General Report, August 1967 to July 1968', Cmnd. 3715 (H.M.S.O., July 1968) para. 47, p. 16.

CHAPTER 23

1. Cf. Lewis, in 'Manchester School' (May 1954 and Jan 1958). Note, however, that Lewis is concerned with real wages and does not specifically consider the implication of monetisation of wages.

2. Ibid., where the difference between the real wages obtained in the subsistence sector and the monetised sector are referred to as 'the cliff'.

3. Ibid.

4. This statement is not incompatible with substantial female employment in the cotton industry even before 1914, since it refers to the national position. See Census data.

5. The chief example is typing and other automated office work. See Chapter 19 above.

6. N. Kaldor, 'Causes of the Slow Rate of Economic Growth of the United Kingdom' (Cambridge U.P., 1966) p. 4.

7. Ibid.

8. Ibid.

9. Ibid., p. 25 (Verdoorn's Law).

10. Ibid., pp. 3, 31.

11. Ibid., p. 35.

12. Derived from London and Cambridge Economic Service, 'Key Statistics of the British Economy, 1900-1966', and 'National Income Blue Books'. 1967 and 1968 are omitted because of the devaluation which took place in November 1967.

CHAPTER 24

1. Between 1901 and 1965, the total number in civil work increased by 45 per cent, or approximately 0.7 per cent a year. Derived from London and Cambridge Economic Service, 'Key Statistics of the British Economy, 1900-1966', Table E.

2. Department of Economic Affairs, 'The National Plan', Cmnd. 2764 (H.M.S.O., 1965) Appendix 4, Tables A1 and A2.

3. The example in mind is the Rolls-Royce–Lockheed deal of 1967.

4. See, e.g., C. P. Kidleberger, 'International Economics' (Irwin, Homewood, Ill., 1968) chap 9.

5. It is not difficult to find exceptions and to point to British exports of herrings and coal as well as to British imports of, say, electrical goods. But here the concern is only with the net balance of trade in the broad commodity groups mentioned.

6. 'Raw materials' in the trade returns of 1907-53, 'basic materials' and 'fuels' in subsequent trade returns.

7. 'Food, drink and tobacco'.

8. 1907 is chosen as the first year, because classification of imports started then. See 'Retained Imports' in 'Trade and Navigation Accounts', now 'Overseas Trade Accounts of the United Kingdom'.

9. Excluded are 1914-19 and 1939-45.

10. Alternatively, the rate of unemployment was 5 per cent or less.

11. See above, note 6. In 1907-53, refined fuels were classed as manufactures. The share of fuels in total imports does not vary much, and their inclusion under raw materials does not substantially affect the argument.

12. Source: Department of Employment and Productivity.

13. Cf. E. A. G. Robinson, 'The Problem of Living within our Exchange Earnings', in 'Three Banks Review' (Mar 1954) p. 12.

14. For a detailed analysis of imports until 1955, see M.FG. Scott, 'A Study of United Kingdom Imports' (Cambridge U.P., 1963).

15. This does not deny that many of these world markets are centred on London and that much British influence can be exerted in world markets.

16. For a fuller treatment and sources, see Chapter 26 below.

17. W. Schlote, 'British Overseas Trade' (Blackwell, 1952) pp. 54-5.

18. W. Beckerman and others, 'The British Economy in 1975' (Cambridge U.P., 1965) pp. 180-1.

19. See above, note 10, and note that in the past an unemployment rate above 5 per cent was an unemployment rate of at least 8½ per cent. Unemployment percentages between 5 and 8½ per cent did not occur at the national level, though they did occur in individual towns and regions.

20. Central Statistical Office, 'United Kingdom Balance of Payments'.

21. These statements are based on a comparison of exports in 1950 and 1964. See also S. J. Wells, 'British Export Performance' (Cambridge U.P., 1964) and National Economic Development Council, 'Export Trends' (H.M.S.O., 1900).

22. Cf. S. J. Chapman, 'The Cotton Industry and Trade' (Methuen, 1905) p. 69.

23. Cf. Brinley Thomas, 'International Factor Movements and Unequal Rates of Growth' in 'Manchester School' (Jan 1961).

24. Statement based on United Nations statistics.

25. Calculated from country tables in 'International Financial Statistics', by method shown in F. V. Meyer, 'The Terms of Trade' (Munksgaard, Copenhagen, 1962) Table 3.

26. There are not sufficient data for years earlier than 1881 to say how much longer.

27. W. Arthur Lewis, 'World Production Prices and Trade', in 'Manchester School' (May 1952).

28. Average of annual percentage growth rates from 1881 to 1950, excluding the war years. For detailed description of method and original sources, see above, note 25, or 'The Terms of Trade of Manufactures', in 'Economic Journal' (Sep 1959). The growth rate of trade in primary products relative to that of manufacturing is slightly lower than that given by Lewis, in 'Manchester School' (May 1952) p. 113. The variation is due to differences in the method of calculation and through linking the League of Nations series, used by Lewis, to United Nations data. The difference is, however, slight and does not affect the argument.

29. Ibid.

30. Calculated from London and Cambridge Economic Service, 'Key Statistics of the British Economy, 1900-1966'; 'Annual Abstract of Statistics'; and Schlote, 'British Overseas Trade'.

31. The 'constant' shown by Lewis, in 'Manchester School' (May 1952), is somewhat below two-fifths. Linked to United Nations data, it comes to almost exactly two-fifths.

32. United Nations data.

33. Average for 1950-65. Derived from United Nations data.

34. See 'Economic Journal' (Sep 1959) and chap 3 of book cited in note 25 above.

35. Statement based on comparison of domestic prices and export prices in the country tables of 'International Financial Statistics'.

36. The term 'Atlantic Economy' was coined by Brinley Thomas in connection with international factor movements. See his 'Migration and Economic Growth' (Cambridge U.P., 1954).

CHAPTER 25

1. Cf. A. H. Imlah, 'Economic Elements in the Pax Britannica' (Harvard U.P., Cambridge, Mass., 1958) Table 4; [W. M. Clarke] Report of the Committee on Invisible Earnings, 'Britain's Invisible Earnings' (British National Export Council, 1967); London and Cambridge Economic Service, 'Key Statistics of the British Economy, 1900-1966'; Central Statistical Office, 'United Kingdom Balance of Payments, 1946-57', and annually from 1964 onwards.

2. Average of 1930-8, including the surplus years of 1930 and 1935.

3. Data for the balance of payments on current and capital account are available from 1952 onwards. Any comparison with earlier data must be confined to the balance of payments on current account. Since this includes merchandise trade and invisible trade, this is the correct comparison in the present context.

4. A drop from £310 million in 1930 to £218 million in 1931, and from £267 million in 1959 to £150 million in 1960.

5. Averages were: 1921-9   £329 million   1953-9 £269 million

                1930-8   £231 million   1960-6 £163 million

6. This is sometimes referred to as the 'private balance', but such terminology would exclude commercial transactions by nationalised industries (such as imports and exports of coal).

7. A Board of Trade estimate, for 1965, shows British ships as carrying the more valuable cargoes in trade, in either direction. Quoted by Clarke Report, Table 35.

8. Average of 1964-6.

9. Cf. Annual Reports of the Liverpool Steam Ship Owners' Association for 1951, 1956, 1961 and 1966 (tables from p. 10 onwards in the 1951 report, and from p. 4 onwards in the other reports); and London and Cambridge Economic Service, 'Key Statistics of the British Economy, 1900-1966, Table K.

10. More precisely, if the tonnage of British exports in 1929=100, then the annual average tonnage in 1964-6 was 41.5; and if the value of British exports (at 1958 prices) in 1929=100, the annual average value of British exports (at 1958 prices) in 1964-6 was 177.0. Since $(41.4 \div 177) \times 100 = 23.4$, the weight of British exports in 1964-6 was, on average, less than one-quarter of what it had been in 1929.

11. Between 1960 and 1966 the tonnage of exports rose by 5 per cent and the value of exports (at constant 1958 prices) by 23 per cent, so that exports became 15 per cent lighter (since $(105 \div 123) \times 100 = 85$).

12. Cf. sources cited in note 9 above.

13. More precisely, if 1929=100, the annual average tonnage of British imports in 1964-6 was 261.5 and the annual average value (at 1958 prices) was 153.8. Since $(261.5 \div 153.8) \times 100 = 170$, imports were over 1½ times heavier.

14. Between 1960 and 1966 the tonnage of imports rose by 28 per cent and the value (at constant 1958 prices) rose by 22 per cent. Since $(128 \div 122) \times 100 = 105$, imports became 5 per cent heavier.

15. Liverpool Steam Ship Owners' Association, sources cited in note 9 above.

16. Source: ibid.

17. Ibid.

18. The implications of the prospects for natural gas, examined in Chap 17, should be related to this point.

19. See sources cited in note 9 above.

20. Details can be derived from the Clarke Report, Table 35 and p. 196, n. 1 (and sources cited).

21. More precisely, 1.4 times. Derived from 'Balance of Payments Pink Books' for 1963 and 1967, Tables 7 and 8 respectively.

22. Based on two crude estimates. One is as follows: freight payments on imports in foreign ships were £230 million and the tonnage 91.9 million, so that the freight per average ton was £2.5; freight receipts from exports in British ships were £161 million and the tonnage 16.8 million, so that the freight per average ton was £9.6; $9.6 \div 2.5 = 3.8$.

An alternative estimate is to divide the 5.5 multiple of payments export tonnage which equal payments import tonnage, by the 1.4 multiple of relevant freight receipts which equal relevant freight payments; the result is 3.9.

23. The space occupied by, say, a motor-car is greater than that occupied by, say, steel bars of identical weight.

24. See sources cited in note 21 above.

25. For details relating to gross earnings of the United Kingdom shipping industry and its contribution to the balance of payments, see Chamber of Shipping of the United Kingdom, 'Annual Reports'. (The relevant tables in the 1967-8 report are on pp. 222-3.)

26. 'Balance of Payments Pink Book, 1968', Table 14.

27. Ibid., and extract from speech by the Governor of the Bank of England (Lord Cromer) to the Confederation of British Industries, in 'Bank of England Quarterly Bulletin' (June 1966) p. 160, which puts those earnings at £200 million.

28. Clarke Report, p. 187, and sources cited there.

29. 'Balance of Payments Pink Books'; 1946-57, Table 1, and 1967, Table 2.

30. Ibid., tables relating to general balance of payments; Clarke Report, Table 3; Imlah, 'Economic Elements in the Pax Britannica', Tables 4 and 8.

31. In the case of the United States, dependence on British capital ceased long before the end of the nineteenth century, and in the case of Canada it ceased in the 1920s. But the difference in costs and prices still persists.

32. 'An Inventory of U.K. External Assets and Liabilities: End-1966', in 'Bank of England Quarterly Bulletin' (Sep 1967) esp. table on p. 266.

33. Cf. Annual Reports of the Bank for International Settlements; 'U.K. Banks' External Liabilities and Claims in Foreign Currencies', in 'Bank of England Quarterly Bulletin' (June 1964); A. T. K. Grant, 'The Machinery of Finance and the Management of Sterling' (Macmillan, 1967) pp. 132-47; Paul Einzig, 'The Euro-Dollar Market', 4th ed. (Macmillan, 1970).

34. See Thomas, in 'Manchester School' (Jan 1961) pp. 9-21.

35. Cf. J. Dunning, 'The Present Roles of U.S. Investment in British Industry', in 'Moorgate and Wall Street' (spring 1961) pp. 29, 32, 36, 37; J. J. Servan-Schreiber, 'Le Défi Américain' (Denoël, Paris, 1967) pt ii, trans. as 'The American Challenge' (Hamish Hamilton, 1968).

36. Cf. W. B. Reddaway, 'Effect of U.K. Direct Investment Overseas: An Interim Report', University of Cambridge Department of Applied Economics, Occasional Paper No. 12 (Cambridge U.P., 1968) pt iii.

CHAPTER 26

1. Suggested further reading:
A. Feavearyear, 'The Pound Sterling', 2nd ed., by E. Victor Morgan (Clarendon Press, 1963).
Sir Ralph Hawtrey, 'A Century of Bank Rate' (Longmans, 1938).
R. Triffin, 'International Central Banking and the International Economy', in 'Review of Economic Studies', xiv (2) (1946-47).
——, 'Our International Monetary System' (Random House, New York, 1968).
L. B. Yeager, 'International Monetary Relations' (Harper & Row, New York, 1966).

2. Except in 1926, the year of the General Strike. Although the balance of payments, calculated in sterling, was even more favourable in the early 1920s, a comparison with the early 1920s is useless on account of wild fluctuations in exchange rates before 1925. For balance of payments data, see London and Cambridge Economic Service, 'Key Statistics of the British Economy, 1900-1966', Table N.

3. The matter is complicated by rising overseas protection, so that it is not certain how far overseas customers could not afford to buy British goods (or any goods) because of impoverishment, and how far they were prevented because of protection.

4. Suggested further reading:
See note 1 above, and
League of Nations, 'International Currency Experience' (Geneva, 1944).
J. M. Keynes, 'Essays in Persuasion' (Macmillan, 1933) pt iii.
A. C. Pigou, 'Aspects of British Economic History, 1918-25' (Macmillan, 1947) pt v.
L. S. Pressnell (ed.), 'Studies in the Industrial Revolution' (University of London Press, 1970); see chap. on 'The Return to Gold in 1925', by R. S. Sayers.

5. Suggested further reading:
See note 1 above, and
League of Nations, 'International Currency Experience'.
Sir Arthur Lewis, 'Economic Survey, 1919-39' (Allen & Unwin, 1949).
F. Machlup, 'International Monetary Economics' (Allen & Unwin, 1966).
E. Nevin, 'The Mechanism of Cheap Money' (University of Wales Press, Cardiff, 1955).
Joan Robinson, 'Essays in the Theory of Employment' (Macmillan, 1937) pt iii.

6. 'H. C. Deb.', 5th series, vol. 468,1949, p. 14.

7. Compare the data in the various Balance of Payments White Papers and the Central Statistical Office's 'Pink Book' on the United Kingdom Balance of Payments, 1968, p. 75.

8. Growth of gross national output at constant prices.

9. (188÷163)x100=115.

10. A 44 per cent increase would have restored the 1949 parity.

11. By Sir Ralph Hawtrey, in 'Incomes and Money' (Longmans, 1967) e.g. on pp. 27, 164, 201-2.

12. Suggested further reading:

Bank of England, 'Quarterly Bulletins'.

'Midland Bank Review', annual monetary reviews.

S. S. Alexander, 'Effects of Devaluation and Trade Balance', in 'International Monetary Fund Staff Papers' (Apr 1952).

——, 'Effects of a Devaluation', in 'American Economic Review' (Mar 1959).

A. R. Conan, 'The Problem of Sterling' (Macmillan, 1966).

D. J. Coppock, 'The Alleged Case against Devaluation', in 'Manchester School' (Sep 1965).

A. C. L. Day, 'Outline of Monetary Economics' Part VI (Oxford U.P., 1957) pt vi.

——, 'The Future of Sterling' (Clarendon Press, 1956).

Sir Roy Harrod, 'The Pound Sterling', Essays in International Finance, No. 13 (Princeton U.P., 1952).

Sir Ralph Hawtrey, 'The Pound at Home and Abroad' (Longmans, 1961).

——, 'Incomes and Money' (Longmans, 1967).

F. Machlup, 'International Monetary Economics'.

R. A. Mundell, 'International Economics' (Macmillan, New York, 1968).

J. O. N. Perkins, 'The Sterling Area, the Commonwealth and World Economic Growth' (Cambridge U.P., 1967).

W. M. Scammell, 'International Monetary Policy' (Macmillan, 1957). Triffin, 'Our International Monetary System'.

Yeager, 'International Monetary Relations'.

13. Percentages derived from International Monetary Fund, 'International Financial Statistics' (Mar 1969) p. 32.

14. This interpretation is based on dollar values, which are the only correct measure of foreign exchange benefits. Sterling values are more relevant as measuring the opportunity costs of exports to the British economy. Comparisons are, however, rendered useless if sterling, the measure, alters in exchange value. For what they are worth, the results are as follows. By value, British exports, were 23 per cent higher in 1968 than in 1967. By 'volume', as measured by constant 1961 values, they were 14 per cent higher; but these estimates of 'volume' are rendered useless by the devaluation which occurred after the base year. For sterling values and volumes, see C.S.O., 'Monthly Digest of Statistics' (Feb 1969) Tables 133 and 134.

15. This point emerges whether dollar values or sterling values are used.

16. Examples are open-market operations; the war-time Treasury deposits, whereby the joint-stock banks had to deposit part of their cash with the Treasury and so could not use it as base for credit; and the special deposits with the Bank of England of the 1960s, whereby the joint-stock banks could be called upon to deposit part of their cash with the Bank of England, which again restricted the credit base.

17. 'The London Discount Market: Some Historical Notes', in 'Bank of England Quarterly Bulletin' (June 1967) esp. p. 147; ibid. (June 1963) Table 7; (June 1968); (Mar 1969) Table 9.

18. Sources: United Nations and C.S.O.

19. Exceptionally heavy withdrawals by Australia (1952) and India (1957) weakened the Area's gold and dollar reserves, but also eliminated those two countries' excess balances.

20. 'The Basle Facility and the Sterling Area', Cmnd. 3787 (H.M.S.O., 1968).

21. League of Nations, 'International Currency Experience'.

Index